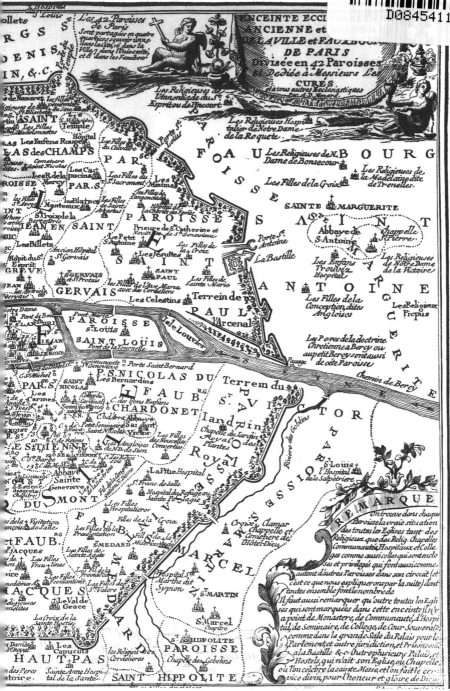

LITURGY, POLITICS, AND SALVATION: THE CATHOLIC LEAGUE IN PARIS AND THE NATURE OF CATHOLIC REFORM, 1540–1630

Ann W. Ramsey

 University of Rochester Press

First published 1999

University of Rochester Press
668 Mt. Hope Avenue
Rochester, NY 14620   USA

and at P.O. Box 9
Woodbridge, Suffolk IP12 3DF
United Kingdom

ISBN 1–58046–031–3

Library of Congress Cataloging-in-Publication Data

Ramsey, Ann W., 1950–
     Liturgy, politics, and salvation : the Catholic League in Paris
and the nature of Catholic reform, 1540–1630 / Ann W. Ramsey.
          p.   cm.
     Includes bibliographical references and index.
     ISBN 1–58046–031–3 (alk. paper)
     1. Paris (France)—Church history—16th century.   2. Sainte Ligue
     (1576–1593)   3. France—History—Wars of the Hugeuenots, 1562–1598.
     4. Religion and politics—France—Paris—History—16th century.   5.
     Calvinism—France—Paris—History.   I. Title.
       DC120.R35   1999
       282'.44361'09031—dc21
                                                                99–17827
                                                                CIP

British Library Cataloguing-in-Publication Data
A catalogue record for this book is available from the British Library

Designed and typeset by ISIS Corporation
Printed in the United States of America
This publication is printed on acid-free paper

CONTENTS

Illustrations

Tables

ACKNOWLEDGMENTS

This study would not have been possible without the generous assistance of several institutions and many individuals. I would like to thank the French government for a Chateaubriand dissertation research grant in 1984–85. The History and Academic Computing Departments at Columbia University provided computer facilities and training in the Statistical Package for the Social Sciences. A summer fellowship awarded by the University of Texas at Austin made it possible to undertake additional archival research in the summer of 1991. A post-doctoral grant from the Society of Fellows in the Humanities at Columbia University in 1991–92 provided the perfect interdisciplinary environment for reconceptualizing my dissertation.

I was extremely fortunate to have attended more than a year of the Paris Seminar of Denis Richet and Robert Descimon in 1984–86. My debts to these two individuals will be evident throughout this study. Robert Descimon introduced me to the *Minutier central*, the notarial archives of the Archives Nationales. Over the years he has shared his extraordinary knowledge; he has read several drafts of this book and has provided guidance and encouragement. His groundbreaking study of the *Seize* has made possible this present work.

On this side of the Atlantic, numerous friends, colleagues, and students have read portions and drafts of this work. I have especially benefited from discussions with and comments from Marsha Colish, Orest Ranum, Lionel Rothkrug, and Moshe Sluhovsky. My colleagues at the University of Texas have been extraordinary in taking time from their demanding schedules to read, to correct, and to entreat. Though all I thank have saved me from many errors and infelicities, some undoubtedly remain, and those are entirely my responsibility.

I am particularly indebted to my "comrades-in-arms," Samantha Worrell, Jara Hill, and Lisa McClain, who assisted with the demanding data entry. I can only salute their endurance and intelligence. Renate Wise was an invaluable editor of several drafts of this work; I would like to thank Sean M.

Culhane, the former Director of the University of Rochester Press, who has been a wonderfully patient and encouraging editor. The manuscript benefited greatly from the copyediting of John W. Blanpied and the extraordinary efforts of Louise Goldberg and Martyn Hitchcock. The anonymous readers' reports have been bracing and insightful.

Over the years of this project a host of individuals have helped with the myriad research and technical tasks without which this book could not have taken shape. I wish to thank them one and all for their skill and commitment, hoping that they realize the extent of my admiration and gratitude for their splendid work. They made this project a much richer experience in every way: Todd Anderson (who reviewed the French of the manuscript), Raina Banu, Bennett Donovon, Andrew McFarland, Chris Mead, Mity Myhr, Anna Otto, John St. Lawrence, Ernest Simmons, Nicole Sitz, Julie Taborsky, and Andrea Winkler. I am also particularly grateful to Irina Rozovskaya for the jacket design because she saw this project at its very inception. I owe a very special thanks to the *conservateurs* and staff of the Archives nationales and to its *Atelier de photographie et microfilmage* for the photography of documents from the *Minutier central*.

On a personal note I would like to thank Stewart White for keeping me moving and to apologize to Katie and Duncan Meisel for not moving more quickly.

It is a pleasure finally to be able to acknowledge the oldest and most abiding of debts: to my teachers, Joan Afferica and Wim Smit, and to Frances Ramsey, Leonard Smith, and Jan Meisel. This book is for them.

A Note on Manuscript Sources and Abbreviations

The actual texts of the sixteenth- and seventeenth-century French manuscript sources cited throughout this work lacked modern French accents, uniform orthography, or punctuation. Ideally, one would wish to change nothing in reproducing these texts. To make these texts more accessible to the modern reader the following additions were made in quoting from the texts when clarity seemed to require it:

1. The French accent *grave* has frequently been added to the preposition *à* to distinguish it from the third person singular of the verb *avoir* (*a*).

2. The accent *aigu* has frequently been added to masculine past participles in the singular and in the plural (e.g., *recommandé*), since the masculine form is more easily confused with finite verb forms than is the feminine.

3. The original spelling has been retained whenever possible. The frequent abbreviations in notarial documents have generally been expanded for clarity. Unless otherwise indicated, all translations are my own.

PREFACE

In 1977 the appearance of the original French version of Denis Richet's article "Sociocultural Aspects of Religious Conflicts in Paris during the Second Half of the Sixteenth Century" signaled a fundamental reorientation in the historiography of the League.[1] Richet proposed more boldly than had others before the thesis that the League was the time when the Catholic Reformation first put down roots in Paris. Few historians of French Catholicism had pursued the origins of "The Century of Saints" into the troubled period of the Wars of Religion. Virtually no historians of the League per se had explored its religious culture.[2]

Above all, Richet stressed that the League "was the beginning of a veritable 'Catholic Action,'" which led to the formation of the *parti dévot* of the seventeenth century.[3] Richet interpreted the "party of the devout" as the direct heir of "zealous" or Leaguer Catholicism. He also argued that Leaguer piety sought to bring Tridentine norms of orthodox belief and new standards of religious decorum and morality to all the population of Paris. In drawing attention to Leaguer piety, Richet broke with centuries of negative League historiography. For Richet, the religious program of the League was as important and certainly more influential than its failed political opposition to royal absolutism.

Two generations of scholarship on the League in Paris, including the work of J. H. M. Salmon, Elie Barnavi, Robert Descimon, Barbara Diefendorf, and Denis Crouzet, among others, have not, however, produced a consensus about the nature, lineages, or legacy of League piety.[4] Recent research, which stresses the autonomy of religious phenomena, presents a powerful challenge to socio-cultural or socio-political interpretations of the Paris League that appeared in the 1970s and early 1980s.[5] Most strikingly absent is any quantitative study of religious beliefs and behavior. This is especially surprising because historians of early-modern France have been pioneers in the use of quantitative techniques for cultural analysis.[6]

Against this background of League historiography, in 1985 I began my dissertation research on the League and the reform of popular culture. Both Denis Richet and Robert Descimon emphasized to me the need to exploit serial sources for the further study of League piety. In Paris, however, unlike Rouen or Lyon, the parish and ecclesiastical archives as well as records of the court of the Châtelet had been decimated, first by the revolution of 1789 and then by the fire that destroyed the *Hôtel de Ville*, or town hall, during the fighting of the Paris Commune.[7] Several individual studies of Parisian parishes were undertaken as master's theses under the direction of Pierre Chaunu and Denis Richet. These have remained unpublished because of the unsatisfactory nature of the Parisian archives themselves.[8] Synodal statutes and parish visitation reports, serial sources that elsewhere serve as centerpieces for the study of religion and society, are also scarce for the city of Paris.[9]

In the context of these strengths and weaknesses in the Parisian archives and in the historiography of the League itself, I turned to Parisian last wills and testaments to study religious mentalities.[10] Based on their observations of soaring numbers of wills during the Great Siege of 1590, Denis Richet and Robert Descimon initially suggested the possibility of a study of the wills of 1590. Their suggestion came at the time Denis Crouzet had begun to publish his early findings on the eschatological fervor of the period, especially as manifest in penitential processions of the 1580s.[11] The initial premises of my research related to the possibility of discovering a dramatic shift in the language or mood of the wills, as a companion phenomenon to the wave of penitential processions and eschatological anguish analyzed by Crouzet. The actual findings for 1590 convinced me to expand the chronology of my study to include the pre-Tridentine period through the first third of the seventeenth century.

Over time, what had begun merely as a very logical step in the evolution of historical methodologies for the study of the League opened new historical domains for me, especially in the field of liturgy. In the liturgical richness of the wills of known League militants, I first began to understand the world-view that Leaguers gave their lives to defend. This discovery initially took me far afield from the problem of the League and popular culture as I had originally conceptualized it. It is tempting to argue that religious culture was the popular culture of the League, if we understand "popular" to mean the broadly shared norms and behaviors that confirm communal identity. The liturgy, with its sense of sacred time and place, its accompanying symbolic modes of thought, and its ludic elements that could be appropriated in so many diverse settings, thus lay at the heart of the League itself. This is an understanding of popular culture too often neglected by general cultural historians. For a time this liturgical culture served as the common bond that bridged the social and factional divisions of Leaguer politics and stood as the foundation of Leaguer political action. The Catholic League was not a unitary or static phenomenon, and thus its religious culture is complex. Last wills and testaments do make clear that religious alliance among Leaguers was inextricably linked to social, cultural, and political loyalties. The pages that follow explore the Catholic League in Paris as a political movement that lived within liturgical time but was also animated by intense contests for social, cultural, and political power.

Introduction

LEAGUE PIETY:
DEFINITIONS AND CONCEPTS

The development of Protestantism in the course of the sixteenth and seventeenth centuries is a part of one of the most significant cultural changes in European history. Only recently has a general recognition emerged that the story of the transition from late-medieval to early-modern forms of worship cannot be told without considering the Catholic variants of this larger process of cultural change. In France, the advent of Calvinism in the first third of the sixteenth century led in the later sixteenth century to decades of civil war, fought ultimately over the very survival of the French monarchy and the right of Henry of Navarre, a Protestant, to succeed to the throne of France. During the most troubled phase of this conflict, the era of the Catholic League, the fiercest struggles were fought between *politiques* (mostly Catholics) and militant or "zealous" Catholics, who under no circumstances were willing to recognize a Protestant as their sovereign. The period is particularly interesting because a long-term cultural struggle about traditional and reformed religion (the Reformation) was intensified by debate over questions of loyalty to the institution of the French monarchy. Under such circumstances, debates over the means of salvation became intimately related to contests over the ultimate boundaries of community and the nature and locus of authority in the world.

In the course of the sixteenth century, throughout Europe a cultural revolution took place in people's understanding of their relations with the sacred. In France, and in Paris in particular, under the conditions of the succession crisis, ritual performance assumed a special significance in the lives of militant Catholics. Anthropologists and historians interested in the social and political functions of religious ritual have long recognized that ritual behaviors are a powerful means of defining the boundaries of community and of signaling membership in it. It is surprising, then, that no study of the Catholic League has systematically examined the relationship between intense liturgical engagement and League political affiliation.

The lack of such a study has much to do with the disincentives for traditional church historians to look to a period of civil war, where Leaguers were accused of treason, for the roots of the flowering of baroque Catholicism. The French monarchy remained Catholic because the most militant Catholics prevailed at critical junctures in the civil wars: at the Massacre of Saint Bartholomew's Day in 1572 and in the lesser-known siege of Paris in 1590, when the Catholic League controlled the capital and resisted the rights of Henry of Navarre to the French throne.

This book offers a new explanation for the successes of radical Catholicism. It presents a study of the way that, at particular historical conjunctures, the liturgy can create and sustain the "collective effervescence" that Emile Durkheim saw as the critical contribution of religion to the coherence of societies.[1] To understand the crisis of the League in Paris, one must understand the civic experience of the liturgy and the ability of the liturgy to link highly politicized but distinct social groups.

Specifically, this book examines the evidence from Parisian wills never before used for a study of the Catholic League. The testamentary analysis seeks both to clarify the historical specificity of League piety and to define its place in long-term changes in the religious culture of Paris in the sixteenth and early seventeenth centuries. Wills are examined primarily in terms of the changing repertoires of symbolic behaviors used by testators from the pre-Tridentine period through the first half of the seventeenth century. This research strategy combines an analysis of the institutions receiving bequests with a careful scrutiny of the language and imagery of the wills.

The chief sources used to investigate the Leaguer understanding of self and of community are all the extant Parisian wills from three sample periods: 1543–44 (159 wills), 1590 (727 wills), and 1630 (344 wills).[2] These years make it possible to track the evolution of the religious culture in three distinct periods: on the eve of the Council of Trent (1545–63); at the height of Leaguer resistance to Henry IV during the siege of Paris in 1590; and in 1630, a still relatively early phase of *dévot* activism in terms of the general population.

The sample of 1543–44 includes a population that came of age religiously when Catholic worship was probably still largely shaped by late-medieval traditions. At this time, however, twenty years of transcendentalist challenges posed by Protestants had intensified intra-Catholic debates about superstition, abuses, and reform. It is thus possible to measure the nature and extent of engagement with these reformist issues in the general testator population. The core of this study, however, is the enormous testator population of 1590. The perilous military situation and the high mortality rates during and immediately following the siege, with its accompanying food shortages and deaths from starvation, undoubtedly contributed to what is at least a tripling of the expected number of wills in a relatively static population.

Finally, selecting a date near the beginning of the social outreach by seventeenth-century Catholic activists makes possible the identification of an avant-garde of Catholic reformers in the testator population. These reformers can then be compared both to the general testator population and to reformers of the League and pre-Tridentine periods. The year 1630, which follows the establishment of the Company of the Holy Sacrament at the Capuchin monastery of Paris in 1629, was a logical choice. This association of lay persons and clerics has long been recognized as one of the most important early initiatives by Catholic activists following the League.[3]

The Research Perspectives and Essential Concepts

The chief aim of this work is to locate the piety of the League era in a broader historical context while at the same time grounding it in the structures of community from which it developed. Three concepts are essential to this study: performativity, immanence, and transcendence.[4] Performativity emerged as the research findings began to indicate that League-related individuals were nearly twice as likely as non-League-related individuals either to provide liturgical detail or to show a particular concern about the ritual aspects of salvation in their wills. This finding about the significance of religious ritual for Leaguers led to a second concept of religious immanence, applied to the sacred and the civic sphere.

Traditional Catholicism was at its core a religion of sacred immanence. This means that the sacred can inhere within the matter of this world. A religion of sacred immanence is acutely sensitive to the physical and bodily locus of the sacred and to religious uses of the body. The body and not just doctrine is essential to religious truth, because religions of sacred immanence depend upon bodily forms of knowing. In the Catholic doctrine of the eucharist, sacred immanence also depends upon belief in the essential unity of sign and symbol and the real presence of Christ in the eucharist. This is, therefore, a system that values a fleshly connection to the sacred.

In a like manner, civic immanence refers to a sense of the sacrality of the enclosed space of the city walls.[5] It not only describes a political culture or set of institutions, but also includes a set of such public, performative practices as civic processions, the rituals of militia service, and the public burning of an effigy of "Heresy."[6] The symbolic dimensions of these performative behaviors define the boundaries of community and one's place in the world. Taken together, these first two concepts, immanence and performativity, emphasize that Leaguers had a particular performative view of community. This Leaguer world-view or ontology depended upon the expressivity and creativity of symbolic behaviors in forging bonds of sacral as well as political allegiance.

Sociologists have suggested conceptual frameworks that can help explain the special meaning of religious ritual to militant Catholics and illuminate why the defense of religious ritual can easily become a matter of debate about the fundamental structures of authority and community. In *The Moral Commonwealth*, Philip Selznick writes that

> Two sources of moral integration compete for preeminence as foundations of community: civility and piety. Civility governs diversity, protects autonomy and upholds toleration; piety expresses devotion and demands integration.[7]

Sociologists have also given us the model of social evolution from "a kin-based world of organic unity" to "an exchange-based world of artificial association." This too is helpful in understanding the sense of community that underlay the loyalties of the Catholic League.

In contrast to performativity and immanence, a third essential concept, transcendence, best describes the redefinition of the sacred in the thought and beliefs of Calvin and the Huguenots of France. Calvinism is a religion of sacred transcendence where the sacred no longer inheres in the world, but, out of reverence, has been displaced to the heavens and shorn of human kinship. During the era of the Catholic League, however, it is important to understand not only differences between Protestants and Catholics. Just as essential to the religious and political struggles of this period were the *politiques*, who were Catholic for the most part. Some *politiques* were inclined to see many forms of religious ritual as non-essential to the foundations of religious truth. In the 1580s and 1590s, *politiques* were much more concerned that conflicts between Leaguers and Calvinists over religious ritual had destroyed the very foundations of legitimate political authority, without which the Church itself could not endure.

In interpreting League piety and the significance of the League era more generally, it is most important to understand the historical relationships between people's concept of the sacred and their notions of legitimate authority in the world. The present study focuses on debates among zealous Catholics, Calvinists, and *politiques*, concerning the place of ritual performance in relation to the sacred. Understanding differing Catholic and Protestant views on "performativity" offers a new way of understanding the issues at stake, not only during the Catholic League but in enduring debates about tolerance, reasons of state, and the imperatives of religious fundamentalism.

Part One

Catholic Militancy and Religious Reform: Tensions between Tradition and Innovation

Chapter 1

The Historical Context: Politics, Religion, and the Emergence of the Catholic League in Paris

This chapter provides a historical introduction to the world of militant Catholicism in sixteenth-century Paris. It offers a chronology of the basic events of this turbulent century in French history and presents a broader interpretive framework to explain the significance of these events for the evolution of militant Catholicism in Paris. Finally, this chapter introduces the reader to testamentary evidence itself by examining two Parisian wills that demonstrate how individual testators helped to shape and were in turn shaped by the great events of this period.

The sixteenth century was the last and arguably the most decisive century of Valois rule in France. The reigns of Francis I (1515–47) and his son Henry II (1547–59) in the first half of the century are associated with the growth of the French state and royal absolutism. In the second half of the sixteenth century, the queen mother, Catherine de Medici, widow of Henry II, was the most enduring political figure. This period is often called the age of Catherine de Medici: she lived through the deaths of three sons, ruled for two of them, and died with the capital in full revolt only a few months before the assassination of the last Valois monarch, her son King Henry III (1574–89).[1]

The reigns of Francis I and Henry II are sometimes viewed as relatively stable periods in contrast to the decades of civil and religious wars that filled the later sixteenth century (1562–98). Nonetheless, the international engagements and domestic policies of these rulers contributed directly to the turmoil of the Wars of Religion. Francis I pursued a ruinous Italian policy that was designed to diminish Hapsburg dominance. Instead he was himself captured at the Battle of Pavia (1525). He incurred enormous state debts and initiated the fateful policy of selling state offices as a means of financing the war against the House of Hapsburg. Francis was also a patron of humanism and, in part for that reason, he failed to take decisive measures when so-called Lutherans first made their appearance in the capital in 1521. It was only during the period of Francis I's Spanish captivity in 1525–26 that authorities in Paris, the *Parlement*, and especially the theology faculty of the Sorbonne, felt free to take measures against what were still termed "Lutherans." In this period of the late 1520s the king was unpopular, and public sentiment suggests that the common people of Paris felt that heresy flourished at court. Significantly, in June of 1528 the first recorded incident of Protestant iconoclasm in Paris took place. In the rue des Rosiers, an image of the Virgin Mary was vandalized. In reaction, in an act of ritual cleansing, all the parishes of the city and the University organized processions to seek forgiveness for this blasphemy. Francis ordered that the broken statue be replaced with a silver one of the Virgin. More importantly, an impressive procession in honor of the holy sacrament carried the new statue to the vandalized site.

Only the Affair of the Placards of 1534, however, seems to have shocked the king into a realization of the extent of Protestant organization and the threat it posed to Catholic culture. Printed broadsheets (placards) attacking the mass appeared in Paris and in key cities such as Orléans and Tours in the early morning hours of Sunday, October 18, 1534. A broadsheet was even placed upon the door of the King's bedchamber at Amboise. As Catholics rose to go to Sunday mass they confronted a searing attack on "the Horrible, Gross, Insufferable Abuses of the Papal Mass." Despite this event, repression remained sporadic. An organized international movement of Catholic reform led by the papacy was not really underway until the convening of the Council of Trent in 1545. By the time the Council closed in 1563, France had already begun its tragic drift into religious warfare.

Only in the final years of his reign did Francis I initiate a harsh policy against religious heterodoxy. The most decisive of these actions came in 1546. In this year both the most unorthodox members of the circle of Meaux reformers and Etienne Dolet were burned at the stake. Meaux had been the first site of sustained Catholic pastoral and parochial reform, so this event called into question the immediate future of Catholic reform itself. Etienne Dolet, one of the most famous humanist publishers, was burned in the heart of the University quarter at the Place Maubert in August of 1546.

Francis I died in March 1547. It thus fell to his son Henry II (1547–59) to begin to bring the state's monopoly of violence to bear upon the emergent movement of French Calvinism. This policy of repression came at least a decade too late to stop the growing popularity of the "reformed" faith. Calvin's own break with Catholicism can be dated to the period of 1533–34. The publication in 1536 of the first edition of his *Institutes of the Christian Religion* established his undisputed position as the leading voice of the French Reformed church. From 1541 until his death in 1564, Calvin would direct the development of the highly organized communities of French Huguenots from his exile in Geneva.

Henry II brought the Hapsburg-Valois wars to a close in April 1559 with the Treaty of Cateau-Cambrésis, but died in a tournament only three months later. The enormous burden of state debt and irreconcilable religious differences between Catholics and Protestants were problems that would dominate the fate of the monarchy in the second half of the century. Henry's oldest son, Francis II (1559–60), succeeded his father at the age of 15. As he had barely reached the age of legal majority, the direction of the government became the object of court struggles. Francis II had married Mary Stuart, Queen of Scots, in April 1558. This union with the Catholic Mary was one of the key elements of a diplomatic policy of international Catholicism. Within France the leading proponents of this emergent international alliance of militant Catholics were the princely houses of Guise and Lorraine, led by Francis, the second duke of Guise (1519–63), and his brother Charles, the Cardinal of Lorraine (1524–74).[2] Uncles to Mary, Queen of Scots, these statesmen were the chief protagonists in the struggle with Catherine de Medici for control of the young king, Francis II.[3] After a troubled reign of only seventeen months, Francis II died. This left the crown to Francis's brother Charles IX (1560–74), who was only ten years of age. In 1560, a formal regency was created for Catherine de Medici, who ruled with the first prince of the blood, Antoine, King of Navarre. Navarre was a region where Calvinism was extremely popular due to the protection it received from Antoine of Navarre's wife, Jeanne of Navarre, an early convert to Protestantism and mother to the future king of France, Henry of Navarre (1589–1610).

By 1560 France was very close to civil war. In the capital, French Calvinism had become a small but organized force. Throughout the 1530s and 1540s Calvinists had been the source of episodic iconoclasm and mockery of Catholic ritual. This created palpable tensions surrounding Catholic processions and religious ceremonies. The other face of Calvinism was, of course, martyrdom. Following the Affair of the Placards, for example, the public burnings had lasted six days and some 120 persons had been condemned and burned at the stake. By the 1550s, the profile of Huguenots in the capital was changing. In 1555, a permanent church was organized according to Genevan regulations in the wealthy outlying quarter of Saint-Germain at the home of a nobleman, sieur de La Ferrière. Most importantly, the appeal of the reformed faith reached into the elite of the state officials in the *Parlement*, and even to the princes of the blood.

In general, the Calvinists of the capital had led a clandestine existence. By 1557, the numbers of persons who gathered for evening assemblies had grown from several dozen to three or four hundred. In this year, in the famous affair of the rue Saint-Jacques, the Catholics of Paris went on the

offensive, spying upon and then attacking Calvinists who had celebrated
the Lord's Supper in a house on this street. Students from the neighboring
college of Plessis had noticed the large gathering. They assaulted the Calvinists who were attempting to leave, and over one hundred persons were
shut in the house until dawn. Royal officials came and made 128 arrests.
Martyrdom at the Place Maubert followed.

Not all Protestant gatherings in Paris were clandestine, however. In
the vast, open, and unguarded spaces of the meadows beyond the city walls,
the *Pré aux Clercs*, where students brawled, Calvinists gathered to sing psalms
as early as 1558. These meetings became popular and well attended, especially by some of the most august nobles of France, who provided an armed
guard at the gatherings. Significantly, in May of 1558, Antoine of Navarre
and his brother, Louis prince of Condé, were prominent among the crowd.[4]

Immediately after the death of Henry II in 1559, the Cardinal of Lorraine
had virtual control of royal policy. The burnings and denunciations in Paris
reached a peak. Calvin, who did not support armed resistance, was warned
by the French Calvinist community that armed conflict was inevitable.
The government of Catherine de Medici was forced to acknowledge the
failure of attempts at theological compromise. This became definitively clear
with the collapse of discussions at the Colloquy of Poissy near Paris in September 1561. This last, great conciliatory effort on French soil occurred at
the time of fateful changes both within the Catholic church and within the
geo-political and confessional disposition of power within Europe as a whole.

A decisive phase in the larger history of the Catholic Reformation was
beginning just as France was sliding into protracted civil war (1562–1629).
Three generations of French men and women fought wars both civil and
religious, which pitted an embattled monarchy against the Huguenots and
ultimately against the armed forces of militant Catholicism. These ultra-
Catholics gradually became completely alienated from the French monarchy because none of its policies brought the desired elimination of heresy
from the kingdom.

Internationally, by the early 1560s, Philip II of Spain, a Hapsburg and
thus traditional enemy of French interests, was prepared to commit resources
to turn back the tide of Protestantism in a much more aggressive manner
than his father, Emperor Charles V. The Jesuits, who had arrived in Paris in
1558, were also at this time emerging as an increasingly potent force in
shaping Catholic culture and society. The papacy in the 1560s assumed
more direct spiritual leadership of a broad movement of Catholic discipline
and renewal. The most potent indicator of this institutional initiative at its
highest level was the meeting of the final and most decisive period of the
Council of Trent, which opened in February 1562 and closed its final ses-

sion in December 1563. This final session, like many Catholics in Paris, regarded the eucharist as a "powerful protection to conquer with vigor all the attacks of the devil."[5] The council also acknowledged the failure of ecumenical efforts due to "the malice of heretics so obdurate that there is nothing they have not infected with error."[6] The principles of dogma were in place and the outlines for a sweeping program of institutional reform had been articulated: "It only remains for the council to charge all princes in the Lord, to give their help and not allow the decrees here made to be abused or violated by heretics, but to see that they are devoutly received and faithfully observed by them and by all."[7]

The government of Catherine de Medici had neither the political will nor the means formally to introduce the Tridentine program of reform into France. Instead Catherine pursued a policy of limited toleration of Protestantism that ultra-Catholics would never accept. There was a third, diffuse group active within French politics at this time, the *politiques*—the name often given to those individuals willing to accept some measure of toleration of Protestantism as a practical necessity essential to the integrity of the French state.[8] For example, figures such as Michel de l'Hôpital, the new chancellor named in 1560 by Catherine de Medici, would argue that although heterodoxy was never desirable, it was necessary to distinguish between acts of political sedition and misbelief. Catherine and her Chancellor believed that concessions to the Protestants were the only way to pacify society. This wager was tragically wrong. In fact, the greatest threat to the French state within the next three decades was not Protestantism but militant Catholicism itself. In the 1580s and 1590s, adherents of the Catholic League used the term *politique* only as a bitter pejorative for those who placed national or any family loyalty above loyalty to the Roman Catholic Church. For militant Catholics, the *politiques'* toleration of "heresy" was as damning as heresy itself.

In July of 1562, following Catherine's initial edict of toleration in January, the first of the Wars of Religion broke out. Before the founding of the first Catholic League of 1576, five civil wars were fought between Catholics and Protestants.[9] The most famous and horrifying event of this period is the Massacre of Saint Bartholomew's Day, which took place in Paris in August of 1572.

In mid-August 1572, the greatest nobles of France, including the military leaders of the Protestants, gathered in Paris to celebrate the marriage of Catherine de Medici's youngest daughter, Marguerite of Valois, with the Protestant Henry of Navarre. A strategic marriage alliance had already been arranged for Catherine's eldest daughter, Elizabeth of Valois, who became the child bride and third wife of Philip II of Spain in June 1559.[10] In the

later part of August 1572, the most eminent of the Protestant leaders who
were in Paris for the marriage festivities, Admiral Coligny, was struck but
not mortally wounded by a would-be assassin, probably acting with Guise
complicity. This event so enraged the Protestant nobles that during the night
of August 23rd Catherine de Medici feared an uprising. She and Charles IX
conferred with a small circle of confidants: Catherine's youngest son, the
duke of Anjou, plus the duke of Nevers, the count of Retz, the duke of Tavannes,
and René Birague, the keeper of the seals. Tremendous debates still rage
about the responsibility for what then occurred. Catherine and Charles IX
had surely wished to have Coligny assassinated, and most likely had entrusted this deed to Henry, the second duke of Guise, and his entourage,
since the young duke had wanted revenge for the death of his father, duke
Francis, who was killed in 1563, at the end of the first war of religion. The
frustrations of the people of Paris, who had for decades endured the presence of "heretics" within their midst, exploded in an orgy of violence that
followed the assassination of Coligny and killed as many as 3,000 persons in
Paris alone. The massacres continued in the provinces for several weeks,
during which some 10,000 victims fell to the violence of Catholic crowds.[11]

The Massacre of Saint Bartholomew's Day served as a tragic indication
of the volatility of religious passions and the extent of religious tensions
within Paris. The relation between this manifestation of militant Catholicism and what is often called the spirit or piety of the League era (*L'Esprit
ligueur*) has been much disputed and is discussed in greater detail in the
chapters that follow.[12]

The Disaffection of the Capital after the Peace of Monsieur

"Zealous" Catholics were gravely disappointed by the terms of the Peace of
Monsieur and the conclusion of the fifth war of religion in 1576. This peace
finally granted Protestants the right to have temples and to hold religious
services in any location at any time, with the exception of the region of
Paris. For the Guise-led Catholic forces as well as for large numbers of fervent Catholics all over France, and especially in the capital, this peace
aggravated their growing disaffection with the king. This disillusionment
with the king and his religious policy also inflamed a growing social conflict within Paris. The common people were ardent Catholics and included
artisans, petty merchants, and minor functionaries of the massive law-court
system. These groups, along with many of the great merchant families of
Paris, came to resent bitterly the wealthy officials of the *Parlement* who had
registered the provisions of the Peace of Monsieur.

The Peace of Monsieur obligated Henry III to pay large sums of money that could only be collected by violating the fiscal privileges and municipal liberties of his Parisian subjects. Municipal traditions allowed for a certain amount of debate and bargaining surrounding most levies. The actual apportionment of the levies was customarily decided by municipal elites meeting at the Hôtel de Ville.[13] In 1576, Henry III instead created a commission of presidents drawn from the highest courts (the highest magistracy of the *Parlement, chambre des comptes,* and the treasurers general) to whom he entrusted the collection of his new levy.

The highest municipal official, the *prévôt des marchands,* presented a remonstrance to the king declaring that he and the other town officers, the aldermen (four *échevins*) were unable to grant the levy because it had not been submitted to a municipal assembly. The text of the remonstrance clearly indicates what municipal privileges were at stake here:

> [The town officials] are not able to accord or consent to anything, humbly entreating his Majesty to permit an assembly in the accustomed manner in the town hall with bourgeois and residents to let them hear what it has pleased your Majesty to propose and say, and in order to make known to the said sire the king the response and resolution [of the assembly].[14]

The municipal protest had no effect, and the levy was assigned to the royal commission in the Louvre palace. Posters protesting this special commission had already appeared throughout the city. The text of one of these posters is especially interesting for what it tells us about the social animus and religious values that animated critics of both the king and his chief officials in the *Parlement.* The text contained "threats of massacre and sacking" directed at two of the highest judges of the *Parlement,* the *présidents* De Thou and Séguier. The cultural policy of these august officials was literally seen as a plague upon the community, since the text directly characterized them as "ancient and destructive pests of the legal system."[15] They were accused

> of having approved the introduction of the so-called reformed religion into the kingdom and in this way, of having accepted a pact already made with the enemies of God that brought total confusion to the church.[16]

The wording of threats against the magisterial elite, "massacre and sack," evokes the memory of popular Catholic violence during Saint Bartholomew's Day and suggests that the perceived leniency of the courts in uneven prosecution of the Huguenots was viewed as harshly as heresy itself. Such details about the disputes over the Peace of Monsieur indicate that the fiscal exactions and the policy of the Edicts of Toleration deepened the very social and cultural fault line that had been created by decades of friction between king and common people over fundamental issues of community definition. There had been long-standing debates over the ritual uses of public space and the maintenance of public order. That these had become more divisive issues was due, in part, to the presence of Protestants who challenged the traditional ritual system of Catholicism with all of its performative elements. The outcome of all these tensions was that the king was separated from his city while the bourgeois and common folk became more hostile toward the elite of the courts.

The Significance of the League of 1576

The turning point came in 1576, in the formation of the first Catholic League. The ultra-Catholics had begun to take the initiative ever since the massacres of Saint Bartholomew's Day in 1572. Given the absence so far of any clearly defined succession crisis, Henry III was able to defuse the movement and check Guise political ambitions by placing himself at the head of this new, national anti-Protestant coalition. While the League of 1576 was thus essentially co-opted and rendered harmless, its very appearance exposed three essential features of the emerging religious and political landscape.

First, Henry III, on the throne barely two years, and initially seen as a strong ruler, had lost the confidence of key elements among the Catholic elite and among local notables in Paris. Second, in this period the aims, ambitions, and organizing capabilities of the duke of Guise emerged more clearly than ever before. Henry, the second duke of Guise, regarded the House of Guise, whose ancestry he traced to Charlemagne, as a legitimate dynastic alternative to the ruling House of Valois. To preserve the catholicity of the realm and to extirpate Protestantism, the duke of Guise was prepared to work in close alliance with the forces of international Catholicism. Third, local Catholic notables in Paris had created a rudimentary network to link zealous Catholics in their neighborhoods with the Guise clientage system, as well as with strategic communal and international institutions.

The Gathering Forces of Militant Catholicism

The protagonists of militant Catholicism at this time included Philip II of Spain, the papacy, the Catholic princes of Guise, Lorraine, and Savoy, and transnational religious orders.[17] Among the religious orders that ultimately sided with the Catholic League were both new and old institutions. The

orders recently introduced into the capital as part of Catholic reform included the Jesuits, the Capuchins, and the Feuillants. Among the older
orders that had deep ties to the urban commune were the four original, so-
called mendicant orders of the capital: the Augustinian friars, the
Franciscans, the Dominicans, and the White Friars, called Carmelites. These
were closely associated in different ways with the University of Paris and its
theology faculty, the Sorbonne, which was the most militant voice of Catholicism within the capital. Within the roughly forty parishes of the city,
local religious associations known as confraternities also developed and
played an essential part in the conflict of the League of 1585. The most
militant of these were the Holy Sacrament confraternities and the confraternity of the Holy Name of Jesus, founded at Saint-Gervais parish. The
role that all of these institutions played in the Catholic League and in the
shaping of Catholic reform in Paris is complex. The analysis of testamentary evidence sheds much new light on this subject by revealing the place
these institutions had in the individual economies of salvation of Parisian
Catholics at the time of the greatest conflict between the monarchy and
the capital.[18]

The geographical distribution of these institutions within the city is
important in understanding the organization and development of militant
Catholicism following the League of 1576. The capital was divided into
three parts: the *Ile de la Cité*, the *Ville*, and the *Université*. Beyond these,
unenclosed by the ancient ramparts of the city and thus difficult to defend,
were the suburbs or *faubourgs*, *faulxbourgs* in the parlance of the period.[19]
The *Ile de la Cité* was the ancient center of the capital. On this island in the
middle of the River Seine were the cathedral of Notre-Dame and many
small parishes whose curates mobilized for the League. The right bank of
the Seine, known as the *Ville*, was the mercantile center of the city. On the
Left Bank was the University quarter, where, among the dense network of
parishes, were located the various colleges of the University and the great
houses of the four mendicant orders.[20]

The Institutions of Catholic Renewal and the
Spirit of the League

For Paris, the period from 1577 to the organization of the League in 1585
was a phase of relative calm amid the storms of civil war. The sixth war of
religion broke out in March 1577 and lasted only until September, when
the Peace of Bergerac ended the fighting. The seventh war of religion, which
began and ended in 1580, was fought principally in southern France, where

the Huguenot forces were concentrated. Within this general time period and slightly thereafter, institutions crucial to both religious renewal and the militant Catholicism of the League era appeared in Paris. The most important of these were the religious orders of the Jesuits, the Capuchins, and the Feuillants, and reformed Holy Sacrament confraternities. No unified history of all these movements and institutions exists because many of their activities were carried on in secrecy, despite their public flamboyance. Testamentary evidence makes it possible to understand how these movements and institutions became part of the religious experience of Parisians during the transition from late-medieval to early-modern forms of worship. To tell the larger story of the transformation of late-medieval Catholicism in Paris, this book will thus also have to explain the history of the Catholic League of 1585–94, which played a decisive but much disputed role in the shaping of early-modern Catholicism.

The League of 1585–94 was a complex phenomenon of magnate revolt and urban insurrection linked together by a movement of militant Catholicism. Although motivated by varying social and political interests, this Catholic coalition, often called The Holy League or *La Saincte Union*, was unified by the desire to restore the catholicity of the kingdom and to extirpate the Protestant heresy. The growing estrangement of ultra-Catholics (Catholics *zélés*, as they came to be called) from the monarchy in the person of Henry III (1574–89) stems directly from their particular understanding of the relation between sacral and political community.

During the 1580s the Catholic opposition focused on King Henry III's failure to pursue a vigorous campaign against Protestantism and ultimately his inability to ensure a Catholic successor to the throne. In May 1588, the Day of the Barricades, a popular uprising supported by the forces of the princely House of Guise (the leading magnate faction) and the *Seize* (the most militant urban faction), forced Henry III to flee from the capital. He would never return. Henry's revenge for the Day of the Barricades was the assassination of the Guise brothers in December 1588. Henry III was himself assassinated in August 1589 by a Dominican monk just as his army was poised for an attack on the capital. The forces of the League in Paris and cities all across France continued their struggle against Henry's Protestant successor, Henry of Navarre. Only Henry IV's conversion to Catholicism in July 1593 made the defeat of the League inevitable. Paris was formally restored to monarchial rule with Henry's entry into the capital on March 22, 1594.

During its six years of opposition (1588–94), when various factions of the Catholic League ruled in Paris, the city was galvanized by a complex series of forces. The magnate factions included the charismatic leadership of the princely houses of Guise and Lorraine and their clientage networks. The communal wing of the League was dominated by the organizational skill (some would say terror) of the *Seize* and their ability to mobilize local elites wishing to restore their social preeminence and to obtain a greater measure of municipal independence from the growing influence and control of the absolute monarchy. Interwoven with each of these factors was a multifaceted movement of Catholic renewal. This was in part a traditional mobilization against heresy. But it was also partly a reforming effort by new religious orders and zealous laypeople led by the highest prelates of the French church like the Cardinal of Lorraine, and reinforced from below by a spirit of popular militant Catholicism. In political terms, however, the Holy Union, *La Saincte Union Catholicque*, represented the most serious challenge to the French monarchy between the Hundred Years War (1338–1453) and the French Revolution of 1789.

To place this chronology of events in a broader historical context, four issues deserve closer analysis. The first issue, Parisian attitudes to heresy, and the second, the development of eucharistic and penitential piety in the context of the threat of heresy, take us back to the Paris of the 1520s, and reactions to Protestant iconoclasm. The third issue embraces the social and cultural changes accompanying the development of royal absolutism, especially social conflicts arising from efforts to reform popular religion and culture in the face of mounting public disorder caused by religious heterodoxy. The fourth and final issue relates to expectations of rulership and the attitudes of Parisians to the last Valois and to Henry of Navarre.

Catholicity in Kin and Kingdom: the Goals of a War against Heresy

For the contemporary reader, French Calvinism is scarcely a heresy, so it is necessary to examine the shared perceptions and behaviors that shaped the Catholic League's war against the religion it regarded as a heresy.

The plea of a young Catholic nobleman, dictating his will in Paris in 1590 as his death drew near, tells us much of what is necessary for understanding ultra-Catholic perceptions of religious nonconformity. In naming the executors of his will, Jehan de Peyere, a squire from "Lencung" in distant Languedoc, addresses a final appeal to save the soul of his brother and to preserve the natural order of succession in his family:

> . . . to his executors hereafter named he wishes that they might exhort and admonish his brother to withdraw from . . . the party of the heretics and embrace that of the Catholics, because the testator himself is at the

point of death, and, having concern for the soul of his brother, [the testa-
tor] implores, exhorts and admonishes his brother, fraternally in the name
of our savior Jesus Christ, that it may please him to leave and abandon
the heretics . . . because he is daily in danger of losing his soul, and so that
he may take the side of the Catholics and place himself in the service of
Messieurs les Mareschal et duc de Joyeuse. And if he does this, let it
please his mother not to choose any heir other than his brother, since he,
for whom the testator has always had brotherly love, is the closest and
most fit to succeed, if only he were not following the party of the heretics
thus rendering himself unworthy.[21]

As captured in his will by the notary Jourdan, the final thoughts of
Peyere form a seamless web: matters of the soul and its salvation are inseparable from convictions about the maintenance of social order and the duty
of a Catholic to serve his party's cause. Some Catholics engaged in elaborate legal subterfuges to keep family property together despite the apostasy
of a family member. Not so Peyere. There is a militancy of conviction that
organizes his thoughts and culminates naturally in the wish that his brother
actively serve the Catholic cause. For militants, the existence of Protestants within a kingdom that had a very special sense of its Christian identity created an unnatural state that imperiled the salvation of one's soul and
the natural order of succession in the world. The family was simply the
microcosm of the kingdom itself, where it was unthinkable that a heretic
could ascend the throne of France. In this religious and political culture,
toleration could never be a social norm.

The legitimacy of rulers depended upon their efficacy in defending the
faith. The sacral responsibilities of all those in power thus transcended any
other aspect of their authority. Historians' understanding of these cultural
expectations of rulership have created a new history of the Wars of Religion in France. For example, such forms of collective action as religious
riots and massacres, which once seemed senseless acts of cruelty and destruction, have been reinterpreted by analyzing their combination of religious motivation and collective political perceptions. For the Catholic
League, however, more conventional forms of political action, such as magnate revolt and urban insurrection, have specific religious, symbolic, and
liturgical components that remain unexplored. Moreover, with a few important exceptions, the ecclesiastical history of the League era has not been
integrated into the political history of the League itself.

Given these lacunae, this chapter will demonstrate the ways in which
political and religious forms of association are experientially part of a con-
tinuum of behaviors, like Peyere's seamless web. In the League era, special
links between piety and politics grew from a matrix of late-medieval tradi-

tions of public performance as varied as religious mystery plays, public preaching, and civic as well as religious processions. The sense of obligation to defend the faith actively, in a public manner, in performance of public action, and in public enactment of belief, thus depended upon long-standing traditions of civic and religious practice.[22]

Across the time span of the sixteenth century, several forces collectively called into question many of these traditional practices that had defined and celebrated membership in a sacral urban commune. The first of these was the growth of royal absolutism, which transformed the balance of social groups within the city by creating a privileged elite who became ennobled by purchasing royal offices in the sovereign courts in Paris.[23] This practice of sale or venality of offices was essential to the growth of royal absolutism. It helped to provide revenues for the insatiable fiscal appetites of an expanding state. Just as important, it was the foundation of a cultural and political alliance between the monarchy and a rising class of humanist-educated office-holders.

The consolidation of this new elite, idealized during the Wars of Religion in the figure of the "perfect magistrate," was the second factor that contributed to the erosion of traditional urban solidarities.[24] The social and political system of the late-medieval urban commune was based on a flexible hierarchy of unequals, the permeability of social boundaries, and a shared sense of loyalties to the municipality as well as to the monarchy. The high price of ennobling offices and the distinctive cultural identity, which this new elite cultivated with humanistic learning, created new and insuperable barriers to social mobility. Furthermore, many of the largest mercantile fortunes were invested in offices and rural estates, thus driving a wedge between former members of a loosely defined Parisian bourgeosie.

Thirdly, in combination with the above factors, divisive economic developments with an especially negative impact on the middle and lower reaches of Parisian society also weakened solidarities within the traditional urban commune. The sixteenth century was a period of growing luxury accompanied by a steep rise in prices.[25] Wages did not keep pace, which created tensions within the relatively privileged world of the guilds and craft production. From 1539 onward, royal legislation sought to break up the closed world of the great merchant and especially artisan corporations.[26] The royal government blamed the guild system for fomenting monopolistic conspiracies and thus driving up prices. Trade guilds were dominated by a rigid system of costly masterships. As a result, relations between guildmasters and their workers, or young *compagnons*, deteriorated. From the 1560s through the 1580s, armed conflicts took place between masters and their workers who were no longer joined with them in extended family units of production and sociability. The most corrosive result of these changes was an unparalleled increase of the poor in French cities. Journeymen (*compagnons*) unable to rise to masterships slid into poverty and were joined by an unparalleled influx of rural poor displaced into French cities. The traditional parish-funded system of poor relief proved inadequate. Two fundamental changes occurred as a result. From the 1530s onward, the municipality began to take over poor relief from the church. At the same time the first laws against public begging were enacted. The poor had, after all, once been God's most blessed, sure to inherit the kingdom of heaven. Now, among some citizens, they instilled social fear.[27]

In short, the culture of absolutism and the economy had in complex ways weakened the bonds between *officiers* and the middle and lower strata of the urban commune. In Paris, the dense concentration of legal institutions and their personnel gave a particular shape to socio-cultural and political conflicts. The social and cultural tensions that ultimately led to the formation of the Catholic League of 1585 were most pronounced between ennobled office-holders, such as magistrates of the most prestigious court, and the lesser men of the law, loosely termed the *basoche*. These lesser legal professionals included, at the upper ranges, attorneys, solicitors, and notaries. At the lower levels there were significant numbers of lesser court personnel such as clerks, ushers, and door-keepers. These various *gens de loi* had traditionally enjoyed neighborhood notability. The best examples of this during the League period are the notaries Hilaire Lybault in the parish of Saint-Merry and François Herbin in the parish of Saint-Gervais. These notaries were deeply implicated in League politics and religious mobilization. In 1590, both men served as notaries for several major *Seize* and other ultra-Catholics discussed in detail throughout this book. These notaries also drew up the exile procurations for the most extreme Leaguers of 1594, whom Henry IV banished because of their refusal to cooperate with the new regime.[28]

In the later sixteenth century the *gens de loi* as a group increasingly lacked the means to succeed in the higher-stakes competition for expensive venal offices. This produced a growing social and political disenfranchisement of a significant middle stratum of the urban commune. Richet identified this middling elite as a group of "intermediate classes" strongly mobilized for the League and close enough to the truly popular classes to rally them to defend traditional religion and traditional urban social structure and culture.[29]

Historians have presented the dissatisfactions of this middling elite primarily in social and political terms. They have argued that the middling elite was a "second bourgeosie" resentful of the emerging hegemony of the "first bourgeosie" composed of *officiers*.[30] In this view, the political mobilization of the middling elite for the League was rooted in frustrated social ambition; these men and their families were unable to rise socially in the more rigidly hierarchial urban system created by the growth of royal absolutism and the sale of offices in particular.[31]

New attitudes toward the poor combined with these tensions between magistrates (*officiers*) and the *basoche* to foster a new and increased scrutiny of public behaviors by clerical and lay elites alike. There were, for example, broad changes in ways of thinking about the etiquette of public, ludic, festive, and sacred behaviors. Historians have identified the increase of canon and civil laws focusing on public order and religious decorum throughout Europe from the late fifteenth century onward as part of a massive attempt by elites to "reform popular culture."[32] The timing and evolution of rulings by the *Parlement* from the early sixteenth century onward bear witness to this growing preoccupation. Office-holders in the *Parlement* exercised significant oversight functions for the maintenance of public order, *la police*, in the parlance of the times.[33] The rulings of *Parlement* thus cover a wide range of behaviors, which are useful barometers of changes in traditional patterns of urban sociability.[34] Examples of this legislation include an *arrêt* or law banning the sale of festive masks on April 27, 1514, because of "the many obscene and filthy things that monstrously take place."[35] The same theme of the improprieties caused by masking becomes associated, in the course of the sixteenth century especially, with restraints on festive and ludic behaviors sponsored by confraternities.

Confraternities are one of the most elusive yet strategic sites where elite desires to reform popular culture intersect with broadly held Catholic desires for a more intense religious experience. Despite the paucity of confraternal archives in Paris, other evidence makes clear that attitudes toward these mixed religious, trade, and political associations are a key to understanding the socially complex strands of Catholic militancy that emerge from the 1540s onward. Confraternal reform, which includes the suppression of banquets, rowdy processions, play-acting societies, and dancing, as well as masking became a political and cultural project that governmental and clerical elites pursued in different ways throughout the sixteenth century. The history of these projects offers prime examples of the reform of popular culture. In their full scope, however, these reform efforts are also intimately bound up with the emergence of militant Catholicism and the formation as well as dissolution of the Catholic League in Paris.

A brief analysis of a treatise on confraternal reform written toward the end of the sixteenth century will clarify how social tensions between *officiers* and the *basoche* spawned demands for the reform of popular culture while complicating enormously the cultural work of Catholic reform and the chances for harmony among the different factions of the Catholic League in Paris.

In Paris in 1604, Jean Savaron, an *officier* and magistrate in the *cour des aides* in Auvergne, published his *Traitté des confrairies*, followed in 1610 by a sequel opposing masking.[36] The *Treatise on Confraternities* exemplifies how changing cultural attitudes towards licit ludic behaviors on the part of a humanist-educated elite could fuel social hostilities among unequal members of the urban community. Savaron vents his social animus against the festivities of the law clerks of the *basoche*, while defending the sober gatherings of the magistrate's confraternity of Saint Yves to which he belongs. Savaron explains that at one time the *basoche* and lawyers were joined under the patronage of Saint Nicolas, who had been the original patron saint of lawyers.[37] In the later Middle Ages a division occurred, because at the festivities for Saint Nicolas students (*escholiers*) and clerks (*clercs*) took up masking and held raucous processions dressed as "kings," "dukes," "captains," and "soldiers," or "sometimes even dressed as bishops with crozier and miters."[38]

The lawyers found these representations offensive; they abandoned Saint Nicolas, banned lascivious dancing offensive to the modesty of women ("pudicité des femmes") and held a separate banquet "tempered by a joyful sobriety."[39] The lawyers' ball was noted for its "seemly gentility" deemed suitable even "for virgins and young ladies . . . and befitting to "good manners" ("sortable aux bonnes moeurs"). Savaron is anxious to expose his humanist learning and Stoic values, while emphasizing the social inferiority of the *basoche*. He provides a Greek etymology for this term and asserts that in French, *basoche* is related to "*basse souche*," literally, "low class." To clinch his argument about the superiority of the magistrates' and lawyers' confraternity, he asserts that "at the balls of his confraternity not even Cato could take offense."[40] Savaron had stated in the opening of his treatise that the guiding principle in his discussion of confraternities was the distinction between "religion" and "superstition." According to his definition:

> Religion is the thing that takes us closest to understanding of our creator, provided that it is not mixed with any superstition.[41]

"Natural reason," he concludes, tells us that "overzealous and indiscrete religion" becomes "superstition." This treatise is a good example of the way social tensions between *officiers* and the *basoche*, ultimately so essential to the formation of the *Seize*, could be part of a much larger debate about the nature of "true religion" and the public behaviors that were appropriate expressions of devotional sensibilities.

These same tensions between the *officiers* and the *basoche* also fanned the passions of popular Catholicism and thus complicated the tasks of religious reform as envisioned by social elites both lay and clerical. The presence of Protestantism in Paris made these intra-Catholic cultural wars all the more volatile at the same time that it made their resolution more urgent. Not surprisingly given the ritual life of the late-medieval and sixteenth-century city, many of these three-sided contests were fought over the proper uses of public spaces. It is at this juncture that the reform of popular culture and resistance to Protestant heresy became most problematic. In hindsight it is easy to see how the growing appeal of Protestantism in Paris was facilitated by the slow erosion of cultural consensus among Catholics about the appropriate use of public space. This breakdown of cultural consensus can be traced at least to the later Middle Ages.

The Challenges of Catholic Reform

The traditional forms of "social effervescence" that had sustained the late-medieval commune were founded upon a blending of the sacred and the profane. It is precisely this interweaving of religion and society that made it possible for testators of the 1540s to speak of honoring the escutcheons of the passion. Like Peyere in the 1590s, who prayed that his brother would serve the Catholic cause in the service of the Mareschal of Joyeuse, so city folk could speak of devotion to the arms of the passion. The difficulty of Catholic reform was that the very militancy necessary to defend the faith depended upon social forms and cultural values that the partisans of transcendence had called into question. Catholic militancy was thus a difficult subject for the clergy because, particularly during the League, it entailed "effervescent" behaviors that conflicted with reformist religious ideals. For example, the clergy made great efforts in Paris to thoroughly Christianize the celebration of the summer solstice, called Saint John's Eve.

Celebrations in Paris, at moments during the League, involved a union of civic and sacral performativity. This fusion of civic and sacral identity is the true "spirit of the League." The early acts of the revolutionary government included the addition of a large effigy of "Heresy," filled with fireworks, which was burned as part of the traditional festive fires of Saint John's Eve on June 23, 1588.[42] Another great performative moment was the famous Armed Procession of May 14, 1590, which celebrated the unlikely success of Parisians in repelling the attack of Henry IV during the early days of the great siege of 1590.

Such events were no mere epiphenomenon. Catholic militancy was dependent upon the very forms of late-medieval association such as confraternities and magnate leagues where the sacred and the profane were unsegregated. It is known that confraternities were ultimately "reformed" so that they were limited to their religious functions, as the Tridentine Decrees sought. In Paris this did not occur until after the defeat of the League. At the height of the League, religious associations such as Holy Sacrament confraternities, companies of penitents, and several special associations such as the Confraternity of the Holy Name of Jesus were militarized, making them the primary cells of League religious and political mobilization.[43]

The roots of these dual functions lie not only within the mixed civic and religious character of confraternities. They are profoundly embedded in late-medieval religious culture per se. Thinking back to Jehan de Peyere's plea to his brother to enlist in the Catholic cause, we might find analogous forms of "enlistment" in the way ardent Catholics of earlier generations thought about their kinship with the Holy Family. To express these sacred loyalties, late-medieval religion was replete with forms of allegiance where liturgy and militancy were linked.

Devotions that appear only in the 1540s wills suggest the soil in which these hybrid behaviors were nourished. The will of Yolland Bonhomme, dated 1544 from the University quarter of Paris, provides the example of devotion to the escutcheons or "Arms of the Passion," a popular late-medieval devotion in which the notion of kinship loyalties are combined with the imagery of putting on the livery of Christ.[44] The essential point is that in late-medieval Catholicism the available forms of enlistment were rich and varied and grew from the experience of both kinship with and combat for the sacred.

The Evolution of Forms of Combat against Heresy

The practice of defending the faith through honoring the real presence of Christ in the eucharist emerged as one of the earliest forms of communal mobilization to repair the damage of heresy. A slow and complex evolution took place in the forms of public devotion to the eucharist. These practices offer some of the best examples of behaviors where for a time socio-religious and political forms of action and association could be expressed and experienced as a relatively unproblematic whole.

Expiatory processions of the eucharist were among the very first public and collective actions taken in Paris in response to Protestant iconoclasm. As contemporary historians have become more attuned to the significance of public rituals and the special place of public enactment in late-medieval Catholicism, detailed descriptions of these expiatory processions have become familiar. One of the earliest reported processions took place on June 6, 1528, following the destruction of a statue of the Virgin in the rue des Rosiers. Félibien reports the "great scandal and enormous event" in which the statue was demolished and explains that a new statue made of silver was carried in the procession for the Feast of the Holy Sacrament on the following Thursday. The procession departed from the friary of the Mathurins located in the heart of the University quarter, soon to become infamous to some for its Catholic militancy. It wound its way across the Seine to the *Ville* or Right Bank of Paris to its destination at Sainte-Catherine du Val des Escoliers. The procession route passed the place "where the terrible event had occurred and prayers were offered to calm the ire of God and also in order to incite devotion in the people who had been so scandalized."[45] Félibien's reference to God's anger draws attention to the powerful penitential motives and need for atonement that surrounded eucharistic piety in this period. Heresy endangered the relationship of each and every individual with God. Protestant sacrilege against the Virgin attacked people's most beloved intercessor with Christ and necessarily brought God's wrath upon the entire community. Both guilt and its expiation took a collective form, the procession, and mobilized the most concentrated site of the sacred, the body of Christ as it had been transformed by the sacrifice of the altar.[46]

In the 1530s, the sacramentarian character of French Protestantism emerged clearly. This position entailed denial of the real and bodily presence of Christ in the eucharist. This critique, embraced by Calvin, struck at the immanentist core of Catholic ritual, the celebration of the mass. Priestly consecration of the host in the mass offered laypeople a bodily experience of their community with each other and with the sacred.[47] The mass was thus essential to the experience of living in a sacral commune. The events known as the Affair of the Placards of 1534, and especially reaction to it, show us the ways this was true.

Historians who have examined the impact of the Affair of the Placards agree that it forms a turning point for the practice of orthodox Catholicism in the capital. The real shock value of the broadsheets lay not so much in the verbal violence of the text or in any insistence upon salvation by faith alone.[48] The text challenged the efficacy of an entire ritual system by denying Christ's real presence in the eucharist and by damning the idea of the mass as a reiterative sacrifice. The author, Antoine Marcourt, saw the mass as the foundation of a defective society. His tract condemned the division of the human community into a privileged priestly class and a crowd of poor sinners who depended upon the mediation of priests as "worthless sacrificers" to reach God.[49] Why should the death of Christ be repeated? demanded Marcourt. Was the historic death of Christ in itself not adequate for the salvation of humankind? As for the real presence, Marcourt boldly asserted that "never was a real body in more than one place at once." From the Catholic perspective this new logic mocked the mystery of the eucharist and challenged the doctrine of transubstantiation, which since the high Middle Ages had provided a learned explanation of the sacrament.

The Spirit of the League and the Transformation of Eucharist Devotion

To conclude this contextualization of Catholic militancy, there is no better testimony than that of members of Holy Sacrament confraternities, the traditional associations that were galvanized during the League. Pierre de L'Estoile, who ridiculed the *Seize* as a "holy confraternity" (*saincte confrérie*), also ridiculed the religion of Pierre Delamer, a zealous Catholic and member of one of the most famous Holy Sacrament confraternities of the League era.[50] Delamer's will speaks eloquently of the "spirit of the League."

Delamer's will was drawn up at his sickbed in his house in the rue Saint-André-des-Arts on the 23rd of December 1590. The *minute* was signed by the notaries de Troyes and Bruyère. Delamer must have been very near death, for Descimon gives 1590 as his date of death. The precise timing of this will—it is essentially a deathbed document—tells us something important about the meaning of the testamentary act in Delamer's own economy of salvation and perhaps also in the religious culture Delamer shared with other testators whose wills were dictated *gisant au lict malade*, from their sickbed. It has been puzzling that so many testators, whose pious bequests evidence considerable religious scrupulosity, should wait until sickness to draw up their last will and testament, especially given the institutional insistence of the church that it was a fundamental Christian obligation.[51]

Delamer's will makes it clear that the very preparation for death was itself yet another site for the negotiation of meaning—the negotiation of salvation between laity and clerics. For so many testators the testamentary act could assume its full meaning only in a very personal eschatological context, that is, at the moment of one's own death. It is possible that the perplexing unevenness of testamentary evidence is not due to the haphazard approach of so many potential testators to the preparation for death. Rather, the meaning of the act is precisely the opposite: its full meaningfulness to individual Christians was as a true "last will" that could be such only

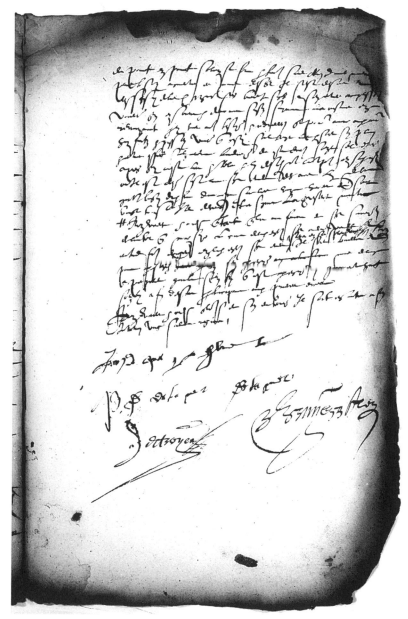

Figure 1. Signature page from the will of Pierre Delamer signed a few days before his death. (Centre historique des Archives nationales. MC/Etude CXXII, 1184.)

as the true last moments approached. This then explains from another perspective why the unexpected death was the greatest curse, because it rendered impossible all the acts that should truly be among the last things of
this world: the testament, the last confession, and the last communion.
Again there appear the age-old tensions between institutional requirements
and individual economies of salvation: institutional eschatology and personal eschatologies are always sites of negotiation and interaction between
laity and clergy.

To seek in this personal way to situate the testamentary act among the
very last things of this world is, of course, a wager—a wager seemingly characteristic of the older religious culture generally. Our healthy testators with
a predominance of pious motivations must thus be understood as having a
different conception of the testamentary act, one that may perhaps be seen
as more in conformity with the institutional requirements of the church.[52]
Understanding the function of the old personal eschatology, with its inherent risks of correctly gauging the moment of death, may help explain some
of the unevenness of testamentary behavior. This notion of the weight of
the older personal eschatology also clarifies why the new clerical initiatives
embodied in the *ars moriendi* functioned as a countervailing tactic in the
negotiation of the preparation for death.

And how is it that Delamer's will drives home this point so clearly? It is
precisely because of the extant *minute* (notarial copy) of his wife's will, dictated "en sa maison rue et paroisse Saint-André-des-Arts," "lying on her
sick bed" (*gisant au lict malade*), dated 22 October 1590 and signed by the
notaries Mathieu Bontemps and Marc Bruyère. Pierre Delamer surely could
have made his preparations in October with the notaries in his own home.
Why did such a zealous Catholic (*zélé*) choose not to do so? The answer lies
in understanding this very personal and very dangerous negotiation, which
was designed to maximize, at whatever risk, the meaningfulness of the last
will and testament—an act of negotiation that, by definition, could not, in
the older religious culture, be institutionalized outside of one's own
eschatological time and space.

Delamer's signature, written with obvious difficulty and barely legible,
is further evidence that his end is very near. No shortening of the preamble
or invocation occurs, however, and the formulas characteristic of the notary Bruyère are given in full, with the significant reference to the merit of
Christ's "saincte mort et passion." The body of the will is very brief. After
the election of burial in his parish church of Saint-André-des-Arts "in front
of the image of the crucifix," the essential funeral arrangements are left to
Delamer's executors, with the stipulation that they do their duty "according to his station in life" ("selon sa qualité").

Given this laconic structure to the will,[53] there is every reason to believe that Delamer treats in detail only the most essential elements of paramount personal importance. First come the final things of the *saeculum*, in the order in which (one is tempted to say) they weighed upon him and also because they impinged upon his own salvation. He deals first with the education of his son, which for him is clearly a matter of religious importance, both because of the choice of the Jesuit college and because of the oversight he asks of Christophe Aubry, adamant Leaguer and his curé:

> [The testator] wishes and requires that if it pleases God to call him away from this world that . . . his son be placed in the Jesuit college of the city of Paris or in another fitting place so that he may continue his studies. . . . [And the testator] to this end prays *Monsieur* his curate to act so that his son may be placed in the aforesaid college of the Jesuits . . . [and that *Monsieur* his curate] may keep an eye out that his aforesaid son be well and duly instructed there.[54]

There follow five clauses regarding debts he owes: for merchandise; for the funeral costs of his wife;[55] and for medical care from a nun ("une garde qu'il l'a pensé, une religieuse").

Then comes a typically formulaic closing: the election of executors *noble homme maistre* [blank space in the document], *advocat*, and *maistre* Jacques Bazin, *commissaire et executeur ordinaire du Parlement*. But before returning to the conclusion of Delamer's will, we must examine how this will as a whole relates to the central themes of this chapter.

Zealous Religion without "Science"

This remarkable will of *noble homme maistre* Pierre Delamer, a doctor and regent in the faculty of medicine and a known *Seize*, demonstrates more than the connections between Holy Sacrament confraternities and Leaguer politics. The directions he leaves for the education of his son in a Jesuit college reveal direct links between the League piety of the father and the religious socialization of the son, and thus show us a set of concrete mechanisms for change within the religious culture. This will demonstrates how individual religious and political engagement become social, even intergenerational, social action. In the father-son relationship, a quintessentially Leaguer religious institution, the Holy Sacrament confraternity, is connected in the most human terms to the institution of the Jesuit college. This will calls into question the stark distinctions that some historians have made between the late-medieval traditions of Leaguer piety and the rigor of

Jesuit scholasticism. Pierre de L'Estoile described Delamer in the following scathing terms:

> A doctor from the committee of the Nine [a Leaguer executive body] who had at least some zeal for God, but not of the scientific sort.[56]

Delamer's will with its bequest to the confraternity of "Saint Sacrement de l'Autel" in the parish of Saint-André-des-Arts, combined with his provisions for the schooling of his son with the Jesuits, when taken together with the 1590 will of Delamer's second wife, *honorable femme* Catherine Tronson, and the 1580 will of his first wife, Guillemette Belanger, suggests a network of relations woven of marriage, friendship, neighborhood, schooling, profession, clientage, Leaguer politics, and notarial practice.

Pierre Delamer, who is one of the few parishioners of Saint-André-des-Arts among the testators of the 1590s, in his will poses some problems for the canons of statistical sampling. In this case, a research strategy that focuses on all extant wills of a particularly strategic year offers the satisfaction of clarifying Labitte's comment in passing about Aubry's stirring up "the traditional spirit of the religious associations," which historians have found so perplexing.[57] These particular comments of Labitte require a gloss precisely because they take us directly to the intersection of piety and politics where, during the League, community and religion are most intensely felt among Catholic militants.

The all-important clause in Delamer's will in which he makes a bequest to the Holy Sacrament confraternity is actually the penultimate clause of the will. It is followed by a request for a *salve regina* on the day of his burial. The placement of these two pious requests outside the structure of the notarial formulas highlights their significance (hatch marks within the body of the will indicate where these two requests were to be inserted). This evidence, striking in its placement, in all likelihood captures the final recorded thoughts of a zealous Catholic concerning the provisions he could make for his salvation. The two directives need to be understood relationally not only in the context of the will as a whole but in relation to each other and to the institutions and rituals of immanentist piety.

First, the confraternity of Christ's body:

> [The testator] requires that the confraternity of the Holy Sacrament of the altar be given and paid by his aforesaid heirs four *sous* a year in order to be included in the prayers of the aforesaid confraternity, which *Monsieur* the curate of the church of Saint-André wishes and intends to honor in the aforesaid church of Saint-André and to bring it to its splendor.[58]

Then on the day of burial of his own body:

> [The testator] desires and requires that on the day of his burial there may be said for him a *salve regina*.[59]

In this closing, League time and reform time are joined in a personal eschatology where mother and son, body of self and body of Christ, holy league, holy confraternity, and universal church are made one once and in the perpetual prayers of his *confrères*. The reformist impulse is articulated in Delamer's desire to support the *curé* Aubry's efforts to "restore" devotion to the Holy Sacrament to its full splendor. Finally, the notion of splendor, with its visual resonance, anticipates the baroque epistemology defined at Trent. To understand the "science" of religion by which Pierre de L'Estoile ridiculed the spirit of the League, it is necessary to turn now to Jean Calvin.

Part Two

Calvin, the Council of Trent, and Zealous Catholicism

Chapter 2

CALVIN AND THE
CRITIQUE OF PERFORMATIVITY

Calvin's Short Treatise on the Holy Supper
of Our Lord Jesus Christ

Ironically, the Protestant Calvin introduced the standards by which zealous Catholicism would long be judged. Calvin's doctrine of the eucharist made the profound differences between the new Huguenot religion of transcendence and traditional Catholicism in Paris in the 1540s tragically clear. That these differences about the eucharist were part of a revolution in attitudes toward religious uses of the body has not been amply addressed by historians of the Reformation.[1] This chapter examines the language of Calvin's treatise on the eucharist and its confounding impact upon zealous Catholics in order to analyze the distinctive gestural cultures of Calvinists and Catholics.

The account of public disorders in Paris in the 1530s and 1540s revealed that veneration of the eucharist and celebration of the mass were the most inflammatory issues separating Catholics from Protestants. In the old religion of immanence, the eucharist had become the most perfect and powerful example of the connectedness of things (signs) and their actual referents (the signified). The longing for this unity is one of the dynamic forces in religions of immanence, particularly when they become destabilized by critiques that mock ritual acts or desecrate sacred objects, as so often occurred in Reformation Paris.[2]

Furthermore, for Catholics, the bread and wine of the mass could become the body and blood of Christ only through ritual performance, the act of consecration. In this sense the mass was the preeminent example of the creative power of ritual and one of the most concentrated forms of effervescent sociability, where performance brought together the body social with the body of God. Common terms in French expressed this profound reality: the term *lever-Dieu* (to lift up God) was used in the 1540s perhaps more than the more formal term, *élévation*, for the act when the priest turned to the congregation and raised high the consecrated host, which was Christ. The cleric, whose office it was to carry the host for the last communion of the sick and dying, was called simply a *porte-dieu*, one who "carries God."[3]

One of the most accessible and revealing of Calvin's writings on the eucharist is the *Short Treatise on the Holy Supper of our Lord Jesus Christ*.[4] Calvin penned the text in French from the safety of Geneva when he was attempting to heal the disputes between his reformed doctrine and that of Luther and Melanchton in 1542. Calvin begins by trying to define the eucharist in terms that might leave the door open for compromise with the Lutherans. Only in the second half of the treatise, devoted to perceived Catholic abuses, does Calvin show his hand. His scathing criticism and satire of the celebration of the Catholic mass lay bare his affective and visceral reactions to the "abuses" in the mass far more than do his purely formal texts, such as his *Institutes of the Christian Religion*. The tone and images in the second portion of his treatise thus bring us much closer to the tensions and conflicts between Catholics and Huguenots in the streets of Paris in the 1540s. The language of Calvin's discussion of Christ's eucharistic presence and Calvin's searing critiques of the mass as a reiterative and propitious sacrifice are especially revealing. His approach to these elements of doctrine raises questions about the experiential dimensions of religions of transcendence and religions of immanence. Comparison of these experiences provides a new way of examining debates about "true religion" in the Reformation. New interpretations of testamentary discourse also become possible because such a comparison underscores the sense of performance and sacred theater that was so essential to an immanentist experience of the mass. In other words, Calvin's satire inadvertently restores the mass to its place among a wide range of "effervescent" experiences that created the sacral and civic bonds of community in late-medieval cities.

The *Short Treatise on the Holy Supper of our Lord Jesus Christ* begins with an explanation of Christ's eucharistic presence and the believer's access to it. Calvin attempts to take conciliatory positions by stressing that there is actual participation in the body and blood of Christ. His close identification of Christ with the Word, however, transforms a palpable experience into one that is spiritual.[5] In fact, because of the preeminence of the spiritual Word in Calvin's understanding of the eucharist, and the resulting language, which derives from this understanding, his argument continually frustrates those seeking to understand the modalities of that actual participation, or "true communication." For example, Calvin states, " . . . we will confess, without a doubt, that to deny that a true communication of Jesus Christ is presented to us in the Supper, is to render this holy sacrament frivolous and useless—an execrable blasphemy unfit to be listened to."[6] His constant reiteration, however, of the terms "representation,"[7] "sign,"[8] and "figure,"[9] when speaking of Jesus in the sacrament itself, is warning enough that he rejects the immanentist concept of a palpable physical presence, which is the *sine qua non* of sacramental performativity.

Speaking Nominally

Although Calvin asserts that the Lord's Supper presents a "true communication of Jesus Christ," his language can only perplex those with an immanentist understanding of the eucharist. For proponents of the real and fleshly presence of Christ in the eucharist, Calvin baffles when he introduces the terminology of instruments:

> Now, if it be asked whether the bread is the body of Christ and the wine his blood, we answer, that the bread and the wine are visible signs, which represent to us the body and blood, but that this name and title of body and blood is given to them because they are as it were instruments by which the Lord distributes them to us.[10]

Calvin stresses that this figuration "by visible signs" is merely a concession to our human weakness:

> the communion which we have in the body and blood of the Lord Jesus ... is a spiritual mystery which can neither be seen by the eye nor comprehended by the human understanding. It is therefore figured to us by visible signs, according as our weakness requires, in such manner, nevertheless, that it is not a bare figure but is combined with the reality and substance. It is with good reason then that the bread is called the body, since it not only represents but also presents it to us.[11]

Trying to be conciliatory toward Melanchthon, Calvin uses the language of nominalism but seeks to deny the nominalist implications of his language. For the immanentist, mere instrumental figuration, as a concession to human weakness, belongs to an alien experience and understanding of the sacred. To the immanentist mind, when Calvin speaks of "names" and "titles," he talks about signs and not about the signified itself, the real and present body of Christ. For Catholics, to combine such figurative language with an argument for a real and palpable contact with Christ in "true communication" (*vraye communication*) created cognitive confusion. The lingering dualism between the sign and referent posed for them a terrifying prospect.

The specifically Leaguer frustration and incomprehension when faced with a battery of such abstract terms[12] can again be seen in reference to a Bordeaux treatise of 1577. This manual was written for members of the Holy Sacrament confraternity of Bordeaux that Catherine de Medici banned because of its militant opposition to the Peace of Monsieur. The unknown author of the treatise writes with genuine consternation about those like Calvin who say that:

> the body of our Lord is given to us [in the eucharist] only by sign and figure, by faith, and by thought and by fantasy and imagination and who knows what sort of substance of the body of our Lord they think they can distill as an extract from heaven in their Supper.[13]

Even without arguing that Calvin is fundamentally a nominalist, it is apparent that to Leaguers and immanentists his language operates in that mode.[14] It is striking that the term "imagination" in the Bordeaux treatise is precisely the term of complaint and critique that proponents of the promulgation of the Decrees of Trent used.[15] The concept of a figurative presence of Christ in the eucharist had come to have, in the late Middle Ages and in the sixteenth century, no meaning for all those who held to an immanentist understanding of the sacred.

The passionate objection in the Bordeaux treatise to Calvin's reliance on the reality of the figurative is evident in the sarcastic use of scientific imagery in "they think they can distill as an extract from heaven in their Supper."[16] Here the tables are turned, as "science" becomes fraudulent performance. The emotional chord struck by the terms "fantasy" and "imagination" (which is echoed by de Soulas, an advocate of the Tridentine decrees) lays bare the emotional realities. The term "imagination" and the Bordeaux treatise's satiric view of Calvin underscore the affective as well as cognitive challenge of Calvin's arguments. Again mocking Calvin's learning, de Soulas asks: "Tell me heretic, great lover of scripture, where have you found it written (that Christ says) 'figure' of my body. . . ."[17] This sarcastic challenge refers, of course, to the New Testament scriptural foundation for the eucharist: "Take, eat. This is my body. . . ."[18]

Calvin is said to be "inconstant" in speaking about Christ's presence in the eucharist:

> One minute he is a Lutheran, the next, in contrast, he takes on the personage of a Zwinglian, and like a juggler, a buffoon, now he says he is inside, now he affirms that he is outside.[19]

Clearly, amusements from popular pastimes make powerful images of deceit, fraudulence, and impropriety for militant Catholics, just as they do for Calvin himself. This is an important reminder of the dual contexts, the reform of popular culture as well as elite acculturation, in which Catholic reform and the complexities of League piety must be understood. These lines from the Bordeaux treatise are a telling example that the "popular" was becoming associated with the nonrational within some militant Catholic discourse as well. Indeed, after the defeat of the League, the critique of "popular" modes of performativity worked to create a cultural consensus among reforming elites who were otherwise separated by doctrine and devotional styles.[20]

The Bordeaux treatise also attacks Calvin and Luther simply as part of a long history of ancient, transcendentalist heresies. Catholics had their own very firm understanding of the historical place of Calvin, and two very different conceptions of history were at stake. Calvin is included in the attack on the Manichean belief that the flesh of man was created by the devil and "that Jesus Christ did not have a true humanity but a fantasy body."[21] The treatise critiques the heresies of Marcion for the same reason and sees Calvinist and Lutheran beliefs simply as a repetition of these ancient heresies.[22] The Bordeaux treatise provides a rare insight into the more strictly theological differences that Leaguers perceived between themselves and the Calvinists. The treatise goes on to argue that Calvin's position on the humanity of Christ was as heretical as the views of "Eunumius" [Eunomius], the Simoniens, the Carpocratistes, the Valentiniens, the Appollinarists, and finally, Berengar of Tours.[23] The essence of the Leaguer criticism attributes to Calvin the heresy of the Anomoeans (another Arian sect associated with Eunomius in the fourth century), who argued that *agennesia*, or "innascibility," was part of the essence of God and that Christ could not be like God since Christ, in his incarnation, lacked this quality.

Moreover, this treatise sheds new light on the theological and affective links between Leaguer circles of the 1570s and the *dévot* milieu in Paris in the first decades of the seventeenth century. For example, Pierre Bérulle, the intellectual center of Parisian Catholic renewal, is best known for his devotion to the incarnation of Christ. Bérulle's devotion to the full humanity of Christ expressed itself in adoration to the "incarnate Word." As is well known, Bérulle has been associated with adoration of a transcendant God. The Leaguer critique of Calvin makes it possible to offer a broader contextualization of Bérulle's true place within the immanentist world-view of the French school of spirituality.

Knowing and understanding from the immanentist perspective depended upon a real and stable cathexis with Christ in his body: upon a bodily presence, and a performative act.[24] Calvin goes on to assert the complete superiority of the spiritual over the physical. His passing disdain for the body sends the fatal signal:

> To maintain us in this spiritual life, the thing requisite is not to feed our bodies with fading and corruptible food, but to nourish our souls on the best and most precious diet.[25]

Spiritual bread is identified with the Word of Christ, his promise of salvation, which in the end becomes the most important component of the sacrament:

> But just as God has placed all fulness of life in Jesus, in order to communicate it to us by his means, so he ordained his word as the instrument by which Jesus Christ, with all his graces, is dispensed to us.[26]

Calvin's Critique: Divergent Concepts of Time and Knowing

When Calvin, in the second half of his treatise, addresses the abuses he perceives in Catholic practice, he focuses on "errors on the supper."[27] It becomes clear that his more general attack on performativity derives from this. Calvin views the passion of Christ as the one and only "one unique sacrifice,"[28] which occurred once in the historical past and which was and is fully adequate for the redemption of all sins. Calvin brings a radical historicity to sacred time, in which the past can only be accessed through imagination and understanding, not through gesture, utterance, intercessors, or performance.[29] The liturgical or performative concept of sacred time, on the other hand, depends upon localized and moveable objects, utterance, and gesture. The liturgical time that Calvin rejects is anchored in immanence, and in this way permits a powerful fusion of past, present, and future that is effected in ritual performance, in the use of evocative symbols, and in the adaptability of ceremonies to fit the needs of the human community. Liturgical time thus is the *sine qua non* for the construction of communities of sacred immanence and lies at the heart of traditional "effervescent sociability."[30]

For Calvin, the sacred past should be honored only in memory and understanding (*intelligence*), not in any form of bodily memory or ritual. Calvin, in effect, discerns two contrasting forms of understanding: "spiritual" understanding (a term he would acknowledge) and what may be called "bodily knowing," in which memory of a sacred past is evoked by place, time, gesture and physical utterance. Physical evocation through gestures and symbolism, such as liturgical number symbolism, has enormous power in making the past present and in infusing the sacred into the world and into the things of this world.[31] There is an immanentist epistemology, or way of knowing the sacred, that may be called bodily knowing. Bodily knowing mobilizes all the senses so that the experience of the sacred is grounded in the palpable and ascends, through the aid of symbols, to higher invisible truths. As the analysis of the Tridentine decrees on the eucharist will show, for Catholics, truth in the world remained essentially performative.[32]

The Meaning of Sacrifice

Calvin explains that the ancient fathers spoke of the Supper as a "sacrifice,"[33] and the reason they gave was,

> because the death of Christ is represented in it. Hence their view comes to this—that this name is given it merely because it is a memorial of the one sacrifice, at which we ought entirely to stop. And yet I cannot altogether excuse the custom of the early Church. *By gestures and modes of acting* [my emphasis] they figured a species of sacrifice, with a ceremony resembling that which existed under the Old Testament, excepting that instead of a beast they used bread as the host. As that approaches too near to Judaism, and does not correspond to our Lord's institution, I approve it not.[34]

He adds, " . . . for under the Old Testament during the time of figures the Lord ordained such ceremonies until the sacrifice should be made in person. . . . Since it was finished it remains for us to receive the communication of it. It is superfluous, therefore, to exhibit it any longer under figure."[35] This remarkable passage, with its sense of finality and historical distance with respect to the passion and death of Christ, delegitimizes an entire mode of human interaction with the sacred: the performative. The telling words in the passage above are "by gestures and modes of acting." For Calvin, after Christ's historical sacrifice, the very nature of figuration clearly changes. Figuration (as a mode of representation) no longer needs to be performative, nor should it be. At the heart of Calvinist critiques of the old gestural culture, in all its manifestations, is this new sense of historicity that requires a new mode of experiencing the sacred (the spiritual or interior). For Leaguers, however, denying performative figuration was equivalent to removing the sacred itself. Surely, this is part of the pathos of the penitential processions of the League era, which can be seen as one example of the supercharging of the gestural systems available in religions of immanence in order to attempt to restore sacrality to the commune through performative action.[36] It is also striking that the only wills of testators in the 1543–44 cohort that echo the anxiety surrounding such doctrinal debates in Paris in the 1540s come precisely from the cultural milieu of the University and the lesser men of the law who make up the largest group of *Seize* activists, the most militant wing of the League. The *avocat honorable homme* Valerend Choquet, whose will is discussed in more detail below, specifically states that the *basses messes* accompanying his services should be performed "every one with sacrifices."[37] While no statistical significance can be attached to this unusual detail, its presence in the will of an *avocat* from Péronne, the site of d'Humières's rising in the first League of 1576, raises interesting questions. Choquet is clearly on business in Paris and turns to the services of the notary Mussart, who drew clients from the University milieu. This suggests the existence of a sub-culture of militant Catholicism with roots going back to the early public clashes of Protestants and Catholics in Paris. That such a milieu existed is extremely likely, but the kind of social and cultural history that notarial archives make possible has not been carried out. This is especially true for the critical period of the 1530s and 1540s, when laypeople were galvanized by events like the 1534 Affair of the Placards both to defend and to reform their church's practices. Valerend Choquet is clearly defending the doctrine of real sacrifice, but he may be a reformer as well, protesting against the practice known as the *messe seche*, or literally, "dry mass." This practice of celebrating mass without consecration of the host and without priestly communion is denounced as an abuse at the Council of Trent. Valerend Choquet's will suggests that the relations between militancy, tradition, and reform could be complex and that they had deep roots in the social world of the University where the culture of scholasticism was married to civic traditions.[38]

Calvin's Critique of Transubstantiation

Besides his objection to the notion of sacrifice, Calvin's attack on the Catholic mass focused on the scholastic doctrine of transubstantiation, which the church had formally adopted as dogma only in the course of the thirteenth century. Transubstantiation from that point on became essential to the logic of the Catholic mass. Using Aristotelian distinctions between accidents (appearance) and substance (inner reality), Thomas Aquinas formulated the classic version of this doctrine in his *Summa Theologiae*.[39] Transubstantiation offered a scholarly explanation of precisely what took place at the moment of consecration, when the priest, during the Canon of the Mass, uttered "Take, eat. This is my body. . . ."[40] and declared the bread and wine to be the true body and blood of Christ.[41] The form of bread and the form of wine were but accidents, non-essential aspects of mere appearance. Priestly consecration, the essential performative act of the mass, had transformed the visible bread and wine into the true substance of Christ's body. Apart from the valuable but indirect evidence of Catholic preaching in this period, it is very difficult to know what ordinary laypeople thought about transubstantiation.[42] The word never appears in testamentary discourse

examined for the present study, not even in the often lengthy wills of clerics who value terminological distinctions. The terms *élévation, lever-Dieu,*
and *sacrifice* appear rarely, and only among the 1543–44 cohort of testators.
It will become clear that the League period is one of complex transition,
while references to taking "communion" do become much more common
by the time of the 1630 wills. Calvin's critique of transubstantiation embraces his rejection of the priestly office and his fundamental opposition to
the place of ceremonies in Catholic worship. Aside from his argument that
there is no scriptural foundation for transubstantiation (as there also is none
for the reiterative/performative sacrifice), his chief objection to transubstantiation is that it pretends to bring down a sacred body from its glory in
heaven, and in so doing entrains an endless series of ceremonies, involving
idolatry and superstition.[43] From Calvin's perspective, the notion of Christ's
bodily "local presence," conjured up by ancient doctors of the Sorbonne,[44]
opens the door to endless and abominable species of performativity. He
explicitly decries "carnal adoration," which he associates with the act "to
prostrate ourselves before the bread of the Supper.[45] He also condemns "other
superstitious practices, such as carrying the sacrament in procession through
the streets once a year or at another time making a tabernacle for it and
keeping it to the year's end in a cupboard to amuse the people with it, as if
it were a god."[46] The tone of this critique amplifies his objections to ritual
performance in Catholic ceremony. He goes on to compare the papal mass
to "une pure singerie et bastelerie"—that is, to buffoonery and apish tricks—
all mocking terms, which further deride popular amusements and drive home
the association of the popular and the irrational.[47]

Inherent in Calvin's attack on the mass is an explicit critique of
sacerdotalism. Calvin's objection here is that "the office of Christ has been
transferred to those whom they name priests." Priests commit an abomina-
tion, he argues: "For it is not merely said that the sacrifice of Christ is one,
but that it is not to be repeated, because its efficacy endures forever."[48] From
the perspective of sacred immanence, however, the very mode of the mass's
efficacy depends upon the metaphysical status of the priest. Sacerdotal performance introduces into the world a mode of action, the exercise of which,
Calvin believes, pretends to transfer to human beings powers that God alone
can exercise. The confusion of boundaries between the sacred and the profane thus emerges in Calvin's thought as the most execrable of human pre-
tensions. From the perspective of Catholic reformers, this transfer of metaphysical agency into persons and things that are *in* this world (though not
fully *of* this world)—priests or the host, for example—had created the possibility for profound confusion in minds not adequately trained in the science of religion.

Chapter 3

Sacred Performance and the Tasks of Tridentine Reform

The Condensation of Sacred Immanence

The primary goal of the Tridentine decrees was to provide a new doctrinal clarity about the nature of the sacred and about proper access to it. The church fathers at the Council ultimately decided that a more rigorously defined and vigorously applied sacramental system, including all seven sacraments defined at the Fourth Lateran Council in 1215, offered the most powerful reforming tool. The foundations of such a remedy were the mass and the sacerdotal office. Implicit in such an approach is what can be termed a condensation of sacred immanence. This entailed a strict hierarchial reordering of all that was sacred in the world and the condensation of all the sacred into primarily sacramental channels through which the laity would now have a more carefully supervised access.[1] Those experiences of the sacred that remained, but were not truly sacramental (for example, the intercession of saints, veneration of the Virgin, pilgrimages, and the use of "holy things" such as candles), would have to have their sacred status clarified in the language and logic of the Decrees. This task, as undertaken by the Council of Trent, required negotiation of a difficult passage between "tradition" and a newly defined sovereignty of doctrine.

Embracing Scripture and Tradition: the Complexities of Performative Reality

In one of its most famous pronouncements, the Council revealed the complexity of its task by acknowledging the value of "tradition" as well as "scripture" in defining sacred truth. The decrees from session 4 (April 1546) make clear that salvation is to be sought within the institution and the practices of the church. It also alludes to a special relationship between practice and sacred truth, a relationship that no Protestant reformer could acknowledge:

The council clearly perceives that this truth and rule are contained in written books and in unwritten traditions which were received by the apostles from the mouth of Christ himself, or else have come down to us, handed on as it were from the apostles themselves at the inspiration of the Holy Spirit. Following the example of the orthodox fathers, the council accepts and venerates with a like feeling of piety and reverence all the books of both the Old and the New Testament, since the one God is the author of both, as well as the traditions concerning both faith and conduct, as either directly spoken by Christ or dictated by the Holy Spirit, *which have been preserved in unbroken sequence in the catholic church* [my emphasis]. . . . [2]

In its effort to articulate a viable institutional means to salvation, the Council was aware that it faced multiple challenges. First, it had to take note of the humanist interpretation of the sacred that defined the Gospel or Word as the sole source of sacred truth.[3] For Calvin, it must be remembered, sacred history in the world had been displaced from the present and was now located in a closed moment of past time. The Council met this challenge of acknowledging the historicity of the sacred by asserting an alternative paradigm of religious truth. The Tridentine position recognized the centrality of the Gospel as preached by Christ but added to this principle its own performative understanding of religious truth based on "unwritten traditions" and grounded in liturgical time.[4] It is crucial to understand this alternative vision as something more than a mere strategy for institutional survival. There are obvious difficulties in arguing that these traditions "have been preserved in unbroken sequence." This chapter will focus mainly on the implications this argument had for Catholic reform of a performative and immanentist reality. This understanding of reality, or ontology of the sacred, has important epistemological consequences and experiential attributes that histories of the Catholic League and Catholic reform have ignored.

The Council's teachings and canons on the mass in particular had enormous potential significance for testators because of the central place the mass had generally attained in individual economies of salvation. There were, for example, ancient and complex traditions of prayers for the dead that had developed in widely diverse local settings. Such prayers could be offered in a variety of settings: in monasteries and lay devotional associations, by the poor, by prisoners, by friends and family. The office for the dead, originally a monastic development, became one of the most important elements in the evolution of liturgical piety and the emergence of the concept of a community of the dead that depended for its salvation on the prayers of the living.[5] In the course of the Middle Ages, there emerged a cultural consensus that the most effective form of prayer for the dead was the mass offered by priests exercising their sacerdotal function.

The mass by no means displaced other forms of ritual action that testators might wish performed on their behalf. An ancient religion of immanence, where salvation depended upon performance in this world, opened wide the doors to lay participation in the overall economy of salvation. The evolution of testamentary discourse and practice offers one of the richest possible records of the actual gestures through which the community of the living and the community of the dead interacted with each other and with the institutional church. These communities were united in defending a constantly evolving performative truth about the proper means of salvation. This performative quality of "truth" within the Catholic church meant that unlike Protestants, who sought to rely solely on the Word (truth embodied in Scripture), Catholics necessarily had to embrace and clarify performative traditions. The truth of performative tradition, by its very nature, acknowledged that human beings do participate in their own salvation and bring something of their own to it. This was a logical proposition directly in conflict with Calvin's concepts of sacred time and sacred truth, and with the doctrine of predestination in particular.

The historical difficulties for Catholic reformers, however, went far beyond problems of "works theology," free-will, and the inevitable diversity of practice in different times and places. Juxtaposed to the truth of scholastic logic (which itself implied a variety of experiences of the sacred) were the multiple realities of lay religious experience itself, which inhered within the "reality" of performative truth. Immanence and performativity were nourished in a visual, oral, and ritual culture. Their adaptation or reform by the Council of Trent posed great difficulties, not only in the context of a truly folkloric religious culture in the countryside, but also within late-medieval and sixteenth-century urban religious culture. Late-medieval and early-modern society entailed a complex overlapping of oral, written, and gestural cultures. Under these cultural conditions, distinctions among sacred spaces and sacred things, even for learned laypeople, were derived from visual and aural experience or, at best, the most casual contact with the written logic of the schoolmen, whose "truth" Calvin so derided. Strict hierarchical distinctions among varieties of the sacred were inevitably hard to convey or to maintain in the traditional religious culture of urban Catholicism.

Moreover, late-medieval Christianity may have been at a particularly difficult juncture in human relations with the sacred due to the plethora of devotional options available to the laity. The unparalleled availability of the sacred—precisely because it was the result of a performative understanding of the sacred—had begun to draw attention to the very nature of the sacred, i.e., to performativity itself. At the same time, clerical reformers within the late-medieval church were beginning to channel the sacred toward sacramental settings or sites where lay interaction with the sacred could come under more intense clerical supervision.[6] This is one clerical source of the intense scrutiny of manners, behavior, and decorum often labeled a general reform of popular culture.

Tridentine Solutions to the Proliferation of the Sacred: The Preeminence of Christ and the Eucharist

The Council of Trent met over a period of eighteen years (1545–63) in a total of twenty-five sessions, interrupted by numerous postponements, transfers, and intense behind-the-scenes debates conducted through commissions of scholarly specialists. The participants carried out a vast correspondence with interested parties all over Europe—all punctuated by the hope of some possible compromise with a range of sectarian positions. The discussion of the eucharistic real presence and the writing of canons on this subject came only in session 13, which began in October 1551. In session 13, devoted to "the most holy sacrament of the eucharist," the decrees used the term *latria* to emphasize the hierarchial preeminence of worship owed to the body and blood of Christ. *Latria* was distinguished from the special honor accorded to the Virgin in *hyperdulia* and the reverence accorded to the saints in *dulia*. *Latria* designated that form of devotion or "adoration which is due to the true God."[7] This in turn depended upon the doctrine of the real presence of Christ in the eucharist:

> In the first place, the holy council teaches and openly and without qualification professes that, after the consecration of the bread and the wine, our Lord Jesus Christ, true God and true man, is truly, really and substantially contained in the propitious sacrament of the holy eucharist under the appearance of those things which are perceptible to the senses. Nor are the two assertions incompatible, that our Saviour is ever seated in heaven at the right hand of the Father in his natural mode of existing, and that he is nevertheless sacramentally present to us by his substance in many other places in a mode of existing which, though we can hardly express it in words, we can grasp with minds enlightened by faith as possible to God and must most firmly believe.[8]

The teaching on the real presence, "the reality of Christ's flesh and blood" in the eucharist,[9] became the cornerstone of a devotional style, articulated more clearly and powerfully than ever before on the preeminence of the eucharist and on the correct devotion owed to this most "sublime and venerable" of all the sacraments.[10] In the case of the eucharist, the performative view of the sacred was at one with itself and was most perfect. Scholastic logic, in the doctrine of transubstantiation, asserted the perfect unity of sign and symbol.

The Eucharist as the Sacrifice of the Altar

The second pillar of Tridentine sacramental theology was the teaching on the priesthood and its performative relationship to Christ. In the Tridentine decrees on the "sacrament of order" (ordination), a particularly Tridentine theory of performance was articulated that begins to suggest the power that symbolic thought retained even within a reformed performative tradition. Issued only toward the very end of the Council, in session 23 on July 15, 1563, the first chapter on the office of the priesthood illustrates the inextricable relations between the sacerdotal function and performative reality:

> Sacrifice and priesthood are so joined together by God's foundation that each exists in every law. And so, since in the new covenant the catholic church has received the visible sacrifice of the eucharist from the Lord's institution, it is also bound to profess that there is in it a new, visible and external priesthood into which the old has been changed. The sacred scriptures show, and the tradition of the catholic church has always taught, that this was instituted by the same Lord our Saviour, and that power was given to the apostles and their successors in the priesthood to consecrate, offer and administer his body and blood, as also to remit or retain sins.[11]

This excerpt points to the two sites, the eucharist and sacerdotal office, where form and function—form and performance—are perfectly linked, without contradiction. But, how does the Tridentine idiom reflect an awareness of the ways in which the traditional immanentist and performative practices of the church entail the possibility for plural and participatory understandings of symbolism and the theories of representation upon which they depend? We encounter great difficulties in practice when trying to limit the application of the performative theory of representation to the performance of the mass alone. From an institutional perspective, the opportunities for local appropriation of the sacred and the inherent multiplicities of meaning that flow from the presence of the sacred in this world constitute perhaps the biggest obstacle for an ancient religion of immanence founded on traditions of performativity. The immanential view of the sacred also powerfully suggests that visible signs have a performative realism. Visually and experientially, thus, it is extremely difficult to maintain strict distinctions between the sacramentally performative that possesses metaphysical efficacy and the merely didactic power of symbolic thought. For example, to differentiate between mass and the eucharist versus other embodiments of the sacred (candles or holy water) that have no sacramental status demands a necessarily more deocentric focus and a more careful distinction between things sacred and things of this world. Such conceptual distinctions are not at all incompatible with the doctrine of sacred immanence but do require some condensation of the sacred into much more carefully circumscribed settings where the hierarchical ordering of the sacred is made explicit.

In the decrees themselves, these boundaries between the domains of practice and experience are also blurred in the language of the text. The opening passage of session 22 asserts that the eucharist is "a true and unique sacrifice," which remains unique in each instance of its performativity. Such an assertion of unique repetition logically requires the existence of a sacramental mode of performance in which time itself is liturgically transformed in ways that Calvin explicitly denied in his version of the historical uniqueness of Christ's sacrifice. For Calvin, Christ's sacrifice occurred only once. Calvin placed this historical understanding of the passion over and above any liturgical representation of Christ's sacrifice.

The language of the Council of Trent in session 22 on the mass stresses that Christ's passion and sacerdotal sacrifice share a performative reality. In chapter 1 of session 22, there are passages that suggest a veritable identity between Christ's sacrifice and the offering of the mass. The eucharist and the priesthood are explained in the following terms:

> And so he, our Lord and God, was to offer himself once to God the Father on the altar of the cross, a death thereby occurring that would secure for them eternal redemption. But his priesthood was not to be eliminated by death. So, in order to leave to his beloved spouse the church a visible sacrifice (as human nature requires), by which that bloody sacrifice *carried out* [my emphasis] on the cross should be represented, its memory persists until the end of time, and its saving power be applied to the forgiveness of the sins which we daily commit; therefore, at the last supper on the night before he was betrayed, as the catholic church has always understood and taught, he announced that he had been appointed for ever a second priest in the order of Melchisedech, offered his body and blood to God the Father under the forms of bread and wine, and handed them to the apostles under the same material symbols to be received by them (whom at that point he was making priests of the new covenant), and he commanded them and their successors in the priesthood to offer them by the words: Do this in remembrance of me.[12]

The text of the decrees demonstrates the power of symbolic modes of thought such as metonymy. In the phrase "the altar of the cross," metonymy creates a close association of eucharist and passion. In the passage below, this is heightened by employing the same verb for the "unique" sacrifice.

In the very next segment of session 22, there is a repetition of the verb *peragere*, which thus links Christ's supreme performative act of sacrifice on the cross and the sacrifice of the mass:

> In this divine sacrifice which is performed in the mass, the very same Christ is contained and offered in a bloodless manner who made a bloody sacrifice of himself once for all on the altar of the cross. Hence the holy council teaches that this is a truly propitiatory sacrifice. . . . For it is one and the same victim here offering himself by the ministry of his priests, who then offered himself on the cross: it is only the manner of offering that is different. For the benefits of that sacrifice (namely the sacrifice of blood) are received in the fullest measure through the bloodless offering, so far is this latter in any way from impairing the value of the former. Therefore it is quite properly offered according to apostolic tradition not only for the sins, penalties, satisfactions and other needs of the faithful who are living, but also for those who have died in Christ but are not yet fully cleansed.[13]

If the argument appears to waver between symbolic identity and a veritable ontological identity of the two sacrifices, this is because there was far from unanimity among the theologians at Trent on this central but difficult question. Such a lack of learned consensus only reinforces the likelihood that theological distinctions between hierarchies of the sacred were difficult for the laity to make in "a late-medieval world saturated with sacramental possibility," as Gail McMurray Gibson very appropriately puts it.[14] The measures ordered by the Tridentine fathers to eliminate abuses, misunderstandings, and superstitions regarding the sacred were attempts to address the ambiguities about the precise locus of the sacred in the world. A definition of this locus had long engaged Catholic reformers, and the unresolved ambiguities surrounding this question contributed greatly to the ferment of the Protestant reformation over such issues as justification and the source of sacred truth. Under such circumstances, where Catholic reformers themselves had not reached a consensus, many historians have understandably either avoided the question of lay understanding of the precise locus of the sacred, or had difficulty in determining the experiential awareness of these boundary-setting tensions among Catholic lay persons.

The following passages from drafts of the decrees make clearer the centrality of performativity in understanding the action of the mass than do the decrees themselves:

> Besides, Christ understood by the words "Do this," not only that they should enact the memory of the supper but that they should enact the

memory of the offering carried out on the cross. Just as, if we do not eat, we do not represent that supper of Christ, so if we do not make an offering and sacrifice, we do not represent the sacrifice made on the cross. For Christ did not say "Say this" but "Do this," as he signified a commemoration to be done not by words but by an action.[15]

The passage brings us the famous concept of the working of the sacrament "by virtue of the work having been performed" (*ex opere operato*), which, in its passive construction, suspends *in abstractum* the question of how one should understand the relations between orders of being and between the sacred and the world (*operato* is a form of the past participle). In noting here the grammatical absence of a true subject, one sees that sacramental action by the instrument of grace raises many practical questions about the agency of the sacred in the world.

René Benoist on the Power of Symbolic Thought

In 1564, just after the formulation of the decrees on the priesthood from session 23, René Benoist published his *Traicté de la messe qui est le sacrifice evangelique*, dedicated to Marie Stuart.[16] Benoist's text provides an example of how easily, from the experiential perspective of the lay observer, symbols and their epistemological value of leading from the visible to the invisible could become intertwined with notions of the metaphysical efficacy of the symbolic things themselves. Such distinctions are particularly hard to maintain within systems governed by a performative understanding of the sacred, especially if the experiential frame of contact with the sacred is primarily visual and unshaped by written doctrinal precepts or inculcated by religious education. Benoist opens his argument by declaring that the priest, in his exterior manner and actions, represents the passion of Christ. In detail he goes on to explain the ways in which the vestments of the priest represent Christ, for whom the priest is minister.

> For in the first place the priest wears vestments which signify and represent that which happened to our Lord in the passion: that is to say the miter signifies the way he was violated and struck in the face: the alb signifies and represents the way he was mocked and cast down in a white robe in the house of Herod. . . . The cloth, the stole, and the cord signify the way he was bound up to be whipped: the chasuble signifies the purple robe in which he was shown to the people. . . . In this way the evangelical priest, thus dressed in the vestments of the chuch, represents our Lord Jesus Christ for whom he is a minister.[17]

Benoist's description of priestly vestments reveals the tensions and richness of relations between immanentist epistemology, which is inherently and necessarily performative, and the sacramental performativity of the priest in the mass. Benoist carefully explains the meaning, symbolism, and significance of each element of priestly vestments and thereby demonstrates the power of symbolic modes of thought in the sixteenth century. From the experiential perspective of one looking at the celebration of the mass, how would one differentiate between symbols that are sacramentally charged and symbols that *only* connect orders of reality and hence only enhance understanding but not being?

Only sacramental teaching that provides clear distinctions between the sacraments and other ceremonies and sacramentals can cognitively reorient the impression made by sacred performance.[18] While some would argue that Trent sought to make such distinctions unambiguous in the visual and experiential frame of the laity, in religions of immanence this is a difficult task. The appeal of the transcendentalist solution, which compartmentalizes the world in order not to compartmentalize the sacred, is evident. For Catholics, however, such compartmentalization clearly could involve a wrenching loss of cathexis with the sacred in the world. Leaguers resist the compartmentalization of the human community for precisely these reasons.

Distinguishing between performative actions of fundamentally different powers—the sacramental as opposed to the merely symbolic—is experientially and visually a demanding task. The complexity of this task is obvious from the quotation above. The last lines of the passage cited describe a sacramental act, since the basic reference is to the priest who "represents our Lord Jesus Christ." Yet the context introduced by *ainsi orné* ("thus dressed") refers to vestments, which merely enrich the symbolism of the visual frame without themselves being essential to sacramental performance. Benoist adds that all the signs made by the priest signify the crucifixion of Christ. Here again we see the ambiguity of performative representation, because even the signs that are part of the consecration (although the words actually consecrate) are enclosed in a space where multiple forms of symbolism are intermingled. The logic by which laypeople organize visual perception may be quite different from the written logic with which schoolmen expressed their scholastic understanding of the sacred. The distinctions occurring within liturgical performance are inevitably hard to discern for the laity unless vernacular explanation is provided either during the ceremony or through sustained educational efforts.[19]

If the Tridentine text on the mass is juxtaposed with Benoist's text on the priest and his vestments, it can been seen that, experientially, sacramental performance occurs precisely in conjunction with what might be called the merely symbolically performative. Both texts refer to phenomena that occupy the same experiential or visual frame, sacerdotal celebration of the mass. The obstacles to implementation of Tridentine reforms are thus located in the domain of lay experience of the sacred and are not merely a matter of doctrinal clarification, although the two are, of course, connected. The transcendentalist "solution" is simply not an option; it is the "other" ontology. Performativity in a context where human agency of some sort is acknowledged can only with difficulty be declared objective. The concept of *ex opere operato*, "by virtue of the work having been done," postulates that sacraments work objectively. This discrepancy calls for two different theories of performativity and, thus, depends upon the acceptance of hierarchies of the sacred inscribed in new boundaries and new hierarchies of the sacred. *Ex opere operato* does not really provide an experientially oriented explanation, yet it is the lay experience of the sacred that Trent inevitably confronted and desired to change. Benoist acknowledges some of these difficulties in his *Catholicque et utile discours des chandelles, torches et tout autre usage de feu en la profession de la foy et religion chrestienne* of 1566. Addressing the objections of heretics to the use of lights, his response speaks to both ontology and experience: "we are not able to be perpetually in abstraction."[20]

His statement about the reality of lay experience clarifies the profundity of the objections to a "communion par imagination," which Catholics frequently raised. Based on an understanding of the different conceptions of time and theories of representation uncovered in the analysis of Calvin's treatise and our analysis of Trent, two additional and interrelated issues emerge. The first concerns the inherent logical and historical complexities that Tridentine reform confronted in defending "tradition," in addition to Scripture, as a source of religious truth. This by no means denies the complexities and contradictions in the notion of Scriptural truth. Catholic reformers, however, faced particular and local traditions of ritual performance where lay religious experience was largely unshaped by scholastic distinction. The second issue that deserves our attention is how the Council of Trent tried to deal with this divergence of lay traditions from newly enunciated norms of doctrinal truth and new norms of ritual decorum. One approach, which has sometimes led critics of Tridentine reforms to speak of the "apotheosis of clericalism," was to focus on the affinity between Christ and the priesthood. The Council fathers at Trent stressed that the priest is transformed in ordination so that he may replicate, in a performative sense, Christ's sacrifice of the cross and the giving of communion in the Last Supper. Thus, only the strictest enforcement of hierarchical distinctions governing the nature of the sacred and forms of ritual performance could serve as the basis for the condensation of sacred immanence that Tridentine reformers perceived as necessary. The Tridentine "sanctification" of the priesthood thus represents a response to ontological necessities, which were, in turn, linked to choices about hierarchy and boundary-setting in the broadest sense and with regard to the nature of the sacred in the world.[21]

Difficulties arise, however, because the immanential view of the sacred powerfully suggests that visible signs have a performative realism. The model (the pure performative ontology) is, of course, the eucharist itself: the visible signs of bread and wine are the true body and blood of Christ. This is the most radical example of a performative theory of representation. Problems arise, however, if the same logic is applied to the requirements of performative realism in the function and figure of the priest. In that case, the distinctions between performative representivity, in which a true metaphysical efficacy inheres, and other less potent forms of symbolic presence become less clear, despite Tridentine efforts at boundary-setting and definition.[22]

The Importance of the Festival of Corpus Christi

The explication of the Festival of Corpus Christi, which arises in the context of the discussion of *latria*, represents one of the most revealing examples of the Tridentine approach to devotional reform. One can think of the foundation of the Festival of Corpus Christi in 1264 as the ancient performative roots of the condensation of sacred immanence. The newly instituted festival celebrated the growing preeminence of eucharistic devotion. The history of this festival would provide a history of performativity itself in the high and late Middle Ages. In this period, confraternities of the holy sacrament were founded so that their members could march in the festival's procession. As seen in the Bordeaux Treatise of 1577, these same confraternities led the way for both militant Catholicism and intensified eucharistic devotion. During the period of the League, in these processions, the bonds of brotherhood corresponded with the deepening of eucharistic devotion. In Tridentine reform the hierarchical impetus of Catholic reform overcame the effervescent sociability of the League.

The Council of Trent thus articulates its epistemology and ontology of the sacred, amid competing pressures for popular performativity, transcendent spirituality, and a more exclusively sacramental performativity. That there is almost no discussion of the liturgical calendar in the decrees only emphasizes the importance given to this particular festival. The Festival of Corpus Christi is singled out for discussion in a way that makes clear that the triumphant eucharistic processions of the *Fête-Dieu* are both the symbol and embodiment of Christ's victory over death. The parallelism and interdependence of the public triumph of eucharistic adoration and the Church's triumph over heresy are made explicit:

> And thus indeed must truth the victor, celebrate a triumph over false-hood and heresy so that, confronted with so much splendor and such great joy of the universal church, her enemies weakened and broken may fall into decline or, touched by shame and confounded, may in time come to repentance.[23]

The Latin phrase *triumphum agere* states perfectly the performative and public nature of the truth that the Corpus Christi festival celebrates. The text makes evident that the procession is intended to evoke awe and reverence, as well as personal introspection about one's inward state of preparedness to approach the sacrament and to receive it with "great reverence and holiness."[24] The didactic elements even in the processional setting are striking, and serve to tie this most powerful affective symbol directly to the sacramental system. In this way the cultivation of an inward state of purity becomes a precondition for even visual access or proximity to the body of Christ. In the emerging vocabulary of baroque piety, "splendor" is both symbol and reality of the victory of Christ over heresy. This duality, which is also unity, represents and enacts the triumph of an immanentist and performative understanding of the unity of sign and symbol and is a source of dynamic tension in the baroque.

The *Fête-Dieu* is a perfect example of the delicate process of reforming sacred immanence. In embracing the *Fête-Dieu*, the Council of Trent understood that the victory of immanence over transcendence required the performative recapturing of public space. But much of Tridentine reform did not grow out of a need to meet a transcendentalist challenge. Indeed, both the reform of immanence and the assertion of an ontology of sacred transcendence grew out of ontological and experiential tensions within the religious culture of the late Middle Ages. Catholic reforms of devotional practices relating to the eucharist were not simply a response to perceived abuses in popular religion. To focus exclusively on the reform of popular culture misses the great ontological drama, which was inherent within the system of sacred immanence itself.

It is crucial to emphasize that ontological dilemmas were scarcely an abstract problem for men and women of the sixteenth century when confronted with the question of their salvation. For our testators it is a question of how one knows Christ and how one best establishes a relationship with Christ in crafting a will. The testators of sixteenth-century Paris were not confused about the source of salvation.[25] Some have made the argument that the uniquely sacramentally performative (the sacrifice itself) fell from sight at the end of the Middle Ages.[26] While one expects to find a picture of orthopraxis in testamentary discourse, it is worth noting that there are remarkable examples of cognitively acute, as well as affectively powerful, forms of devotion to the eucharist that may accompany an expansive votive orientation.[27] In other words, a strong christocentric orientation in the language of a will may include an extremely long list of saints whose intercession the testator seeks. Tridentine reform did, however, raise a complex set of questions for those steeped in the culture of sacred immanence and the profusion of forms of performative symbolism. Does one know Christ in word or in gesture, and if in both, how is one to express those combinations of understanding? How do testators negotiate the questions of boundaries between the multiple relations to the sacred offered by the traditions of immanence and performative truth?

Chapter 4

LEAGUER ZEAL AND
Politique RATIONALITY: GESTURE AND
COMPETING VISIONS OF AUTHORITY

From Gestural Culture to Epistemology and Politics

The view of *politiques* examined in this chapter shows us how a change in the norms of acceptable performativity created the preconditions for the triumph of *homo politicus* and set the stage for the defeat of the traditional culture of sacred immanence. Three of the founding fathers of the *politique* tradition of historiography—Pierre-Victor Palma Cayet (1525–1610), Estienne Pasquier (1529–1615), and Pierre de L'Estoile (1546–1611)—were highly critical of the League. These writers' assessments of the League give new insights into the socio-cultural and political conflicts that conditioned the transition from late-medieval to early-modern forms of worship in Paris. A close textual analysis of their writings reveals the profound differences over structures of authority and attitudes toward the sacred that separated them from their Leaguer opponents. Of the three writers considered, only Palma Cayet was a latter-day convert to Catholicism. Pasquier and L'Estoile were loyal Catholics, ardent defenders of the Gallican church and its traditional liberties, and enemies of superstition and ceremonial superfluities in matters of religion. Examining the values and sensibilities that underlay their hostilities towards the League offers a more nuanced understanding of the tensions within Catholic reform and the clash of social and political interests that shaped the local dynamics of the Catholic reformation in Leaguer Paris. This analysis will, in turn, reveal that the contests fought out amongst Catholics at the time of the League had enduring consequences for the construction of boundaries between the sacred and the profane.

Politique historiography of the League is important since *politique* texts, like *politique* action, depended upon the creation of boundaries between the sacred and the profane. This act of compartmentalization is of historic significance because it established the basis for a new standard of rationality that was openly hostile to religious enthusiasm. The *politique* critique of League religiosity redefined sacrality and legitimized the new epistemological status of "reasons of state." There is thus a direct line of descent from the defeat of the League to the Day of the Dupes and France's entry into the Thirty Years' War against Catholic Spain.[1]

What may appear in the *politique* writings as local debates over social status and processional decorum are, in fact, furious contests for power: power to shape the boundaries of community, power to decide the norms of behavior considered rational, and power to shape a new epistemology for narrative truth. Although as individuals, *politiques* may be well known only to specialists in French legal and political history, it would be difficult to overestimate their significance in shaping the political culture of *ancien régime* France. At one of the most critical junctures in French national development, at the close of the sixteenth and the beginning of the seventeenth century, *politiques* provided the cultural counterbalance to the religious fundamentalism of Leaguers. The way in which *politiques* rallied to the cause of the French monarchy, in the person of Henry IV, arrested the growth of centrifugal forces, regionalism, urban particularism, and magnate ambitions, which Leaguer ultramontanism and ties to Spain would surely have nourished.[2] The historical boundaries of France and the degree and nature of national integration were all far less decided in the late-sixteenth century than subsequent history would lead us to think. In this sense, subsequent history has obscured the importance of *politique* opposition to the forces of the League and veiled the contingent and even unstable character of French national development during the Wars of Religion.[3]

Because it is unwise to generalize about a cohesive *politique* party throughout the decades of the civil wars, the analysis here focuses on the *politiques* of the late 1580s and 1590s. During this period one may speak of a certain unity among those who rallied to Henry of Navarre, opposed the League, and accepted, in many cases reluctantly, the necessity of religious toleration.[4] Although Palma Cayet, Pasquier, and L'Estoile are diverse in background, they were hostile toward the League and adamant in their defense of the rights of succession of Henry of Navarre. Their accounts, written largely contemporaneously with the events themselves, lend particular significance to their views. Their works and their wide reception were largely responsible for passing down to posterity specific, profoundly negative evaluations of the League.[5] In the *politique* tradition, misunderstanding and *mépris* of the Catholic League are rooted in three historical judgments: 1. a denial of the religious motivation of the League; 2. a deliberate misrepresentation of its social recruitment, particularly by ridiculing as "rabble" its urban and more "popular" faction, the Paris Sixteen; and 3. a profound cultural distrust and rejection of the League's strong Italian and Spanish influences, not only in matters of high politics. More significantly, this distrust entailed an intense antipathy toward the exteriorized and somatic qualities of Leaguer piety that were identified as Spanish or Italian. This antipathy was rooted in a north-south cultural conflict that expressed itself in sixteenth-century France in acute cultural xenophobia that is carried forward into ambivalence about the baroque and Italian and Spanish cultural models in particular. When analyzing the three misunderstandings in *politique* tradition of League historiography, it is necessary to recognize at the outset that, although they may be presented as analytically distinct, they are profoundly interdependent. Even the language of one of these authors serves to unmask meaning in another. In fact, the ways in which each of these three judgments flows into the others accounts, in large measure, for the persistence of negative evaluations of the League.[6]

The first judgment—denial of the religious motives of the League—is in many ways the most complex phenomenon because it is simultaneously cause and effect of the negative evaluations of the League. The examination of Palma Cayet, Pasquier, and L'Estoile will show that they deny the religious content of the League in many ways. Exploring this often venomous "denial" reveals a complex and fascinating debate among Catholics about what constitutes "true religion," and about rationality as opposed to "idolatry," "superstition," and "zeal." By examining the way *politique* texts generate these dichotomies, it is possible to gain a direct and experiential understanding of the competing visions of authority, Leaguer and *politique*, that shaped the transition from late-medieval to early-modern Catholicism in Paris.

Palma Cayet's Denial of the League's Religious Content

Politique historians have been most emphatic and scathing in denying the religious motivations of Leaguers. The best introduction to this particular misunderstanding of the League comes from the histories of Pierre-Victor Palma Cayet, who was a learned humanist and royalist historian with close personal ties to the new monarch, Henry IV (1589–1610). A student of Theodore de Beza (Calvin's successor), a tutor of Henry of Navarre, and pastor to Henry's sister, Palma Cayet reentered the Catholic church as a priest in 1595. His career as religious and political partisan exemplifies many complexities of the period; his own confessional evolution matches that of the monarch he served.

Palma Cayet, as *chronologue de France*, pronounced with epigrammatic certainty on the struggle of the League against Henrys III and IV. The very term *chronologue*, a chronologist, or describer of the times, anchors his account in an objective dimension completely at odds with Leaguer conceptions of time and sacred history.[7] His judgment that "This was a war for the State and not a war for religion"[8] was the most damning possible statement that could be made about the militant Catholic cause, since it denied the religious component of the movement altogether. Palma Cayet focuses principally on the political ambition of the Guise and what he views as the treasonable willingness of the parties to *La Saincte Union* to ally themselves with Spain and the forces of international Catholicism, thereby, in his view, subordinating French to Spanish and Italian interests.

In the following passage, Palma Cayet identifies a series of offending parties. Each of them in his view has transgressed the boundaries of legitimate authority, and thus offended the sovereignty of God:

> under pretext of their rank or office, popes, kings, princes, bishops and doctors are not permitted to do indecent things. All zealous people are not good: the holy scripture does not advocate those who are rash, presumptuous, and desperate, because God alone creates miracles and makes judgments which are his alone.[9]

In Palma Cayet's view, popes (and by extension their legates such as Caetano), kings (the Leaguer King Charles X), princes (the Guises and their princely allies), bishops (the Leaguer bishops, such as Guillaume Rose), and doctors (the doctors of theology from the University of Paris) have done *choses indécentes*.[10] This conception of "indecent" deeds depends upon *politique* judgments concerning things that are unfitting and inappropriate to the perceived real domain and authority of these individuals. Implicit in his condemnation of Leaguer activists is an emergent, not always consciously articulated, conception of a separation of the domains of secular and religious authority that rests on an even more fundamentally held conviction about the behaviors appropriate to each domain of authority. As shall be seen, the perception of such a boundary is one of the sources of a new set of norms and sensibilities concerning public decorum and religious uses of the body.[11]

Politique Boundary Perceptions and Conceptions of Rationality

Palma Cayet's term *inconsiderez* on its own, in a denotative sense, means rash or unadvised.[12] However, in Estienne Pasquier's use of this word we may detect a more precise *politique* connotation. This usage, in turn, reveals more of the assumptions implicit in the unacknowledged ways *politiques*, whether of Calvinist or Catholic provenance, triumphed in defining the parameters of permissible action and proper comportment. From Pasquier's *Pour-parler du Prince*, Huguet cites the following passage:

> this great king of kings, produced so many strange and unheard of measures to lead events to their preordained end.[13]

The context in which Pasquier uses *inconsiderez* depends upon a clear dichotomy between the sacred and the profane based on distinctions between the means appropriate to God and those appropriate to human beings. This distinction emerges from the special force of the sixteenth-century word *estrange*, which conveys a quality of being alien and entirely other and associated with the miraculous. *Estrange* thus echoes the assertion in Palma Cayet's passage above that "on his own God alone creates miracles." The limiting and confining of the domain of the miraculous, but not necessarily its denial, is an essential feature of the *politique* compartmentalization of experience.

Palma Cayet's passage clearly tells us that the nature of the transgression committed by each of the Leaguer figures is their irrational failure to observe this basic distinction between orders of reality: the transcendental (God's domain) and the merely mortal, that is, the eternal as opposed to the perpetual, as in Boethius' sense of the two separate spheres of time: one human and one pertaining to God. Moreover, the alleged irrationality of Leaguer actions is suggested by the particular use of *outrecuidez*, which could be used to mean *déraisonnable*, literally, without reason.[14]

Another passage from Palma Cayet dealing with the political importance of forgetting further shows how different conceptions of time relate to the distinctions between *politique* and Leaguer experiences of order and reality. In the preface to the *Chronologie novenaire*, Palma Cayet wrote:

> What is the purpose, some could say to me, of calling to mind in the present all that the most Christian Kings Henry III and Henry IV did against the Catholic princes of the League, their subjects? It is a thing of the past; the peace says that these things should not be remembered . . . but it is not prohibited to write down for posterity how these things came about, because the princes and the people who rebelled against their sovereign shouldn't have done it if they did not want it talked about; and they shouldn't themselves have talked of it and published it if they didn't want posterity to know.[15]

Palma Cayet was convinced that "posterity needs to know how things happened." However, the Edict of Nantes (1598)—the *paix* of which Palma Cayet speaks—had declared that forgetting was crucial to the establishment of civil peace. Palma Cayet's text reveals an unresolved conflict between the concepts of time that are dictated by state edicts and the competing senses of sacred time that inflamed the passions of the religious wars. The Edict of Nantes sought to create a new historical memory, which would convey a legal line of succession from Henry III to Henry IV. This new sense of time, dependent upon the legislative authority of the state, would thus help establish a new chronology and a new narrative truth grounded in the principles of state sovereignty and the unquestioned legitimacy of Henry IV's authority as "the most Christian King."

Historiographical tradition has generally seen the extraordinarily complex Edict of Nantes as an act of religious toleration, and has thus labeled it a rational solution to the vicious passions of the Wars of Religion. Many of its measures were, in fact, never fully implemented and cannot be construed as ending the Wars of Religion in any practical or definitive way.[16] It thus becomes all the more necessary to unmask the world-view that has long defined the historical representation of the League and its historical other, the Edicts of Toleration.

Palma Cayet and the Truth Claims of National and Methodological Transcendence

Palma Cayet defends his history, claiming impartiality. We can see now one of the ways in which this *politique* position makes his *chronologie* of France a partisan document of a kind of methodological transcendence. He presents his chronology of the League as a value-neutral and merely factual record of historical events. This very notion of a value-neutral narrative underpins and sustains the larger unstated assumptions that Palma Cayet makes about the primacy of politics over religion. Proof of this lies in his unwavering assertion that the League was a war "for the State and not a war for religion." The notion that the events of the League took place within only one frame of reference, that of power politics, proclaims the triumph of *homo politicus* over *homo religiosus*. *Politique* histories of the League, and the period of the League itself, are thus landmarks in the creation of a specific French national identity compatible with the evolution of the absolutist state. By associating the League with both disorder and irrationality, *politique* historians, and those who have followed in their footsteps, in effect deny the possibility of religious narratives of this period because such narratives had lost their connections with transcendence. The differences that separated Leaguers and *politiques* thus not only concerned conceptions of human motivation and the concept of the state, but involved a fundamental dispute about the nature of the sacred itself.

Palma Cayet's Critique of Transgressive Zeal

We may now articulate the silent equation between God and the legitimate kings of France, Henrys III and IV, which is the structural foundation of Palma Cayet's critique of Leaguer popes, kings, bishops, and doctors. The previous passage cited from Palma Cayet explicitly invokes God's sovereign majesty: "on his own God creates miracles and makes judgments which are his alone."

Palma Cayet uses the terms *indecentes, inconsiderez, outrecuidez,* and *desesperez* to denounce Leaguers' "false" authority. The lineage and connotations of these terms belonged to a rationalist discourse. This analysis reveals how *politique* historical narratives sought to establish their own unimpeachable transcendence. In the same way, Leaguer actions in the world offended the rational sensibilities of these new partisans of transcendence. Sensibilities are more difficult to study than constitutional principles; yet it is the clash of sensibilities and their powerful alignment with competing constitutional principles that gives the contest between the Leaguers and the *politiques* such historical importance. In other words, the logical structure of Palma Cayet's history depicts Leaguers as offending God's sovereign authority by challenging, excommunicating, and assassinating the legitimate monarchs of France. Leaguers also offended Palma Cayet's rationalized religious sensibilities with their transgressive religious zeal. *Politique* critiques of League religiosity become an invective against popular religious culture. These critiques underscore, from a new perspective, the way in which cultural wars of the sixteenth century over norms of religious comportment are closely tied to the compartmentalization of religion and politics. This compartmentalization was accompanied by a profound change in emotional attitudes toward the sacred. In changing the behavioral norms within the traditional religious culture, forms of "collective effervescence" were necessarily abandoned as a prelude to the triumph of *homo politicus*. A concrete example of this change is the way the decline of municipal assemblies is accompanied by a decline in popular festival days.[17] The conversion of King Henry IV and the reform of popular culture together made a new alliance of religion and the state possible: key elites could ally with a now transcendentally rational state. In the clash of fundamental loyalties created by the succession crisis, the Leaguer vision of the law of God lost its legitimacy not so much by traditional standards of high treason against the state, nor even by the new norms of sovereignty, as important as these were. Rather, a new standard of transgression had emerged in behavioral norms defined by *bienséance* (seemliness) and *modestie* and a hostility to religious enthusiasm. To the charges of treason and the libel of social inferiority were ultimately added the indictment of irrationality. In the French, one could say the standards of *lèse majesté* were trumped by *bienséance* and *pudicité*.

The Social Misidentification of the *Seize*

For the *politiques*, the first step in creating a fundamentally new kind of authority required fabricating the myth of the "popular," lower-class leadership of the *Seize*. Estienne Pasquier will serve as a guide to the second historical misunderstanding of the League: the deliberate social misidentification of the local Parisian Leaguers most identified with urban radicalism. Pasquier's account of the *Seize* stranglehold on Paris in the winter of 1588–89 clarifies not only the social, but more importantly, the cultural tensions underlying Palma Cayet's critique of Leaguers' transgressive zeal. A close structural analysis of the historical narrative in Pasquier's letters from 1588–89 will reveal these complex motivations. This approach thereby clarifies how much Protestant debates about religious comportment heightened intra-Catholic social and political conflicts.[18]

The *politique* understanding of League piety and the relationship between this understanding and the conflict between *officiers* and lesser *gens de loi* will become clearer as Pasquier's own background is analyzed, along with a now famous letter that has become the *locus classicus* of the social misidentification of the *Seize* as "men of low condition." Pasquier is, of course, one of the major figures of French humanism. His *Recherches de la France* is among the most important monuments of a self-consciously national revival of vernacular literature and historical legal scholarship that formed one of the dominant strands of French humanism. Unlike Palma Cayet, Pasquier remained a "fils de l'Eglise Romaine,"[19] an institution he defended according to his own vision of its Gallican liberties and independence. Besides his humanist endeavors and his activity as a minor poet of the *Pléiade*, Pasquier made his reputation as a lawyer in 1565 when he argued the case against the licensing of the Jesuit College at the University of Paris. At issue in this case, according to traditional interpretations, was the defense of Gallicanism against ultramontanism in all of its Italian and Spanish manifestations. The struggle of the Jesuits to gain permission to establish the Jesuit college of Clermont at the University has been largely interpreted within a politico-legal context as an ultramontane challenge to the traditions of Gallicanism.[20] The result is a lack of a cultural history of ultramontanism in France, particularly for the League era, when such a cultural perspective is sorely needed to contextualize attitudes to Catholic reform.

Pasquier's discourse on the social inferiority of his Leaguer opponents offers a starting point for a broader cultural perspective on the clash of devotional sensibilities among Catholics during the League era. Pasquier's training as a lawyer, the cases he fought, and his family, as well as professional ties to the world of the courts and *officiers*,[21] all served to place him at the eye of the storm of the greatest urban, social, and cultural conflicts of his day, which were themselves the product of a volatile admixture of humanism, cultural nationalism, and desires for religious renewal. Pasquier's career and writings demonstrate how, under the pressure of the growth of absolutism and its social and cultural system, these complex cultural movements worked their way into the social and institutional fabric of Paris. Pasquier thus provides an opportunity to contextualize further the *politique* social misidentification of the *Seize* and its long-term import for the understanding of the differences among Catholic reformers at a critical moment of transition for *ancien régime* society, culture, and politics.

The immediate source of friction between the judicial elite and the lesser legal professionals was the high cost of venal offices, as seen in Chapter 1. Even more fundamentally, however, the growth of the cultural hegemony of the *officiers*, of largely *politique* persuasion in the 1590s, changed the patterns of urban sociability within the *bonnes villes* or great urban communes of France.[22] This destabilized the older urban civic culture.[23] At the same time, the rise of this *officier* elite played an essential part in the growth of the absolutist state: fiscally, as a source of revenue through the purchase of offices; strategically, as a counter-weight to the authority of the nobility; and ideologically, through its legal scholarship and humanistic training. The rise in the social and political preeminence of these office-owning, bourgeois gentlemen created complex divisions within the traditional urban commune. Robert Descimon has argued that civic life had once depended on a wide (if still unequal) distribution of social honors among several segments of the bourgeoisie, including especially the middling elites of the *basoche* who were notables at a neighborhood level. As a sign of these changing times, the office-owning elite began, in the later sixteenth century, to monopolize municipal honors as well. Moreover, the personal nobility conferred by their venal offices set them a class apart from other elements of the bourgeoisie.[24] These complex changes in social structure and political culture are important for the way they severed the bonds to the older civic culture. The impact is evident in the policing of traditional behaviors in public, which came under new and intense scrutiny especially by *Parlement*, the institutional arm of the *officiers*.

The most incisive interpretation of how the comportment of elites (mostly *officiers*) themselves changed is Colin Kaiser's invaluable study of the records of the disciplinary sessions of the *Parlement*.[25] These documents permit Kaiser to recount in detail how, in the second half of the sixteenth century, *officiers* of the sovereign courts imposed upon themselves an ever more probing and explicitly Catholic moral and behavioral code. Kaiser emphasizes the attention given to questions of permissible physical gestures as part of a general disciplining of comportment. Kaiser concludes that for the elite of the sovereign courts, a process of self-acculturation took place. The cultural result, which was not clearly articulated at the beginning of the process, was the production of "the perfect magistrate," a cultural ideal that permitted persons ennobled by the purchase of office to forge a political and social identity distinct from both the nobility of the sword and the rest of the Third Estate, especially the middling elites. This movement, which was a fundamental component of the reform of popular culture, destroyed the patterns of sociability upon which the traditional urban commune had depended.

The magistrates studied by Kaiser cultivated a "professional asceticism," which censored gestures such as smiling or scratching by a "good judge." Formal manuals such as those by La Roche-Flavin provided the minute details of a code of behavior that was then reinforced in seventeenth-century "hagiographies" of perfect magistrates. Kaiser argues that 1577 marked a turning point in the disciplinary uses of these special sessions of *Parlement*, the *mercurial*. From that point on a new scrutiny of the behavior of *officiers* took place in the disciplinary sessions. These meetings ceased to carry out purely technical and routine examinations of *officier* behavior and became more intrusive into the domestic lives of the *officiers*, their recreations, and their leisure pursuits. Most important, however, was the emphasis placed on strict public display of confessional conformity. Kaiser links this evolution directly to the growing influence of the League.[26]

The sober and grave public presentation of the self by *officiers* had far-reaching ramifications. Kaiser speaks of a "system of signs" entailing a rigorous set of self-imposed rules, "*autocontraintes*," which, "given the intensity of urban life, required a rejection of the temptations of a rich sociability. . . ."[27] This is another example of the ways in which "collective effervescence" was subdued in the marriage of Catholic reform and the culture of absolutism.

The way Kaiser helps us to understand the changing sensibilities of the *officiers* can now be applied directly to the problem of explaining *officier* hostility toward what historians conventionally call the "flamboyant" and "exteriorized" aspects of League piety. Let us listen now to Pasquier as he inveighs against the *Seize* takeover of power and at the same time reveals to us his basic apprehensions about the ways *Seize* piety mixes religion and politics. His analyses of two processional moments—that of Bussy le Clerc, a zealous *procureur* (a lesser legal professional, loosely speaking a member of the *basoche* in Descimon's terminology) leading several magistrates to the Bastille, and that of the penitential processions that gripped Paris in the wake of the Guise murders in December 1588—display perfectly the different gestural cultures separating zealous Catholics from the *politiques*.

We may focus on *Lettre IX* of Pasquier's *Lettres historiques*, written to his son Maistre Nicolas Pasquier, a counselor and *maistre des requestes ordinaire du roy*.[28] In this one brief letter there are three powerful passages that connect Pasquier's perception of multiple disorders resulting from the *Seize* seizure of power. His description of events begins immediately following Henry III's execution of the Guise brothers at Blois on December 23–24, 1588. The executions, intended by the king as a necessary preemptive strike against the League and its leadership, instead led to an insurrection engineered in Paris by the *Seize*. Pasquier provides the following account of these events:

> The name of king is no longer known in Paris. Not only is it not known, but worse, it is detested and abhorred. . . . As soon as they heard the news of the death of the two brothers there was a general revolt on the very day of Christmas. The next day in a veritable tumult, the duke of Aumale was made Governor of Paris in the mayor's palace. This choice was confirmed two or three days later right in the *Parlement* where an oath of loyalty was sworn by the duke; on the seventh of January [1589] the theologians assembled at the college of the Sorbonne in a formal capitulary declared that because of the events which had taken place at Blois, the subjects were not only free and released from any oath of loyalty or obedience that they might have taken to the King; but that also, without any harm to their conscience, they could arm themselves, unite and raise monies against him; all of this was first and foremost the work of the Holy See. His Holiness' advice was not actually sought; but this was done with false information from some seditious preachers and treated as a formal resolution, and so arms were taken up within a day. The *Parlement* [was] led by the likes of a Bussi le Clerc and his confederates from the Palais [Palais de justice] to the Bastille, where they picked a few choice seigneurs as it suited them to lock up there. . . . But just think, I beg of you, just how much the words 'de Bussi' and 'le Clerc' have been fatal and ruinous to Paris; because the person who, during the reign of Charles VI, introduced the captain of 'Isle-Adam' on behalf of the Burgundians did so by the gate of Bussi and his name was le Clerc.[29]

Before turning to a description of the furor in the provinces, Pasquier offers one last parting shot at the events in Paris, saying, "I have just recounted to you the Parisians' debauch."[30]

Accompanying the *Seize* political ascendancy were mass penitential processions expressing grief at the loss of the League's leaders and eschatological anguish and despair at God's wrath, which seemed to presage a terrible, impending Last Judgment.[31] Pasquier conveys his perception of multiple disorders in one of the most powerfully revealing *politique* accounts of these penitential processions of the winter of 1588–89. He gives us a narrative, filled with tension, that reveals contradictions that have profoundly shaped both the social imagination of the *ancien régime* and our understanding of the connections between late-medieval religion and the development of absolutism—the preeminent terrain of contested boundaries.

Two striking elements in *Lettre IX*, when read dynamically and in relation to each other, demonstrate the evolution of a *politique* world-view and reveal the values shaping Pasquier's understanding of the turbulent winter of 1588–89, when the diverse forces of *la Saincte Union* took control of Paris. This letter goes far beyond a mere slanderous social misidentification of the *Seize*. It also permits us to understand the clash of Leaguer and *politique* religious sensibilities from a social and cultural and, ultimately, experiential and ontological perspective. The first striking element is Pasquier's description, in precise and historically resonant terms, of one of the most significant socio-cultural conflicts of the League period: the confrontation between the worlds of the *officiers* and the *gens de loi*.[32] The second arresting element in *Lettre IX* is Pasquier's description of the mass penitential processions of 1588–89, which he interprets as an effort by "penitents" to move God to avenge the Guise murders. The theme of vengeance, which will be discussed in more detail later, forms the unspoken link between Pasquier's narrative of the socio-political conflict (*basoche* vs. *officiers*) and the processional fervor. It becomes clear that he equates the penitential processions with social disorder and a flagrant violation of boundaries that should separate the sacred from the profane. In his eyes, the processions represent an unbridled presumption by men and women who attempt to invoke God's wrath against their social betters.

Overall, then, the letter's leitmotif is the disorder associated with the *Seize* insurrection *and* with the mass penitential processions. The subtitle of the letter refers to "les désordres en province" following the Guise murders when, in fact, Pasquier focuses first on events in Paris. In his opening comments on the *Seize* assumption of power, Pasquier's choice of adverb, *tumultuairement*,[33] makes his position clear:

> There was a general revolt on the very day of Christmas. The next day in a
> veritable tumult, the duke of Aumale was made Governer of Paris. . . .[34]

Pasquier inveighs against the Sorbonne decree of January 7, 1589 ("theologiens assemblez au College de Sorbonne"), which released the nation from obedience to Henry III. For this he blames the Pope and especially the radical preachers of Paris.[35] The actions of these clerical agents of the League are but a brief introduction to other events in Paris. Just as Palma Cayet introduced us to the *politique* image of forces of international Catholicism, so Pasquier has given us the *politique* view of the world of the *Seize* and the penitential processions, which he presents as two interrelated and transgressive processional events: the arrest procession led by Bussy le Clerc, described below, and the penitential processions of the winter of 1588–89.[36] These structural associations in the text effectively link political and religious performance (the processions), condemning both as illegitimate modes of Leaguer activism since they violate a particularly *politique* sense of social and religious decorum and the proper uses of public space and public power.[37] The hallmark of this *politique* view is the nascent compartmentalization of piety and politics, which takes here the form of an attack on the exteriorized religious rituals of the Leaguer processions, which are seen as a form of counterfeit piety masking base political ambition.

The denouement of Pasquier's Paris narrative introduces the famous social misidentification of the *Seize*:

> It has been said that the Sixteen, among the most seditious in Paris and men of the lower class, have usurped all authority and power and they are called the Council of the Sixteen. It is a true anarchy. . . . [38]

By conflating the *Seize* with what one might term the lower classes ("the people/*le peuple*"), Pasquier manages to misrepresent thoroughly the political, social, and cultural realities of Parisian communal traditions.

Within a narrative framework that opens with the tumultuous revolt and ends with a gloss of the Parisian events as a *desbauch*, two remarkable passages are linked by the theme of vengeance. These show how a discourse on social difference, scathing about the *Seize*, is deployed in the service of rationalized religion, with its particular emphasis on God's transcendence. Both passages are devoted to processional events, each of which assails Pasquier's sense of right order in the universe. They are decisively interrelated and have long discouraged serious study of League piety in traditional accounts of history. The first passage addresses the *basoche/officier* conflict, while the second provides a satire of the penitential processions. The *basoche* seeking personal vengeance against their social superiors become conflated with the vengeance-seeking penitents, whom Pasquier, as a learned humanist, views from the perspective of his own invidious version of an ancient (Aristotelian) discourse on the natural superiority (and orderliness) of those born to command and the learned men who serve them. Pasquier's evocation of the social conflict shows a sharp definition of the social fault lines, which are activated during the League, while, at the same time, it shrewdly suggests that Bussy le Clerc's "procession" taking *officiers* off to the Bastille is nothing more than wanton violence:

> The Parlement, [was] led by a [by the likes of a] Bussi le Clerc and his confederates/companions from the Palais [Palais de justice] to the Bastille, where they picked a few choice seigneurs as it suited them to lock up there. . . . [39]

The multiple tensions verging on contradiction in this passage merit close examination. Pasquier manages both to name and to obscure his opponents—a rhetorical device used with skill by the author. As in the passage from Palma Cayet, our understanding depends on our ability both to identify the precise historical referents in the text and to read the underlying structures organizing the passage and then relate this material to the rest of the narrative. The most profound tension comes from the dismissive and derisive depiction of Bussy le Clerc and the denial of any rational motives for his actions ("qu'il leur a pleu . . .") when juxtaposed to what is now known (thanks to the research of Robert Descimon) about who "un Bussi le Clerc" is. The satiric deprecating force of "one" dissolves in the acid bath, as it were, of quantitative social research on the social recruitment of the *Seize*: Bussy le Clerc is a *procureur* in the *Parlement*, a member of a group, associated with the *basoche* and the *gens de loi*, who supplied some forty percent of the known *Seize* leaders.[40] Descimon's analysis, as we shall see, is far more subtle and dynamic than my initial simplified presentation.[41] "Un" Bussy le Clerc points to a socio-cultural fault line: *Parlement* vs. *basoche* where the boundaries of community were being redrawn according to diverging criteria of virtue. Pasquier has also given us what we may call an "inversion ritual" in his description of the procession of Bussy le Clerc to the Bastille: the lowest leads the highest.[42] This rhetorical deployment of carnival imagery is a grave form of social, cultural, and political critique. What do we really know about Bussy le Clerc and why is he leading the *Parlement* to the Bastille? On January 16, 1589, Bussy le Clerc, who had given the keys to the Porte Saint-Antoine to the duke of Guise during the Day of the Barricades in 1588, was named by Guise as governor of the Bastille. L'Estoile tells us sarcastically that Bussy le Clerc "était estimé fort brave soldat pour un procureur et fort zélé à la cause de la Ligue."[43] In fact, his League activism and participation in Catholic violence can be traced at least as far back as 1587 and his participation in the *journée de Saint-Séverin*, a reaction to the King's order to remove the immanentist memorial site to English Catholic martyrdom, commissioned by Catherine, Duchess of

Montpensier, sister to the slain Guise brothers. We also should note the corporal specificity of Bussy le Clerc's "verbal" aggression against the participants in the 1590 *politique* riot: "Who are these traitors who speak of peace? *I want to rip out their hearts with my hands* [my emphasis]."[44]

Bussy le Clerc's procession may be said to have begun a generation before he presented himself in the Grand Chamber of the *Parlement* in January 1589 to lead off the *premier président* Harlay to the Bastille. Richet has carefully uncovered the background to Bussy le Clerc's revenge. From Richet's work we know that, as early as 1559, the voices of popular Catholicism were raised among the *gens de loi*, who accused the *officiers* of the *Parlement* of tolerance toward the Protestant heresy. The landmarks in this growing antagonism between the *gens de loi* and the parlementary magistrates, which Richet calls "a sharp conflict over social and cultural hegemony between two unequally matched segments of the Parisian bourgeoisie," are now well known. In 1562 the *procureur* Fichard accused the *president* of the *Parlement* Harlay of being a hypocrite: "Look at him now, going to mass. He's a big hypocrite. He's one of the biggest Huguenots."[45] It is precisely the son of this Achile de Harlay, also a first *président* in the *Parlement*, whom Bussy le Clerc leads off to prison.[46]

When "un" Bussy le Clerc assumes his rightful place in this tradition of popular Catholic activism (and among the forty percent of *Seize* who were *gens de loi*, who in turn can be associated with a systematic defense of an alternative communal order), the force of "un" loses its derisive intent and becomes instead part of a set of revealing tensions. A wonderfully ironic reading is now possible because of what is now known about the statistical significance of "un" Bussy le Clerc. In other words, what Pasquier intended as the most dismissive element in the passage, the denial of any elevated rationality in *Seize* motivation, can now be turned on Pasquier himself. His suggestion of a wanton, that is, spiteful, vindictive, and haphazard arrest can no longer be sustained in the light of Descimon's political sociology of the *Seize*.

The partisan quality of this passage emerges from the contradiction between Descimon's precise identification of Bussy le Clerc and Pasquier's suggestion of wanton violence, as expressed in the phrase "a few choice *seigneurs* as it suited them (*qu'il leur a pleu*)." This phrase evokes an image of violence anchored only in its own spiteful and dissolute promiscuity: in a word, "debauched." Going far beyond memoirs and eyewitness accounts, Barnavi and Descimon in particular have restored Bussy le Clerc to history with quantitative precision. What is furious, mad, insensible, bedlam-like disorder for Pasquier now becomes an emblem of the structures of the sociocultural conflict that erupted during the League.

The *Politique* Construction of
Rational Politics and Rational Religion

In Pasquier's analysis, the theme of vengeance forms a bridge between his social deprecation of the *Seize* and his understanding of the penitential processions of the winter of 1588–89. *Letter XI* provides what may be the most significant *politique* account of the processional fervor that gripped Paris following the execution of the Guises. Like Palma Cayet, Pasquier defines the essence of the conflict unfolding during the League period, and helps to reveal the contrasting mental universes of Leaguers and *politiques*:

> It is no longer a matter of waging war against the new Religion; the entire goal of Paris is vengeance. . . . For this devotion [to vengeance/and to the Guises] men and women process in mere shirts, receive their Creator every Sunday, attend divine services from morning to night, not to appease the ire of God but rather to provoke it against their king, having no other faith and religion in their hearts than passion, not the Passion of our Lord Jesus Christ, but rather their own, in their fury thinking that the same passibility [fury and emotion] could be found in our great and impassible God [transcendent; unmoved].[47]

The assumptions implicit in this passage depend, as was the case with Palma Cayet, upon a series of unspoken equations: the combined disorders of the *Seize* takeover of power and the penitential processions constitute rampant social vengeance in the form of "la desbauche du Parisien"—a Parisian debauch. The most powerful contrasts are expressed in the tension between *passibilité* and *impassible*. These terms resonate within the Christian tradition in arguments about the nature of the incarnate Christ and his susceptibility to sensation and pain. Moreover, they also echo a debate over the properly somatic or nonsomatic character of religious passion and religious experience.[48] According to Pasquier, the *Seize* and the penitents are moved by their desire for furious revenge. He implicitly insists that they both completely misunderstand the transcendent nature of God. According to him, the *Seize* are false zealots because their religion is a mask for personal vengeance; the penitents, in seeking God's direct intervention in their cause, completely misunderstand the purpose and modes of God's intervention in the world. As Palma Cayet would say, "il a ses merveilles a soi"—he works his own miracles.

Pasquier's discomfort with the phenomenon of the processions goes far beyond social satire and the ridicule of vengeance as the personal motivation for processional and penitential engagement. Just as was seen in Palma Cayet's narration, the disorder Pasquier condemns is the confusion of orders of reality, which he sees as transgression against God's transcendence (his impassibility). From Pasquier's perspective it is the Leaguer, especially the *Seize*, projection of their human community and its *agita* into their vision of the sacred that most offends him. In other words, the characteristic Leaguer fusion of the sacred, political, and social, as embodied in the *Seize* movement or the project of the Holy Union, is a fundamentally transgressive and irrational "other" embodying a misunderstanding of the sovereignty of God and kings. As was the case with Palma Cayet's evaluation of Leaguer religiosity, Pasquier's critique of the processional culture of the League leads us to the heart of the debate over sacred immanence and sacred transcendence and the problem of the definition of rational behavior. The Leaguer culture of religious immanence, which required an enactment of palpable connections to the sacred, was inextricable from Leaguer expressions of political engagement, which were, in turn, based in a particular sacral understanding of *polis* and politics. In Pasquier, it is the horror of a true partisan of transcendence that underlies and motivates his satire of League devotional practices and Leaguer political engagement.

In the *politique* view of rationalized religion voiced by Pasquier, the *Seize* transgression consists not simply of a projection of *their* emotions onto a transcendent and impassible God. It is rather the act of projection itself that constitutes the transgression. Yet the projection of the human community onto the Holy Family was at the heart of medieval religion, which depended on a sympathetic permeability and interweaving of the sacred and profane.[49] This binding together of the spheres of the sacred, the profane, and the civic lay at the core of late-medieval lay piety and urban experience. Pasquier's vision of God's impassible sovereignty was thus a profound critique of Leaguer social and political relations as well. For *politiques* like Pasquier, the social, political, and religious values of the *Seize* represented an offense to a transcendent God as well as to the transcendent sovereignty of the institution of the monarchy.

Pierre de L'Estoile's Denigration of the Exteriorized Piety of the League

Like Pasquier, Pierre de L'Estoile was a *politique* and a Catholic. He was closely tied to the same privileged circles of the emergent state bureaucracy, the *Parlement*, and the social world of the *officiers*. In the 1560s, after studying law at Bourges, he purchased the office of *audiencier à la Chancellerie de France*, which he retained until 1601.

Pierre de L'Estoile will show us in detail how *politiques* rejected the League's strong Italian and Spanish elements that entailed ultramontane loyalties and exteriorized piety. L'Estoile kept a nearly daily journal for the period of 1574 to 1610 and created an invaluable collection of satiric sheets and ephemera of the period.[50] L'Estoile's lasting influence on historical conceptions of the League is due only in part to the detailed and extensive nature of his memoirs, which are among the richest journals in French history. A remarkable convergence of conceptions about politics, rationality, and French national identity, which L'Estoile has often appeared to embody, explains why his judgments of League piety were until relatively recently so persuasive. To understand his influence in League historiography, the myth of L'Estoile, as impartial witness assisting at the birth of modernity, must be debunked.

L'Estoile actually had a rather complex reaction to the League, and it is possible to identify three strata in his reaction. First, as a *politique*, his views are based on the primacy of politics and the needs of the French state. This means that he tends to be scathingly critical of most things connected with the League, associating the League almost exclusively with sedition and political disorder. This overtly political aspect of L'Estoile has most strongly influenced the whole course of League historiography. A second, related strand in his view of the League concerns his characterization of the *Seize* as seditious hispanophiles in matters of devotion and politics. Basically, until the political contest with Spain became somewhat diffused by the peace of Vervins in May 1598, it was difficult to advocate openly Spanish models of religious devotion. This fact has deeply influenced interpretations of the sixteenth-century origins of the seventeenth-century French school of spirituality. There is also a third strand in L'Estoile's views on Leaguer, especially *Seize*, piety. Denis Richet first called attention to L'Estoile's praise of League-sponsored reforms of processional comportment. This third element in L'Estoile's analysis of *Seize* piety identifies a trend toward devout self-discipline. This assessment stands in direct contradiction to L'Estoile's more pervasive attack on the exteriority of League piety. This contradiction reveals the logical and interpretive flaw in any analysis of League piety that posits a simple binary opposition between so-called traditional exteriorized piety and the more "interiorized" piety of the seventeenth century. The religious behaviors spawned during the League were far more complex than this simple binary scheme suggests.

L'Estoile's self-contradiction reveals that this is so. The following passage cited by Richet presents L'Estoile's favorable view of Leaguer Mardi Gras processions in February 1589: "Throughout the day there were in Paris fine and devout processions instead of the dissolution and trash of mascarades and Shrove Tuesday revelries with which people besotted themselves during previous years." Thus, in L'Estoile there is a fundamental ambiguity about the nature and legacy of Leaguer religious zeal.[51] L'Estoile's memoirs, and an analysis of their influence, permit an exploration of a powerful and enduring set of values affecting the study of the Catholic reformation: the denigration of the highly physical, exteriorized piety of the League and an emphasis on interiorization of piety as a progressive stage in the evolution of Catholic reform and modernity. The complexity of L'Estoile's own views has greatly hampered historians trying to understand the relationship between the League and Catholic reform.

The Advent 1598 Procession of Corpus Christi and Its Critique by "all men of intellect"[52]

L'Estoile provides a telling example of the conflation of exteriorized piety with political sedition in a critique he makes of innovation in an Advent procession of the eucharist. He describes this as a dangerous novelty and attempt to introduce into Parisian parishes, at a particularly volatile moment, a Spanish-inspired, gesturally flamboyant eucharistic devotion, usually reserved for the Festival of Corpus Christi (*la Fête-Dieu*). His account from late December 1598 stresses the disorders that the new-style procession caused, the volatile character of Advent-season preaching, and the critique of this liturgical innovation by "all persons of intellect" ("tous les hommes d'esprit").[53] He goes on to note that the *Parlement* of Paris issued an edict ordering the Bishop of Paris "de se contenter de faire observer les anciennes traditions et cérémonies de l'Eglise, sans y rien innover ni changer."[54] The new-style celebration persisted in the parishes of Saint-Séverin, Saint-Étienne-du-Mont, and Saint-Benoît—all parishes surrounding the University that had been ardently pro-League. L'Estoile stresses not only all the immanential details of this new sacred performance (bell-ringing, lighting, bowing in respect), but also the disorders that occurred in the rue de la Harpe when the valet of a gentleman—although a Catholic—failed to dismount as the sacrament passed by and the surrounding crowd forced their torches into his face and pushed him to his knees.

This combination of detail suggests that the atmosphere L'Estoile describes is charged with the ontological tensions between immanence and transcendence. Other events further expose tensions inherent in *politique* associations of transcendence with monarchical order and immanence with local disorders. For example, the Edict of Nantes had just been registered by the *Parlement* (the mode of civil time and forgetting) while militant Catholics were talking of the need for a *Saint Barthélemy* (a new massacre). In evoking the tinderbox atmosphere stirred up by militant preachers who

were calling for the new Advent procession ("quelques predicateurs de
Paris"), L'Estoile's account also stresses the role of the Capuchin Brulart as
instigator of the new form. The mention of the Capuchin and the identity
of the three parishes where the procession persisted suggest a strong continuity with the known sources of religious activism in 1590. They also point
to the mixed religious culture of the League, which galvanized late-medieval preaching traditions and simultaneously embraced the new reformed
religious orders such as the Capuchins.

The Advent example is also particularly interesting because changes
in eucharistic piety introduced under the auspices of the Capuchins were
among the most important modifications in devotional practices during
the League. One of the best examples of such innovation is the Forty Hours
eucharistic devotion introduced into Paris by Bellintani da Salò, the first
general of the Capuchins, who arrived in 1572. This devotion played a
crucial role in sustaining morale during the siege of 1590, and just as important, Pasquier has also satirized this League-associated devotional practice.
During the long period of the Wars of Religion, Advent, the festival cycle
preceding the Nativity, had become an especially contentious time of year
because of the intensity of provocative preaching associated with the onset
of one of the holiest and most joyous religious seasons and also a period of
heightened religious tensions. Since inflammatory preaching at Advent time
had been a cause of religious and civic disorder throughout the Civil War
period, L'Estoile was particularly likely to oppose such provocative forms of
devotion/sedition in this period. Again, we can discern another unspoken
equation between the seditious quality of Advent preaching during the
League, and the Spanish-style Advent procession, which L'Estoile terms "à
la mode d'Espagne." Revealing his Gallican views on the independence of
the French church, L'Estoile concluded that this was "a ceremony of sedition more than of devotion."[55] These statements stress, by emphasizing the
opinion of hommes d'esprit, that the critique of the ceremony was both rational and in the interests of public order.[56]

The Armed Procession of the Monks of the League:
"A Parade to Delude Vulgar Minds"

We are now ready to consider the Armed Procession of May 14 as represented in politique satire and the traditions derived from this mode of representation. To celebrate their victory in repulsing an attack by the armies of
Henry IV in the early days of the Great Siege of 1590, more than one thousand armed monks, friars, priests, devout laymen, and students marched in

a form of military review and sacred procession intended to culminate in a benediction by the papal legate, Enrico Caetano. The identities of many who participated in the "Armed Procession of the League" are preserved in numerous eyewitness accounts, in ruthless satires of the phenomenon of the armed monk-citizen, and in several remarkable paintings. This armed procession brought together the forces of local popular Catholicism, international and ultramontane Catholicism, and representatives of the *Seize*. The procession also presents zealous Catholics in one of their most characteristic activities, the ritualized use of public space in actions at once sacral, militant, and civic.

The journals of Pierre de L'Estoile provide one of the most detailed descriptions of the participants. Guillaume Rose marched first as captain and commander. Recently named bishop of Senlis (1584), he had ties to Paris through the University, where he served as professor and then *grand-maître* at the college of Navarre, a theological faculty known for its austerity. Numerous ecclesiastics followed four by four; then came other "captains," the *curés* of the various parishes most supportive of the League. From the University parish of Saint-Côme came Jean Hamilton, a Scot, who had received his doctorate in theology in Paris in 1586, shortly before his nomination as *curé*. Jullien Pelletier, whose intimate connections to the *Seize* are amply documented, processed as the *curé* of the parish of Saint-Jacques-de-la-Boucherie, located in the *Ville*. There followed representatives of the religious orders that provided the largest contingents: the Chartreux, the Feuillants (Reformed Cistercians), the Capuchins, and the Carmelites (White Friars), as well as the other older mendicant orders. At the head of each column marched the *chef* or prior of each order, carrying a crucifix in one hand and a weapon in the other. Leading the Feuillants was the fiery orator Dom Bernard de Montgaillard, who would flee Paris in 1594. The Carmelites of the Place Maubert near the University were led by their prior, Simon Fillieul, who ultimately joined Guillaume Rose on the list of exiles in 1594. The Capuchins, the reformed third order of Franciscans brought to Paris from Italy in 1572, were also present together with monks from the Order of the Chartreux and their prior, who committed large sums to finance the *Seize*.[57] The other great mendicant houses were represented as well: the Dominicans of the rue Saint-Jacques; the Augustinians, on the Left Bank of the River Seine, where the revolutionary government of Paris regularly met; the Minims, who had a number of students marching among them; all accompanied by "quelques bourgeois de la ville qu'on appelait catholiques zélés."[58]

As a performative embodiment of the phenomenon of the "monk-citizen," the procession violated the *politique* understanding of a necessary

compartmentalization of the sacred from the profane. To nullify this processional disorder, *politiques* again responded with a campaign of satire and
ridicule. L'Estoile reports a *quartrain* circulated in Paris at the time of the
procession by persons he terms *méchants politiques*:

> You may be sure, Sirs, that in mid-May, this procession was a Mardi-gras
> out of season that created an attitude of Lenten (i.e., penitential) arro-
> gance. . . . [59]

These words express outrage at multiple disorders of time and decorum, and
at the transgression of boundaries, and thus alert us again to divergent perceptions of reality dividing *politiques* from zealous Catholics. Most importantly, the biting thrust of this critique raises the question of how participants in such a procession, so many of whom came from religious orders
associated with the Catholic reformation, can be understood as advocates
for religious reform, while at the same time they have been so thoroughly
associated with treason, mayhem, and ignorance. This, of course, is part of
the puzzle of the Janus face of the League.

L'Estoile himself clearly relishes recounting the embarrassing conclusion of the event, when, just as the papal legate Caetano was offering his
blessing, a shot fired by a cleric unaccustomed to bearing arms, resulted
(purportedly) in the death of a member of the legate's entourage. In choosing to emphasize the military maladroitness of the cleric, L'Estoile is taking
an ontological stance in his implicit condemnation of the cleric as an arms-
bearing citizen. The dichotomy of sacred and secular gestures underlies his
own scathing account of the procession and its fatal outcome:

> Hamilton, of the Scottish nation, and curate of the parish of Saint-Côme
> [in the University quarter] acted as a sergeant lining up his men to march,
> and then, from time to time, stopping them so they could sing hymns;
> sometimes he ordered them to fire their muskets. Many people rushed to
> see these novel displays, which according to the "zealous Catholics" [i.e.,
> particularly religiously engaged Leaguers], represented the Church Mili-
> tant. The [papal] Legate also came to meet the procession and, by his
> presence, gave approval to this demonstration which was both truly ex-
> traordinary and at the same time utterly laughable. When one of these
> new "soldiers" wished to fire a salute to the Legate, who was in his car-
> riage, he fired upon it and killed one of the clerics in the Legate's entou-
> rage, who turned out to be his chaplain. [60]

L'Estoile's remarks are emblematic of a confused satirical tradition in which
the Armed Procession of clerics is recounted with an emphasis on the acci-
dental firing of a shot, which kills one of the legate's men. Just as Calvin
saw the mass as the foundation of a disordered society, *politiques* saw the

May 14, 1590, procession as a fundamentally disordered event. The message in their polemics was that Leaguers kill their own, and that Leaguer clerics make a deadly mockery of citizenship as well as of clerical office.

Another more explicitly satirical account of the Armed Procession can be found in a manuscript collection entitled *Histoire des singeries de la Ligue*.[61] Here, the Armed Procession of May 14 is misdated to July 1590 (although it is entirely possible that another Leaguer procession may have taken place on that date as well). The term *singerie* labels the Leaguer activities as a counterfeit form of piety likened explicitly to a *mommerie*. The unknown author begins:

> It was around the month of July of the year 1590, that a large number of priests and monks (I don't say religious persons) and novices dressed as soldiers' boys turned out along with the *Seize* accompanied by a crowd of pedants, the whole lot of diverse orders and nations of the university. [They were] lightly armed on the upper body as if in Catholic antiquity, just like those who watch over the sepulchre in Avignon. They were dancing to the sound of the tambourine of Biscaye in imitation of Mardi Gras so that all of Paris could see this laughable and mad assemblage which filled the streets to the great regret and displeasure of upstanding persons.
>
> Following after them and making up a rear guard was a pretty wretched fellow who was said to be a barrister gone mad, armed in the same fashion as if on this very day he had to fight savage pygmies against whom the wrens and other fledglings of the sky wage brutal war.[62]

There follows a description of more bizarre figures:

> . . . a troop sergeant with a cornet de verre hanging in his belt who was said to have brought from Saint Mathurin some copper wire with which he was driving a horde of fools of Paris of which well nigh half were drunk with the stories which little by little and with a tone of disharmony foretold the following—that this mummery was nothing other than the sign and signal of an infinite number of miseries and misfortunes to come.[63]

The details of persons and places are revealing: a deranged *avocat* foolishly armed; a pun upon Saint Mathurin, the physician of mad fools, also the name of an order of mendicants, the Mathurins, who played an important role in militant Catholicism (for example, as the site from which the eucharistic procession, in response to Protestant iconoclasm, departed in 1528). The satiric details are presented as harbingers of even greater disorders and as explicit threats to the order prized by *gens de bien*, or upstanding members of the community, true citizens, not madmen and fools. The most damning critiques of Leaguer performativity are raised in the mockery of Leaguers' understanding of Christian antiquity (i.e., superstitious tra-

ditionalism rather than scripturally derived traditions) and in the ap- plica-
tion of the term *mommerie*, a convention of satiric discourse that condemns
through the use of the language of carnival. The passage thereby attempts
both to disarm the power that carnival possesses to reassert the right order
in the world and to delegitimize the religious traditionalism of Leaguer devotional practices. The charge of *mommerie* is thus a further example of
what Descimon calls "the fable of the popular League." This royalist version of the Leaguer past not only denies the participation of *gens de bien*
with the *Seize* movement, it "renders unthinkable the reproduction of the
older system of the medieval town."[64]

The Ultimate Sources of Hostility to the
Exteriority of League Piety

Politique accounts of the "Armed Procession of the League" show that the
conventions of anti-League satire degraded League piety by applying to it
derogatory terms descriptive of disorderly popular performances, including
sacred theater, preaching, and communal processions not considered consonant with civil order. The *politique* use of terms like *mommerie* is similar to
Calvin's critique of a priest in the act of consecration as a juggler or circus
performer, a *bateleur*. This same hostility was also present in Palma Cayet's
term *outrecuidant* (extravagant, without limits, beyond reason—*déraison*)
and in Pasquier's horror at the penitents' projection of their affect onto a
transcendental God. L'Estoile, however, maintains two contradictory views
of League processional culture: a negative view of its excesses and disorder,
and a more positive perception of the League's place in Catholic reform as
a stimulus to devout comportment. Common to all these *politique* reactions
is, nonetheless, a particular constellation of rationality, social hegemony,
and royal absolutism whose cultural values have given us the myth of progressive modernity in its first early-modern French embodiment.

Religious Ceremony and the Boundaries of the
Sacred and the Profane

At his death in 1611, L'Estoile was buried in his parish church, Saint-André-
des-Arts, which had been a focal point of Leaguer activism. The journal
L'Estoile kept for the period of 1574–1610 and the collection of satiric sheets
and ephemera of the period provide our most detailed accounts of the League
from a *politique* perspective.

L'Estoile certainly carries forward Pasquier's critique of the League's conflation of the boundaries of the sacred and the profane. His accounts of League preaching show what *politiques* found most offensive in the *Seize* projection of human relations onto the domain of the sacred. L'Estoile's curate was Christophe Aubry, one of the most radically politicized of the League preachers.[65] L'Estoile's accounts of Aubry's defense of traditional sacred immanence show how *politiques* perceived projection and boundary transgression in *Seize* religion and politics. Nowhere is this Leaguer projection of human emotions onto the sacred made more clear than in L'Estoile's description of the communal vows of Easter 1591, undertaken to protect the Leaguer-held town of Chartres, which was under siege:

> That very day, on the advice of all of those at the Theology faculty of Paris a pilgrimage to Notre-Dame of Chartres was announced, where all would go on foot, assuming that the town had not been taken [by Henry IV], because if the town had been taken all virtue of that good Virgin would be exhausted because she would have changed parties and become a *politique*.[66]

L'Estoile goes on to recount how his curé Aubry led the parishioners of Saint-André on a procession to the Leaguer parish of Saint-Jacques-de-la-Boucherie in the *Ville*. He notes scathingly that the purpose of this action was "to entreat this good saint [Saint-Jacques] to use his pilgrim's staff to crack the head of the devil from Béarn [Henry IV] and kill him on the spot."[67]

In this same Easter week of 1591, when the fate of the town of Chartres hung in the balance, Aubry gave one of his more rousing sermons, predicting the desecrations of sacred ceremonies that would occur if Leaguers were foolish enough to accept Henry as king:

> But my friends, said he [Aubry], I assure you that if ever this evil relapsed heretic who has been excommunicated, if he should ever enter this city, no matter by which gate, he'll take away from us our religion, our holy mass, our beautiful ceremonies, our relics; he will make stables for his horses of our beautiful churches; he will kill your priests and make of our [liturgical] ornaments and copes, breeches and livery for his pages and lackeys. And I know this is as true as I know that it is truly God that I am about to eat and receive in the eucharist, and I warn you of this, so that you may take measures to protect yourselves. These words greatly offended many of the upstanding parishioners of Aubry's parish [Saint-André-des-Arts].[68]

One of the most striking aspects of this passage is the interweaving of the paraliturgical with the more specifically sacramental. In this account,

Leaguers such as Aubry could not conceive of a value-neutral domain of the adiaphora, things "indifferent" to salvation.[69] On the contrary, ornaments, relics and ceremonies have a sacral and emotional reality that is as powerfully charged as the sacrifice of the mass itself. This passage, when set alongside of the views of the Chancellor Michel de l'Hôpital, conveys the widest possible divergence among Catholics about the place of rituals and liturgical performance in an economy of salvation:

> We should not adore the unique, eternal God, who knows the depths of our hearts, from whom no mystery escapes, by elegant supplications, by the varied concert of our songs, by harmonious poems praised by the masses; we celebrate His grandeur, His sanctity, His immortality better in the glowings of a soul candid and simple like Himself. Our style must be simple, without preparation, without refinement, without ornaments, but filled with a serious dignity. It is enough to express the sentiments innate in our hearts under the inspiration of a natural sincerity; the refinements and the graces of form . . . are useless.[70]

Part Three

Immanence and Sacred Performance
in League Piety

Chapter 5

The Quantitative Analysis of Symbolic Behavior

The State of Research on Parisian Wills

Given the legal and religious culture of sixteenth- and seventeenth-century Paris, last wills and testaments of this period offer an unparalleled record of the symbolic behaviors that testators wished performed on behalf of their salvation.[1] In the majority of extant wills, testators are content to fulfill their canonical obligations to leave a will by commending their soul to God, leaving a customary five *solz* to their parish, designating a place of burial and an executor, and perhaps by requesting, in formulaic terms, a funeral service.[2] Nearly half the surviving wills, however, do not fall into this minimalist category.[3] French historians in particular have made last wills and testaments a staple of quantitative study of religious mentalities and beliefs and attitudes toward death.[4] None of this historiography has focused on the quantification of gesture *per se* or movements of the body as specified by the testator. Furthermore, in analyzing requests for religious services, no existing studies have ever engaged the detail, variety, or complexity found in Parisian wills. In testamentary analysis, the importance of the body at the end of life has been relatively ignored in favor of matters of the spirit: how testators understood the fate of their soul.[5]

Historians have thus never attempted to analyze the full range of symbolic behaviors that testators mention in their wills.[6] The reasons for this have never been purely technical. Rather, no one has focused on the full implications of sacred immanence and performativity in late-medieval and early-modern Catholic religious culture. Most crucially, the forms of historical agency available to testators through the uses of symbolic behaviors had fallen from sight: because historians have assumed that the language and imagery of wills is largely formulaic, they have overlooked how much the testators revealed about themselves in the documents. To remedy these problems, in addition to developing the conceptual framework presented in Parts I and II, it was essential to employ techniques adequate for the analysis of a religion of sacred immanence and performativity, where every detail has import. The most important and novel methodological decision made for this project was the commitment to code "pious requests." The aim was to capture and to quantify all the detail in the will regardless of whether it constituted a bequest involving a stated sum of money. This entailed development of a very different sort of code book where the testator's words were treated as a choreography describing the precise movements of the testator's body from the deathbed through the moment of interment. This involved assigning a numeric value to all nuances of words, gesture, timing, sacred place, and liturgical details, rather than simply coding aggregate numbers of masses or the amounts and recipients of bequests. This chapter introduces the basic quantitative techniques that were developed to analyze the performative reality in which testators lived and thought about death and salvation. Applying this methodology allows us to pinpoint those pious gestures that were characteristic of known League militants and of socio-professional groups, such as the *gens de loi*, who were known for their League militancy.

The chief finding of this new approach to symbolic behaviors is that, in their wills, individuals and social groups who can be linked to the League are nearly twice as likely to demonstrate distinctive patterns of performativity and immanential religious engagement than are testators without likely League affiliation. Table 5.1 offers a summary of these findings by indicating the higher percentage of performative testators in League-identified populations.[7]

The Creation of the Subpopulations for Analysis

In Table 5.1 the testator population of 1590 is divided into a reference group of testators who had no known link to the League and are compared to key subpopulations. The findings on the social identity of League militants in the work of Barnavi, Descimon, Richet, and Salmon helped to demarcate subpopulations. The first individual subpopulation of ninety-one League-related testators was created by using the standard primary and secondary sources of League historiography and all of the information provided in the will, in the civil as well as religious clauses. These ninety-one testators met one or more of the criteria listed in Table 5.2.[8]

A second subpopulation, "University Milieu," includes all individuals who were related to the University by profession and education, by bequests made to the University, and by use of a notary located in the University quarter. A third subpopulation comprises all 1590's testators belonging to the professional milieu of the *gens de loi*.[9] These were grouped together because of the consensus in League historiography that this professional group was the most highly politically mobilized for the League and for the *Seize* in particular. The *gens de loi* were further subdivided into those associated with the University through notary location and through bequests to the University and those not affiliated with the University. This subdivision makes it possible to see if ritualized performance (performativity, as specified in the gestures, or gestural economy, of the will) is higher for those *gens de loi* with University connections.

The decision to group together all testators making bequests to the Jesuits, the Capuchins, and the Feuillants was based on two factors: first, these new or reformed religious orders were closely associated with political support for the League; and secondly, a considerable number of well-known Leaguers made bequests to these three religious orders.[10] Finally, a total of eight persons among the testators of 1590 were associated with religious reform in their wills. The figures for the last two columns show that no individuals in the reference population made bequests to the new or reformed religious orders or were associated with reformist bequests. Among the 727 testators of 1590 only those with links to the League engaged in reformist behaviors. These testators are discussed in detail in Chapter 7 along with the criteria used to identify "reformist behaviors."

Measuring Religious Behavior

To analyze religious behaviors in wills, over two hundred variables were created.[11] As Appendix K shows, many of these variables permit the coding of the most basic will data concerning the identity of the testator, the will, and the notary. While the details of the coding scheme are reported in Appendix K, it is worthwhile to understand here that the computerized version of each will consists of a number of records. For coding purposes the information in each of the major sections of a will was placed in a separate record. The first section of the will (approximately half of the first page) is usually referred to as the preamble. It opens with an identification of the two notaries present and provides a usually very complete identification of the testator. For those above the status of craftsman or ordinary merchant, first name and family name (women always kept their family name) are usually preceded by honorary epithets known as *qualités*, which immediately give some idea of the social status and professional group of the testator. The actual profession follows. Or, in the case of many bourgeois, only the terms *bourgeois de Paris* or *marchand et bourgeois de Paris* appear, indicating

Table 5.1
Performativity in the 1590 Testator Population
[ ] indicates numbers of testators

Population	% of Testators Showing Performativity	% of Testators Showing Immanence	% of Testators Mentioning Body of Christ	% of Testators with Liturgical Details	% of Testators Bequesting/ Belonging to Jesuits, Capuchins or Feuillants (i.e., JCF)	% of Testators Concerned with Reform
I. Reference Population [437] (all except Key Subpopulations)	36.6% [160]	16.5% [72]	6.2% [27]	4.1% [18]	0.0% [0]	0.0% [0]
II. All Key Subpopulations [290] (Leaguers, University Milieu, Gens de Loi, JCF)	42.7% [124]	24.8% [72]	11.0% [32]	5.9% [17]	9.0% [26]	2.4% [7]
A. Leaguers [91]	56.0% [51]	28.6% [26]	15.4% [14]	11.0% [10]	18.7% [17]	6.6% [6]
B. University Milieu [162]	40.7% [66]	27.8% [45]	12.3% [19]	6.2% [10]	6.8% [11]	2.5% [4]
by profession [31]	32.3% [10]	32.3% [10]	6.5% [2]	3.2% [1]	19.4% [6]	6.5% [2]
by bequest** [14]	85.7% [12]	42.9% [10]	35.7% [5]	14.3% [2]	21.4% [3]	0.0% [0]
by notary location [118]	38.1% [45]	24.6% [29]	11.0% [13]	5.9% [7]	1.7% [2]	1.7% [2]

Table 5.1, cont'd
Performativity in the 1590 Testator Population
[ ] indicates numbers of testators

Population	% of Testators Showing Performativity	% of Testators Showing Immanence	% of Testators Mentioning Body of Christ	% of Testators with Liturgical Details	% of Testators Bequesting/ Belonging to Jesuits, Capuchins or Feuillants (i.e., JCF)	% of Testators Concerned with Reform
C. *Gens de Loi* [97]	41.2% [40]	22.7% [22]	6.2% [6]	4.1% [4]	2.0% [2]	0.0% [0]
University** [17]	52.9% [9]	29.4% [5]	0.0% [0]	11.8% [2]	0.0% [0]	0.0% [0]
non-University [80]	38.7% [31]	21.2% [17]	7.5% [6]	2.5% [2]	2.5% [2]	0.0% [0]

** Indicates University connection is associated with higher performativity.

Table 5.2
Criteria for League-Identified Testators in 1590

# of Testators	Criteria
3	Testator is a known League cleric.
4	Testator has a League affiliation mentioned in Descimon or Barnavi.[1]
1	Testator made a bequest to an individual listed in Descimon or Barnavi.
1	Testator's spouse made a bequest to an individual listed in Descimon or Barnavi.
7	Testator has a relative mentioned in Descimon or Barnavi.
15	A League cleric attended the testator's funeral.
5	The testator made a bequest to a League cleric.
2	Testator's executor or witness is mentioned in Descimon or Barnavi.
7	The Guise family employed the testator or his/her spouse.
9	The testator has probable League connections.[2] (Special will language or use of a League-related notary.)
1	The executor of the will is connected to the Mayenne family.
6	The testator has ties to a noble in the League.
5	The testator is employed by a noble in the League.
2	The witness to the testator's will has ties to a noble in the League.
1	The testator is a soldier in the army of the Catholic Union.
19	Testator uses Raoul Bontemps, a League-affiliated notary.
2	Testator is a Foreign Catholic noble soldier.
1	Executor is a Seize curé.
91	Total # of League Testators[3]

1. Robert Descimon, *Qui étaient les Seize? Mythes et réalités de la Ligue parisienne* (Paris: Klincksieck, 1983); Elie Barnavi, *Le Parti de Dieu: Etude sociale et politique des chefs de la Ligue parisienne* (Brussels, Louvain: Nauwelaerts, 1980).
2. This group is examined in detail below.
3. League testators throughout this book refers only to these ninety-one individuals designated as Leaguers because they meet the criteria in Table 5.2. The more important outcome of this study, however, is that many more than these ninety-one individuals could also be considered Leaguers by virtue of the religious criteria analyzed in this book. Such an expansion of the population deemed Leaguer is a hypothesis to be tested in a separate study. For example, many of the testators of the "University milieu" may well be Leaguers, but further corroborating evidence is required. Other researchers may wish to do such prosopographical research using Appendix H, Testator Members of the University Milieu.

that the testator is a privileged person and member of the city's burgher class.[12] Women are also identified by their marital status and the name and profession of present or previous husbands. Immediately following, the notary indicates the health of the testator. It is significant that in the overwhelming majority of cases the testator is in ill health. This is usually indicated with the phrase "lying in his/her sickbed" ("gisant au lict [lit] malade") followed by a formulaic statement attesting to the mental competence of the testator. That the 1590's wills were overwhelmingly composed at the testator's sickbed, indicates that even though a cleric is not present, for most people, recourse to wills had not yet become routinized but was still a part of very old death rituals put in place with the church's efforts at Christianization throughout the Middle Ages. The notary plays a double and intermediary role. On the one hand, he represents the secularizing influence of the state, which takes a greater interest in regulating the authenticity of the documents, for example by requiring signatures. On the other hand, through the language the notary employs he also invokes the authority of the church and the specifically Christian purposes for which the will first evolved under the close direction of the medieval church.

Immediately after the indications of testator health and mental competence a variety of formulaic phrases follow, indicating the motivations for making the will or recalling the Christian obligation to leave a will. These are clearly derived from notarial practice but suggest that the notary acts as an intermediary between the church and the testator, since the formulas are most often of a religious coloration. These formulas are usually repeated for all the clients of a given notary regardless of social attributes of the testator, although there are some interesting exceptions. This general rule strongly suggests that when examining the language of wills for changes in mentality or religious beliefs, as Vovelle has done for mentality and Chaunu for belief (i.e., the Christocentric piety of the Counter-Reformation), it must be remembered that these changes occur in part via the cultural intermediacy of the notary. The role of the notary will be considered now in detail by looking at two parts of the will in particular: the invocation (along with the related question of the presence of a cleric) and then the commendation.

The most highly religiously charged language of the will is found in the invocation, which usually closes the preamble, and in the *commendatio animae*, which usually immediately follows the invocation. It is these two sections of the will that entitle Chaunu to speak of the will as a prayer. An invocation and a commendation appear in the overwhelming majority of the 1590 cases, and as Chiffoleau has shown for the region of Avignon they are clear evidence of the way the church sought to sacramentalize the will itself.[13] It would be very important to know when the invocation first appeared in wills. It is clearly one of the very first sacralizing gestures incorporated into the document and is probably coeval with the emergence of the religiously motivated wills of the early Middle Ages. Originally, the invocation literally embodied the gesture of crossing oneself and the repetition of some form of the phrase, "Au nom du père, du fils, et du sainct esprit." With the exception of League-related notaries, by the sixteenth century these words reoccur only in holograph wills.[14]

Since one of the main functions of the will is to organize one's funeral, a large record was devoted to the information that every testator provided in more or less detail. In order to capture all symbolic gestures in the will, a distinct record was created for coding all pious requests over and above the testator's description of the funeral. Thus, while every testator has records with biographical and literacy data, a will record, and a record for notary data, only testators who make what are termed "pious requests" receive a distinct record reserved for this information on pious requests. In the testator population of 1590, roughly one-quarter of testators made no detailed pious requests. Table 5.3 ranks testators according to the number of pious requests made. The most interesting finding in Table 5.3 results from a comparison of the number of bequests made by 91 Leaguers and a reference population of non-Leaguers (636 testators). Leaguers are two times less likely to have wills without detailed pious requests than are non-Leaguers. Leaguers are also more than two times more likely to leave wills with more than eleven pious requests than are non-Leaguers.

A pious request generally corresponds to a discrete event. For example, a testator specifies: "as my body is placed in the ground sing Ave Maria"; another testator says: "[I] wish to have my curate and his vicar attend the funeral"; or another request is, "on the day of burial [I] wish to have the poor who are present given 3 écus vingt solz." Each testator will have one record for each of these pious requests. The number of pious requests made, however, is only the most general indicator of symbolic behaviors. The content of the actual behaviors is coded in far more nuanced variables that actually make it possible to classify and count different expressions of immanential, performative, and reformist behaviors.[15]

An Introduction to the Performativity Index: Augustin Gueret, Master *Charcutier* of Saint-Gervais Parish

The primary tool for analyzing the symbolic behaviors of testators is the Performativity Index. An extensive search for a simple set of pious behav-

Table 5.3
Comparison of Number of Pious Requests in Three Testator
Populations and between Leaguers and Non-Leaguers

Number of Requests	1543–44		1590		1630	
	Number of Testators	% of Testators	Number of Testators	% of Testators	Number of Testators	% of Testators
no requests	26	16.4%	171	23.5%	73	21.2%
1–5 requests	49	30.8%	322	44.3%	136	39.5%
5–10 requests	36	22.6%	148	20.4%	72	20.9%
11–20 requests	36	22.6%	71	9.8%	42	12.2%
more than 30 requests	12	7.5%	15	2.1%	21	6.1%
Total	159	100%	727	100%	344	100%

Number of Requests	1590 Leaguers		1590 Non-Leaguers	
	Number of Testators	% of Leaguers	Number of Testators	% of Non-Leaguers
no requests	11	12.1%	160	25.2%
1–5 requests	44	48.4%	278	43.7%
5–10 requests	14	15.4%	134	21.1%
11–20 requests	15	16.5%	56	8.8%
more than 30 requests	7	7.7%	8	1.3%
Total	91	100%	636	100%

iors that Leaguers shared found no basic social indicators, nor any pattern of religious institutional loyalties shared extensively by all 91 Leaguers. Instead, the data revealed that well-known League militants and the larger populations known in the literature to be League-related shared an unusual attachment to ritual and liturgical details that was expressed in often highly idiosyncratic ways. For this reason the Performativity Index, conceived initially as an intuitive response to the lack of a simple series of behaviors Leaguers shared, became the most important interpretative tool in this study. In other words, Leaguers shared a variety of performative behaviors that revealed intensely personal religious engagement. That this ritual engagement was particularly intense derives from the nonstereotypical character of the individual pious requests associated with Leaguers.[16]

At the most primitive level the larger number of pious requests League-related individuals make is the first indicator of this intensely felt ritual attachment. It is crucial to emphasize that the number of pious requests is not crudely related to testator wealth, but rather results from will language. A detail as simple as the request that services be said "devoutly" is significant for several reasons. First, only seven testators out of 727 make a request of this nature.[17] The addition of this one word to a will does not in any significant way increase the cost of the document, since notaries charged by the line. Second, very wealthy testators had other means at their disposal to make the crucial point that all rituals be performed devoutly.[18]

Tracing the coding of a specific will may best illustrate how the Performativity Index identifies the wide variety of intensely felt forms of League piety. The will of a master *charcutier* from Saint-Gervais parish was selected for a variety of reasons. Augustin Gueret has never appeared under his own name in any history of the League in Paris. Many historians of the popular roots of the League in Paris have, however, imagined this historical actor: a master artisan associated with the butchers and meat trades that have a long tradition of political activism in Paris, Gueret is in the subpopulation of Leaguers and of Reformers. The curate of Gueret's parish was the Leaguer Jehan Gincestre, who seized control of Saint-Gervais in May of 1588 following the Day of the Barricades. The parish of Saint-Gervais is known for its League activism. One historian of this parish has argued that the parish assemblies at Saint-Gervais underwent a certain democratization in the League period, although this evidence is still debated. If such "democratization" took place, then a master artisan with a generation or more of ancestors buried in the parish, who signs his name to his will in May of 1590, might have participated in this process. The parish assemblies of the League period may also be instances of the intense collective experience of the sacred, similar to the "collective effervescence" that Durkheim associated with the sacred in group totemic practices.

The first instance of performativity in Gueret's will occurs in the record giving information about the funeral. Every testator has a funeral record, but most give terse and rather standardized information. For this reason, the variable "funeral package" was developed when testators requested a group of typical behaviors relating to their funeral.[19] Gueret, however, provides rich detail on when and how the bell of the parish church is to be rung for him. He asks for "the ringing of the two large bells only, which should be pulled each three strokes, in the evening and in the morning, and at the end let them be rung together throughout one half-hour." In one sense, this request has no aggregate statistical significance, since no other testator makes the same request. The statistical significance emerges only as all the information on performativity in the entire will is slowly aggregated into the variables that capture all the various forms of performativity.

As the case of Gueret demonstrates, performativity is first coded in its physical specificity: bell-ringing, *sonnerie*. Of primary importance is that the sounding of the parish bells is of special significance to this testator because of the detailed attention he gives to it. The bell announces his death in the evening of its occurrence, on the morning after, and brings closure after the burial itself. Bell-ringing (*sonnerie*) is one of six initial variables with values that are aggregated into a number in the Performativity Index. The variable in this case is value 6 of the Performativity Index, "Aural and Visual Symbolic Community" (Table 5.4). This means that the behavior mentioned by the testator creates, either aurally or visually, a symbolic community. The other five initial variables that were considered to work in the performative manner of a request for the sounding of bells were: 1) any request for an announcement of the death at the time of bidding prayers (*prosne*); 2) any request for a crier to call out the death through the streets; 3) any request that the name of the dead person be inscribed into the parish book of the dead; 4) special requests: great bell-ringing (*grosse sonnerie*), inscription into the book of the dead of a confraternity, and the lesser bell-ringing (*petite sonnerie*); and 5) any request for bell-ringing when the viaticum is carried to the sick, any mention of intense bell-ringing (*la grosse sonnerie à grande branle*), and requests for bell-ringing by the confraternity. This aggregation was done in a blind fashion without foreknowledge of the aggregate outcome. The result is captured in Tables 5.4 and 5.5.

Table 5.4 shows us that twenty-four testators in 1590 asked for gestures producing "Aural and Visual Symbolic Community" and that eight of these twenty-four testators met the criteria for Leaguers. Table 5.5 tells us that these eight Leaguers represent thirty-three percent of 1590's testators who requested this type of performativity. With less than thirteen percent of the testators being Leaguers, they are overrepresented among the 1590's testators who request a gesture that produces an "Aural or Visual Symbolic Community." In evaluating the testator's request for bell-ringing within the economy of salvation of Leaguers, it is also significant that the ringing of the "tocsin" was the alarm signal sent by ringing the parish bells. This behavior plays a potent role in the history of militant Catholicism itself: the tocsin was sounded at the beginning of the massacres of Saint Bartholomew's Day, and it was sounded to gather the crowds to protest the removal of the panels in Saint-Séverin parish that depicted the torture and death of Mary, Queen of Scots (1587).

Other performative elements in Gueret's will are found in a long clause where he states that he "wishes and bids that at the time of the laying out of his body in rest in front of the crucifix there should be sung *Vexilla regis prodeunt* and three times *O crux ave spes unica*, all done with devotion, and [as] his body is placed in the ground sing *Salve regina*, also seemly and devoutly." As Appendix K indicates, this clause was coded in two separate records (#7 and #8) of his pious requests,[20] because Gueret is speaking about

Table 5.4

Performativity Index for the Three Sample Periods, Including a Breakdown of the 1590 Leaguer Population

Types of Performativity and Symbolic Behaviors	1543–44 Testators		1590 Testators		1590 League Testators		1630 Testators	
	% Testators Prescribing	# of Test	% Testators Prescribing	# of Test	Leaguer % of Total Population	# of Leaguers	% Testators Prescribing	# of Test
1) Decoration of a Sacred Object	0.6%	1	0.1%	1	0.1%	1	0.3%	1
2) Banquet	2.5%	4	0.3%	2	0.3%	2	0.3%	1
3) Pilgrimage Vows	0.6%	1	1.8%	13	0.1%	1	1.5%	5
4) Extraordinary Detail on Funeral Cortege	3.1%	4	0.3%	4	0.0%	0	0.3%	1
5) Above Average Number of Lights [12+]	21.4%	34	7.6%	73	1.9%	14	14.0%	48
6) Aural and Visual Symbolic Community	11.9%	19	2.8%	24	1.1%	8	5.8%	20
7) Sign of Cross (Symbolic Act Sacralizing Document)*	7.2%	11	5.8%	42	2.1%	15	2.7%	9
8) Verbal Performativity	8.8%	14	1.2%	10	0.3%	2	2.3%	8
9) Bodily Performativity	13.8%	22	20.6%	155	3.7%	27	29.7%	102
10) Aspersion with Holy Water	1.3%	2	0.7%	7	0.4%	3	3.8%	13
11) Liturgical Performativity in Detail	19.5%	31	9.2%	68	2.0%	15	16.9%	58
12) Offertory Procession (Lay Participation, Vernacular Prayers)**	1.3%	2	1.4%	9	0.3%	1	1.5%	5
13) Celebrant of Symbolic Importance	0.6%	1	0.3%	2	0.1%	1	0.0%	0
14) Strict Comportment of Celebrant	4.4%	7	0.4%	5	0.5%	4	1.2%	4
15) Bequests to Prisoners (Symbolic Value of Their Prayers)	0.0%	0	0.1%	1	0.0%	0	0.9%	3

Table 5.4, cont'd
Performativity Index for the Three Sample Periods, Including a Breakdown of the 1590 Leaguer Population

Types of Performativity and Symbolic Behaviors	1543–44 Testators		1590 Testators		1590 League Testators		1630 Testators	
	% Testators Prescribing	# of Test	% Testators Prescribing	# of Test	Leaguer % of Total Population	# of Leaguers	% Testators Prescribing	# of Test
16) Special Clerical Intervention without Testator's Presence	3.1%	5	0.4%	3	0.3%	2	3.2%	11
17) Sacraments Taken	3.8%	6	4.5%	34	1.2%	9	3.8%	13
18) Intelligibility of Service and/or Educational Bequests	0.6%	1	1.1%	9	0.7%	5	1.2%	4
19) Entrance into a Monastery	0.0%	0	0.3%	2	0.3%	2	2.0%	7

* Does not include holographic (privately composed) wills. For an explanation and a detailed analysis, see Table 5.6.
** For a fuller explanation and detailed analysis, see Table 5.7.

Table 5.5

Performativity Index: 1590 Population Compared with 1590 League Population Percentages

Types of Performativity and Symbolic Behaviors	1590 Testators		1590 League Testators	
	% Testators Prescribing	# of Testators	League % of each Performative Population	# of Leaguers
1) Decoration of a Sacred Object	0.1%	1	100%	1
2) Banquet	0.3%	2	100%	2
3) Pilgrimage Vows	1.8%	13	7%	1
4) Extraordinary Detail on Funeral Cortege	0.3%	4	0%	0
5) Above Average Number of Lights [12+]	7.6%	73	19%	14
6) Aural and Visual Symbolic Community	2.8%	24	33%	8
7) Sign of Cross (Symbolic Act Sacralizing Document)*	5.8%	42	36%	16
8) Verbal Performativity	1.2%	10	20%	2
9) Bodily Performativity	20.6%	155	17%	27
10) Aspersion with Holy Water	0.7%	7	43%	3
11) Liturgical Performativity in Detail	9.2%	68	22%	15
12) Offertory Procession (Lay Participation, Vernacular Prayers)**	1.4%	10	20%	2
13) Celebrant of Symbolic Importance	0.3%	2	50%	1
14) Strict Comportment of Celebrant	0.4%	5	80%	4
15) Bequests to Prisoners (Symbolic Value of Their Prayers)	0.1%	1	0%	0
16) Special Clerical Intervention without Testator's Presence	0.4%	3	67%	2
17) Sacraments Taken	4.7%	34	27%	9
18) Intelligibility of Service and/or Educational Bequests	1.1%	9	56%	5
19) Entrance into a Monastery	0.3%	2	100%	2

*   Does not include holographic (privately composed) wills. For an explanation and a detailed analysis, see Table 5.6.

**   For a fuller explanation and detailed analysis, see Table 5.7.

two separate events: the laying out of his body in front of the crucifix and the placing of his body into the ground. Since his body is mentioned in each request he receives two counts for "Bodily Performativity" on the Performativity Index. Since he mentions by name three specific hymns, one of which is not common, he receives one count for liturgical performativity. Gueret asks that at each of the events that concern his body and its placement "everything" (*tout*) be done "devoutly" and "seemly and devoutly." The use of the word "devoutly" is captured each time by the initial variable "Honest/Devout." In the creation of derivative variables, "Honest/Devout" works in two different ways: first, each occurrence counts as an instance of the variable "Reform," where it is value 5, "concern with clerical discipline or exactitude in performance of liturgical duties." Secondly, "Honest/Devout" counts as an instance of value 14 in the Performativity Index, "strict comportment of celebrant."

Gueret is a good example of the way in which intense concern with liturgical detail reveals a complex experience with the sacred. Liturgy and the body together are part of a particularly intensely felt piety that has both disciplining and reformist components in a very immanentist context. Gueret also received 1 count for the derivative variable "immanence" because of the importance he attached to the relationship between his body and the sacred object of the "crucifix." Absent from Gueret's will are any indications of the condensation of sacred immanence into especially sacramental settings. His request for masses at the mendicant orders was coded, but did not trigger any of the performativity variables. This is important to emphasize because the requests retained had to meet criteria of particular intensity or detail, or possess a uniqueness that could be interpreted as evidence of intense feeling, such as Gueret's repetition that aspects of his funeral ritual be carried out "devoutly."

Bequests of Performative Objects (Value 1)[21]

The types of performative behaviors in the "Performativity Index" are organized in a hypothetical hierarchy, with 19 distinctive values, representing increasingly performative attitudes. The values begin with testators' gifts of "performative" objects intended for liturgical or paraliturgical use.[22] Testators made such bequests in order to construct an active and efficacious, hence performative, relationship between themselves and the sacred. This raises the question of the votive, or the devotional, orientation of the bequest. For example, a testator of 1543, *noble et discrète personne maistre* Leon Le Cyrier, *commandeur* de Brie Comte Robert, gives a red velvet robe to adorn the Virgin, while a testator from 1590 gives a pound of silver to have a liturgical ornament made upon which the Holy Sacrament is to be placed in order for it to be carried in processions along with reliquaries.[23] Without prejudging the devotional orientation of these bequests, one can at least say that the first gesture has a Marian and nonsacramental focus, while the second gesture is an expression of reverence for the Holy Sacrament in a processional context. The first bequest is emblematic of a particular Marian worship that constructs an anthropomorphic and more horizontal relationship to a clothed and adorned Virgin.[24] The act of dressing clearly is a human activity, even if we know that it can become highly ritualized and, thus, become a symbolic behavior with great representational and even transformative powers. Here, dressing also has a reciprocal context as a form of gift-giving or exchange in which Le Cyrier seeks the patronage or intercession of the Virgin in his salvation. In the case of the second bequest of a liturgical ornament, the gift has a clearly sacramental referent and it occurs in a carefully regulated processional context.

René Benoist's analysis of the symbolic meaning of priestly vestments examined in Chapter 4 also relies upon the performative function of clothing. His treatise, however, underscores the sacramental referents of the clothing being described (ordination and the sacrament of the altar). The symbolism of the priestly vestments that recall the stages of the passion itself facilitates understanding that the priest "represents" Christ. Furthermore, vestments, so crucial to the sacrament of ordination, in a realist sense, represent the transformed nature of the priest and signify his entry into a separate *ordo* or metaphysically distinct class of human beings.

With Benoist the experiential frame of vestments/clothing has become more sacramental and passion-centered, or Christocentric, as compared to the bequest in 1543 by the cleric Le Cyrier, who leaves a robe of velvet to clothe the Virgin. While adhering to an immanentist view of the sacred, Benoist shifts the axis of the experiential frame from a horizontal to a more vertical orientation, thus giving us an example of the condensation of sacred immanence, that is, the centering of the sacred within a more exclusively sacramental framework, and here, within a sacerdotal context. The condensation of sacred immanence in priestly vestments in the Benoist treatise entails the same movement toward more sacramentally focused gifts of sacred objects that occurs in 1590 and 1630. One may think of this process as a gathering of the widely (horizontally) dispersed relations to the sacred and their reorganization into a more narrowly (clerically) defined vertical or hierarchal axis where unambiguous distinctions between *latria*, *hyperdulia*, and *dulia* govern devotional behaviors and facilitate a more methodical application of the sacramental system.

In 1630, very personal gifts of clothing persist, usually as bequests to the poor. Although the evidence is far from conclusive, the sole bequest of a religiously performative object is striking and suggestive of a new and decorous intimacy with the eucharist. A 1630's reformer, Damoiselle Françoyse de Verneuil, "a young woman having attained the age of legal majority, resident in the *hôtel* of Madame de Ville and in her service," gives to the Minims "her petticoat of wrought velvet with a white background to be used to make a canopy to be held over the holy sacrament."[25] Some form of bodily intimacy seems present in the gift of a petticoat to increase the splendor of eucharistic processions. To use a Tridentine vocabulary, however, the petticoat is an instance of a deocentric performance of *latria* (or eucharist adoration) while Le Cyrier's gift of a dress for devotion is an expression of *hyperdulia* to the Virgin.

Banqueting Behaviors and Pilgrimages (Values 2 and 3)

The next values of the Performativity Index deal with traditional forms of performativity such as banqueting (value 2) and pilgrimages (value 3). Pilgrimages and banqueting are symbolic behaviors that produce temporary states or, in medieval pilgrimages, temporary changes in personal status.[26] At the apex of the hierarchy of values for the Performativity Index is entrance into a monastery, which was intended as a permanent change of status, a literal death to the world. The behaviors in banqueting and pilgrimages introduce the question of how performativity creates community as well as transforms identities.

To answer this question, it is essential to place the terminology of the wills in the long-term historical context of actual behaviors or requests. There are quite literally archaeological layers of meaning to be discovered in wills, of which banqueting is a perfect example. The services in the early church were originally composed of a service of the Word and a separate eucharistic supper, sometimes formally called a liturgical meal. These eucharistic meals, commonly held on Wednesdays and Fridays, were separated from the eucharist proper, and they persisted as a distinct feast, or *agape*, until their disappearance in the early part of the fourth century. The separation of "dining" from the service of the Word is generally considered a response to Gnostic criticism of the sacrality of substances.[27] The opposition between early Christian orthodoxy and Gnosticism is a good example of the way fundamentally different alternative ontologies of the sacred are linked to an alternative conception of the church as a community, and to radically different views of the agency of men and women within the church.

Rituals, which depend in large measure on the vitality of collective memory in a given community, not only reflect social and political arrangements; they are also used to reshape or resist the social and political order.[28] This is especially true of the League period, where the gestural economy of Leaguer wills is part of an alternative social and political vision and a different collective memory. The *politiques*, of course, had insisted upon the necessity of forgetting in order to construct a new civil order.

The earliest debates over the eucharist at the time of the institutional origins of Christianity demonstrate that the Word and sacred and performative sociability were often considered mutually exclusive domains. The very act of separating the eucharist from the *agape* entails a condensation of sacred immanence. It represents an attempt to respond to spiritualist and transcendentalist critiques while still living with the sacred in the world and maintaining a performative understanding of salvation and immanence. The long-term dynamics set in motion by the condensation of sacred immanence, and by the more careful regulation of performative behaviors that accompanies the condensation of sacred immanence, are not simply a linear and uninterrupted process. In the high Middle Ages the condensation of sacred immanence proclaimed the unique status of the eucharist among a plethora of sacred things. But, as the sacramental system emerged clearly from the pronouncements of the Fourth Lateran Council of 1215, the eucharist became an ever more concentrated and affectively powerful locus of the sacred.

In sixteenth-century Catholic religious culture we have seen intense pressures to regulate sacred performance. The same energies produced attempts to regulate the ludic and festive activities at lay and clerical gatherings, including the reform of confraternal banqueting. Reform of dining practices, as part of the general effort of ecclesiastical and lay authorities to regulate performative behaviors, took on particular urgency in the sixteenth century. This brief evaluation of "banqueting" shows just how much was at stake in the civil and ecclesiastical legislation regulating this kind of performative behavior. Confraternal banqueting in practice created hundreds of microsites of access to the sacred and bonds of fellowship (horizontality), which traditionally escaped parochial or episcopal regulation. Tridentine legislation in session 22 concerning confraternities aimed at establishing parochial and episcopal control over devotional confraternities by reinforcing authority in vertical bonds, which would facilitate control over the multitude of horizontal, communal, and family loyalties.[29]

In a similar manner, this attempt to regulate the performativity associated with the banquet expresses a desire to elevate and clarify the status of the eucharist. Behaviors that have a symbolic relationship to the eucharist, such as the ancient, actual association of the eucharist with feasting, were especially strategic targets for reform. In the case of banqueting, however, the condensation of sacred immanence is not simply a regulatory effort by authorities. The wills of all years demonstrate the different and often creative ways by which testators themselves sought through banqueting to establish a direct relationship between themselves (their own bodies) and the salvific body of Christ.[30] Leaguers, in particular, dwell on the details of banquets or specify that only the "truly poor" should be invited to feast in memory of the testator. Some details of their bequests suggest testators themselves sought a heightening of their relation to Christ through a reform of banqueting mores.

When certain forms of performativity such as banqueting are more strictly regulated or redefined to conform to a more Christocentric norm, such redefinitions are inevitably related to a changing vision of right order in the Christian community. The information in wills about the performative orientation of the testator can, then, add to our understanding of what symbolic behaviors tell us about a testator's broader vision of the human community. The analysis of symbolic and performative behaviors thus uncovers the classic boundary issues of a culture and a polity in transition.

Lights and Sexual Purity (Values 4, 5, and 12)

Value 4 of the Performativity Index, which is so crucial in helping track this evolution in symbolic behaviors, deals with performative aspects of the funeral cortege where issues of community and liminality are interwoven. Values 4, 5, and 12 are related. While value 4 signals extensive details in the testator's prescriptions for the funeral cortege, value 5 deals with various directives and requests for the use of candles in the funeral cortege and at services, especially where some particular activity with symbolic significance is specified. Value 12 analyzes details concerning the offertory procession. The events tracked by these values are linked as processional moments where the use of lights has particular significance. Candles have long had an important symbolic place in liturgical piety.[31] René Benoist has written on lights, demonstrating how even this Christian symbol was part of debates linking performativity to "superstition."[32] In fact, the way in which Benoist connects legitimate and appropriate performativity to sexual purity in his treatise on lights helped structure the Performativity Index in a way that reveals the connections between the desire to regularize and control access to the eucharist and the deeply felt cultural need to control female sexuality.

Benoist makes a fascinating argument about the appropriateness of candles for the celebration of the feast of the purification of the Virgin. His premise is that legitimate performativity (that is, nonsuperstitious use of lights) is directly connected to sexual purity. First he contrasts the purity of the Virgin to the "impurities, weaknesses, imperfections and blemishes common to other women." Then he presents what appears to be a novel and strange argument about the purity of wax that makes sense only when one extrapolates from the narrowly stated subject of the use of the candles for the feast of the Virgin to the more general logical referent of his argument, which is legitimate performativity more broadly construed. Thus, Benoist argues that there is nothing

> more appropriate to signify the sanctity of Jesus Christ, and the purity of the Virgin, than the candle, whose substance is made without mixing, of male and female . . . just as the sacred humanity of Jesus Christ was formed from the Virgin without any copulation and defilement.[33]

Moreover, the title of Benoist's essay suggests a general connection between varieties of performativity and the act of "profession de foy." Such a connection was already implicit in the Tridentine understanding of the performative truth of eucharistic splendor, as seen in the ever more elaborate processions of the *Fête-Dieu* that became a triumphant profession of faith.[34] Benoist's argument, which exposes the latent connections between nonsuperstitious performativity, sexual purity, and profession of faith, offers further evidence about the general anxiety about performativity and its relation to the control of female sexuality. The goal of a more carefully defined access to the eucharist (that is, the condensation of sacred immanence in the eucharist and in sacramental or carefully regulated paraliturgical settings) is thus directly related to the desire for a more guarded ordering of gender relations. Both involve more carefully regulated performativity and the canalization of votive behaviors into Christocentric and Marian settings. The theory that clerically sanctioned Marian devotions underwent a profound change from the late Middle Ages to the early-modern period is convincingly presented in a recent article by Ellington, who uses sermons from the late fifteenth through the early seventeenth century to trace the transformation of Mary's relation to the passion.[35]

Wills provide an additional and untapped source for understanding the manner in which anxieties about the locus and votive orientation of performative behaviors are connected to notions of communal and sexual purity, and how these anxieties actually transform social behaviors and shape communities.

Requests Affecting the Creation of a Liturgical Community (Value 6)

Continuing with the analytical theme of community formation and performativity, value 6 deals with a range of directives that effect the creation of a ritual or liturgical community. As the discussion of Gueret's will demonstrates, behaviors or gestures included under value 6 are explicit requests for bell-ringing, payments for criers to announce the testator's death through the streets of Paris (to elicit prayers and summon the poor), and requests for inscription into the book of the dead kept at the parish church so these past members of the parish will be remembered collectively in perpetuity in the parish prayers.[36]

Sacralizing Gestures: Making Sacred Time and Space (Value 7)

Value 7 addresses the performativity of the sacralizing gestures that a testator may make at the time of the actual writing down of the will. These gestures, such as making the sign of the cross or asking for a special sacral heading (*in nomine domini*, Jesus + Maria) or the inscription of a simple mark of the cross at the top of the document, are essentially performative and immanentist since they sacralize the moment of the testamentary act as well as the document itself. Table 5.5 reveals the direct correlation of value 7 (use of sacralizing headings) with League affiliation and thus emphasizes the interweaving of the immanential and the performative in the League-affiliated population. In Table 5.5, see the row next to the heading "Sign of the Cross," where Leaguers represent thirty-six percent of all testators using sacralizing headings.

Sacral headings are used in both holograph wills (that is, private wills written by the hand of the testator and subsequently brought to the notary for safekeeping and/or transcription) and in nonholographic (that is, notarial or public) wills. One of the most powerfully probative indices revealing changes in the religious culture is the changing use of sacralizing headings and their transfer from the public notarial will to the privately composed will. Table 5.6 analyzes the changing setting in which sacralizing headings occur in wills over the three sample periods.

This table distinguishes between wills drawn up in a public setting by a notary and wills drawn up in a private or domestic setting by the testator. In 1543–44, there were eleven notarial wills with sacralizing headings, and the eleven testators represent about seven percent of a general testator

Table 5.6
From Public to Private: Sacred Performance

	1543–1544	1590		1630
Notarial (public) wills	11	42	(15)**	9
with sacral headings	[69%]	[93%]		[48%]***
as a percentage of GTP*	7%	6%	(2.06%)	3%
Private wills with sacral	5	3	(1)	10
headings	[33%]	[7%]		[52%]
as a percentage of GTP	3.14%	0.41%	(0.14%)	2.91%
Total wills with sacral	16	45	(16)	19
headings				
as a percentage of GTP	10.06%	6.19%	(2.20%)	3.52%

*   General Testator Population

**   Parentheses contain the numbers of Leaguer wills with sacral headings and their percentages within the GTP. Of the 42 notarial wills with sacral headings in 1590, for example, 15 were Leaguer wills.

***   Brackets express the public or private wills as a percentage of the wills with sacral headings.

population of 159 persons. In 1590, forty-two wills with sacralizing headings were drawn up in a public setting. Of these forty-two wills, fifteen were the wills of Leaguers. That Leaguers represent less than thirteen percent of the general testator population, but drew up fifteen (roughly one-third) of the forty-two notarial wills that have sacralizing headings, means that Leaguers were much more likely to use sacralizing gestures in a public setting.

In 1630, the absolute number of notarial wills decreases, as would be expected in a testator population much smaller than that of 1590. Yet, it should be noted that the overall percentage of testators using sacralizing headings in a public setting has decreased compared to 1543–44 as well as to 1590. By 1630 the sacralizing gesture itself has not only become rarer, but it has become more a feature of private wills, as can be seen in Table 5.6. In 1543–44, thirty-three percent of all wills with sacral headings were private. In 1590, however, only seven percent of all wills with sacral headings were private, meaning that ninety-three percent of all wills with sacral headings were dictated in a public setting to a notary. By 1630, the percentage of wills with sacral headings that were dictated in a public setting falls to fifty-two percent, while the private setting for the use of sacralizing headings now accounts for forty-eight percent.

The contours of the transformation of Parisian religious culture from the pre-Tridentine period to the Enlightenment are thus reflected in Table 5.6. By 1630 the sacral gesture becomes confined to the private space in a condensation of sacred immanence that, at the same time, drives the penitents from the streets and outlaws their confraternities. The most powerful sacral gesture in 1630 now involves a separation from the world (entering a monastery) rather than an act that invests public space, as some of the most characteristic forms of League piety once did. For Leaguers in 1590, however, sacral behaviors (such as making the sign of the cross at the top of the will) were carried out in public domains such as the office of a notary, just as the oath of the League profession of faith was taken in public. League piety filled urban space in 1590 just as the penitential processions had filled the streets of Paris in 1588–89 and the roads of Champagne in 1583–84.

Verbal Performativity (Value 8)

The testator's use of symbolic referents or explanatory wording, such as "in honor of the passion" or "in honor of the five wounds" or "in the name of the 13 apostles," when making a bequest or stating accompanying pious directives is represented by value 8, "verbal performativity." The significance of these phrases lies in the clues they provide about how the testator understands his or her pious request. In combination with other structures of the will, this symbolic wording can serve as a guide to the relative symbolic density of the will—that is, the webs of symbolic meaning that the testators construct between themselves and the sacred, whatever its embodiment.

Bodily Performativity: Body of Self (Value 9)

Value 9 of the Performativity Index deals with expressions relating to bodily performativity. Any pious directives in which the location of the testator's body, its presence, or its precise treatment or movement is indicated are considered instances of bodily performativity. The precise meaning to the testator of the details specified under this category of directives may vary considerably from case to case, and may, in fact, never be fully known. Examples range from requests to be buried in the habit of a religious order to directives concerning timing ("before the body leaves the house") to indicators of the movement of the body ("as the body is placed in the ground"). Most of these expressions serve to designate in a spatial or temporal sense critical moments that begin as death nears and attain some degree of resoluton at the time of burial. All of these expressions make the body the focal point of the experiential frame. The distinctiveness of "bodily performativity" as a mode of characterizing a particular moment in time becomes perceptible when contrasted with value 11, "liturgical performativity," and especially with value 18, "educative or intelligibility" stipulations as part of a directive. This contrast will also provide an opportunity to point to a very long-term shift from a highly immanential to a more transcendental understanding of the relationship to the sacred that is most conducive to salvation.

Thanks to the enormous upsurge of interest in the history of death, general historians have become more familiar with material that was once the preserve of liturgical specialists and some anthropologists and ethnographers.[37] Historians have become more aware that conceptions of the "good" death underwent significant variations within the Christian tradition throughout the Middle Ages and the early-modern period. A careful analysis of the types of performativity that testators invoke for their final moments provides further understanding of the negotiation between clergy and laity about the nature and locus of the sacred and about access to it, particularly in the crucial liminal period of mortal sickness and impending death.[38]

In the earlier Middle Ages it was believed that the most perfect death was the death at the very moment of reception of the last communion or viaticum. The believer desired literally to die with the host in the mouth. There is no more unambiguous expression of an immanentist understanding of the sacred than this, when body of self and body of Christ become one.[39] The moment of approaching death is structured according to a very personal eschatology by many of the League-affiliated testators, such as Genevieve Rolland. She requests a priest to be present with her constantly from the moment she has received the last communion and also requests that her body not be moved for twenty-four hours following her death. Leaguers had widely divergent attitudes toward the treatment of their bodies after death, but they were far from indifferent. For example, *honorable femme* Tassine de Compans, from one of the most prominent Leaguer families, specifically requests that her body not be cut open[40] while *honorable femme* Margueritte Dugué requests that her heart be cut out, encased in lead, and buried by the Holy Sacrament.[41]

The Offertory Procession and the Liturgical Construction of Community (Value 12)

In liturgical memory, it can be argued that the offertory procession is particularly associated with lay participation in a liturgical community. Historically, the prayers associated with the offertory procession were retained in the vernacular longer than any other component of the mass. The directives relating to the offertory[42] merit a distinctive performativity value because of the historical evolution of the ancient offertory procession in the early Christian liturgy. Theodore Klauser, a historian of liturgy, has argued that, in the first centuries of the church,

> each according to his means and following an ancient and widespread custom, used to bring their own contributions to the evening meal. After the separation of the eucharist from the *agape*, they continued to bring their gifts to each of the two liturgical meals; and in this custom, as well as in the regular practice of the ancient world, whereby members of the community themselves presented the sacrificial offerings, lie the roots of the so-called offertory procession, i.e. the presentation of gifts by the faithful.[43]

This passage is directly related to the communal interpretation of the League developed by Robert Descimon. Descimon sees in the political engagement of the *Seize*, in particular, a defense of the ancient rough equality of all "bourgeois," that is, members of the urban commune who, though divided by levels of wealth, nevertheless understood themselves to be part of a community. In this view, the *Seize* and their supporters were galvanized in the cause of the Holy Union not only to defend "integral Catholicism" but also to challenge the legitimacy of a system of venal office with its attendant privileges of nobility that increasingly posed insurmountable barriers to social mobility and destroyed the fabric of the traditional urban commune. Descimon's argument of the equality of the *bourgeois* becomes even more powerful when considered in relation to Leaguer conceptions of the cleric as "citizen" (*citoyen*) that were evident in the petition presented by Leaguer clergy to the duke of Mayenne.

Furthermore, the analysis from the wills of 1590 presented in Table 5.7 reveals the liturgical evidence supporting a communal interpretation of League, especially *Seize*, piety. "The Offertory Procession and the Leaguer Construction of a Liturgical Community" (Table 5.7) shows that 1590's testators mentioning the offertory procession in their wills are clearly linked to the Leaguer milieu by a variety of criteria, including the parish of their residence and the notary they selected. These findings allow us to associate the lay, participatory, and publicly performative quality of the ancient offertory procession with the political and religious engagement of League-affiliated testators, thus underscoring the particular communal orientation of performativity among League militants. The roots of this performativity lie in shared forms of cultural memory that are sustained by liturgical behaviors such as a particular attachment to the offertory procession. The association of this symbolic behavior with several indices of League affiliation

Table 5.7
The Offertory Procession and the Leaguer Construction of a Liturgical Community

Name & Sex		Social Group	Male Profession	Notary	Parish of Residence	Persons Asked to Attend Offertory	Main Purpose	Total # of Bequests
NOEL, Marie	F	Artisan	*Marchand Maistre Boucher*	Arragon	St. Jacques de la Boucherie	13 poor women	On the day of her death, the poor are to attend a *basse messe*, go to the *offrande* with 1 *chandelle ardente*, each gets one *petit pain*, and 12 *deniers tz*. and pray for her to God.	4
HOTMAN, Blanche	F	Honorable/ Bourgeosie	Widow of *Marchand Joyallier*	Arragon	St. Jacques de la Boucherie	"*Tous les pauvres de la paroisse*"	On day of burial give to each of the poor of the parish 1 lighted candle to take to the offertory and give each 12 *deniers* to pray for her soul, her deceased friends, and relatives.	12
POLAIR, Claude	F	Honorable/ Bourgeosie	Wife of a *Marchand Orfevrier*	Arragon	St. Barthelemy	"*Aux pauvres qui se trouverront*"	To the poor who gather on the day of her burial give bread made from "*ung septier de bled, lesquelz pauvres seront tenuz auparavant led. distribution assister à une basse messe qui sera dicte en ladicte eglise par l'ung des quatre ordres mandians, et aller à l'offrande d'icelle avecq une chandelle ardente en la main, qui seront tenuz prier dieu pour l'ame de lad. testatrice et ses parens et amiez trespassez.*"	30

Table 5.7, cont'd
The Offertory Procession and the Leaguer Construction of a Liturgical Community

Name & Sex	Social Group	Male Profession	Notary	Parish of Residence	Persons Asked to Attend Offertory	Main Purpose	Total # of Bequests
GASTELLIER, Catherine F	Honorable/ Bourgeosie	Wife of a *marchand espicier & bourgeois de Paris*	Arragon	St. Jacques de la Boucherie	The poor of St. Jacques de la Boucherie	To the poor . . . 1 *écu 2 tiers* and for this that they may take to the *offrande une chandelle ardente* and let there be said one *basse messe* and the poor should pray God for her.	8
HEBERT, Denis M	Day Laborer	*Gagne-Denier*	Thévenin	St. Nicolas des Champs	24 *pauvres*	"*Item ordonne qu'il soit donner à 24 pauvres à chaschun trois deniers lesd. pauvres yront à l'offrande à la dernière desd. trois messes.*"	4
PLASTRIER, Charlotte F	Honorable/ Bourgeosie	Wife of *marchand espicier de Paris & Quartenier*	Filesac	St. Nicolas des Champs	200 *pauvres de sa paroisse*	"*3 écuz soleil 20 solz pour estre distribuer à d'eulx ung sol tz. et auquelz sera baille une chandelle de cire pour aller à l'offrand de ladicte messe qui se dira en la chappelle du st. sacrement.*"	11
POIGNANT, Jehan[1] M	Honorable/ Bourgeosie	*Marchand et bourgeois*	Mahieu	St. Jacques de la Boucherie	50 *pauvres of the parish*	Who will attend his services and go to the offertory of the church on the day of his burial to each 1 *sol tz.* and pray God for him.	9

Table 5.7, cont'd

The Offertory Procession and the Leaguer Construction of a Liturgical Community

Name & Sex	Social Group	Male Profession	Notary	Parish of Residence	Persons Asked to Attend Offertory	Main Purpose	Total # of Bequests
FRANCISQUE, F Genevieve[2]	Soldiers	*Archer des gardes du roy*	Leroux	St. Eustache	*100 pauvres*	To attend each of her services at the Bons Hommes at the couvent filles Dieu and give each *ung chandelle et 3 deniers pour l'offrande* and also give each poor 12 deniers that they pray God for her; also requests 13 *basses messes*.[3]	16
BAUDRY, F Blanche	Artisan	*Faiseur d'estuves*	Troyes	St. Eustache	*100 pauvres*	*"1 chandelle ardente à la main et les admonestes . . . de prier dieu pour l'ame d'elle testatrice et de ses pere et mere, parens et amyes trespasses et que a chascun d'iceulx pauvres leur soient baillé et distribuez et aulmosnez deux deniers pour tous payes et a chascun ung pain de la valleur de douze deniers."*	8

1. "And the testator has said that he thanks God for the six children of which three are sons and three are daughters it has pleased God our creator to give him in marriage to honorable femme Anne Doublet, his wife, and he entreats our Lord and creator to give them the grace to be good people and to always have the fear of God in front of them and he wishes and charges the afore said children to always obey and have honor and reverence for their mother as good children are obliged to do and if these children or any one of them do the contrary he wishes and orders that his wife give to the l'Hostel Dieu de Paris the part and the portion that would belong to the disobedient ones among them."
2. "As she is leaving Paris to go to Bouy near the town of Provins and also due to her old age and fearing that she might become ill on the road or worse than she might encounter someone of the party opposing the Holy Catholic Union, and that they might treat her badly in her person."
3. The request for 13 *basses messes* is a forbidden form of liturgical number symbolism.

reveals the full hypothetical scope of the interrelations of civic and sacral immanence that guided the development of the Performativity Index.

Of the nine testators mentioning the offertory procession, all selected poor persons to participate in the procession. Seven of the nine testators were from ardent Leaguer parishes, that is, Saint-Jacques-de-la-Boucherie, Saint-Nicolas-des-Champs, and Saint-Barthélemy. The will of Genevieve Francisque, one of the two testators from the parish of Saint-Eustache, a *politique* parish, contains a rare and remarkable revelation that she is a supporter of the Holy Union. The other testator from Saint-Eustache parish, Blanche Baudry, the wife of an artisan, went out of her parish to the University quarter to have her will drawn up by the clearly League-connected notary Claude de Troyes. De Troyes' practice, located in the Leaguer parish of Saint-André-des-Arts, included four Leaguers, among them young *noble homme* Pierre Hennequin, who made bequests both to the Jesuits and to the Feuillants and Sebastien Megaly, the former aumoner of Mary, Queen of Scots, then "presently aumoner to the duke of Mayenne." De Troyes also had the very highest performativity ranking of all notaries based on the consistent use of the sacralizing heading "Jesus Maria" found with the sign of the cross at the top of his clients' wills.[44] These interconnections strongly suggest that for Blanche Baudry, de Troyes was a notary of conviction.

Finally, four of the nine testators who were from League-affiliated parishes and who mentioned offertory processions chose the notary Louis Arragon. Arragon is a particularly interesting League-affiliated notary. Denis Pallier, a specialist on printers during the League, has identified Arragon as one of the notaries frequented by Leaguer printers, as Table 5.8 shows. Arragon's parish was Saint-Jacques-de-la-Boucherie, whose curate was the *Seize* militant Jacques Pelletier. He also had two clients in 1590 who were members of the highly politicized confraternities of the Holy Sacrament. In subsequent chapters we will see that all the other notaries listed in Table 5.8 have special attachments to the League that are apparent in all of their clientele, not simply their clientele of printers.

Entering a Monastery (Value 19)[45]

Value 19 in the Performativity Index permits us to track the changing patterns of monastic professions from 1543–44 to 1630 and to relate this behavior to changes in other performative behaviors. This analysis provides a new perspective on the well-known general trend toward increased monastic professions in the seventeenth century. Although the data does not concern large numbers of cases, they are consonant with the distinct feminization of

Chapter 6

Paris Ligueur, 1590: The Fusion of the Civic and the Sacred

What is La Saincte Union Catholicque?

Recent historians of the Paris League would agree that a special fusion of the civic and the sacred is one of the most striking features of the Catholic League, or the Holy Union (*La saincte Union catholicque*). There is much less consensus about how to characterize the relations between the civic and the sacred and how to explain the mechanisms of their fusion. In part, these problems persist because no historian has systematically examined the relations of the civic to the sacred across the entire period of militant Catholicism. The magnitude of such a task inevitably means that each historian privileges certain sources and certain time periods.[1] An even more fundamental difficulty arises because historians of the League differ about the role of socio-political factors in defining the Holy Union. There are also disagreements over how to develop socio-professional or socio-economic categories and apply them to the League movement over time. After a high-point of radicalism in 1591 under *Seize* leadership, many defections from "the party" of zealous Catholics took place. From this point the more conservative princely League led by Charles, duke of Mayenne, began to vie with the *Seize* wing of the League for control of Paris. There also remained a silent and perhaps even majoritarian segment of the population, the *politiques*. By 1593 the *politique* position in favor of recognizing Henry of Navarre as king began to assert itself, especially after Henry's conversion to Catholicism in July 1593. This growing royalist force known as the *semoneux* (from the French verb *semondre*, to summon) ultimately gained complete control of the city with Henry IV's entry into Paris in March 1594.[2]

The Warriors of God: Crouzet and the Phenomenological Analysis of Leaguer Gestural Culture

One of the goals of Denis Crouzet's study of the League is to restore both "God" and "the people" as agents in the historical process.[3] From this perspective, Crouzet regards the League, or Holy Union, as "a prophetic and mystical union with God."[4] Even more significantly, Crouzet designates two historical moments as an intense "complete imbrication of the Civic and the Social. . . . "[5] Thus, although Crouzet regards the League as "a collective enchantment," he does provide a historical context for this interpretation. The two historical periods of special significance in Crouzet's arguments are the fifty-five-day mourning period in Paris for the Lorrain princes lasting from the end of December 1588 through February 1589, and the assassination of Henry III by Jacques Clément in August 1589.

The duke and cardinal of Guise had been assassinated on the king's order in the night from December 23 to December 24, 1588. The news of this act reached Paris on Christmas day and triggered an unparalleled outpouring of anguish and a sense of calamity for the Catholic cause. Intensifying this sense of peril and impending final judgment was the memory of the failed Armada of November 1588 in which the hopes for a Catholic reconquest of England were dashed.

Crouzet's treatment of two events in the mourning period for the Guises deserves close analysis for what it reveals about his essentially phenomenological treatment of the fusion of the civic with the social. He regards the funeral service in Notre-Dame cathedral for the slain Guises as a time when, as he says, "it is by the striving towards God, in the celebration of the funerals of the Lorraine princes and in the penitential piety [expressed at this moment] that the [Catholic] Union is consummated."[6] Crouzet argues that the emotional intensity of the mourning processions and services induced a state of "desubjectification," "desocialization," and "deritualization."[7] In this remarkable view the gestural culture of Leaguers lies beyond ritual, and certainly beyond merely institutionally imposed ritual.[8] For Crouzet, League time is "mythic," not liturgical time.[9] Although he mentions liturgy frequently, he does not intend to explore its effects as a prime channel for sacred action in the world. The other great apogee of sacral action in a history that is "outside of history" is the regicide of Henry III by Jacques Clément, which Crouzet regards as a virtual sacramental "sacrifice" uniting all of the people of Paris.[10]

Crouzet's Interpretation of Catholic Militancy and Violence

Crouzet's interpretation of the League as a mystical experience is riddled with tensions about the social identity of the participants in this intense search for purification and expiation. He posits a unity of the bourgeoisie that depends upon "the eschatological unity of the city,"[11] and argues that the "League" antedates the social tensions usually seen as the engine of the League movement.

Nonetheless, Crouzet is also interested in the relationship between the two groups that have long been the focus of attention in social and political analyses of the movement: the "clerical League" (the League of the preachers) and the *Seize*. In his insistence that religious engagement is not a matter of social cleavages, he argues that the clerical League and the *Seize* are one. "The clerical League is indissociable from the League of laymen. . . . The *Seize* have, in themselves, the very same sacral power that the preachers possess. . . ."[12] The difficulty of this argument is its approach to historical agency and its reliance on historical sources that seem to take on a life of their own. As a companion to this approach to the agency of words is a view of the sacred as completely otherworldly rather than deeply social. The League for Crouzet is an "ordre surnaturel."[13] As such, it could never simply be the work of ecclesiastical elites and a "second bourgeosie."[14] Rather the League is a "prophetic consciousness" and the result of a "mechanism of anguish."[15] In the mind of the participants in this sacred crusade the project of the League is authored by God. In this way, Crouzet is able to speak of sacral consciousness as a historical force.[16]

Connected to this approach is a particular interpretation of the relationship between the League of the *Seize* and violence.[17] Crouzet distinguishes sharply between the period of the Saint Bartholomew's Day Massacres (a failure, in his view) and the subsequent interiorization of violence that occurs during the League period itself.[18] This view of the gestural culture of Catholicism reinterprets the physically expressive characteristics of League piety as a form of interiorization. It becomes possible to speak of the violence of prayer ("violence orante") as an introjection of otherwise exteriorized violence.[19] This places the League in a direct relationship to the flowering of seventeenth-century French mysticism.[20] Thus, in Crouzet's history, the body of the penitent holds an ambiguous place. At one moment Crouzet stresses the physical desire to join with God.[21] But he also has interpreted the white sackcloth of the penitent as an expression of the desire to transcend the body.[22] Moreover, Crouzet regards the violence against the life of Henry III as an expression of mystical adoration, "a mystic love that is collectively experienced; the Catholic Union attains its soteriological fulfillment in him."[23]

In discussing the phenomenon of Catholic militancy, Crouzet insists upon the existence of two phases of the experience of zealous Catholics that he regards as very different in nature. The first phase is "collective enchantment" and the millenarian and mystical pursuit of atonement, cleansing, and unification with God. In a "second phase," that of "militancy," social, economic, and political factors do play a role where earlier they did not.[24] Crouzet does not follow up this distinction, but it is clearly an important one essential for understanding militant Catholicism.

Social and Civic Fusion from the
Perspective of Testamentary Evidence

This chapter uses the wills of 1590 to map Leaguer loyalties in their social, political, and especially liturgical specificity. The motive forces of the League, and the *Seize* in particular, were indeed closely tied to aspirations for salvation. In this sense Crouzet's vision of the "soteriological" essence of the Holy Union is entirely justified. For the known League militants and individuals whose wills give clear evidence of Leaguer loyalties, the eschatology of millenarian mysticism was clearly not the only path to salvation. Testamentary evidence naturally tends to give a view of "orthopraxis" in the sense that Eamon Duffey has used this term. That does not, however, disqualify this evidence. Rather, the intense liturgical and social bonds this chapter documents reveal that more than one eschatology and more than one vision of salvation prevailed in Leaguer Paris. In the economies of salvation presented below, liturgy becomes "the royal road" to understanding the consciousness and behaviors of supporters of the Holy Union.

The following analysis thus attempts to bridge the differences between the socio-political and phenomenological interpretations of the League by examining the geography of Leaguer loyalties as mapped by testamentary evidence.

The Cultural Mapping of Leaguer Economies of Salvation[25]

In large measure, the key to *Paris ligueur* in 1590 lies in discovering the ways in which the University resonated throughout the city. Crouzet draws attention to this dynamic when he speaks of the fusion of the civic and the sacred.[26] There is still a need, however, for a social and institutional analysis that focuses on the locus of the sacred in the world. At the center of such an analysis must be the world of the League preachers, who were products largely of the University's two theology faculties, the college of the Sorbonne, and the less well known and more austere College of Navarre. The authority of these clerics had deep roots within the civic and religious culture of the city. Claude de Seyssel, in his famous portrait of the late-medieval French monarchy, wrote about the power of preaching as one of the three bridles upon the king.[27] The influence of these doctors and bachelors of theology upon civic life was assured by their roles as Parisian curates or as members of the great monastic communities that were intimately involved in the lives of ordinary Parisians in a myriad of ways. The Capuchins, for example, new to the city from Italy, first became broadly popular only after they ministered to the sick in the plague years of the 1580s. The sacral space of the monastery often served as civic space as well.

At the center of the map, then, lies the world of the University as Leaguers understood it: a dense network of traditional mendicant orders and associated educational institutions whose social and institutional histories became intimately intertwined as the mendicant orders, in particular, became both the preeminent teachers and students of scholasticism and, in effect, the chief missionaries to a growing urban population.[28] In 1590 the religious and political militancy of League preachers and their allies among the *Seize* grew directly from these deep, affective, and at times contradictory bonds that developed in a volatile blend of scholasticism and popular religion that characterized much of urban piety of the high and especially the late Middle Ages. Speaking generally, in each of these periods, as well as during the League, one can find an urban population anxious about its salvation in a world shaken by profound cultural changes, whether these be associated with the commercial revolution of the high Middle Ages that first brought the mendicants to the cities, the aftershocks of the Black Death, or the cataclysmic shattering of confessional unity in the Europe of the sixteenth century.

A closer look at the map of Leaguer Paris reveals the great monastic houses near the University, in whose meeting rooms the League was conceived.[29] On the present *Quai des Augustins*, on the Left Bank of the Seine, was the house of the Augustinians; the Dominicans of the rue Saint-Jacques, also known as the Order of Preachers, or the Black Friars, were also called the Jacobins because their monastery was located on the rue Saint-Jacques, the most prominent street of the University quarter. This was a neighborhood shared by clerics, booksellers, notaries, students and, in 1590, by soldiers and nobles as well. Jacques Clément, the assassin of Henry III, was a monk of this friary. His superior, Edmond Bourgoing, who praised this act, was himself drawn and quartered. The Carmelites, or White Friars, were located on the Place Maubert,[30] the site where heretics were regularly burned. The prior of the Carmelites would be forced into exile in 1594, at the time of Henry IV's triumphant entry into Paris. The last of the great mendicant orders were the Franciscans (or Cordeliers), founded originally in the parish of Saint-Côme in 1230. At this same parish, the Scot, Hamilton, fresh with his doctorate of theology from the Sorbonne, became one of the most vocal of the *Seize* curates in the heart of the University quarter.[31]

Among medievalists the cultural forces that brought the mendicants to the cities in the thirteenth century are well known, as is the story of how these preaching orders became intimately involved with the learned population of the schools, which served as a recruiting ground for the mendicants. Further, the strategic role that these preeminent preaching orders played in addressing the rising religious aspirations of a growing urban population riddled with anxieties about the incompatibilities of money-making and salvation is also familiar.[32] A very similar basis for interaction between the mendicants and an anxious laity existed at the time of the League just as it had during the commercial revolution of the twelfth and thirteenth centuries. The parallels extend further since the challenges facing the mendicant orders and the difficulties confronting traditional colleges of the University were heightened by royal absolutism and the tensions within reformed and reinvigorated Catholicism. Like the culture of *basoche*, and the trade corporations of the city, traditional mendicant piety faced new cultural and social norms when the traditional civic culture in which their religiosity had flourished was transformed by Catholic reform and the reinvigorated monarchy.[33]

Did a new understanding of monasticism and the role of lay apostolicity reach Paris with the arrival of the Jesuits, the Capuchins, and the Feuillants? Bernard Chevalier, for example, has come closest to defining the importance of the mendicants in the urban culture of the late Middle Ages.[34] He offers a penetrating evaluation of conflicting attitudes toward the mendicant orders, whom he describes as "the sole mediators between the learned Church [of scholasticism] and popular piety [la piété commune]." The understanding of the fusion of sacral and civic immanence that emerges in testamentary analysis indicates there is much more to be learned about the bonds between the University, the mendicants, and the urban laity. The activism of the mendicant orders during the period of the League indicates the influence of the same forces that shaped the civic identity of the laity.

One of the most important figures of the League period is the armed monk-citizen who marched in the May 14, 1590, procession. The context and meaning of this great performative moment have been much misunderstood and distorted. Historians have failed to explore the figure of the armed cleric as citizen and defender of civic values. To interpret the significance of the armed cleric, we need to consider the Leaguer (or *Seize*-specific) perception of ecclesiastics as citizens. This perception emerges clearly in a petition presented by the clergy of Paris to the Duke of Mayenne in 1590. The clergy and the University insist that every person holding an office or benefice be required to take an oath to uphold the Catholic religion. This explicit equation of governmental/civic offices and benefices is of fundamental importance. The petition emphasizes the public and performative setting of this fundamental oath of allegiance calling for a "public confession by each *bourgeois*, whether ecclesiatic or lay."[35] This petition reveals a powerful underlying equation between the *Seize* protest against venality of office and clerical abhorrence of simony. The fact that both lay and clerical members of the League objected to a commercialization of offices both public and sacred points to key values concerning the sacred and the civic that both groups shared. The petition of the clerics to the Duke of Mayenne is explicit in considering ecclesiastics as "cytoyens" as they argue for a universal requirement to take the "Serment d'Union":

> It shall be prohibited for any ecclesiastical court or jurisdictional authority, any chapters and colleges, and congregations whether founded in the universities or recognized bodies to receive any office or benefice prior to having taken the oath of the Union like all other citizens. . . . [36]

Is it significant that the Jesuits did not process in the May 14th armed review? The military role of the Jesuits during the siege of Paris is well known. Their armed contingent was alone responsible for turning back a surprise attack by Henry of Navarre on the 9th and 10th of September 1590 just after the siege had been lifted. Thus, the argument cannot be made that the Jesuits refused to bear arms on behalf of the Catholic Union. Chevalier, however, sees the role of the Jesuits as a decisive break with these popular and antiquated traditions of the Middle Ages. He thus makes a fundamental contrast between the mixed religious culture fostered by the mendicants and the "purification" of old-style religion by the Jesuits.[37] There is, however, a strong performative element in Jesuit religious culture, apparent in the figure of someone like Henry III's ascetic Jesuit confessor, Emond Auger, who wrote the statutes for the king's company of White Penitents founded in 1583 at the Augustinian friary, as well as an important treatise on penitence, *Metanoeologie*.[38]

The ties between the *Université* and the *Ville*, as revealed in testamentary evidence, suggest some of the ways these bonds defined the boundaries of civic identity while simultaneously linking the city to the wider world of militant Catholicism. There are three excellent examples. First, Jehan Gincestre, the young bachelor of theology from the University who seized control of the curacy of Saint-Gervais,[39] who was one of the League's most inflammatory and anti-royalist preachers, deposited his 1590 will with the Leaguer notary François Herbin. Second, Pierre Christin, the "Demosthenes of the League," left a 1590 will with the Leaguer notary Hilaire Lybault. Third, the holograph will of Jehan Hervy, the curate of Saint-Jean-en-Grève, deposited with the Leaguer notary Monthenault in the parish of Saint-Gervais, recasts our understanding of this curé's character and party loyalties.[40] Although there appears to be no testamentary evidence for him, François Pigenat, who was also trained at the University, and gave the funeral oration in Notre-Dame cathedral for the slain Guise brothers, seized control of the parish of Saint-Nicolas-des-Champs, a parish with an activist confraternity of the Holy Sacrament.[41] An examination of the clients of the notaries Herbin and Lybault, along with Lamiral, Cothereau, and Raoul and Mathurin Bontemps permits a more detailed understanding of the links between the *Ville* and the *Université*, the new and old religious orders and confraternities central to League mobilization.[42]

Although Denis Richet stressed the close ties between the lesser *gens de loi* (the *basoche*) and the League preachers, little has been learned about this alliance and what sustained it. In an effort to explore this question, the next portion of this chapter examines the notaries who prepared the wills of the lesser men of the law and of the "University milieu," the two groups most highly mobilized for the League, and especially for the *Seize*. Table 6.1 shows the notaries used by testators from the social milieu of the *gens de loi*. We have already encountered Hilaire Lybault and François Herbin in Chapter 1 as notaries for the most intransigent Leaguers exiled in 1594. In 1590, Lybault drew up the will of the League preacher, Pierre Christin, and had sixteen other testators. Seven of these testators (over forty-one percent of all of Lybault's wills for 1590) are of the milieu of the *gens de loi*.

The mendicant orders, as already emphasized, were an integral part of the University milieu. For example, as Table 6.2 shows, a broader social spectrum of individuals asked to be buried at the mendicant orders in 1590, which suggests the particular nature of the University's attraction during the highly politicized period of the League.[43] Because the University was intimately engaged with the mendicant orders, it is interesting to see precisely which testators from the University milieu integrated the mendicant orders into their economies of salvation.

Next in importance as notaries for the *gens de loi* are Philippe Cothereau and Raoul Bontemps.[44] Table 6.3 shows that the notaries Philippe Lamiral, Raoul Bontemps, and François Herbin had the largest numbers of clients from the University and liberal professions. A closer look at these notaries who were most important for the testators of the University milieu will help pinpoint the sites and behaviors that brought the University milieu together with strategically situated individuals and groups in the general testator population, especially those known for their League affiliations. Here many important Leaguers can be recognized.[45] It should be remembered that one of the League's most radical curates, Jehan Gincestre, from Saint-Gervais, chose Herbin to draw up his will.[46] The patterns of testamentary practice revealed in these notarial clienteles will show the way the bonds of performativity linked the *Ville* and the *gens de loi* to the world of the League preachers and to the *Université*. These ties form the matrix from which the fusion of civic and sacral immanence developed in 1590.

Table 6 .1
1590 Notaries Used by *Gens de Loi* Testators

Notary Name	Number of Testators Categorized as *Gens de Loi*	Percent	Cumulative Percent
Lybault	7	7.2%	7.2%
Cothereau, P.	6	6.2%	13.4%
Bontemps, R.	5	5.2%	18.6%
Levasseur	5	5.2%	23.7%
Bergeon	4	4.1%	27.8%
Jacques	4	4.1%	32.0%
Labarde	4	4.1%	36.1%
Lusson	4	4.1%	40.2%
Chapelain, S.	3	3.1%	43.3%
Chapellain, J.	3	3.1%	46.4%
Charles	3	3.1%	49.5%
Fardeau, J.	3	3.1%	52.6%
Peron	3	3.1%	55.7%
Tulloue	2	2.1%	58.8%
Arragon	2	2.1%	60.8%
Bernard	2	2.1%	62.9%
Bontemps, M.	2	2.1%	64.9%
Bruyère	2	2.1%	67.0%
Chartain	2	2.1%	69.1%
Filesac	2	2.1%	71.1%
Herbin	2	2.1%	73.2%
Leroy	2	2.1%	75.3%
Monthenault	2	2.1%	77.3%
Muret	2	2.1%	79.4%
Périer	2	2.1%	81.4%
Poche	2	2.1%	83.5%
Saint Vaast	2	2.1%	85.6%
Thevenin	2	2.1%	87.6%
Goguyer	1	1.0%	88.7%
Haultdesens	1	1.0%	89.7%
Lamiral	1	1.0%	90.7%
Babynet	1	1.0%	91.8%
Mahieu	1	1.0%	92.8%
Maigret	1	1.0%	93.8%
Robinot	1	1.0%	94.8%
Rossignol	1	1.0%	95.9%
Saint-Fussien	1	1.0%	96.9%
Trouvé	1	1.0%	97.9%
Troyes	1	1.0%	99.0%
Viard	1	1.0%	100.0%
Total	97	100%	

Table 6.2
Role of the Mendicant Orders in Economies of Salvation

Social Group	1540		1590		1630	
	Number of Testators	% of Total Mendicant Burial Requests	Number of Testators	% of Total Mendicant Burial Requests	Number of Testators	% of Total Mendicant Burial Requests
Nobles	1	50%	5	20%	1	20%
Honorables bourgeois	1	50%	4	16%	2	40%
University/liberal professions			4	16%	1	20%
Merchants					1	20%
Artisans			4	16%		
Middle/lower officials			2	8%		
Laboureurs			2	8%		
Clergy			1	4%		
Noble office/epithet			1	4%		
Gens de Loi			1	4%		
Soldiers			1	4%		
Total # of Testators	2	100%	25	100%	5	100%
Testators as a percentage of the General Testator Population		1.2%		3.4%		1.4%

Table 6.3
1590 Notaries Used by University/Liberal Professional Testators

Notary Name	Number of Testators from University/ Liberal Professions	Percent	Cumulative Percent
Lamiral	7	22.6%	22.6%
R. Bontemps	5	16.1%	38.7%
Herbin	3	9.7%	48.4%
Bruyère	2	6.5%	54.8%
Chauvet	2	6.5%	61.3%
Bernard	1	3.2%	64.5%
Charles	1	3.2%	67.7%
Fardeau	1	3.2%	71.0%
Jacques	1	3.2%	74.2%
Babynet	1	3.2%	77.4%
Lybault	1	3.2%	80.6%
Maigret	1	3.2%	83.9%
Monthenault	1	3.2%	87.1%
Périer	1	3.2%	90.3%
Saint-Vaast	1	3.2%	93.5%
Thévenin	1	3.2%	96.8%
Troyes	1	3.2%	100.0%
Total	31	100%	

Pierre Brotin's Testament: Not Just a Will but a Paradigm

To understand this alliance of the *Seize* and the clergy, there is no better place to begin than in the *étude* of the notary Clément Bernard to whom, on May 3, 1590, a young man of 18, still below the age of legal majority, came to dictate his will. Bernard's practice lay in the heart of the University quarter in the parish of Saint-Séverin, one of the main Leaguer parishes, and one of the sites where international Catholicism was most at home in Paris. We have only to recall the riots in this parish in 1587 protesting the removal of the *Tableau of Madame de Montpensier*, which depicted the martyr's death of Mary, Queen of Scots, to be reminded of the volatile combination of Guise loyalties and passionate local attachments to international Catholicism that filled the neighborhoods of the University quarter. The furor over the publication of the Bull *In Coena Domini* [*At the Lord's Supper*] that Gallican historians of the French church have been loath to explore also ignited not far from there in 1580.[47]

Our young testator Pierre Brotin, a resident of the neighboring University parish of Saint-Benoît, where the impassioned Leaguer Jehan Boucher was *curé*, identified himself as the son of the deceased Pierre Brotin, a "*marchand et habitant*" of the city of Dijon, a Leaguer stronghold, and of Guyette Lourdaye, now married to *honorable homme* Jehan Darmacourt, a *marchand et Bourgeois de Paris.*[48] As it is customary in the preamble of a will to indicate one's motivations and the state of one's health, Brotin reveals that he is about to depart for Burgundy and then journey on to Rome. With a clear sense of the danger of travel in such calamitous times, he refers directly to the "guerres civilles" that daily augment sickness and misery throughout the kingdom.[49] Then, instead of the simple formula "allant et venant" to describe his good health, Brotin provides an unusually detailed and revealing description of himself:

> going and coming daily through the streets of this city of Paris and to churches to hear the word of God and to attend his divine service.[50]

The performative element in this excerpt originates in the idea of accumulating salvific benefits by daily attending services at several churches. Perhaps this passage also echoes the late-medieval practice of seeing as many elevations of the host as possible in the belief that there is salvific efficacy in this form of ritual participation. What is striking in this preamble from Brotin's will is the precision of the verb *ouyr* (to hear) and the careful liturgical distinction the testator makes between the two clearly defined parts of the religious ceremony: the Service of the Word ("*la parolle de Dieu*") and the mass or eucharist ("*son divin service*").[51]

Brotin's obvious hunger for the Word of God and his daily attendance at mass convey the consolation of the liturgy and the personal impact of the Leaguer *curés* and preachers in sustaining Leaguer morale.[52] Brotin's will thus reveals the affective impact of these preachers, so many of whom were Leaguer clerics and a constituent element of the University as a *habitus*, as Bourdieu would use this term. The sparse but direct testimony of Brotin's will, "faict, nommé et dicté de sa propre bouche"—a rarely encountered phrase in the 1590s wills—counters the almost universally polemical or sarcastic accounts of the role of Leaguer *curés* and preachers during the siege and underscores their central role in the Leaguer understanding of salvation and right order in the world.[53] While Brotin clearly acknowledges the dangers of civil war, he is preoccupied with the problem of his salvation. Brotin's conjunction of thoughts about matters of a more "civil" nature and matters of salvation is a salutary warning to historians about the limitations of isolated words ("civil war") in conveying the fullness of experience. Brotin surely did not understand the *politique* dichotomy between civil and sacred because both domains were integral to his religious experience and his ontology of self.

Although his will is quite unremarkable in its actual pious provisions
(he leaves all arrangements to his mother), it is arresting in the way it
contextualizes the central performative reference in the will, that is, Brotin's
intense devotion to hear the Word of God as preached and as celebrated
through the liturgy. His itinerary from Burgundy to Rome in the early days
of the siege is the only other unique feature in this testament. When placed
together, however, these bits of information draw our attention to the cultural interaction between the preachers of the League and zealous Catholics of Paris and contextualize this relationship within the twin poles of its
Guisard and ultramontane loyalties. Brotin's journey thus evokes the sacred
geography of an ancient Christian empire where the Middle Kingdom of
Burgundy linked the Franks to Rome. Also recognizable are the boundaries
of a dynastic dream, which the Houses of Guise and Lorraine sought to
realize with claims of family lineage traced to Charlemagne. In strict geo-
political terms, Brotin's journey follows the "Spanish Road,"[54] which stretched
from Italy to the Low Countries. The testamentary evidence of 1590, however, concretizes these broader loyalties within the local boundaries of a
vital Leaguer subculture in which sacred and political geography were inseparable. The performative relations between the preacher and his audi-
ence that are at the core of Brotin's economy of salvation become a paradigm
pointing us to the local, performative, social, and political bonds that conveyed
membership in La saincte Union.[55] Our task at hand, then, is to extrapolate
from the evidence on notarial clienteles that documents actual social or political alliances between the preachers and clerics of the League and specific
segments of the Parisian population. This permits a broader contextualization
of Brotin's relationship to the preachers and clerics of the League.

The Mobilization of the University Milieu: The World of Philippe Lamiral

A brief investigation of some of the testaments of the notary Philippe Lamiral
allows us to see these patterns even more clearly. Lamiral's practice was
located in the University quarter on the rue Saint-Jacques where he was
active as a notary from 1555 through 1590. Of all the notaries of the 1590s,
Lamiral has a clientele with the highest concentration of University-related testators and the highest proportion of clerical testators. Table 6.4
lists Lamiral's clients by profession and gives their rankings on the key cluster variables that offer an index of performativity. A great deal is known
about Lamiral the man. Robert Descimon documented the marriage of
Lamiral's daughter Marie to the Seize activist Claude Garlin, a procureur by

Table 6.4

Performativity Rankings for Testators of Notary Philippe Lamiral

Surname	Profession (see below)	# Times Shows Performativity	# Mentions of Body of Jesus Christ	# Immanentist Gestures	# Mentions of own Body	# Uses of Liturgical Detail	# Uses of Liturgical Calendar	# Bequests to Jesuits/ Capuchins/ Feuillants	# Reformist Gestures
Legoux	7	1	0	1	0	0	0	0	0
Richer	1	0	1	1	0	0	0	0	0
Mollert	9	0	0	0	0	0	0	0	0
Laurent	5	7	2	0	3	3	0	0	0
Eloy	8	0	0	0	0	0	0	0	0
Mallemen	6	0	0	0	0	0	0	0	0
Debucholic*	7	0	0	0	0	0	0	0	0
Faure	7	0	0	0	0	0	0	0	0
Durant	1	1	2	1	0	0	0	0	0
Prevost	9	0	0	0	0	0	0	0	0
Devillers	7	0	0	2	0	0	1	0	0
Faber	7	0	0	1	0	0	0	0	0
Forgeais	2	2	0	1	0	0	0	0	0
Prevost	7	0	0	0	0	0	0	0	0
Rolland	5	11	1	9	2	2	0	1	1
Dufour	7	0	0	0	0	0	0	0	0

Table 6.4, cont'd
Performativity Rankings for Testators of Notary Philippe Lamiral

Professional Categories of Testators

Professional Category	Number of testators	Percent	Cumulative Percent
university/liberal professions	7	43.8	43.8
clergy	2	12.5	56.3
honorables bourgeois	2	12.5	68.8
artisans	2	12.5	81.3
nobles	1	6.3	87.5
gens de loi	1	6.3	93.8
mixed merchants	1	6.3	100.0
Total	16	100.0	100.0

* brother of Georges Bucholicq, who uses the notary Ph. Cothereau. See Table 6.5.

profession who took his oath in the Leaguer militia in July 1588, participated in the Brisson affair, and was one of those exiled from Paris in 1594 by
Henry IV.[56] Descimon wrote of Garlin with a poignant insight, especially
when we contemplate the evidence that has accumulated only after his
prosopography appeared: "The deep political roots of the Holy Union in
Paris depend upon this reserve of a second line of leaders of the *Seize* of
which Garlin is representative."[57] Applying our theory allows us to demonstrate the extent to which this political implantation was in so many cases
inextricable from a form of religious conviction that necessarily expressed
itself in immanentist and performative religious as well as political comportment. Garlin belonged to the socio-professional milieu with the highest rate of *Seize* affiliation. He lived in the parish of Saint-Séverin, which,
as already mentioned, was known for its traditional defense of international
Catholicism. This was, in fact, the parish to which Mademoiselle de
Montpensier belonged despite her residence in the quarter of the Louvre
(her version of the "pull factor," one might say).[58] The marriage of Lamiral's
daughter to Garlin demonstrates the nature of the social ties that mirror
the political and religious alliance of the *gens de loi* with the Leaguer clerics.
In other words, the marriage alliance with Garlin is related to the composition of Lamiral's notarial clientele (its heavily clerical and University component) and even more importantly to the type and distribution of
performative and immanential behavior among Lamiral's clients. It is important to note that the laymen and laywomen, and not the clerics, among
Lamiral's clients engage in performative or reformist gestures. In other words,
by their professional identities and institutional loyalties the clerics among
these notarial clienteles literally embody an identity that the lay people
enact through the gestural economies of their wills. Indeed, the notion of
shared meanings and feelings would be less convincing if the clerics' wills
were primarily responsible for the high performativity rankings and markers of special pious engagement, while the lay clients' wills were unexceptional in their performativity. This dimorphism reveals the distinct but reciprocal bonds between clerics and religiously engaged laity at the time: the
clerics embody sacral immanence in their metaphysical transformation in ordination; the laity are drawn in their own powerful way to enact immanence in their pious requests and higher rates of testamentary performativity.

Les Mathurins, Pères de la Trinité, or de la Rédemption des Captifs: A Microsite of Zealous Catholicism

As Table 6.4 indicates, the two of Lamiral's testators with the highest general indicators of performativity are *honorable femme* Marye Laurent and

honorable femme Genevieve Rolland, both laywomen in good health.[59] Examining the identity, devotional loyalties, and gestural economy of the first of these testators, Marye Laurent, takes us closer to yet another microsite of Leaguer activism: the monastery of the Mathurins, also known as the Fathers of the Trinity or Fathers of the Redemption of Captives. The latter name is an interesting echo of the crusading period that the League itself resembled in so many ways. Laurent shared bonds to this order with the Leaguer notary Lamiral, who selected burial there. Laurent was also a member of the confraternity of Saint John the Evangelist, located at the Mathurins.[60] The neighborhood of this monastery is a site where booksellers, *gens de loi* such as Lamiral (and Saint-Vaast), and the clerics of the schools, churches, and monasteries of the University quarter met and shared deeply felt bonds of civic and religious loyalties.

In addition to having a high general performativity level (7), Marye Laurent is one of only two of Lamiral's testators who lived outside of the University quarter.[61] She was clearly a client of conviction for whom Lamiral represented a notary of conviction practicing in a neighborhood to which she, despite her current residence, had close ties. She was the widow of *honorable homme* Pierre Ricouart, whose profession of *marchand libraire* clearly suggests the nature of the ties his widow would have to the University quarter. Laurent lived in a house known by the sign of the Dolphin on the Bridge of Notre-Dame in the parish of Saint-Jacques-de-la-Boucherie. Her husband came from a family of printers directly tied to the University and at one time had exercised the charge of *messager-juré de l'Université*. Their marriage took place in 1539, and after her husband's death sometime before 1558 she succeeded him in the charge of *libraire-juré de l'Université* until approximately 1572. At the time of her will she must have been in her seventies. Her Leaguer loyalties cannot be questioned: in addition to her close ties to the University, she specifically asks that the *curé* of her current parish in the *Ville*, Julien Pelletier, one of the clerics most intimately involved with the *Seize*, personally participate in her funeral cortege along with all the priests of her parish, Saint-Jacques-de-la-Boucherie. Underscoring for us her close relationship with Pelletier, she also asks that, if possible, Pelletier himself should celebrate "la grande messe de son enterrement." She then bequests to Pelletier, in addition to his "droitz" (or normal fee), the additional sum of one *écu soleil*.[62]

Table 6.4 shows that Marye Laurent has a high general performativity level. Three of her specific performative directives occur under the category of "mentions liturgical detail."[63] First she requests her masses with unusual detail: namely, for her burial service she stipulates that there should be a "service complect de vigilles, laudes et recommendaces à diacre et soubzdiacre et coristes" and that on the day following her burial a similar service should also be celebrated. Furthermore, she specifically states that at the beginning of each mass there should be said "à hault voix, *domine non secundum pecata nostra.*"

Furthermore, Laurent receives a total of three counts for the performativity she mentions in relation to her own body.[64] First, she explicitly requests that "with her body in front of the crucifix [she] wishes the *vexilla regis prodeunt* [the hymn of the passion, as it was known in 1540] to be said and sung by the priests who will attend her cortege and burial."[65] Second, Laurent receives a performativity count relating to her body by requesting that "as soon as her aforesaid body is buried . . . let there be prayers for her soul and those of her relatives, both living and dead, and at the same instant say and sing out loud *salve regina domine non secundum, de profundis,* and the customary prayers."[66] Third, Laurent requests that her *curé* celebrate "la grande messe de son enterrement," when her body would be present.

Our attention to these details discloses the way in which Laurent experiences each moment of a liminal process, marked by the movements of her own body and projected to a point of closure as the body is lowered into the ground. This is the moment which Laurent explicitly designates for the *salve regina,* which the Dominicans had popularized in the twelfth century, as well as the moment in which she remembers the community of the living and the dead closest to her. This liturgy in honor of the Virgin and the psalms for the dead, which the mendicants had done so much to popularize, had the power, in 1590, both to unite and to polarize. We have only to remember the request of Augustin Gueret who clearly feared the disturbance that the appearance of the mendicants in his cortege might create. This capacity to divide and to unite is the most revealing evidence there is of the centrality and the paradox of the liturgy in an era of cultural change, when, inexorably, an ancient symbolic community was being transformed by politics in a new key. We shall see again that Leaguers lived with and through their bodies in sacred time in very particular ways: both in immanence and in transcendent aspiration, since the body of self has multiple meanings as part of the community that is the body of Christ. We see these multiple meanings expressed as Laurent's body is lowered into the ground and passes from the community of the living to the company of the dead. In her will, Laurent expresses this transition and complex self-identity, evoking in one undifferentiated memory the Virgin, her own relatives living and past, and her aspiration for salvation, expressed in the *de profundis.*[67]

It is essential to note, by looking at Table 6.4 as a whole, that none of the other testators of Lamiral besides Laurent and Genevieve Rolland make such detailed pious directives. This coding system is a first step in permitting us to tap individual religious consciousness and understand its political dimensions in the contested terrain of *Paris ligueur*.

Lamiral's Economy of Salvation

Philippe Lamiral has left what may well have been a death-bed will since he is known to have died in 1590. This document, dated November 2, 1590, was drawn up at the home of Lamiral, rue Saint-Jacques in the parish of Saint-Benoît, by the notary Jacques de Saint-Vaast, whose practice was also located on this street. The two notaries not only knew each other and had practices located on the rue Saint-Jacques but also signed together, since all notarized documents required two notarial signatures.[68] Lamiral's will is a rich document providing crucial information about his devotional orientation and his material circumstances.

Among the fifteen Saint-Vaast testators, Lamiral, when requesting intercession, includes five saints who are not named by the other fourteen testators of Saint-Vaast. Following on the recommendation of his soul to God and to Christ "savior and redeemer," and the standard mentions of Saint Michael, "angel and archangel," and Peter and Paul, we find Saint Jehan Baptiste, Saint Estienne, Saint Nicolas (patron of notaries), Saint Genevieve (the patron saint of Paris), and Saint Catherine. Intriguing in Lamiral's will is that, in addition to its expansive votive orientation, it limits the funeral ceremony itself.[69] This request for limitation, which might be taken as a sign of "interiorization," is nonetheless combined with very explicit directions for the procession for his dead body and its liturgical treatment. These funeral directives, accompanied by strict limitations on more worldly pomp (especially the escutcheons), make clear that what have often been taken as indicators of interiorization can, in fact, be very much part of a richly immanentist, performative, and votive piety—a piety that allots profound importance to the body in its articulation of worldly devotional (institutional) loyalties and in the expression of an understanding of salvation. Lamiral requests to be buried in the nave of the church of the Mathurins at the entrance to the chapel of Saint Roch. Before his body is carried to the church of the Mathurins, he wishes that it first be carried to his parish church of Saint-Benoît, brought into the choir, and placed in front of the crucifix. He asks for one complete service to be said for him at Saint-Benoît the morning of his burial and, if he is buried in the evening, he requests additionally that the *placebo* be said. He also specifies that the canons of the chapel in Saint-Benoît say the psalms of the dead and the *vexilla regis prodeunt* with his body present. He gives to the *oeuvre et fabrique* of Saint-Benoît one and a half *écus*; to his *curé*, Jehan Boucher, one *écu*; to the vicar, one *écu*; and, to one hundred poor who gather on the day of his funeral, one hundred *solz*. All other funeral matters relating to lights and to other services and masses he leaves in a standard formula to his executor Garlin.

The will concludes with several civil bequests that give us even more insight into Lamiral's worldly circumstances: he leaves to Jacquette, a servant, two *écus*, "his Sunday robe," with "chausses, soulloirs and pantouffles," and her wages for helping during his illness. To the nurse of his grandson, Claude Garlin, he gives one-half *écu* for her to pray for him. The will ends with the careful enumeration of four debts: most tellingly, a debt of three *septier de bled*, which bespeaks both the hardships of the siege and the ability of many to find extraordinary resources despite the hard times. As evidence of his financial difficulties, Lamiral states that the rent (a sum unnamed) on his house is due "aux messieurs de la Sorbonne." Lamiral's will attests to the multiple ties that bound Lamiral, himself a member of that most politicized group, the *gens de loi*, to the world of the University. His lodging clearly placed him in an economic relationship with the administrators of the vast real estate holdings of the Faculty of Theology (the Sorbonne) throughout the University quarter.[70] Moreover, his devotional loyalties, which can be read in the liturgical spaces through which his body moves and in which it finally comes to rest, are all located close to the University, on its great North-South axis: the rue Saint-Jacques. His bequests to the parish of Saint-Benoît, a site of much "inflammatory" preaching, and specifically his request for the canons to be present as his body is brought to the crucifix in the choir, indicate personal ties to this highly politicized group of clergy. His choice of burial in the church of the Mathurins bespeaks his neighborhood ties and points to a microsite in the University quarter where the kinds of cultural production and social interactions so essential to zealous Catholicism took place. For example, the treatise of de Soulas, examined in Chapters 2 and 3, was printed by the publisher Jehan Petit-pas located in the rue Saint-Jacques, at the sign of the L'Escu de Venise, "pres les Mathurins."[71]

Philippe Cothereau and His Client Bucholicq: Feasting in the Company of the White Penitents

In an examination of the notary Philippe Cothereau (see Table 6.5), yet another related world of League piety is discovered: a world where mendicants

Table 6.5
Performativity Rankings for Testators of Notary Philippe Cothereau

Surname	Profession (see below)	# Times Shows Performativity	# Mentions of Body of Jesus Christ	# Immanentist Gestures	Mentions of own Body	Uses of Liturgical Detail	Uses of Liturgical Calendar	# Bequests to Mendicants	# Bequests to Jesuits/ Capuchins/ Feuillants	Reformist Gestures
Debraye	6	1	0	1	1	0	0	0	0	0
Allard	2	0	0	0	0	0	0	1	0	0
Paulleau	6	0	0	0	0	0	0	0	0	0
Gadeau	5	2	0	0	1	0	0	1	0	0
Davelle	5	0	0	0	0	0	0	0	0	0
Tache	9	0	0	0	0	0	0	0	0	0
Despreaux	9	0	0	1	0	0	0	0	0	0
Leger	6	0	1	0	0	0	0	0	0	0
Jacquerye	5	2	0	1	0	0	0	1	0	0
Matrop	9	0	1	0	0	0	0	0	0	0
Moreau	5	1	1	0	0	0	0	1	0	0
Catin	6	1	2	0	0	0	0	0	0	0
Dizane	2	0	1	0	0	0	0	0	0	0
Tannaix	6	0	1	0	0	0	0	0	0	0
Fricquant	5	0	1	0	0	0	0	0	0	0
Decastres	5	1	0	0	0	0	0	3	0	0
Delahaye	8	0	0	0	0	0	0	1	2	0
Dufriche	9	1	1	0	0	0	0	1	0	0
Pichon	6	0	1	2	0	0	0	2	2	0
Breton	9	2	0	2	0	0	0	1	1	0
Ymbert	1	4	2	2	0	0	0	1	0	0
Broussault	1	1	0	0	0	0	0	0	0	0
Debucholicq*	2	3	1	1	1	1	1	20	0	0
Rossect	5	0	0	0	0	0	0	1	0	0
Leboeuf	5	0	0	0	0	0	0	0	1	0
Rocheret	5	1	1	0	0	0	0	0	0	0
Passart	5	0	0	1	0	0	0	1	0	0

*brother of de Bucholic who uses the notary Ph. Lamiral. See Table 6.4.

Table 6.5, cont'd
Performativity Rankings for Testators of Notary Philippe Cothereau

Professional Categories of Testators

Professional Category	Number of testators	Percent	Cumulative Percent
honorables bourgeois	10	37.0	37.0
gens de loi	6	22.2	59.3
all artisans	5	18.5	77.8
nobles	3	11.1	88.9
clergy	2	7.4	96.3
mixed merchants	1	3.7	100.0
Total	27	100.0	100.0

Type of *Gens de Loi*	Number of testators	Percent	Cumulative Percent
Gens de Loi: avocat	2	33.3	33.3
Gens de Loi: procureur	2	33.3	66.7
Gens de Loi: huissier & sergent	2	33.3	100.0
Total	6	100.0	100.0

(the Augustinians in particular), Jesuits, penitential confraternities, and civic leaders commingled.[72] The Jesuit Emond Auger wrote the statutes for the Confraternity of the White Penitents (*La Congrégation des penitents de l'Annonciation de Notre-Dame*), founded in 1583 by Henry III, at this Augustinian monastery in Paris. This provides further evidence for the multiple channels of influence that shape the performativity of the League era.[73] The White Penitents were an expression of the fraternalism of the meridional religious culture from which the League drew so heavily and which served, simultaneously, to galvanize Jesuit asceticism as public performance in the specific religious conjuncture of the League era. The crucial point to note—and here I differ with Chevalier who, as we saw, regarded the Jesuits as a rupture[74] with the traditional religious culture fostered by the mendicants—is that in the unique conjuncture of the League the Jesuits joined hands, so to speak, with those who would dance the dance of penitents through the streets of Paris. This same dance made Henry III, too, briefly both a penitent and a Leaguer, in the sense that the League can be understood as a complex gesture of atonement.[75] In 1585 Henry could not and did not place himself at the head of the League as he had done in 1576. Thanks to the assassin Jacques Clément, in 1589, Henry III became the vehicle of atonement itself. The king was thus an immanentist object of immolation whose death paradoxically assured the future of politics in a new key: that is, the compartmentalized politics of *raison d'état* (*Staatsraison*) embraced by the *politiques*.[76] Frances Yates has herself spoken of "Auger's 'basteleur' technique of converting street-corner theater and street masquerade to virtuous uses."[77] The essential point to make is that for the generation of Jesuits, like Emond Auger, the strict separation of the sacred and the profane was not yet a reality.

We can see how in Paris in the 1580s and 1590s these Jesuits of the sixteenth century represent the same commingling of popular culture and piety with spiritual revival. Such interconnections among the mendicants (the Augustinians, in particular), Jesuits like Auger, and penitential confraternities of the League are evoked in the will of the Cothereau testator *noble homme* Georges Bucholicq, *gentilhomme de la chambre de feu Monseigneur le reverendissime et illustrissime Jehan Cardinal de Lorraine*. His will gives testimony to the particular bonds, both solemn and festive, that linked noble elites to the mendicant orders of the University and to the Jesuit-sponsored White Penitents of the League period. Bucholicq's close ties to the Augustinian monastery, the site of political meetings of the *Seize*, exemplify the interconnection between these friars, the University, and the early generation of Jesuits such as Auger. Bucholicq identifies himself as a native of Clessa in Dalmatia, and thus points to the far-flung international aspects of

Lorraine influence and clientage networks. It is important to note that Bucholicq may be one of our oldest testators: the Cardinal of Lorraine whom he served died in 1574, and the notary Philippe Cothereau tells us that Bucholicq cannot sign, having lost his sight some two years ago. This information about his age is pivotal when interpreting the pious provisions of his will.

Bucholicq, who mentions his home in the *Faubourg* Saint-Germain and gives his home parish as Saint-Sulpice, is one of dozens of testators displaced by the armies of Henry of Navarre during the *Toussaint* (All Saints' Day) attack of November 1, 1589, when the defenses of the *Faubourg* Saint-Jacques were penetrated and the Abbey of Saint-Germain was taken by Navarre himself. This testator, like so many others who were uprooted by Navarre's military operations, gives a temporary address: "presently in a room in a house at the foot of Saint-Michel bridge," which is located in the University quarter. Bucholicq's closest religious ties besides those to his parish of Saint-Sulpice, where he mentions his *banc*, are to the Augustinian monastery where he wishes to be buried near the main door to the chapel of the Conception of Notre-Dame, the site of what was the most popular confraternity in all of the wills of 1543–44.

Bucholicq's will gives us privileged insight into both the political and religious culture of the Augustinians and the League itself, since in its institutional life the monastery reproduces the "structures of meaning and feeling"[78] that shaped Leaguer political and religious sensibilities. Consider that this monastery not only served as the site of the founding of the White Penitents under Auger's guidance, but also was the home of devotion to the Conception of Notre-Dame. We can see the very venues in which immanence met transcendence in what Auger would call the *branle* [dance] of penitence.

The older devotion to the Conception of Notre-Dame expresses a quintessentially late-medieval religious worship, where immanence literally meets transcendence. The corporeality of conception is transformed by the miraculous in a way that renders one of the most universal and foundational of organic and social processes, that is the founding of a (holy) family, as Christian mystery.[79] The sacred as miraculous elevates the Virgin to the status of "mère de Dieu"—a phrase frequently used in calling for her intercession in the invocations of wills—while, at the same time, locating the Virgin in an anthropocentric experiential frame for those who sought her intercession. Bucholicq expresses the depth of his Marian piety in many of the details of his bequests to this Augustinian monastery, preeminently in asking to be buried at the door to the chapel of the Conception of Notre-Dame, and including the Day of the Ascension of the Virgin among the other holy days for which he provides for meals (*repas*) in his memory for all the Augustinian friars.

The Cardinal of Lorraine, whom Bucholicq served, was himself a White Penitent, and, in fact, the cardinal is said to have died from a cold caught while processing as a penitent in the rain in Avignon.[80] There is certainly reason to speculate that Bucholicq was himself a White Penitent.[81] What is more important, however, concerns the sensibilities shared with Emond Auger and Bucholicq when the former was writing the Statutes for the Confraternity of the Annunciation of Notre-Dame, the formal name of the White Penitents, and the latter was bequesting to the Augustinian monks.[82] The very nature and scale of Bucholicq's bequests to the Augustinians are, in every way, a high water-mark of performativity in a richly late-medieval tradition, in which Marian and penitential overtones coexist in what may seem an unstable combination. Yet, this apparent instability is a manifestation of the process of a cultural transformation itself in which immanence and performativity were undergoing permutations in concrete devotional sites and practices.

A closer look at Bucholicq's bequests to the Augustinians reveals yet another site where immanence and transcendence meet, further inducing transformations in the fabric of Parisian life and religious culture. Bucholicq leaves the general disposition of his funeral and the question of lights and candles to his executors, asking only that his obsequies be done "honorably and without excess."[83] He provides additional details dealing with matters that were of particular importance to him; he requests the presence of all the mendicant orders and the children of the three main charity hospitals in whatever numbers his executors should choose, but stipulates that all of the priests and monks of the Augustinian order should be present. The rest of the will is devoted chiefly to a perpetual foundation for the *repas* and for a *basse messe* to be said daily for him by the regent of the monastery, who, as he notes, is a "docteur en la sainte faculté de théologie." This small detail in Bucholicq's will evokes the multiplicity of relationships between the friars and the Theology Faculty. Such multiform bonds were essential to the dramatic chain of events leading from the Sorbonne Decree of January 1589 to the assassination of Henry III by the Dominican Jacques Clément. These ties find confirmation in the Dominicans' prior Edmond Bourgoing's eulogy of Clément's "martyr's deed," and in his treatise praising the assassination.

The testaments of 1590 make it possible for the cultural historian to begin to situate the constitutional crisis of the League within the framework of religious experience, thus bringing us closer to both the fundamental structures of the period and the more elusive fabric of human experience. Historians of the early Christian era, who share with specialists on the League an interest in the question of how change in a religious culture actually takes place, have identified "dining" or "dining scenes" as strategic social and religious sites where personal and religious identity are shaped in one of Christianity's most potent symbolic moments.[84] With this broad framework in mind, consider what symbolic meanings Bucholicq understood and experienced as he made testamentary provisions for perpetual annual feasts to be celebrated in his memory by the community of Augustinian monks. We know that in the late Middle Ages communal feasting occurred frequently and in a wide range of settings, although mostly in the strategic small-group setting of the confraternity and at funeral banquets where friends, family, participating clerics, and the poor would be invited to dine together. From the perspective of the testator, banquets for the Augustinian friars—literally *repas*, because reformist tendencies had already brought the traditional banquet into ill repute—offer a highly charged symbolic site where the commemoration of the testator's death becomes simultaneously a work of charity (love, *agape*, love feast) and a commemoration in perpetuity of the Last Supper. Symbolically, the funeral banquet (as a distant relative of the *agape*) recalls, and in a performative sense reenacts, Christ's Last Supper with his disciples. This act of recalling the salvific death of Christ—his promise to his disciples, and to all others, who dine "in remembrance of me" that death may become everlasting life—gives the words of Bucholicq's testament a meaningful force that transforms the pious directive into a powerful mode of symbolic action within the framework of a personal eschatology. How else can one understand the phenomenon of so many deathbed wills and wills of testators, otherwise scrupulous in performing their Christian obligations, postponed until the very last moments of life? Such documents are part of an older eschatology where control still eluded the institutional church, and the testator had a rich symbolic vocabulary for expressing very personal understandings of the relation of his own death to the death of Christ.

It is also well known that dining customs, as they developed from the late-antique through the medieval period, acquired many levels of cultural meaning. In the early Christian understanding of the sharing of bread and wine, classical pagan traditions as well as the pagan and communal traditions of non-Roman peoples were interwoven. These multilayered dining traditions carried a powerful affective impact on the construction of communal and civic identity and on the shaping of palpable and symbolic bonds of kinship groups, whether in blood ties or in associations of both trade and devotional confraternities, at the meetings of officers of medieval corporations, and when the king dined with the municipal officeholders of Paris. Banqueting of the kind provided for in Bucholicq's will gives transcendent meaning to bodily consumption and, therefore, exemplifies perfectly the way in which Leaguer sociability was interwoven with transcendence.

We can detect, moreover, the moralizing tendencies in this will that will ultimately lead to the disappearance of this shared sociability. The performativity of banqueting was intermittently criticized by church councils when the tone of such gatherings indicated that the foundational Christian grounding of the ritual had become lost. As part of the general late-medieval anxiety about performativity in the world, banquet scenes came under increasingly harsh criticism by city-fathers and clerical reformers alike. The significance of the carefully chosen word *repas*, which introduces one of the most important cultural dynamics that a careful language analysis of wills can illuminate, is herein discovered. Words are more easily censored than behaviors. Bucholicq avoids the term "banquet" but insists on memorial feasting in a distinctly sacralized setting that reconnects communal feasting with its original meaning. In his choice of language and explicit detailed directives, Bucholicq expresses his understanding of Christ's words and their connection to his own death. The economy of feasting is thus recentered within the economy of salvation and its performativity is enhanced by the testator's own understanding. We also see now why historians must pay more attention to the nuance and choice of wording in testamentary discourse, for the testator's words, even if conveyed by the pen of the scribe, represent one of the most important forms of agency within the framework of death and salvation. The dynamics of this agency involve what is, in most cases, a negotiation of meaning conveyed by the choice or avoidance of certain words, as well as by careful directives that serve ultimately to reshape the gestural culture of sixteenth-century Catholicism.

Bucholicq's bequest for commemorative meals reveals how this form of religious sociability becomes closely realigned with the sacrament of the commemorative masses, which the testator has ordered, as well as with other essentially immanentist paraliturgical acts such as the recitation of psalms beside the grave of the testator. In choosing Marian and Christocentric dates from the liturgical calendar for the celebration of his memorial banquets, Bucholicq further underscores the alignment of his own death with the salvific death of Christ. He then shares with the liturgical community of the Augustinians a common perspective of sacred time and memory, for the dates he has chosen, Christmas, Easter, and the Ascension of the Virgin, anchor the economy of feasting within a triad of Christian mysteries that have prosopoetic force. The referents, the nascibility of Christ, his passibility (which Pasquier found so troubling), unspoken but understood in the choice of Easter, and finally the ascension of Mary, celebrated on *Mi-*

aoust (August 15th), complete the Christian family cycle and also link banqueting to its ultimate referent, the Last Supper.

On each day that the memorial meal is held, the testator provides for the following foods:

> a leg of lamb and for the priests as well as the novices a white bread weighing twelve ounces and a pint of wine and something additional for the prior and for the doctors and officers of the aforesaid convent, as much as fifteen *écus soleil* will provide for each of the aforesaid meals.[85]

There may well lie a powerful symbolism in the choice of the foods offered: Lamb is associated with sacrifice; the twelve ounces (an unusual size of bread) may represent the twelve disciples who shared the Last Supper with Christ; and even the fifteen *escuz* expressed as three times five may symbolize the Trinity and the Five Wounds. The Council of Trent explicitly expelled this kind of number symbolism from the domain of the strictly liturgical (numbers of masses) and the paraliturgical (numbers of candles). Bucholicq and other testators discussed in Chapter 8, however, transfer this symbolism to the domain of charity. Given his very old age, Bucholicq had come of age in a world saturated with such sacred symbolism. He was engaging in a kind of negotiation with Tridentine prescriptions that permitted him to avoid officially proscribed gestures and even terminology such as the word "banquet" itself, while still expressing his own understanding of the relation of his death to Christ's death and the place of both in the liturgical community of the Augustinian monastery.

We must remember that Bucholicq chose as the site for this negotiation the monastery where the Conception of Notre-Dame was revered along with the Annunciation, where the *Seize* organized for the defense of communal liberties as they understood them, and where the rector himself embodied, through his office, the legitimacy of the University as the ultimate arbiter of the loyalties of zealous Catholics. Bucholicq thus expresses in one act of affective force and cognitive clarity the powerful imbrication of sacral and civic immanence so characteristic of League piety. Bucholicq's religious sensibilities, his understanding of sacred agency, and his comprehension of his own relation to Christ are all governed by a performative logic in which the concept of boundaries between the sacred and the profane have no substance or experiential reality. Bucholicq did not understand his salvation independent of very specific performative gestures that had to be associated with a liturgical community. He further sacralizes the *repas* by requiring that on the day of each feast a *De profundis* and other prayers for the dead must be said at his grave, or in the chapel of the Conception of

Notre-Dame. The words *De profundis*, which open the 129th psalm,[86] the best known of all prayers for the dead, mark the trajectory for all immanentist aspiration: from the depths toward the heavens. Thus with this gesture and these words Bucholicq also expresses transcendent aspiration within its corporate and corporeal frame, reminding us, as do the penitents who filled the streets of Paris, that the sinner like the pilgrim indeed has a body.

A remarkable passage, to which Frances Yates called attention in her analysis of processional life in Paris, speaks of the White Penitent processions in the following terms:

> Entering into the dance of Penitence, we wouldn't follow this cadence of the Holy Spirit for very long before [our procession] had brought into the world a holy harmony of many good works. [87]

This excerpt, with its reference to the "dance of penitence" [*branle de Penitence*], reveals direct links between the varieties of performativity, enacted in a corporate setting, in memory of the liturgical dancing that once filled the church itself before either saints or sinners had learned to experience the unequivocal boundaries of the partisans of transcendence.[88]

The Defense of Immanence: A Patriotism beyond National Boundaries

The wills of 1590 reveal another League geography mapped partly by what is known of the life and death of Claude Blosseau. Blosseau was a lieutenant of a company of foot soldiers, part of a regiment commanded by the sire of Mortilly "for the service of the 'unyon des Catholiques.'" A casualty of the skirmishes of the early days of the siege, Blosseau was wounded on May 12, 1590. Twelve days later, as he lay dying, he had his will drawn up by the notary Mathieu Bontemps. Among the provisions of the will he requested that a small pot of holy water be placed beside his grave next to his wife's, along with the following epitaph that he dictated:

> Here lies Claude Blosseau, a lieutenant of captain Saint-Just, wounded by musket in the *faubourg* of Saint-Laurent, the twelfth day of May of the year 1590, from which wound he died for the defence of our holy religion and for the defence of his homeland.[89]

His words remind us that zealous Catholics were patriots as well, in an alternative order of reality beyond the boundary-setting authority of the *politique* state. Blosseau's understanding of his own life and death, "pour la defense de notre saincte religion et de sa patrye," epitomizes the Leaguer fusion of politics and piety.

Mendicant Activism and League Piety

The testamentary evidence from the notaries analyzed in this chapter illustrates how ultramontane religious influences became part of the fabric of urban life. The language of this interaction, from the very formation of the alliances between the mendicant orders and the urban population, was liturgical as well as homilitic, just as Brotin told us. The evolution of the liturgy of the Dominican order in Paris provides a valid example for this cultural interaction: The statutes of the thirteenth century indicate that the offices were to be sung "shortly" (*breviter*, in Latin, hence the Breviary) so that the monks might have time for their studies.[90] As the integration of the orders with the schools increased, so did the conscious effort of the mendicants to draw the laity into the monastic churches of the University quarter. The monks who were students were released from the obligation to be present for the performance of the daily offices except compline, which would be performed when laymen quit work for the day. The Dominicans converted this aspect of their liturgical obligations into a public service sung when the workday was over. To further rouse the laity's interest, the Dominicans added the *salve regina*, which became one of the most beloved components of offices with which the urban laity became familiar, and which they mention in their wills.[91] The long-term organic relations between the University, the mendicants, and the urban laity thus provide a starting point for placing League piety in its full historical perspective.

Table 6.2 ("Role of the Mendicant Orders in Economies of Salvation") compares the populations for the three sample years who requested burial at the mendicants. The table shows clearly that in 1590 a much broader segment of the testator population was connected, in these different ways, to the world of the University via their bonds to the mendicant orders.[92] This information on the place of the mendicants in the economies of salvation of testators from all three sample periods reveals yet another way in which the University, via the mendicants, exerted an unparalleled influence on the piety of the League era.

The most important finding, however, concerns the distinctive patterns of religious engagement that, as we can see now, are characteristic of two different but related circles of League piety. There are two distinct Leaguer populations: one drawn to the world of the mendicants and the University (in which the *gens de loi*, artisans, and more-modest merchants are predominant) and another (examined in the next chapter) drawn to the world of the new religious orders.[93] The gestural economies of the two groups are quite distinct, with traditional religious attachments more characteristic of the first population.[94] The testators of the notary Raoul

Bontemps, in particular, link the world of the University to the activist, didactic piety sponsored by the Jesuits. Raoul Bontemps served as the notary not only for the University milieu, but also for the most highly politicized *Seize* who in June of 1590 went to the *étude* of Bontemps to draw up the now famous *Seize* loan document known as the *Emprunt*. The varied functions fulfilled by this Leaguer notary are the best examples of the links of *Seize* activism with ties to religious orders both old and new.

Although we may think of these two poles of League piety as the traditionalism of "la commune" versus the innovation of the new (Jesuit) and the reformed orders (Capuchins, or reformed Franciscans, and the Feuillants or reformed Cistercians), such a binary opposition is, in fact, inaccurate and fails to account for the confluences between these groups and the interchanges and links, which actually show us how religious change occurs. To understand these more complex patterns of association and cultural change at work we are obliged to think in terms of a broadly shared ontology and many diverse patterns of performativity that, together, explain the activism of the League period and the transition to Catholic Reform in the seventeenth century.[95] Herein lies an explanation of how League piety drew on late-medieval traditions of sacral and civic immanence while, at the same time, laying the foundations for the cultural and behavioral changes associated with *dévot* and even baroque piety.

Chapter 7

THE LEAGUE AND THE DEFINITION OF CATHOLIC REFORM: AN EXPERIENTIAL APPROACH

Tools to Identify Reformist Testators

The opening words of the Decrees from the very first session of the Council of Trent on December 13, 1545, speak directly of the need for a "reform of the clergy and the Christian people."[1] It is exceedingly rare for Parisian testators to speak so directly about Catholic reform, yet their wills make clear that in a myriad of ways they were living, and often themselves shaping, the experience of Catholic reformation. This chapter uses the testamentary evidence from all three sample periods to explore the changing nature of that experience.

The chapter focuses primarily upon a small but strategic group of testators who explicitly voice reformist concerns in their wills. In tracking the evolution of zealous Catholicism in Paris there is particular value in mining the wills of those rare testators who chose to address reformist issues explicitly and often at length. Their wills are important because they reveal an avant-garde of Catholic reformers whose identity and personal experience would otherwise be unknown. Their wills also furnish clues about the social and cultural worlds they inhabited. This chapter will first highlight those extraordinary individuals whose wills offer rich details about the world of zealous Catholicism in Paris. There is another larger group of 1590's testators whose wills indicate strong but indirect evidence of affiliation with Catholic reform, either by having mentioned taking the sacraments or by having made bequests to their confessors. The comparison of the case studies with the aggregate study of this larger population offers a new way of understanding the lineages and legacy of League piety and its longer-term relationship to Catholic reform.

A variable with seven values for types of specific reformist requests identified a total of twenty-nine reformist testators from all three sample years.[2] The first part of this chapter presents a concise comparative overview of testators from the three sample periods (1543–44, 1590, and 1630) who made such reformist requests in their wills. The most striking finding

Table 7.1
Reformist Testators in Three Sample Periods

Indicators of Reform	1543–44 # of reformist bequests	1543–44 Testator's name	1590 # of reformist bequests	1590 Testator's name	1630 # of reformist bequests	1630 Testator's name
Cognitive concerns and educational investment	1	Choquet, Valerend	4	[L] de Mombron, René [L] Marion, Jehan [L] Thibault, Jehan [L] Malescot, Laurens	5	Ferrand, Magdelain Fayet, Anthoine Petit, Claude de Verneuil, Françoyse Marchant, Jehanne
Investment in administration of the sacraments	0	none	2	[L] de Mombron, René [L] Marion, Jehan	2	Perot, Marie
Building or improving church or chapel	0	none	2	[L] de Mombron, René de Fleury, Anne	3	Tronson, Margueritte Mareschal, Olivier de Terneau, Lucelle
Confraternity reform	0	none	1	[L] Marion, Jehan	2	Lefevre, Margueritte Leboiteux, Marguerite
Clerical discipline	1	Bonhomme, Yolland	2	[L] Marion, Jehan [L] Gueret, Augustin	0	none
Morality or competence of celebrant valued by testator	4	Noel, Martine Delafontaine, Magdaleyne Devendosine, François Morel, Martine	2	[L] Rolland, Genevieve [L] Thiersault, Marye	4	Villain, Jeanne Muletz, Marguerite du Boys, Germain Tronson, Margueritte
Reverence of sacred object	1	Lecoq, Charles	1	[L] Marion, Jehan	0	none
Total Number of Reformist Requests	7		14		15	
Total Number of Reforming Testators	7		8		14	
Total Number of the General Testator Population	159		727		344	
Percentages of the General Testator Population Who Are Reformers	4.4%		1.1%		4.1%	

[L] indicates League affiliation

for understanding League piety and its relation to seventeenth-century reform is that in 1590, seven of the total of eight reformers have clear League affiliations, particularly to the *Seize*.

Table 7.1 shows that in all three sample periods reformers were most interested in augmenting the cognitive, moral, or material quality of relations with the sacred and with their clergy. There are a variety of ways to compare the reforming populations from the sample years. Perhaps the most striking feature, aside from the clear predominance of Leaguers among the 1590's reformers, is the progressively wider range of reformist concerns testators express. Also notable is that of the fourteen reformers of 1630, ten are women.[3]

Table 7.2 compares the three reforming populations, showing the part of town where their notaries practiced, the part of town where they lived, any indicators of ultra-Catholic connections, their sex, their (or their spouse's) occupation, their health at the time of will, whether they were able to sign their will, and the overall number of pious requests they made. While the number of testators involved is small, three striking features emerge in comparing the three sample years. First, by 1630, far fewer reformers have links to the university milieu based on the notary they used or the part of town in which they lived.[4] Second, the following micro-portraits illuminate the most striking features of the reformist populations in each of the three years. Both in 1543–44 and in 1590, the majority of reformist testators reside in the University quarter or have other significant connections to the University itself. Finally, by 1630, Catholic reformers, social elites, and new and reformed monastic orders and charitable institutions fill a once-open landscape in the *faubourgs*, the physical space where a reform of popular culture is carried out.[5] The *faubourgs* had been the domain of a succession of groups destined to become increasingly marginalized. Student brawls, once common in *faubourgs* near the university, decreased as part of a general censure of violence committed by young men. In a parallel manner, Protestant prayer meetings in the meadows of the *faubourg* (*Pré aux Clercs*) were banned as part of the triumph of religious orthodoxy. Ironically, the more stringent code of public decorum that Protestants themselves sought to enforce silenced the crowds of hymn singers who used to gather in these open spaces.

The Reformers of 1543–44: The Will of Valerend Choquet of Péronne: Traditional and Reformist Directives Underscore the Dilemmas of Tridentine Reform

In 1543–44, the testators' reformist intentions focus primarily on the morality or competence of the priest who will celebrate their services (four testators; see Table 7.1), and on the related issue of enforcing clerical discipline (one testator, Yolland Bonhomme). These concerns are consistent with the emphasis on clerical discipline and reform articulated in the opening session of the Council of Trent in 1545. One testator, *honorable homme maistre* Valerend Choquet, is a particularly significant reformer because he combines educational and cognitive concerns with a deep and discerning attachment to the very forms of symbolic behaviors (liturgical number symbolism) that the Council of Trent would condemn in the decrees from session 22 in September 1562. Such a testamentary juxtaposition of divergent devotional norms lie at the foundations of the Janus face of League piety, where tradition and innovation are side by side, not simply in different factions of the political movement, but within individual testators, reformers included.

The bequests Choquet made to the chief schoolmaster of his hometown of Péronne (the founding site of the first League of 1576) offer an overall context for the interpretation of Choquet as a reformer:

> And the testator wishes and orders that the day of his aforesaid service there should be one hundred *sous* sent to the principal master of the main school of the aforesaid Pérronne so that he can distribute this money to poor students whom he should choose in a fair manner and let these alms stimulate the students to pray for the soul of the aforesaid testator and also give the school master ten *sous*.[6]

In 1543, the educational investment made by Choquet was still closely tied to very old traditions of prayers for the dead. Thus, it is important to be cautious and look for further clues. Before determining that Choquet's choice of a schoolmaster and schoolchildren to say these prayers is an indicator of reform, one must ask if his request fostered educational goals. Further clues about the testator's religious sensibilities emerge from other bequests in the will and from a comparison of how the bequests for educational purposes change over the sample periods.

The most convincing indicator that Choquet is particularly concerned with interrelated pedagogical and cognitive aspects comes in a pious directive concerning his desire to receive the last sacraments while still in full possession of his faculties:

> Next, the aforesaid testator gives one *écu* to the cleric or vicar who will administer the sacraments to him and prays that the sacraments be administered early to him and before he has lost the use of his reason and let the cleric exhort him concerning the faith and concerning the passion of our Lord and things salutary and let there be said at his death the aforesaid passion.[7]

In its explicit wording, this clause is unique in all of the wills examined, although two other 1543–44 testators discussed below share, if somewhat less explicitly, Choquet's concern for cognitive clarity about doctrine, ritual, and most particularly about sacramental behaviors.

Equally important, this remarkable directive with its focus on the passion[8] demonstrates how much the testator's conception of his own end is tied to the concepts of the passibility of Christ and the mass as a reiterative sacrifice.[9] This understanding of the mass represents the culmination of centuries of liturgical and doctrinal evolution and helps explain why the mass became accepted as the most efficacious form of prayer for the dead.

The extent to which the testator uses the number symbolism of five, accompanied by symbolic and explanatory wording, reveals the cognitive and affective power that number symbolism holds for him. Choquet's divergent—traditional and reformist—devotional directives exemplify the complexity of the Tridentine reforming task from session 22, which issued "Canons on the most holy sacrifice of the mass" and a "Decree on things to be observed and avoided in celebrating mass." After requesting burial at a local parish "in the church in front of the crucifix," Choquet makes discerning distinctions between efficacious and superfluous forms of ritual behaviors:

> Also, the testator wishes and orders that his burial and services should be done without any worldly pomp and as simply as possible and let there be invited thirty poor persons of good character and from these his executors should choose in a fair manner the five poorest who shall each be given a large candle and one *écu* and to the remaining of the aforesaid poor give five *sous* to each in honor of the five wounds [of Christ].[10]

The symbolism of the five wounds that Choquet reiterates through his use of both fives and multiples of five (the twenty-five remaining from the thirty) must be seen as a form of cognition and thus of agency that permits him to express his own comprehension of Christ's life and death, and thereby place his own death in the framework of a larger salvation history.[11]

Choquet's expressed desire to receive the sacraments while fully sentient is juxtaposed to his use of an ancient mode of symbolic thought (number symbolism). His concern about the timing of the reception of his last communion appears to represent a clarion break with the older tradition of the perfect death, in which one sought to die with the host in one's mouth. Choquet's case, however, exemplifies the coexistence of multiple ways of knowing Christ in one person's own religious experience. Although this testator seems to reflect a long-term shift from bodily knowledge to a closeness with Christ through understanding, there is no evidence that the notion

Table 7.2
Comparison of 1543–44, 1590, and 1630 Reformers

Variables	1543–44 Reformers [7]		1590 Reformers [8]		1630 Reformers [14]	
Notary's Part of Town						
université	14.3%	[1]	37.5%	[3]	28.6%	[4]
ville	85.7%	[6]	37.5%	[3]	57.1%	[8]
cité	0		25%	[2]	7.1%	[1]
Testator's Part of Town						
université	42.9%	[3]	62.5%	[5]	7.1%	[1]
faubourg parishes	0		12.5%	[1]	28.6%	[4]
ville	28.6%	[2]	25%	[2]	50.0%	[7]
League Connection (i.e., ultra-catholic connections)						
yes	N/A		87.5%	[7]	7.1%	[1]
no	N/A		12.5%	[1]	92.9%	[13]
Sex						
male	42.9%	[3]	62.5%	[5]	28.6%	[4]
female	57.1%	[4]	37.5%	[3]	71.4%	[10]
Occupation						
honorables bourgeois	42.9%	[3]	25%	[2]	28.6%	[4]
gens de loi	28.6%	[2]	0		7.1%	[1]
univ./liberal profs.	0		25%	[2]	0	
clergy	0		12.5%	[1]	7.1%	[1]
noble office/epithet	0		12.5%	[1]	14.3%	[2]
middle/lower officals	0		0		14.3%	[2]
nobles	14.3%	[1]	12.5%	[1]	21.4%	[3]
artisans	0		12.5%	[1]	0	
unclassifiable	14.3%	[1]	0		7.1%	[1]
Health[1]						
healthy	57.1%	[4]	62.5%	[5]	64.3%	[9]
sick	N/A	[3]	37.5%	[3]	35.7%	[5]

Table 7.2, cont'd
Comparison of 1543–44, 1590, and 1630 Reformers

Variables		1543–44 Reformers [7]		1590 Reformers [8]		1630 Reformers [14]	
Signing Information[2]	yes	0		100%	[8]	100%	[14]
	no	100%	[7]	0		0	
Number of Pious Requests	more than 20	57.1%	[3]	50%	[4]	42.9%	[6]
	11–20	42.9%	[4]	0		21.4%	[3]
	5–10	0		25%	[2]	28.6%	[4]
	1–5	0		25%	[2]	7.1%	[1]

1. Health data was not available for these 3 wills of 1543–44.
2. In the general testator population of 1543–44 only 8 out of the total of 159 testators signed their wills.

of a clear dichotomy between physical knowing and ratiocination can be substantiated at all for this period—it may simply be a matter of projecting modern-day mind-body dichotomies on to the past. Nonetheless, the notion of interiorization or spiritualization is all too easily invoked to characterize the emergence of a more intellectualized religion in the early-modern period. The analysis of Choquet's will underscores the conceptual bias of contrasts that are often drawn between "rational" and ritualized or immanentist forms of symbolic behaviors and thus demonstrates the need for a more nuanced set of categories with which to analyze religious change.

Choquet's will offers insight not only into the religious imagination but also into the institutional loyalties and social milieu of pre-Tridentine reformist testators in Paris. The pronounced passion-centered language in the preamble and his choice of the notary Mussart suggest that Choquet may have had ties to the University milieu where this affective language of the passion was most favored. Mussart's practice was located near les Halles (in the *Ville*), but he appears to have had clients who were linked to the milieu of the University. Another Mussart client, *noble homme* Jehan Paluau, a *bourgeois de Paris*, shows these university connections through his profession as a *messaiger juré en l'Université de Paris* and through the richly passion-centered imagery and liturgical specificity of the extraordinary holographic will that he brought to Mussart to transcribe. Jehan Paluau, like Choquet, is also deeply attached to the number symbolism of five.[12] Paluau also speaks of the terrible temptations that can shake faith at the moment of death, and he also emphasizes his attachments to "Rhomme," thanking God for "the churches and temples in Rome and elsewhere where the name of Christ is honored."[13] These details from Paluau's will bring us closer to the embattled world of international Catholicism in Paris in the 1540s and shed light on the religious culture of the University milieu with its ties to mendicant-sponsored forms of piety.

Yolland Bonhomme: A Paradigm of a Testator from the University Milieu

The will of *honorable femme* Yolland Bonhomme, widow of *honorable homme* Thielman Kerver I (a native of Koblenz in the Rhineland) takes us to one of the early sources of ultra-Catholicism and to the future site of ardent support for the League. Bonhomme's husband was a *marchant libraire juré en l'université* and a *bourgeois de Paris*.[14] At the time she made her will, Yolland Bonhomme was in good health and a resident of Saint-Benoît parish, which, as the discussion of the notary Philippe Lamiral revealed, had close institu-

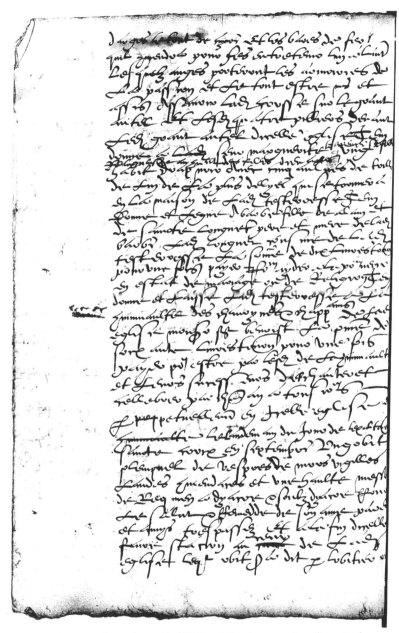

Figure 2. A bequest from the will of Yolland Bonhomme for a liturgical ornament decorated with the escutcheons (*armoiries*) of the passion. (Centre historique des Archives nationales. MC/Etude LXXIII, 5.)

tional affiliations with both the University and the monastery of the Mathurins. It is important to remember that the first procession of the holy sacrament to repair the profanation of Protestant iconoclasm in 1528 set out from this monastery. There are several features in her will that demonstrate the intensity of her religious sensibilities. The preamble of her will begins with the signing of the cross.[15] Like Choquet, Bonhomme emphasizes the need to exercise reason in order to resist temptation at the approach of death. In her own preparation for death, the memory of Christ's passion is central. The especially vivid and affective quality of her passion-centered concept of redemption is clear in her emphasis on the merits of Christ's painful death and passion ("le merite de sa douloureuse mort et passion"). This significant wording in the recommendation of her soul (recommendatio animae) concludes with the explicit statement of "Amen." These are both features closely associated with Leaguer notaries and their clients in 1590.[16]

Bonhomme's attachments to the monastery of the Mathurins further reveal a line of continuity with the sites of Catholic action that have been identified for the League period among printers, notaries, their clients, and the Mathurins. In 1590, the Leaguer notary Philippe Lamiral, who worked closely with the League-affiliated notary Saint-Vaast,[17] wished to be buried at the Mathurins. One of Lamiral's clients, Marie Laurent, widow of the printer Pierre Ricouart, requested, like Lamiral,[18] burial at the Mathurins where she indicated that her husband, her mother, and her father were also buried. Bonhomme's mention of John the Evangelist in her request for intercession may well signal membership in the confraternity dedicated to John the Evangelist, which, as seen in the will of Marie Laurent, was located at the Mathurins.[19] Bonhomme makes a remarkable bequest of five hundred livres to the Mathurins:

> [the monies] are to be employed in making a cross mounted on four pillars and decorated with angels, all of this made of copper but with supports of iron so that it may be kept at one or another altar, and the angels should bear the escutcheons of the passion and all of this should be placed on the main altar of the aforesaid church.[20]

In her liturgical directives Bonhomme displays highly immanentist traits, including a particular devotion to the cross. First, she gives sixty livres to celebrate in perpetuity a solemn obit on the eve of or the day after the day of exaltation of the holy cross in the month of September. Secondly, Bonhomme specifically requests that the stations of the cross be performed at the obit occurring on the memorial of the day of her death. She also explicitly calls for aspersion of holy water over her grave following each low mass (*basse messe du jour*) to be said for her daily by a priest of the Mathurins in the year following her death.[21] Moreover, she requests that the community of the church of Saint-Benoît

> inscribe and register the aforesaid *obit* into the book of the dead of the community for perpetual commemoration . . . and all of the clerics of the church should attend her *obit* from the reading of the first lesson until the very end of the entire *obit* and if some or any one of the clerics are not present at the aforesaid *obit* they may not receive any monies.[22]

She adds that if any cleric should leave before the service is over, his money would go to the others who stayed for the whole service.[23] Along with this reformist concern for clerical discipline, Bonhomme, like Choquet, also uses liturgical number symbolism.

These cases of Choquet and Bonhomme are part of the aggregate data about the geography of reform in 1543–44. In the reference population of 152 testators who are not reformers, only fifteen percent reside in the University quarter. Among the seven reformers of 1543–44, three are residents of the University quarter and all are parishioners of Saint-Benoît, the future parish of Jehan Boucher, who embodied the interconnections between the University and the *Seize*. By 1630, only one reformer of a total of fourteen resided in the University quarter. This change may reflect a decline in the University's cultural influence in the world of seventeenth-century reform.

Jehan Marion:
In Defense of Tridentine Order

Compared with the reformers of 1543–44, those of 1590 voice a broader range of reforming interests and often express multiple reforming goals. Most significant for the argument of this book, these testators constitute a small avant-garde of seven individuals, with six of them closely linked to the League by a variety of criteria, including their choice of notary, their institutional affiliations to the University, and especially their links to the new religious orders—the Jesuits, Capuchins, and Feuillants.[24]

In 1590, the most notable change in the orientation of reform is an increase in investments in education fostered by the rise of new religious orders. A close examination of the will of Jehan Marion illustrates in detail sev- eral of the most important catalysts for religious reform in the Leaguer movement in 1590. The evidence in his will and particularly the circumstances of its composition reveal trajectories of macro-cultural change that transformed the spontaneous, Southern-influenced penitential piety of the

League era into a more strictly institutionally circumscribed and more sacra-mentally channeled network of relations with the sacred. A figure such as Jehan Marion clearly acts as a cultural intermediary, and represents one of the channels by which *occitan* penitential piety was transplanted to Paris during the period of the League.

His will was made not at his imminent physical death, but at his "civil death," that is, as part of his preparation to take vows with the Feuillants, the very religious order that Pigafetta's account of the May 14 Procession described as the most ascetic and austere of the new reforming orders. It is likely that Marion was among those whose very bones were visible through their coarse monastic robes as they processed with their weapons in the armed review of May 14, 1590. Given the very civic character of the pro-cession of May 14, the conventional notion of the monastic vow as "civil death" is belied by the reality of the monk-citizen who acts as defender of both a communal and a universal sacred order. "Civil death" thus appears as an artifact from an alien world-view where the sacred and the profane were dichotomous orders of reality.

Marion's will was drawn up on February 5, 1590, by the notary Claude Jourdan, whose practice was on the rue Saint-Honoré and who had another southern testator, the nobleman Jehan de Peyere from Languedoc, a mem-ber of the entourage of the Joyeuse family, all zealous Catholics.[25] Marion describes himself as a "prebster, novice en l'Oratoire Monseigneur Saint Bernard, fondé à Paris ès Faulxbourg Saint Honoré." He notes that he was previously a canon in the cathedral church of Carcassonne, and the *curé*, or parish rector, in the church of Notre-Dame de Fanjeaux. Fanjeaux is lo-cated thirty kilometers from the city of Carcassonne, and approximately seventy kilometers from Toulouse, where the Catholic *Parlement* dominated the city's political culture, and where the first French foundation of the reformed Cistercians known as the Feuillants was established in 1577. Marion is the only individual in the entire corpus of testators who specifi-cally mentions the need to adhere to the reforming Decrees of Trent. He prescribes five different sorts of reforming directives that reveal his institu-tional loyalties and reforming intent. Marion's background as a secular cleric is of telling significance, for it counters historians who, in their eagerness to explore lay piety, sometimes forget that the front line of militant and re-forming Catholicism came from within the church itself.

In his first bequest, Marion remembers his former parish of Fanjeaux in a clearly reforming directive aimed at augmenting the reverence and splen-dor of the eucharistic procession, the moment that best represented the triumph of Catholic orthodoxy and defense of the doctrine of sacred imma-nence, as affirmed in the Decrees of the Council of Trent. It is important to note that Protestants were numerous in Fanjeaux. Marion's bequest indicates that he wanted to increase respect and decorum in the treatment of the sacred in the world. His solicitude embraces the most universal embodiment of the sacred—the Holy Sacrament—as well as the most particular forms of sacred embodiment—the local relics in the sacristy of the parish of Fanjeaux, which Marion felt were not yet properly housed. The reverence for these local parish objects is an enactment of the doctrine of the communion of saints. This doctrine refers to the creation of a transcendent community connecting concrete, local sites of immanence and the members of the body of Christ through the efficacity of ritual performance located throughout the world. Marion's bequest takes us to the experiential setting of that doctrine, which was so thoroughly denigrated by Protestant theologians from the sixteenth century onward:[26]

> As for his worldly goods first of all [the testator] has left and given in legacy to the parochial church of Our Lady in Fanjeaux the sum of twenty *écus* in one payment to be used to purchase a pound of silver suitable for bearing the holy sacrament when it is carried in procession, along with a reliquary in which should be placed the relics of Saint Ganderic and any others that are in the sacristy of the aforesaid church of Fanjeaux that have still not been encased and all this should be done with the best material and in the best manner possible. . . . [27]

Marion emphasizes the significance of this bequest within his own understanding of reform. The phrase "En premier lieu" is the best guide to what reform in the world meant to Marion, second to his own decision to serve, "perserverer en service," by his entry into the Feuillant order. His reforming intent is also focused simultaneously on two different levels: First, he supports tangible investments designed to foster cognitive as well as behavioral changes in parishioners' relations with the sacred; secondly, he promotes incentives for a more responsible pastoral presence by the local clergy.

The next reforming clause of Marion's will attempts both to augment the divine service in his parish of Fanjeaux and, in his words, "to incite the priests of this church to be resident there and to carry out their obligations."[28] Marion establishes at Fanjeaux parish a foundation of matins, lauds, and the daily office, followed by vespers and ending with the choir singing ("tout hault") a *libera* and a *de profundis*. These psalms were traditionally found in the office for the dead, and a testator might select holy days for the perpetual celebration of these ceremonies. The combination of feast days Marion chooses is unique among the 1590's testators and offers special insight into the relationship between liturgical loyalties and the personal meaning of reform for the testator. Marion begins with the feast of the circumcision of Christ, followed by Passion Sunday and Ascension Sunday, and the most immanentist festival of "l'Invention de la Saincte Croix" (the Discovery of the Sacred Cross). Next, Marion chooses the Marian feasts of the Annunciation and the Conception of the Virgin, and finally, both the birth-date of John the Baptist and his festival (celebrated on the 24th of June). The days chosen represent a powerful Christocentric and Marian focus, but Marion's devotion to John the Baptist deserves special attention.

Jehan Marion:
From Penitence to Charity

Marion's devotion to John the Baptist needs to be understood in the context of Marion's membership in the Confraternity of Divine Mercy (*la Confrérie de la Miséricorde*).[29] This confraternity, one of the many penitential confraternities popular in meridional culture, exercised a powerful influence on League piety. Devotion to John the Baptist (especially to "John the Baptist *Décollé*, Beheaded") was central to the penitential movement of the sixteenth century, and therefore its immediate significance to Jehan Marion must be understood on several levels. For example, it is increasingly clear, thanks to the work of Denis Crouzet in particular, how the religious imagination of the sixteenth century was steeped in prophecy and astrological prediction, eschatological preaching, and a penitential consciousness rooted in preparation for the approaching end of time and the Last Judgment.[30] This was not necessarily a panic mentality limited to a small group. In the League era, the sense of living at the end of time was shared by elites and the popular classes, and it became a potent source for religious reform whose effects were felt not only in an apocalyptic framework but also, paradoxically, in enduring institutional reforms. In fact, tensions between apocalyptic visions and recognition of the need to institutionalize the *imitatio Christi* have been present in Christianity since its inception. Awareness of this polyvalence and paradox within the apocalyptic mentality itself is essential to understanding League piety and League connections to later Catholic reform. The cathexis with new liturgical forms such as the Forty Hours eucharistic devotion demonstrates one of the powerful capacities of liturgy to institutionalize the apocalyptic component of reforming periods. The awareness of the devotion to John the Baptist and its polyvalent elements is key to that understanding.

Devotion to John the Baptist has a special appeal within the context of both prophecy and the prefiguration of a messianic mood, or Second Coming. John the Baptist foretold the coming of Christ and Judgment Day (Matthew 3:12). Moreover, Marion's emphasis on the celebration of the nativity of John the Baptist is clearly related to the parallels established in the account of the First Chapter of Luke between the birth of John the Baptist, prophesied by angels, and the birth of Christ announced by the angel Gabriel.[31] John the Baptist's life as an itinerant preacher who called for repentance before the end of time sent a message with which sixteenth-century Catholics could immediately identify. Marion may well have understood his own entrance into the Feuillant order as a preparation for the coming final judgment. Mattia Bellintani da Salò, the head of the Capuchins in Paris, understood the reform of his Franciscan Third Order in similar terms as a stage in perfection immediately preceding the Second Coming.[32]

It is easy to see the historical, narrative, and experiential bonds that made John a central devotional figure for penitential confraternities and for ascetic practices such as those associated with the Feuillant order in particular. Through John the life and death of Christ become more accessible for those who identify with the consummate moment of penitential suffering and its transformation into a transcendent charity ("For God so loved the world . . ."). The cultural work of penitential confraternities in the sixteenth century underlies and facilitates the emergence of their charitable functions in the seventeenth and eighteenth centuries.[33]

Marion's bequest provided a clear message that the way to Christ was through penitential fraternalism and repentance. Just as important are the disciplining and reformist conditions Marion places on the financial arrangements for clergy who would be expected to be present at the celebration of the ceremonies requested in his foundation. Marion leaves very careful instructions that reveal how penitence has in his own mind become connected to charity. He specifies that only clergy actually residing in the parish and attending the prescribed ceremonies may receive any payment from the income of the foundation. Crucially, he adds that the part that would go to those absent should be given to the sick poor rather than increase the portion of those present.[34] The interrelations of penitence and charity in Marion's economy of salvation manifest the personal and shared experiences that create change in broad social trends and beliefs. Specifically, Marion's will demonstrates the permutation of values that facilitates the charitable movements of Catholic action in seventeenth-century Paris.

The next of Marion's reformist gestures is a didactic directive that further transforms traditional memorialization into an occasion for discipline and learning:

> At the same time the testator founds and wishes that on each of these
> days there be composed and delivered a sermon on the solemnity of the
> day by the regent or some of the priests of the aforementioned church,
> [or] by some monk of the Convent of Saint Dominic or of another . . . ,[35]

The second clause makes even clearer that Marion conceives of memorialization in a didactic and charitable context, for he gives the more traditional foundation a transformative social power to heighten the awareness of all present about the meaning and significance of each festival day. What might have been passed over in other testamentary analyses as simply the particular devotional sensibilities of one testator constitutes a transformative social action. Marion expresses his belief that penitence and repentance are the path to Christ and to the Virgin while, simultaneously, censoring absent clerics and providing for an instructive "service of the word" (as Pierre Brotin would have spoken of the sermon) to accompany the celebration of the divine service. A close analysis of these various elements of Marion's foundation thus demonstrates how liturgy could become the language for social change as well as for political movements.

Marion also places in perspective the nature of the urban revolution produced by mendicant preaching. His preference that a Dominican offer the sermon of edification, in addition to a later bequest he makes to the Dominican Confraternity of the Rosary (*Confrérie Notre Dame des Chappeletz*), highlights a direct line of descent from the liturgical and preaching revolution of the thirteenth century (carried out in the cities by mendicant orders like the Dominicans) to the liturgical and didactic modes of Leaguer activism in 1590. The new religious orders of the Catholic reformation to which Leaguers and reformers are so strikingly drawn in 1590 thus continue the mendicant legacy of a revival of preaching and the enrichment of the liturgy through new devotional forms.

The third clause of Marion's will identifies some of the specific contexts in which cultural change takes place. These changes engage the laity's senses, aesthetic sensibilities, and affect or emotions. In his next bequest, Marion requires his heirs to purchase the oil necessary to keep a lamp constantly lit in the choir (particularly in front of the image of the Virgin Mary). The significance of the vespers services becomes even more clear because of Marion's solicitude for having the lamps kept lit in front of the image of the Virgin through the end of vespers, which is precisely when the working laity would have finished their labors and could seek solace in the ceremonies inside the mendicant and other churches. Marion's concern to have the *libera* and the *de profundis* sung "tout hault" by the choir after vespers can be understood in this larger context, as well.

The Cistercians (the order of Cîteaux, from which the Feuillants are derived), as well as the Dominicans, were known not only for their doctrinal learning and dramatic preaching, but also for their leading position in the propagation of the cult of the Virgin Mary. Marion's own strong connection to Marian piety is evident throughout the will. The order that he joined in Paris took the name Notre-Dame des Feuillants. His choice of Marian feast days for his foundation and his desire that a lamp be lit by the image of the Virgin during the vesper hours, are further evidence of this devotion. The lamp and the sermon of explication are complementary elements of the renovated religion of immanence, since both illuminate the structure of meaning and feeling in a Leaguer economy of salvation that linked Brotin to Marion, Fanjeaux to Paris, and all to Rome and to Christ in the holy alliance called the Catholic League.

Further, as seen in the case of the *Confrérie de la Miséricorde*, pious associations, where laity and clergy established personal relationships, were one of the primary ways in which a universal economy of salvation took concrete and local form. The Tridentine fathers were acutely sensitive to the need to spell out distinctly the hierarchy of devotional loyalties. This hierarchy began in *latria* (adoration) of Christ (Marion's very first reforming directive, namely, the procession of the Holy Sacrament), descended to the *hyperdulia* of Marian veneration, and finally also incorporated local loyalties. In Marion's will this last level is represented in three elements: 1. his concern for the parish relics, 2. his confraternal membership in a penitential company of *miséricorde*, and 3. his bequest to a Marian association of a Dominican foundation, the *Confrérie Notre Dame dicte du Chapellet*—the Rosary. The careful ordering of Marion's bequests moved through the full range of salvific bonds, which are hierarchically articulated by the testator (the force again of "en Premier lieu"). Marion's will demonstrates how, in a reformed religion of immanence, the local and palpable were united with the universal in a reformed religion of immanence. Thus, for example, the touch of the fingers to the rosary bead (the *chapellet*) is further sacralized through association of symbolic numbers of sequences for recitation. Through symbolic numbers of recitations a gesture can be elevated so that it physically links prayer to liturgical memory through symbolic understanding.

In Marion's will the process of condensation of sacred immanence can be detected through a canalization of loyalties into sacramental sites and into the above-mentioned focus on Christocentric and Marian holy days. Moreover, the effort to increase participation in the sacraments is the focus of Marion's fourth reforming directive:

> Next [the testator] wishes and orders that the rectors of Fanjeaux, present and future, should, when leaving the church to go to carry extreme onction to a sick person, have some bell sounded to announce to the people that the bell ringing means that they should pray to God for the sick person to whom the aforementined extreme unction is being carried.[36]

This is yet another processional moment that occurs in a directly sacramental context: the ceremony of bringing the last sacrament and extreme unction to the sick and dying. Marion is concerned not only with the didactic issue that the villagers know why the church bells toll, but also with what is, in effect, an increase in sacramental participation. This request strives to ensure communal prayers that will unite the living and the dying in one economy of salvation.

The final reformist directive of Marion's will is the one most concerned with the educational needs of the entire community. He gives two hundred *écus* to purchase land for a perpetual endowment for the salary of a schoolmaster or regent who would be able "to instruct well and thoroughly the youth of the aforesaid town of Fanjeaux."[37] The sign of the times may be found in the concern for orthodoxy and a broad educational mission that combines traditional liturgical elements with catechism teaching for the youth and increased church attendance by the whole community. In this bequest, which comprises several directives, the Council of Trent is mentioned as the guiding force in shaping a self-conscious orthodoxy and in setting a new moral tone for the community. Marion dictates in detail the procedures he wishes to be set in place for hiring the schoolmaster, and he delineates the functions he expects this individual to carry out:

> And at the time of his induction [the schoolmaster] will be required, besides the usual examination of his doctrine and character, to make a profession of faith according to the content of the Holy Council of Trent in front of the rector or his vicaires and in the presence of the consuls [of the town] or the judges and administrators. . . . Further, the schoolmaster will similarly be required during the period of his appointment to take the schoolchildren or have them taken to hear the mass and at entering their school they should be made to say a *veni creator* and on departing a *salve regina*, also the aforesaid schoolmaster shall be responsible for teaching [the schoolchildren] some catechism on Fridays and on Sunday after vespers [he shall] take them in front of the rector in the presence of the vicars, the other priests, and the people who wish to be present, so that they may show what they have learned from the aforesaid catechism, [and] the rector, vicar or priest shall make a brief exposition or instruction out of this both for the schoolchildren and for the people.[38]

What does Marion's will and his place in League piety say about the interrelations of traditional forms of performativity and their adaptation to the reformist goals embraced both by Marion and by the Decrees of Trent? Most importantly, that his local performative loyalties are combined with his embrace of Tridentine standards of orthodoxy. For so many Catholics of the "Century of Saints," these mixed loyalties passed through such intermediaries as John the Baptist and membership in penitential confraternities that gave universal loyalties a more immediate local reality.

A final point of analysis is the processional element in Marion's will, which begins and ends by emphasizing the power of processional moments in defining his own experience of reform. Having establishing a more sacred enclosure for the host in the local parish processions, which affirms a triumphant eucharistic real presence, he moves toward the conclusion of his will by focusing on the communal and universal experience of processions bearing extreme unction to the sick and dying.

The discussion of Marion's will has sought both to show the hierarchically ordered elements of the will and to reveal the personal, experiential settings through cultural change occurring from the sixteenth to the seventeenth century. Although these experiential settings were founded in the penitential performativity of the League era, they led to a reform of behavior and cognitive relations to the sacred that are considered more characteristic of the seventeenth-century Catholic Reformation itself and the process of the condensation of sacred immanence. To elucidate this process of cultural change it is important to look more carefully at the emergence of those concrete institutional sites where Leaguer piety becomes Catholic Reform.

How can the meaning of Marion's decision to enter the Feuillants be understood more clearly? Like the procession of the Feuillants from Toulouse to Paris in July 1587—when sixty-two monks of this order walked two by two for twenty-five days with bare feet and without relaxing the most rigorous discipline—Marion's decision to enter the order was itself a penitential act and an expression of deep asceticism. Marion's life, as captured in his will at the moment of monastic profession, thus represents one point of the initiation of the profound cultural change whereby *imitatio Christi* undergoes a process of institutionalization revealed in the flowering of monastic professions in the seventeenth century.[39]

Marion takes us to the locus of "a silent revolution." Richet employed this term to indicate that a revolution in religious sensibilities had taken place between the 1570s and the 1590s that few had noticed because of the sound and fury of dynastic crisis and political factionalism. Marion's place

Table 7.3
Monastic Professions in the Three Sample Periods

Year	Testator's Name and Sex		Notary & notary part of town	Testator Profession/socio-professional background	Special heading	Holograph	Institutional affiliation
1544	Frère Loys de Challencon	M	Cartault place Maubert, Université	*"religieux non profes en l'eglise et abbaye de Saint Anthoine le Petit"*	no	no	abbaye de Saint-Antoine le Petit à Paris
1590	Marion, Jehan	M	Jourdan rue Saint-Honoré Faubourg	prebstre-novice; brother and executor: *conseiller au Parlement de Toulouse*	Jesus . . . Maria	no	Notra-Dame des Feuillants (Reformed Cistercians)
	Leboindre, Philippe	M	Bontemps, R. rue des Canettes, Cité	most recently: *"serviteur de monsieur l'evesque de Renes"* [the Leaguer bishop of Rennes, Aimar Hennequin]	A cross at the top of the page	no	*"les freres mynimes au couvent de Nigeon lèz Chailiot pres la ville de Paris"* *("... et estant sur le point de ladicte profession")*
1630	Frère Jourdain de Paris, nommé au monde Pierre Rousselet	M	Bruneau rue du Temple, Ville	*religieux novice* His uncle and executor, Pierre Rousselet: *advocat au Parlement*	no	no	Couvent Notre Dame de Grace du Tiers crdre Saint François de Picquepusse *("... qu'il est prest de se retirer du monde par la profession qu'il espera moyennant la grace de Dieu de faire ... pour y vivre et mourir")*
	Frère Pierre Blondel	M	Collé rue des Arcis, Ville	*religieux novice*	no	no	*"Couvent Nostre Dame de Longpont, ordre de Clugny"*

Table 7.3, cont'd
Monastic Professions in the Three Sample Periods

Year	Testator's Name and Sex		Notary & notary part of town	Testator Profession/socio-professional background	Special heading	Holograph	Institutional affiliation
1630	Rouillé, Claire (soeur Marie-Claire)	F	Cousinet (delivered to the notary "au parloir dudict couvent") rue Saint-Avoie, Ville	religieuse novice, "au monde, vetue de feu Jean Tronçon, escuier sieur de Couldray, conseiller du roy et correcteur en sa chambre des comptes"	Cross at the top of each page; special heading "Vive Deus"	yes	couvent de la visitation Nostre Dame au faulxbourg Saint-Jacques
	Soeur Elisabeth Bellina	F	Fieffé rue Saint-Antoine, Ville	religieuse novice et non professe	no	no	couvent et l'hospital de la Charité Nostre Dame
	Gourgue, Marie (Marie de Jesus)	F	Haultdesens rue de la Verrerie, Ville	religieuse novice, (father is Monsieur le premier president Gourgue in the Parlement at Bordeaux; mother is dame Marie Séguier; and uncle is Monsieur le president Séguier in the Parlement of Paris)	Jesus + Maria, then at top: "au nom de la tres saincte trinité, pere, filz et sainct esprit. . . ."	yes	la monastere de l'Incarnation de l'ordre des Carmelites
	Frère Anthoine Germinot, nommé de religion Frere Samuel age: 22	M	Charles* place Maubert, Université	presently: religieux non-profece	no	no	au couvent des pères Capucins au faubourg Saint-Jacques "estant sur le point de sa profession"
	Frère Claude Thome, nommé du religion Frere Ambroise age: 22	M	Charles* place Maubert, Université	presently religieux non-profex "estant sur le point de faire profession"	no	no	au couvent des Reverends peres Capuchins fondé faubourg Saint-Jacques

* Jean Charles of place Maubert (dates of practice: 1581–1635) had five League-related testators in 1590. The presence of Frère Amboise among his clients in 1630 suggests the ongoing ties of Jean Charles with the religious avant-garde.

in the larger movement of religious change, however, can be pinpointed after examining the micro-portraits of the 1630's testators and exploring the options they exercised in their quest for religious reform. Some clues to the seventeenth-century context of reform are already evident: for example, the emergence and, later, dominance among seventeenth-century reformers of the robe or *officier* (office-holding magistracy) milieu from which Marion is descended in Toulouse. Geographical clues accompanied the rise of this social elite, as Marion's monastery was founded in the *Faubourg* Saint-Honoré, in the territorial circumscription of the parish Saint-Germain-l'Auxerrois, the most elite of the Parisian parishes. These clues strongly suggest that the defining characteristics of Marion's reforming milieu with its powerful meridional, penitential outlook had a strong affinity with what has been termed the growing "professional asceticism" developing in the *officier* and robe class of the *Parlements* and sovereign courts.[40]

As the portraits of two other 1590's reformers will demonstrate, part of the cultural world of the University had formed bonds of loyalty to the new religious orders such as the Jesuits, Capuchins, and Feuillants. This milieu within the University, represented by Genevieve Rolland, Lamiral's most performative testator, was beginning to form a cultural alliance with the rising class of the *noblesse d'office*. The full significance of this cultural and social shift can be seen best among the 1630's reformers. Some elements of this disciplined and ascetic religious engagement can be found in the two female testators of 1590 whose reformist concerns were focused on the morality and competence of the celebrant of their services.[41]

Marye Thiersault's Family Ties

In 1590, *noble damoiselle* Marye Thiersault left a remarkable will. The social ties revealed in the will, combined with what is known about the Thiersault family and its marriage alliances, illustrate that she belonged to the highest echelons of the robe nobility who possessed both direct and multi-generational connections to one of the most important figures of seventeenth-century Catholic renewal, Michel de Marillac. These family alliances are one starting point for exploring the social, cultural, and institutional sites where personal religious engagement begins to shape the Janus face of League piety.

Thiersault was a widow of two marriages. She first married an *avocat en Parlement*, *noble homme maistre* Regnault de Bailly. Her second marriage was with *noble homme maistre* Robert de Sainct Germain, a *conseiller*, *notaire* and *secrétaire du roi*, who was one of the four notaries and secretaries of *Parlement*, and was thus a member of the robe nobility. This second marriage made Thiersault a relative of Marie de Sainct Germain, the second wife of Michel de Marillac, whom Thiersault calls her niece in the quotation below.[42] Thiersault's 1590 will establishes for the first time the long-standing personal and religious nature of these family ties. A detailed bequest to Marie de Sainct Germain makes this point:

> Next [the testator] gives the wife of the aforesaid sire, president Amelot, a cross of gold in which there are ten diamonds with a pearl at the end of the cross, as a token of the friendship she has for her and also to assure that she will remember her in her prayers, just as [the testator] asks of her with all her heart.[43]

Marie Thiersault names four nephews among the executors of her will, including *noble homme maistre* Pierre Thiersault, *sieur* d'Essisses. This nephew Pierre has been identified as a member of the *Seize* with strong ties to Mayenne.[44] Furthermore, Pierre married *damoiselle* Marie de Nully, the daughter of Estienne de Nully, one of the most controversial and most prominent of the *Seize* leaders in *Parlement* whom L'Estoile reckoned to have "a Spanish soul."[45] In 1612, Pierre Thiersault's daughter Marie married *noble homme maistre* Loys Chantereau-Lefebvre, *avocat* in *Parlement*, the son of the *Seize* François Chantereau-Lefebvre.[46] The signatures on this marriage contract reveal more *Seize* alliances to the Lecoigneux and Sainctyon families.[47]

Thiersault takes the unusual step of naming two further individuals to assist the five named executors. Each of these individuals has significant Leaguer connections. For example, the first named is *sieur president* Amelot (the first husband of Marie de Sainct Germain). Amelot receives several carefully described items of jewelry—all "les plus beaux"—in return for his assistance and prayers. To assist Amelot, Thiersault designates *noble homme maistre* Jehan Bacquet, "conseiller et advocat du roy en la Justice du Trésor," whose daughter Magdelaine Bacquet married the *Seize*, *noble homme maistre* Antoine Charpentier, an *avocat* who was executed in the Place de Grève in 1597 on charges of spying for Spain.[48]

From Thiersault to the Dames de Charité: Bringing the Eucharist to the Sick and Poor

Thiersault's will demonstrates a highly personal and intricate economy of salvation that includes most facets of League piety analyzed in this book. It needs to be emphasized, however, that this document is particularly important as an example of a deeply devout and intimate lay appropriation of liturgy and attention to liturgical detail. For Thiersault, death and salvation, like life itself, were inconceivable without the bonds of religious ritual and shared articles of faith that united her to church, family, and friends. This will demonstrates how family and political ties were embedded in a religious matrix that defined the boundaries of loyalty and trust. Her very personal engagement in religious ritual requires a reconceptualzation of the "âme espagnole" from a perspective other than that of the interests of state. Following the initial *recommendatio animae*, like so many of the *Seize*-identified wills, Marye Thiersault's begins "apres avoir fait profession de sa foy, religion catholicque, apostolique et romaine en laquelle elle veult par la grace de dieu comme bonne chrestienne vivre et mourir. . . ." The two senses in which the notion of "faire profession" can be encountered, the taking of monastic vows and the public profession of faith, have a powerful affinity in the way they both refer to public performative acts defining self-identity in relation to a communal/confessional affiliation. During the League the communal and the confessional were one in the Leaguer mental universe. Thiersault's will opens with a uniquely worded request for pardon that emphasizes a deeply penitential view of the self:

> In the first place [the testator] has recommended and recommends her soul to God our creator, saviour, and redeemer in all humility and reverence, thanking him humbly for the infinity of goods she has received in this mortal world especially for the participation in his Holy Sacraments, confessing that she has gravely offended him by several great and grave sins, she hopes that by the beneficence of the holy passion of Jesus Christ his son our saviour and by the intercession of the holy and sacred virgin Mary his mother and by all the saints of paradise her sins may be pardoned such that Satan may overcome neither her soul nor her.[49]

When characterizing Thiersault's penitential piety, it is crucial to note the sacramental reference that precedes the admission of grave sin and the expression of hope founded on "le benefice de la saincte passion" that follows and precedes the request for intercession. What distinguishes her sacramentally channeled and more hopeful penitential piety from the anguished penitential piety of the earlier processions of the 1580s is her confidence in the redemptive power of the passion as re-enacted in the mass and eucharist.[50] The language of Thiersault's commendation of her soul suggests a fundamental cultural shift from the penitential piety of the street processions to the sacramentally channeled piety of the post-League period, where penitence is either confined to the inside of homes, churches, and monasteries or transformed into charitable Catholic action permeating the city.[51] In the transition from the sixteenth to the seventeenth century two very different structures of penitential piety (which are based on temperamentally different understandings of the passion) are apparent.[52] The processional piety of the earlier period is focused on the connections between the immense suffering of Christ during his passion and the immensity of human sin: the appeal for divine mercy (*miséricorde*) is not tempered by great confidence in institutional solutions.[53] Sacramentally channeled penitential piety, on the other hand, requires not only confidence in institutions but several underlying pre-conditions: access to knowledgeable and compassionate clergy and affectively and cognitively powerful settings for sacramental and liturgical experiences, such as the Forty Hours eucharist devotion. For the *dévot* of the seventeenth century, these relationships could be powerfully charged. One of the chief challenges of "reform," from the perspective of the *ecclesia*, is to find ways of institutionalizing the imitation of Christ in ways that join individual aspirations to social and institutional needs, and engender confidence in institutional practices and behavior. The growing popularity of the Capuchins, and Thiersault's special attachment to them, may be in part explained by the particular way Franciscan piety had traditionally fused the devotion to the Passion with devotion to the eucharist.[54] Thiersault's will embodies this fusion, and its potential to facilitate actual social transformations. These transformations include the Catholic action associated with the charitable missions of the *Dames de Charité*, who bring the eucharist into the homes of the sick and poor as part of the *Dames'* own penitential and devotional engagement.

The processional as opposed to sacramental expressions of penitential piety also create different structures of community. The anguished processional form of penitential piety is oriented toward the "communitas" of liminal states and to times of crisis such as the epistemological rupture within which the contest between Leaguers and *politiques* was enacted. It is unstable and not easily controlled by official hierarchy.[55] Sacramentally structured penitential piety, on the other hand, reinforces hierarchy and the status of the priestly intermediary and also creates a different religious experience. However, Thiersault's will can tell us still more about the role liturgy plays in the religious experience of the time.

Thiersault's Lay Appropriation of Liturgy

The liturgical precisions of Thiersault's will are its most striking feature. Fully seventy-five percent of her eighty pious directives deal with requests for a wide range of services, usually specified in minute detail. Despite the length of her will, Thiersault is selective in her demands, and her emphases provide a good indication of which ritual features are most important to her as she contemplates death, funeral services, burial, and the requirements of salvation. After choosing burial in her parish church of Saint-Germain-l'Auxerrois, she leaves nearly all the details of her funeral arrangements to the discretion of her heirs "assuring herself that they will carry these out decently and as would be appropriate."[56] Thiersault does, however, request that her body be present in the church for her service. The first place she pauses in order to provide detail comes at what signifies for her a crucial liminal moment: the actual burial of her body. She asks that her body not be moved for twenty-four hours following her death. Then, she requests that at the time her body is placed in its sepulchre the prayers *domine non secundum, salut regina, Deus qui nos patrem et matrem,* and the *de profundis* be said or chanted "en faulx bourdon."[57] This kind of liturgical precision involving musical sophistication and the constant repetition of so many well-known parts of the liturgy for the dead forms a pattern throughout the will. It has profound significance in understanding not only League piety but also for understanding the emergence of baroque ceremonial. Thus it is important to consider both the meaning and function of the richness of liturgical detail in Thiersault's will. Her will is first and foremost an affirmation of the salvific value of liturgical ritual.[58] For Thiersault, as the high performativity associated with Leaguers in general shows, religious ritual literally creates and sustains the boundaries of community and meaningful order in the world. This testator provides an excellent example for Victor Turner's theory that symbolic and ritual action have an ontological status.[59] How can the practical effects of Thiersault's enormous investment in liturgical detail be understood in experiential terms?

Thiersault's list of prayers promotes a particular aesthetic sensibility. Her wealth and social position combined with her cultural interests permit her to create meaning in very specific ways. Her investment in ritual must be viewed in the light of her equal investment in intellectual religious comprehension. She insists upon the choice of a priest "who understands what he says." In one of her most personalized service requests she establishes a perpetual foundation for a daily low mass "de jour" to be said at "precisely 9 A.M." in the chapelle des Troys Roys (the Chapel of the Three Kings) by her *chappelain ordinaire maistre* Jehan Bernard, assisted by an *enfant du coeur* to say the responses. After the death of *maistre* Bernard, Thiersault requests that the service be said by *maistre* Fremin Geoffroy, *chappelain au coeur.* Then, she requests that her heirs, assisted by *monsieur le president* Amelot, select a replacement: "ung homme d'eglise habitué en icelle eglise St. Germain, homme de bien et qu'il entende ce qu'il dira [et] bien vivant . . ."[60] In one telling comment, Thiersault not only emphasizes her deep cognitive engagement, but also shows her keen awareness of the epistemological—or on a more pragmatic level, the didactic—function of ceremony. Thiersault's insistence on a priest who understands what he says goes to the heart of the Tridentine educational initiatives that accompany the defense of ceremony and include the banning of the use of symbolic numbers (as a form of superstition). The Council of Trent's insistence upon the connection between ceremony and understanding, of course, also stressed the need for an educated clergy capable of explaining the central rituals to the laity. This need was clearly reflected in the foundation Marion established for a sermon to be given to explicate the significance of the festival days chosen for his masses. Also, if ceremony is created to honor God—its other primary function—then the moral and intellectual qualities of the celebrant must be adequate to the task.[61]

This analysis can be taken one step further if the debates about "ceremonies" at the time of the Council of Trent are considered and then the cultural consequences of such a pronounced emphasis on ceremony as an epistemology of the sacred are examined.[62] While the didactic functions of ritual have always been present, a deeper look into Thiersault's detailed liturgical prescriptions raises the question of how reception of baroque ritual differed among social groups. The great patrons of the liturgical arts, such as Thiersault, who could establish costly endowments surely experienced the baroque ritual in a different way than did the much larger mass of more common parishioners who may have felt a loss of local liturgical traditions in exchange for receiving a more standardized and uniform Tridentine ritual order.[63]

What forms of local knowing, and hence participation, may have been lost? The beginnings of an answer to this question emerge from analysis of the trend toward greater liturgical standardization shown in Table 7.4. The most powerful correlation with the trend toward a narrower range of liturgical choices is the decline in the use of number symbolism in testators' requests for services and masses over the three sample periods. It is possible that the creative ontological force of the liturgy was increasingly eclipsed by its didactic functions later in the seventeenth century, because at this time the didactic role of liturgy was emphasized. Crucial debates on the precise role of ceremony took place in Catholic circles at the time of the Council of Trent. For example, Braun stressed in *De ceremoniis* that all ceremonies have been instituted to signify a certain mystery. Jerome Emser argued that all Christian ritual ultimately leads back to the central mystery of Christianity, namely, to the meaning of Christ's life and death. The various modalities of symbolic action, such as the use of sacred objects or demarcation of sacred time and space, are thus pathways to higher and more

Table 7.4

Liturgical Standardization and Its Relation to the Decline in Number Symbolism in the Three Sample Periods

Year	I. Total number of distinctive verbal expressions GTP* required in requesting any and all services and masses	Year	II. Number of distinctive verbal expressions GTP* required in requesting services and masses containing number symbolism
1540	172 verbal expressions	1540	51 verbal expressions
1590	113 verbal expressions	1590	12 verbal expressions
1630	102 verbal expressions	1630	10 verbal expressions

*   GTP=General Testator Population

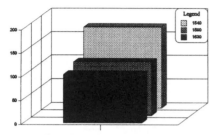

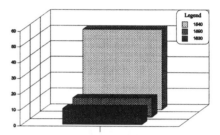

I.   Total number of distinctive verbal
     expressions.

II. Number of distinctive verbal
     expressions.

secret mysteries. Emser wrote, "that which is secretly and mysteriously symbolized by vestments, ceremonies, and ornaments is the mystery of Christ's passion and the mystery of his whole life."[64] Ceremony and ritual, with the attendant visual experience, became a method of sacred knowing.

There are, of course, other important functions of ceremony. It can affirm particular structures of authority and community. This was one of the most important findings to emerge from the analysis of *politique* texts in Part Two. To defend ceremony, Thiersault, however, not only affirms the importance of liturgical tradition; she is also on the leading edge of a particular kind of liturgical innovation: the establishment of foundations for meticulously detailed *saluts* for various holy days. Although certainly not unknown earlier, this lay appropriation of the liturgy, by elites in particular, in pursuit of personal salvation becomes most popular in the second half of the seventeenth century.[65] While this proliferation of ceremony, which occurred at the height of what might be called baroque piety, is a sign of religious engagement on the part of the elite, by the eighteenth century the church became overburdened with these liturgical demands. Some historians have described the expansion of a more formal and standardized ceremony as a possible cause of the unresponsiveness of the church in a new age.[66] This can be seen as part of the paradox of the baroque and its unintended consequence: liturgy lost some of its traditional ontological force (its power to create sacral communities across class lines) as it became ever more preoccupied with epistemological and aesthetic functions in defense of new standards of decorum and permissible forms of performativity. Note, for example, how much of baroque ceremonialism confined processions to the inside of churches and how carefully canalized popular participation in exterior processions became.

Thiersault, with her ritual construction of community, was keenly aware of what her social position allowed her to do. She was also cognizant, however, that salvation required humility, which she expressed primarily through charity and by turning to the poor as intercessors. About fourteen percent of the pious directives in Thiersault's will were addressed to the poor and to charitable institutions. Beyond her desire that her cortege be conducted "honestement," her only further directive dealing with this central aspect of funeral ritual concerned the role of the poor in the cortege. The directives concerning poor persons were marked by scrupulous detail, and reveal the testator's desire for the poor to play very specific and active intercessory roles. The only instance of any form of number symbolism in Thiersault's will was the choice of "thirteen truly poor persons" ("treize vrays pauvres") who were given detailed instructions to participate in her cortege and attend her services. She stated:

> Next [the testator] wishes and orders that at her aforesaid cortege and burial thirteen truly poor persons should be dressed, giving to each of them a robe and a hat of black cloth valued at one *escu* per *aulne* which they will wear while they participate in the cortege carrying one large candle each, which also will be given to them and when the aforesaid cortege has ended, they [must] leave the aforesaid robes and hats in the house of the aforesaid *damoiselle* testator and to each them should also be given ten *sous tournois* and after eight days the aforesaid *damoiselle* wishes that her service *du bout de l'an* be said both in the choir and at the parish altar of the aforesaid [church of] Saint-Germain [l'Auxerrois] where the aforesaid thirteen truly poor persons, dressed as above, shall each attend her services and at their conclusion they may take with them their robes and hats and there shall be given to them ten *sous tournois*.[67]

Thiersault is unique in designating "vrays pauvres," although there is a growing tendency among testators to specify the truly needy, "les plus necessiteux." She directs that each poor person is to carry a torch and be given one *sol*, a *robe*, and a *chaperon de drap noir* costing one *écu* per *aulne* to wear to the funeral service. At the end of the service these poor persons are required to return the mourning clothes to Thiersault's house and to appear again in eight days to put on the mourning clothes anew to attend Theirsault's "bout de l'an."[68] Only at the end of this ceremony may they keep the clothes and be given an additional ten *solz* each.

The desire for more than a merely perfunctory association with the poor is demonstrated again in her bequests to prisoners in the *Grand* and *Petit Châtelet* and at the episcopal prison of *Fort L'Evesque*. Thiersault gives twenty *escuz* to each of the Châtelet prisons, and thirty-three *escuz ung tiers* to the *Fort L'Evesque*. Half the sum bequeathed to *Fort L'Evesque* is to be used to say a low mass every Sunday for the year following the testator's death, a service that includes a *de profundis* to be said following each mass "à haute voys" by the priest and the prisoners in attendance. The remaining sum is to be distributed to the prisoners. Each person receiving alms is required by the will to say a *de profundis* for the testator's soul.

What is striking about Thiersault's bequests to the poor is the duration of time the poor are required to be engaged on behalf of the testator's soul. The greatest difficulty comes in trying to evaluate the nature of the bonds or social relations that such pious requests create. In this respect, it is also important to note the variety of ways Thiersault's will continues to evoke penitential themes. This occurs in her in-kind bequest to the Capuchins, which also includes what might be considered another use of number symbolism. She gives to the Capuchins two *muidz* of wheat (*bled*) to remember her in their prayers and adds:

> and pray that when they are advised of her death and passing that during seven consecutive days they say the seven psalms with the carols and prayers.[69]

Thiersault's specification has particular resonances with Capuchin views of piety. Gifts in kind were more in keeping with Capuchin asceticism and vows of poverty than were gifts of money. Moreover, Capuchin reform was interpreted by its founders and early generals in an eschatological light as a final and most perfect reform.[70] Bellintani da Salò, whose writings were well known in devout circles, had been particularly drawn to the *Historia septem tribulationum ordinis minorum* of Ange Clareno in writing his history of the Capuchin order. Thiersault might have been influenced by this symbolic understanding of the number seven as well.[71] Bellintani da Salò argued that the Franciscan order had to pass through seven stages of tribulation before attaining its final perfect reform. Thiersault might easily envision the procession of her own body this way. Capuchin asceticism also gave its spirituality particularly strong affinities with penitential piety. Although recitation of the seven penitential psalms was a traditional intercession for the dead, that Thiersault particularly asks this of the Capuchins and no other order suggests her special receptivity toward Capuchin spirituality and her desire for a closer association with this penitential mode of monastic piety.[72] Thiersault's concordant use of number symbolism (thirteen poor and seven days) suggests that even among the religious elite, number symbolism still had particular resonance. There is every reason to believe that testators understood the power of this form of symbolism that permitted them to make connections not only between themselves and Christ, but between their penitential selves and the poor. Despite her association with some forms of number symbolism, however, Thiersault does not use the number five, with its allusion to the five wounds, which had been popular in the wills of 1543–44. For the most popular types of liturgical number symbolism used by testators who still use such proscribed practices, see Table 8.2: "The Most Popular Service-Related Number Symbolism over Three Sample Periods." Instead, she further expresses her penitential sensibilities through requests for masses on Fridays (four times), and Wednesdays and Fridays (three times, a total of seven). She also makes repeated requests for the "vexilla regis prodeunt" (*salut de la passion*). Most particularly, as part of the service she requests for the Chappelle des 'Iroys Ruys, she asks that, following each mass on Wednesday and Friday, there also be said "la passion de Jésus Christ."

Overall, Thiersault's will reveals a creative lay appropriation of religious ritual to express and reproduce on a personal level larger structures of order and meaning. By employing a symbolic mode of understanding, Thiersault attempted to overcome the problems of maintaining an authentic community. These efforts on her part came at a time when growing social divisions and liturgical changes were making the preservation of that community even more difficult. The abundance of detail makes the point, easily overlooked in the more formulaic wills, that this maintenance of community and personal expression of larger structures is one of the prime functions of a will. At the center of the will is an ontology, not just an epistemology. In both her creativity and use of liturgical traditions Thiersault brings order and structure to a liminal process in which social actors of vastly different social provenance are brought together in ever more ritualized ways. In Leaguer wills, death and salvation remain part of a communal process in which the living and the dead are bound together through strategic intercessions and participatory rituals. Thiersault shows us an economy of salvation organized around four fundamental concepts: the merits of the poor as displayed in their role in the convoy, devotion to the Virgin as displayed in the *saluts*, belief in the salvific function of the Passion as symbolized through sacred time (Wednesdays and Fridays), and liturgical reiteration of the Passion.

The symbolic action in which Thiersault invests is actually socially programmatic in its emphasis on the ritual construction of community through intercessions and through the liturgy. Her will may imply less direct transformative social action than, for example, the will of Marion. But, ritual and its creative elaboration lie at the heart of the new aesthetic of the baroque. The most socially programmatic detail, which allows us to comprehend how Thiersault understands the sacred, is her emphasis upon the relationship between personal morality, active cognition, and the performance of ritual on the part of the priest who will say her "basse messe du jour" in the Chapel of the Three Kings. Finally, conceptualized in these terms, it is clear how Thiersault's bequest to the Capuchins can be seen to involve the most dynamic cathexis of her spiritual values and programmatic social action. In the Capuchin mission, spirituality, asceticism, and transformative social action were inextricably interwoven. There is undoubtedly tension between Capuchin asceticism and the baroque investment in immanence and spectacle that needs to be better understood. The acculturating missions of the Capuchins may be thought of as a Catholic mode of Weber's paradigm of a worldly means of asceticism. To focus exclusively on the Protestant model that privileges transcendence and relies upon a very particular notion of market-oriented rationality obscures the creative relationship between Catholic religious experience and socio-cultural and aesthetic change.

The Jesuit Affiliations of Laurens Malescot, Jehan Thibault, and Raoul Bontemps: A *Seize* Reforming Milieu

The 1590's testators of Raoul Bontemps leave reformist directives for educational purposes, aimed at cognitive change. The Leaguer and particularly *Seize*-centered specificity of this type of reforming concern begins to become even more clear. The two testators, *noble et discrete personne maistre* Laurens Malescot and *maistre* Jehan Thibault, both chose Bontemps, the most prominent *Seize* notary, to draw up their wills. Bontemps is for each testator a notary of conviction. Both testators, in good health and thus able to exercise a full range of options, lived or lodged in the University quarter, but selected Bontemps' practice on the *Ile de la Cité*.

First, it is important to examine the Jesuit connections of these two reformers and their reforming bequests. Then the nature of the Jesuit affiliation in League piety can be assessed, and it will be possible to explore what this may say about the broader question of the nature of Catholic reform in Paris. Laurens Malescot, a priest and doctor of canon law at the University of Paris, was also a resident at the College of Calvi near the Sorbonne within Boucher's parish of Saint-Benoît. On March 16, 1590, only two days after the disastrous defeat of the Catholic armies at Ivry, Malescot dictated a remarkable eight-page will to Raoul Bontemps that was co-signed by the Leaguer notary Mathieu Bontemps.[73] The handwriting of the document is unlike any other of the testators of Raoul Bontemps: the recommendation structure of the will is unmistakably of University provenance, and its language is focused on the Passion of Christ and the sacramental manifestation of Christ's compassion, that is, the possibility of redemption that begins in baptism:

> And first of all as a Christian redeemed by the blood and by the passion of our lord savior and redeemer Jesus Christ, regenerated by holy baptism in his church [the testator] has recommended his soul to God through prayer to the most sacred and glorious Virgin Mary, mother of God, and to his good angel and to monsieur Saint Laurens and Saint Genevieve, his intercessors, so that he may for the time that he dwells below in his body and from the time he attains glory ever be transported into the eternal beatitude of his body, coadjutor with his soul in the aquistion of the glory of heaven.[74]

From Malescot's request to be buried in the cathedral church of Notre-Dame in Le Puy in Vellay, in the tombs reserved for canons, it is apparent that he, like Marion, had served in the office of canon, which during the Reformation had become a target of harsh criticism because it offered a source of income but entailed no pastoral duties. Malescot's professional background thus further explains all the safeguards Marion included in his foundation to ensure that no absent cleric should participate in the income of the foundation. It is fair to say that both men knew abuses at first hand, and such knowledge can produce a zealous desire for reformation. In his reforming directive Malescot gives an annual *rente* of sixteen *écus deux-tiers* to the college in the town of Le Puy to found in perpetuity "a public lecture on moral dilemmas in the sacrament of confession,"[75] which would be open to the public and clergy alike in order to edify them in the fine points of confession. This is a specific educational and sacramental focus that cannot be found in any of the wills of clerics in 1543–44. The remaining clauses in this will expose Malescot's close ties to the Jesuits. He leaves a portion of his books to the Jesuit College of Clermont in Paris or to the College at Tournon, and leaves a *rente* to support a Jesuit Marian congregation founded at the College of Clermont.

The final educational reformer of 1590 is *maistre* Jehan Thibault. In his will of September 4, 1590, he identifies himself only as a "cytoyen de la ville de Lyon," presently lodged in the rue du Foing, parish Saint-Séverin. It is difficult to imagine a person in good health residing in Paris in the

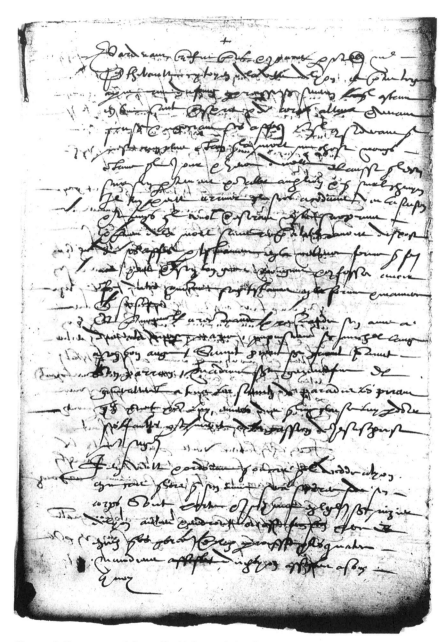

Figure 3. First page of the will of Jehan Thibault, "citizen of the city of Lyon," with a small cross marked at the top. Notary Raoul Bontemps. (Centre historique des Archives nationales. MC/Etude XXIII, 95.)

month of the highest mortality following the siege for any other reason than Leaguer business. Thibault's choice of the notary Raoul Bontemps, in any case, leaves no doubt of his motivations. The pious and reforming directives he makes in his will tell us even more about the reforming commitments of such a politically mobilized individual. For example, he specifies that if he dies in Lyon, his body should be carried by the four mendicant orders of Lyon and by the priests of his parish of Saint-Nizier, where he wishes to be buried near his deceased relatives. In his reforming directive Thibault gives to

> the congregation of Our Lady at Lyon,
> where the Jesuits assemble, 12 *écus soleil*
> to be used for little catechisms and for
> rosaries to be distributed to the poor. . . . [76]

Evident in the will is the ever more characteristic juxtaposition of the educative and the liturgical (where mind and body are joined in prayer, and learning is designed to form not only a socially but also an anthropologically integrated economy of salvation that plays on reason, affect, and bodily senses). Neither of these two wills is lengthy and neither makes many bequests, but the orientation of the bequests toward educational efficacy is their most striking feature. Their choice of the notary Raoul Bontemps makes clear that groups among the *Seize* were deeply committed to Jesuit piety and educational reform, despite L'Estoile's disparaging remarks about the lack of science in the religious zeal of a Leaguer such as Pierre Delamer.

The World of Genevieve Rolland: A Nexus between the University and the New Religious Orders

To pursue the connections between the new religious orders and League piety, it will be useful to examine the extraordinary will of *honorable femme* Genevieve Rolland. In making bequests to reformed religious orders of the League era, Rolland's loyalties lie exclusively with the Feuillants, unlike Thiersault, whose bequests to the reforming orders went exclusively to the Capuchins. Interestingly, in contradistinction to the many Leaguers who bequest to two or more orders among the Jesuits, Capuchins and Feuillants, each of the 1590 reformers presents a more concentrated set of loyalties, since each makes bequests to only one of these three orders. Rolland returns us to a very special milieu within the world of the University, in which a profound Christocentrism, expressed in penitential piety, has become allied with personal asceticism. This combination ultimately will foster traits of social discipline through new and very structured relations with the poor and through charitable outreach in general. In the discussion of her notary, Philippe Lamiral, many clues to the social and cultural world with which Rolland is associated have already been encountered. Her will permits us to assemble these fragments of evidence into a more comprehensive analysis.

Rolland is herself a resident of the University quarter in the *Seize* parish of Saint-Séverin. She chooses as her notary Philippe Lamiral, who co-signs with Jacques de Saint-Vaast, a strongly League-identified combination that has already been frequently encountered. It is important, however, to recall that Lamiral requested in his own will that there be no pomp and superfluity in his funeral ceremony. This modest request assumes a broader significance now as the connections between Rolland, the ascetic piety of the Feuillants, and the emergence of a very disciplined charitable engagement with the poor are explicated. This evidence will provide another model, besides that represented by Marion, of how zealous penitential piety became the Catholic action of the seventeenth century.

The indications of "zeal" in Rolland's own will are a good place to begin. She is among the strategic group of testators for whom it can be argued that the will is a response to the disastrous defeat of Mayenne and the Catholic forces at the Battle of Ivry on March 14, 1590. For these testators, the will becomes a first line of militant defense for the soul itself, imperiled perhaps more than the body by Henry IV's now inevitable assault on the capital. In good health at the time, Rolland has her will drawn up on March 29, 1590, in the *étude* of Philippe Lamiral. She identifies herself as the widow of *honorable homme* Pierre LeDoyen, a *bourgeois de Paris*, and most certainly an *homme de loi*, and probably a *procureur*, given the epithets and what was learned of Rolland's two previous marriages. In the civil clauses of her will, she mentions previous marriages, each to a *procureur au Parlement*. To the children of her first husband, deceased *maistre* Philippe Brunel, *procureur en la cour de Parlement*, she gives six hundred livres "because of the good conduct, honor, and friendship he has shown towards her."[77] To Charles Frassier, the son of her deceased second husband *maistre* L. Frassier, a *procureur en la cour de Parlement*, she gives an annual *rente* "to aid in the costs of schooling and for their other needs."[78]

Other civil clauses provide more crucial information about the social, cultural, and political milieu to which Genevieve Rolland belonged. She is related through her third and present husband, *honorable homme* Pierre LeDoyen, to the family of the notary Jacques Fardeau. Fardeau was deeply connected to the League milieu of the University and co-signed wills with Jacques Saint-Vaast, just as Lamiral did in his practice.[79] Rolland ratifies a *donation* to Marie Fardeau, the daughter of *honorable homme maistre* Jacques

Fardeau, *notaire au Chastellet*, and makes a *donation* to Fardeau's wife, Marie Le Doyen. Marie is obviously related to Rolland, and is perhaps a sister of Rolland's present husband. Additional civil clauses reveal more University connections: in a codicil of August 1, 1590, Rolland asks that the children of deceased Catherine Brunel (the family of Rolland's first husband) be able to participate equally in the inheritance of their mother. The children's father, *maistre* Simon La Fille, is identified as "previously an official functionary" (*cy-devant suppôt de l'Université de Paris*).

Genevieve Rolland is clearly related to Nicolas Rolland, who proclaimed Aumale the Governor of Paris following the May 1588 Leaguer coup of the Day of the Barricades, when Henry III was forced to flee his capital. Even more pertinent in the context of Leaguer piety is the fact that Nicolas Rolland, at the time the chief alderman (*échevin*) of Paris and a relative of the testator, held the posthumously born son of the slain duke of Guise at the baptism font.[80] Significantly, this ceremony occurred in the midst of the mourning period for the slain Guises that extended throughout the months of January, February, and March of 1589.[81]

Rolland and the Art of Dying

The remarkable text and provisions of Rolland's will demonstrate the complexities and contradictions of reformist engagement, and thus bring us much closer to an experiential understanding of how local, civic, and deeply personal penitential piety were interwoven with Tridentine prescriptions redefining the boundaries of orthodoxy. The *recommendatio animae* conveys the intensity of the testator's religious engagement, and is unlike any of the quite striking commendations of the soul of other Lamiral testators, some of whom were clerics of the University milieu:

> And in the first place as a good and true catholic [the testator] has recommended and recommends her soul to God, our father, creator, saviour, redeemer, Jesus, in all devotion and humility, calling upon, entreating, and imploring his omnipotence and infinite goodness asking that her sins and offenses committed and perpetuated during her life be pardoned, and when her poor soul becomes separated from her body she begs God to receive it and to grant her eternal beatitude. . . . [82]

She concludes by asking for the prayers and intercessions of the more typical saints but reiterates, showing her deep penitential sense of self, that she desires "pardon and mercy for her sins and offences, giving thanks to God for the property given and loaned [to her] in this mortal life."[83] The will continues with striking influences from the literature on the art of dying (*ars moriendi*), so that this will can be seen as focused on the preparation for death, which is, of course, a deeply penitential vision of life itself.

This perspective is encapsulated in the detailed directives Rolland leaves about the suffrages to be undertaken on her behalf before her death, as her end approaches. Rolland begins her detailed prescriptions with the moment of her final communion:

> Immediately after she has received the body of our saviour, let a priest be sent to her, a man of good character, who will stay with her at all times and admonish her concerning salvation right up until the moment that she dies. And let this same priest say and celebrate, for the salvation of her soul, a mass each day, and for this [she] requests that during all this time this priest should be well fed and given a place to sleep and let him also be given a candle of white wax with a payment of 20 *livres tournois* for each day that he is with her including the mass that he says for her. [The testator] wishes and orders that the aforesaid priest select another priest to stay with her during the time that he will be saying and celebrating her mass. And let this other priest also be paid 10 *sous tournois* for his presence with her.[84]

The passage is important and fascinating for what it reveals about the depth of the bond between the priest and this penitent. Rolland's desire for a sacerdotal presence, combined with her fastidious adherence to the Tridentine prescriptions that masses should no longer be celebrated in private dwellings, show us a side of Leaguer piety that is culturally already traveling in a different affective path. It no longer shows the despair of the penitential processions that had filled the streets of Paris only a few months earlier. The passage thus presents us with a clear example of the condensation of sacred immanence where the most direct control over the sacred is restored, as Thiersault would say, to a priest who understands what he says.

The Reformers of 1630:
The Emergence of Two Salient Paths for Reform

Among the testators of 1630 two salient paths for reform emerge. The first includes a greater investment in administration of the sacraments. Moreover, sacramental participation takes a striking new form. This can be seen in the pious directives of the 1630's will of *honorable femme* Jehanne Marchant, who requests communities of religious orders and a group of poor girls receiving dowries to take communion in memory of the testator. This novel bequest further channels the sacred into sacramental settings while binding the testator to two symbolic communities through actual partaking of the eucharist. Traditional memorialization has become completely sacramentalized through the testator's act of charity to the poor and the testator's desire for a vicarious yet performative union with the monastic life through the very body and blood of Christ.

The second prominent path of reform involves a transformation of the self and the boundaries of one's community by entering the monastic life, whose flowering in the seventeenth century in Paris reflects a renewed channel of reform with a myriad of new institutional options. The testaments of 1630 reveal the extent of new monastic foundations, which become vital centers for the transformation of Parisian religious culture in the first third of the seventeenth century. Also significant in the 1630's wills is the absence of any reforming directives that anticipate clerical abuses, such as absenteeism from the testator's services. In fact, the holograph will of the 1630's reformer Germain du Boys clearly reflects rising expectations of the clergy, since he specifies his wish to have his *annual* service said by "an extremely devout cleric" ("ung homme d'eglise fort dévot.") Du Boys also shows the way in which the behaviors having peak values in the Performativity Index have begun to account for a more significant portion of instances of performativity.[85] He gives the enormous sum of one thousand *livres* "to redeem and liberate some poor prisoners . . . who will be taken to my place of burial . . . and exhorted to pray for the salvation of my soul. . . ."[86] This chapter concludes with a discussion of the two wills that best express these religious experiences as the institutionalization of the *imitatio Christi*.

Jehanne Marchant, the widow of *noble homme* Michel Chapin, who was a *vallet de chambre ordinaire du roy*, is counted as a reformer by virtue of her extraordinarily expressive investment in the administration of the sacraments. Her bequests in effect create performative relationships with five religious communities of women, each of whom she asks to take communion in her memory. This is an entirely new request not encountered in the other sample years. Each of Marchant's directives demonstrates a testamentary evolution in which the performative has become increasingly sacramental and charitable, sustaining new forms of community that are combined by Marchant into one economy of salvation.

In her first bequest to a religious community she states:

> . . . [the testator] makes a legacy and gives to madame de Montmartre the sum of 60 *livres* for the work of her monastery entreating her most humbly to have all of the nuns take communion in the name of the testator on the day of or the day after her death and each year on this same day throughout the life of the aforesaid lady of Montmartre.[87]

Her next bequest is to the "peres Feuillants Faubourg Saint-Honoré" of whom she asks only to be remembered in their daily prayers. In a second request to a religious community of women she gives 30 *livres* to the nuns of the Passion [the new house of *Capucines* founded in 1604/1606] with the request that on the day of her death, or the following day, all of the nuns will take communion in her name. To the long-established and very popular "filles religieuses de l'Ave Maria" [the female Franciscans or Poor Clares] she gives thirty *livres* as well "so that they will pray God for her soul and will take holy communion in her memory once a week for the period of a year."[88] The *Religieuses Pénitentes* (originally, at their founding, the result of a preaching campaign to reform the lives of prostitutes by having them form a religious community, the *Filles pénitentes*) receive a bequest in which the testator asks their good mother superior pray God for the salvation of her soul and have them also take communion for this purpose once a week. Finally, in a directive using the symbolism of the five wounds, Marchant joins these communities to the recipients of her most intricate charitable bequest in the following way:

> In honor of the five wounds of our lord, [she] gives and makes a legacy of the sum of 250 *livres* to five young girls who are to be chosen by her aforesaid executors, this makes for each of them, 50 *livres*, so that on the Friday before or after they marry a mass of the passion may be celebrated or that the passion may be said and they shall also take holy communion and pray to God.[89]

Marchant's pious gestures demonstrate the persistent power of the symbolic framework of Passion-centered language and its application to the domain of charity (away from the primarily liturgical uses in regards to services that had predominated). The result emphasizes the inextricable bonds between charity, the Passion, and the eucharist in ways that demonstrate the social dimensions and programmatic creativity of symbolic thought.

Monastic Profession as Performative Transformation

The holograph will of *damoiselle* Marie de Gourgue, drawn up in her own hand on May 7, 1630, in connection with her entry into the Carmelite order, takes us to the apex of the Performativity Index.[90] This order, brought to Paris from Spain in 1610 thanks to the efforts of many zealous Leaguers, now called *dévots*, embodies the institutionalization of Leaguer spirituality. The opening lines of the will state directly the testator's intentions and reveal, in a voice quite different from that of Jehan Marion, the thoughts and emotions accompanying this religious profession of 1630.

VII may
Jesus (cross) Maria

In the name of the most holy trinity, father, son and holy spirit, giving
thanks for his infinite goodness and for the many favors received from his
holy and generous hand and also [giving thanks] that it has pleased him
to give knowledge of and desire for his service and in honor of Jesus Christ
our lord and in honor of the poor and humble life he led desiring to imi-
tate him in this way of life scorning worldly goods and commodities in
order to give myself to his word and to the desire which he instills in
me to abandon and renounce these things for the love of him. And to
this end I surrender fully all my goods in this final act and testament as
follows . . . [91]

Marie de Gourgue, who becomes Marie de Jesus with her entry into the
Carmelite Order, belonged to the highest nobility of the robe.[92] Her mother
was *dame* Marie de Séguier. Her uncle was thus Pierre Séguier, the *président*
of the *Parlement de Paris*. The next clause of her will, which clarifies the
social milieu to which she belongs, is addressed to him.

First, I give and will to Monsieur Seguier, the president, my uncle, in
recognition of the singular affection he has always shown for me, all the
furniture, items considered to be furniture and belonging to me along
with all acquired property and a third of my property considered my inheritance all of which I received from the estate of my deceased father
the president de Gourgue and generally all that which I may by law give
away from the aforesaid estate in which legacy I intend to include the
sum of one hundred thousand *livres* which it pleased the King to bestow
by letters patent upon my deceased father, the first president, in recognition of his office of first president.[93]

In the next brief clause she leaves all her other "biens paternels" to her
paternal uncle, monsieur de Gourgue *trésorier général de France*, asking that
her other aunts and uncles and their children from this side of her family be
content with but one *escu* each: "wishing that they be content with this."
To receive equal shares as heirs of her maternal property she names monsieur le doyen Séguier, her uncle, and her aunt madame de Ligny.

The second page of the will also bears the sign of the cross at the top of
the page. Here with suitable humility she asks Pierre Séguier to undertake
the responsibilities of executor of her will. There are no pious clauses whatsoever. The three persons present at the signing of this will already occupy
a liminal space. The final lines of the document bring us very close to the
experience of this moment. The testator notes that the document once
signed is to take effect as a last will and testament caused by her death.

Legally this disposition of all personal property upon entering a monastery was termed "a civil death" in the sense of death to this world.[94]

The will is signed: "Marie de Gourgue, presently sister Marie de Jesus, unworthy novice and Carmelite."[95] The document closes with a notarial hand describing what has just transpired between the notaries and Marie de Gourgue, "religieuse novice en la monastere de l'Incarnation de l'ordre des Carmelites": that she has declared this to be her last will and testament written in her own hand and signed "au parloir dudict monastere." The testator signs once more indicating the transitional nature of the moment: "Marie de Gourgue, s[oeur] Marie de Jesus." There follow the notarial signatures of Laurent Haultdesens and Pierre Blosse.[96]

Thoughts on Last Things

This will evokes a pervasive sense of liminality. The juxtaposition of the dual identities of the testator is striking: unworthy ("indigne") yet forced to address for one last time the question of her property and her status in the world. The scene witnessed is itself located on a boundary between the monastery and the world: the *parloir*, parlor, or visitors' room of the monastery. The will that Marie de Gourgue gives to her notaries is signed one generation after the last penitential processions had filled the streets of Paris. These, too, have been described as a liminal experience.[97] Moreover, there is evidence that laywomen dressed as *moniales* (nuns) participated in these processions. An episcopal *mandement* of 1589 expressly forbade these women to engage in these behaviors, which the hierarchy of the Parisian church regarded as a violation of the proper boundaries separating the lay from the clerical estate. The wave of monastic foundations of the early seventeenth century suggests that zealous laymen and laywomen found new ways to negotiate their relationship with the clerical estate. This relationship of laypeople to the clergy is often at the center of tensions within every movement for religious reform. This is inevitable as laywomen and laymen seek a life of apostolic renewal through various forms of renunciation of the world. In a relative sense Marie de Gourgue had apparently great freedom with which to negotiate the proper relationship between the two cities, of this world and the next. For other penitents, this would not always be the case. Gourgue's choice of a monastery for her *imitatio Christi* signaled in surprising ways a decisive break with the older public and processional penitential culture of the League. The nature of this caesura is explored further in the Epilogue to this book.

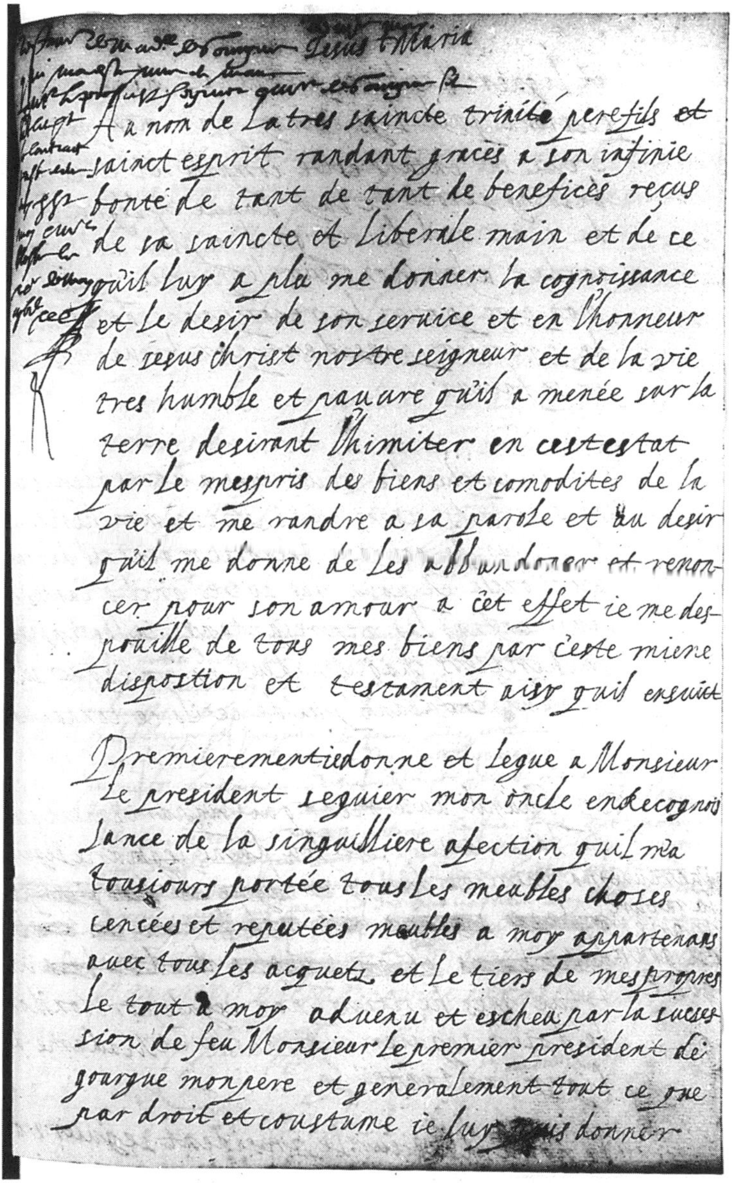
Jesus + Maria

A u nom de La tres saincte trinité pere fils et
sainct esprit randant graces a son infinie
bonté de tant de tant de benefices reçus
de sa saincte et Liberale main et de ce
quil luy a plu me donner la cognoissance
et le desir de son seruice et en lhonneur
de jesus christ nostre seigneur et de la vie
tres humble et pauure quil a menée sur la
terre desirant lhimiter en cest estat
par le mespris des biens et comodites de la
vie et me randre a sa parole et au desir
quil me donne de les abbandoner et renoncer pour son amour a cet effet ie me despouille de tous mes biens par ceste miene
disposition et testament ainsy quil ensuict

Premierement ie donne et legue a Monsieur
Le president seguier mon oncle en recognois
sance de la singulliere afection quil ma
tousiours portée tous les meubles choses
censées et reputées meubles a moy appartenans
auec tous les acquets et le tiers de mes propres
le tout a moy aduenu et escheu par la succes
sion de feu Monsieur le premier president de
gourgue mon pere et generalement tout ce que
par droit et coustume ie luy puis donner

Figure 4. First page of the holograph will of Marie de Gourgue, with the words "Jesus Maria" separated by a small cross at the top of the page. Marginalia in the hand of the notary identifying the document. (Centre historique des Archives nationales. MC/Etude LIV, 515.)

Towards an Aggregate Perspective:
Leaguers and the Nature of Catholic Reform

The reformist traits in the preceding case studies suggest links to a more broadly defined world of testators who are also part of a movement for the renovation of personal piety. In other words, there are many ways to experience and express reformist sentiment. The Decrees issued from session 2 of the Council of Trent, which met after the Feast of the Epiphany on January 7, 1546, set forth with clarity the behaviors expected of all the faithful assembled to define a program of Catholic reform:

> . . . all of the faithful gathered in the city of Trent are to be exhorted . . . to free themselves of the evils and sins which they have hitherto committed and for the future . . . to be urgent in prayer, to confess more often, to receive the sacrament of the eucharist [and] visit churches frequently.[98]

These norms define in the simplest terms the goals of Catholic reform and describe the very behaviors by which zealous Catholics sought to sustain themselves through the hardships of the Siege of 1590. At the heart of these reforms is the call for more sustained sacramental interaction between the laity and clergy. Along with testamentary evidence, these norms also help identify the larger contours of the Catholic reform movement in Paris. While few testators tell us as directly as Pierre Brotin of the solace they received from frequent attendance at the divine service, wills do provide diverse criteria for identifying testators who sought out the reiterative sacraments of confession and communion or had close ties to the clergy in a pastoral context. Table 7.5 identifies a total of thirty-four testators in 1590 who were not previously identified as reformers. Their wills indicate that they have taken the sacraments.

According to the criteria of League affiliation (Table 5.2, "Criteria for League-Identified Testators in 1590"), nine of these thirty-four testators were Leaguers. Tables 7.6 and 7.7 show that these thirty-four individuals belong to a group whose members used League-affiliated notaries and resided in parishes known to be strongly mobilized for the League.

The strong presence of testators from Saint-Gervais parish takes on further significance when it is remembered that its *curé* was Gincestre, a bachelor of arts from the University, who seized control of the curate after the Day of the Barricades in May of 1588. The choice of the notary Monthenault is also particularly significant since this notary was part of a Leaguer network centered around the parish of Saint-Gervais. In addition, the social groups represented by these thirty-four testators fit closely the social profile of the *Seize* as identified by Robert Descimon.

Table 7.5

1590: Comparison of Eight Reformers with Various Groups of Testators

Variables		Reform Testators [8]		Testators Who Took Sacraments [34]		Testators Who Bequested to Confessors [45]		General Testator Population [727] (missing values not included)	
Notary's Part of Town (when known)	*université*	37.5%	[3]	35.3%	[12]	11.1%	[5]	18.6%	[135]
	ville	37.5%	[3]	64.7%	[22]	77.8%	[35]	59.8%	[435]
Testator's Part of Town	*université*	62.5%	[5]	29.4%	[10]	13.3%	[6]	22.0%	[160]
	ville	25%	[2]	67.6%	[23]	82.2%	[37]	63.1%	[459]
League Connection	yes	100%	[8]	25.6%	[9]	11.0%	[5]	13.1%	[95]
	no	0		73.5%	[25]	88.9%	[40]	86.9%	[632]
Sex	male	62.5%	[5]	55.9%	[19]	24.4%	[11]	49.0%	[356]
	female	37.5%	[3]	44.1%	[15]	75.6%	[34]	50.8%	[369]
Occupation	honorables bourgeois	25%	[2]	23.5%	[8]	48.9%	[22]	24.8%	[180]
	gens de loi	0		17.6%	[6]	13.3%	[6]	13.3%	[97]
	all artisans	1		14.7%	[5]	2.2%	[1]	18.6%	[135]
	univ./liberal prof.	25%	[2]	8.8%	[3]	2.2%	[1]	4.3%	[31]
	clergy	12.5%	[1]	5.9%	[2]	0		4.4%	[32]
	noble office/epithet	12.5%	[1]	5.9%	[2]	4.4%	[2]	3.2%	[23]
	servants	0		5.9%	[2]	2.2%	[1]	2.3%	[17]
	laboureurs	0		5.9%	[2]	0		6.9%	[30]
	nobles	12.5%	[1]	2.9%	[1]	6.7%	[3]	5.1%	[37]
	mixed merchants	0		2.9%	[1]	8.9%	[4]	5.8%	[42]
	soldiers	0		2.9%	[1]	0		2.5%	[18]
	other	0		0		11.1%	[5]	6.4%	[39]
	unclassifiable	0		2.9%	[1]	0		2.5%	[18]

Table 7.5, cont'd
1590: Comparison of Eight Reformers with Various Groups of Testators

Variables		Reform Testators [8]		Testators Who Took Sacraments [34]		Testators Who Bequested to Confessors [45]		General Testator Population [727] (missing values not included)	
Health	healthy	62.5%	[5]	11.8%	[4]	11.1%	[5]	12.0%	[87]
	sick	25%	[2]	88.2%	[30]	88.9%	[40]	86.8%	[631]
Signing Information	yes	100%	[8]	50.0%	[17]	57.8%	[26]	55.2%	[401]
	no	0		23.5%	[8]	20.0%	[9]	31.6%	[230]
Number of Bequests	more than 20	50%	[4]	5.9%	[2]	2.2%	[1]	2.1%	[15]
	11–20	0		20.6%	[7]	24.4%	[11]	9.8%	[71]
	5–10	25%	[2]	14.7%	[5]	44.4%	[20]	20.4%	[148]
	1–5	25%	[2]	50.0%	[17]	28.9%	[13]	44.3%	[322]
	no bequests	0		8.8%	[3]	0		23.5%	[171]

Table 7.6
Notaries Used by Testators Who Have Taken the Sacraments

Name of Notary		Number of Testators	Percent
Monthenault	[L]	6	17.6
Chartain	[L]	3	8.8
Bergeon	[L?]	2	5.9
Charles	[L]	2	5.9
Fardeau	[L]	2	5.9
Lybault	[L]	2	5.9
Trouve	[L]	2	5.9
Troyes	[L]	2	5.9
Bernard	[L]	1	2.9
Bontemps, M.	[L]	1	2.9
Chazeretz		1	2.9
Contenot		1	2.9
Ferrant		1	2.9
Lamiral	[L]	1	2.9
Babynet	[L?]	1	2.9
Motelet		1	2.9
Perier		1	2.9
Poche		1	2.9
Rossignol		1	2.9
Saint Vaast	[L]	1	2.9
Thévenin		1	2.9
Total		34	100.0

[L] League affiliated
[L?] Strong presumption of League affiliation

In examining Tables 7.8 and 7.9, which list the forty-five individuals who made bequests to their confessors, we find that a similar pattern emerges, suggesting the League affiliation of testators with closer and more direct ties to their clergy.

In summary, by comparing the data from the micro-portraits with the data from the larger testator populations who engage in reformist behaviors, we can see how League affiliation was spread to the *ville*, especially to parishes with strong affiliations to the University through their *curés*: for Saint-Gervais, through Gincestre; for Saint-Jean-en-Grève, through Hervy; and for Saint-Nicolas-des-Champs, through Pigenat.[99]

The aggregate evidence on reformers and testators mentioning the sacraments or their confessors raises again the question of how individuals integrated the normative aspirations of the Council of Trent into the fabric

Table 7.7
Parishes of Testators Who Have Taken the Sacraments

Testator's Parish		Number of Testators	Percent
St Gervais	[L]	5	14.7
St Paul		4	11.8
St Jean en Grève	[L]	4	11.8
no location specified		3	8.8
St Benoist	[L]	3	8.8
St Germain l'Auxerrois	[L]	3	8.8
St Séverin	[L]	2	5.9
St Eustache		2	5.9
St Merry		2	5.9
St André des Arts	[L]	1	2.9
St Etienne du Mont		1	2.9
St Nicolas du Chardonnet		1	2.9
St Leu/St Gilles	[L]	1	2.9
St Jacques de la Boucherie	[L]	1	2.9
St Nicolas des Champs	[L]	1	2.9
Total		34	100.0

[L] League affiliated

of their lives. The final chapter explores the changing role of number symbolism in the wills of all three sample periods in order to understand more about the actual unfolding of the religious changes advocated in the Tridentine Decrees.

Table 7.8
Notaries Used by Testators Who Have Made Bequests to Confessors

Name of Notary		Number of Testators	Percent
Parque		5	11.1
Peron	[L?]	5	11.1
Herbin	[L]	4	8.9
Mahieu	[L?]	4	8.9
Bernard	[L]	3	6.7
Bergeon	[L?]	2	4.4
Chazeretz		2	4.4
Cothereau, P.	[L]	2	4.4
Landry	[L]	2	4.4
Lybault	[L]	2	4.4
Charles	[L]	1	2.2
Chartain	[L]	1	2.2
Chefdeville	[L?]	1	2.2
Desquatrevaulx		1	2.2
Doujat	[L?]	1	2.2
Dunesmes	[L?]	1	2.2
Ferrant	[L]	1	2.2
Goguyer		1	2.2
Labarde	[L]	1	2.2
Le Camus		1	2.2
Babynet	[L?]	1	2.2
Lusson	[L?]	1	2.2
Monthenault	[L]	1	2.2
Saint-Fussien		1	2.2
Total		45	100.0

[L] League affiliated
[L?] Strong presumption of League affiliation

Table 7.9
Parishes of Testators Who Have Made Bequests to Confessors

Testator's Parish		Number of Testators	Percent
St Eustache		8	17.8
St Germain l'Auxerrois	[L]	5	11.1
St Gervais	[L]	4	8.9
St Jean en Grève	[L]	4	8.9
St Séverin	[L]	3	6.7
St Lou/St Gilles	[L]	3	6.7
St Jacques de la Boucherie	[L]	3	6.7
St Nicolas des Champs	[L]	3	6.7
St Paul		3	6.7
St Etienne du Mont		2	4.4
St Merry		2	4.4
St Benoist	[L]	1	2.2
St Sauveur		1	2.2
Ss Innocents		1	2.2
St Christophe		1	2.2
Ste Marine		1	2.2
Total		45	100.0

[L] League affiliated

THE BOUNDARIES OF COMMUNITY AND THE BODY OF CHRIST: CULTURAL MEANING IN THE ASCENDENCY OF FIVE OVER THIRTEEN

Symbolic Behaviors Prior to the Council of Trent

Before the Tridentine reforms, testators had at their disposal a vast array of symbols to construct a relationship between themselves and the sacred and to express their understanding of how the believer can be saved. The widespread use of symbolic numbers was one of the most characteristic behaviors of the pre-Tridentine cohort of testators. Of all of the ritual behaviors encountered in testamentary discourse, the use of number symbolism underwent the most radical change. While there has been very little discussion of how to interpret the change, it is clear that censorship of this behavior was an important part of a much wider campaign on the part of the ecclesiastical hierarchy to change fundamentally the way testators thought and behaved in their relations with the sacred. The question of symbolic numbers, as a particular form of performativity, thus deserves a place at the center of historians' debates about the religious culture of late-medieval Catholicism and the nature of Catholic reform. Clerical reformers of the period condemned the practice of asking for a special number of masses or candles. The assumption of reformers seems to have been that such requests necessarily entailed a belief in the greater salvific value of such ritual performances. Such requests were therefore censored as "superstitious" because they suggested an attempt by laypeople magically to influence sacramental efficacy and tamper with the working of grace. The campaign to eliminate the superstitious use of symbolic numbers thus reflected heightened clerical sensibilities about the nature and locus of the sacred in the world and the correctness of lay beliefs and behaviors toward the sacred.

Eamon Duffy has argued, however, that "it is impossible to talk of a single experience of the Mass."[1] So too it should be impossible to speak of a uniform superstition. Rather, an investigation of the multiple meanings of symbolic gestures to laypersons and clerics alike is required. This returns us to one of the questions central to historical understanding of performativity in League religious culture and in religious engagement and change more generally: how can one analyze the forms of agency that individuals possess in a richly symbolic environment?

The Prohibition of Liturgical Number Symbolism at the Council of Trent

The Council of Trent, and subsequent liturgical legislation enjoined by it, set in motion a formal process of censorship of the laity's traditional use of a whole range of performative and immanentist expressions of religious symbolism. Of special importance in the analysis of testamentary discourse is the Tridentine prohibition of symbolic numbers in requests for masses in particular times, places, and quantities, as part of a quest for salvation. Canon One of the reforming decrees of Session 22 declares:

> Finally, to leave no room for superstition, they [bishops] are to ensure by edict with accompanying penalties that priests do not celebrate at other than the proper times, nor use in the celebration of mass rites or ceremonies and prayers other than those approved by the church and traditional from long and praiseworthy usage. They should banish from the church any idea of a particular number of masses and candles which derives more from the cult of superstition than from true religion, and teach the people the nature and source of the very precious and heavenly effect of this most holy sacrifice.[2]

The Council of Trent's pronouncements on the celebration of masses and other paraliturgical details (numbers of candles, for example) challenged directly the use of symbols to enhance the efficacy of the mass. This censorship of certain symbolic modes of thought is a phenomenon of profound cultural significance; yet, there has been little discussion of this problem, apparently even among historians of the liturgy.[3] The issue of the use of symbolic numbers presents a new index to evaluate the religious culture of the League era and its relation to Catholic reform. This analysis also takes us to the heart of the most difficult tasks the church was facing: development of a practical set of teachings concerning the nature of performativity within a newly reformed regime of sacred immanence. At the same time, lay people sought a range of participatory roles in the pursuit of salvation. For some this included an aspiration for greater spiritual perfection by engaging in the *imitatio Christi*. The individual forms and meanings of *imitatio* were undergoing profound changes in the course of the Catholic and Protestant reformations and following the League in particular. Marie de Gourgue, for example, spoke in 1630 of her gratitude for God's gift to her of, not only the desire, but also the "the knowledge of . . . his service." The search for a science of *imitatio* had begun to take on new and specific forms that prioritized understanding and redefined "desire" and aspiration.

The Decline in the Use of Number Symbolism

There is, furthermore, a lingering sense, in looking back on the portions of the wills of Thiersault and Rolland that dealt with the role of competent priests, that the foundations for a didactic regime of lay tutelage were slowly taking shape. Historical analysis of the related issues of agency, understanding, and desire are in this respect central to the broader contextualization of League piety and of Catholic reform that this book has sought to present. A closing look at the specific forms of performativity entailed in number symbolism demonstrates the cultural complexities at the heart of League piety in 1590 and points to the need for the further study of liturgy and the paraliturgical in shaping social and political relations in *ancien régime* society.

Examination of testators' choices for services and masses over the three sample periods reveals that the smallest testator population (1543–44; 159 testators) expressed the greatest diversity of liturgical preferences and used the widest range of verbal expressions in making their requests for services and masses. The other striking feature of the 1543–44 liturgical preferences was the frequency with which particular numbers of masses (low masses or *basses messes*) were requested as an accompaniment to the standard funeral service or *service complet*. The virtual disappearance of particular numbers in liturgical directives of the later sample years suggested it was possible to quantify the extent and nature of compliance with the Tridentine ban on so-called superstitious numbers.

The Tridentine instructions to bishops from Session 22 had, without further definition, stated that bishops should "banish from the church any idea of a particular number of masses and candles which derives more from the cult of superstition than from true religion."[4] This laconic prohibition in the Decrees gave little indication of the range and importance of the issues at stake in definitions of "true religion" and "the cult of superstition."[5] Symbolism offered pre-Tridentine testators a powerful tool of lay agency in the making of meaning and constructing relationships between themselves and the sacred. This chapter quantifies compliance with the Tridentine proscriptions of what had been a vital domain of lay self-expression in order to suggest some of the broader cultural changes associated with the declining use of number symbolism.

Table 8.1 indicates a radical decline in the use of service-related number symbolism. In 1543–44, forty-one percent of all testators making

Table 8.1

Decline in Number of Testators and Bequests That Employ Service-Related[1] Number Symbolism

Year	The Defined Universe	Total Number of Testators in That Universe	Number of Testators Who Employ Number Symbolism in Requesting Services/Masses	Percentage of Testators Who Employ Number Symbolism	Number of Service-Related Bequests That Employ Number Symbolism	Percentage of Service-Related Bequests That Employ Number Symbolism
1543–1544	General Testator Population	159 testators	55 testators	35% of the GTP	138 bequests	Does not apply.
	Population Making Bequests	133 testators	55 testators	41% of bequesting testators	138 bequests	11% of all bequests
	Population Making Service-Related Bequests	118 testators	55 testators	43% of testators requesting services	138 bequests	24% of service-related bequests
1590	General Testator Population	727 testators	21 testators	3% of the GTP	27 bequests	Does not apply.
	Population Making Bequests	556 testators	21 testators	4% of bequesting testators	27 bequests	0.78% of all bequests
	Population Making Service-Related Bequests	418 testators	21 testators	5% of testators requesting services	27 bequests	2% of service-related bequests.

Table 8.1, cont'd
Decline in Number of Testators and Bequests That Employ Service-Related[1] Number Symbolism

Year	The Defined Universe	Total Number of Testators in That Universe	Number of Testators Who Employ Number Symbolism in Requesting Services/Masses	Percentage of Testators Who Employ Number Symbolism	Number of Service-Related Bequests That Employ Number Symbolism	Percentage of Service-Related Bequests That Employ Number Symbolism
1630	General Testator Population	344 testators	16 testators	5% of the GTP	32 bequests	Does not apply.
	Population Making Bequests	271 testators	16 testators	6% of bequesting testators	32 bequests	1% of all bequests
	Population Making Service-Related Bequests	217 testators	16 testators	7% of testators requesting services	32 bequests	3% of service-related bequests

1. "Service-related" refers to funeral and memorial services and to masses.

bequests employed number symbolism in requesting services or masses. In 1590 this figure plummeted; only four percent (or twenty-one testators out of a population of 727 testators) used number symbolism in requesting services. The synodal legislation for Paris in this period is silent on the issue of number symbolism. The Tridentine prescriptions may well have caused testators to alter their behavior. The channels of transmission are unclear. Therefore the question remains: how did testators come to alter their behavior? By 1630, the figure rebounds somewhat. The increases are due entirely to renewed use of five and its multiples in requesting services. This may well occur because the Christocentric number symbolism of fives (for the five wounds of Christ) was more compatible with the overall Christocentric movement inherent in Tridentine reform.[6]

As we saw in Table 7.4, there is a relationship between the decline in the diversity of verbal expressions and the virtual disappearance of certain key numbers that had been tremendously popular among the testators of 1543–44 when requesting services and masses.[7] This finding is especially important, as it emphasizes one of the avenues through which cultural standardization took place.

Defining Symbolic Numbers and Their Historical Significance

The analysis focused on the changing uses of the numbers 5, 25, 13, 33, and 40, and their multiples when the latter seemed contextually justified. The chief criteria governing the selection of these "symbolic numbers" were: *1.* the widespread popularity of a number in 1543–44; *2.* the radical change in usage of a number over the sample years; and *3.* a testator's explicit indication of a symbolic meaning attached to a given number. Excluded from the analysis are numbers that either had no particular role in relation to requests for services and masses or whose usage remained so pervasive both in ecclesiastical and secular culture that it would be difficult to construe any particular significance in their use.[8] The numbers 5 and 25 fit the three criteria because they were frequently encountered in liturgical directives in 1543–44. As Table 8.2 shows, the use of the numbers 5 and 25 by testators still using service-related number symbolism rose to fifty-nine percent in 1630, although the ten individuals are in a small minority of persons still using liturgical number symbolism. However small, these numbers are one of our best guides to the symbolic worlds the Council of Trent set out to transform. Moreover, explanatory wording explicitly associates 5 and its multiples with explanatory phrases such as "en l'honneur des cinq plaies," referring to the five wounds of Christ, a very popular late-medieval devotion.

Table 8.2
The Most Popular Service-Related Number Symbolism over Three Sample Periods
Symbolic Numbers: 5 & 25, 13 & Its Multiples, 33, and 40

Symbolic Numbers Employed:

Year	Total Number of Testators Using Service-Related Numeric symbolism	5 & 25		13 & multiples		33		40	
		Total Number of Testators	Percentage of Testators	Total Number of Testators	Percentage of Testators	Total Number of Testators	Percentage of Testators	Total Number of Testators	Percentage of Testators
1540	55 testators	12	22%	43	78%	9	16%	2	4%
1590	21 testators	5	27%	12	57%	2	9.5%	2	9.5%
1630	17 testators	10	59%	3	18%	3	18%	1	6%

Symbolic Numbers Employed:

Year	Total Number of Testators Making Service-Related Bequests	5 & 25		13 & multiples		33		40	
		Total Number of Testators	Percentage of Testators	Total Number of Testators	Percentage of Testators	Total Number of Testators	Percentage of Testators	Total Number of Testators	Percentage of Testators
1540	118 of a GTP[1] of 159	12	10%	43	36%	9	8%	2	2%
1590	418 of a GTP of 727	5	1%	12	3%	2	0.5%	2	0.5%
1630	217 of a GTP of 344	10	5%	3	1%	3	1%	1	0.4%

1. GTP = General Testator Population.

The Cultural Significance of the Number Thirteen

Particularly intriguing was the use of the number 13, the most popular symbolic number in 1543–44, which underwent a precipitous decline in liturgical use and was, moreover, associated with only one very unexpected instance of explanatory wording found in the will of Michel Vincent. In May of 1543 *noble homme* Michel Vincent, *chauffecire de la chancellerie de France*, dictated his will from his sickbed to the notary René Contesse. He made the most extraordinary uses of the number 13, requesting for his cortege thirteen priests of his parish of Saint-Germain-l'Auxerrois, thirteen choir priests, and thirteen priests and thirteen novices from each mendicant order. He also requested complete services with thirteen *basses messes* in his parish and at Saints-Innocents. In one directive for the four mendicant orders he asked for "a complete service with thirteen low masses, vigils, lauds and the recommendation [of his soul to God] in the name of the thirteen apostles."[9] Nothing in the testamentary evidence from any other will explicitly conveyed the meaning that 13 held for the other testators from all sample years who used the number 13 in requesting services.[10]

The occurrence of other symbolic numbers such as 33 and 40 was extremely rare. Thirty-three represents the number of years Christ is believed to have lived on earth, and interestingly, was requested by Marguerite Dugué, a Lybault testator, as part of her extraordinary devotion to the body of Christ.[11] Forty was included because of its biblical associations. Aside from its connection to the resurrected Christ, 40 is associated with ascetic experience (wandering in the desert) and with trials, such as the flood of forty days. The Forty Hours eucharist devotion was introduced into Paris by Bellintani da Salò, the Capuchin general, and was extremely important as a source of moral encouragement during the League.

The Persistence of Number Symbolism among Leaguers

The use of symbolic numbers in requesting masses persisted among two small but strategic populations of testators who are some of the most important League-identified testators of 1590. First, a group of twenty-one testators (see Appendix I) continues to use service-related number symbolism in 1590. Secondly, fourteen League-related testators use number symbolism in bequests to the poor. In the first group, for example, we find Genevieve Rolland, one of the key reformers with ties both to the clerical milieu of the University and to the new order of the Feuillants;[12] Claude Blosseau, a soldier for the Holy Union who was wounded in Henry IV's failed assault on the capital on May 12; and Marguerite Dugué, a *bourgeoise de Paris* whose heart was to be buried near the Holy Sacrament.[13]

Genevieve Rolland asked for two complete services, each including thirteen *basses messes*.[14] This use of number symbolism represents one of Rolland's most important liturgical requests, since each of the complete services was to be said on the day of her death or the day after, one in the church where she is buried and the other at the Church of Saints-Innocents, directly adjoining the Cemetery of Saints-Innocents. She asks the *curé* of Saints-Innocents and "all the priests of Saints-Innocents" to attend this second service. In selecting the Church of Saints-Innocents, Rolland associates herself with one of the most powerful immanentist sacred sites of Paris, the equivalent of a communal graveyard, located in the heart of the *Ville*. Thus, her request for thirteen *basses messes* as a part of her complete service joins her symbolically with the community of the dead of all Paris.[15] Her fellow Leaguer, Blosseau, requested a complete service consisting of one high mass and thirteen low masses, to be said the day of his death or the day after, just as Rolland did. Also among the testators requesting thirteen masses was Genevieve Francisque, who asked one hundred poor persons to attend the offertory procession, and who was identified as a Leaguer based on the evidence she gives for drawing up the will.[16]

From Penitence to Charity: The Roots of Cultural Standardization

There are some distinct social and cultural differences between the two groups of testators using number symbolism in 1590. The first group of twenty-one testators (see Appendix I) have strong League affiliations but lower rates of signing signatures than the second group of fourteen testators who limit their use of number symbolism to the realm of charity (Appendix J). There are only two overlaps between these two populations: Genevieve Rolland and the famous Leaguer Tassine de Compans.[17]

An examination of the 1590's testators who confine their use of traditional number symbolism to the domain of charity and bequests to the poor thus shows another face of the League: René de Mombron, the young noble attending the college of Lisieux who was one of the 1590's reformers, leaves ten poor persons a total of five hundred *écus*. Further, two Jesuit testators of the League-affiliated notary Raoul Bontemps both use the symbolic number 10. The first is *maistre* François Auzanet, a student in the Jesuit college of Clermont in Paris, who makes bequests to dower ten poor girls and ten boy orphans. *Maistre* Baltasar Chavasse, a regent of the University living in the Jesuit college of Clermont, dowers ten poor girls. These bequests involving multiples of 10 all come from the University milieu and especially the Jesuit college where one would expect close familiarity with the Tridentine decrees that discouraged the use of number symbolism.

The Tridentine Decrees did not take a position concerning the use of number symbolism in bequests to the poor. The population of fourteen testators (Appendix J) using number symbolism in bequests to the poor consists of three distinct groups. A group of six testators uses strictly multiples of 5 (five use the number 10, and one uses the number 20). Who can tell us what this group of six testators intended with these numbers? Do their bequests still resonate with the memory of the wounds of the body of Christ? Have they forsaken the explicit reference to the body of Christ, which would require the use of the number 5, in order to accommodate the new Tridentine norms of "true religion"?

There is a second group of seven testators among the fourteen users of number symbolism in bequests to the poor who exclusively employ the number 13 in such requests. It is possible to suggest that there was a strong penitential association with the number 13. In the entire corpus of wills the only explanatory wording that ever accompanies the use of the number 13 occurs in the 1540s when a testator requests thirteen masses in honor of the thirteen apostles. In this case, the association is probably with Judas Iscariot, sinner among a world of sinners. By 1590, Marye Thiersault, one of our most elite Leaguers and a reformer, has renounced the proscribed liturgical symbolism. In place of a request for thirteen masses she makes a bequest to thirteen poor persons. She understands her community with the poor through the traditional number of 13 rather than with the Jesuit-influenced group of Bontemps testators who understand the bonds of community with the poor through even, and what might be characterized as more rational, numbers, such as 10 and 20. Finally, in the group of fourteen users of symbolic numbers in bequests to the poor is Tassine de Compans. She, like Genevieve Rolland, engages in the forbidden practice of service-related number symbolism but also uses a unique expression for the five wounds of Christ by bequesting to five hundred poor persons.

Baroque Flamboyance and Deocentric Standardization

As Tables 8.3 and 8.4 show, testators in 1590 and 1630 who specify numbers of recipients in making bequests choose larger and more even numbers of persons in their wills.[18] Even more interesting however is the evolution of testators' liturgical preferences and their uses of number symbolism in suggesting the modern character of the baroque. A comparison of the changing liturgical fate of the numbers 13 and 5 reveals the negotiated and interactive dynamic of religious reform at work. The origins of the popularity of these

Table 8.3
Most Frequently Used Numbers
for All Recipients of Pious Bequests[1]

Number of Recipients	1543–44	1590	1630
1	190	349	340
2	35	27	9
3	1	3	
4	8	22	14
5	4		**4**
6	14	13	5
7	1		1
8	1	3	1
9	1		
10	3	12	2
12	26	41	21
13	7	12	4
14		1	
15	1	1	1
16	1	1	3
18	5	1	2
19	1		
20	8	8	7
21	2		
24	4	6	1
25	2	2	1
30	3	2	3
36	1	2	
40	3	2	5
50	1	4	2
52		2	
60	2	5	4
63			1
75		1	
100	3	23	12
104	1		
120	2	4	2
160	1		
180		2	
200	1	3	2
240		1	2
300		1	2
360		1	1
500		1	
600		1	
900			1
Total of bequests with specified # of recipients	333	561	459

1. Note, by 1630, testators' choice of even, more uniform numbers, which are also multiples of 5.
2. The numbers bolded in the first column have been defined as symbolic numbers in this chapter or explicitly so by testator language.

Table 8.4
Most Frequently Used Numbers
of Persons in Bequests to the Poor[1]

Number of Poor Recipients	1543–44	1590	1630
1	17	27	20
2		4	2
3		3	2
4		1	2
5	3		3
6		1	3
7		1	
8		1	
9	1		
10		6	1
11		1	
12	3	5	14
13	1	9	2
14		1	
18	2		
20		1	3
21	1		
24		2	
25	1		
30		1	2
36	1		
40	1		3
50		4	1
60	2	5	2
63			1
75		1	
100	3	23	11
120	1	4	2
180		2	
200	1	3	2
240		1	2
300		1	2
360		1	1
500		1	
900			1
Total of bequests with specified # of poor recipients	40	111	79

1. Note, by 1630, testators' choice of even, more uniform numbers, which are also multiples of 5.
2. The numbers bolded in the first column have been defined as symbolic numbers in this chapter or explicitly so by testator language. The numbers 10 and 20 are bolded because they are multiples of 5 and are used by likely League-related testators.

two numbers seem to lie in two vastly different cultural domains. Both numbers have clear reference points in salvation history. Thirteen may be thought of as symbolizing the number of persons who sat down to the Last Supper. One might conclude that 13 was therefore a rich eucharistic symbol, full ultimately with hope and thus a powerful way of connecting one's own death with the paschal drama and the promise of salvation. There is, however, a major problem with this interpretation: no sources consulted present such a Last Supper correlation. Instead commentators always make the point that the sources for the meaning of this number are unclear or obscure, virtual code words for "forever lost in the mists of popular, oral culture."[19] Even if one accepts a direct reference to the Last Supper, the symbol is clearly polyvalent because of its strong association with misfortune and betrayal. This is very much in tension with a hopeful eucharistic message.[20] One can almost capture the essence of the transition from late-medieval to early-modern religious culture through the exploration of these two numbers.

The experiential trajectories of League piety are far more diverse than historians have been able to demonstrate to date. Some individuals look back to the ancient communal roots of liturgical tradition in their use of the symbolism of 13.[21] Others, however, clearly of a younger generation, envision a more hierarchically and uniformly ordered world, still deeply moved by the Passion but now more focused upon its sacramental manifestations (the eucharist) and more channeled into new religious institutions, such as the Jesuits, whose pedagogy, at least publicly, carefully circumscribed the body of Christ into sacramental settings.[22] By 1630 the *imitatio Christi* is especially found in monastic professions such as that of Mademoiselle Gourgue (analyzed in Chapter 7 as a paradigm for monastic profession as a mechanism for the condensation of sacred immanence)[23] or in charity to the poor. In the case of Marguerite Dugué, who requested three high masses and thirty low masses (3+30=33), her Christocentrism is itself polyvalent: her body was to be buried beside the crucifix and her heart beside the Holy Sacrament.

Thus in 1590 *imitatio* was found in a different range of penitential behaviors that not only filled the streets of Paris but also shaped new boundaries of community through palpable appropriations of the body of Christ in which the social and the political self were reflected. Dugué, Rolland, Compans, Thiersault, Mombron, the Jesuits, and the soldier Blosseau each offer another facet of League piety. Their divergent, yet allied, gestures reproduce—both at the level of the single individual and at the level of social structures—the tensions within the League itself that find some measure of resolution in an emerging, new *ancien régime*.

We now can see how the change in symbolic systems can facilitate powerful cultural changes and express very real exchanges of power as well.

Out of the deocentric impulse, paradoxically, is born both the trend toward standardization and the phenomenon of baroque flamboyance that is distinct from the phenomenon of late-medieval (ideocentric, local, personal, communal) flamboyance. The changing uses of number symbolism reveal one form of change in symbolic behaviors that leads to the "rationality" of uniformity and standardization. By 1590, virtually all of the testator population had accommodated the Tridentine proscriptions against the liturgical uses of number symbolism. In fact the most sweeping and dramatic change taking place between the era of the pre-Tridentine testators and that of the Leaguers is the dramatic decline in testators' use of number symbolism. This close correlation between the declining use of number symbolism and the onset of standardization is one demonstration of a much broader cultural phenomenon. The prohibition of a whole range of performative and symbolic behaviors was one of the most important forces reshaping the early-modern world and the forms of community that Leaguers had tried, often in unique ways, to preserve. The radical decline in the liturgical use of the number 13 and the relative increase in the use of 5 (and especially its even multiples) is another manifestation of the condensation of sacred immanence with its stricter hierarchies of *latria* (adoration of Christ) and regal veneration of Mary (*hyperdulia*). Five and its multiples can be understood as the triumph of a powerful deocentrism over the penitential sense of community represented by the local, traditional use of the number 13.[24]

Liturgical Use of the Number 13 in 1630

A comparison of the two wills in 1630 where we find the liturgical use of the number 13 is instructive for what it reveals about the circumstances in which the traditional liturgical symbolism critiqued at Trent continued to be used. Admittedly by 1630 we are dealing with a very marginal phenomenon. But this is precisely why it is interesting, because it sheds light on the social and individual circumstances that placed certain aspects of personal piety beyond the reaches of ecclesiastical reform.

Both of these 1630 testators are widows and both request 13 *basses messes* to be said in the church where they request burial on the day of their death or as soon after death as possible. The first of these testators is Dame Marguerite Chippard, the widow of an *avocat* in the Parlement of Paris, who is a non-signer because of blindness, which certainly suggests old age is a factor in her traditionalism. What is interesting in her case, however, is a very substantial gift of thirty *livres* to her confessor whom she names. This confessor at least cannot be seen as a successful enforcer of liturgical reforms since he fails to eradicate Chippard's typically pre-Tridentine and sanctioned liturgical gesture. This should caution us against assuming that a strengthened and regularized penitential system always functioned in a monolithic way to enforce new liturgical norms.

Our second 1630 testator to request thirteen *basses messes* takes us to a very different social milieu. Anne Baslé, the widow of a tailor, is one of the ninety-six testators in 1630 who were non-signers. Like the widow Chippard, Anne Baslé requests thirteen *basses messes* to be said in the church where she requests burial (her parish, Saint-Méderic) "as soon as possible after her death." The totality of the religious and secular clauses in this will underscore Baslé's very modest social status and her significant pious commitments.[25]

Baslé's civil bequests are all within the popular milieu: for prayers and for care during her illness Baslé gives the contents of two coffers to Anne Noirelair, "her neighbor." She is owed ten *livres par promesse* by Roch Tranier, a *gagne denier à Paris*. Her only other detailed pious bequest is to the Augustins—four *livres*, ten *solz*, for one complete service. Finally, Baslé leaves the surplus of her property to the *maistre cordonnier* Jacques Tutin, whom she names as executor "a la charge de faire prier dieu pour elle." Baslé is thus an interesting example of a non-signing woman from the popular milieu who makes a small number of pious bequests and gives every indication of a very sincere pious engagement. In the aggregate, however, in 1630, there is weak correlation between illiteracy, low social status, and liturgical gestures that have been critiqued by ecclesiastical reformers as "superstitious."

With the two exceptions of Baslé and Chippard, which in a sense prove the rule, we can conclude that, overall, traditional number symbolism in a strictly liturgical setting (relating to numbers of masses or candles) was no longer seen as a desirable practice by the vast majority of testators.

Symbolism and the Sacrament of Communion in 1630

Finally, it is necessary to recall the extraordinary will of Jehanne Marchant, which suggests an essential aspect of the overall nature of the transformation of symbolic behaviors between the sixteenth and seventeenth centuries. Her notary was Jean Fontaine, who served as notary for the convent Notre-Dame-de-la-Charité, the Feuillentines, or female branch of the most austere Cistercian reformed order. As was seen this testator made important bequests to the Feuillants, *faubourg* Saint-Honoré, and to the "filles de la Passion," as the newly founded order of the Capucines was popularly known.

Her request for a memorial communion in her memory might be thought of as encapsulating the transformation of the religious culture that we have been witnessing in the analysis of number symbolism. In this pious directive the testator moves from strictly liturgical commemoration to communion itself, both the most symbolic and most participatory of all religious rituals from the perspective of the laity in this phase of the Catholic reformation. The structures of community that sustained the penitential piety of the League era has undergone complex changes.

In the context of the present work it has only been possible to begin to suggest the richness of the material and its analytic challenges and rewards. Further work in the notarial archives that focuses on the quantitative analysis of performativity should look to the use of research teams, an approach at the heart of much of the quantitative work in the 1970s. Statistical methodologies such as those used by Philip Hoffman become appropriate usually when the sample sizes of the subpopulations increase.[26] This present study will have fulfilled its purpose if it stimulates such further research. Only the further refinement and the application of the quantitative techniques used in this study to larger testator populations will produce subpopulations large enough to make more sophisticated statistical techniques meaningful. Some readers may argue that much of the evidence about the League population remains in the Appendixes of this present work. It needs to be remembered that in analyzing and contextualizing the Catholic League, this work has sought to focus on long-term cultural change. The material of the Appendixes and of the notarial section of the bibliography is intended to ease the way of future researchers as they embark, collectively or individually, on these new adventures.

In conclusion, however, the complex strands of the argument of this book need to be summarized with regard to the analysis of Leaguer piety and the problem of Catholic reform. This book has presented two broad perspectives on League piety and Catholic reform using the analysis of performativity. The first perspective from which League piety and Catholic reform have been viewed rests on an interpretation of the significant role of notaries as important members of the gens de loi. Although further statistical correlations should be sought, it is possible to suggest that the political conjuncture of the League made key notaries particularly apt cultural intermediaries. One thinks of the practices of Raoul and Mathieu Bontemps, Hilaire Lybault, Philippe Cothereau, Lamiral, Monthenault, and de Bruyère in particular as the starting point for a network analysis. The findings of this work on rates and types of performativity and reformist behaviors have laid a foundation upon which to explore the actual social distribution of the various types of performativity over time. From this analysis one may then ask what precise combinations of social, political, and cultural or ideological interests propel change in a religious culture and in dominant epistemologies more generally.

The second perspective may be thought of as the larger cultural perspective for the contextualization of League piety. Here the performativity associated with groups known for League affiliation provides a new tool for understanding the culture Leaguers sought to defend. This analysis established the broad parameters for a more detailed study of the precise range and variety of performative behaviors associated with specific social groups. Performativity may also ultimately be correlated statistically not only with social identity but also with parish affiliation. This chapter has also suggested that generational differences account for the results obtained about Leaguer performativity. Wills, however, do not provide more than the most occasional and approximate sense of the age of testators. This is yet another reason for larger-scale research into the evolution of specific notarial practices.

Conclusion

ECONOMIES OF SALVATION
CA.1540–CA.1630:
THE NATURE OF THE SACRED
AND THE POWER TO MAKE MEANING

Throughout Reformation Europe, wherever religious change was contemplated, the arrangements of political power and social order implicitly came under scrutiny as well. The present history of the Catholic League and the complexities inherent in Catholic reform has deliberately focused on the problem of religious change during a time of acute social and political conflict. The royal succession crisis in the 1580s and 1590s threatened to bring a Protestant to the throne of France precisely at a time when the monarch's failure to eradicate heresy had already compromised the institution of the monarchy itself. Under these circumstances, the earliest historians of the League emphasized the purely political nature of the conflict between the Catholic League and the *Politiques*, or royalists.

This book, however, has been primarily concerned with exploring the ways in which the experience of the liturgy gave birth to the Catholic League. This change of focus has made it possible to expose the larger cultural stakes inherent in the partisan politics of the League era. The most important new finding of this work is that affective investment in liturgical ritual can, under specific historical conditions, generate the most fundamental bonds of community and galvanize individuals to political action.

To summarize this finding for Paris in the period from ca.1540 to ca.1630, it is useful to think in terms of competing economies of salvation, which structured late-medieval and early modern Parisian society, culture, and politics. The term "economies of salvation" emphasizes that in the sixteenth and seventeenth centuries, the liturgy was an essential site for the production of meaning, social order, and authority relations. Part of the creative capacity of liturgy, often overlooked by historians, is that it can, in times of crisis such as the Wars of Religion, express people's most fundamental notions of right order in the world. Further, the notion of economies of salvation underscores that historical contests are fought over control of and access to the production of meaning.

In thinking about the competing economies of salvation embraced by Calvinists, moderate Catholics (*Politiques*), and militant Catholics in Paris, this book has also emphasized that religious doctrines entail gestural cultures. This approach ultimately exposes the link between gestural culture, politics, and the sacred. Doctrines elicit, proscribe, and prescribe, more or less strictly, habits of worship. Habits of worship are actions in the world, and as such, they necessarily enjoin cognitive, corporal, and emotional stances toward the sacred. The preceding analysis of the ways liturgical preferences in Parisian wills were associated with political party and social identity must not be divorced from these cultural attributes of ritual practice.

Accordingly, throughout this book three central concepts—transcendence, immanence, and performativity—have informed the discussion of competing attitudes toward religious rituals. These three concepts not only describe attributes of the sacred, they also help explain how bodies engage in social, political, and religious action. The book has thus both clarified Calvinism's challenge to traditional Roman Catholic practice and illuminated cultural and political stakes in intra-Catholic rivalries.

Calvin's doctrinal position of separating things sacred from things of this world created a religious culture of transcendence. In emphasizing "this worldly asceticism" of Calvinism, Reformation historiography for a long time provided a strangely disembodied analysis of the habits of the believer. This literature focused on how a mental revolution in doctrine (Calvin's soteriology and ecclesiology) reshaped the productive (economic) forces in the world. Max Weber's writing on the Protestant work ethic is the classic statement of this economic interpretation of religious cultures. Instead, Chapter 2 in the present book showed that Calvin's position on the eucharist was inseparable from a new gestural culture of liturgical asceticism, a product of excluding the miraculous from everyday life.

Chapter 3 of this book examined the Decrees of the Council of Trent, whose implementation has long been viewed as a goal of Leaguer politics. Analysis of the language and syntax of the Tridentine decrees disclosed an unexpectedly complex relationship between the immanence and performativity envisioned at Trent and the liturgical experience of Parisians as revealed in their last wills and testaments. By exposing the tensions, both semantic and historic, in the gestural culture promoted by Catholic reform, this book has shown that it is no longer possible to regard the League as the moment when Tridentine reform first took root. The text of the Tridentine decrees presented a historical diversity of belief and behavior as an "unbroken sequence" of doctrine and practice. In focusing on the multiple tensions between the textual representation of tradition in the Decrees and the lived experience of the liturgy exposed in Parisian wills, this book has brought to light important paradoxes inherent within both Catholic reform and Leaguer aspirations for salvation.

The state of the archival evidence to date has made it impossible to identify with certainty an adequate corpus of *politique* wills suitable for quantitative analysis. Thus, to explore these paradoxes, Chapter 4 concentrated on *politique* historians' visceral reaction against the intensely performative religious culture of Leaguers. Like Chapter 3, Chapter 4 thus employed discourse analysis in order to highlight unexplored cultural dimensions of the political and social conflict between royalists (*politiques*) and militant Catholics of the League. Before demonstrating the relationship between testamentary discourse, liturgy, and political engagement, it was first necessary to focus upon the connections between language and gestural culture. Taken together, the chapters in Part Two laid the groundwork for examining the changing content and significance of early modern Parisian Catholicism as a doctrine and practice of immanence and performativity.

At the heart of such an analysis is the question raised so powerfully in the work of Denis Crouzet: How do words become actions? The present book has approached this central problem of historical inquiry by asking how immanentist doctrines became action in the world. Specifically, Part Three presented a quantitative cultural analysis of how doctrine became worship for three cohorts of Parisian testators. The wills studied ranged from 1543–44 to 1630. The analysis, however, centered on the more than seven hundred testators of 1590. These individuals crafted their economies of salvation at the height of the confrontation between Henry IV and the League-controlled capital.

Chapter 5 presented a new model for quantitative cultural analysis in order to describe and interpret the performative characteristics of League piety. These performative characteristics form the core of the difference between religions of immanence and those of transcendence. The creation of a Performativity Index in Chapter 5 provides researchers from a variety of disciplines with a historically grounded technique for quantifying and categorizing symbolic behaviors. Chapters 6, 7, and 8 used both aggregate quantitative analysis and microportraits of notaries and their clients. These chapters documented the particular relationships between notaries, their clients, and the complex and changing expressions of militancy and reform in Parisian society.

The detailed case studies of the wills of ultra-Catholic notaries and their testators in Chapter 6 sought to combine a history of liturgy and of testamentary practice with the findings from recent socio-political analysis of the Catholic League. This chapter offered a new socio-cultural analysis of Leaguer and especially *Seize* militancy. It did so by focusing on the way testators and notaries shared liturgical loyalties and ties to specific religious institutions and especially to religious orders. The analysis throughout this book has been animated by the conceptual force of a question Natalie Davis posed nearly twenty years ago when she asked: "Where is the sacred in the sixteenth-century French city?" This question signaled a conceptual revolution that has brought historians to the point of a new and sympathetic understanding of the distinctions between religions of immanence and religions of transcendence. We have not begun to exhaust the potential of this question, which directs the historian to investigate the palpable and bodily locus of the sacred in the world. In this spirit, Chapter 6 showed the relationship between a practical geography of the sacred in Leaguer Paris and manifestations of the sacred in testamentary discourse. This revealed a greater symbolic density in the words and gestures of wills of individuals linked to League political activism. This close analysis of the performative gestures that testators specified for their funerals, memorial masses, and works of charity thus provides a novel demonstration of the ways ritual and liturgy shape human communities. By exploring the manifold connections between League-affiliated groups and individuals and wills rich in symbolic gestures, a previously unknown dynamic shaping League-era social and political conflicts has come to light.

Chapter 7 turned to the broader chronology of the gestural culture of ultra-Catholicism. Although further study is required, the role of the University of Paris appears especially significant among reformist testators of the 1540s and 1590. This discussion of the continuities and discontinuities in the residence patterns, social identity, and symbolic gestures of testators with reformist interests developed new criteria for identifying the lineages and legacies of League piety and its relation to Catholic reform.

Chapter 8 demonstrated the challenge and the potential for further quantitative studies of symbolic behaviors in testamentary evidence. The Decrees of the Council of Trent explicitly banned the very widespread late-medieval practice of requesting masses or candles in special symbolic numbers such as five, thirteen, and thirty-three. Parisian wills show that this practice, so popular among the testators of 1543–44, was virtually eliminated by 1590. The study of number symbolism makes possible a particularly targeted investigation of sites of resistance as well as social sites of creative cooperation with Tridentine reforms. There were important surprises in this evidence that suggest some paradoxes at the heart of Catholic reform and Leaguer political activism. The use of number symbolism persisted among

some of the most devoted League militants. Among other probable Leaguers associated with notaries having strong ties to the Jesuits, there appears to be a deliberate rationalization of the use of number symbolism.
These notaries and testators move away from a traditional preference for
the number thirteen and toward multiples of five and larger, even numbers.
The evidence from the micro-portraits thus reveals that the religious culture, particularly of known Leaguers, was not always in harmony with the
Tridentine desire to eliminate lay appropriation of sacred symbols through
the use of symbolically expressive numbers. This raises the most fundamental questions about the transformation of religious cultures and the power
of believers to make meaning in their own way through the appropriation
of liturgical symbolism.

Tridentine reforms may well have fostered a longer-term cultural process of secularization in which standardization of the liturgy diminished the
older creative power of testators to shape very personal and idiosyncratic
relations with the sacred. This conclusion grows out of the analysis of
Tridentine reforms of the mass that was presented in the discourse analysis
of the Decrees of the Council of Trent in Part One of this book. Tridentine
reforms of the mass, discussed in Chapter 3, accompanied limits on a whole
range of other traditional performative behaviors. The range of activities
and world-views embraced banqueting and the virtually kin-like relationship between laity and the Sacred Family with its myriad of saintly intercessors. The concentration of performativity in more strictly sacramental
behaviors represents a condensation of sacred immanence and is a general
characteristic of the aims of Tridentine reform. In this way, Tridentine reforms preserved the immanentist core which lay at the center of sacerdotal
practice and eucharist celebration. It also stripped away practices that suggested the unregulated authority of lay people to make sacred meaning in
extra-sacramental forms. Such a limitation on symbolic behaviors is in direct conflict with traditional modes of performativity. The persistence of
liturgical number symbolism among some League-affiliated testators suggests the need to rethink the analysis of exteriority and interiority in characterizing League piety. Leaguer aspirations for salvation spawned multiple
economies of salvation. It is necessary to conclude that the religious cultures of the League and the ultimate triumph of Tridentine standardization
and didacticism stand in an unexpected historical tension. The older, more
public, affectively charged and varied expressions of League piety were at
odds with the didactic uniformity and sacerdotalism fostered in the logic of
the Tridentine Decrees.

Finally, we see that the competition between the cultural and gestural
systems of Calvinism and of traditional Catholic practices produced its own

impetus for religious and cultural change. There is thus a parallel between the liturgical asceticism of Calvin and the reduction in the liturgical options available to testators adhering to the Tridentine proscription of number symbolism. The creative agency that the laity had possessed within the traditional rituals of "orthopraxis" was diminished with the introduction of Tridentine reforms. Thus, in their attack on "superstition," the Decrees of Trent participated in what has been perceived as Calvin's cultural revolution.

This kind of religious history of the Catholic League had long remained, with a few important exceptions, an unexplored domain. *Politique* historians and their secularist successors in the French Revolution and the Third Republic long determined the dominant historical interpretation of the period. This victors' version of history was profoundly secular, and it oversimplified the multiple transformations of late-medieval religious practices. More specifically, when earlier generations of historians focused on Leaguer obscurantism and the movement's abuse of clerical power, an important history of private devotion and its once public and shared meaning fell from sight. Thus metanarrative and secular imperatives at the heart of modern history marginalized a whole series of topics connected with religions of sacred immanence. This obscured essential complexities in the transitions from late-medieval to early modern forms of religious practice.

By working out the relationship between testamentary discourse, liturgy, and political engagement, this book has sought to bridge these gaps in the historiography of religious change. It has also laid to rest notions about the merely formulaic nature of testamentary discourse. This very misperception is the product of a secularist view of history. Most surprisingly, in searching for the locus and nature of the sacred in the world, this study has heightened awareness of the historicity of reason itself. This history has demonstrated how the culture wars of the sixteenth century, which were fought over the question of performativity, necessarily transformed the possibilities for making meaning in the world. No purely bi-confessional model can convey the complexity of this process in which Leaguers and *Politiques* also played important roles. Multiple battles transformed the always plural relations between meaning and performance. In setting the investigation of Catholic reform and the Catholic League in the broader perspective of a history of performativity, this book has also underscored that the defeat of the League and the triumph of Trent were paradoxically allied. Together, and in unanticipated ways, all these parties created a historic caesura in the power to make meaning in the world.

Epilogue

The Triumph of Transcendence: Science and *Homo Religiosus* on the Eve of the Enlightenment

In order to clarify the long-term cultural changes at work in the rationalization of ritual behaviors, this Epilogue examines a late-seventeenth-century debate over the merits of religious self-flagellation. In this early-Enlightenment contest over permissible forms of religious performativity, we may observe how processional behaviors, which once filled the streets of Paris in the League era, are driven into obscurity. Flagellants and the explicit, sixteenth-century symbolic association of priestly vestments with Christ's flagellation fall from sight in ritual life. Eighteenth-century medical discourse comes to regard both as "alien" and thus as deviant and irrational. Such medicalization of penitential behaviors offers the final key to understanding the lineage of the problem of League piety: the body of Christ and the body of the believer cease to share a symbolic field of public and performative interrelations, except in carefully regulated circumstances. Eudaemonism triumphs over penitential piety just as transcendent rationality displaces sacred immanence to the margins of history. The disappearance of the penitent from public space is recapitulated in the discursive triumph of the pursuit of happiness and its alliance with a nascent psychiatric epistemology of the sacred. With this epistemological shift, the ultimate transfer of League piety beyond the boundaries of national memory is thus foreordained and then consummated in nineteenth-century French republican historiography with its particular canons of narrative truth inherited from *politique* conceptions of social order, *science*, and national identity.

The discourse analysis of Parts One and Two made clear that the history of the League—history as both events per se and as their recounting— was inseparable from a larger debate about permissible forms of public performativity. The epistemological divisions of the late Middle Ages, which came most dramatically to focus on the nature of Christ's presence in the eucharist, only widened and made more grave the localized debates occurring all over Europe about permissible forms of public behaviors. To view these local conflicts as part of a growing campaign to reform popular culture diverts historians' attention to social and political conflict before the full extent of the cultural, religious, and intellectual crisis can be adequately evaluated or their interrelations understood.

The evidence presented in this book shows that until we find more adequate ways of talking about the nature of the transition from the late Middle Ages to the early-modern period, and the role of symbolic systems in that change, we will lack powerful tools for a further understanding of League piety. Opening the field of inquiry and placing at its center the meaning of contests over performativity and their relationship to definitions of rationality (*vraye intelligence* or *science*, as Calvin or L'Estoile would say) is a fundamental step in the study of League piety. The relationship between the League and Catholic reform must be seen as a problem of long-term cultural, social, and political change. For this reason, it is necessary to carry this analysis forward to the eve of the Enlightenment. A brief history of a debate over the legitimacy of religious self-flagellation and the changing attitudes towards penitential behaviors that led up to this controversy will reveal the importance of this broad framework in comprehending the lineages and the legacies of League piety.

A learned dispute carried on by two seventeenth-century French clerics, Jean-Baptiste Thiers and the Abbé Boileau, makes clear just how much is at stake in divergent readings of symbolic behaviors and processional moments. In 1701 Abbé Boileau published his treatise *Histoire des flagellans ou l'on fait voir le bon et le mauvais usage des flagellations parmi les Chrétiens*.[1] Two years later, Abbé Jean-Baptiste Thiers responded to Boileau's attack on the merits of voluntary flagellation in his own work on this subject.[2] Their debate clarifies the changing attitudes to flagellation across the seventeenth century and, when properly contextualized, brings additional clarity to the "problem within a problem" in studying League piety. Boileau's condemnation of religious self-flagellation signals a radical epistemological rupture and discloses the meaning of the triumph of transcendence for the telling of the history of the League. His critique of voluntary flagellation as pathological sexual arousal transfers one of the most powerful performative and symbolic forms of *imitatio Christi* from the domain of soteriology to that of pathology and deviant psychology. This medicalization of what was formerly a religious discourse about the uses of the body and religious symbols discloses the failure of a system of critical thought to interpret the symbolic systems of the past. Herein lies the "problem within a problem" in writing the history of League piety.

Much can be learned by listening to Boileau and the counter-arguments of Thiers. Boileau was both a cleric and doctor at the Sorbonne as well as a medical doctor. Of the two authors, Abbé Thiers is the better known to historians now because he was "rediscovered" in the late 1960s and in the 1970s as an ardent proponent of the reform of popular culture and religion. In works like his *Traité des jeux . . .* (Paris, 1686) and *Traité des superstitions qui regardent les sacramens* (Paris, 1679), he gave detailed accounts of the popular practices he sought to reform, thus providing crucial ethnographic data for historians of popular culture.[3] His treatise defending voluntary flagellation, however, has been completely neglected in the modern literature.[4] For our purposes, this oversight simply underscores the modernist bias in writing about the reform of popular culture. It further reveals the extent to which lack of a broad cultural, intellectual, and religious framework for understanding performative behaviors, especially the liturgically performative, has deprived historians of the tools needed to understand the high stakes involved in reading symbolic moments. Much less is presently known about our innovator Abbé Boileau. At the outset of his work, Boileau signals that he is writing from the perspective of a new genre that he calls simply "la Critique," noting that this is more suitable to the subject matter than "la science sublime de la Théologie." *Critique* is, of course, at the heart of coming Enlightenment ideas of reason and rationality, and thus Boileau begins on a note of radical epistemological reorientation. The birth of this new and medicalized discourse on what had been understood as meritorious ascetic behaviors in imitation of Christ reorders the boundaries of the sacred and the profane and transforms the religious understanding of the body.[5]

Boileau argues for a new ethic on the religious uses of the body based on the key concepts of "pudeur," "bienséance," and "superstition." The superstition condemned by Thiers was that found in folkloric rural Christianity. Boileau instead redefines the concept of superstition and applies it this time to learned Christianity itself, whenever it has praised the flamboyant and highly exteriorized practice of flagellation. Boileau's model is based on the need for "la componction interieur" where behavior is guided by the norms of "pudeur" (sexual modesty) and "bienséance" (propriety). Although Boileau does not mention the word "civilité," his terms "pudeur" and "bienséance" are drawn from an essentially secular discourse on "civilité" that since the Renaissance had been profoundly reshaping norms of behavior.[6] This discourse on civility, whose norms are so much more familiar and "reasonable" to us, has helped obscure the ongoing importance of penitential piety as a source of social discipline, especially in the seventeenth century. The great virtue of the Boileau-Thiers debate is to throw into relief the coexistence of two radically different sources of social discipline in the seventeenth century, "civility" and "penitential piety." Only in the eighteenth century did the new medical discourse of speculative and empirical anatomy and then psychiatry challenge the pious understanding of flagellation and begin to assert its theoretical hegemony over the body of the believer.

Each author offers his own history of the uses of voluntary self-flagellation. As a critic, Boileau seeks to demonstrate what limited use and approval self-flagellation has had in the Christian tradition. He refutes the arguments that self-flagellation was practiced among the early Christians or advocated in early monastic rules. He ascribes the introduction of self-flagellation to Peter Damien in the mid-eleventh century. The great penitential wave of 1260 is described as a dangerous "superstition" practiced by a "sect" that clearly ran the risk of heresy by arguing that flagellation was as cleansing an experience as auricular confession.[7] Boileau takes the side of Gerson, whose fifteenth-century treatise *Against the Flagellants* condemned the revival of flagellant practices by Vincent Ferrare. Boileau claims that Gerson approved of flagellation under only the most limited of circumstances: that it be administered on the order of a superior, and that it be moderate, without scandal and ostentation and the shedding of blood.[8] Boileau then discusses the revival of the sect at the end of the sixteenth and beginning of the seventeenth century.[9] Boileau's account begins to shed light on the transition from the highly exteriorized piety of the League period to the more interiorized piety of the seventeenth century. Boileau actually turns to historians of the League, agreeing with their denunciations of flagellation as a violation of the proper interiorization of piety.[10] Boileau approvingly describes the 1601 ruling by *Parlement* that prohibited assemblies of the Blue Penitents in Bourges and signaled the legal abolition of the penitents in the north of France.

The arguments in favor of voluntary flagellation were presented by the Abbé Jean-Baptiste Thiers, whose very name evokes strong penitential associations. At first Thiers' stance seems at odds with what we might expect from an advocate of discipline and order and an avowed opponent of superstition in any form. His position forces us to rethink the psychological roots of critiques of popular performative behaviors. In reading his defense of voluntary flagellation it becomes clear that self-flagellation has been practiced and advocated particularly by individuals and religious orders that have been especially associated with the reform of popular culture, such as Cardinal Borromeo of Milan or the Capuchins, whose seventeenth-century missions into the countryside are well known.[11]

This suggests that from the beginning the ascetic impulses of the elite penitents of Paris were hostile to the irreverent practices of popular culture—for example, the abuses of Carnival and the failure to adhere to Lenten strictures. In mobilizing popular religious fervor, there was an entire medieval ascetic tradition of penitential piety upon which the penitents of the League could and did draw. We now need to develop even closer and more finely nuanced readings of penitential behaviors that can tell us more about the performative traditions that these behaviors drew upon. The dance of penitence of which Emond Auger spoke follows an even more complex cadence than we may have realized.

Until now it had always been confusing to argue that the League looked back to medieval traditions of popular piety because, since the advent of the literature on the reform of popular culture, we have become accustomed to associate the popular traditions of medieval piety with rowdy mixtures of the sacred and the profane and a host of popular superstitions. What now becomes clear is that the League was heir to popular traditions of medieval asceticism, not simply to popular trends of medieval piety. But the ascetic tradition bears within itself, through its own performative body, a conflicted inheritance, which requires much more study from the perspective of a history of the body and of performativity and symbolic behaviors.

The results of the analysis of number symbolism in Chapter 8 thus provide some additional information for this history of attitudes toward performa- tivity and the conflicted inheritance of League piety itself. The testators who continued to use the prohibited number symbolism of 13 for their service requests in 1590 are not drawn from the reforming elite, but they are nonetheless, as a group, strongly associated with League radicalism (Claude Blosseau; Margueritte Dugué, a member of a Holy Sacrament Confraternity; Genevieve Francisque, the wife of a League soldier). This suggests a cultural and social division within the League itself in relation to the question of symbolic and performative behaviors. Even more interestingly for what it says of attitudes about performativity, the numbers used by testators of 1630 to designate the numbers of recipients of bequests are overwhelmingly even numbers and the symbolic multiples of 5. In this sense we may say that in Paris the Catholic Reformation represented the triumph of five-ness over thirteen-ness with all of its full symbolic implications of the orderly triumph of deocentrism over the multiple realities of communal and individual economies of salvation. Implicit in this victory is a Passion-become-sacramental-sacrifice in which the majority of believers, those not engaged in ascetic practices, receive Christ's body as the sacrament of the altar but no longer reenact for themselves his suffering on the cross.[12] In turning to the domain of charity in the seventeenth century, the *dévots* thus transform the penitential inheritance of the League and its forms of performativity.

There is a strong parallel among the trajectories of the various performative behaviors, attitudes to self-flagellation, and uses of number symbolism. The appearance of this parallel suggests the emergence of a powerful normative drive that finds its most striking expression in Boileau's condemnation of voluntary self-flagellation. Penitential behaviors, including flagellation, had been a powerful form of sacred performance.[13]

In the late sixteenth century, one of the most important advocates of self-flagellation within a tradition of penitential piety was Cardinal Borromeo of Milan, who founded a penitent confraternity whose statutes were included as part of the Second Provincial Council of Milan in 1569 and approved by Pope Gregory XIII.[14] Cardinal Borromeo is known to have himself practiced flagellation and to have approved of the confraternity of "disciplinés/disciplinati" as the most pious in his diocese.[15] The confraternity is known to have emphasized charity as the expression of divine love. Flagellation was undertaken "in imitation of the life of Christ." The characteristics of this confraternity suggest some of the emphases that may have been particularly important in the sixteenth century. Flagellation occurred on all the Sundays of Advent, during the weeks leading up to Easter, and on carnival days when, as Borromeo's regulations stated, "God was more specially offended."[16]

Borromeo's statutes praised the same sort of discipline and modesty in processional behavior that L'Estoile had come to appreciate in the penitential processions of Paris.[17]

[Borromeo] enjoined [the members of these confraternities] to see that all the members participated in the procesions with modest and orderly comportment, and that out of devotion they disciplined themselves with lashes rather than substituting another person to do this for them.[18]

The changes in penitential behavior and especially in flagellation in the course of the seventeenth century also raise interesting questions about the inter-relation of Protestant and Catholic reforms. Although Borromeo had recommended the use of flagellation on carnival days precisely to counter popular excesses, there is some suggestion that flagellation itself became disdained as dangerous and excessive for laypeople. It is known that the "disciplinati" had influenced religious theater, especially enactments of the passion in street processions. Some of these same processions were condemned both by Protestants and by Catholics, like L'Estoile, as excessive and undisciplined displays. Properly reformed versions of these passion plays were used by the Capuchins in their missions of the seventeenth century to reconvert Protestant strongholds.

There remained, however, many contexts in which flagellation was praised and continued to be practiced in the seventeenth century. Discipline in moderation, especially on Fridays in memory of Christ's passion, remained widely recommended in the constitutions of monastic institutions for both men and women.[19] Flagellation also remained a practice associated with the intensification and perfection of one's spirituality, but increasingly the practice was to be limited to tightly controlled situations in which the necessary distinctions between sacred and profane were maintained. In his *Spiritual Exercises*, Loyola counseled its use by those on spiritual retreat. François de Sales also recommended its moderate use to stimulate the appetite for devotion, but this was in the context of his work that addressed the super-pious, *Introduction à la vie dévote*.[20] Flagellation also continued to be practiced by the various Marian Congregations that have been the focus of Chatellier's study.[21] It is particularly interesting to note that in the example Chatellier provides, both the members of the Holy Sacrament confraternity and the members of the Congregation of the Holy Virgin participate as flagellants in a procession enacting the passion. It is also known that flagellation was practiced at the secret Marian Congregation meetings called the Aa. One of the most important defenses of flagellation was published by the Jesuit Gretzer. It is particularly important to note that so many figures and movements so essential to *dévot* piety were part of what seems to be an ongoing tradition of penitential piety that included flagellation.

Thiers also shows, however, that there was a growing sense of sexual modesty ["pudicité"] that accompanied flagellation in the seventeenth century, which helps account for the secrecy in which the practice occurred. This attitude toward sexual modesty is also a hallmark of debates over the publicly permissible forms of performativity.

Charges of the immodesty and deviant sexual behavior associated with flagellation were first leveled by Boileau, whose Enlightenment sensibilities led him to characterize flagellation as an irrational and medically destructive practice.[22] Flagellation becomes, symbolically speaking, an echo of thirteen in a world of five-ness: that is, a deviant and proscribed symbolic behavior.

The following passage from Thiers also shows the connections between a growing concern with "pudicité" and the growing secrecy surrounding flagellation.

> And it is for that reason [modesty] that today monks and nuns take "discipline" on their shoulders, on their loins, or on their thighs completely naked, but out of sight of the brothers or sisters which is in private in their cells or at the door of their cells . . . but with all the windows closed and all the lights extinguished: which removes the indecency which could exist in giving oneself "discipline". . . . [23]

At some point much later in the seventeenth century, flagellation also came to be considered too dramatic and external a form of piety. From that point on an entire discourse about the devotional benefits of flagellation became obscured, and the organic links between the penitential piety of the League and important currents of seventeenth-century *dévot* piety were lost. One of the ways that this process occurred was through the medicalization of what had been a religious discourse about the benefits of flagellation.

We can see this medicalization in the treatise written by Boileau. Boileau argues that flagellation lacks antiquity within the Christian tradition and is a practice "opposed to veritable piety and even to modesty."[24] To Boileau's mind flagellation is "a fruit of idolatry and superstition."[25] He also connects flagellation with the religion of ignorant persons. For example, Boileau blames the "ignorance and grossness" of painters who are "les livres des ignorans" for having so frequently portrayed flagellation that it is mistakenly assumed to have been deeply rooted in the Christian tradition. We can see an Enlightenment redefinition of religion and aesthetics underway in which superstition, flagellation, immodesty, and illiteracy characterize a religious tradition that is opposed to "veritable piety."

Boileau particularly condemns the work of Auger, arguing that the practices of the League were prejudicial to royal authority. He thus condemns the League by using the political standard of absolute monarchy and the religious criteria of the new, more rationalized, less expressive, and more internalized piety. Enlightenment historiography on the League transmitted this view of the League to the anti-clerical, republican, and nationalistic traditions of nineteenth-century historiography. Several generations of confusion about the nature of League piety resulted, because the essence of the movement ran counter to the predominantly secular and rationalistic development of Western culture in which a highly affective religion was condemned as superstition. The remarkable conclusion to Boileau's treatise launches into a detailed medical description of flagellation as a form of deviant behavior. This is the final stage in a long process whereby the religious traditions of the League were calumniated and finally completely obscured by a rationalist critique that was redefining true religion by Enlightenment standards. The empirical and medical detail and the very cadence of Boileau's description of what actually takes place as flagellation occurs is a shock and alone provides enough of a comment on the sea change that had occurred in religious sensibilities.

> The study of physiology teaches us that all the nerves of the human body proceed from the brain and that they form a sort of marrow which passes by the canal of vertebrae of which the spine is composed. . . . Anatomists have observed that there is a pair of nerves located after the fifth vertebra which is connected with the shoulders. . . .

He then elaborates a theory of "vital spirits" that in effect displaces the problem of evil from the moral or religious sphere to that of medical science.

> This having been stated it is clear that blows by sticks or whips dull the flow of these vital spirits and send them back to the brain where they have come from where they become entirely dissipated: in such a manner that this continual accession of spirits and the dissipation which results can only weaken the optic nerve causing damage to the eyes.

To counter the suggestion that the loins can be whipped without danger, thus sparing damage to the eyes, he points out that

> anatomists observe that the loins extend as far as the three exterior muscles of buttocks, the large, the medium and the small; and that there are three internal or one large muscle which is called the muscle with three heads, or the triceps, because it originates in three places of the pubic bone: the upper, median and lower. This having been said it is absolutely unavoidable that when the loin muscles are whipped with sticks or with a whip the animal spirits are violently forced back toward the pubic bone and that they excite immodest movements because of their proximity to the genital parts: these impressions go to the brain and paint there vivid images of forbidden pleasures which fascinate the mind and with their tempting charms reduce chastity to dissipation.[26]

Boileau thus offers us an entirely new epistemology of religious passion and redefines beyond recognition the penitential tradition of medieval asceticism that characterized both the League and much of *dévot* piety.

The public uses of flagellation and the nexus between charity (and its association with the number 13) and this form of penitential behavior became so obscured that the broad connections between penitence and charity were emptied of their original meaning. During the League the direct connection between "good works" and flagellation was available to people. The public penitential processions kept this connection in view. During the seventeenth century, the first important change was that these public manifestations disappeared from the north of France. The effects of this across the seventeenth century are twofold: 1) although flagellation continued to occur, partly in private, the meaning of this flagellation was largely lost from sight;[27] 2) partly as a result of this loss of visible connection, the historiography of charity lost an explanation of the powerful affective content of the seventeenth-century impulse to charity. The deep connections between penitence and charity were simply generalized into such concepts as, for instance, the seventeenth century as an "Augustinian century." Even in the work of one of the most astute analysts of the connections between charity and discipline, Michel Foucault, the original meaning of "discipline" as flagellation has received no sustained discussion. In the course of the seventeenth century, charity seems for many to have become a sublimation of ideas about the worthless and sinful nature of human beings.

Sect, Sectarian Politics, and Culture Wars from the Reformation to the Enlightenment

The religious experience of the League was discredited because as a symbolic system it no longer had an ontological integrity in the eyes of its opponents who, if they could read its meanings, deliberately chose not to do so or to do so only in a satiric mode. As the religious discourse on flagellation became medicalized, the original religious and reformative aspects of penitential piety also became obscured. Changing attitudes towards voluntary self-flagellation provide a key to understanding the profound changes in seventeenth-century religious sensibilities. It is essential to establish when and under what circumstances voluntary flagellation first became obscured and then was completely discredited. This history finally takes us beyond the system of religious values and behaviors that were activated during the League. In doing so the perspective gained in this Epilogue finally frames League piety in its broadest and most revealing context. Seventeenth-century and early-eighteenth-century reactions to the uses of voluntary flagellation in turn throw into relief the forces that helped discredit the religious legacy of the League, since the flagellant movement had been a particularly visible aspect of League piety.

In 1703, Jean-Baptiste Thiers offered a counter-argument that flagellation is an ancient, still widely respected, and widely practiced custom. He collected excerpts to that effect from seventeenth-century monastic constitutions, penitentials, and confraternity statutes. Thiers's material suggests what specific penitential practices were used in the seventeenth century.

The examples Thiers gives range from the *Rituel d'Evreux* in 1606 to a *Rituel* from Alet in 1667, including a *rituel* from Paris in 1645. All agree that penitence consists of three elements: prayer, fasting, and alms. Aside from the close connection between penitence and alms, and thus charity, that the trilogy makes clear, the important point to emerge from these texts is that fasting was a generic expression for mortification of the body that emphatically included voluntary flagellation throughout the seventeenth century. The comparison of four examples from four *rituels* establishes this beyond a doubt. The first is taken from Evreux in 1606; the second is from Arras in 1628 about the time of the founding of the Company of the Holy

Sacrament; a third is in French from Orleans in 1642. The fourth text demonstrates the possibilities for control of the body that could be obtained with the perfection of penitence, where, to use Auger's phrase, the world was a school for penitence. It is from Alet in 1667.

> [Evreux:] Omne satisfactionis genus ad hac tria praecipue refertur orationem scilicet, jejunium et eleemosynam. Per jejunium, non oportet solum intelligere ciborum abstinentiam sed corporis disciplinas et castigationes, cilicia, peregrinationes et alia omnia opera poenalia.

> [Arras, 1628:] Triplex poenitentiarum genus communiter assignatur, videlicet, oratio, jejunium, et eleemosnya. Ubi per jejunium quoque intelliguntur omnia quae ad castigationem corporis valet ut abstinentia cibi vel potus, disciplinarum, usus et cilicii, vigiliae, peregrinatio, humi cubatio, etc.

> [Orleans, 1642:] Les oeuvres qu'on a coûtume d'ordonner pour les penitences se reduisent à trois, à l'aumône, à l'oraison, et au jeûne. Sous le jeûne sont comprises toutes les oeuvres de misericorde, qui regardent les austerités et macerations du cors, comme les cilices, les disciplines, les veilles, les pelerinages et autres semblables.

> [Alet, 1667:] Le jeûne par lequel on satisfait à Dieu pour les pechés, comprend-il seulement l'abstinence des viandes et de la nourriture corporelle? Non, mais il comprend aussi toutes les mortifications et toutes les austerités qui peuvent abatre le cors, et lui faire souffrir quelque peine et quelque incommodité comme les haires, les cilices, les disciplines, coucher sur la dure, se mortifier dans l'usage des plaisirs, même licites comme dans l'usage de la vûë, de l'ouïe, de l'odorat.[28]

The most important aspect of these passages is the psychology they reveal, the desire for a total control of the senses: sight, sound, and smell. Such concepts were not easily conceivable outside the context of penitential piety. To state the problem more positively, penitential piety formed the psychological underpinnings for the new theories of mental and physical discipline that gave a new intensity to the centuries- old task the church set itself of reforming popular culture. But the crucial point to make is that this was not simply or even primarily a debate of elites against the people. The idea of a reform of popular culture is perhaps a misguided term—the discursive result of the effort to legitimize a particular view of rationality by associating it with cultural progress, which then only "popular" disorder hindered.

The debate between Boileau and Thiers shows us that across the seventeenth century, the religious culture of the Catholic Reformation, in choosing to make secret its Leaguer inheritance, became quite unintentionally a religious culture where fundamental questions of ontology were becoming essentially epistemological problems and where, for practitioners of the new discourses of "critique," such as Boileau, the forms of knowing no longer included an understanding of the ascetic uses of the body. A vital site for the *imitatio Christi* was shamed into silence. Before silence, however, came satire, and for this we may finally thank the historians who were such adamant opponents of the League, who made this history of League piety possible. I turn at last to Jacques-Auguste de Thou who may now, unmasked, have the last word on the League:

> il s'etoit élevé une secte de gens qui peu satisfaits de témoigner leur re-pentance par la componction interieure, en vouloient donner des marques au dehors par un principe d'orgueil et se couvroit d'un sac suivant la coûtume qui se pratiquoit dans les dueils sous ancienne loy: fondez aussi sur un passage mal expliqué du psalmiste, ou il dit, je me prépare pour le foüet. . . . [29]

> [There arose a sect of persons who were little satisfied to demonstrate their repentance by interior contrition, wishing, out of the sin of pride, to show contrition through outward signs, and they covered themselves in sackcloth according to the custom of mourning practices found in the Ancient Law: (the custom was) founded on a passage ineptly expressed by the psalmist, who wrote, I prepare my body to receive the whip. . . .]

The triumph of transcendence, from Calvin, to the *Politiques*, to parties within the Enlightenment itself largely shaped League historiography. Caught between and at times a party to these culture wars, Catholic reformers had the difficult task of recasting the celebration of the sacred in a world of radically altered understandings of the boundaries of the sacred and the profane and of profanation itself.

House of Valois

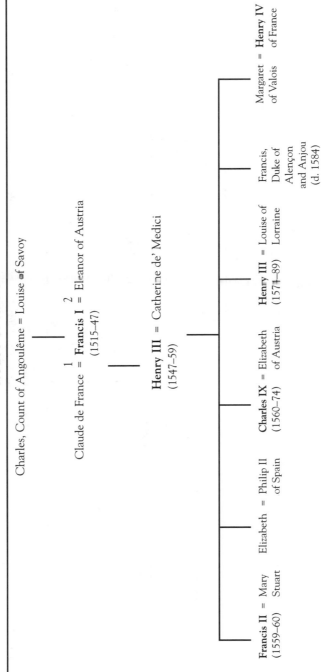

Charles, Count of Angoulême = Louise of Savoy

Claude de France =¹ **Francis I** =² Eleanor of Austria
(1515–47)

Henry III = Catherine de' Medici
(1547–59)

Francis II = Mary Stuart
(1559–60)

Elizabeth = Philip II of Spain

Charles IX = Elizabeth of Austria
(1560–74)

Henry III = Louise of Lorraine
(1574–89)

Francis, Duke of Alençon and Anjou
(d. 1584)

Margaret of Valois = **Henry IV** of France

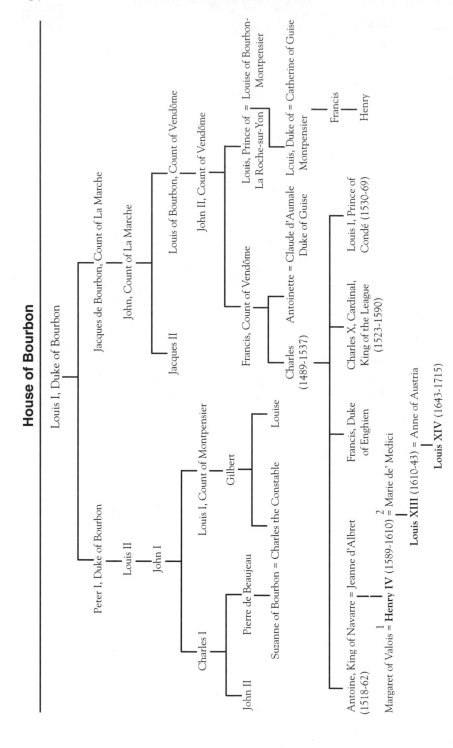

House of Bourbon

Appendix B
Houses of Guise and Lorraine

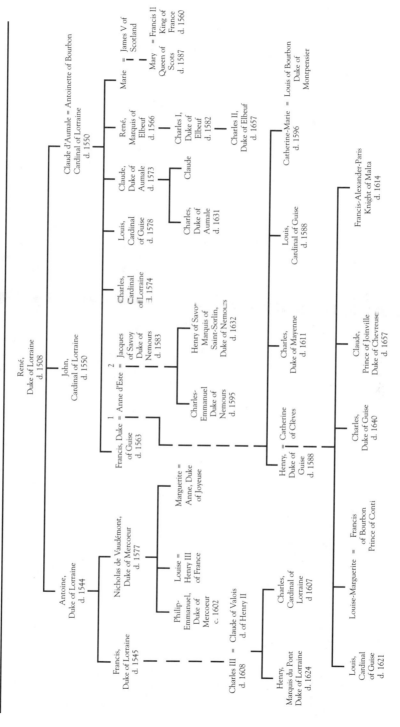

Appendix C
Eight Variables to Analyze Performativity

Type of performative behavior	Quotes

I. The Performativity Index (19 types of pious requests)

1. Decoration of a sacred object

   ". . . *la somme de vingt escuz soleil . . . pour estre employee en l'achapt d'une livre d'argent propre pour servir à mectre le sainct sacrement pour porter en procession ensemble ung reliquare . . .*" n. Jourdan (1590)

2. Banquet

   ". . . *qu'il soit donné . . . à treize aultres pauvres . . . ung pain de la valleur d'un sol . . . une chopine de vin, et de la viande selon le jour . . . à ce qu'ils prient Dieu pour les trespassez et sans que l'on face aultre banquet ny assembee en sadicte maison . . .*" n. Lamiral (1590)

3. Pilgrimage vows

   ". . . *veult qu'il soit faict à son intention deux voiages à nostre dame de Liesse qu'elle y a vouéz et qu'il soit chanté à chacun voiage une messe . . . et au retour d'icelle il passe aussy par nostre dame de la victoire . . .*" n. Cartier (1630)

4. Extraordinary detail on funeral cortege

   ". . . *appellez les prebstres . . . avec les vicaires et clerc et ledict clerc avec la grande croix et pour lumiere six torches du poix de livre et demy piece . . .*" n. Le Tellier (1543)

5. Above average number of lights (more than 12)

   Each child shall carry "*une chandelle ardente avec deux et demi douzaine de torches et quatre cierges de livre piece pour la presentation avec deux aultres pour le grand autel de trois quarteron piece avec six aultres cierge d'ung quarteron piece pour l'autel du sainct sacrement . . . avec ung cierge blanc pour l'offrande.*" n. Croiset (1590)

6. Aural and visual symbolic community

" . . . *sortans de l'eglise pour aller porter l'extreme onction à quelque malade faire tainter quelque quelque cloche pour advertir le peuple que c'est pour leur signifier de prier Dieu pour quelque malade* . . . " n. Jourdan (1590)

7. Sign of Cross (symbolic act sacralizing document)

"*Jhesus Maria*" at -op, " . . . *en se signant du signe de la croix et disant par luy in nomine, patris et filii et spiritus sancti, amen.*" n. Crozon (1544)

8. Verbal performativity

One basse messe every week on Friday during one year, " . . . *en memoire de la passion de nostre seigneur.*" n. Robinot (1590)

9. Bodily performativity

"*Item veult et ordonne que son coeur soict mis et enchassé en plombe et porté dans l'eglise Notre Dame de Poissy et icelluy mectre dans une petite chapelle qui est deriere le grand autel d'icelle en laquelle est et repose le saint sacrement.*" n. Lybault (1590)

10. Aspersion with holy water

"*Item veult et ordonne qu'il soit dict . . . à perpetuite en ladicte eglise St. Leu St. Giles une autre messe basse de requiem et que à la fin d'icelle le prestre qui la celebra asperge de l'eau benoist sur la fosse de ladicte testateur.*" n. Bruyère (1590)

11. Liturgical performativity in detail

" . . . *pour sa pouvre ame à l'autel de la parroisse . . . ung service complect assavoir vigils à neuf pseaumes et neuf lecons, laudes, recommandaces et trois haultes messes à diacre et soubzdiacre l'une du saint esprit, l'autre de nostre dame, l'autre de requiem avec la prose des trespassez et trente basses messes.*" n. Le Roy (1543)

12. Offertory procession (lay participation, vernacular prayers)

" . . . *lesquelz pauvres seront tenuz auparavant ladicte distribution . . . aller à l'offrande d'icelle [église] avecq une chandelle ardente en la main.*" n. Arragon (1590)

13. Celebrant of symbolic importance

"*Je veux que aux cordelliers, jacobins, carmes et augustins soient dictes et cellebrees aux chacuns desdictz quatre ordres cestassavoir ausdictz cordelliers et jacobins à chacur d'iceulx trente basses messes qui sont soixante basses messes et ausdictz carmes et augustins à chacun d'iceulx vingt basses messes qui sont cent*

Type of performative behavior	Quotes
	esses dont en chacun d'iceulx couventz l'on dira cestassavoir aux cordelliers dix messes de la trinite, dix du sainct esprit, cinq de nostre dame et cinq de requiem, aux jacobins dix de tous sainctz, dix des anges, cinq des apostres et cinq de toutes vierges, aux carmes cinq de tous martres, cinq de sous confesseurs, cinq de la croix, et cinq des apostres, aux augustins cinq de la passion, cinq de l'asension nostre seigneur, cinq du sainct sacrement et cinq de l'epifanye et que lesdictes basses messes soient dictes par les plus pouvres religieux au cheoix et eslestion des gardiens et prieurs d'iceulx couventz et pour chacune messe soit baillé deux solz parisis et non point moings." n. Mussart (1544)
14. Strict comportment of celebrant	*" . . . lesquelz services elle prie estre faitz et dictz le plus honestement et devotiement que faire ce pourra . . ."* n. Cruce (1540)
15. Bequests to prisoners (symbolic value of their prayers)	*" . . . donne et legue aux pouvres prisonniers la somme de dix livres distribuee en livres argent ou aultres choses à eulx necessaires . . ."* at discretion of executors. n. Poutrain (1540)
16. Special clerical intervention without testator's presence	*" . . . veult et ordonne que durant trente jours commerçant le jour que l'on verra ladicte veufve commencee aux assaulx de la mort et que l'on espere plus sa mort que sa vie ou tost apres son trespas veult estre dictes et cellebrees en l'eglise du couvent des cordelliers à Paris trente basses messes au nom de Jhesus et que à chacune desdictes messes y ayt une chandelle de cyre ardante de deux deniers tournois piece et qu'il soit paié pour chacune messe trois solz tournois."* n. Champin (1540)
17. Sacraments taken	*" . . . desire . . . mourir en bonne Catholicque apostolicque et romaine comme elle y a vescu et entende vivre le reste de ses jours et estre munye à sa mort des saincts sacremens de l'eglise . . ."* n. Belin (1630)
18. Intelligibility of service and/or educational bequests	*" . . . à la congregation Nostre Dame de Lyon qui s'assemble aux Jesuistes . . . douze ecus pour employer en petitz catheschismes et chappelletz . . ."* n. R. Bontemps (1590)

19. Entrance into a monastery

"Au nom de la tres saincte trinite pere, fils et sainct esprit randant graces a son infinie bonté de tant le tant (sic) de benefices recus de sa saincte et liberale main et de ce qu'il luy a pleu me donner la cognoissance et le desir de son service et en l'honneur de Jesus Crist nostre seigneur et de la vie tres humble et pauvre qu'il a menee sur [la terre] desirant l'himiter (sic) en ceste estat par le mespris des biens et comoditees de la vie et me rendre a sa parole et au desire qu'il me donne de les abbandoner et renoncer pour son amour a cet effet ie me despouille de tous mes biens par ceste mienc disposition et testament aisy (sic) qu'il ensuict." n. Haultdesens (1630)

II. Indicators of Immanence

1. Sacred object below saint in hierarchy

To *" . . . l'Eglise Notre Dame de Liesse deux chandelliers d'argent vallant cent cinquante livres piece pour servir à l'autel . . ."* n. Le Gay (1630)

2. Sacred object devoted to saint

" . . . soit baillé par son executeur une cotte verte pour le paremens de l'image de Madame Ste. Anne estant à St. Etienne du Mont." n. Garnon (1630)

3. Sacred object devoted to Mary

" . . . à la confrerie du St. Sacrement fondee en l'eglise St. Estienne, sa vierge garnie d'argent avec la somme de deux escuz pour estre participant aux prieres . . ." n. Charles (1590)

4. Sacred object devoted to Christ

The testator gives to the *" . . . oeuvre et fabrique . . . pour participier aux prieres et bienfaictz d'icelle eglise St. Séverin [et] pour employer par les marguilliers d'icelle fabrique en la couverture qu'il conviendra pour couvrir d'argent le baston de la croix de ladicte eglise que on a de coustume porter es processions d'icelle eglise . . ."* The testator wishes this legacy to be entered in the martyrologe. n. Champin (1540)

5. Sacred place below saint in hierarchy

Wishes to be buried in the chapel of the *" . . . College de Sorbonne à coste du grand autel vis à vis l'image des onze mil vierges."* n. Lamiral (1590)

Type of performative behavior	Quotes
6. Sacred place related to a saint	Wishes to be buried " . . . *hors et vis à vis la porte de chapelle St. Francois.*" n. Tulloue (1630)
7. Sacred place related to Mary	" . . . *chapelle notre Dame de Pitie devant le grand autel.*" n. P. Cothereau (1590)
8. Sacred place related to Christ	" . . . *eglise de l'hospital St. Denis devant le crucifix.*" n. Peron (1590)
9. Sacred place within economy of salvation (e.g., Purgatory)	" . . . *ordonne . . . à l'instant de sondict enterrement estre chanté 'in purgatoris' avec l'oraison . . .* " n. Paisant (1630)
III. Mentions of the Body of Christ (in any form)	
1. Decorative item for the celebration of the Eucharist	" . . . *faire paindre et enrichir le simbolle au corporellier de boys ou repose le tres precieulx corps de nostre seigneur Jhesus Christ . . . si ne le faire paindre devant mon trespas.*" n. Boissellet (1540)
2. A gift is an element in the Eucharist (i.e., Wine and Bread)	" . . . *soyt porté à l'offrande quy se fera à chacune desdictes messes une pinte de bon vin et deux petis pains . . .*" n. Crozon (1540)
3. Liturgical reference to the *Fête-Dieu* (Festival of Corpus Christi)	"*Veult et entend que le service qu'elle a fait dire . . . depuis le decedz de deffunct son mary en ladicte eglise St. Croix pendant l'octave du St. Sacrement soict apres son decedz dit celebré et continué à perpetuite . . .*" n. Cousinet (1630)
4. Burial of body near Holy Sacrament	" . . . *son corps mort estre porté en l'eglise St. Gervais sa paroisse ou sera fait le service et de là transporté en l'eglise St. Jehan en Greve pour y estre inhumé et enterré entre les fondz et la chapelle neufve du St. Sacrement.*" n. Grandrye (1630)
5. Liturgical performance including the Holy Sacrament (e.g., specific mention of "elevation of Host")	Asks that the first Sunday of every month " . . . *à la fin du salut ordinaire de la confrarye du Rosaire il sera chanté à perpetuite devant le sainct sacrement en ladicte eglise une antienne de la vierge selon le temps avec une libera et de profundis et les oraisons acoustamés pour les mortz à l'intention dudict Caillon et ladicte femme.*" n. Saint-Vaast (1630)

6. Explicit requirement for religious services in honor of the Holy Sacrament

In church where buried, testator requests every year in perpetuity "... *le jour de la grande feste de dieu apres vespres un salut du sainct sacrement.*" n. Sainct-Fussien (1630)

7. Holy Sacrament administered by priest

"... *au prebstre qui lui a administré des saintz sacrements pendans sa malladye, un escu sol.*" n. Charles (1590)

8. Bequest to an institution honoring the Holy Sacrament

"... *Confrairie du Saint Sacrement fondee en ladicte eglise de Monstreul, dix solz.*" n. Poche (1590)

9. Gift to increase lay reception of Eucharist

"*Plus donne ... à cinq pauvres filles en l'honneur des cinq playes de nostre seigneur ... à la charge que le vendredy devant ou apres qu'elles seront mariees elles feront celebrer une messe de la passion ... et feront la saincte communion et prieront Dieu pour le salut de son ame.*" n. Fontaine (1630)

10. Request for prayers by an individual who will take communion in memory of the testator

"*Veult et ordonne ladicte damoiselle testatrice estre baillé payé et continué audit sieur de Montereal douze livres dix solz de rente par chacun an à compter du jour du decedz d'icelle damoiselle testatrice pour estre par ledict curé distribuez à celluy qui donnera la saincte communion en ladicte eglise Sainct Sulpice les jours des festes solempnelles seullement affin qu'il ayt soins de recommander ladicte damoiselle aux prieres et oraisons des communicans ...*" n. Marreau (1630)

11. Mention in testator's will of receiving communion at time of will

Signs will in the presence of "*maistre Estienne de Jouye prebstre porte dieu ...*" n. Morthenault (1590)

IV. Mentions of Testator's Own Body

1. Mention of testator's body

"... *vingt et une paouvres escolliers pour conduire mon corps jusques aux sainctz innocens chacun en leur main ung petit cierge ardant lesquelz yront apres le corps et sans leurs pseaulmes et le lendemain se trouveront au service quy se fera en ladicte eglise sainct eustache pour assister audict service et auront chacun escollier deux solz tournois cestassavoir douze deniers tournois pour le convoy du*

Type of performative behavior	Quotes
	corps et douze deniers tournois pour assister audict service le lendemain auquel service ilz porteront à l'offrande chacun leursdictz cierges lesquelz cierges ilz seront tenuz rapporter du jour de l'enterrement au service du lendemain et pour trouver lesdictz paouvres escolliers fauldra prier le maistre de l'hospital sainct gervais à Paris les fournir parce que l'on m'a dict qu'il en cognoist beaucoup." n. Mussart (1540)
V. Indicators of Liturgical Detail	
1. Mix of liturgical detail	" . . . *vigilles, recommendances et cinq hautes messes, la première de la trinité, la seconde des cinq playes, la tierce du sainct esprit evec la collecte des anges la quatre de nostre dame avec la collecte de omnibus sainctes, la cinquieme de requiem et pareillement tant de basses messes à qu'il se trouveront de prebstres ayant devotion de celebrer.*" n. Mussart (1540)
2. Mass in honor of entity lower in the sacred hierarchy than saints (e.g., confessors, virgins)	"*Veult et ordonne . . . deux autres messes basses des apostres en l'eglise des celestins . . .*" n. Dupont (1540)
3. Mass in honor of a saint	" . . . *un trentain de sainct Augustin à couvent des Augustins faubourg St. Germain.*" n. Paisant (1630)
4. Mass in honor of angels	" . . . *messe des anges . . .*" n. Bergeon (1540)
5. Liturgical or paraliturgical ceremony in honor of Mary and Christ	" . . . *aux minims de vye sayne* (to say every Thursday in perpetuity) *une haute messe du saint sacrement à diacre et souüz diacre et* (after the mass) *un salut regina ou immolata ou ave maria stella et une libera et apres vespres dudict jour un salut du saint sacrement.*" n. J. Chapellain (1590)
6. Mass in honor of Mary	" . . . *vingt-cinq messes basses de la vierge . . .*" n. Delacroix (1630)

7. Other liturgical/paraliturgical ceremony in honor of Mary and Christ

"*Veult et ordonne que quant son corps sera en l'eglise pour estre inhumé soit dict chanté en ~ entrant devant le crucifix l'himne vexilla regis prodeunt, une orai~on de la croix, salut regina, une oraison de la vierge marie, le pseaulme de profundis . . . et durant que son corps sera en l'eglise y soient cin~ petits cierges . . . ardent devant le crucifix.*" n. Champin (1540)

8. Liturgical/paraliturgical ceremony other than Mass, in honor of Christ

"*. . . passion selo~ saint Jehan . . .*" before the Mass. n. Champin (1540)

9. Mass in honor of Christ

"*. . . 33 basses m~sses assavoir . . . trois aultres messes de la nativité nostre seigneur, trois de l~ circonsyion, trois de la passion, trois de la resurection, trois de la assention, tr~is de la pentecoste . . .*" n. Parque (1590)

10. Mass in honor of Trinity or Holy Spirit

"*. . . une [haute m~esse] du sainct esprit . . .*" n. Trouvé (1590)

VI. *Use of Liturgical Time and Calendar*

1. Day of week specified with no condensation of sacred immanence implied

"*. . . une basse m~esse de requiem par chacune sepmaine le jour de lundi . . .*" n. Lenorm~nt (1540)

2. Day of week and festival specified with no condensation of sacred immanence implied

Gives "*50 solz t~ de rente annuelle à l'eglise de Fleury*" for commemoration of testator and her friends and for saying every Sunday and solemn day a "*l~era*" on testator's grave. n. Perier (1590)

3. Festival, no condensation of sacred immanence

"*. . . seront son~ez tant la veille que lesdictz jours des cloches de ladicte eglise*" on 24 August, 2 September, 6 October and "*le jour des trespassez . . .*" n. Motelet (1630)

4. Festival in honor of saint

"*. . . une libera, une salve regina et les oraisons y accoustumez*" on testator's grave on the fe~tival of All Saints. n. Muret (1590)

Type of performative behavior	Quotes
5. Day of week in honor of Mary	" . . . par chascun jour de samedi . . . une salve regina les oraisons nostre dame . . ." n. Thurer (1540)
6. Marian festival	" . . . le jour de l'assumption de nostre dame un salut de la vierge . . ." n. Paisant (1630)
7. Day of week: hybrid	Three basses messes requested each week for one year "le lundy [du] sainct esprit, le jeudy du saint sacrement de l'authel et l'autre le vendredy de la passion de nostre saulveur et redempteur . . ." n. Mahieu (1590)
8. Day of week and festival: hybrid	The chaplain should say mass all Sundays and "festes de l'annee les mercredy et vendredy . . ." n. Saint-Vaast (1630)
9. Festival: hybrid	At each "des quatres bonnes festes de l'an, Pasques, Penthecoste, Toussainctz et Noel [distribute to] pauvres gens . . . quatre solz [each] . . ." n. Le Roy (1540)
10. Day of week and festival in honor of Mary and Christ	Prebstre is to say "tous les mois au jour de vendredy et aux quatre festes solempnelles de nostre dame . . . une basse messe . . . avec une salve regina . . ." n. Parque (1630)
11. Festival in honor of Mary and Christ	Two obits each year on day testator dies and on "jour des festes d'assencion de nostre seigneur, nativite, nostre dame, conception nostre dame et dernier jour de la purification . . ." n. Bontemps, R. (1590)
12. Day of week in memory of Christ	" . . . par chacune sepmaine le jour de vendredy une basse messe . . . et en la fin de chacune desdictes messes estre dit la passion nostre seigneur . . ." n. Leclerc (1540)
13. Day of week and festival honoring Christ	The masters and governors of the church must say "une haulte messe" each year in perpetuity on Friday "des Quatre temps" just before Christmas Day. n. Lybault (1590)

14. Festival honoring Christ

Wants said by *margulliers* on Easter of each year immediately after midday and after vespers, two *salutz*, one in front of the crucifix and the other at the altar of the virgin. n. Desquatrevaulx (1590)

VII. Bequests to Jesuits, Capuchins, and/or Feuillants

1. Any Jesuit institution bequest

To "*peres jesuites de saint Louis 150 livres tournois* . . ." n. Bourgeois (1630)

2. Any Capuchin institution bequest

To her nephew François Charlet who took a vow at the order of Capuchins, bequests eleven "*ecus soleil*" for his needs and that they may pray for her. n. Mahieu (1590)

3. Any Feuillant institution bequest

" . . . *deux services complets aux feullantans* . . . " n. P. Cothereau (1590)

4. Capuchin or Feuillant bequest

" . . . *que lors qu'il sera aux agonies de la mort ou incontinent apres son decedz il soit dit à son enterrement le trentain saint gregoire à l'eglise des Capucins ou aux Feuillans* . . . " n. Moufle (1630)

VIII. Reformist Behaviors

1. Cognitive concerns and educational investments

"*Item la dite testateur veult et entend qu'il soict baillé deux cents livres au procureur du colege des peres jesuites laquelle somme sera emploiee par ledict procureur pour la nouriture et entretenement de quelques pauvres enfans pour leur ayder à faire leur estudes en leur College de Clermont* . . . " n. Bourgeois (1630)

2. Investment in administration of the sacraments

" . . . *supliant . . . ladicte dame de faire communier toutes ses religieuses à l'intention de ladicte testatrice le jour ou le lendemain de son deces et tous les ans* . . . " n. Fontaine (1630)

3. Building or improving church or chapel

" . . . *jusques à ce que la chappelle ou eglise que ledict testateur et sa femme se doivent faire bastir à Mouy pour les religieux dudict tiers ordre saint Francois soit construite et ediffiee* . . . " n. Jolly (1630)

Type of performative behavior	Quotes
4. Confraternal reform	"... à la confraternité sainct Charles Boromée ... en l'eglise Sainct Jacques de la Boucherie la somme de huict cens livres ... employee en acquisition de rentes ou heritages ... [pour] estre ... employés aux fraiz du service divin qui se faict ... le jour de la feste et solempnité dudict sainct Charles qui est le quatre novembre de chacune annee." [newly founded confraternity] n. Gerbault (1630)
5. Clerical discipline	(re: a distribution) "... que ceulx qui auront este assistans ausdictes offices des matines et laudes de telle sorte que la pars des absens ne soit donnee ne distribuee aux presens mais qu'elle soit donnee pour dieu aux pauvres malades ..." n. Jourdan (1590)
6. Morality or competence of celebrant valued by testator	"J'ordonne encores ung annuel de messes des trespassez pour le repos et salut de mon ame ... en l'eglise ou je seray inhumé par ung homme d'eglise fort devot ..." n. Perier (1630)
7. Reverence of sacred object	Gives a livre of silver to make a reliquary in which to carry the Holy Sacrament in procession and wishes the reliquary to be made "de meilleure matiere et facon qu'il se poura faire pour la somme susdicte selon l'advis des recteur et marguilliers de ladicte eglise." n. Jourdan (1590)

Appendix D
Leaguers: Criteria for Identification and Basic Testator Data, 1590
(Alphabetized and Grouped by Notary)
For column totals see Appendix L

Notary; Parish;* Part of Town; (Second Notary to sign when known)	Testator	Testator's Parish	State of Health	Special Burial Institution Requested	Location for Burial Requested	Sacralizing Headings	Examples of Performativity	Evidence of League Connections	Socio-Professional Category and (Profession)
Arragon; Saint-Jacques-de-la-Boucherie; Ville	De la Duriere, Anthoine	Saint-Jacques-de-la-Boucherie	Sick	Saints-Innocents	Where executor chooses	none	none	Guise employed testator. Notary Arragon identified in Pallier as a notary frequented by Leaguer printers.	Soldier (archer of the guards of Monseigneur the Duke of Mayenne, Lt. General of the royal state and the Crown of France)
Bergeon; Saint-Merri; Ville	Michel, Jehan	Saint-Méderic[1]	Sick	Sainte-Croix-de-la-Bretonnerie Monastery	none	none	Bodily performativity; Liturgical performativity	Descimon[2] Barnavi[3]	Gens de Loi (attorney in Parlement)
Bernard; Saint-Séverin; Université	Brotin, Pierre[4]	Saint-Benoît	Healthy	Left to executor	Left to executor	none	"Allant et venant journellement par les rues de ceste ville de Paris et aux eglises pour ouyr la parolle de dieu et assister à son divin service."	Travels to Rome via Dijon	Merchant

Notary; Parish;* Part of Town; (Second Notary to sign when known)	Testator	Testator's Parish	State of Health	Special Burial Institution Requested	Location for Burial Requested	Sacralizing Headings	Examples of Performativity	Evidence of League Connections	Socio-Professional Category and (Profession)
Bernard; Saint-Séverin; Université	Delorrain, Marie	Saint-Séverin	Sick	Saint-Séverin	none	none	Lights; Liturgical performativity	Bequest to League cleric	Honorable/ Bourgeosie (Clothier)
Bontemps, M.; Saint-André-des-Arts; Université	Barbin, André	Saint-André-des-Arts	Sick	Saint-André-des-Arts	none	none	none	In the service of the duke of Mayenne	Supply master for the duke of Mayenne's army (vivandier)
Bontemps, M.; Saint-André-des-Arts; Université (Bruyère)	Blosseau, Claude	Saint-André-des-Arts	Sick	Saint-André-des-Arts	none	none	Symbolic construction of community; Aspersion of holy water	Solcier in the Catholic Union	Soldier (lieutenant of a company of soldiers in the regiment of the sieur de Mortilly for the service of the Catholic Union)
Bontemps, M.; Saint-André-des-Arts; Université (Bruyère)	Dubuisson, Pierre	Saint-André-des-Arts	Sick	Non-Parisian church or parish	none	none	none	Ties to a noble of the League	Noble (squire, governor of a duchy and captain of a castle)
Bontemps, M.; Saint-André-des-Arts; Université (Bruyère)	Dufay, Claude	Saint-André-des-Arts	Sick	Abbey Saint-Victor	none	none	none	Witness has ties to a noble of the League	Noble (chevalier of the order of the king)

						In nomine domini, amen	Symbolic act sacralizes		
Bontemps, R.; La Madeleine; Cité (holograph)	Auberry, Jehan	No location given	Sick	Unknown	none	none	none	League cleric at funeral: Michel Aucelin, curate of La Madeleine parish	Unknown
Bontemps, R.; La Madeleine; Cité (Bontemps, M.)	Auzanet, François	Saint-Benoît	Sick	No	Testator omits all burial information	none	none	Bontemps is notary	University/Liberal professions (student at Jesuit College of Clérmont)
Bontemps, R.; La Madeleine; Cité (Dumarc)	Balotin, Jehanne	Saint-Christophe	Sick	Saint-Christophe	Wants to be buried where she usually sits in church	none	none	Bontemps is notary	Middle/Lower Offical (officer that gathers money for the collations of the gentlemen of the court of Parlement (*buvetyer*)
Bontemps, R.; La Madeleine; Cité (Dumarc)	Blanchard, Jehan	No location given	Healthy	No	Testator omits all burial information	none	none	Bontemps is notary	University/Liberal professions (student at the Jesuit College of the University of Paris)
Bontemps, R.; La Madeleine; Cité (Lybault)	Boucher, François	Sainte-Croix	Sick	Sainte-Croix	none	none	none	Uncle is the Leaguer preacher Boucher, curate of Saint-Benoît	Gens de Loi (barrister in the Parlement)

Notary; Parish;* Part of Town; (Second Notary to sign when known)	Testator	Testator's Parish	State of Health	Special Burial Institution Requested	Location for Burial Requested	Sacralizing Headings	Examples of Performativity	Evidence of League Connections	Socio-Professional Category and (Profession)
Bontemps, R.; La Madeleine; Cité (Dumarc)	Chavasse, Baltasar	Saint-Benoît	Healthy	Jesuit College of Clermont	none	none	none	Bontemps is notary; lives at the Jesuit college	University/Liberal professions (regent, College Saint Barbe; University of Paris)
Bontemps, R.; La Madeleine; Cité (Bontemps, M.)	Cheval, Geneviève	La Madeleine	Sick	La Madeleine	Named chapel of an institution	Cross at the top of the page	Symbolic act sacralizes; Lights; Bodily performativity; Symbolic construction of community	Bontemps is notary	Gens de Loi (attorney in the Parlement)
Bontemps, R.; La Madeleine; Cité (Bontemps, M.)	Daumeau, Michèle	Sainte-Croix	Sick	Sainte-Croix	none	Cross at the top of the page	Bodily performativity; Symbolic act sacralizes	Bontemps is notary	Profession unknown; "agee de cinquante-cinq ans usant et jouissant de ses droitz"
Bontemps, R.; La Madeleine; Cité (Bontemps, M.)	Deplane, Pierre	Saint-Méderic	Sick	Sainte-Geneviève-des-Ardents	none	Cross at the top of the page	Bodily performativity; Liturgical performativity; Symbolic act sacralizes	Bontemps is notary	Honorable/Bourgeoisie (marchand et bourgeois de Paris)
Bontemps, R.; La Madeleine; Cité (Dumarc)	Desmarosy, Gelayne	Saint-Christophe	Sick	Left to executor	Left to executor	none	none	Bontemps is notary	Servant

Witnesses	Name	Location	Health	Burial	Burial Info	Symbol	Sacralization	Notary	Status
Bontemps, R.; La Madeleine; Cité (Dumarc)	Durant, Marie	Sainte-Croix	Sick	Saint-Paul	none	none	Bodily performativity; Liturgical performativity	Bontemps is notary	Rural Worker (wine grower)
Bontemps, R.; La Madeleine; Cité (Bontemps, M.)	Egert, Mathurin	La Madeleine	Sick	La Madeleine	none	none	Bodily performativity	League cleric at funeral	Gens de Loi (attorney in the Parlement)
Bontemps, R.; La Madeleine; Cité (Labarde)	Garnier, Eustache	Saint-Christophe	Sick	Saint-Christophe	none	none	none	Bontemps is notary	Gens de Loi (commissioner and examiner at the Châtelet)
Bontemps, R.; La Madeleine; Cité (Dumarc)	Guerin, Magdelaine	Saint-Pierre-aux-Boeufs	Sick	Saints-Innocents	Near chaise	none	none	Bontemps is notary	Honorable/ Bourgeoisie (marchand et bourgeois de Paris)
Bontemps, R.; La Madeleine; Cité (Dumarc)	Leboindre, Philippe	No location given	Unknown	No	Testator omits all burial information	Cross at the top of the page	Entering a monastery (the Minims of Nygeon); Symbolic act sacralizes	Bontemps is notary; in the service of the known-Leaguer, bishop of Rennes	Clergy (formerly the servant of the bishop of Rennes and also a religious)
Bontemps, R.; La Madeleine; Cité (Bontemps, M.)	Malescot, Laurens	No location given	Healthy	If dies in Vellay, in Cathedral Nostre Dame de Puy	Tomb of the canons	none	Provides for religious education; concerned about intelligibility of the sacraments	Bontemps is notary	University/ Liberal professions (doctor in a university faculty)
Bontemps, R.; La Madeleine; Cité (Dumarc)	Massé, Asdrubal	No location given	Sick	Saint-Christophe	none	none	none	Bontemps is notary; member of a crusading order with close ties to Philip II of Spain (see Appendix G)	Clergy (chevalier of the order of Saint John of Jerusalem)

Notary; Parish;* Part of Town; (Second Notary to sign when known)	Testator	Testator's Parish	State of Health	Special Burial Institution Requested	Location for Burial Requested	Sacralizing Headings	Examples of Performativity	Evidence of League Connections	Socio-Professional Category and (Profession)
Bontemps, R.; La Madeleine; Cité (Dumarc)	Mesteryer, Jehanne	Saint-Barthélemy	Sick	Saint-Barthélemy	"In front of the image of Our Lady . . . behind the Holy Sacrament"	none	Liturgical performativity	Bontemps is notary	Honorable/Bourgeosie (goldsmith)
Bontemps, R.; La Madeleine; Cité (Bontemps, M.)	Rosmeau, Ysabeau	La Madeleine	Sick	La Madeleine	none	Cross at the top of the page	Symbolic act sacralizes	Bontemps is notary	Artisan (carpenter)
Bontemps, R.; La Madeleine; Cité (Dumarc)	Sicry, François	No location given	Healthy	Unknown	Testator omits all burial information	Cross at the top of the page	Symbolic act sacralizes	Bontemps is notary	University/Liberal professions ("priest of the Company of Jesus, resident in the college of Clermont")
Bontemps, R.; La Madeleine; Cité (Dumarc)	Theault, Perette	Saint-Christophe	Sick	Saint-Christophe	No special location indicated	none	Bodily performativity	Bontemps is notary	Gens de Loi (attorney in the Parlement)
Bontemps, R.; La Madeleine; Cité (Four signatures)	Thibault, Jehan	Saint-Séverin	Healthy	If dies in Lyon, in église Saint Nizier	none	Cross at the top of the page	Bodily performativity; Symbolic act sacralizes; Provides for religious education/concerned about intelligibility of the sacraments	Bontemps is notary	Honorable/Bourgeosie (citizen of the city of Lyon)

Bruyère; Faubourg	Delamer, Pierre	Saint-André-des-Arts	Sick	Saint-André-des-Arts	Near the crucifix	none	Requests *salve regina* and placement of body in front of the crucifix	In Decimon/Barnavi: identified as a Leaguer	University/Liberal professions (regent in the faculty of medicine)
Bruyère; Faubourg	Lenoir, Geneviève	Saint-André-des-Arts	Sick	Saint-André-des-Arts	none	none	Celebrant has symbolic importance	League cleric at funeral	Gens de Loi (barrister in the Parlement)
Bruyère; Faubourg (Bontemps, M.)	Thomas, Noel	Saint-André-des-Arts	Sick	Cordeliers	none	none	none	Ties to a noble of the League	Noble (squire, soldier)
Bruyère; Faubourg (Bontemps, M.)	Tronson, Catherine	Saint-André-des-Arts	Sick	Saint-Leu/Saint-Gilles	Behind the aforementioned church where her forebears were buried	none	Lights; Bodily performativity; Aspersion of holy water	Bequest to League cleric	University/Liberal professions (master, doctor, or regent in faculty of medicine)
Charles; Saint-Etienne-du-Mont; Université	Courtes, Joseph	Saint-Etienne-du-Mont	Sick	Jacobins	In the chapel of Our Lady of Rosaries founded in the church of the convent of the Jacobins	none	none	Foreign Catholic noble soldier	Nobility (squire, soldier in the company of Don Octavio of Aragon, captain in a company of horsemen for his majesty in the Catholic army)
Charles; Saint-Etienne-du-Mont; Université	De Champaigne, Marie	Saint-Etienne-du-Mont	Sick	Saint-Etienne-du-Mont	In front of the chapel of Our Lady	none	none	Guise employed testator's spouse	Soldier (archer of the guards of the late Duke of Guise, the grandfather)

Notary; Parish;* Part of Town; (Second Notary to sign when known)	Testator	Testator's Parish	State of Health	Special Burial Institution Requested	Location for Burial Requested	Sacralizing Headings	Examples of Performativity	Evidence of League Connections	Socio-Professional Category and (Profession)
Charles; Saint-Etienne-du-Mont; Université	Hoyau, Jacqueline	Saint-Benoît	Sick	Saint-Benoît	Under the charnel house of the church of Saint-Benoît	none	none	League cleric at funeral	Master Artisans (master locksmith)
Charles; Saint-Etienne-du-Mont; Université	Janotin, Barbe	Saint-Séverin	Sick	Saint-Séverin	none	none	none	League cleric at funeral	Honorable/ Bourgeosie (bourgeois de Paris)
Charles; Saint-Etienne-du-Mont; Université	Rillon, Nicolas	Saint-Etienne-du-Mont	Sick	Abbey Sainte-Geneviève	none	none	none	Ties to a noble of the League	Nobility (squire, governor of Passy in Normandy (royal administration))
Chartain; Saint-Eustache; Ville	Le Goix, Pierre	Saint-Germain-l'Auxerrois	Sick	Saints-Innocents	none	none	Sacraments taken; Bodily performativity	Relative in Descimon/ Barnavi identified as a Leaguer	Gens de Loi (sergent à verge priseur juré de biens en la ville et prevosté de Paris)
Chartain; Saint-Eustache; Ville	Lesellier, Marie	Saint-Germain-l'Auxerrois	Sick	Saints-Innocents	In a named chapel	none	Sacraments and Oath of League taken	Asks Père Confesseur to attend funeral procession	Honorable/ Bourgeosie (cloth merchant)
Chartain; Saint-Eustache; Ville	Perdrinel, Claude	Saint-Eustache	Sick	Saint-Eustache	Near his wife	none	Sacraments and Oath of League taken	Possible League connections	Gens de Loi (attorney in the chambre des comptes)

Source; Origin; Quarter	Name	Parish	Health	Church	Burial location		Performativity	League connection	Social status
Chefdeville; Saint-Germain-l'Auxerrois; Ville (Levasseur)	Debarde, Marguerite	Saint-Jacques-de-la-Boucherie	Sick	No	none	none	none	League cleric at funeral: Julien Pelletier, curate of St.-Jacques-de-la-Boucherie	Artisan (wood turner or master white wood worker)
Contenot; Unknown; Ville	Dampmartin, Jehan	Saint-Germain-l'Auxerrois	Sick	Saints-Innocents	none	none	Bodily performativity; Liturgical performativity; Sacraments taken	In Descimon/ Barnavi: identified as a Leaguer	Honorable/ Bourgeosie (marchand et bourgeois de Paris)
Cothereau, P.; Unknown; Cité	Catin, Marie	Saint-Germain-Le-Viel	Sick	Saint-Germain-Le-Viel	In front of the chapel of Sainte-Anne	none	Symbolic construction of community	Relative in Descimon/ Barnavi identified as a Leaguer	Gens de Loi (usher in Parlement)
Cothereau; Unknown; Cité	Debucholicq, Georges	Saint-Sulpice	Sick	Augustins	"... in front of the great door of the chapel of the Conception of Our Lady, his body to be put in a wooden coffin and stone tomb . . ."	none	Bodily performativity; Banquet; Verbal performativity	Guise employed testator or testator's spouse	Noble (gentleman of the chamber of the former John Cardinal of Lorraine)
Cothereau; Unknown; Cité	Leger, Guillaume	Saint-Séverin	Sick	Saint-Séverin	Chapel of Saint-Masnier	none	none	Executor or witness to will in Descimon/ Barnavi identified as a Leaguer	Gens de Loi (attorney in Parlement)
Cothereau; Unknown; Cité	Pichon, Loys	Saint-Séverin	Healthy	Saint-Séverin	In the chapel of Our Lady of Piety in front of the great altar	none	none	Member of confraternity of Black Penitents	Gens de loi (priest and attorney in Parlement)

Notary; Parish;* Part of Town; (Second Notary to sign when known)	Testator	Testator's Parish	State of Health	Special Burial Institution Requested	Location for Burial Requested	Sacralizing Headings	Examples of Performativity	Evidence of League Connections	Socio-Professional Category and (Profession)
Croiset; No parish given; Cité	De Compans, Tassine	Sainte-Croix	Healthy	Sainte-Croix	choir	none	Bodily performativity; Liturgical performativity	Spouse bequest to someone in Descimon/Barnavi corpus identified as a Leaguer	Honorable/Bourgeosie (clothier)
Croiset; No parish given; Cité	Defontaines, Magdelaine	No location given	Sick	Ave Maria	none	none	Bodily performativity	Ties to a noble of the League	Noble office/epithets (demoiselle of the duchess of Nemours)
Croiset; No parish given; Cité	Du Ru, Anne	Saint-Pierre-des-Arcis	Healthy	church and monastery of Ave Maria of this city of Paris	No special location, but did mention a time, morning	none	Bodily performativity; Lights; Liturgical performativity	League cleric at funeral	Honorable/Bourgeosie (spice merchant, apothecary)
Croiset; No parish given; Cité	Lecammus, François	No location given	Sick	Saints-Innocents	In the family tomb	none	Symbolic construction of community	Executor connected to Mayenne	Clergy (canon of the Sainte-Chapelle, King's Chapel)
Croiset; No parish given; Cité	Massere, Balthazard	Saint-Pierre-des-Arcis	Sick	Our Lady of the Fields	"... in front of the choir next to the sepulchre of the late Doctor Massere, his brother ..."	none	none	Guise employed testator	Middle/Lower Offical (formerly the controller in the house of the late Cardinal de Guise recently deceased)

Croiset; No parish given; Cité	Pastey, Banigne	Saint-Séverin	Sick	Cordeliers	At the chapel of Saint-Claude	none	none	Employed by a noble of the League	Middle/Lower Offical (treasurer and receveur général des finances of madame the duchess and monseigneur the duke of Nemours)
Doujat; Saint-Germain-l'Auxerrois; Ville	Fustel, Charles	Saint-Eustache	Sick	Saints-Innocents	"In front of . . . the most beautiful image in the most lovely place joining the large tomb . . . where the *salut* is ordinarily sung"	none	none	In Descimon/Barnavi: identified as a Leaguer	Honorable/Bourgeosie (marchand et bourgeois de Paris, marchand frippier)
Dunesmes; Unknown; Ville	Derosny, Jehanne	Saint-Germain-l'Auxerrois	Sick	Saints-Innocents	none	none	none	Bequest to League cleric	Honorable/Bourgeosie (bourgeois de Paris)
Dunesmes; Unknown; Ville (Saint-Fussien)	Mosnier, Jacques	Saint-Germain-l'Auxerrois	Sick	Unknown	none	none	none	Employed by the Leaguer Archbishop of Lyon	Servant (wine steward of the Archbishop of Lyon)
Fardeau, J.; Saint-Séverin; Université (Belot)	Ledanoys, Nicole	Saint-Etienne-du-Mont	Sick	Saint-Etienne-du-Mont	none	Cross after preambe	Bodily performativity; Symbolic act sacralizes	Relative in Descimon/Barnavi identified as a Leaguer	Gens de Loi (attorney in Parlement)

Notary; Parish;* Part of Town; (Second Notary to sign when known)	Testator	Testator's Parish	State of Health	Special Burial Institution Requested	Location for Burial Requested	Sacralizing Headings	Examples of Performativity	Evidence of League Connections	Socio-Professional Category and (Profession)
Fardeau; Saint-Séverin; Université (Belot)	Saultier, Aymé	Saint-Benoît	Sick	Saint-Benoît	Testator did not specify a special location	"In nomine patris et filii et spiritus sancti, Amen."	Sacraments taken at time of will; Symbolic act sacralizes	Native of Savoy; probable League connections	Escuyer (squire, presently a student in the University of Paris, native of Savoy)
Ferrant; Unknown; Ville (Contenot)	Aubertin, Jehanne	Saint-Germain-l'Auxerrois	Sick	Saint-Germain-l'Auxerrois	none	none	none	League cleric at funeral	All Artisan (tailor)
Ferrant; Unknown; Ville (Contenot)	Legras, François	Saint-Nicolas-des-Champs	Sick	Ave Maria	none	none	none	League cleric at funeral	Noble office/ epithet (councilor to the king, corrector in his chambre des comptes)
Ferrant; Unknown; Ville (Contenot)	Nepueu, Robert	Saint-Germain-l'Auxerrois	Sick	Saints-Innocents	none	none	Bodily performativity	League cleric at funeral	Honorable/ Bourgeosie (clothier)
Herbin; Saint-Gervais; Ville	Debasanier, Geneviève	Saint-Gervais	Sick	Eglise de Bue (or at Saints-Innocents with ancestors if cannot get to Bue)	Chapelle de Notre Dame	none	Pilgrimages, vows	Guise employed the testator or testator's spouse	Nobility (Squire, sieur de Bue, seigneur) (a governor and ...captain of the Chateau of Pompierre)

Herbin; Saint-Gervais; Ville (Girault, Alexandre)	Gincestre, Jehan	Saint-Gervais	Sick	Saint-Gervais	In the great chapel of Our Lady	none	none	League cleric	Clergy/University/Liberal professions (priest, curate, doctor of theology)
Herbin; Saint-Gervais; Ville (Jablier, Thomas)	Gueret, Augustin	Saint-Gervais	Sick	Saint-Gervais	In the cemetery of the church of Saint-Gervais on the side where candles are usually placed at the location where his ancestors have been buried	none	Bodily performativity; Liturgical performativity; Celebrant comportment important	League cleric at funeral	Master Artisan (pork butcher, sausage and cold cuts maker)
Herbin; Saint-Gervais; Ville	Larcher, Pierre	Saint-Gervais	Sick	Monastery/convent of Sainte-Croix	none	none	none	Executor or witness in Descimon/Barnavi identified as a Leaguer	Noble office/epithet (councilor of the king and maistre ordinaire in the chambre des comptes)
Herbin; Saint-Gervais; Ville (Jablier, Thomas)	Lottin, Marguerite	Saint-Gervais	Sick	Saint-Gervais	none	none	Liturgical performativity	Relative in Descimon/Barnavi identified as a Leaguer	(councilor to the king at his *cour des aides*)
Jourdan; Unknown; Ville (Aymeray)	Delamothe-L'aubespine, Joseph	Saint-Germain-l'Auxerrois	Sick	Saint-Germain-l'Auxerrois	none	none	Bodily performativity	Ties to noble in the League	Noble (Seigneur, bailly and governor of Auxerre)

Notary; Parish;* Part of Town; (Second Notary to sign when known)	Testator	Testator's Parish	State of Health	Special Burial Institution Requested	Location for Burial Requested	Sacralizing Headings	Examples of Performativity	Evidence of League Connections	Socio-Professional Category and (Profession)
Jourdain; Unknown; Ville (Beaufort)	Depeyere, Jehan	Saint-Germain-l'Auxerrois	Sick	Saint-Germain-l'Auxerrois	none	none	Lights	Ties to noble in the League	Noble (squire, seigneur of Lencung, maître d'hôtel de madame la maréchale de Joyeuse)
Jourdain; Unknown; Ville	Marion, Jehan	Faubourg Parishes	Healthy	Will for Civil Death (i.e., entrance into a monastery); therefore omits burial specifications	Will for Civil Death (i.e., entrance into a monastery); therefore omits burial specifications	Jesus † Maria	Lights; Symbolic construction of community; Symbolic act sacralizes; Celebrant comportment important; Provides for religious education/concerned about intelligibility of the sacraments; Enters a monastery; Calls for the enforcement of Trent	Enters Feuillant monastery in Paris	Clergy (priest-novice)
Lamiral; Saint-Benoît; Université (Saint-Vaast)	Debucholic, Nicolas	Saint-Barthélemy	Healthy	Augustins	In the family tomb	none	none	Witness to will has ties to noble of the League	University/ Liberal professions (bachelier in the law faculty)

Lamiral; Saint-Benoît; Université (Fardeau)	Dufour, Toussainct	Saint-Etienne-du-Mont	Healthy	Left to executor	Left to executor	none	none	Executor is Seize curate	University/Liberal professions (regent, College Sainte Barbe, Université of Paris)
Lamiral; Saint-Benoît; Université	Laurent, Marye	Saint-Jacques-de-la-Boucherie	Healthy	Saints-Innocents	Near her husband	none	Bodily performativity; Liturgical performativity; Sacraments taken	League cleric at funeral	Honorable/ Bourgeoisie (bookseller)
Lamiral; Saint-Benoît; Université	Prenost, Marie	Saint-Etienne-du-Mont	Sick	Unknown	Testator omits all burial information	none	none	In Descimon/ Barnavi: identified as a Leaguer	Artisan (cord/rope maker)
Lamiral; Saint-Benoît; Université	Rolland, Geneviève	Saint-Séverin	Healthy	In parish church where she dies	none	none	Clerical intervention without testator; Bodily performativity; Liturgical performativity; banquet, concern for intelligibility of sacraments, symbolic construction of community	Relative in Descimon/ Barnavi identified as a Leaguer	Honorable/ Bourgeoisie (bourgeois de Paris)
Landry; No parish given; Ville	Lynden, Théodore	Saint-Germain-l'Auxerrois	Sick	Unknown	Testator omitted all burial information	none	none	Foreign Catholic noble soldier; Executor is the duke of Parma	Titled Nobility (viscount of Dorvial, "gentleman of the chamber of the duke of Parma, Lt. Governor and captain general of his Catholic lord in . . . the Low Countries")

Notary; Parish;* Part of Town; (Second Notary to sign when known)	Testator	Testator's Parish	State of Health	Special Burial Institution Requested	Location for Burial Requested	Sacralizing Headings	Examples of Performativity	Evidence of League Connections	Socio-Professional Category and (Profession)
Landry; Ville (Levasseur)	Thiersault, Marye	Saint-Germain-l'Auxerrois	Healthy	Saint-Germain-l'Auxerrois	In the family tomb	none	Lights; Bodily performativity; Liturgical performativity; Provides for religious education/ concerned about intelligibility of the sacraments; Symbolic construction of community	Bequest to someone identified in the Descimon/Barnavi corpus as a Leaguer	Noble office/ epithet (councilor, notary, secretary to the king, and one of four notaries and secretaries of Parlement)
Le Roux; Saint-Eustache; Ville	Francisque, Geneviève	Saint-Eustache	Healthy	Saint-Eustache	"In the masonry work of the church. . . near the place where Father Jehan was accustomed to stand"	No special heading	Lights; Bodily performativity; Liturgical performativity; Offrande	Detailed attention paid to material organization of funeral; Masses at each church of the four mendicant orders for one year	Soldiers (archer of the king's bodyguards)
Leroy; Saint-Germain-l'Auxerrois; Ville	De Pomereau, Marguerite	Saint-Germain-l'Auxerrois	Sick	Saints-Innocents	Near the Virgin, beside her mother, in front of the image of Our Lady	none	Clerical intervention requested without Testator's presence required	Bequest to League cleric	Middle/Lower Offical (paymaster of the sieur of Brissac)

Lusson; La Madeleine; Cité	Petit, Françoise	Saint-Gervais	Sick	Sainte-Croix	Left to executor	No special heading	Lights	Gives painting of Crucifix and Passion	Artisans (daughter of a deceased master butcher)
Lybault; Saint-Merri; Ville	Christin, Pierre	Saint-Jean-en-Grève	Sick	Augustins	none	none	none	League cleric	University/Liberal professions (doctor of theology in the theology faculty)
Monthenault; Saint-Gervais; Ville (Motelet)	Hervy, Jehan	Saint-Jean-en-Grève	Sick	Saint-Jean-en-Grève	Place for curés	none	Sacraments taken	League cleric: curate of St.-Jean-en-Grève	University/Liberal professions (priest, curate, doctor of theology)
Peron; Saint-Etienne-du-Mont; Ville	Delacourt, Ysabel	Saint-Leu/Saint-Gilles	Sick	Saint-Nicolas-des-Champs	Near the chapelle de saint Denis	none	Bodily performativity; Lights	League cleric at funeral	Honorable/Bourgeosie (marchand et bourgeois de Paris)
Robinot; Saint-Nicolas-des-Champs; Ville (Thibert)	Debriays, Gabriel	Saint-Nicolas-des-Champs	Sick	Saint-Nicolas-des-Champs	none	none	none	Employed by a noble of the League	Soldier (marshal in charge of the accommodations for the army of the duke of Mayenne)
Saint-Vaast; Saint-Benoît; Université (Lamiral)	de Mombron, René	Unknown	Sick	College de Lisieux	" . . . in the chapel of the aforementioned college of Lysieux . . . "	none	Sunday school classes and Eucharist for seigneurial parish	Native of Brittany, probable League connections	University/Liberal professions (escuier, seigneur, "presently a student")

Notary; Parish;* Part of Town; (Second Notary to sign when known)	Testator	Testator's Parish	State of Health	Special Burial Institution Requested	Location for Burial Requested	Sacralizing Headings	Examples of Performativity	Evidence of League Connections	Socio-Professional Category and (Profession)
Saint-Vaast; Saint-Benoît; Université	Lamyral, Philippe (Lamiral)	Saint-Benoît	Sick	Mathurins	"... in the nave of the church of the Mathurins, at the door and entrance of the chapel of Saint-Roch..."	none	Bodily performativity	Bequest to League cleric	Gens de Loi (notary of the king at the Châtelet)
Troyes; Saint-André-des-Arts; Université (Chauvet)	Brunet, Marye	Saint-André-des-Arts	Sick	Saint-André-des-Arts	none	Cross at the top of the page	Bodily performativity; Liturgical performativity; Symbolic act sacralizes	League cleric at funeral	Gens de Loi (barrister in the Parlement)
Troyes; Saint-André-des-Arts; Université	Debonacoursy, Laurens	Saint-Séverin	Sick	Cordeliers	In the choir near the cloister	Cross at the top of the page	Sacraments taken; Symbolic act sacralizes	League cleric at funeral	Clergy (abbot)
Troyes; Saint-André-des-Arts; Université (Chauvet)	Galloys, Barbe	Saint-Sulpice	Sick	Saint-Sulpice	none	Jesus ... Maria	Symbolic act sacralizes	Employed by a noble of the League	Soldier (in the guards of a high noble)
Troyes; Saint-André-des-Arts; Université	Hennequin, Pierre	Saint-André-des-Arts	Sick	Saint-André-des-Arts	none	Jesus ... Maria	Symbolic act sacralizes	Has relative in Descimon/Barnavi identified as a Leaguer	Noble office/epithet

| Troyes; Saint-André-des-Arts; Université (Chauvet) | Megaly, Sébastien | Saint-Séverin | Sick | Saint-Séverin | none | Cross at the top of the page | Symbolic act sacralizes | Employed by a noble of the League | Clergy (priest, former chaplain of Mary Queen of Scots) |

* As this book was going to press, additional parish addresses were supplied but could not be included.
1. Testator spelling of Saint-Merri.
2. Descimon, Qui, 164.
3. Barnavi, Le Parti, 370.
4. See detailed discussion of this testator in Chapter 6.

Appendix E
Mastery Notary Chart, 1590

Notary Name Dates of Practice (* indicates notary with 9 or more testators)	Notary Address	Notary Parish	Total Wills	Number League Testators[1]	League Status of Notary	Used by League Printers[2]	Exite Procurations of 1594[3]	Co-Signs With League Notary	Performativity Ranking	In 1540 or 1630
Arragon, Louis* 1587–1622	rue Saint-Jacques-de-la-Boucherie	Saint-Jacques-de-la-Boucherie	22	1	Strong League presumption	Yes	No	No	73%	No
Aymeray, François 1585–1594	près l'église Saint-Eustache, puis à Saint-Denis-en-France	Saint-Eustache	0	0	?	—	—	—	—	—
Beaufort, Claude de 1568–1605	rue Saint-Honoré, paroisse Saint-Germain-l'Auxerrois	Saint-Germain-l'Auxerrois	6	3	Strong League presumption	No	No	Nicolas Leroy	Fewer than 9 clients, not ranked	No
Becquet, Jean 1585–1590	rue Saint-André-des-Arts	Saint-André-des-Arts	1	0	?	No	No	No	Fewer than 9 clients, not ranked	No
Belot, Pierre 1586–1594	rue Saint-Jacques	Saint-Séverin	0	0	?	Yes	—	—	—	—
Bergeon, François* 1573–1630	rue Saint-Denis, paroisse Saint-Merri, puis rue Barre-du-Bec	Saint-Merri	17	1	?	No	No	R. Bontemps	53%	Yes
Bernard, Clément* 1582–1600	rue de la Harpe	Saint-Séverin	12	1	Strong League affiliation presumption	No	No	No	67%	No

Name / dates	Address	Parish			League status			Relationship	Percent	
Bontemps, Mathieu* 1585–1621	rue Saint-André-des-Arts	Saint-André-des-Arts	13	4	League-affiliated	No	No	Marc Bruyère	25%	No
Bontemps, Raoul* 1569–1617	rue des Canettes, paroisse de la Madeleine	La Madeleine	22	2	Emprunt of 1590, *Seize* financing[5]	No	No	B. Dumarc, H. Lybault, M. Bontemps	59%	No
Bruyère, Marc* 1583–1591	à Saint-Germain-des-Prés	faubourg Saint-Germain	10	4	League-affiliated	No	No	M. Bontemps	50%	No
Chapelain, Sébastien 1586–1612	rue Saint-Martin, au coin de la ruelle de Venise	Saint-Merri	5	0	?	No	No	No	Fewer than 9 clients, not ranked	No
Chapellain, Jean* l'aîné, seigneur de Billy et de Louainville 1580–1623	pointe Saint-Eustache	Saint-Eustache	19	0	?	No	No	—	53%	No
Charles, Jean* 1581–1635	place Maubert	Saint-Etienne-du-Mont	34	5	League-affiliated	No	Yes	—	21%	Yes
Chartain, Lambert 1553–1590	rue Saint-Honoré, place aux Chats	Saint-Eustache	3	3	Strong League presumption	No	No	—	Fewer than 9 clients, not ranked	No
Chauvet, François 1582–1591	au bout du pont Saint-Michel	Unknown	5	0	?	No	No	—	Fewer than 9 clients, not ranked	No
Chazeretz, Jean 1577–1605	rue Saint-Denis	Unknown	6	0	?	No	No	—	Fewer than 9 clients, not ranked	No
Chefdeville, René* 1577–1602	près les Halles	Saint-Eustache	10	1	?	No	No	—	20%	No

Notary Name Dates of Practice (* indicates notary with 9 or more testators)	Notary Address	Notary Parish	Total Wills	Number League Testators[1]	League Status of Notary	Used by League Printers[2]	Exite Procurations of 1594[3]	Co-Signs With League Notary	Performativity Ranking	In 1540 or 1630
Contenot, Nicolas* 1587–1603	rue Saint-Honoré, au coin de la rue Tirechappe	Unknown	10	1	?	No	No	—	40%	No
Contesse, René II 1586–1644	rue des Fossés-Saint-Germain-l'Auxerrois	Saint-Germain-l'Auxerrois	2	0	?	No	No	Tulloue	Fewer than 9 clients, not ranked	Yes
Cothereau, Jean 1583–1597	rue de la Harpe	Unknown	1	0	?	Yes	No	—	Fewer than 9 clients, not ranked	No
Cothereau, Philippe* 1578–1613	rue de la Calandre	Unknown	27	4	Strong League presumption	Yes	No	—	44%	Yes
Croiset, François* 1559–1601	rue de la Vieille-Draperie	Unknown	10	6	Strong League presumption	No	No	—	30%	No
Des Quatrevaulx, Antoine* 1579–1617	rue de l'Arbre-Sec, au coin de la rue d'Avron	Saint-Germain-l'Auxerrois	13	0	?	No	No	Montherault	23%	No
Doujat, Pierre 1583–1623	rue Comtesse d'Artois	Unknown	6	1	?	No	No	—	Fewer than 9 clients, not ranked	No
Dumarc, Barthélemy 1569–1590	rue Saint-Jacques	Saint-Benoît	1	0	?	No	No	Yes	Fewer than 9 clients, not ranked	No

Name	Address	Parish			League affiliation			Clients	%	
Dunesmes, Jacques II 1590–1596	rue de l'Arbre-Sec près la Croix-du-Trahoir	Unknown	7	2	?	No	No	Des Quatrevaulx, Monthenault	Fewer than 9 clients, not ranked	Yes
Fardeau, Jacques* 1581–1629	rue Saint-Jacques	Saint-Séverin	9	2	Strong League presumption	Yes	No	Belot, Saint-Vaast	56%	Yes
Ferrant, Charles 1582–1611	rue Saint-Honoré, au coin de la rue des Bourdonnais	Unknown	5	3	Strong League presumption	No	No	Contenot	Fewer than 9 clients, not ranked	No
Filesac, Claude* 1589–1611	rue Saint-Martin	Saint-Nicolas-des-Champs	19	0	?	No	No	Herbin, Peron	21%	Yes
Girault, Alexandre 1588–1604	rue des Marmousets	La Madeleine	6	0	?	No	No	—	Fewer than 9 clients, not ranked	No
Goguier, Henri* 1576–1591	place Baudoyer	Unknown	19	0	?	No	No	Le Roux	11%	No
Haultdesens, Laurent 552–1596	rue de la Fontaine-Maubué	Unknown	4	0	?	No	No	Thevenin	Fewer than 9 clients, not ranked	Yes
Herbin, François* 1569–1592	rue Saint-Antoine	Saint-Gervais	22	5	League affiliated	No	Yes	Girault, de Poche, Monthenault, Lenormant	41%	No
Jacques, Martin* 1581–1605	rue des Marmousets	La Madeleine	19	1	?	No	No	—	37%	No
Jourdan, Claude 1576–1606	rue Saint-Honoré	Unknown	5	3	Strong League presumption	No	No	Filesac, Leroy	Fewer than 9 clients, not ranked	No

Notary Name Dates of Practice (* indicates notary with 9 or more testators)	Notary Address	Notary Parish	Total Wills	Number League Testators[1]	League Status of Notary	Used by League Printers[2]	Exite Procurations of 1594[3]	Co-Signs With League Notary	Performativity Ranking	In 1540 or 1630
La Barde, Simon de* 1588–1604	rue Saint-Christophe, puis au Marché-Neuf	Saint-Christophe	13	0	?	Yes	No	Girault, Filesac	0%	No
Lamiral, Philippe* 1555–1590	rue Saint-Jacques	Unknown	16	5	League affiliated	Yes	No	Saint-Vaast, Fardeau	31%	No
Landry, Jacques* 1568–1600	rue de la Tabletterie, au coin de la rue de la Harengerie.	Unknown	12	2	Strong League presumption	No	No	—	42%	No
Le Camus, Jean/Chantemerle, Denis, son beau-père 1578–1601	rue des Prouvaires, à la Corne de cerf (en association)	Saint-Eustache	8	0	?	No	No	Yes	Fewer than 9 clients, not ranked	No
Lemoyne, Olivier/Babynet, Hugues 1580–1590	rue Saint-Séverin	Saint-Séverin	8	0	?	No	No	—	Fewer than 9 clients, not ranked	No
Lenormant, Jean le jeune 1586–1618	place Baudoyer	Unknown	1	0	?	No	No	de Poche	Fewer than 9 clients, not ranked	No
Le Roux, Pierre 1589–1630	pointe Saint-Eustache	Saint-Eustache	7	1	?	No	No	—	Fewer than 9 clients, not ranked	Yes

Name	Address	Parish								
Leroy, Nicolas 1571–1610	rue Saint-Germain-l'Auxerrois	Saint-Germain-l'Auxerrois	8	1	?	No	No	—	Fewer than 9 clients, not ranked	Yes
Le Vasseur, François* 1582–1620	rue du Temple	Saint-Nicolas-des-Champs	15	0	?	No	No	—	13%	No
Lusson, Jean I* 1566–1599	rue des Marmousets, au Chef Saint-Jean	La Madeleine	18	1	?	No	No	—	22%	No
Lybault, Hilaire* 1580–1621	rue Barre-du-Bec	Saint-Merri	17	1	League affiliated	No	Yes	Bergeon	35%	Yes
Mahieu, Martin* 1569–1612	rue des Arcis	Saint-Pierre-des-Arcis	13	0	?	No	No	—	39%	No
Maigret, Jérôme 1575–1596	cloître Sainte-Opportune	Sainte-Opportune	3	0	?	No	No	—	Fewer than 9 clients, not ranked	No
Monthenault, Laurent de* 1579–1619	rue de Barres	Saint-Gervais	11	1	Strong League presumption	No	No	Yes	73%	Yes
Motelet, Jean 1588–1614	rue de la Verrerie, près le Petit-Saint-Antoine, puis au carrefour Guillori	Saint-Jean-en-Grève	10	0	?	No	No	—	0%	No
Muret, Jean* 1585–1614	rue Saint-Côme, puis rue Comtesse d'Artois	Saint-Côme	10	0	?	No	No	—	50%	No

Notary Name Dates of Practice (* indicates notary with 9 or more testators)	Notary Address	Notary Parish	Total Wills	Number League Testators[1]	League Status of Notary	Used by League Printers[2]	Exite Procurations of 1594[3]	Co-Signs With League Notary	Performativity Ranking	In 1540 or 1630
Parque, Edme* 1565–1603	rue de la Ferronnerie	Unknown	23	0	?	No	No	—	35%	Yes
Peron, Cléophas* 1555–1599	rue aux Ours	Unknown	41	1	?	No	No	—	29%	No
Périer, Mathurin* 1589–1626	place Maubert, au Cheval blanc	Saint-Etienne-du-Mont	15	0	?	Yes	No	—	20%	Yes
Poche, Jean de* 1579–1598	à la porte Baudoyer	Saint-Gervais	21	0	Strong League presumption	No	No	Yes	71%	No
Privé, Nicolas 1581–1604	rue Saint-Antoine, près le cimetière Saint-Jean	Saint-Jean	6	0	?	No	No	—	Fewer than 9 clients, not ranked	No
Robinot, Nicolas* 1588–1546	rue du Temple	Saint-Nicolas-des-Champs	10	1	?	No	No	Yes	20%	Yes
Rossignol, Pierre de 1578–1613	rue Saint-Antoine	Unknown	6	0	?	No	No	Goguyer, de Poche	Fewer than 9 clients, not ranked	No
Saint-Fussien, Valeran de 1585–1610	rue de l'Arbre-Sec	Saint-Germain-l'Auxerrois	3	0	?	No	No	Des Quatrevaulx, Machevelle	Fewer than 9 clients, not ranked	Yes
Saint-Vaast, Jacques de* 1589–1637	rue Saint-Jacques	Saint-Benoît	15	2	Strong League presumption	Yes	No	—	27%	Yes

Name	Address	Parish								
Thevenin, Jean* 1588–1631	rue aux Ours, puis rue Saint-Martin	Saint-Merri	10	0	?	No	No	—	50%	Yes
Trouvé, Claude* 1566–1606	rue Saint-Antoine	Saint-Paul	10	0	?	No	No	Goguyer	50%	Yes
Troyes, Claude I de* 1583–1625	rue Saint-André-des-Arts	Saint-André-des-Arts	11	5	Strong League presumption	No	No	Yes	82%	Yes
Tulloue, Philippe* 1576–1618	rue Saint-Germain-l'Auxerrois, au coin de la rue de Lavandières	Saint-Germain-l'Auxerrois	17	0	?	No	No	—	29%	Yes
Vachot, Philippe 1586–1604	rue de la Chanvrerie	Unknown	3	0	?	No	No	—	Fewer than 9 clients, not ranked	No
Viard, Pierre 1588–1623	rue Saint-Antoine	Saint-Paul	3	0	?	No	No	Babynet, Thevenin, Goguyer	Fewer than 9 clients, not ranked	No

1. Leaguer status of clients only as determined by criteria for Leaguers in Table 5.2.

2. See Denis Pallier, *Recherches sur l'imprimerie à Paris pendant la ligue (1585–1594)* (Geneva: Librairie Droz, 1976), 196, who lists those notaries consistently used by League printers. See Table 5.8, "Notaries Listed in Denis Pallier," for further details.

3. In 1594 Henri IV exiled the most intransigent Leaguers from Paris. Before they left the city, they needed to draw up procurations, or documents that allowed others to conduct their business in their stead. Two League-affiliated notaries, François Herbin and Hilaire Lybault, drew up these exile procurations.

4. The percentages indicate what percentage of a notary's testators had at least one occurrence of performativity. Only notaries with 9 or more testators were included in this calculation. See Appendix F for "The Overall Performativity Rankings for Notaries, 1590."

5. R. Bontemps drew up loan documents, which helped to finance the *Seize* movement in the summer of 1590. See Robert Descimon, *Qui étaient les Seize? Mythes et réalités de la Ligue parisienne (1585–1594)* (Paris: Klincksieck 1983), 80 n. 124, for these loans ("*Emprunts*").

Appendix F
Overall Performativity Ranking for Notaries, 1590

(Thirty-seven of 72 notaries had nine or more cases. Percentages reflect numbers of clients with at least one instance of performativity.)

Notaries	Number of Testators	League affiliation in clientele	General Performativity	Show of Immanence	Mention of the Body of Jesus Christ	Mention by Testator of Own Body	Liturgical Details	Use of Liturgical Calendar	Connected to Jesuits, Capuchins or Feuillants	Reformist Traits
Averages for Performativity			39%	21%	9%	18%	6%	8%	4%	1%
Arragon	22	1	73%	23%	9%	23%	5%	5%	0%	0%
Bergeon	17	1	53%	18%	6%	18%	0%	0%	6%	0%
Bernard[l]	12	2	75%	17%	17%	25%	17%	8%	0%	0%
Bontemps, M.	12	4	25%	0%	0%	8%	0%	8%	0%	0%
Bontemps, R. ‡[2]	22	22	59%	27%	5%	27%	5%	5%	27%	9%
Bruyère ‡	10	4	50%	20%	10%	27%	10%	10%	0%	0%
Chapellain, J.	19	0	53%	16%	11%	32%	5%	11%	0%	0%
Charles	34	5	21%	24%	6%	0%	0%	3%	3%	0%
Chefdeville	10	1	20%	10%	0%	10%	0%	10%	0%	0%
Contenot	10	1	40%	10%	10%	30%	10%	10%	10%	0%
Cothereau, P.	27	4	44%	48%	7%	19%	0%	4%	7%	0%
Croiset	10	6	30%	0%	20%	20%	10%	0%	10%	0%
Desquatrevaulx	13	0	23%	15%	0%	8%	8%	8%	0%	0%
Fardeau, J.	9	2	56%	11%	22%	22%	5%	0%	0%	0%
Filesac	19	0	21%	11%	5%	11%	5%	0%	0%	0%
Goguyer	19	0	11%	11%	0%	0%	0%	0%	0%	0%
Herbin	22	5	41%	27%	0%	14%	9%	18%	9%	0%
Jacques	19	[1]	37%	26%	0%	21%	16%	11%	0%	0%
Labarde	13	0	0%	0%	0%	0%	0%	0%	0%	0%

Lamiral	16	5	31%	44%	25%	13%	13%	6%	6%	6%
Landry	12	2	42%	50%	33%	25%	17%	33%	17%	8%
Levasseur	15	0	13%	7%	33%	0%	13%	7%	0%	0%
Lusson	18	1	22%	0%	6%	11%	0%	6%	6%	0%
Lybault	17	1	35%	12%	6%	18%	0%	6%	0%	0%
Mahieu	13	0	39%	23%	8%	85%	8%	23%	8%	0%
Monthenault	11	1	73%	9%	37%	18%	0%	9%	9%	0%
Muret	10	0	50%	30%	0%	50%	10%	10%	0%	0%
Parque	23	0	35%	17%	4%	0%	4%	13%	4%	4%
Périer	15	0	20%	60%	7%	7%	7%	12%	0%	7%
Peron	41	1	29%	17%	10%	24%	0%	0%	0%	0%
Poche	21	0	71%	5%	10%	10%	10%	5%	0%	0%
Robinot	10	1	20%	10%	0%	20%	0%	10%	0%	7%
Saint-Vaast	15	2	27%	60%	13%	7%	13%	10%	0%	0%
Thévenin	10	0	50%	33%	10%	40%	0%	20%	0%	0%
Trouvé	10	0	50%	20%	10%	10%	10%	10%	0%	0%
Troyes	11	5	82%	27%	0%	18%	0%	0%	9%	9%
Tulloue	17	0	29%	29%	6%	12%	6%	6%	0%	0%

1. *Italics* = University location.

2. ‡ = University-affiliated notary.

Appendix G
The World of Leaguer Preachers and Clerics

LEGEND

1. Name of testator and dates of birth and death
    1 Testator's parish
    2 State of health
    3 Education
    4 Socio-professional status
    5 Reputation as orator
    6 Ties to the League
    7 Date of the will
    8 Notary, notary's parish, number of Leaguer testators
    9 Co-signing notary and/or witnesses
    10 Executor
    11 Notable bequests
    12 Other sources
    13 Burial location

1. HERVY, Jehan (?–June 1590)

1. Saint-Jean-en-Grève (*Ville*)
2. Healthy
3. *Docteur en théologie (faculté de Paris)*
4. *Curé* of Saint-Jean-en-Grève
5. Not available
6. Nature of ties to League
    1 Use of notary Monthenault in Leaguer parish Saint-Gervais
    2 Witness: Guillaume Rose, Bishop of Senlis
    3 Recipient of 50 *écus* from Madame Guise
7. 17 May 1590 (this is a holograph will)
8. Monthenault, Saint-Gervais, 1 Leaguer testator
9. Witness Guillaume Rose
10. His brother, Sire Andre Hervy and "*mon bon ami et voisin*" Sieur Givery
11. Notable Bequests:
    1 To Feuillants, "*50 écus owed him by Madame Guise*" (see L'Estoile below)
    2 Bureaux des Pauvres; Hôtel Dieu
    3 To Collège de Navarre (sum not quantified) to purchase a silver cross for processions
12. "*Il n'était que pédant, mais la race félonne*
    De rebelles Guisards s'armant contre leurs rois,
    Sa fortune grandit, et l'éclat de sa voix
    Servit à ébranler l'Etat et la couronne. . . .
    . . . Il devint de dépit malade et furieux,
    Et d'une prompte mort il prévint, malheureux,
    L'honneur qui l'attendait d'être évêque en chemise"
    (L'Estoile, *Journal*, June 1590, p. 53) (and see entry for Pigenat below)
13. Parish church in place for "*curés*"

2. GINCESTRE, Jehan

1. Saint-Gervais (*Ville*)

2. Sick
3. *Docteur en théologie*
4. "*Prebstre, docteur en théologie et curé de la cure de l'église Monsieur Saint-Gervais*. . . ."
5. See L'Estoile
6. The chief link between the University and the parish of Saint Gervais in the *Ville*
7. 10 September 1590
8. Herbin (Herbin and Lybault drew up the exile procurations of 1594), Saint Gervais, 5 Leaguer testators
9. Senault (famous Leaguer whose descendant becomes a priest of the *Oratoire*)
   1 Will dictated "*au nom de la saincte Trinite*"
10. Executor—*noble homme* M. *Pierre Acarye, conseiller du roy*
11. Notable bequests:
    1 *Oeuvre et fabrique* "50 escus d'or soleil"
    2 "*Jour de son trespas soit . . . donné aux pauvres de la paroisse la somme de trois escus vingt solz tz*"
    3 *l'Hôtel Dieu de Paris 20 écus*
    4 Wants returned all the books given him by the *commissaire* Le Norman
    5 Also return the chest of books loaned him by *maistre* Anthoine Cartier
12. Not available
13. Parish church "*en la grande chappelle nostre dame*"

3. CHRISTIN, Pierre

1. Saint-Jean-en-Grève, presently
2. Sick
3. *Noble et scientiffique personne, docteur en theologie*
4. See above
5. "The Eloquence of Demosthenes," Pierre Cornéio, *Siege de Paris, 1590*
6. All funeral arrangements left to "*Madame la duchesse de Nemours, sa maistresse*"
   1 Use of notary Lybault creates a link to the world of the basoche (Gens de Loi); see Table 6.1 for socio-professional status of Lybault clients
7. 7 October 1590
8. Lybault, (drew up the exile procurations of 1594 with notary Herbin), St-Merri, 1 Leaguer testator
9. Bergeon
10. *Noble homme maistre Anthoine Hennequin, seigneur d'Assy*
11. Notable Bequests:
    1 Regarding the sum of 2,000 *livres* from the revenues of the archbishop of Auch, he demands nothing and let any available amount be used "*à oeuvres pyes ou pour prier dieu pour l'âme dudict testateur*"
12. Not available
13. Augustinian monastery, Paris (linked to Mendicants)

4. MASSE, Asdrubal (dates unknown)

1. Saint-Jean-en-Grève
2. Sick
3. Not given
4. "*Chevalier de l'ordre de Saint Jehan de Jherusalem, natif de la ville de Rome aage de vingt cinq ans ou plus*"
5. Not available

6.   See 12 below: on his crusading order
7.   6 November 1590
8.   R. Bontemps, La Madeleine, 22 Leaguer testators (chief Leaguer notary)
9.   Dumarc (Saint Benoît)
10.   His brother, Cimo Massé
11.   Notable bequests:
       1   Masses at Nostre Dame de Lorette
12.   Other sources:
       1   The commander of his crusading order, Jean Moreo is said to be "a special agent of Philip II." Moreo is described as "*consommé dans l'art d'acheter les volontes, [and] sut gagner le duc de Guise et le rendre espagnol de coeur*" (L'Estoile, *Journal*, 1590, p. 8)
13.   Parish of Saint Christopher

5. PIGENAT, François (?–June 1590)

1.   Saint-Nicolas-des-Champs
2.   Not known
3.   Not available
4.   *Curé* of Saint-Nicolas des Champs (seized control of this parish after the Day of the Barricade)
5.   Gave the funeral oration in Nôtre-Dame Cathedral for the slain Guise brothers
6.   Trained at the University of Paris
7.   Not available
8.   Not known
9.   Not known
10.   Not known
11.   None
12.   Other sources:
       1   "*En ce mois, moururent à Paris Pigenat, curé de Saint-Nicolas des Champs, un des tonnants prédicateurs de la Ligue et des confidents et appointés de madame de Montpensier et du légat; auquel tint compagnie le curé de Saint-Jean de même ligue et humeur; et furent tous deux plaisamment pasquillés et honorés dessuivants tombeaux. . . .*" (see Hervy, Jehan above) (L'Estoile, *Journal* vol. I, pp. 52–53)
       2   "*Le curé de Saint-Jean mourant*
           A témoigné sa sodomie,
           Et Pigenat mourut criant:
           Je n'ai prêché que menterie!"
           (L'Estoile, *Journal*, June 1590, p. 53)
13.   Not available

6. MEGALY, Sebastien

1.   Saint-Séverin
2.   Sick
3.   "*Prebstre, aulmosnier de la feue Royne d'ecosse et de monseigneur le duc de Mayne*"
4.   *Venerable et discrette personne me*
5.   Not given
6.   Employed by a league noble, i.e., the leader the Duke of Mayenne
7.   10 November 1590
8.   Claude Troyes, Saint-André-des-Arts, 5 Leaguer testators

9. Chauvet
10. *Noble homme* Claude de Ryeeux
11. Notable Bequests:
    1 Declares he gave for safekeeping to noble homme maistre Ph. le Meau *"secretaire du deffunct cardinal de Guise 5 coffres de bahutz"* containing clothing, books, etc.
    2 Sell all these items for execution of this will and any left over goes to this executor for their good services and aid during his illness
    3 As for the rest of his *"biens, meubles, et immeubles,"* gives them to his brothers and sisters, natives of Tourbye near town of Nisse and pray to God for him, *"parens et amyes trespasses"*
12. Not available
13. Present parish or Saint-Séverin or whatever parish executors recommend

Testator Members of the University Milieu

Testator Name	Testator Parish and Part of Town	Testator Notary and Notary Address	Testator Socio-Professional Category and Profession	Testator League Status
University profession/affiliated				
David, Vincent	Saint-Christophe	Jacques; Cité	University/liberal professions (*sieur*)	No League connection
Lefebvre, Jacques	Saint-Benoît	Thevenin; Ville	University/liberal professions (*prebstre docteur theologe*)	Notary has probable League affiliation
Regnault, Simon	Saint-Etienne-du-Mont	Périer; Université	University/liberal professions (*maistre es arts*)	No League connection
Lemaire, Jacques	Saint-Leu Saint-Gilles	Maigret; Ville	University/liberal professions (*escolier, estudiant*)	No League connection
Symony, Richard	Saint-Etienne-du-Mont	Babynet; Université	University/liberal professions (*escolier, estudiant*)	No League connection
Massot, Augustin	Saint-Séverin	Chauvet; Université	University/liberal professions (*estudiant*)	No League connection
Certain, Pierre	Saint-Séverin	Chauvet; Université	University/liberal professions (*petit bedeau*)	No League connection
Legoux, Pierre	Saint-Benoît	Lamiral; Université	University/liberal professions (*prebstre curé, grand bedeau fac. theologie*)	Uses Leaguer notary, Lamiral
Debucholic, Nicolas	Saint-Barthélemy	Lamiral; Université	University/liberal professions (*bachelier en la faculté de droit*)	Witness ties noble League
Faure, Francoyse	Saint-Benoît	Lamiral; Université	University/liberal professions (*lecteur es droitz*)	No League connection
DeVilliers, Jacques	Saint-Etienne-du-Mont	Lamiral; Université	University/liberal professions (*maistre es arts université de Paris, boursier, theologien et procureur college des Choletz*)	League-affiliated notary
Faber, Jacques	Saint-Benoît	Lamiral; Université	University/liberal professions (*docteur regent faculté theologie*)	League-affiliated notary
Gincestre, Jehan	Saint-Gervais	Herbin; Ville	Clergy; University/liberal professions (*prebstre curé docteur theologie*)	League cleric; uses Herbin as notary
Barne Ville, Pierre	Saint-Benoît	Herbin; Ville	University/liberal professions (*maistre es arts, teacher petite ecole*)	Herbin did exile procurations of 1594
Bertrault, Jehan	Saint-Jean-en-Grève	Herbin; Ville	University/liberal professions (*regent au college du couvent des Billettes*)	Herbin did exile procurations of 1594
Saultier, Ayme	Saint-Benoît	Fardeau; Université	University/liberal professions (*escuyer, de present escolier estudiant*)	Possible League connections
Courtes, Gabriel	Saint-Benoît	Charles; Université	University/liberal professions (*estudiant*)	League-affiliated notary

Name	Parish	Notary	Profession	Notes
De Mombron, René	Unknown	Saint-Vaast; Université	University/liberal professions (*estudiant, escuyer, seigneur*)	League-affiliated notary
Prenost, Pierre	Saint-Benoît	Lamiral; Université	University/liberal professions (*prebstre et chapelain*)	League-affiliated notary
Dufour, Toussainct	Saint-Etienne-du-Mont	Lamiral; Université	University/liberal professions (*regent, college Sainte-Barbe université de Paris*)	Executor is a *Seize curé*
Delamer, Pierre	Saint-André-des-Arts	Bruyere; Faubourg	University/liberal professions (*maistre docteur, regent, faculté de médecine*)	In D/B[1]
Tronson, Catherine	Saint-André-des-Arts	Bruyere; Faubourg	University/liberal professions (*maistre docteur, regent, faculté de médecine*)	Bequest to League cleric; wife of Delamer
Christin, Pierre	Saint-Jean-en-Grève	Lybault; Ville	University/liberal professions (*docteur en la faculté de théologie*)	League cleric; uses Lybault as notary, who has highest concentration of *gens de loi* as clients
Hervy, Jehan	Saint-Jean-en-Grève	Monthenault; Ville	Clergy; University/liberal professions (*prebstre curé docteur theologie*)	League cleric
Darmys, Pierre	Saint-André-des-Arts	Troyes; Université	University/liberal professions (*es droits et precepteur*)	League-affiliated notary
Blanchard, Jehan	Unknown	Bontemps, R.; Cité	University/liberal professions (*escolier, estudiant*)	Raoul Bontemps is notary
Sicry, Francoys	Unknown	Bontemps, R.; Cité	University/liberal professions (*prebstre*)	Raoul Bontemps is notary
Chavasse, Baltasar	Saint-Benoît	Bontemps, R.; Cité	University/liberal professions (*regent, college université*)	Raoul Bontemps is notary
Malescot, Laurens	Unknown	Bontemps, R.; Cité	University/liberal professions (*docteur of a university faculty*)	Raoul Bontemps is notary
Auzanet, François	Saint-Benoît	Bontemps, R.; Cité	University/liberal professions (*escolier, estudiant*)	Raoul Bontemps is notary
Auvray, Pierre	Saint-Séverin	Bernard; Université	University/liberal professions (*prebstre-boursier*)	Notary with probable League affiliation

Bequests to University individual or organization

Name	Parish	Recipient	Profession	Notes
Cercellier, Claudet	Saint-Eustache, Ville	Doujat, Pierre; rue Comtesse d'Artois, Ville	Honorable/bourgeois (*marchand-espicier*)	No known League status
Christianon, Nicolas	Saints-Innocents, Ville	Parque, Edme; rue de la Ferronnerie, Ville	Clergy (*prebstre, curé*)	Curé of Saints-Innocents
Daubonnet, Marie	Saint-Eustache, Ville	Contenot, Nicolas; rue Saint-Honoré, au coin de la rue Tirechappe, Ville	Mixed merchants (*fripier*)	No known League status

Testator Name	Testator Parish and Part of Town	Testator Notary and Notary Address	Testator Socio-Professional Category and Profession	Testator League Status
Debucholicq, Georges	Saint-Sulpice, université	Cothereau, Philippe; rue de la Calandre, Cité	Nobles (*gentilhomme de la chambre de feu J. Cardinal de Lorraine*)	Employed by League
Dechampaigne, Marie	Saint-Etienne-du-Mont, université	Charles, Jean; place Maubert, Saint-Etienne-du-Mont, Université	Soldiers (*archer des gardes*)	Guise employs testator's spouse
Decompans, Tassine	Sainte-Croix	Croiset, François; rue de la Vieille-Draperie, Cité	Honorable/bourgeoisie (*drapier*)	Spouse is famous Leaguer
Duru, Anne	Saint-Pierre-des-Arcis	Croiset; Cité	Honorable/bourgeoisie Corps de Marchands (*grocer, apothecaire*)	League cleric at funeral; bequest to League cleric
Jacquemye, Jehanne	Saint-Séverin	Cothereau, P.; Cité	Honorable/bourgeoisie (*marchand and bourgeois de Paris*)	No League connection
Ledanoys, Nicole	Saint-Etienne-du-Mont	Fardeau; Université	Gens de loi (*avocat en parlement*)	Relative in D/B[1]
Moreau, Claude	Saint-Jacques-de-la-Boucherie	Cothereau, P.; Cité	Honorable/bourgeoisie (*bourgeois de Paris*)	No League connection
Parque, Claude	Saint-Gervais	Herbin; Ville	Honorable/bourgeoisie (*marchand et bourgeois de Paris*)	No League connection
Thibault, Jehan	Saint-Etienne-du-Mont	Charles; Université	Soldier; honorable/bourgeoisie (*epicier, apothecaire*)	No League connection
Ymbert, Marye	Saint-Paul	Mahieu; Ville	Middle & lower nobility; Nobles (squire and lt. in the artillery)	No League connection

Notary's part of town is University

Testator Name	Testator Parish and Part of Town	Testator Notary and Notary Address	Testator Socio-Professional Category and Profession	Testator League Status
Desgrange, Nicolle	Sainte-Opportune	Fardeau; Université	Artisans (*tondeur*)	No League connection
Debremes, Marthe	Saint-Séverin	Fardeau; Université	Honorable/bourgeoisie (*Corps de Marchands*) (*drapier*)	No League connection
Rochette, Marguerite	Saint-Séverin	Fardeau; Université	Gens de loi; Procureur (*practicien au palais*)	No League connection
Perrier, Julien	Saint-Séverin	Fardeau; Université	Master artisans (*tailleur d'habitz*)	No League connection
Macott, Marie	Saint-Séverin	Fardeau; Université	Independent female occupation; Servant	No League connection

Name	Parish		Occupation/Status	League connection
Levasseur, Guillaume	Saint-Nicolas-du-Chardonnet	Fardeau; Université	Clergy (*prebstre chanoine-caron*)	No League connection
Fournier, Gilles	Saint-Nicolas-du-Chardonnet	Charles; Université	Honorable/bourgeoisie (*marchand libraire*)	No League connection
Anevel, Martin	Saint-Nicolas-du-Chardonnet	Charles; Université	Honorable/bourgeoisie (*bourgeois de Paris*)	No League connection
Poutteau, Jacquette	Saint-Etienne-du-Mont	Charles; Université	Rural worker (*vigneron*)	No League connection
Buisson, Nicolle	Saint-Etienne-du-Mont	Charles; Université	Merchant (*marchand de chevaux*)	No League connection
Combault, Claude	Saint-Etienne-du-Mont	Charles; Université	Artisan (*mareschal*)	No League connection
Janotin, Barbe	Saint-Séverin	Charles; Université	Honorable/bourgeoisie (*bourgeois de Paris*)	League cleric at funeral
Blanchon, Loyse	Saint-Etienne-du-Mont	Charles; Université	Honorable/bourgeoisie (*marchand de vin*)	No League connection
Assart, Michel	Saint-Etienne-du-Mont	Charles; Université	Rural worker (*vigneron*)	No League connection
Hoyau, Jacqueline	Saint-Benoît	Charles; Université	Master artisans (*serrurier*)	League cleric at funeral
Broutesaulge, Anne	Saint-Etienne-du-Mont	Charles; Université	Mixed merchants (*boucher*)	No League connections
Nyon, Claude	Saint-Hilaire, Faubourg	Charles; Université	Artisan (*passementier-rubanier*)	No League connections
Lampereur, Marye	Saint-Etienne-du-Mont	Charles; Université	Master artisan (*tapissier*)	No League connections
Budé, Magdelene	Saint-Etienne-du-Mont	Charles; Université	Gens de loi; procureur (*procureur au Chastelet*)	No League connections
Symon, Claude	Saints-Innocents	Charles; Université	Mixed merchants (*marchand-ferronier*)	No League connections
Godet, Michel	Saint-Etienne-du-Mont	Charles; Université	Master artisan (*patissier-oublieur*)	No League connections
Courtes, Joseph	Saint-Etienne-du-Mont	Charles; Université	Middle/lower nobility (*escuyer, homme d'armes & capitaine d'une compaignie . . . pr sa majesté en l'armee catholicque*)	Foreign Catholic noble soldier
Maigret, Marcel	Saint-Etienne-du-Mont	Charles; Université	Honorable/bourgeoisie (*marchand et bourgeois de Paris*)	No League connections
Symeau, Marye	Saint-Etienne-du-Mont	Charles; Université	Honorable/bourgeoisie (*marchand de vin*)	No League connections
Nicolle, Christienne	Saint-Etienne-du-Mont	Charles; Université	Mixed merchants (*verrier-vendeur de verre et bouteilles*)	No League connections
Guyot, Jehan	Saint-Etienne-du-Mont	Charles; Université	Master artisan (*barbier-chirurgien*)	No League connections
Pinart, Jacques	Saint-Benoît	Charles; Université	Honorable/bourgeoisie (*Corps de marchands*) (*drapier*)	No League connections
Quartier, Anne	Saint-Etienne-du-Mont	Charles; Université	Honorable/bourgeoisie (*marchand de vin*)	No League connections
Bugnehain, Philippe	Saint-Etienne-du-Mont	Charles; Université	Honorable/bourgeoisie (*bourgeois de Paris*)	No League connections
Delaunay, Jehan	Saint-Etienne-du-Mont	Charles; Université	Gens de loi; Avocats (*avocat en parlement*)	No League connections
Rillon, Styppane	Saint-Etienne-du-Mont	Charles; Université	Titled nobility (*escuyer, gouverneur de Essy, royal administration*)	Ties noble League

Testator Name	Testator Parish and Part of Town	Testator Notary and Notary Address	Testator Socio-Professional Category and Profession	Testator League Status
Pocquart, Paulle	Saint-Etienne-du-Mont	Charles; Université	Master artisan (*potier d'etaing*)	Possible relation of *Seize*, nr. 187 in Decimon[1]
Laurens, Adrian	Saint-Etienne-du-Mont	Charles; Université	Honorable/bourgeoisie (*marchand et bourgeois de Paris*)	No League connections
Richard, Renée	Saint-Etienne-du-Mont	Charles; Université	Honorable/bourgeoisie (*bourgeois de Paris*)	No League connections
Langloix, Catherine	Saint-Séverin	Charles; Université	Soldier (*soldat*)	No League connections
Ruau, Gilette	Saint-Hilaire, Faubourg	Charles; Université	Master artisan (*tissutier-rubanier*)	No League connections
Constantin, Francoyse	Saint-Etienne-du-Mont	Charles; Université	Gens de loi; Procureur (*procureur en parlement*)	No League connections
Cruchot, Pierre	Saint-Benoît	Saint-Vaast; Université	Mixed merchants (*marchand/marchant*)	No League connections
Lamyral, Philippe	Saint-Benoît	Saint-Vaast; Université	Gens de loi; Notary & commissioner (*notaire au chastelet*)	Bequest to League cleric
Delalande, Anthoine	Saint-Benoît	Saint-Vaast; Université	Honorable/bourgeoisie (*Corps de Marchands*) (*marchand maistre espicier*)	No League connections
Charles, Jehanne	Saint-Benoît	Saint-Vaast; Université	Gens de loi; Notary & commissioner (*notaire*, outside Paris)	No League connections
David, Edme	Saint-Etienne-du-Mont	Saint-Vaast; Université	Rural worker (*vigneron*)	No League connections
Delahaye, Philippe	Saint-Benoît	Saint-Vaast; Université	Laboureur	No League connections
Lambert, Marie	Saint-Hilaire, Faubourg	Saint-Vaast; Université	Artisan (*barbier-chirurgien*)	No League connections
Ladvocat, Geneviève	Saint-Etienne-du-Mont	Saint-Vaast; Université	Honorable/bourgeoisie (*bourgeois de Paris*)	No League connections
Coullon, Jehan	Saint-Séverin	Saint-Vaast; Université	Laboureur (*laboureur en vigne*)	No League connections
Challmyer, Estienette	Saint-Benoît	Saint-Vaast; Université	Honorable/bourgeoisie (*imprimeur*)	No League connections
Daimall, Jehanne	Saint-Benoît	Saint-Vaast; Université	Independent female occupation; Servant	No League connections
Moreau, Claude	Saint-Benoît	Saint-Vaast; Université	Honorable/bourgeoisie (*marchand et bourgeois de Paris*)	No League connections
Brigrand, Francoys	Saint-Nicolas-des-Champs	Saint-Vaast; Université	Middle/lower official (*suivant les finances*)	No League connections
Chambaude, Loys	Saint-Benoît	Saint-Vaast; Université	Soldier (*homme d'armes de la compaignie de . . .*)	No League connections
Caille, Margueritte	Saint-Etienne-du-Mont	Périer; Université	Laboureur	No League connections
Arnoul, Julliene	Saint-Etienne-du-Mont	Périer; Université	Artisan (*boucher*)	No League connections
Boissy, Claude	Saint-Etienne-du-Mont	Périer; Université	Laboureur	No League connections
Langlois, Jehanne	Saint-Nicolas-du-Chardonnet	Périer; Université	Mixed merchants (*marchand/marchant*)	No League connections

Name	Parish	Affiliation	Status/Occupation	League connections
Defleury, Anne	Saint-Etienne-du-Mont	Périer; Université	Titled nobility (*maître d'ho=el ordinaire de sa majesté*)	No League connections
Haultemps, [illegible]	Saint-Etienne-du-Mont	Périer; Université	Gens de loi; Procureur (*pro=ureur en parlement*)	No League connections
Coulonque, Claude	Saint-Etienne-du-Mont	Périer; Université	Master artisan (*patissier-oublieur*)	No League connections
Censier, Nicolas	Saint-Etienne-du-Mont	Périer; Université	Honorable/bourgeoisie (*marchand et bourgeois de Paris*)	No League connections
Delaporte, Jouanpaule	Unknown	Périer; Université	Soldier (*soldat*)	No League connections
Massotin, Marie	Saint-Etienne-du-Mont	Périer; Université	Honorable/bourgeoisie (*marchand et bourgeois de Paris*)	No League connections
Chairet, Jehan	Saint-Côme	Périer; Université	Servant (*marchand/marcha=t*)	Possible political connections
Tornet, Romaine	Saint-Etienne-du-Mont	Périer; Université	Day Labourer (*manouvrie=*)	No League connections
Dolliboy, Jehan	Saint-Etienne-du-Mont	Périer; Université	Gens de loi; Avocats (*avoc=t en parlement*)	No League connections
Parent, Perrette	Saint-Etienne-du-Mont	Babynet; Université	Gens de loi; Notary & commissioner (*commissaire et examineur du roy au Chastelet*)	No League connections
Dollet, François	Saint-Nicolas-du-Chardonnet	Babynet; Université	Honorable/bourgeoisie (*bo=rgeois de Paris*)	No League connections
Chofflart, Marie	Saint-Etienne-du-Mont	Babynet; Université	Honorable/bourgeoisie (*chirurgien du roy juré*)	No League connections
Lemaistre, Guillaume	Saint-Séverin	Babynet; Université	Honorable/bourgeoisie (*marchand de drap de soie = marchand de soie*)	No League connections
Delatour, Georges	Unknown	Babynet; Université	Middle/lower nobility (*esc=yer*)	No League connections
Pirou, Anne	Saint-Séverin	Babynet; Université	Master artisan (*cordonnier=*)	No League connections
Demedelin, Martin	Saint-Séverin	Babynet; Université	Master artisan (*chapelier*)	No League connections
Delacroix, Ignace	Saint-Germain-le-Viel	Cothereau, J.; Université	Soldier (*maistre & pair de =a gendarmerie de France*)	No League connections
Richer, Gilles	Saint-Séverin	Lamiral; Université	Clergy (*prebstre*)	No League connections
Mollert, Simon	Saint-Benoît	Lamiral; Université	Master artisan (*tonnelieur*)	No League connections
Laurent, Marye	Saint-Jacques-de-la-Boucherie	Lamiral; Université	Honorable/bourgeoisie (*marchand libraire*)	League cleric at funeral
Eloy, Loys	Saint-Etienne-du-Mont	Lamiral; Université	Mixed merchants commer=e: *sans états* (*facteur*)	No League connections
Mallemen, Jehan	Saint-Séverin	Lamiral; Université	Gens de loi; Procureur (*procureur en la cour de parlement*)	No League connections
Durant, Guillaume	Saint-Benoît	Lamiral; Université	Clergy (*prebstre vicaire*)	No League connections
Prevost, Marie	Saint-Etienne-du-Mont	Lamiral; Université	Artisan (*cordier*)	Mentioned in D/B
Forgeais, Jehan	Saint-Nicolas-du-Chardonnet	Lamiral; Université	Middle/lower nobility (*no=-escuyer seigneur de or sieur de . . .*)	No League connections

Testator Name	Testator Parish and Part of Town	Testator Notary and Notary Address	Testator Socio-Professional Category and Profession	Testator League Status
Rolland, Geneviève	Saint-Séverin	Lamiral; Université	Honorable/bourgeoisie (*bourgeois de Paris*)	Relative in D/B
Delacoupelle, Perette	Saint-Merri	Becquet; Université	Middle/lower official (*conseiller du roy au tresor*)	No League connections
Demoras, Michel	Unknown	Bontemps, M.; Université	Unclassifiable	No League connections
Regnault, Marye	Saint-André-des-Arts	Bontemps, M.; Université	Master artisan (*cordonnier*)	No League connections
Dufay, Claude	Saint-André-des-Arts	Bontemps, M.; Université	Titled nobility (*chevalier de l'ordre du roy*)	Witness ties noble League; related noble League
Blosseau, Claude	Saint-André-des-Arts	Bontemps, M.; Université	Soldier (*lieutenant d'une compagnye de gens de guerre au regiment du sieur de Mortilly pour le service de l'unyon des Catholicques*)	Catholic Union Soldier
Blancheteau, Marie	Unknown	Bontemps, M.; Université	Laboureur	No League connections
Girault, Denise	Saint-André-des-Arts	Bontemps, M.; Université	Gens de loi; Huissiers & sergeants (*huissier au chastelet*)	No League connections
Dubuisson, Pierre	Saint-André-des-Arts	Bontemps, M.; Université	Middle/lower nobility (*escuyer, sieur de . . . , seigneur, gouverneur of a duché & capitaine of a chasteau*)	Ties noble League
Chrinadelle, Perette	Saint-André-des-Arts	Bontemps, M.; Université	Independent female occupation (*boulanger*)	No League connections
Poincteau, Janie	Saint-André-des-Arts	Bontemps, M.; Université	Artisan (*chirurgien juré, université de Paris*)	No League connections
Lechantre, Pierre	Saint-Séverin	Bontemps, M.; Université	Gens de loi; Huissiers & sergeants (*huissier/sergent, palais*)	No League connections
Regnier, Marye	Saint-André-des-Arts	Bontemps, M.; Université	Titled nobility; Noble office/epithet (*escuyer, comiss. artil.*)	No League connections
Barbin, André	Saint-André-des-Arts	Bontemps, M.; Université	Mixed merchants; Commerce: *sans etats* (*vivandier de l'armee*)	Guise employ testator/spouse
Garent, Magdelane	Saint-André-des-Arts	Dumarc; Université	Master artisan (*tailleur d'habitz*)	No League connections
Delivaigres, Gaspard	Unknown	Troyes; Université	Honorable/bourgeoisie (*concierge de la maison of high Noble/cardinal*)	No League connections
Hennequin, Pierre	Saint-André-des-Arts	Troyes; Université	Noble office/epithet	Relative mentioned in D/B

Debonacoursy, Laurens	Saint-Séverin	Troyes; Université	Clergy (*abbé*)	League cleric at funeral
Galloys, Barbe	Saint-Sulpice	Troyes; Université	Soldier (in *gardes* of a high Noble)	Employed noble League
Baudry, Blanche	Saint-Eustache	Troyes; Université	Artisan (*faiseur d'esteues*)	No League connections
Hanoys, Guillaume	Saint-Séverin	Troyes; Université	Mixed merchants (*marchand/marchant*)	No League connections
Ginguard, Claude	Unknown	Troyes; Université	Honorable/bourgeoisie (*marchand et bourgeois de Paris*)	No League connections
Megaly, Sébastien	Saint-Séverin	Troyes; Université	Clergy (*prebstre aulmosnier reine d'escosse*)	Employed noble League
Brunet, Marye	Saint-André-des-Arts	Troyes; Université	Gens de loi; procureur (*procureur en la cour de parlement*)	League cleric at funeral
Defrotte, Françoise	Saint-André-des-Arts	Troyes; Université	Noble office/epithet	No League connections
Poirot, Jeanne	Saint-Benoît	Bernard; Université	Master artisan (*maçon tailleur de pierres; maistre juré es l'art et mayssonerie*)	No League connections
Delorrain, Marie	Saint-Séverin	Bernard; Université	Honorable/bourgeoisie (*Corps de Marchands*) (*drapier*)	Bequest to League cleric; possible League connections
Baron, Pierre	Saint-André-des-Arts	Bernard; Université	Clergy (*prebstre habitue*)	No League connections
Myot, Jacques	Saint-André-des-Arts	Bernard; Université	Honorable/bourgeoisie (*marchand et bourgeois de Paris*)	No League connections
Gourgoueron, Magdaleine	Saint-Benoît	Bernard; Université	Gens de loi; Procureur (*procureur en la cour de parlement*)	No League connections
Berthin, Jehan	Saint-Séverin	Bernard; Université	Honorable/bourgeoisie (*marchand et bourgeois de Paris*)	No League connections
Bourgoing, Denise	Saint-Côme	Bernard; Université	Unclassifiable	No League connections
Danisy, Catherine	Saint-André-des-Arts	Bernard; Université	Gens de loi; huissiers & sergents (*huissier des requestes du palais*)	No League connections
Bourdonnoys, Nicolas	Saint-Séverin	Bernard; Université	Honorable/bourgeoisie (*Corps de Marchands*) (*drapier*)	No League connections
Baron, Jacques	Unknown	Fardeau; Université	Gens de loi; Avocats (*licencier en droit, advocat en parlement*)	No League connections

1. D/B corpus=individuals mentioned as Leaguers in the corpus of individuals in Robert Descimon, *Qui étaient les Seize? Mythes et réalités de la Ligue parisienne (1585–1594)*, Mémoires de la fédération des sociétés historiques et archéologiques de Paris et de l'Ile-de-France, vol. 34 (Paris: 1983), and Elie Barnavi, *Le Parti de Dieu: Etude sociale et politique des chefs de la Ligue parisienne 1585–1594* (Louvain: Nauwelaerts, 1980).

Appendix I

Twenty-one Testators Using Service-Related Number Symbolism, 1590
[P=*Politique* curé at parish; L=Leaguer curé at parish; N=neutral curé at parish]

Testator Name, Parish, and Signature Information	Notary, Notary Part of Town, Number of League Testators	Testator's Age and/or Marital and Health Status	Testator's or Spouse's Profession	League Connections or Indices of Zealous Catholicism	Symbolic Number Used for Services/ Masses	Type of Service/Mass and Location for Celebration
LEDANOYS, Nicole Saint-Etienne-du-Mont [P], non-signer	Fardeau *Université* 2 Leaguers	one generation removed from Leaguer nephew; widow, 1 spouse named; sick	*avocat en la cour de Parlement* [i.e., *Gens de loi* high-rate League affiliation]	Nephew is Jehan Louchart[1]	13	"*1 service complect avec vigilles, laudes, recommendaces, et 3 hautes messes et 13 basses messes*" to be said in chapel of St. Denis in home parish of Saint-Etienne-du-Mont
CAVE, Marguerite Saint-Nicolas-des-Champs [L], non-signer	Peron *Ville* 1 Leaguer	widow, 1 spouse named sick	*marchand*	Strong emphasis on ritual performance	13	"*1 service complect dans Saint-Gervais avec vigilles, laudes, recommendaces et 3 hautes messes, libera, et oraisons accoustumés et 13 basses messes*"
LEBOUC, Marguerite Saint-Nicolas-des-Champs [L], non-signer	Peron *Ville* 1 Leaguer	widowed, 2 previous spouses healthy	*laboureur* (living in the country village of Aubervilliers, Parisian banlieue)	No	3+10=13 5	4 complete services each of "*3 hautes messes et 10 basses messes avec vigilles, laudes et recommandaces dans l'église Haubervilliers*" for 5 years for her soul and her friends'
DAILLY, Sebastienne no parish specified, non-signer	Peron *Ville* 1 Leaguer	married	not specified	*Recommendatio animae* includes 11 saints including John the Baptist and Marie Magdalene	5	"*5 services completz*" in whatever churches her executor decides

Name	Marital status / Health	Occupation	Notes	No.	Service description
GOULIART, Etienne Noisy le Sec, non-signer	widower sick	*marchand et laboureur "refugie . . . au cloistre et parroisse Saint-Mederic"*	No	5	*"5 services completz"* as executor wills
MOREAU, Claude Saint-Benoist [L], non-signer	married sick	*marchand et bourgeois de Paris*	No	5	*"5 services completz et solempnels en la maniere accoustumée"*
BRAIERE, Catherine Orly, non-signer	widow, 1 spouse named sick	*laboureur de vignes*	*Recommendatio animae* includes 17 intercessors including John the Baptist and *"tous les martyrs et tous les confesseurs"*	5	*"5 services completz pour remede de son ame"*
GOMBAULT, Barbe Saint-Nicolas-des-Champs [L], non-signer	widow, 1 spouse named healthy	*marchand et bourgeois de Paris*	Invocation stresses God's *"bonne iustice en vertu de la passion de nostre seigneur"*	13	*"3 hautes messes et 13 basses messes"* with body present in the parish church of Saint-Nicolas-des-Champs
FOURNYER, Regnault Saint-Leu-Saint-Gilles [L], signs	unknown healthy	*Greffier et controlleur du guet de ceste ville de Paris*	Invocation requests of God: father, son, and holy spirit *"le supplians d'avoir pitié de luy en faveur du merite et passion . . . de Jesu-Christ interpellant . . . les merites de la sacree vierge"*	13	*"Service complect et solempnel de 3 hautes messes et 13 basses messes avec vigilles, laudes, et recommendaces"*
PREVOST, Geneviève Saint-Nicolas-des-Champs [L], non-signer	widow, 1 spouse named healthy	*marchand et bourgeois de Paris*	Strong emphasis on ritual performance and ritual ornaments; *Recommendatio animae* includes John the Baptist, St. Magdalene, and St Geneviève	13	*"3 hautes messes avec vigilles, laudes et recommendaces et 13 basses messes"* in perpetuity once a year on day of death
FRANCISQUE, Geneviève Saint-Eustache [P], non-signer	widow, 1 spouse named: Nicolas Acelin healthy	*archer des gardes du corps du roy soubz la charge de monsieur Richelieu*	Preamble mentions her fear that she may *"devenir mallade sur le chemin ou bien qu'elle ne rencontrast aulcuns tenans le party"*	13	*"1 service complect de bons hommes avec 1 haute messe de requiem et 13 basses messes de requiem et 1 service complect à convent filles*

Testator Name, Parish, and Signature Information	Notary, Notary Part of Town, Number of League Testators	Testator's Age and/or Marital and Health Status	Testator's or Spouse's Profession	League Connections or Indices of Zealous Catholicism	Symbolic Number Used for Services/ Masses	Type of Service/Mass and Location for Celebration
				contraire de la Sainte Union Catholique et qu'ilz ne lui feisent aulcun mauvais traitement en sa personne et aussi considerant par elle que briefs soit les joures de toute humayne creature"; "Amen" at end of preamble; strong emphasis on lights; body present for service; offertory procession		*dieu avec 1 haute messe de requiem et 13 basses messes de requiem*"; "3 *services complects avec 3 haultes messes, l'une de l'office notre dame, autre Saint Esprit et autre de requiem avec 13 basses messes*"
PERCHERON,[2] Jehanne Saint-Eustache [P], signs	Parque Ville 0 Leaguers	wife of François Coquin healthy	*marchand et bourgeois de Paris*	*Recommendatio animae* includes supplication to God, to Jesus Christ, "*notre salveur et redempteur*," to "*la benoiste et tres sacrée vierge Marie, sa mere*," and to 10 named saints plus angels, archangels, and all saints in Paradise	33	33 *basses messes* in churches and monasteries at the discretion of the executors
DE COMPANS, Tassinne Sainte-Croix [N], signs	Croiset Cité 6 Leaguers	widow, 1 spouse named healthy	*marchand drappier*	Widow of Robert Le Goix, League leader; Executor is a Leaguer, Jehan de Compans; strong emphasis on ritual performance; Lengthy request for intercession from God, Christ, Mary, and numerous named saints refers to "*la doulourense mort qu'il a soufferte en l'arbre de la croix pour noz pechez*"; request for burial near chapel du Saint Sacrement and specifically requests	13	"13 *basses messes*" on day of burial or the day following

RICHER, Gilles Saint-Séverin [L], signs	Lamiral *Université* 5 Leaguers	single male, no parent data healthy	*Prebstre habitue en église Sainct-Benoist*	lighting at altar of Saint Sacrement in the chapel Notre Dame & St. Nicholas; Attached to parish of Saint-Séverin despite other religious ties	13	"13 basses messes" as executors decide
RABACHE, Jehanne Saint-Gervais [L], signs	Trouvé *Ville* 0 Leaguers	widowed, 2 previous spouses healthy	*conseiller, notaire et secretaire du roy maison et couronne de France*	Intercession "*implorant la benoiste et glorieuse vierge Marie,*" John the Baptist, John the Evangelist, and other named and unnamed saints, angels, and archangels to intercede for him; strong emphasis is on ritual performance	25 50	On day of death or day after at Ave Maria, wants one complete service with *vigilles*, *recommendaces* and 4 named *haultes messes* (Notre Dame, Sainct Esprit, Anges, requiem) plus 50 *basses messes de requiem* saying "*la passion*" after each *basse messe* on her tomb "*et gecte de l'eau benoiste en la fin de chascune messe*" and a similar complete service plus 50 *basses messes* "*a la huictaine apres son deces*"; on the day after the first above service, wants another service as decribed above but with 25 *basses messes*; for *bout de l'an*, wants same complete service plus 50 *basses messes* as she had after death. Wants passion said after each *basse messe* (and the next day) on her *fosse*
BLOSSEAU, Claude Saint-André-des-Arts [L], signs	M. Bontemps *Université* 4 Leaguers	widower sick	*lieutenant d'une compagnye de gens de pied au Regiment du sieur de Mortilly pour le service de l'unyon des Catholicques*	Soldier in the Catholic Union; strong emphasis on ritual performance; wants "*une brnestier*" attached to his "*sepulture*" "*pour mettre eaue brnoiste pour jecter sur leursdrtez sepulture*"	13	"*1 service complect de 3 hautes messes et 13 basses messes avec vigilles, recommandances, oraisons accoustumées dans l'église Saint-André-des-Arts*" on the day of burial or day after burial

Testator Name, Parish and Signature Information	Notary, Notary Part of Town, Number of League Testators	Testator's Age and/or Marital and Health Status	Testator's or Spouse's Profession	League Connections or Indices of Zealous Catholicism	Symbolic Number Used for Services/Masses	Type of Service/Mass and Location for Celebration
LECONTE, Thomas Saint-Leu-Saint-Gilles [L], signs	Bruyère *Faubourg* 4 Leaguers	married healthy	*tourneur en boys*	Invokes God, Christ and "*le suppliant que par le merite, prieres, et intercessions de la glorieuse et tres sacrée vierge Marie,*" John the Baptist, John the Evangelist, and other named and unnamed saints, angels, and archangels	13	"3 *services complets avec 3 hautes messes and 13 basses messes avec vigilles, recommandances and oraisons accoustumées*" at 1. parish, 2. Cordeliers, 3. Augustins
DE COCQUEREL, Nicolle Saint-Eustache [P], signs	Ferrant *Ville* 3 Leaguers	wife of Nicolas Quelault sick	*marchand et bourgeois de Paris*	Strong emphasis on ritual performance; Preamble stresses doctrinal precision "*au nom du pere, du fils et du Saint Esprit, trois personnes en Unite, un seul Dieu, une mesme essence*"; Invocation to God, Christ, "*la benoiste et tres sacrée vierge Marie*", and St. Eustache and companions, St. Agnes and companions, St. André, St. Denis and companions, and to all martyrs, Sts. Nicholas and Clare and their confessors and to St. Geneviève and all virgins, etc.	10/40	"*60 basses messes des trespassez pour le salut et remede de sa pauvre ame et de ses pere et mere et tous ses bons amis trepassez: 10 en l'église des mynimes, 10 au monastere ave maria,*" and 10 in each church of 4 mendiants (10+10+40=60)
DROUYN, Ambroyse Saint-Jean-le-Rond, signs	Labarde *Cité* 0 Leaguers	single male, no parent data sick	*prebstre habitué en l'église notre dame de Paris*	Leaguer *curé de la Fosse* reports in May 1576 canons of Notre-Dame refuse to say the *Te Deum* ordered by Henry III after Peace of Monsieur	10 40	"*1 service complect dans Saint-Jean-le-Rond et 1 haute messe à Nostre Dame Panthuise et 10 basses messes*" at each of the 4 mendicant orders

DUGUE, Marguerite Saint-Jean-en-Grève [L] signs	Lybault *Ville* 1 Leaguer	widow, 1 spouse, Jehan Michel, named healthy	*bourgeois de Paris*	Strong emphasis on ritual performance	3+30=33	3 complete services of 3 *hautes messes* and 30 *basses messes* in *église Saint-Jehan-en-Grève* 1 day of burial or day after, 1 after 8 days, and 1 at *bout de l'an* which all ultra-Catholics think concede too much to Protestants; suggests that clergy of Notre-Dame harbor long-standing resentments against peace with Protestants
ROLLAND, Geneviève Saint-Séverin [L], signs	Lamiral University 5 Leaguers	wife of Pierre Le Doyen; healthy	*bourgeois de Paris*	Uses Leaguer notary Lamiral; Sister-in-law Marye Le Doyen is married to notary Jacques Fardeau, a notary popular with Leaguers and listed by Pallier[3] as a notary frequented by Leaguer printers; Testator uses notary Lamiral, whose daughter married a Seize; Emphasis on performative ritual—requests one *basse messe* each day *"en avant icelle la passion . . . selon St. Jehan"* and during the passion *"l'on sonne . . . des cloches de ladicte église à son intention et pour le salut de son ame . . ."*	13 twice	Requests 2 services, each containing *"3 hautes messes avec 13 basses messes"*

1. (*gens de loi*) cited as Descimon, nr. 151. Robert Descimon, *Qui*, p. 181.
2. *Honorable femme* Jehanne Percheron, wife of *honorable homme* François Coquin (a May testator in good health, requested thirty-three *basses messes* "assavoir trois de l'annunciation nostre dame par l'ange Gabriel, trois aultres messes de la nativité nostre seigneur, trois de la circomsyion, trois de la passion, trois de la resurrection, trois de l'assention, trois de la penthacouste, trois de la trinité, trois de l'assumption nostre dame, trois de sa nativité, trois de sa nativité, trois de sa conception . . ."
3. Pallier, *Recherches*, 196.

Appendix J

Fourteen Testators Using Symbolic Numbers in Bequests to the Poor, 1590
[P=*Politique* curé at parish; L=Leaguer curé at parish; N=neutral curé]

Testator Name, Parish, and Signature Information	Notary, Notary Part of Town, Number of League Testators	Testator's Age and/or Marital and Health Status	Testator's or Spouse's Profession	League Connections or Indices of Zealous Catholicism	Symbolic Number Used for Poor	Number and/or Type of Poor (Designated by a Symbolic Number and the Location of the Poor)
ROYER, Jacqueline Saint-Eustache [P], non-signer	Peron *Ville* 1 Leaguer	married, wife of Loys Delarendoete; 1 previous spouse healthy	*archer des gardes du corps du roy*	Requests burial in Saint-Nicholas-des-Champs, a Leaguer parish, *"pres le bureau des pauures"*; Invocation asks for intercession *"par les merites de la passion de son filz notre seigneur saueur et redempteur Jesus Christ. . . ."*	20	Gives 12 *deniers* each to 20 poor of the parish where she dies
MOMBRON, René de Saint-Benoist [L], signs	Saint-Vaast *Université* 2 Leaguers	young single male, *"22 ans ou environs"* sick	*escuier, seigneur de Souche et Saint-Aignan de Nantes en Bretagne, estudiant en l'université de Paris college de Lysieulx*	Requests every Friday in perpetuity 1 high requiem mass in the parish of Saint-Aignan; 1 low requiem mass every Wednesday and Friday in perpetuity; Close ties to four mendicant orders in Nantes; Requests 300 low requiem masses at Saint-Aignan parish and at the churches of the Cordeliers, Jacobins, and Minims of Nantes; Makes educational investment; *Rente* of 500 *escus* for a perpetual foundation "for instruction of the children of the parish" who must say *"ung salut en ladicte escolle et ung de profundis"*; Purchases for Saint-Aignan	10	10 poor girls *de ladicte paroisse "que la rente qui prouiendra de ladicte somme [500 escuz soleil] soit distribuée chascun an par lesdictz marguilliers et curé . . . à dix pauores filles . . . pour subuenir à les marier et à ce qu'elles prient dieu pour ledict testateur"*; gives 5 *solz* each to all the poor of Saint-Aignan parish who are in the church at time of his first service

Name	Executor / Residence	Status	Occupation	Details	No.	Charity
NOEL, Marie Saint-Jacques-de-la-Boucherie [L], non-signer due to health	Arragon¹ *Ville* 1 Leaguer	widow, 1 spouse named, sick	*boucher*	parish "*calice, chandelles, buvettes d'argent, parements d'hostie . . . chappes, ung chasuble . . . et linge pour le pain [et] hostie*"; Rente for communion bread and wine of the parish of Saint-Aignan in perpetuity; Notary Arragon is identified by Pallier as being a notary frequented by the Leaguer printers	13	13 poor women
FOURNYER, Regnault Saint-Leu-Saint-Gilles [L], signs	Thevenin *Ville* 0 Leaguers	unknown healthy	*Greffier et contre-rolleur du guet de ceste ville de Paris* (The *guet* or town watch was essential to town security during siege of 1590.)	Invocation requests of God: father, son, and holy spirit "*lui supplians d'avoir pitié de luy en faveur de la merite et passion . . . du Jesus Christ interpellant . . . les merites de la sacree vierge*"; Emphasis on ritual performance	13	13 poor are given 20 *solz parisis* to pray for testator
L'HERI, Therrye Saint-Merry [P], non-signer	Motelet *Ville* 0 Leaguers	wife of Jehan Salvy sick	*manouvrier*, native of Arcy, near Compiègne	Asks pardon of all whom she may have offended in her home parish	13	13 poor who assist at her convoy and burial
de COMPANS, Tassine Sainte-Croix [N], signs	Croiset *Cité* 6 Leaguers	widow, 1 spouse named, Robert Le Goix healthy	*marchand drappier*	Widow of Robert Le Goix, a Seize activist; Executor is a Leaguer, Jehan de Compans; strong emphasis on ritual performance; Lengthy request for intercession from God, Christ, Mary, and numerous named saints; refers to "*la douloureuse mort qu'il a soufferte en l'arbre de la croix pour noz pechez*"; request for	500	"*à cinq cens pauvres, au nom des cinq playes de nostre seigneur à chacun pauvre XII (solz) chacun. . . .*"

Testator Name, Parish, and Signature Information	Notary, Notary Part of Town, Number of League Testators	Testator's Age and/or Marital and Health Status	Testator's or Spouse's Profession	League Connections or Indices of Zealous Catholicism	Symbolic Number Used for Poor	Number and/or Type of Poor (Designated by a Symbolic Number and the Location of the Poor)
				burial near chapel of Holy Sacrament and specifically requests lighting at altar of Holy Sacrament in the chapel Nostre Dame & St. Nicholas; In a previous (1579) will, Compans requests "Qu'il ne soit porté à sondict convoy aucunes armoiries ne fait pompes funebres et mondaines et que tout soit à l'honneur de Dieu." In 1590, Compans requests, "Item defend que par expres que à sondict convoy et enterrement sortent portent ne mises à la maison et eglise aucunes armoiries ny faict pompes mondaines mais que le tout soit conduict modestement à l'honneur et gloire de Dieu et que sondict corps soit cryé . . . sans aucunes armoiries . . ."; Asks brother's children to attend cortege: "qu'elle ne desire si grandz hommes mondaines après sondict corps"		
ROLLAND, Geneviève Saint-Séverin [L], signs	Lamiral Université 5 Leaguers	wife of Pierre Le Doyen healthy	bourgeois de Paris	Uses Leaguer notary Lamiral; Husband Pierre Le Doyen's sister, Marye, married to notary Jacques Fardeau,[2] a notary popular with Leaguers and listed by Pallier as being a notary frequented by the Leaguer printers; Testator uses a notary, Lamiral, popular with other Leaguers;	13 twice	24 prisoners of the Conciergerie, 5 solz each; "... veult et ordonne à l'issue de son premier service ... treize pauvres qui se trouveront en eglise aussy veult & ordonne qu'il soit donné et distribué à treize aultres pauvres apres les susdictz deux services"

Name	Notary / Type / League	Status	Occupation	Notes	No.	Bequest detail
				Emphasis on performative ritual—requests one basse messe each day "en avant icelle la passion . . . selon St. Jehan" and during the passion "l'on sonne . . . des cloches de ladicte église à son intention et pour le salut de son ame . . ."		*faictz et celebrez estant son deuil en retour à sa maison à chacun d'eulx ung pain de la valleur d'un sol piece une chopine de vin, et de la viande selon le jour . . .*
LEMAÇON, Anne Saint-Paul [P], signs	Trouvé *Ville* 0 Leaguers	widow, 1 spouse named, Guillaume Belle, healthy	*conseiller du roy en son chastelet*	Emphasis or performative ritual ("*voiage* to St. Claude")	10	"à dix pauvres honteux et vielles personnes" gives a demi ecu to each; 33 escuz 1 tiers to Hostel Dieu
MORIN, Gabriel Saint-Germain-l'Auxerrois [L], signs	Contesse *Ville* 0 Leaguers	married twice sick	*marchand bourgeois de Paris*	Emphasis or performative ritual; wants to be buried "*devant l'ymage Notre Dame*"; vow to church of Nostre Dame de Vertus; Bequest to the confraternity *des archers de ville* (one of the oldest communal institutions thus an example of the combination of civic and sacral performativity)	13	13 poor of the testator's *banlieue* village, to each, 12 deniers
THUE, Huguette Saint-Jean-en-Grève [L], non-signer	Monthenault *Ville* 1 Leaguer	widow, 1 spouse named, Daniel Despersine sick	*maistre doreur*	Uses League-related notary Monthenault; 8 Augustinian monks to carry her body in her cortege	13	"13 pauvres au retour de son enterrement pour dieu," i.e., in honor of God/for love of God
GIRARD, Pierre Saint-Paul [P], signs	de Poche *Ville* 0 Leaguers	married sick	*marchand boulanger*, resident of "*Montreul sur le boys de Vincennes estant reffugie en ceste ville de Paris*"	Notary de Poche consistently uses sacralizing readings, in this case In nomine domini. Amen. Invocation implores "l'intercession de la benoise, glorieuse et sacrée vierge Marie" as well as many saints and angels named and unnamed (i.e., many intercessors)	10	"à dix des plus pauvres hommes habitans" of home parish

Testator Name, Parish, and Signature Information	Notary, Notary Part of Town, Number of League Testators	Testator's Age and/or Marital and Health Status	Testator's or Spouse's Profession	League Connections or Indices of Zealous Catholicism	Symbolic Number Used for Poor	Number and/or Type of Poor (Designated by a Symbolic Number and the Location of the Poor)
CHAVASSE, Baltasar Saint-Benoist [L], signs	R. Bontemps Cité 22 Leaguers	single male, no parent data, healthy	regent au Collège de la Compagnie de Jesus dict de Clermont fondé l'Université de Paris	Testator uses a notary, R. Bontemps, very popular with Leaguers; makes sign of the cross on will; Invocation "suppliant par le merite de sa sainct mort and passion (of Christ his redeemer)"; requests burial in closest college or maison of Jesuits; emphasis on performative ritual	10	"10 pauures filles" of legitimate birth
AUZANET, François Saint-Benoist [L], signs	R. Bontemps Cité 22 Leaguers	young, single male sick	estudiant en l'Université de Paris au collège de Clermont	Testator uses a notary, R. Bontemps, very popular with Leaguers; Invokes "le merite de sa sainct passion"; Large bequest to Jesuit college of Clermont	10 twice	"Dix pauures filles neez en loyal mariage natifves de ladicte ville de la Soubzterraine" and to "dix garçons orfelins aussi nez en loyal mariage de ladicte ville de Soubzteraine"
THIERSAULT, Marye Saint-Germain-L'Auxerrois [L], signs	Landry Ville 2 Leaguers	widowed, 2 previous spouses, Regnault de Bailly & Robin du Sainct Germain healthy	avocat en la court de Parlement	Names two Leaguers, Jehan Amelot and Jehan Bacquet, to aid her executors; Strong emphasis on performative ritual; Services requested show strong emphasis on Christ's Passion, including mention of a procession in front of the crucifix; Strong attachment to Mary as well	13 twice	13 "vrays pauures"; 13 "vrays pauures"; 33 escuz un tiers to the prisoners of Fort L'Eveque (the episcopal prison)

1. This notary (Aragon) is listed in Pallier, *Recherches*, 196, as used habitually by Leaguer printers.
2. Fardeau's Leaguer clients are Nicole Ledanoys and Ayme Saultier.

Appendix K
The Coding of a Will

Because of the novel approach to coding in this book the conventional word "bequest" is herein termed request. This is because money is not always bequested with every pious request.

There are three types of variables:

1) Initial Variables which are the most numerous and have the greatest number of values to capture slight differences in wording

2) Derivative Variables, which draw together specific values from different Initial Variables or from other Derivative Variables to explore different hypotheses or perform specific analyses

3) Counting Variables, which sum up the number of occurrences of different types of performativity coded by Initial and Derivative variables, thus giving a measure of a testator's performative engagement

Record Type 1: Testator Identification

Variable	Value	Value Label
ID	003	Testator ID number
Surname	Gueret	Testator surname
Given name	Augustin	Testator given name
Sex	1	Male
Marital Status	3	Married
Health	1	Sick
Will month	5	May
Will day	26	Day will signed
Will year	1590	Year will signed
Testator's present parish	13	Saint-Gervais
Testator's home region	1	Native Parisian

Variable	Value	Value Label
Part of town in which testator lived	1	Ville
Profession	101	Charcutier (pork butcher and cold-cut maker)
Professional modifier	2	Master
Professional category	9	All artisans
League Affiliation	6	Requested Leaguer curé, Jehan Gincestre, attend his funeral. Gincestre seized control of Saint-Gervais following the Day of the Barricades in 1588.
Spouse's surname	Guyot	Surname of spouse
Spouse's given name	Claude	Given name of spouse

Record Type 2: Information on Notary used by Testator

Variable	Value	Value Label
Notary	33	Herbin
Part of town in which notary lived	1	Ville
Parish location of notary's practice	13	Saint-Gervais
Street on which notary lived	Stanto	Street name (rue Saint-Antoine)
Beginning date of notary's practice	1569	Year in which notary began practice
Ending date of notary's practice	1592	Year in which notary ended practice

Record Type 10: Literacy Information

Variable	Value	Value Label
Literacy	3	Signs will

Record Type 14: Information on Burial (*Indicates a value which generates a count for performativity. See pp. 308ff.)

Variable	Value	Value Label
Burial location requested	3	Present parish cemetery
Special location for burial within a given institution	15	Other special location: "on the side of the church where they place the tapers at the place where his ancestors have been buried."
Institution at which testator requests burial	13	Saint-Gervais
Testator requests to be buried alongside	28	Ancestors
Does testator request formulaic standard funeral package?	4	No, does not specify wants standard package; provides own detail on some items.
Does testator give special burial instructions?	2* [one count for bodily performativity]	Yes, special ceremony requested: requests "when his body is placed in the earth, sing *Salve regina*, also with devotion."
Limitations on funeral cortege	3	Testator asks that specific persons not attend, but pays them. Gueret asks that the four mendicant orders not process in cortege "because of the troubles." Nonetheless Gueret paid each order 1 *écu soleil* for each to say one service, a high mass with deacons, subdeacons, bread, wine and lights.
Limitations on bell-ringing or special detail (*sonnerie*)	6* [one count for performativity: the detail on bell-ringing generates value 6 in the Performativity Index: Aural and Visual Symbolic Community] See Table 5.4	Limits and details amount of bell-ringing. Gueret asks "two large bells only be rung three times in the evening and morning following death, and at the end the bells are to be rung together for one half hour."
Requests lights at funeral	1	Detailed for cortege and/or burial
First type of light requested	1	Torches
Number of first type of light requested	24* [one count for performativity: Value 5 in the Performativity Index: Above Average Number of Lights (12+)]	Actual number of lights requested
Size of each light requested	1	1 lb. each

Record Type 15: Specific Pious Requests

Gueret made 8 specific Pious Requests.

#1

Variable	Value	Value Label
Who shall perform action requested?	170	Parish, *curé* (Jehan Gincestre) and vicar
Institution where action is to occur	13	Saint-Gervais [Leaguer parish]
Type of institution	1	Parisian parish [14 possible derivative values were established after recoding of type of institution.][1]
Classification of institution	2	Parish[2]
Was institution in home parish?	1	Yes [This derivative variable helps determine whether testators were abiding by Tridentine attempts to tie Catholics more closely to their home parishes.]
Main purpose of request	2	Attend cortege and/or services
Number of persons requested	2	

#2

Variable	Value	Value Label
Who shall perform action requested?	162	Priests who have been provided with a living from the church (*habitué*)
Institution where action is to occur	13	Saint-Gervais [Leaguer parish]
Type of institution	1	Parisian parish
Classification of institution	2	Parish (See note 2)
Was institution in home parish?	1	Yes
Main purpose of request	2	Attend cortege and/or services
Number of people requested	999	All. Gueret requests all priests provided with a living by his parish church participate in his cortege.

#3

Variable	Value	Value Label
Who shall perform action requested?	95	Four mendicant orders
Location of institution	95	Four mendicant order houses
Type of institution	2	Parisian monasteries
Classification of institution	3	Monastic (See note 2)
Was institution in home parish?	2	No
Mendicant orders	1	Bequest to at least one of the mendicant orders[3]
Main purpose of request	3	Provide services
Sub-purpose (more specificity)	101	1 complete service of 1 high mass with deacon and subdeacon
Total number of services requested	4	
Was a lump payment made to multiple recipients?	999	Yes
Total expenditure on request	4	
Denomination of currency	e	*écu*
Purpose of lump payment	2	Services

#4

Variable	Value	Value Label
Who shall perform action requested?	148	Parish vestry [*oeuvre* and *fabrique*]
Institution where action is to occur	13	Saint-Gervais
Type of institution	1	Parisian parish
Classification of institution	2	Parish (See note 2)
Was institution in home parish?	1	Yes
Main purpose of request	1	General gift (non-specific charity)
Total expenditure on request	1	
Denomination of currency	e	*écu*

#5

Variable	Value	Value Label
Who shall perform action requested?	800	Poor
Type of poor	67	"The poor who are present [at the church] on the day of burial."[4]
Sex of poor	3	Unspecified sex[5]
Special type of/role of poor	9	STP1, poor present at church[6]
Type of institution	10	Unknown (Gueret does not require the poor of any specific institution.)
Classification of institution	1	Charitable bequest (See note 2)
Was institution in home parish?	2	No (Gueret's poor could have been from any parish.)
Main purpose	1	General gift (non-specific charity)
Beginning time and/or other limiting/descriptive conditions	06	Day of burial[7]
Particular time specified at which request to be carried out	16	Day of burial[8]
Total expenditure on request	3	
Denomination of currency	e	écu
Additional payment	20	sols

The final 3 requests (#6,#7 and #8) were coded from the following large and multi-faceted clause in Gueret's will:

"[Gueret] wants and orders that his body be laid out in front of the crucifix and that there be sung *Vexilla regis prodeunt* and three times *O crux ave spes unica*; all with devotion, and when his body is placed in the earth sing *Salve regina* also devoutly."[9]

#6

Variable	Value	Value Label
Who shall perform action requested	150	Church
Specific institution	13	Saint-Gervais
Type of institution	1	Parisian parish
Classification of institution	2	Parish (See note 2)
Was institution in home parish?	1	Yes

Main purpose	3	Provide services, religious ceremony
Sub-purpose (service)	187	Gueret wants and orders that his body be laid out in front of the crucifix and that the "Salutation to the Passion" be sung [Vexilla regis prodeunt]
Service expresses christocentrism	1	Yes[10]
Liturgical detail	9* [one count for performativity, Value 11 on Table 5.4]	Christocentric detail other than request for Christocentric mass[11]
Immanence	5	Gueret's request that his body be placed in front of the crucifix indicates belief in the special sacred nature of an object associated with Christ, here the crucifix.[12]
Testator mentions body	1	Yes[13]
Bodily performativity	9* [one count for performativity: Value 9 on Table 5.4, Bodily Performativity]	See immediately above
Liturgical performativity	11* [one count for performativity: Value 11 on Table 5.4, Liturgical Performativity]	Shows liturgical performativity[14]
Beginning time and/or other limiting/descriptive conditions	258	Any request for services to be said with special care and devotion. [See note 7]
Reformist Behaviors	5*[15] [one count for performativity: Value 14 on Table 5.4, Strict Comportment of Celebrant]	Clerical discipline or absenteeism (Gueret requests the hymns be sung with devotion.)[16]

#7

Variable	Value	Value Label
Who shall perform action requested?	150	Church
Specific institution	13	Saint-Gervais
Type of institution	1	Parisian parish

THE CODING OF A WILL

Variable	Value	Value Label
Classification of institution	2	Parish
Was institution in home parish?	1	Yes
Main purpose	3	Provide services, religious ceremony
Sub-purpose (more specificity)	169[17]	Hymn: O crux ave spes unica. Gueret asks that O crux ave spes unica be sung three times with his body still in front of the crucifix.
Beginning time and/or other limiting/descriptive conditions	121	In front of the crucifix
Service expresses Christocentrism	1[18]	Christocentrism in service request
Liturgical detail	9	Christocentric detail other than mass. (See note 12)
BODY2	1	Yes[19]
Bodily Performativity	9* [one count for performativity: Value 9 on Table 5.4, Bodily Performativity]	See immediately above
Liturgical Performativity	11* [one count for performativity: Value 11 on Table 5.4, Liturgical Performativity]	Testator specifically mentions a liturgical hymn
Beginning time and/or other limiting/descriptive conditions	258	Any request for services to be said with special care or devotion: Gueret asks that the three O crux ave spes unicas be sung "with devotion."
Concern for Honesty/Devotion	3	Testator mentions devotion or special reverence
Reformist Behaviors	5* [one count for performativity: Value 14 on Table 5.4, Strict Comportment of Celebrant]	Clerical discipline or absenteeism mentioned: Gueret requests the hymns be sung with devotion (see note 7)
Performativity Index	14	Strict comportment of celebrant: Gueret requests the hymns be sung with devotion.

#8

Variable	Value	Value Label
Who shall perform action requested	150	Church

Specific institution	13	Saint-Gervais
Type of institution	1	Parisian parish
Classification of institution	2	Parish (See note 2)
Was institution in home parish?	1	Yes
Main purpose	3	Provide services, religious ceremony
Sub-purpose (service)		Salut or Salve regina (Gueret requests a Salve regina, also to be sung.)
Liturgical detail	6* [one count for performativity, Value 6 on Table 5.4, Aural and Visual Symbolic Community]	Marian detail other than request for Marian mass (Gueret requests the Marian hymn Salve regina.)
Beginning time and/or other limiting/descriptive conditions	122	As his body is placed in the ground
Testator mentions body	1	Yes
Bodily performativity	9* [one count for performativity: Value 9 on Table 5.4, Bodily Performativity]	See immediately above
Liturgical performativity	11* [one count for performativity: Value 11 on Table 5.4, Liturgical Performativity]	Shows liturgical performativity[20]
Beginning time and/or other limiting/descriptive conditions	258	Any request for services to be said with special care and devotion. [See note 7]
Reform	5[21] [one count for performativity: Value 14 on Table 5.4, Strict Comportment of Celebrant]	Clerical discipline or absenteeism (Gueret requests the hymns be sung with devotion.)[22]

Aggregate Data from the Counting Variables

Because the above data often breaks down single will "Items" into multiple Pious Requests (each a Record Type 15) in order to capture the rich data within the single request (see Gueret's Pious Bequests #6–#8 from one will Item), it was necessary to aggregate the data to ensure that a particular testator was not overrepresented in his desire for performative acts, liturgical precision, reform, etc. The following variables count the actual number of times the testator mentions specific words or phrases or asks for specific items in his will. This means that a wealthy testator making many requests need not be overcounted, but the detail of that will can also be captured. In Gueret's case the mention of "devout" did not require any significant financial investment.

Number of Times Testator Shows Concern for Liturgical Detail: 2

The counting variable LITURG# counts the number of occurrences for any value of the variable "Indicators of Liturgical detail." See Appendix C for this variable.

Although Gueret gives detail on *two* hymns he would like sung in front of the crucifix, he clearly conceives of the two hymns as part of one event—the presentation of his body prior to burial. He also gives detail when he specifies the *Salve regina* be sung later as his body is placed into the ground (a separate event from the presentation of the body in the church).

This Counting Variable counts the number of times actual detail (other than requests for generic services) is provided during what the testator perceives as different liturgical events.

Number of Times Testator Shows Concern for Reform: 2

Gueret twice requests in his will that certain hymns be sung with devotion: the two hymns in front of the crucifix and the hymn as his body is placed in the ground. The Counting Variable (REFORM#) counts the number of times the testator exhibits reformist tendencies in his will.

Number of Times Testator Sets Limits on His Burial: 2

Gueret limits attendance at his convoy when he requests the four mendicant orders not attend and he limits the bell ringing that is to accompany his burial service. The Counting Variable (LIMIT#) counts the number of limits a testator places on performative, public aspects of the burial. It would also capture limits on lights, display of coats of arms (*armoiries*), services, etc., if these had occurred in Gueret's will.

Number of Bequests Involving the Mendicant Orders: 1

Although Gueret requests a service at each order, he requests this in one will item and issues a lump sum payment for the four services. He conceives of this as one bequest. (MEND#)

Number of Bequests in Which Testator Reveals Belief in the Immanentist Nature of the Sacred (sacred residing in material world): 1

Gueret asks for the presentation of his body in front of the crucifix. (IMMAN#)

rung to signal his neighbors to pray for his soul, thereby tying them into a public, sacred community of believers.) PIN6#, Value 6 on the Performativity Index.

Bodily Performativity: 2 (Gueret asks for his body to be laid out in front of the crucifix and for a special hymn to be sung as his body is placed into the ground.) PIN9#, Value 9 on the Performativity Index.

Liturgical Performativity: 2 (Gueret is concerned with how the liturgy is performed when he asks for specific hymns at two moments in his service and actual burial: when he requests specific hymns after the presentation of his body in the church and at the moment his body is placed into the ground.) *Emphasis on the Comportment of the Celebrant:* 2 (Gueret asks twice that his hymns be sung with devotion.) PIN14#, Value 14 on the Performativity Index.

Number of Bequests Involving Special Attention to Testator's Body: 2

Gueret requests his body be laid out in front of the crucifix and that a special hymn be sung as his body is placed in the ground.
The Counting Variable BODY2# was designed to capture the importance testators attached to their physical body and the bodily or physically performative rituals associated with death and burial.

Summary: Number of Times Each Type of Performativity is Displayed in Will

Display of Lights: 1 (Gueret makes one request for 24 lights weighing one pound apiece.) PIN5#, Value 5 on the Performativity Index (Tables 5.4 and 5.5.

Construction of Sacred Community: 1 (Gueret asks for bells to be

2. The possible values for the variable INST3, classification of institution are as follows: *1* charitable bequests (to poor people, collection boxes for money for the poor, *boîtes*, charitable institutions Parisian and non-Parisian, prison and Cappelle); *2* bequests to the parish (Parisian and non-Parisian parishes, personnel, vestry *œuvre* and *fabrique*, other (chapels); *3* monastic bequests (all Parisian and non-Parisian monasteries, Jesuits); *4* confraternal bequests (all Parisian and non-Parisian confraternities, confraternal chapels); *5* vows (all); *6* other bequests.

3. This derivative variable, MEND, was created to capture how testators conceived of their connection to the four mendicant orders: *–8* no relation to mendicant order; *1* bequest: at least one of the mendicant orders; *2* buried at one of the mendicant orders'; *3* body carried in cortege by one or more of mendicants; *4* testator is professionally associated with one of the mendicants.

4. Value 67 is one of values for the variable STP (Special Type of Poor) that classifies the poor in 202 possible ways.

1. The Derivative Variable INST1 sorts and recodes all individually named institutions. There are 14 possible values: *1* Parisian parish; *2* Parisian monasteries; *3* banlieue and diocese of Paris; *4* non-Parisian parish; *5* non-Parisian monasteries; *6* Parisian charitable institutions; *7* non-Parisian charitable institutions; *8* Parisian colleges; *9* special locations; *10* unknown locations; *11* prisons; *12* pilgrimage sites (vow institutions); *13* non-Parisian colleges; *14* defies all rules. The variables INST1–INST6 were created. The next step determined which institutions were "strategic" for a given year. For the present work, the most important strategic institutions were the mendicant orders. The variable MEND analyzes a testator's relationship with a mendicant order; see Table 6.2, for some results. The other "strategic" institutions were the Jesuits, the Capuchins, and the Feuillants, not mentioned by Gueret. See Table 5.1 the variable JCF, which is strongly associated with Leaguers and reformers in 1590.

5. The value labels for the variable STPSEX are: –5 cases with no Rec15s; –6 STP, not these types; –8 case without STP; 1 male poor specified; 2 female poor specified; 3 no sex specified.

6. The value labels for the variable STP1 are: –5 cases with no special pious requests; –6 STP, not these types; –8 case without STP; 1 honteux; 2 enferme, renferme; 3 aged; 4 malades; 5 estudiants; 6 clergy; 7 prisionniers; 8 mendians; 9 poor who take part in death/burial.

7. Value 06 is one of the values that identify beginning time and/or other limiting/description conditions (BTLC).

8. Value 16 is one of 33 possible values of the derivative variable BTLCTIME which regroup the timing of an event so that the urgency or priority of the request can be determined from the perspective of the testator.

9. Will of Augustin Gueret, notary Herbin, CVIII, 23 p./folio VI xx xii: "Veult et ordonne que la presentation soit delaisse en repos devent le crucifix et qu'il soyt chanté Vexilla regis prodeunt et trois fois O crux ave spes unica, le tout avec devotion et son corps mis en la terre chante salve regina aussi bien et devotement."

10. Value 1 is one of ten possible values for the derivitive variable XTHEME which identify all instances of Christocentrism generated by many different initial variables (NBTLC, BOUT, SPECIAL, SPECIAL2, INK1, INK2, MP, INST, NFREQ, NSERV, DURAT, SPLOC, NSPHEAD, PERSON# and SERV#) and classifies them thematically. 1 Passion, Crucifix, Fridays, Penitence (focuses on the penitential, sacrificial and corporal aspects of the crucifixion); 2 number 5, Cinq Playes (all uses of the number 5 and references to the 5 wounds of Christ); 3 hybrid; 4 Holy Sacrament; 5 Number Symbolism (any number symbolism not connected to the number 5 [which is covered in XTHEME 2]: thirty-three, the number of years Christ lived on earth, or forty, the number of days Christ was in the wilderness or the number of days Christ returned to earth following the resurrection; 6 Corps Notre Seigneur (specific mention of the body (corps), as opposed to other word choice such as sacrament or communion; See Appendix C: "Mentions of the Body of Christ (in any form)" opposed to the sacrament of the body, or the bread); 7 Generic Christocentric Reference (not covered by any other specific theme— this category codes instances where Christ is obviously important to the testator, but it is not clear in what way Christ is important, i.e. sacramentally, penitentially. For example, a testator requests a *basse messe en nom de Jhesus* or wishes to be buried *devant l'ymage de Notre Sauveur.*" Christ plays a role in these testators' concerns about death, but it is not clear in what manner: Christ is important—as sacrifice, as saviour?); 08 Cross/Easter/Nativity (focuses on the redemptive and hopeful aspects of Jesus's life, his resurrection and his assumption); –5 no special Pious Requests; –8 no Christocentrism.

11. Value 9 is one of 11 values for the variable LITURG. See Appendix C analyzing how the testator uses liturgical detail in his will.

12. For the values of the variable IMMAN, see Appendix C, "Indicators of Immanence."

13. One is one of three values for the variable BODY2: 1 testator mentions body; –5 no bequest made; –8 body not mentioned.

14. The derivative variable LITURGICAL PERFORMATIVITY captures testators' perception of the power of the liturgy. Gueret's attention to the interplay of the musical motif of the passion, and the placing of his body before the crucifix, suggest his understanding of liturgy as a way to create a symbolic association of his body with the body of Christ, thus creating a salvific relationship. See Appendix C: "Mentions of Testator's Own Body."

15. One of 8 values of the variable REFORM. See Appendix C: "Reformist Behaviors."

16. See note 16 above.

17. The sub-purpose here refers to the variable SERVICE which has 327 types of services or liturgical song, chant or prayers. See Table 7.4. p. 000 on the reduction in the variety of liturgical requests.

18. One of three values of the variable XSERVICE: –5 no special pious request; –8 no Christocentric service; 1 Christocentrism through service or ceremony.

19. See note 14 above.

20. See note 15 above.

21. See note above.

22. See Appendix C, for the values for the variable REFORM.

Appendix L
Comparison of Leaguers with a Reference Population of Non-Leaguers, 1590

Leaguer Population of 1590 (91 Testators)

Parish of League Testators at the Time of Will

Parish	Frequency	Percent	Cumulative Percent
Saint-Germain-l'Auxerrois	13	14.3%	14.3%
Saint-André-des-Arts	10	11.0%	25.3%
No Location Specified	8	8.8%	34.1%
Saint-Séverin	8	8.8%	42.9%
Saint-Benoît	8	8.8%	51.6%
Saint-Gervais	6	6.6%	58.2%
Saint-Etienne-du-Mont	5	5.5%	63.7%
Saint-Christophe	4	4.4%	68.1%
Sainte-Croix	4	4.4%	72.5%
Saint-Jacques-de-la-Boucherie	3	3.3%	75.8%
Saint-Eustache	3	3.3%	79.1%
La Madeleine	3	3.3%	82.4%
Saint-Sulpice	2	2.2%	84.6%
Saint-Nicolas-des-Champs	2	2.2%	86.8%
Saint-Merry	2	2.2%	89.0%
Saint-Jean-en-Grève	2	2.2%	91.2%
Saint-Barthélemy	2	2.2%	93.4%
Saint-Pierre-des-Arcis	2	2.2%	95.6%
Saint-Nicolas-du-Chardonnet	1	1.1%	96.7%
Saint-Leu-Saint-Gilles	1	1.1%	97.8%
Saint-Pierre-aux-Boeufs	1	1.1%	98.9%
Saint-Germain-le-Viel	1	1.1%	100.0%
TOTAL	91	100.0%	100.0%

Burial Location of League Testators, 1590

Location	Frequency	Percent	Cumulative Percent
Non-Parisian Area Parish	25	27.5%	28.1%
Saint-André-des-Arts	6	6.6%	34.8%
No Location Specified	5	5.5%	40.4%
Saint-Germain-l'Auxerrois	4	4.4%	44.9%
Saint-Christophe	4	4.4%	49.4%
Sainte-Croix	4	4.4%	53.9%
Saint-Séverin	3	3.3%	57.3%
Saint-Etienne-du-Mont	3	3.3%	60.7%
Saint-Gervais	3	3.3%	64.0%
La Madeleine	3	3.3%	67.4%
Augustinian Monastery	3	3.3%	70.8%

Cordeliers Monastery	3	3.3%	74.2%
Missing	3	3.3%	75.9%
Saint-Benoît	2	2.2%	78.1%
Saint-Nicolas-des-Champs	2	2.2%	80.3%
Ave Maria Convent	2	2.2%	82.5%
Sainte-Croix-de-la-Bretonnerie Monastery	2	2.2%	84.7%
Illegible	2	2.2%	86.9%
Saint-Sulpice	1	1.1%	88.0%
Saint-Leu-Saint-Gilles	1	1.1%	89.1%
Saint-Paul	1	1.1%	90.2%
Saint-Jean-en-Grève	1	1.1%	91.3%
Saint-Barthélemy	1	1.1%	92.4%
Sainte-Geneviève-des-Ardents	1	1.1%	93.5%
Jacobin Monastery	1	1.1%	94.6%
Mathurin Monastery	1	1.1%	95.7%
College de Lisieulx	1	1.1%	96.8%
Saint-Victor Abbey	1	1.1%	97.8%
Jesuit College de Clermont	1	1.1%	98.9%
Sainte-Geneviève Abbey	1	1.1%	100.0%
TOTAL	91	100.0%	100.0%

Special Burial Location of League Testators, 1590

Location	Frequency	Percent	Cumulative Percent
No special location	52	57.1%	57.1%
In, near, or in front of a chapel in a specific church or monastery	11	12.1%	69.2%
Does not apply, no burial information	8	8.8%	78.0%
Other special location	4	4.4%	82.4%
Family tomb	3	3.3%	85.7%
Choir	2	2.2%	87.9%
Other monument or section in the cemetery of the Innocents	2	2.2%	90.1%
In a specifically named chapel of an institution	2	2.2%	92.3%
Near the Virgin	1	1.1%	93.4%
Near or in front of a crucifix	1	1.1%	94.5%
Under the charnel house	1	1.1%	95.6%
Where the executor chooses	1	1.1%	96.7%
In or near any saint's altar or chapel	1	1.1%	97.8%
In the cemetery of the Innocents near a chaisse	1	1.1%	98.9%
By the regular seat of the testator	1	1.1%	100.0%
TOTAL	91	100.0%	100.0%

Sex of League Testators, 1590

Sex	Frequency	Percent	Cumulative Percent
Male	54	59.3%	59.3%
Female	37	40.7%	100.0%
TOTAL	91	100.0%	100.0%

Health of League Testators, 1590

Health	Frequency	Percent	Cumulative Percent
Sick	74	81.3%	81.3%
Healthy	16	17.6%	98.9%
Missing	1	1.1%	100.0%
TOTAL	91	100.0%	100.0%

Relation of League Testators to the University Milieu, 1590

Relation	Frequency	Percent	Cumulative Percent
Not of the University milieu	54	59.3%	59.3%
Testator used a notary with a practice in the University quarter	18	19.8%	79.1%
Employed in a University profession	13	14.3%	93.4%
Made a bequest to an individual or organization of the University of Paris	6	6.6%	100.0%
TOTAL	91	100.0%	100.0%

Socio-Professional Status of League Testators, 1590

Socio-Professional Category	Frequency	Percent	Cumulative Percent
Honorables Bourgeois	16	17.6%	17.6%
Gens de Loi	15	16.5%	34.1%
University/Liberal Professions	14	15.4%	49.5%
Nobles	11	12.1%	61.5%
All Artisans	7	8.8%	70.3%
Clergy	6	6.6%	76.9%
Noble Office or Noble Epithet	5	5.5%	82.4%
Soldiers	5	5.5%	87.9%
Middle/Lower Officials	4	4.4%	92.3%
Mixed Merchants	2	2.2%	94.5%
Servants	2	2.2%	96.7%
Unclassifiable	2	2.2%	98.9%
Rural Workers	1	1.1%	100.0%
TOTAL	91	100.0%	100.0%

Level of Literacy of League Testators, 1590

Level of Literacy	Frequency	Percent	Cumulative Percent
Signs will	63	69.2%	69.2%
Declares does not know how to sign	15	16.5%	85.7%
Declares cannot sign due to incapacity	13	14.3%	100.0%
TOTAL	91	100.0%	100.0%

Holograph Wills of League Testators, 1590

Holograph Will	Frequency	Percent	Cumulative Percent
No	89	97.8%	97.8%
Yes	2	2.2%	100.0%
TOTAL	91	100.0%	100.0%

Sacral Headings for Wills of League Testators, 1590

Headings	Frequency	Percent	Cumulative Percent
No special heading	75	82.4%	82.4%
Cross is made at the top of the page	10	11.0%	93.4%
"Jesus . . . Maria"	4	4.4%	97.8%
"In nomine domini, amen."	1	1.1%	98.9%
"In nomine patris et filii et spiritus sancti" (with or without cross and "amen")	1	1.1%	100.0%
TOTAL	91	100.0%	100.0%

Notaries of Wills of League Testators, 1590

Name of Notary	Number of Testators	Percent	Cumulative Percent
Bontemps, R.	22	24.2%	24.2%
Croiset	6	6.6%	30.8%
Charles, Jean	5	5.5%	36.3%
Herbin	5	5.5%	41.8%
Troyes	5	5.5%	47.3%
Bontemps, M.	4	4.4%	51.6%
Bruyère	4	4.4%	56.0%
Cothereau, P.	4	4.4%	60.4%
Lamiral	4	4.4%	64.8%
Chartain	3	3.3%	68.1%
Ferrant	3	3.3%	71.4%
Jourdan	3	3.3%	74.7%
Bernard	2	2.2%	76.9%
Dunesmes II	2	2.2%	79.1%

Fardeau	2	2.2%	81.3%
Landry	2	2.2%	83.5%
Saint-Vaast	2	2.2%	85.7%
Arragon	1	1.1%	86.8%
Bergeon	1	1.1%	87.9%
Chefdeville	1	1.1%	89.0%
Contenot	1	1.1%	90.1%
Doujat	1	1.1%	91.2%
Jacques	1	1.1%	92.3%
Le Roux	1	1.1%	93.4%
Leroy	1	1.1%	94.5%
Lusson	1	1.1%	95.6%
Lybault	1	1.1%	96.7%
Monthenault	1	1.1%	97.8%
Peron	1	1.1%	98.9%
Robinot	1	1.1%	100.0%
TOTAL	91	100.0%	100.0%

Part of Town Where Notaries of League Testators Practiced, 1590

Area	Frequency	Percent	Cumulative Percent
Cité	34	37.4%	37.4%
Ville	28	30.8%	68.1%
Université	24	26.4%	94.5%
Faubourg Parishes	4	4.4%	98.9%
Missing	1	1.1%	100.0%
TOTAL	91	100.0%	100.0%

Parish of Notaries of League Testators, 1590

Parish	Frequency	Percent	Cumulative Percent
No Location Specified	37	40.7%	40.7%
La Madeleine	24	26.4%	67.0%
Saint-André-des-Arts	9	9.9%	76.9%
Saint-Gervais	5	5.5%	82.4%
Saint-Eustache	5	5.5%	87.9%
Saint-Germain-des-Prés	4	4.4%	92.3%
Saint-Séverin	2	2.2%	94.5%
Saint-Benoît	2	2.2%	96.7%
Saint-Merry	2	2.2%	98.9%
Saint-Nicolas-des-Champs	1	1.1%	100.0%
TOTAL	91	100.0%	100.0%

Non-Leaguer Reference Population of 1590
(All other testators, 636)

Parish of Non-League Testators at the Time of Will

Parish	Frequency	Percent	Cumulative Percent
Saint-Nicolas-des-Champs	66	10.4%	10.4%
Saint-Eustache	66	10.4%	20.8%
Saint-Germain-l'Auxerrois	64	10.1%	30.8%
Saint-Paul	50	7.9%	38.7%
Saint-Etienne-du-Mont	46	7.2%	45.9%
Saint-Jacques-de-la-Boucherie	46	7.2%	53.1%
Saint-Gervais	37	5.8%	59.0%
Saint-Merry	35	5.5%	64.5%
No Location Specified	31	4.9%	69.3%
Saint-Séverin	29	4.6%	73.9%
Saint Jean-en-Grève	24	3.8%	77.7%
Saint-Benoît	21	3.3%	81.0%
Saint-André-des-Arts	12	1.9%	82.9%
Saint-Christophe	11	1.7%	84.6%
Saint-Germain-le-Viel	9	1.4%	86.0%
Saint-Leu-Saint-Gilles	8	1.3%	87.3%
Sainte-Croix	8	1.3%	88.5%
Saint-Nicolas-du-Chardonnet	7	1.1%	89.6%
Sainte-Geneviève-des-Ardents	7	1.1%	90.7%
Sainte-Laurent	6	0.9%	91.7%
Saints-Innocents	6	0.9%	92.6%
Saint-Côme	5	0.8%	93.4%
Saint-Saveur	5	0.8%	94.2%
Sainte-Opportune	5	0.8%	95.0%
Saint-Barthélemy	5	0.8%	95.8%
La Madeleine	5	0.8%	96.6%
Missing	4	0.6%	97.2%
Saint-Pierre-aux-Boeufs	4	0.6%	97.8%
Saint-Hilaire	3	0.5%	98.3%
Notre-Dame-de-Paris	3	0.5%	98.7%
Saint-Pierre-des-Arcis	2	0.3%	99.1%
Sainte-Marine	2	0.3%	99.4%
La Sainte-Chapelle	1	0.2%	99.6%
Saint-Germain-des-Prés	1	0.2%	99.8%
Saint-Josse	1	0.2%	100.0%
TOTAL	636	100.0%	100.0%

Burial Location of Non-League Testators, 1590

Location	Frequency	Percent	Cumulative Percent
Non-Parisian Area Parish	310	48.7%	48.7%
Saint-Nicolas-des-Champs	28	4.4%	53.1%

Saint-Paul	24	3.8%	56.9%
Saint-Séverin	21	3.3%	60.2%
Saint-Etienne-du-Mont	21	3.3%	63.5%
Saint-Eustache	21	3.3%	66.8%
Saint-Gervais	18	2.8%	69.7%
Saints-Innocents	17	2.7%	72.3%
Saint-Benoît	14	2.2%	74.5%
Saint-Jean-en-Grève	14	2.2%	76.7%
Saint-Germain-l'Auxerrois	10	1.6%	78.3%
Saint-Jacques-de-la-Boucherie	9	1.4%	79.7%
Augustinian Monastery	7	1.1%	80.8%
Saint-Germain-le-Viel	6	0.9%	81.8%
Carmelite Monastery	6	0.9%	82.7%
Ave Maria Convent	6	0.9%	83.6%
Saint-Anthoine	6	0.9%	84.6%
Saint-Sulpice	5	0.8%	85.4%
Cordeliers Monastery	5	0.8%	86.2%
Saint-André-des-Arts	4	0.6%	86.8%
Saint-Merry	4	0.6%	87.4%
Saint-Barthélemy	4	0.6%	88.1%
La Madeleine	4	0.6%	88.7%
Sainte-Croix-de-la-Bretonnerie Monastery	4	0.6%	89.3%
Saint-Nicolas-du-Chardonnet	3	0.5%	89.8%
Saint-Christophe	3	0.5%	90.3%
The Church of the Temple	3	0.5%	90.7%
Non-Parisian Area Parish/Church Not Found	3	0.5%	91.2%
No Location Specified	2	0.3%	91.5%
Saint-Côme	2	0.3%	91.8%
Saint-Saveur	2	0.3%	92.1%
Sainte-Opportune	2	0.3%	92.5%
Sainte-Geneviève-des-Ardents	2	0.3%	92.8%
Vitry sur Seine	2	0.3%	93.1%
Champigny sur Marne	2	0.3%	93.4%
Billetes Monastery	2	0.3%	93.7%
Enfants-Rouges	2	0.3%	94.0%
Subtotal	598	94.0%	94.0%
(The remaining 6% of the non-Leaguer population of 1590 consisted of 38 individuals who specified 36 different places in which to be buried.)	38	6.0%	100.0%
TOTAL	636	100.0%	100.0%

Special Burial Location of Non-League Testators, 1590

Location	Frequency	Percent	Cumulative Percent
No special location	390	61.3%	61.3%
In, near, or in front of a chapel in a specific church or monastery	55	8.6%	70.0%
Does not apply	51	8.0%	78.0%

Location	Frequency	Percent	Cumulative Percent
Other monument or section in the cemetery of the Innocents	28	4.4%	82.4%
Other special location	26	4.1%	86.5%
Under the charnel house	15	2.4%	88.8%
Near the Virgin	11	1.7%	90.6%
Where the executor chooses	9	1.4%	92.0%
Near a crucifix	8	1.3%	93.2%
Near a preacher	6	0.9%	94.2%
In front of the image of Our Lady	6	0.9%	95.1%
In the nave in front of the crucifix	5	0.8%	95.9%
Near his customary seat	4	0.6%	96.5%
Family tomb	4	0.6%	97.2%
Near a cross (not in the cemetery of the Innocents)	4	0.6%	97.8%
Near a statue or image of a saint	3	0.5%	98.3%
Choir	3	0.5%	98.7%
Under the portal	2	0.3%	99.1%
Near the customary seat of one's spouse	2	0.3%	99.4%
Near the common grave for the poor (fosse aux pauvres)	2	0.3%	99.7%
Cemetery of a monastery or convent	1	0.2%	99.8%
Chapel of an institution	1	0.2%	100.0%
TOTAL	636	100.0%	100.0%

Sex of Non-League Testators, 1590

Sex	Frequency	Percent	Cumulative Percent
Female	332	52.2%	52.2%
Male	302	47.5%	99.7%
Mutual Will	2	0.3%	100.0%
TOTAL	636	100.0%	100.0%

Health of Non-League Testators, 1590

Health	Frequency	Percent	Cumulative Percent
Sick	557	87.6%	87.6%
Healthy	71	11.2%	98.7%
Missing	8	1.3%	100.0%
TOTAL	636	100.0%	100.0%

Relation of Non-League Testators to the University Milieu, 1590

Relation	Frequency	Percent	Cumulative Percent
Not of the University milieu	511	80.3%	80.3%
Testator used a notary with a practice in the University quarter	100	15.7%	96.1%
Employed in a University profession	17	2.7%	98.7%
Made a bequest to an individual or organization of the University of Paris	8	1.3%	100.0%
TOTAL	636	100.0%	100.0%

Socio-Professional Status of Non-League Testators, 1590

Socio-Professional category	Frequency	Percent	Cumulative Percent
Honorables Bourgeois	164	25.8%	25.8%
All Artisans	127	20.0%	45.8%
Gens de Loi	82	12.9%	58.6%
Laboureurs/Well-to-do Peasant Farmers	50	7.9%	66.5%
Mixed Merchants	40	6.3%	72.8%
Clergy	26	4.1%	76.9%
Nobles	26	4.1%	81.0%
Noble Office or Noble Epithet	18	2.8%	83.8%
Middle/Lower Officials	18	2.8%	86.6%
University/Liberal Professions	17	2.7%	89.3%
Unclassifiable	16	2.5%	91.8%
Servants	15	2.4%	94.2%
Rural Workers	15	2.4%	96.5%
Soldiers	13	2.0%	98.6%
Day Laborers	6	0.9%	99.5%
Skilled Independent Workers	3	0.5%	100.0%
TOTAL	636	100.0%	100.0%

Level of Literacy of Non-League Testators, 1590

Level of Literacy	Frequency	Percent	Cumulative Percent
Signs will	338	53.1%	53.1%
Declares does not know how to sign	215	33.8%	86.9%
Declares cannot sign due to incapacity	83	13.1%	100.0%
TOTAL	636	100.0%	100.0%

Holograph Wills of Non-League Testators, 1590

Holograph Will	Frequency	Percent	Cumulative Percent
No	634	99.7%	99.7%
Yes	2	0.3%	100.0%
TOTAL	636	100.0%	100.0%

Sacral Headings for Wills of Non-League Testators, 1590

Headings	Frequency	Percent	Cumulative Percent
No special heading	607	95.4%	95.4%
"In nomine domini, amen."	16	2.5%	98.7%
"Jesus . . . Maria"	5	0.8%	98.7%
Cross is made at the top of the page	5	0.8%	99.5%
"Au nom du père du filz et du Saint-Esprit. Amen Jesus."	1	0.2%	99.8%
Sign of cross made following the preamble	1	0.2%	99.9%
"Making the sign of the cross upon myself"	1	0.2%	100.0%
TOTAL	636	100.0%	100.0%

Notaries of Wills of Non-League Testators, 1590

Name of Notary	Number of Testators	Percent	Cumulative Percent
Peron	40	6.3%	6.3%
Charles, Jean	29	4.6%	10.8%
Cothereau, P.	23	3.6%	14.5%
Parque	23	3.6%	18.1%
Arragon	21	3.3%	21.4%
Poche	21	3.3%	24.7%
Chapellain	19	3.0%	27.7%
Filesac	19	3.0%	30.7%
Goguyer	19	3.0%	33.6%
Jacques	18	2.8%	36.5%
Herbin	17	2.7%	39.2%
Lusson	17	2.7%	41.8%
Tulloue	17	2.7%	44.5%
Bergeon	16	2.5%	47.0%
Lybault	16	2.5%	49.5%
Levasseur	15	2.4%	51.9%
Périer	15	2.4%	54.2%
Desquatrevaulx	13	2.0%	56.3%
Labarde	13	2.0%	58.3%
Mahieu	13	2.0%	60.4%
Saint-Vaast	13	2.0%	62.4%
Lamiral	12	1.9%	64.3%
Bernard	10	1.6%	65.9%
Landry	10	1.6%	67.5%

Monthenault	10	1.6%	69.0%
Muret	10	1.6%	70.6%
Thevenin	10	1.6%	72.2%
Trouve	10	1.6%	73.7%
Chefdeville	9	1.4%	75.2%
Contenot	9	1.4%	76.6%
Robinot	9	1.4%	78.0%
Bontemps, M.	8	1.3%	79.2%
Le Cammus	8	1.3%	80.5%
Babynet	8	1.3%	81.8%
Fardeau	7	1.1%	82.9%
Leroy	7	1.1%	84.0%
Beaufort	6	0.9%	84.9%
Bruyère	6	0.9%	85.8%
Chazeretz	6	0.9%	86.8%
Girault	6	0.9%	87.7%
Leroux	6	0.9%	88.7%
Prive	6	0.9%	89.6%
Rossignol	6	0.9%	90.6%
Troyes	6	0.9%	91.5%
Saint-Chapelain	5	0.8%	92.3%
Chauvet	5	0.8%	93.1%
Doujat	5	0.8%	93.9%
Dunesmes	5	0.8%	94.7%
Croiset	4	0.6%	95.3%
Haultdesens	4	0.6%	95.9%
Jourdan	3	0.5%	96.4%
Maigret	3	0.5%	96.9%
Motelet	3	0.5%	97.3%
Saint-Fussien	3	0.5%	97.8%
Vachot	3	0.5%	98.3%
Viard	3	0.5%	98.7%
Contesse	2	0.3%	99.1%
Ferrant	2	0.3%	99.4%
Becquet	1	0.2%	99.5%
Cothereau, J.	1	0.2%	99.7%
Dumarc	1	0.2%	99.8%
Lenormant	1	0.2%	100.0%
TOTAL	636	100.0%	100.0%

Part of Town Where Notaries of Non-League Testators Practiced, 1590

Area	Frequency	Percent	Cumulative Percent
Ville	407	64.0%	64.0%
Université	111	17.5%	81.4%
Cité	80	12.6%	94.0%
Missing	32	5.0%	99.1%
Faubourg Parishes	6	0.9%	100.0%
TOTAL	636	100.0%	100.0%

Parish of Notaries of Non-League Testators, 1590

Parish	Frequency	Percent	Cumulative Percent
No Location Specified	327	51.4%	51.4%
Saint-Nicolas-des-Champs	43	6.8%	58.2%
Saint-Eustache	42	6.6%	64.8%
Saint-Germain-l'Auxerrois	41	6.4%	71.2%
La Madeleine	41	6.4%	77.7%
Saint-Gervais	38	6.0%	83.6%
Saint-Merry	37	5.8%	89.5%
Saint-André-des-Arts	16	2.5%	92.0%
Saint-Séverin	15	2.4%	94.3%
Saint-Benoît	14	2.2%	96.5%
Saint-Paul	13	2.0%	98.6%
Saint-Germain-des-Prés	6	0.9%	99.5%
Sainte-Opportune	3	0.5%	100.0%
TOTAL	636	100.0%	100.0%

Population of 1543–44 (159 Testators)

Parish of Testators at the Time of Will

Parish	Frequency	Percent	Cumulative Percent
No Location Specified	65	40.9%	40.9%
Saint-Germain-l'Auxerrois	18	11.3%	52.2%
Saint-Etienne-du-Mont	10	6.3%	58.5%
Saint-Jacques-de-la-Boucherie	9	5.7%	64.2%
Saint-Eustache	8	5.0%	69.2%
Saint-Merry	8	5.0%	74.2%
Saint-Gervais	6	3.8%	78.0%
Saint-Benoît	5	3.1%	81.1%
Saint-Séverin	4	2.5%	83.6%
Saint-Leu-Saint-Gilles	4	2.5%	86.2%
Saint-André-des-Arts	3	1.9%	88.1%
Saint-Paul	3	1.9%	89.9%
Saint-Nicolas-des-Champs	2	1.3%	91.2%
Saint-Côme	1	0.6%	91.8%
Saint-Nicolas-du-Chardonnet	1	0.6%	92.5%
Saint-Hippolyte	1	0.6%	93.1%
Saint-Laurent	1	0.6%	93.7%
Saint-Jean-en-Grève	1	0.6%	94.3%
Saints-Innocents	1	0.6%	95.0%
Saint-Barthélemy	1	0.6%	95.6%
La Madeleine	1	0.6%	96.2%
Saint-Germain-le-Viel	1	0.6%	96.9%
Saint-Christophe	1	0.6%	97.5%
Saint-Médard	1	0.6%	98.1%

Saint-Etienne-des-Grez	1	0.6%	98.7%
Illegible	1	0.6%	99.4%
No Value	1	0.6%	100.0%
TOTAL	159	100.0%	100.0%

Burial Location of Testators, 1543–44

Location	Frequency	Percent	Cumulative Percent
Saints-Innocents	68	42.8%	42.8%
Non-Parisian Area Parish	22	13.8%	56.6%
Saint-Etienne-du-Mont	9	5.7%	62.3%
Non-Parisian Church or Parish	9	5.7%	68.0%
No Location Specified	7	4.4%	72.4%
Saint-Séverin	7	4.4%	76.8%
Saint-Gervais	5	3.1%	79.9%
Saint-Benoît	3	1.9%	81.8%
Saint-Nicolas-des-Champs	3	1.9%	83.7%
Saint-Paul	3	1.9%	85.6%
Saint-André-des-Arts	2	1.3%	86.9%
Saint-Hyppolyte	2	1.3%	88.2%
Cordeliers Monastery	2	1.3%	89.5%
Hospital in Church of the Trinity	2	1.3%	90.8%
Parish Where Individual Dies	2	1.3%	92.1%
Saint-Côme	1	0.6%	92.7%
Saint-Eustache	1	0.6%	93.3%
Saint-Merry	1	0.6%	93.9%
Saint-Laurent	1	0.6%	94.5%
Saint-Saveur	1	0.6%	95.1%
Saint-Jean-en-Grève	1	0.6%	95.7%
Saint-Germain-le-Viel	1	0.6%	96.3%
Mathurin Monastery	1	0.6%	96.9%
Bernardin Monastery	1	0.6%	97.5%
Hôtel-Dieu, Paris	1	0.6%	98.1%
Saint-Etienne-des-Grez	1	0.6%	98.7%
Saint-Victor Abbey	1	0.6%	99.4%
College of Cardinal Lemoyne	1	0.6%	100.0%
TOTAL	159	100.0%	100.0%

Special Burial Location of Testators, 1543–44

Location	Frequency	Percent	Cumulative Percent
No special location	105	66.0%	66.0%
Other monument or section in the cemetery of the Innocents	12	7.5%	73.6%
No burial information in will	8	5.0%	78.6%
Other special location	5	3.1%	81.8%

Location	Frequency	Percent	Cumulative Percent
Near a crucifix	4	2.5%	84.3%
Where executor chooses	4	2.5%	86.8%
In front of the image of our Lady in the cemetery of the Innocents	4	2.5%	89.3%
In a named chapel	4	2.5%	91.8%
Near the common grave for the poor (*fosse aux pauvres*)	3	1.9%	93.7%
In or in front of a chapel in a church or a monastery	2	1.3%	95.0%
Under the charnel house	2	1.3%	96.2%
Near a preacher	1	0.6%	96.9%
Choir	1	0.6%	97.5%
Near a cross	1	0.6%	98.1%
Near one's customary seat	1	0.6%	98.7%
In Saints-Innocents near the bench where the *salut jeudy absolu* is said	1	0.6%	99.4%
Illegible	1	0.6%	100.0%
TOTAL	159	100.0%	100.0%

Sex of Testators, 1543–44

Sex	Frequency	Percent	Cumulative Percent
Female	80	50.3%	50.3%
Male	78	49.1%	99.4%
Mutual Will	1	0.6%	100.0%
TOTAL	159	100.0%	100.0%

Health of Testators, 1543–44

Health	Frequency	Percent	Cumulative Percent
Sick	75	47.2%	47.2%
Healthy	54	34.0%	81.1%
Missing/Error	30	18.9%	100.0%
TOTAL	159	100.0%	100.0%

Socio-Professional Status, 1543–44

Socio-Professional Category	Frequency	Percent	Cumulative Percent
Honorables Bourgeois	49	30.8%	30.8%
Gens de Loi	23	14.5%	45.3%
Nobles	19	11.9%	57.2%
Mixed Merchants	14	8.8%	66.0%
All Artisans	14	8.8%	74.8%

Clergy	10	6.3%	81.1%
Unclassifiable	10	6.3%	87.4%
University/Liberal Professions	7	4.4%	91.8%
Laboureurs/Well-to-do Peasant Farmers	5	3.1%	95.0%
Middle/Lower Officials	3	1.9%	96.9%
Servants	3	1.9%	98.7%
Soldiers	2	1.3%	100.0%
TOTAL	159	100.0%	100.0%

Level of Literacy of Testators 1543–44

Level of Literacy	Frequency	Percent	Cumulative Percent
Not mentioned in will	151	95.0%	95.0%
Signs will	8	5.0%	100.0%
TOTAL	159	100.0%	100.0%

Holograph Wills of Testators, 1543–44

Holograph Will	Frequency	Percent	Cumulative Percent
No	152	95.6%	95.6%
Yes	7	4.4%	100.0%
TOTAL	159	100.0%	100.0%

Sacral Headings for Wills of Testators, 1543–44

Headings	Frequency	Percent	Cumulative Percent
No special heading	143	89.9%	89.9%
"Jesus . . . Maria"	10	6.3%	96.2%
"Au nom du père du filz et du Saint-Esprit. Amen Jesus."	3	1.9%	98.1%
Cross is made at the top of the page	2	1.3%	99.4%
Cross and other special heading	1	0.6%	100.0%
TOTAL	159	100.0%	100.0%

Notaries of Wills of Testators, 1543–44

Name of Notary	Number of Testators	Percent	Cumulative Percent
Cartault	9	5.7%	5.7%
Contesse	8	5.0%	10.7%
Crozon	8	5.0%	15.7%
Brahier	6	3.8%	19.5%
Champin	6	3.8%	23.3%
Poutrain	6	3.8%	27.0%
Trouve	6	3.8%	30.8%

Name of Notary	Number of Testators	Percent	Cumulative Percent
Boulle	5	3.1%	34.0%
Dunesmes	5	3.1%	37.1%
LeClerc	5	3.1%	40.3%
LeRoy	5	3.1%	43.4%
Viau	5	3.1%	46.5%
Boissellet	4	2.5%	49.1%
Charlet	4	2.5%	51.6%
Cordelle	4	2.5%	54.1%
Cruce	4	2.5%	56.6%
Maupeou	4	2.5%	59.1%
Montigue	4	2.5%	61.6%
Mussart	4	2.5%	64.2%
Nicolas	4	2.5%	66.7%
Payen	4	2.5%	69.2%
Perier	4	2.5%	71.7%
Ymbert	4	2.5%	74.2%
Bergeon	3	1.9%	76.1%
Dupont	3	1.9%	78.0%
Halle	3	1.9%	79.9%
Lenormand	3	1.9%	81.8%
L'Olive	3	1.9%	83.6%
Louvencourt	3	1.9%	85.5%
Roger	3	1.9%	87.4%
Alart	2	1.3%	88.7%
Cousin	2	1.3%	89.9%
Fardeau	2	1.3%	91.2%
LeTellier	2	1.3%	92.5%
Thuret	2	1.3%	93.7%
Turpin	2	1.3%	95.0%
Boulle	1	0.6%	95.6%
Bruslé	1	0.6%	96.2%
Contesse	1	0.6%	96.9%
Filesac	1	0.6%	97.5%
Frenicle	1	0.6%	98.1%
LeCharron	1	0.6%	98.7%
Merault	1	0.6%	99.4%
Palanquin	1	0.6%	100.0%
TOTAL	159	100.0%	100.0%

Part of Town Where Notaries Practiced, 1543–44

Area	Frequency	Percent	Cumulative Percent
Ville	102	64.2%	64.2%
Université	53	33.3%	97.5%
Cité	4	2.5%	100.0%
TOTAL	159	100.0%	100.0%

Parish of Notaries of Testators, 1543–44

Parish	Frequency	Percent	Cumulative Percent
No Location Given	117	73.6%	73.6%
Saint-Benoît	8	5.0%	78.6%
Saint-Nicolas-des-Champs	6	3.8%	82.4%
Saint-Germain-l'Auxerrois	5	3.1%	85.5%
Saint-Eustache	5	3.1%	88.7%
Saint-Jacques-de-la-Boucherie	4	2.5%	91.2%
Saint-Gervais	4	2.5%	93.7%
La Madeleine	4	2.5%	96.2%
Saint-Méderic	3	1.9%	98.1%
Saint-André-des-Arts	2	1.3%	99.4%
Saint-Sauveur	1	0.6%	100.0%
TOTAL	159	100.0%	100.0%

Population of 1630 (344 Testators)

Parish of Testator at the Time of the Will, 1630

Parish	Frequency	Percent	Cumulative Percent
No Location Specified	53	15.4%	15.5%
Saint-Eustache	31	9.0%	24.5%
Saint-Germain-l'Auxerrois	30	8.7%	33.2%
Saint-Nicolas-des-Champs	29	8.4%	41.7%
Saint-Paul	23	6.7%	48.4%
Saint-Méderic	22	6.4%	54.8%
Saint-Séverin	17	4.9%	59.8%
Saint-Sulpice	14	4.1%	63.8%
Saint-Jacques-de-la-Boucherie	13	3.8%	67.6%
Saint-Gervais	13	3.8%	71.4%
Saint-Etienne-du-Mont	12	3.5%	74.9%
Saint-André-des-Arts	10	2.9%	77.8%
Saint-Jean-en-Grève	8	2.3%	80.2%
Faubourg Saint-Jacques	8	2.3%	82.5%
Saint-Benoît	7	2.0%	84.5%
Saint-Médard	6	1.7%	86.3%
Saint-Sauveur	5	1.5%	87.8%
Saint-Leu-Saint-Gilles	3	0.9%	88.6%
Sainte-Opportune	3	0.9%	89.5%
Saint-Barthélemy	3	0.9%	90.4%
Saint-Martial	3	0.9%	91.3%
Saint-Nicolas-du-Chardonnet	2	0.6%	91.8%
Saint-Hippolyte	2	0.6%	92.4%
Saint-Roch	2	0.6%	93.0%
Saint-Landry	2	0.6%	93.6%
Saint-Germain-le-Viel	2	0.6%	94.2%
Sainte-Marine	2	0.6%	94.8%

Parish	Frequency	Percent	Cumulative Percent
Nôtre-Dame of Paris	2	0.6%	95.3%
Saint-Josse	2	0.6%	95.9%
Sainte-Côme	1	0.3%	96.2%
Saint-Hilaire	1	0.3%	96.5%
Saint-Laurent	1	0.3%	96.8%
Saints-Innocents	1	0.3%	97.1%
La Madeleine	1	0.3%	97.4%
Saint-Pierre-des-Arcis	1	0.3%	97.7%
Sainte-Croix	1	0.3%	98.0%
Saint-Jacques du Haut Pas	1	0.3%	98.3%
Rosny	1	0.3%	98.5%
Saint-Denis	1	0.3%	98.8%
Church of Saint-Martin, Faubourg Saint-Marcel	1	0.3%	99.1%
Pré Saint-Germain, Church of	1	0.3%	99.4%
Illegible	1	0.3%	99.7%
No Value	1	0.3%	100.0%
TOTAL	344	100.0%	100.0%

Burial Location of Testators, 1630

Location	Frequency	Percent	Cumulative Percent
Non-Parisian Area Parish	70	20.3%	20.3%
Saints-Innocents	53	15.4%	35.8%
Saint-Séverin	16	4.7%	40.4%
Saint-Nicolas-des-Champs	16	4.7%	45.1%
Saint-Paul	13	3.8%	48.8%
Saint-Eustache	12	3.5%	52.3%
Saint-Merry	12	3.5%	55.8%
No Special Location Given	11	3.2%	59.0%
Saint-Germain-l'Auxerrois	11	3.2%	62.2%
Saint-Jean-en-Grève	10	2.9%	65.1%
Non-Parisian Area Church/Church Not Found	10	2.9%	68.0%
Saint-Etienne-du-Mont	9	2.6%	70.6%
Saint-André-des-Arts	8	2.3%	73.0%
Saint-Gervais	7	2.0%	75.0%
Saint-Sulpice	6	1.7%	76.7%
Saint-Jacques-de-la-Boucherie	6	1.7%	78.5%
Saint-Médard	5	1.5%	79.9%
Faubourg Saint-Jacques	5	1.5%	81.4%
Saint-Benoît	4	1.2%	82.6%
Saint-Sauveur	4	1.2%	83.7%
Saint-Leu-Saint-Gilles	3	0.9%	84.6%
Saint-Roch	3	0.9%	85.5%
Saint-Barthélemy	3	0.9%	86.3%
Saint-Martial	3	0.9%	87.2%
Saint-Nicolas-du-Chardonnet	2	0.6%	87.8%
Saint-Hippolyte	2	0.6%	88.4%
Carmelite Monastery	2	0.6%	89.0%

Cordeliers Monastery	2	0.6%	89.5%
Hospital of the Quinze-Vingts	2	0.6%	90.1%
Carmes Deschaussez	2	0.6%	90.7%
The Convent and Hospital of St. John the Baptist of Charity	2	0.6%	91.3%
Subtotal	314	91.3%	91.3%
30 Other Unique Locations	30	8.7%	8.7%
TOTAL	344	100.0%	100.0%

Special Burial Location of Testators, 1630

Location	Frequency	Percent	Cumulative Percent
No special location	192	55.8%	55.8%
Does not apply	33	9.6%	65.4%
In front of chapel or church	18	5.2%	70.6%
Near one's customary seat	13	3.8%	74.4%
In family tomb	12	3.5%	77.9%
Where executor chooses	12	3.5%	81.4%
Named chapel of an institution	11	3.2%	84.6%
Other special location	10	2.9%	87.5%
In the choir	7	2.0%	89.5%
Other monument or section in the cemetery	6	1.7%	91.3%
In the nave	4	1.2%	92.4%
Near the Virgin	3	0.9%	93.3%
Near the cross	3	0.9%	94.2%
In the Holy Innocents cemetary in a special location	3	0.9%	95.1%
Marian reference other than Virgin	3	0.9%	95.9%
Where the priest chooses	3	0.9%	96.8%
In front of the image of the Virgin	2	0.6%	97.4%
Illegible	2	0.6%	98.0%
Near a statue or image of saint	1	0.3%	98.3%
Near a crucifix	1	0.3%	98.5%
Near a preacher	1	0.3%	98.8%
Near the seat of a relative	1	0.3%	99.1%
Under the charnel house	1	0.3%	99.4%
Near the Holy Sacrament	1	0.3%	99.7%
Where one usually sits	1	0.3%	100.0%
TOTAL	344	100.0%	100.0%

Sex of Testators, 1630

Sex	Frequency	Percent	Cumulative Percent
Female	179	52.0%	52.0%
Male	158	45.9%	98.0%
Mutual Will	7	2.0%	100.0%
TOTAL	344	100.0%	100.0%

Health of Testators, 1630

Health	Frequency	Percent	Cumulative Percent
Sick	218	63.4%	63.4%
Healthy	110	32.0%	95.3%
Missing	16	4.7%	100.0%
TOTAL	344	100.0%	100.0%

Socio-Professional Status of Testators, 1630

Socio-Professional Category	Frequency	Percent	Cumulative Percent
Honorables Bourgeois	71	20.6%	20.6%
All Artisans	58	16.9%	37.5%
Nobles	41	11.9%	49.4%
Gens de Loi	33	9.6%	59.0%
Mixed Merchants	23	6.7%	65.7%
Clergy	19	5.5%	71.2%
Noble Office or Noble Epithet	19	5.5%	76.7%
Middle/Lower Officials	19	5.5%	82.3%
Servants	18	5.2%	87.5%
Unclassifiable	15	4.4%	91.9%
University/Liberal Professions	9	2.6%	94.5%
Soldiers	6	1.7%	96.2%
Day Laborers	5	1.5%	97.7%
Rural workers	4	1.2%	98.8%
Skilled Independent Workers	2	0.6%	99.4%
Laboureurs/Well-to-do Peasant Farmers	2	0.6%	100.0%
TOTAL	344	100.0%	100.0%

Level of Literacy of Testators, 1630

Level of Literacy	Frequency	Percent	Cumulative Percent
Signs will	222	64.5%	64.5%
Declares does not know how to sign	96	27.9%	92.4%
Declares cannot sign due to incapacity	22	6.4%	98.8%
Missing	4	1.2%	100.0%
TOTAL	344	100.0%	100.0%

Holograph Wills of Testators, 1630

Holograph Will	Frequency	Percent	Cumulative Percent
No	331	96.2%	96.2%
Yes	13	3.8%	100.0%
TOTAL	344	100.0%	100.0%

Sacral Headings for Wills of Testators, 1630

Headings	Frequency	Percent	Cumulative Percent
No special heading	325	94.5%	94.5%
Cross is made at the top of the page	13	3.8%	98.3%
Cross is made and other special heading	2	0.6%	98.8%
Cross and "Au nom du père du filz et du Saint-Esprit"	2	0.6%	99.4%
"Jesus . . . Maria"	1	0.3%	99.7%
"In nomine patris . . . Amen.	1	0.3%	100.0%
TOTAL	344	100.0%	100.0%

Notaries of Wills of Testators, 1630

Name of Notary	Number of Testators	Percent	Cumulative Percent
Saint-Vaast	15	4.4%	4.4%
Turgis	15	4.4%	8.7%
Bourgeois	10	2.9%	11.6%
Huart	9	2.6%	14.7%
LeGay	9	2.6%	16.9%
Morel	9	2.6%	19.5%
Paisant	9	2.6%	22.1%
Delacroix	8	2.3%	24.4%
Nourry	8	2.3%	26.7%
Poictevin	8	2.3%	29.1%
Bruneau	7	2.0%	31.1%
Charles, Jean	7	2.0%	33.1%
Cousinet	6	1.7%	34.9%
LeConte	6	1.7%	36.6%
LeRoy, C.	6	1.7%	38.4%
Monthenault	6	1.7%	40.1%
Tulloue	6	1.7%	41.9%
Camuset	5	1.5%	43.3%
Cartier	5	1.5%	44.8%
Dauvergne	5	1.5%	46.2%
Destrechy	5	1.5%	47.7%
Fieffe	5	1.5%	49.1%
Garnon	5	1.5%	50.6%
LeRoux	5	1.5%	52.0%
Lybault	5	1.5%	53.5%
Marreau	5	1.5%	54.9%
Ogier	5	1.5%	56.4%
Perier	5	1.5%	57.8%
Vautier	5	1.5%	59.3%
Vigeon	5	1.5%	60.8%
Caron	4	1.2%	61.9%
Chapellain	4	1.2%	63.1%
Demas	4	1.2%	64.2%
Dubois	4	1.2%	65.4%

Name of Notary	Number of Testators	Percent	Cumulative Percent
Gaultier	4	1.2%	66.6%
Gerbault	4	1.2%	67.7%
Jutet	4	1.2%	68.9%
Lestoré	4	1.2%	70.1%
Moufle	4	1.2%	71.2%
Parque	4	1.2%	72.4%
Richer	4	1.2%	73.5%
Robinot	4	1.2%	74.7%
Troyes	4	1.2%	75.9%
Cresse	3	0.9%	76.7%
Duchesne	3	0.9%	77.6%
Dupuys	3	0.9%	78.5%
Fontaine	3	0.9%	79.4%
Groyn	3	0.9%	80.2%
LeMercier	3	0.9%	81.1%
LeRoy, E.	3	0.9%	82.0%
Marion	3	0.9%	82.8%
Motelet	3	0.9%	83.7%
Parque	3	0.9%	84.6%
Remond	3	0.9%	85.5%
Saint-Vaast	3	0.9%	86.3%
Thévenin	3	0.9%	87.2%
Vassetz	3	0.9%	88.1%
Bauldry	2	0.6%	88.7%
Beauvais	2	0.6%	89.2%
Belin	2	0.6%	89.8%
Blosse	2	0.6%	90.4%
Boucot	2	0.6%	91.0%
Charles, Jacques	2	0.6%	91.6%
Colle	2	0.6%	92.2%
Guerreau	2	0.6%	92.7%
Haultdesens	2	0.6%	93.3%
Herben	2	0.6%	93.9%
LeCamus	2	0.6%	94.5%
LeMoyne	2	0.6%	95.1%
LeVasseur	2	0.6%	95.6%
LeVoyer	2	0.6%	96.2%
Menard	2	0.6%	96.8%
Saint-Fussien	2	0.6%	97.4%
Bergeon	1	0.3%	97.7%
Charlet	1	0.3%	98.0%
Cothereau, Bon.	1	0.3%	98.3%
Grandrye	1	0.3%	98.5%
Guyon	1	0.3%	98.8%
Jolly	1	0.3%	99.1%
LeRoux	1	0.3%	99.4%
Perlin	1	0.3%	99.7%
Petit	1	0.3%	100.0%
TOTAL	344	100.0%	100.0%

Part of Town Where Notaries Practiced, 1630

Area	Frequency	Percent	Cumulative Percent
Ville	213	61.9%	61.9%
Université	88	25.6%	87.5%
Cité	25	7.3%	94.8%
Faubourg Parishes	15	4.4%	99.2%
Missing	3	0.9%	100.0%
TOTAL	344	100.0%	100.0%

Parish of Notaries of Testators, 1630

Parish	Frequency	Percent	Cumulative Percent
No Location Specified	208	60.5%	60.5%
Saint-Benoît	23	6.7%	67.2%
Saint-Nicolas-des-Champs	16	4.7%	71.8%
Saint-Sulpice	15	4.4%	76.2%
Saint-Germain-l'Auxerrois	15	4.4%	80.5%
Saint-Méderic	14	4.1%	84.6%
Saint-Paul	14	4.1%	88.7%
Saint-Séverin	12	3.5%	92.2%
Saint-Pierre-des-Arcis	9	2.6%	94.8%
Saint-Eustache	7	2.0%	96.8%
Saint-Leu-Saint-Gilles	5	1.5%	98.3%
Saint-Jacques-de-la-Boucherie	4	1.2%	99.4%
Saint-Gervais	1	0.3%	99.7%
Saints-Innocents	1	0.3%	100.0%
TOTAL	344	100.0%	100.0%

NOTES

Preface

1. The French original of Denis Richet, "Aspects socio-culturels des conflits religieux à Paris dans la seconde moitié du XVIe siècle," appeared in *Annales: Economies, sociétés, civilisations* 32 (July 1977): 764–90. All citations are from the English translation: Denis Richet, "Sociocultural Aspects of Religious Conflicts in Paris during the Second Half of the Sixteenth Century," in *Ritual, Religion, and the Sacred: Selections from the Annales, Economies, Sociétés, Civilisations*, eds. Robert Forster and Orest Ranum, trans. Elborg Forster and Patricia M. Ranum, vol. 7 (Baltimore: The Johns Hopkins Press, 1982).

2. The exception is the remarkable work of Henri Brémond, *Histoire littéraire du sentiment religieux en France depuis la fin des guerres de religion jusqu'à nos jours* (1923; reprint, Paris: Armand Colin, 1967), who announced his intention to privilege "personal individual experience" and explore the truths of the inner life. See *A Literary History of Religious Thought in France: From the Wars of Religion Down to Our Own Times*, vol. 1, trans. K. L. Montgomery (London: Society for Promoting Christian Knowledge, 1928).

3. Richet, "Sociocultural Aspects," 200.

4. J. H. M. Salmon, "The Paris Sixteen, 1584–94: The Social Analysis of a Revolutionary Movement," *Journal of Modern History* 44 (1972): 540–76; Elie Barnavi, *Le Parti de Dieu: Etude sociale et politique des chefs de la Ligue parisienne 1585–1594* (Louvain: Nauwelaerts, 1980); Robert Descimon, *Qui étaient les Seize? Mythes et réalités de la Ligue parisienne (1585–1594)*, vol. 34, Mémoires de la fédération des sociétés historiques et archéologiques de Paris et de l'Ile-de-France (Paris: Klincksieck, 1983); Denis Crouzet, *Les Guerriers de dieu*, 2 vols. (n.p.: Champ Vallon, 1990); and, among her many works cited below, Barbara B. Diefendorf, "Review Article, The Catholic League: Social Crisis or Apocalypse Now," *French Historical Studies* 15 (Fall 1987): 332–44, and Diefendorf, "Recent Literature on the Religious Conflicts in Sixteenth-Century France," *Religious Studies Review* 10 (October 1984): 362–67, which discuss the controversies. For a major debate, see R. Descimon and E. Barnavi, "La Ligue à Paris 1585–1594: une révision," *Annales: Economies, sociétés, civilisations* 37 (January 1982): 72–128, and a response to Diefendorf by Robert Descimon, "Milice bourgeoise et identité citadine à Paris au temps de la Ligue," *Annales: Economies, sociétés, civilisations* 48 (July 1993): 885–906.

5. Denis Richet, in somewhat of a departure from his preceding work, first spoke of "the autonomy of religious phenomena" in "Politique et religion: les processions à Paris en 1589," in *La France d'ancien régime. Etudes réunis en l'honneur de Pierre Goubert.* (Toulouse: 1984). Reprinted in Denis Richet, *De la réforme à la Révolution: Etudes sur la France moderne* (Paris: Aubier, 1991), 69–82.

6. Foundational is Gabriel Le Bras, *Etudes de sociologie religieuse* (Paris: Presses Universitaires de France, 1955). See also the work of Michel Vovelle, *Piété baroque et déchristianisation en Provence au XVIIIe siècle: Les attitudes devant la mort d'après les clauses des testaments* (Paris: Plon, 1973); Pierre Chaunu, *La mort à Paris: XVIe, XVIIe et XVIIIe siècles* (Paris: Fayard, 1978); Philip Benedict, *Rouen During the Wars of Religion* (Cambridge: Cambridge University Press, 1981); Philip Hoffman, *Church and Community in the Diocese of Lyon, 1500–1789* (New Haven: Yale University Press, 1984).

7. For these losses and the importance of the Châtelet archives for the study of popular religion and culture, see Charles Desmaze, *Le Châtelet de Paris, son organisation, ses privilèges: Prévôts, conseillers, chevaliers du guet, notaires, etc.* (Paris: Didier, 1870). For the highest court, the *Parlement*, see Félix Aubert, "Le Parlement et la ville de Paris au XVIe siècle," *Revue des études historiques* 71 (1905): 225–47, 337–57, 453–87.

8. A number of these master's theses and some Ph.D. dissertations may be consulted at the Centre de recherche historique at Paris IV (the Sorbonne). See also the dissertation by Alain Brunhes on the parish of Saint-Eustache, directed by Denis Richet.

9. For the basic work on pastoral visits, see Dominique Julia, "La réforme posttridentine en France d'après les procès-verbaux de visites pastorales: ordre et résistances," *La società religiosa nell'eta moderna* (Naples: 1973); Marc Venard, "Les visites pastorales dans l'église de France au XVIeme siècle: Evolution d'une institution," *Les églises et leurs institutions au XVIeme siècle, actes du 5eme colloque du centre d'histoire de la réforme et du protestantisme,* ed. Michele Péronnet (Montpellier: Université Paul Valéry, 1978); A. Artonne and O. Pontal, *Répertoire des statuts synodaux des diocèses de l'ancienne France du XIIIe à la fin du XVIIIe siècle* (Paris: Editions du C.N.R.S.: Documents, Etudes et Répertoires, 1963), 343–80; Jacques Gadille, Dominique Julia, and Marc Venard, "Pour un répertoire des visites pastorales," *Revue d'histoire de l'église de France* 55 (January 1969): 49–67; Jacques Gadille, Dominique Julia, and Marc Venard, "Pour un répertoire des visites pastorales," *Annales: Economies, sociétés, civilisations* 25, no. 2 (March 1970): 561–66; Marc Venard, "Le répertoire des visites pastorales (suite)," *Revue d'histoire de l'église de France* 55 (July 1969): 279–89; Nicole Lemaître, "Visites pastorales sous logiciel," *Histoire moderne et contemporaire informatique* 8 (1986): 7–35; Keith Luria, *Territories of Grace: Cultural Change in the Seventeenth-Century Diocese of Grenoble* (Berkeley and Los Angeles: University of California Press, 1991); an older study, Jeanne Ferté, *La vie religieuse: Dans les campagnes parisiennes (1622–1695)* (Paris: J. Vrin, 1962), also made use of pastoral visits. For work on synodal statutes, see Simone Potonniée, "Les confréries dans l'ancien

régime d'après les statues synodaux" (Thèse Faculté de Droit et des Sciences Economiques: 1960). The synodal statutes most useful for Paris were: Pierre de Gondy, *Statuta reverendi in Christo Patris domini Petri de Gondy, episcopi parisiensis edita in synodo anno D. 1582*, Paris, Bibliothèque Nationale (hereafter referred to as the BN); Pierre de Gondy, *Statuta a Petro de Gondy, episcopum Parisiensem, in synodo parisiensi renovata, anno 1585*, Paris, BN; also bound in this volume are *Statuts renouvelez par R. Père François de la Rochefoucault, Evesque de Clairmont: & publiez au S. Synode tenu audict Clairmont le vingtuniésme jour d'octobre 1599*; Henri de Gondy, Cardinal de Retz, *Réglemens faicts de l'authorité de Mgr . . . Cardinal de Retz . . . contenans l'explication de quelques articles des statuts synodaux de son diocèse*, Paris: François Julliot, 1620, in *Synodicon* de 1674, 385–422; also in this volume, François de Harlay, *Statuts publiés dans le synode tenu à Paris le 5e jour de juillet 1674 par Mgr l'Archevesque de Paris . . .* (Paris: François Muguet, 1673), 423–43.

10. Parisian last wills and testaments are housed as part of the Archives Nationales (hereafter referred to as the AN) in the *Minutier central*, which is the largest collection of notarial acts in all of Europe. A guide exists, *Les archives nationales. Etat général des fonds*, vol. 4, *Fonds divers* (Paris: Archives Nationales, 1980).

11. See especially the early publications of Denis Crouzet, "Recherches sur les processions blanches: 1583–1584," *Histoire, économie et société* 4 (1982): 511–63, and "La représentation du temps à l'époque de la Ligue," *Revue historique* 270, no. 2 (1984): 296–388.

Introduction

1. E. Durkheim, *The Elementary Forms of Religious Life* (London: Allen and Unwin, 1961). The concept of "effervescent sociability" lay at the heart of Emile Durkheim's understanding of the more than rational dimensions of religious experience. For a further contemporary discussion of the power of "effervescent sociability," see Philip A. Mellor and Chris Shilling, *Re-Forming the Body: Religion, Community and Modernity* (London: Sage Publications, 1997), 1, 17. Also see M. Richman, "The Sacred Group: A Durkheimian perspective on the Collège de sociologie (1937–39)," in *Bataille: Writing the Sacred*, ed. C. Bailey Gill (London: Routledge, 1995), 60.

2. A total of 1,230 wills were coded and analyzed using the *Statistical Package for the Social Sciences* Release 6.1 (1994), hereafter SPSS. The quantitative data in this book are based on those 1,230 wills, although many more than these were examined in the process of selecting the opening and closing years for the sample periods. For the period 1543–44, 159 testators made 1,332 pious requests; for 1590, 727 testators made 3,642 pious requests; and for 1630, 344 testators made 2,220 pious requests. The number of pious requests per testator

ranged from zero to a maximum of eighty requests in the forty-seven-page will of Marye Thiersault, an ardent Leaguer related by marriage to Michel de Marillac.

3. See Alain Talon, *La Compagnie du Saint-Sacrement (1629–1667): Spiritualité et société* (Paris: Cerf, 1990); Marguerite Pecquet, "Des Compagnies des Pénitents à la Compagnie du Saint-Sacrement," *XVIIe siècle* 69 (1965): 3–36; Raoul Allier, *La cabale des dévots, 1627–1666* (1902; reprint, Geneva: Slatkine Reprints, 1970). Talon's most recent work, *La France et le Concile de Trente (1518–1563)* (Rome: Ecole Française de Rome, 1997), did not appear in time to be considered in the present book.

4. For approaches to sacred immanence, see N. Z. Davis, "The Sacred and the Body Social in Sixteenth-Century Lyon," *Past and Present* 90 (February 1981); Carlos M. N. Eire, *War Against the Idols: The Reformation of Worship from Erasmus to Calvin* (Cambridge: Cambridge University Press, 1986). On immanence, see also Guy E. Swanson, *Religion and Regime: A Sociological Account of the Reformation* (Ann Arbor: University of Michigan Press, 1967). For reactions to Swanson's argument, see the symposium entitled "Reevaluating the Reformation" in *Journal of Interdisciplinary History* 1 (Spring 1971), especially Natalie Z. Davis's response, "Missed Connections: *Religion and Regime*," 381–94. The term performativity has begun to appear in a variety of disciplines. Judith Butler uses performativity in a critical and cultural sense, stressing that performativity refers to the production of the self or subject, which she argues is the result of publicly regulated performances and not an essentialist given. See *Bodies That Matter: On the Discursive Limits of "Sex"* (New York and London: Routledge, 1993), especially 20 and 224ff., for her definitions of performativity. There are both Hegelian and Marxist influences in this view of the production of self and meaning. Similarly, in the realm of literary interpretation, performativity argues against a uniform and stable, and thus reified, meaning in texts. Performativity stresses that the act of reading by the individual reader is a creative interaction or performance, which actively produces meaning. For performativity in the context of the liturgy see Chapter 2 below.

5. The concept has a close affinity with the most recent work of Robert Descimon, who develops the concept of *catholicisme corporatif*, with a strong anthropological orientation. Of League piety he writes: "Cette religion cimenta un sens de la communauté particulièrement fort, une communauté mise en scène par des rituels qui ne sont pas un simple reflet des structures sociales existantes, mais un appel vers le passé (les morts), et vers le futur, en somme, un acte de perpétuation." See Robert Descimon, "Le corps de ville et le système cérémoniel parisien au début de l'âge moderne" (1996). Note especially the filiation between Descimon's description of the scope of this concept and Robert A. Markus's insights into the program of Pope Leo I to establish "a Christian community" entailing "a Christian civic time." See Robert A. Markus, *The End of Ancient Christianity* (Cambridge: Cambridge University Press, 1990), 127. Marguerite Pecquet, "Des Compagnies des Pénitents à la compagnie du Saint-

Sacrement," *XVII Siècle* 69 (1965): 28, has used a related term, *catholicisme intégral.* See also Bernard Chevalier, *Les bonnes villes de France du XIVe au XVIe siècle* (Paris: Aubier Montaigne, 1982), and Yves Barel, *La ville médiévale, système social, système urbain* (Grenoble: Presses Universitaires de Grenoble, 1975).

6. For the burning of an effigy of "Heresy" by the new League government of Paris at the communal celebration of St. John's Eve, see the account in the entry for 23 June 1588 of Pierre L'Estoile's *Journal de l'Estoile pour la règne de Henri III*, ed. Louis-Raymond Lefèvre (Paris: Gallimard, 1948), 564.

7. See Philip Selznick, *The Moral Commonwealth: Social Theory and the Promise of Community* (Berkeley: University of California Press, 1992), 369.

Chapter 1

1. See Appendix A.

2. See Appendix B.

3. See Appendix B.

4. Antoine, first prince of the blood, remained a Catholic. It is reported that on this same day, he also attended mass. His brother Louis of Bourbon, prince of Condé (1530–69), converted to Protestantism and was titular head of the French Protestant movement. See Appendix A.

5. *Decrees of the Ecumenical Councils*, vol. 2, *Trent to Vatican II*, ed. Norman P. Tanner, original text established by G. Albergio, J. A. Dossetti, P.-P. Joannou, C. Leonardi, and P. Prodi, in consultation with H. Jedin (London: Sheed and Ward, Ltd., and Washington, D.C.: Georgetown University Press, 1990), session 25, chap. 10, 780.

6. *Decrees*, 780.

7. *Decrees*, 798.

8. For current debates on the use of the term *politique* and the position of L'Hôpital, see Edmond M. Beame, "The Politiques and the Historians," *Journal of the History of Ideas* 54 (July 1993): 335–60.

9. The first war 1562–63; the second 1567–68; the third 1568–70; the fourth 1572–73; the fifth 1574–76, concluded by the Peace of Monsieur.

10. See Appendix A.

11. These figures come from J. M. H. Salmon, *Society in Crisis: France in the Sixteenth Century* (New York: St. Martin's Press, 1975), 187. The bibliography on the massacres is extensive. See the most recent discussions by Denis Crouzet, *La nuit de la Saint-Barthélemy: Un rêve perdu de la renaissance* (Paris: Fayard, 1994), and J. Bergeron, "Pour une histoire, enfin, de la Saint-Barthélemy," in *Revue historique* 282 (1989).

12. The famous study of the League by Anquetil entitled *L'esprit de la Ligue* (*The Spirit of the League*) has made the term ironic, in much the same way that the spirit of the League has remained elusive. See Louis Anquetil, *L'esprit de la Ligue*

ou histoire politique des troubles de la France pendant les XVIe et XVIIe siècles (Paris: Janet et Cotelle, 1818).

13. See Robert Descimon, "Les assemblées de l'hôtel de ville de Paris (mi-XVie–XViie siècles)" (1987).

14. The town officials "ne pouvoient accorder ne consentir aulcune chose; suppliant très humblement à Saditte Majesté luy permettre de faire, en la manière accoustumée, Assemblée en l'Hostel de la dicte Ville des bourgeois et habitans, pour leur faire entendre ce qu'il avoit pleu à Sa Majesté proposer et dire, pour par après en faire entendre audict Sieur Roy la responce et résolution [of the assembly]." *Reg. BV*, 7:375.

15. The French reads, "antiques pestes de la justice." Paul Robiquet, *Paris et la ligue sous le règne de Henri III. Etude d'histoire municipale et politique* (Paris: Hachette, 1886), 47.

16. As cited in Robiquet, *Paris* 47: "d'avoir introduit par vérification, pacte à pris fait avec les ennemys de Dieu et de roy la prétendue religion en roiaume . . . et mis l'Église de Dieu en confusion."

17. See Appendix B for the genealogy of these families and their interconnections. The ties between these Catholic princes and the *Seize* can be found in the practice of the notaries Marc Bruyère and Claude I de Troyes. For an example drawn from the practice of Marc Bruyère, see the will of the *Seize*, Pierre Delamer, Figure 1.

18. See Ann W. Ramsey, "From Ontology to Religious Experience: Civic and Sacred Immanence in the Holy Sacrament Confraternities of Paris during the Catholic League," in *Confraternities and Catholic Reform in Italy, France and Spain*, Sixteenth Century Essays & Studies, vol. 44, ed. John Patrick Donnelly and Michael W. Maher (1999).

19. The form *fau* or *faulx* is derived from the thirteenth-century phrase *fors bourg*, meaning outside of the burg or city.

20. See endpapers (The Ecclesiastical Map of Paris) for the forty-two parishes of the early seventeenth century, the colleges of the University, and the great religious institutions of the city.

21. Archives Nationales, *Minutier central* (hereafter AN, *Min. cen.*) IV, 17 [Claude Jourdan] (8/6/1590), will of Jehan de Peyere.

22. For an analysis of these traditions on the wane in the eighteenth century, see Robert A. Schneider, *The Ceremonial City, Toulouse Observed: 1738–1780* (Princeton: Princeton University Press, 1995).

23. These institutions formed the highest echelons of the state's legal and administrative apparatus. The sovereign courts were the *Parlement*, the *chambre des comptes*, the *cour des aides*, and the last to be established, the *cour des monnaies* (January 1552). For a discussion of these institutions and their personnel, see Roland Mousnier, *Les institutions de la France sous la monarchie absolue, 1598–1789*, vol. 2, *Les organes de l'état et la société* (Paris: Presses Universitaires de France, 1974), 273ff. His accounts are not always consistent. Compare for example

this discussion with the English edition, Roland Mousnier, *The Institutions of France under the Absolute Monarchy, 1598–1798: Society and the State*, vol. 1, *The Social Structure of France under the Absolute Monarchy*, trans. Brian Pearce (Chicago: University of Chicago Press, 1974), 431ff. (in the French edition of Mousnier, *Institutions*, vol. 1, *Société et état*, 335). The classic study on the sale of royal offices remains Roland Mousnier, *Recherches sur la vénalité des offices: Sous Henri IV et Louis XIII* (Paris: Presses Universitaires de France, 1971). Marcel Marion, *Dictionnaire des institutions de la France aux XVIIe et XVIII siècles* (Paris: Editions A. & J. Picard, 1979), and Gaston Zeller, *Les institutions de la France au XVIe siècle* (Paris: Presses Universitaires de France, 1948), provide concise definitions of the office-holders and the *corps* and *compagnies* they formed. Emile Lousse, *La société d'ancien régime: Organisation et représentation corporatives*, Etudes présentées à la Commission internationale pour l'histoire des assemblées d'états (Louvain: Bibliothèque de l'Université, 1943), discusses the profound effects of corporative thinking on French institutional development.

24. Jonathan Dewald, "The 'Perfect Magistrate': Parlementaires and Crime in Sixteenth-Century Rouen," *Archiv für Reformationsgeschichte* 67 (1967): 284–300.

25. David Hackett Fischer, *The Great Wave: Price Revolutions and the Rhythm of History* (New York: Oxford University Press, 1998).

26. For an overview, see Alfred Franklin, *Dictionnaire historique des arts, métiers, et professions exercés dans Paris depuis le treizième siècle* (1906; reprint, New York: Burt Franklin, 1968), and especially the preface by M. E. Levasseur.

27. See Michel Félibien and G. A. Lobineau, *Recueil des pièces justificatives pour servir à l'histoire de Paris*, vol. 2 of *Historie de la ville de Paris* (Paris, 1725), 599a, for the issuance of an ordinance against vagabonds dated June 3, 1532. There is a vast literature on the poor and poor relief in the sixteenth century. Bronislaw Geremeck summarizes the evidence for Paris in "Paris: Moral Anxiety and Fear," in *Poverty: A History*, trans. Agnieszka Kolakowska (Oxford: Blackwell, 1994), 124–31. For an overview and bibliography, see Robert Jütte, *Poverty and Deviance in Early Modern Europe* (Cambridge: Cambridge University Press, 1994).

28. Both notaries and their clientele are discussed in more detail in Chapter 6. Their names appear as voting members of the Leaguer General Assembly of August 15, 1589, which selected new aldermen. See François Bonnardot, ed., *Reg. BV*, 9:437–42, which reads like a roll-call of the *Seize*. Participation in General Assemblies was an important sign of notability and a classic indicator of cooperation among unequal members of the bourgeosie. See Robert Descimon, "Les assemblées de l'hôtel de ville de Paris," in which he studies these municipal traditions.

29. For this argument about the pivotal role of the lesser notables or "intermediate classes" in the *Seize* wing of the League, see Denis Richet, "Sociocultural Aspects of Religious Conflicts in Paris during the Second Half of the Sixteenth Century," in *Ritual, Religion, and the Sacred: Selections from the Annales, Economies, Sociétés, Civilisations*, eds. Robert Forster and Orest Ranum, trans. Elborg Forster and Patricia M. Ranum (Baltimore: 1982), 183, 196–97, and

199–202. For detailed socio-political analysis of the *gens de loi*, see especially the work of Robert Descimon discussed in more detail in Chapter 4.

30. On the cultural hegemony of the *officiers*, Myriam Yardeni, *La conscience nationale en France pendant les guerres de religion (1559–1598)* (Louvain: Editions Nauwelaerts, 1971), 63, has remarked, "La culture, le monde théologique mis à part, devient essentiellement le patrimoine des robins conquérants. . . . " *Robin* is a term commonly used for the magistrates of the *Parlement*, the "robe nobility" in contrast to the older nobility of the sword. "Culture, with the exception of the world of theologians, essentially became the patrimony of the triumphant men of the robe [*robins*]."

31. Henri Drouot, *Mayenne et la Bourgogne: Etude sur la Ligue (1587–1596)* (Paris: Picard, 1937), first made this argument with evidence on the social support for the League in Burgundy. Richet and Descimon have adapted this model to the Paris League and have begun to define a socio-cultural component in the frustrations of this middling elite. See also Richet, "Sociocultural Aspects," and Robert Descimon, *Qui étaient les Seize? Mythes et réalités de la Ligue parisienne (1585–1594)*, vol. 34, Mémoires de la fédération des sociétés historiques et archéologiques de Paris et de l'Ile-de-France (Paris: Klincksieck, 1983).

32. The literature is massive. The term "reform of popular culture" was coined by Peter Burke, *Popular Culture in Early Modern Europe* (New York: Harper & Row, 1978), 207ff.

33. *La police* should not be translated as "police" in a conventional Anglo-Saxon sense but is more equivalent to the keeping of public order. It included oversight of the poor, theatre and popular pastimes, and the tenor of public preaching, as well as all processional life, both secular and religious. For a fundamental introduction with reference to original sources, see Felix Aubert, "Le Parlement et la Ville de Paris au XVIe siècle," *Revue des études historiques* (1905). See the classic use of "la police" by Claude de Seyssel, *The Monarchy of France*, trans. J. H. Hexter (New Haven: Yale University Press, 1981).

34. Félibien, *Recueil*, and *Reg. BV* were most helpful in reconstructing a general chronology of Parlementary rulings.

35. Félibien, *Recueil*, vol. 2, 630, writes that "plusieurs choses impudiques et vilaines estoit merveilleusement scandaleuses."

36. Jean Savaron, *Traitté contre les masques* (Paris: 1608). There are other examples of just such a combination of cultural critiques of masking, confraternities, and efforts to reform popular culture more generally. See, for example, the *Commentaire sur les edicts et ordonnances du roy contenans les inhibitions et defences des confrairies monopolaires, et les causes pourquoy*, written by the *jurisconsulte* (lawyer) Philibert Bugnyon, Lyon 1585. Bugnyon opposes trade confraternities for their spirit of particularism and monopoly and their masking, banquets, and "assemblies which meet under the guise of religion," 29.

37. Jean Savaron, *Traitté des confraires* (Paris, 1604), 11.

38. Félibien, *Recueil*, vol. 2, 633, provides evidence of a vestige of this cooperation between the clercs of the *basoche* and the magistrates of the *Parlement*:

an entry for February 1, 1514, indicates that the *Parlement* contributed a sum towards the cost of "the games and dances of the *basoche*."

39. Savaron, *Traitté des confraires*, 13.

40. Savaron, *Traitté des confraires*, 15.

41. "La religion est la chose qui nous ramene de plus pres a la cognoissance de nostre Createur . . . moyennant qu'elle ne soit point meslee d'aucune superstition." Savaron, *Traitté des confraires*, 2.

42. "Le 23e juin, au feu de la Saint-Jean, les prévôt des marchands et échevins, firent mettre sur l'arbre la représentation d'une grand furie qu'ils nommèrent Hérésie, pleine de feux artificiels dont elle fut toute brûlée." Pierre de L'Estoile, *Journal de L'Estoile pour le règne de Henri III, 1574–1589*, ed. Louis-Raymond Lefèvre, 6th ed., vol. 2 (Paris: Gallimard, 1943), 564.

43. For a new interpretation, see Christopher W. Stocker, "The Confraternity of the Holy Name of Jesus: Conflict and Renewal in the Sainte Union in 1590," in *Confraternities and Catholic Reform in Italy, France and Spain*, Sixteenth Century Essays & Studies, vol. 44, ed. John Patrick Donnelly and Michael W. Maher (1999). I would like to thank Dr. Stocker for sharing a copy of his paper with me.

44. AN, *Min. cen.* LXXIII, 5 [Jean Cruce] (21/2/1544), will of Yolland Bonhomme.

45. Félibien, *Recueil*, vol. 2, 675. This is the first mention by Félibien of any religiously motivated violence in Paris in the sixteenth century.

46. For a discussion of the Tridentine interpretation of the eucharist as "the sacrifice of the altar," see Chapter 3, p. 48.

47. For the development of the devotion to the host in the later Middle Ages, see Edouard Dumoutet, *Le désir de voir l'hostie et les origines de la dévotion au Saint-Sacrement* (Paris: Gabriel Beauchesne, 1926). For a later example see the case of Marguerite Pommier, a woman who sought a cure for infertility at Ardilliers. While attending mass, at the moment of the elevation of the host, she is said to have cried out twice, "Jésus Maria," and lost consciousness. Jean de Viguerie, *Le catholicisme des français dans l'ancienne France* (Paris: Nouvelles Editions Latines, 1988), 42–43.

48. Lucien Febvre, "Une Date: 1534. La Messe et les placards," in *Au coeur religieux du XVIe siècle*, 2nd ed. (Paris: Ecole Pratique des Hautes Etudes, 1957), 217–30.

49. For an excellent description of Parisian attitudes toward the mass and eucharistic worship in the sixteenth century, see Barbara Diefendorf, "The Most Catholic Capital," in *Beneath the Cross: Catholics and Huguenots in Sixteenth-Century Paris* (New York: Oxford University Press, 1991), 28–48.

50. Pierre de L'Estoile, *Journal de L'Estoile pour le règne de Henri IV, 1589–1600*, ed. Louis-Raymond Lefèvre, 4th ed. (Paris: Gallimard, 1948), vol. 1, 164.

51. For an example of the church's ongoing campaign to ensure that no Catholics died intestate, see (for the beginning of the sixteenth century) Félibien's 1505 comment that "les curés de Paris refusent d'inhumer les morts, avant que

d'avoir veu les testamens." *Recueil*, vol. 2, 619. Lay reformers also embraced this campaign against intestates. See, for example, Jean du Laurier, *De l'estat present du royaume quant à la religion, justice, et police*, Dedicated to Henri II, roy de Navarre, Bearn . . . " premier pair de France" (1583), 118.

52. See Appendix L for the percentage of healthy and unhealthy testators in each of the sample years. Leaguers are more likely to be in good health at the time their wills are drawn up than are testators from the reference population of non-Leaguers in 1590. Compare this with the testator population for 1543–44 and 1630.

53. Immediately above the signature of the notary at the bottom left of the page, we see Pierre Delamer's attempt to sign his name: Pierre de la mer.

54. "Item veult et ordonne s'il plaise a dieu l'appeller de ce monde que . . . son fils soit mis au college des Jesuites en ceste ville de Paris ou en autre bon lieu pour y continuer ses estudes. . . . Priant a ceste fin monsieur le curé de l'eglise de faire en sorte que sondict fils soit mis audict college des jesuites ou en autre lieu . . . et avoir l'oeil a ce que sondict fils y soict bien et deument instruict." AN, *Min. cen.* CXXII, 1184 [Marc Bruyère] (23/12/1590), will of *noble homme maistre* Pierre Delamer.

55. Her will, AN, *Min. cen.* CXXII, 1184 [Marc Bruyère] (22/10/1590), will of *honorable femme* Catherine Tronson.

56. Never one to miss the opportunity for a scathing comment, L'Estoile, who wrote in French, offered up his derision of the university doctor Delamer in Latin: "médecin du conseil des Neuf qui habebat quidem zelum Dei, sed non secundum scientam." The identification of Delamer as a *Seize* comes from Descimon, *Qui*, 129 (no. 54). Descimon signals the 1580 will of Delamer's first wife Dame Guillemette Bellanger, the daughter of *honorable homme* Jehan Bellanger, a secretary to the duchesse of Ferrara. There is an extant will of Delamer's second wife, Catherine Tronson, AN, *Min. cen.* CXXII, 1184 [Marc Bruyère] (22/10/1590), included in the database for 1590. Both wives' wills reveal clientage networks and Italian ties, but neither makes a bequest to a Holy Sacrament confraternity. The practice of the notary Bruyère is an example of the clustering of League sympathizers in particular notaries. See Appendix E. Bruyère co-signs with Mathieu Bontemps who, in turn, also co-signs with Raoul Bontemps.

57. Charles Labitte, *De la démocratie chez les prédicateurs de la Ligue* (1841; reprint, Geneva: Slatkine Reprints, 1971): "la vielle esprit des corporations religieuses."

58. "Item veult et ordonne que tant que la confrarie de Saint-Sacrament de l'autel que monsieur le curé de l'eglise St. André veult et entend faire digner en lad. eglise St. André sera en sa splendeur il soit baillé et paié par sesdictes hoirs [crossed through] à son filz . . . par chacun mois de l'an a perpetuité quatre solz tournois qui est par chacun an quarente huit solz tournois affin d'estre participant aux prieres dicelle." AN, *Min. cen.* CXXII, 1184 [Marc Bruyère] (23/12/1590), will of *noble homme maistre* Pierre Delamer.

59. "Item veult et ordonne que le jour de son enterrement il soit dict a son intention ung *salve regina*." Ibid.

Chapter 2

1. See, however, the remarkable essay of Jacques Heers, "La fête, affirmation des valeurs spirituelles," chapter 2 in *Fêtes, jeux et joutes dans les sociétés d'occident à la fin du moyen-âge* (Paris: Vrin, 1982 (original Conference Albert-le-Grand, 1971)). More recently on theater and religious culture, see Gail McMurray Gibson, *The Theater of Devotion: East Anglian Drama and Society in the Late Middle Ages* (Chicago and London: The University of Chicago Press, 1989). The landmark work on the place of the body in medieval Christianity is, of course, Caroline Walker Bynum, *Holy Feast and Holy Fast: The Religious Significance of Food to Medieval Women* (Berkeley: University of California Press, 1987). See also Caroline Walker Bynum, *The Resurrection of the Body in Western Christianity, 200–1336* (New York: Columbia University Press, 1995); and Jean-Claude Schmitt, *La raison des gestes dans l'occident médiéval* (Paris: Gallimard, 1990), who have brought the body to the forefront of research interests. For the study of the Reformation, see Lyndal Roper, *Oedipus & the Devil: Witchcraft, Sexuality and Religion in Early Modern Europe* (London: Routledge, 1994). See, however, the reintegration of the body into studies of the liturgy: Gerard Lukken, *Per visiblia ad invisiblia: Anthropological, Theological and Semiotic Studies on the Liturgy and the Sacraments*, ed. Louis van Tongeren and Charles Caspers (Kampen, Netherlands: 1994); *Liturgy and the Body*, ed. Louis-Marie Chauvet and François Kabasele Lumbala, *Concilium*, no. 3 (1995). For the new possibilities of electronic databases in the history of liturgy see, for example, *Late Medieval Liturgical Offices, Resources for Electronic Research: Sources and Chants, Subsidia Medievalia,* 24 (Toronto: Pontifical Institute of Medieval Studies, 1996). For a critical and controversial orientation in the historic mind/body dualism of Western culture, see Morris Berman, *Coming to Our Senses: Body and Spirit in the Hidden History of the West* (London: Unwin Paperbacks, 1990). Of signal significance in placing the body at the center of Christian liturgy was M. D. Chenu, "Towards a Sacramental Anthropology," *La Maison-Dieu* 119 (1974).

2. See especially Chapter 5 in Michel de Certeau, *The Mystic Fable*, vol. 1, *The Sixteenth and Seventeenth Centuries*, trans. Michael B. Smith (Chicago and London: University of Chicago Press, 1992), which discusses the experiential effects of nominalism in separating signs from their referents.

3. This term appears in 1590 only, exclusively in the wills of testators who are receiving deathbed communion. They are clients of the notaries Chartain, Monthenault, Lamiral, Charles, Fardeau, and Thévenin. Chartain's testators use the wording from the Leaguer Oath of Allegiance within their wills. The other notaries' League connections are discussed below in chapter 6.

4. The texts consulted were, for the English translation, *Short Treatise on the Holy Supper of our Lord Jesus Christ*, in *John Calvin, Selections from his Writings*, ed. John Dillenberger (New York: Anchor Books, 1971), 507–41, and for the French, the *Petit Traicté de la saincte cene de nostre seigneur Jesus Christ*, in Jean Calvin, *Three French Treatises*, ed. Francis M. Higman (London: University of London,

The Athlone Press, 1970), 98–130. All quotations in French and French page references are from this French edition. The French edition also provides line numbers, abbreviated herein by l.

5. *Short Treatise*, 509–10. For more about the intra-Protestant context in which this treatise was written, Calvin's relationship to Melanchthon, and attempts at healing the breach with Lutherans, see Higman, ed. *Three French Treatises*, Introduction, 8–9.

6. *Short Treatise*, 513. *Petit traicté*, 106, ll.2–5: " . . . nous confesserons sans doubte que de nier la vraye communication de Jesus Christ nous estre presentée en la Cene, c'est rendre ce sainct Sacrement frivole et inutile, qui est un blaspheme execrable et indigne d'estre escouté."

7. *Short Treatise*, 513.

8. *Petit traicté*, 115, l.5.

9. *Short Treatise*, 513.

10. *Short Treatise*, 514. *Petit traicté*, 106, ll.24–29: " . . . si on demande assavoir neantmoins si le pain est le corps de Christ, et le vin son sang, nous respondrons que le pain et le vin sont signes visibles, lesquelz nous representent le corps et le sang; mais que ce Nom et tiltre de corps et de sang leur est attribué, pource que ce sont comme instrumens par lesquelz le Seigneur Jesus nous les distribue."

11. *Short Treatise*, 515. *Petit traicté*, 107, ll.7–14: "Ainsi en est il de la communication que nous avons au corps et au sang du Seigneur JESUS. C'est un mystere spirituel, lequel ne se peult veoir l'oeil, ne comprendre en l'entendement humain. Il nous est doncques figuré par signes visibles, selon que nostre infirmité requiert; tellement neantmoins que ce n'est pas une figure nue, mais conjoincte avec sa verité et substance. C'est donc bon droict que le pain est nommé corps, puis que non seulement il le nous represente, mais aussi nous le presente."

12. For example, "figured to us by visible signs," and, "the bread is given to us to figure the body of Jesus Christ," *Short Treatise*, 515.

13. *Instruction pour les confraires de la confrairie du S. Sacrement de l'autel, estably à Bordeaux, avec les articles, qui doivent estre gardez par tous ceux qui sont de ladite confrairie* (Bordeaux: S. Millanges, 1577), 12. "Le corps de nostre seigneur nous y est donné seulement par signe & figure, par foy, et en esprit, & par fantasie, & imagination & ie ne sçai quelle substance du corps de nostre Seigneur, ils font passer comme par un alambic, & decouler du ciel en leur Cene."

14. Words (and the Word) operate as signifiers in a non-performative understanding of consecration. For Calvin, the function of the Word is as a *promise* [my emphasis] of salvation. The words and gestures of consecration are not intended to effect literally the bodily presence of the signified.

15. G. D. S. de Soulas, *Discours au Roy pour la reception du Concile de Trente: contre ceux qui s'efforcent de l'empescher. Ou il est prouvé que l'un des meilleurs moyens d'arrester le cours des heresies, est de faire valoir Conciles Generaux* (Paris: chez Jean Petit-pas rue S. Iacques l'Escu de Venise pres les Mathurins, 1615), 43. The manuscript consulted (Mazarine, ms. 37202) was bound in a volume bearing

the dates 1546–1690 that contained some twenty items, each a small pamphlet published individually, with the earliest dating from 1546 and the most recent from 1690. The titles included the *Decrees from Session VIIa*, which anathematized key Protestant positions including denial of Christ's institution of seven sacraments, the idea that faith is sufficient for salvation, lay ministry of the word, etc. Other treatises included the *Oration of the Cardinal of Lorraine at the Colloquy of Poissy*, 1561; Charles du Moulin's attack on Trent; and the promulgation of several synodal statutes. These publication details are important because they indicate the dense networks of information—centered particularly in the quarter of the University of Paris (especially, the rue Saint-Jacques, see "rue S. Iacques" above)—that shaped public opinion during the Wars of Religion and beyond.

16. Robert Descimon drew my attention to the scientific imagery in this passage. This scientific imagery, ridiculed in the Leaguer response, makes clear the nature of the contest taking place between two modes of knowing and the two different sets of ontological commitments: zeal vs *science*.

17. De Soulas, *Discours au Roy pour la reception du Concile de Trente*, 80: "Dis moy heretique, grand amateur de l'escriture ou a tu trouvé escrit ce . . . [that Christ says] figure de mon corps. . . . "

18. Matthew 26:26.

19. *Instruction pour les confraires*: "tantost il Lutheranise, tantost au contraire il faict le personnage d'un Zuinglien, & comme un ioueur de passe passe, et bateleur, maintenant il dit qu'il est dedans, maintenant il afferme qu'il est dehors," 170–71. See also Randle Cotgrave, *A Dictionarie of the French and English Tongues* (1611; reprint, Columbia, S.C.: University of South Carolina Press, 1950), s.v. passe-passe, "a iugling tricke."

20. See Denis Richet, "Sociocultural Aspects of Religious Conflicts in Paris during the Second Half of the Sixteenth Century," in *Ritual, Religion, and the Sacred: Selections from the Annales, Economies, Sociétés, Civilisations*, eds. Robert Forster and Orest Ranum, trans. Elborg Forster and Patricia M. Ranum (Baltimore: 1982), 206.

21. *Instruction pour les confraires*: "[que Iesus Christ n'a pas eu une vraye humanité, main un corps fantastique]," 8–9.

22. Marcion was the second-century leader of a sect that rejected the God of the Old Testament and sought, through its interpretation of the apostle Paul, to distance itself as completely as possible from the perceived ritualism of Jewish law.

23. *Instruction pour les confraires*, 101, 103, 140.

24. See the discussion below on Trent, especially concerning the draft material prior to the issuance of the decrees that is quoted by Erwin Iserloh, "Das tridentinische Messopferdekret in seinen Beziehungen zu der Kontroverstheologie der Zeit," in *Wege der Forschung*, vol. 313, *Concilium Tridentinum*, ed. Remigius Bäumer (Darmstadt: Wissenschaftliche Buchgesellschaft, 1979), 363.

25. *Short Treatise*, 509. *Petit traicté*, 102, I.17: "Pour nous sustener donques en ceste vie, il n'est pas question de repaistre noz ventres de viandes corruptibles

et caduques; mais de nourrir noz ames de pasture meilleure et plus precieuse." The once standard translation by John Dillenberger interpolates here adding the adjective "spiritual" to the original "life" of the French. I would like to thank Todd Anderson, whose careful proofreading called my attention to this discrepancy.

26. *Short Treatise*, 509. *Petit traicté*, 102, ll.25–28: "Mais tout ainsi que Dieu a constitué toute plenitude de vie en Jesus, afin de nous la communiquer par son moyen; aussi il a ordonné sa Parolle comme instrument, par lequel Jesus Christ, avec toutes ses graces, nous soit dispensé."

27. *Short Treatise*, 525.

28. "un Sacrifice unicque," *Petit traicté*, 117, l.1–2.

29. Margaret R. Miles, "Theology, Anthropology, and the Human Body in Calvin's *Institutes of the Christian Religion*," in *Harvard Theological Review* 74:3 (1981), 303–23.

30. See E. Durkheim, *The Elementary Forms of Religious Life* (London: Allen and Unwin, 1961); Philip A. Mellor and Chris Shilling, *Re-Forming the Body: Religion, Community and Modernity* (London: Sage Publications, 1997); and M. Richman, "The sacred group: A Durkheimian perspective on the Collège de sociologie (1937–39)," in *Bataille: Writing the Sacred*, ed. C. Bailey Gill (London: Routledge, 1995), 60.

31. See chapter 8 for a discussion of the Tridentine proscription of liturgical and paraliturgical number symbolism.

32. The psychological mood (the affective and cognitive states) and the aesthetic systems associated with each form of knowing (performative knowing versus knowledge of the Word) are quite different, and we will explore this further in our discussion of Trent.

33. *Short Treatise*, 526.

34. *Short Treatise*, 526.

35. *Short Treatise*, 526. *Petit traicté*, 117–18, ll.29–31. "Car en l'ancien Testament, du temps des figures, le Seigneur avoit ordonné telles ceremonies, en attendant que ce sacrifice feust faict en la chair de son Filz bien aymé, lequel en estoit l'accomplissement. Depuis qu'il a esté parfaict, il ne reste plus sinon que nous en recevions la communication. Parquoy, c'est chose superflue de le plus figurer."

36. Crouzet's conclusion on changes in the processional system, however, stresses "l'affaiblessement du système processionel" (the weakening of the processional system) as a result of Protestant critiques. See Denis Crouzet, "Recherches sur les processions blanches: 1583–1584," in *Histoire, économie et société* 4 (1982), 514.

37. The language is unambiguous, "toutes avecq sacrifices." AN, *Min. cen.* XX: 16: [Jacques Mussart] (31/8/1543), will of Valerend Choquet.

38. The will of Valerend Choquet will be further addressed in chapter 7. Choquet is important as an example of doctrinal sophistication combined with extensive use of ritual number symbolism, five and thirteen, condemned by Trent as a "superstition."

39. Thomas Aquinas, *Summa Theologiae III*, *quaestiones 75–77*.

40. Matthew 26:26.

41. The Council of Trent affirmed the validity of the Canon of the Mass and Aquinas's views on transubstantiation. See *Decrees of the Council of Trent*, session 22, chapter 4. For a full description of the Canon of the Mass, see Cheslyn Jones et al. (eds.), *The Study of Liturgy* (New York: Oxford University Press, 1992), 267–69.

42. Larissa Taylor, *Soldiers of Christ: Preaching in Late Medieval and Reformation France* (New York: Oxford University Press, 1992), 135–37.

43. "For if we would place him under the corruptible elements of the world, besides subverting what Scripture tells us in regard to his human nature, we annihilate the glory of his ascension." *Short Treatise*, 530.

44. *Short Treatise*, 529. *Petit traicté*, 120.

45. *Short Treatise*, 531. Compare this with the evolution of the Forty Hours eucharistic devotion discussed in chapter 1.

46. Compare Calvin's criticism of the annual procession of the eucharist (the Festival of Corpus Christi or the *Fête-Dieu*) to Trent's exaltation of this event as discussed in chapter 3.

47. *Short Treatise*, 533; *Petit traicté*, 123. A remarkable satirical treatise written against the processional activity in Paris during the siege of 1590 is entitled "Les singeries de la Ligue." Bibliothèque historique de la ville de Paris, ms. 533: *Recueil des pièces sur la Ligue*.

48. *Short Treatise*, 527. *Petit traicté*, 118, ll.16–19. "Car il n'est pas dict seullement que le Sacrifice de Christ est unicque, mais qu'il ne doit jamais estre reiteré, entant que l'efficace en demeure tousjours."

Chapter 3

1. Freud used this term in writing about the logic of representation in dreams in "The Considerations of Representability," Sigmund Freud, *The Interpretation of Dreams*, trans. James Strachey (New York: Basic Books, 1965), 374–85. He wrote, "[The] pouring of the content of a thought into another mould may . . . serve the purposes of the activity of condensation and may create connections, which might not otherwise have been present . . . ," Freud, *Interpretation*, 379. As a description of religious change the condensation of sacred immanence indicates a gathering of the dispersed affective ties to saints and the Holy Family and a focusing (condensing) of the experience of the sacred within a powerful deocentric vertical axis. See also "The Work of Condensation," in Freud, *Interpretation*, 312–33, and the sections "Bequests of Performative Objects (Value 1)" and "Banqueting Behaviors and Pilgrimages (Values 2 and 3)" in Chapter 5, below.

2. A full treatment of what might be called Tridentine discourse would include not only the full range of the decrees themselves, the work and corre-

spondence of the scholarly commissions of *consultores*, and the correspondence of participants (*diffinitores*) and their opponents, but also the remarkable histories of the Council composed in the sixteenth and early seventeenth century. Despite the vast bibliography on this topic, much of this material could be reexamined from an experiential perspective.

3. This is not to suggest, by any means, that the Word lacks historicity, but humanists of Calvin's stripe would see themselves as something similar to "strict constructionists." To be saved one did not interpret Scripture, one believed the Word. In their broadest claims about Scripture, reformers such as Calvin took a completely nonperformative position about the interaction that occurs between text and reader. The Catholic position on Scripture is also problematic, but the analysis here focuses on performative aspects of the Tridentine text, not Scripture itself.

4. *Decrees of the Ecumenical Councils*, vol. 2, *Trent to Vatican II*, ed. Norman P. Tanner, original text established by G. Albergio, J. A. Dossetti, P.-P. Joannou, C. Leonardi, and P. Prodi, in consultation with H. Jedin (London: Sheed and Ward, Ltd., and Washington, D.C.: Georgetown University Press, 1990), 663.

5. For a broad and useful overview, see Robert James Edmund Boggis, *Praying for the Dead: An Historical Review of the Practice* (London, New York, Bombay, and Calcutta: Longmans, Green, and Co., 1913), and more recently, Megan McLaughlen, *Consorting with the Saints: Prayer for the Dead in Early Medieval France* (Ithaca: Cornell University Press, 1994), who examines the social and geographical differentiation in votive piety and prayers for the dead in the early Middle Ages. Numerous histories of the mass and of liturgy more generally are cited in the Bibliography.

6. An excellent example of the complexities of this process is Charles Zika, "Hosts, Processions, Pilgrimages: Controlling the Sacred in Fifteenth-Century Germany," *Past and Present* 118 (1988).

7. *Decrees*, 695.

8. *Decrees*, 693.

9. *Decrees*, 694.

10. *Decrees*, 695. Under "devotional style" lies a theory of representation, as well as an epistemology and ontology of the sacred. These technical points deserve a separate investigation as part of a historical study of the scholastic study of ontology.

11. *Decrees*, 742.

12. "Is igitur Deus et Dominus noster, etsi semel se ipsum in ara crucis, morte intercedente, Deo Patri oblaturus erat, ut aeternam illis redemptionem operaretur: quia tamen per mortem sacerdotium eius exstinguendum non erat, in coena novissima, qua nocte tradebatur, ut dilectae sponsae suae ecclesiae visibile (sicut hominum natura exigit) relinqueret sacrificium, quo cruentum illud semel *in cruce peragendum* [my emphasis] repraesentaretur eiusque memoria in finem usque saeculi permaneret, atque illius salutaris virtus in remissionem eorum, quae a nobis quotidie committuntur, peccatorum applicaretur: sacerdotum secundum

ordinem Melchisedech se in aeternum constitutum declarans, corpus et sanguinem suum sub speciebus panis et vini Deo Patri obtulit ac sub earundem rerum symbolis apostolis (quos tunc novi testamenti sacerdotes constituebat), ut sumerent, tradidit et eisdem eorumque in sacerdotio successoribus, ut offerent, praecepit per haec verba: *Hoc facite in meam commemorationem*," *Decrees*, chapter 1, session 22, 732–33. Readers may note an unusual translation of the Latin "sacerdotum secundum ordinem Melchisedech" that one would expect to see translated as "according to the order of Melchisedech." I would like to thank Todd Anderson and Martha Newman for their insights into this passage.

13. Et quoniam in divino hoc sacrificio, quod in missa *peragitur* [my emphasis], idem ille Christus continetur et incruente immolatur, qui in ara crucis semel se ipsum cruente obtulit: docet sancta synodus, sacrificium istud vere propitiatorium esse. . . . Una enim eademque est hostia, idem nunc offerens sacerdotum ministerio, qui se ipsum tunc in cruce obtulit, sola offerendi ratione diversa. Cuius quidem oblationis (cruentae, inquam) fructus per hanc incruentam uberrime percipiuntur: tantum abest, ut illi per hanc quovis modo derogetur. Quare non solum pro fidelium vivorum peccatis, poenis, satisfactionibus et aliis necessitatibus, sed et pro defunctis in Christo, nondum ad plenum purgatis, rite iuxta apostolorum traditionem offertur." *Decrees*, 733–34.

14. Gail McMurray Gibson, *The Theatre of Devotion: East Anglian Drama and Society in the Late Middle Ages* (Chicago and London: The University of Chicago Press, 1989, p.b. 1994), 6. "The fifteenth-century commitment to the particularity of religious experience—the adoration of Our Lady of Walsingham or a Madonna in a Book of Hours, rather than an abstract Mother of God—is not so much, it could be argued, an increasing secularization as a growing tendency to see the world saturated with sacramental possibility and meaning and to celebrate it."

15. "Praetera Christus illis verbis: *Hoc facite* non solum intellexit, ut memoriam cenae, sed oblationis in cruce peractae memoriam agerent. Sed quemadmodum, si non cenamus, non repraesentamus illam cenam Christi, sic, si non offerimus et sacrificamus, Christi sacrificium in cruce oblatum non repraesentamus. Et Christus non dixit: Hoc dicite, sed: *Hoc facite*, quasi significaret non verbis, sed facto faciendam commemorationem." From CT VII 389, 7–12; VIII 733, 1, cited by Erwin Iserloh, "Das tridentinische Messopferdekret in seinen Beziehungen zu der Kontroverstheologie der Zeit," in *Wege der Forschung*, vol. 313, *Concilium Tridentinum*, ed., Remigius Bäumer (Darmstadt: Wissenschaftliche Buchgesellschaft, 1979), 363. I would like to thank Martha Newman for her help with the translation, here and elsewhere. Iserloh, 364, stresses: "Daß die repraesentatio in der Eucharistie primär Handlung und nicht Bewußtseinsvorgang ist."

16. René Benoist (1521–1608) was curate of Paris' most populous parish, Saint-Eustache, located in the *Ville*. In the 1560s Benoist may be considered an activist Catholic reformer. Only after the succession crisis of 1584 and the founding of the League did Benoist take up a *politique* position in support of the monarchy.

17. Benoist, *Traicté de la messe*, 10. "Car premierement le Prestre prend les vestemens, qui signifient et represent ce qu'a esté faict à nostre Seigneur en sa passion: c'est à sçavoir La mict qui signifie comme il a esté voilé et frappé sur la face: l'Aube qui signifie et represent comme il a esté mocqué et deiecté avec *une robbe blanche* [my emphasis; cf. "les processions blanches"] en la maison d'Horodes. . . . Le Pharon, l'Estoile, et ceinture, signifient comme il a esté lié pour estre flagellé: et la chasuble, signifie la robbe de pourpre, en la quelle il a esté monstré au peuple . . . tellement que le Prestre Evangelique, ainsi orné des vestemens de l'Eglise, represente nostre Seigneur Iesus Christ, duquel il est ministre."

18. The sacraments, of course, actually effect what they signify, and thus convey grace, while sacramentals distribute the sacred into the world but confer no grace. Sacramentals thus can be seen as ontologically dependent on the weaker rather than the stronger concept of representation. The didactic emphasis among reform-minded testators is examined in chapter 7.

19. J. Froger, "Le concile de Trente a-t-il prescrit de donner des explications en langue vulgaire pendant les cérémonies liturgiques?" in *Ephemerides liturgicae* (1959), 81–115, 161–205.

20. Benoist, *Catholicque et utile discours* . . . , Folio 15: "nous ne pouvons estre perpetuellement en abstractions."

21. In his analysis of the sacerdotal function, Henri Brémond argues that the priesthood is not merely reformed but sanctified as a result of Tridentine reforms. See Henri Brémond, *Histoire littéraire du sentiment religieux en France depuis la fin des guerres de religion jusqu'à nos jours, La conquête mystique, l'école française* (1923; reprint, Paris: Librairie Armand Colin, 1967), vol. 3, part 1: 141ff.

22. See session 23, "Canons on the sacrament of order," canon 1: "If anyone says that in the new covenant there is no visible and external priesthood; or that there exists no power to consecrate and offer the true body and blood of the Lord, and to forgive or retain sins, but only a duty and a mere service of preaching the gospel; or that those who do not preach are simply not priests: let him be anathema." See also *Decrees*, 743 generally, and chapter 4 of session 23: "In the sacrament of order, as in baptism and confirmation, a character is imprinted, which cannot be deleted or removed," 742. In its concreteness and performativity, the notion of an imprinted character is clearly the language of immanence.

23. *Decrees*, 696: Ac sic quidem oportuit victricem veritatem de mendacio et haeresi *triumphum agere*, ut eius adversarii in conspectu tanti splendoris et in tanta universae ecclesiae laetitia positi vel debilitati et fracti tabescant vel pudore affecti et confusi aliquando respiscant" (my emphasis).

24. *Decrees*, 696.

25. This is said to take a clear stand about where to locate the testator population of sixteenth-century Paris in the great debates about the Christian Middle Ages. See James van Engen, "The Christian Middle Ages as an Historiographical Problem," *American Historical Review* 91, no. 3 (June 1986): 519–52; Jean Delumeau, *Le catholicisme entre Luther et Voltaire* (Paris: Presses Universitaires de France, 1971), 4th ed. 1992; Bernard Chevalier, *Les bonnes villes de France du*

XIV au XVIe siècle (Paris: Aubier Montaigne, 1982); Etienne Delaruelle, *La piété populaire au moyen âge*, ed. R. Manselli and A. Vauchez (Turin: Bottega d'Erasmo, 1975).

26. Jacques Toussaert, *Le sentiment religieux en Flandre à la fin du moyen-âge* (Paris: Plon, 1963); Josef Andreas Jungmann, *Missarum Sollemnia: eine genetische Erklärung der römischen Messe* (Vienna: Herder, 1952); Theodor Klauser, *A Short History of the Western Liturgy: an Account and Some Reflections*, 2nd ed., trans. John Halliburton (Oxford and New York: Oxford University Press, 1979).

27. In 1590, however, there is no apparent correlation between the tendency of a notary to have wills with a large number of requests for the intercession of saints and the opening date of the notary's practice. For the sixty-four notaries represented in the 1590 wills, the earliest opening dates of practice were 1552, 1553, and 1555 (three notaries). Nearly one-half of all the sixty-four notaries had practices beginning in 1580 or later. An article in preparation, "The Notaries of the Catholic League," will provide a detailed quantitative cultural analysis of correlations between the age-groups of notaries and indicators of political alignment and will language.

Chapter 4

1. On the Day of the Dupes (November 10, 1630) Louis XIII refused the demand of the queen mother to dismiss Richelieu and instead removed Marillac as Keeper of the Seals. This ruined the opportunity for direct political influence by the party of the *dévots*. France entered the Thirty Years' War in 1635 despite the protests of the party of the *dévots* who insisted, against Richelieu, that confessional principles should determine foreign policy goals.

2. See Nancy Lyman Roelker, *One King, One Faith: The Parlement of Paris and the Religious Reformations of the Sixteenth Century* (Berkeley, Los Angeles, London: University of California Press, 1966), 274, for a brief synopsis directing the reader to the works of J. Russell Major, Robert Harding, and Kristen Neuschel, all of whom have revised our understanding of the degree of royal centralization and its vulnerabilities.

3. Crucial to the debates about definitions of *politiques* and the weight of *politiques'* cultural influence are Donald R. Kelley, *Foundations of Modern Historical Scholarship: Language, Law and History in the French Renaissance* (New York: Columbia University Press, 1970), and Roelker, *One King*. Roelker summarizes the state of the ongoing debates, 325–28. See especially 407–8, where Roelker points out that in "royalist-nationalist historiography" the session of June 28, 1593, which defended the Salic law, and thus Henry IV's right to the French throne, is seen as "the finest hour of the *Parlement* of Paris." For the development of French nationalism, see Myriam Yardeni, *La conscience nationale en France pendant les guerres de religion (1559–1598)* (Louvain and Paris: Editions Nauwelaerts, 1971). For a critical perspective on nation-state-centered

historiography and especially the role of Michelet and Lavisse, see Suzanne Citron, *Le mythe national: l'histoire de France en question* (Paris: Les Editions Ouvrières, 1989). She introduces her work with Michelet's vision of the French national past as a form of salvation history in which youth should be instructed "comme foi et religion." Michelet, *Le peuple* (1846): "Le jour où se souvenant qu'elle fut et qu'elle doit être le salut du genre humain, la France s'entourera de ses enfants et leur enseignera la France comme foi et religion, elle se retrouvera vivante et solide comme le globe."

4. See Roelker, *One King*, 325, for this definition.

5. Roelker, *One King*, 325, argues that De Crue de Stoutz, Michelet, and Ranke were largely responsible for depicting the *politiques* as the essence of "good sense" and bourgeois respectability (De Crue). She emphasizes that "the nineteenth century conception . . . has prevailed uncritically to the present day. . . . " For what *politique* interpretations of Leaguer religious experience illuminate about the nearly universal difficulties of modern Western culture's assessment of movements of religious enthusiasm, see the Epilogue.

6. For the mainstays of the negative judgments besides Lavisse and De Crue de Stoutz, Michelet, and Ranke (note 5 above), see Louis Anquetil, *L'esprit de la Ligue ou histoire politique des troubles de la France pendant les XVIe et XVIIe siècles* (Paris: Janet et Cotelle, 1818), passim, Paul Robiquet, *Paris et la Ligue sous le règne de Henri III: Etude d'histoire municipale et politique* (Paris: Hachette, 1886), and Robiquet, *Histoire municipale de Paris*, vol. 3, *Règne de Henri IV* (Paris: Hachette, 1904).

7. For one analysis of Leaguer conceptions of time and the transcendent sacred, see Denis Crouzet, "La représentation du temps à l'époque de la Ligue," *Revue historique* 548 (1983): 297–388.

8. "Ceste guerre a esté une guerre d'Estat et non pas une guerre pour la religion," Pierre-Victor Palma Cayet, *Chronologie novenaire contenant l'histoire de la guerre et les choses les plus mémorables advenues sous le règne de Henri IV (1589–1598)*, in *Nouvelle collection des mémoires relatifs à l'histoire de France . . .* , ed. Michaud et Poujoulat, vol. 12 (Paris: 1854), 10. Palma Cayet's work was originally published in Paris in 1607.

9. " . . . car, sous ombre d'estre papes, roys, princes evesques ou docteurs, il n'est pas licite de faire choses indecentes. Tous les zeles ne sont pas bons: la saincte Escriture n'advoue ceux qui sont inconsiderez, outrecuidez et desesperez, car Dieu faict ses merveilles luy seul, et a ses jugements à soy propres." *Chronologie novenaire*, 10.

10. See Appendix G.

11. Chapter 2 and the Epilogue examine, from different perspectives, how this boundary perception is related to the critique of ritualized performance and strongly somatic or exteriorized piety.

12. Randle Cotgrave, *A Dictionarie of the French and English Tongues* (1611; reprint, Columbia, S.C.: University of South Carolina Press, 1950), s.v. "inconsideré" (hereinafter, "Cotgrave").

13. "Tant produit ce grand roy des roys d'estranges et inconsiderez moyens, pour conduire les choses à leur effect préordonné." Estienne Pasquier, *Pour-parler du prince* (I, 1025), in *Les oeuvres d'Estienne Pasquier* (Amsterdam, 1723), cited by Edmond Huguet, *Dictionnaire de la langue française du seizième siècle*, vol. 4, 596.

14. Further structures of meaning may be mentioned: the root of *outrecuider* is composed of *outre* and the old French *cuider*, which was the popular form of *cogiter*, to think. See also Alain Rey, ed., *Dictionnaire historique de la langue française* (1994), and Frédéric Godefroy, *Dictionnaire lexique de l'ancien français* (1990). Such deep structures are carried forward in a series of discourses, which include, of course, Descartes. Foucault's structural analysis of *déraison* still requires a sequel on the historical domain of *raison*. The full resonance of the original French edition, *Folie et déraison: Histoire de la folie à l'âge classique* (Paris, 1961), was lost in the severely edited English translation, *Madness and Civilization: A History of Insanity in the Age of Reason* (New York, 1973). The tensions between the baroque and classicism as two different epistemologies are, for example, lost, as is the connection between Gothic and baroque. For a very suggestive cultural analysis of one pillar of the rationalist world view, see Susan R. Bordo, *The Flight to Objectivity: Essays on Cartesianism and Culture*, SUNY Series in Philosophy (Albany, N.Y.: State University of New York Press, 1987).

15. "A quel propos, pourront me dire quelques-uns, de rememorer à present tout ce que les rois très-chretiens Henri III et Henri IV ont fait contre les princes catholiques de la ligue leurs subjects? C'est un faict passé; par la paix il est dit qu'il ne faut plus s'en souvenir . . . mais il n'est pas defendu de laisser par escrit à la posterité comme ces choses sont advenus, car ces princes et les peuples qui se sont rebellez contre leur souverain ne le devoient faire s'il ne vouloient qu'on le dist; ils ne devoient eux-mesmes le dire et faire publier, s'ils ne vouloient que la posterité le sceust." Palma Cayet, *Chronologie*, 10. Much more could be said about the textual strategy of this passage. Note especially the careful linking of the names of Henrys III and IV, which gives an impression of dynastic continuity and the close association of "Catholics" as "subjects" in the same phrase. Henry IV's policy was directed at securing the loyalty of his Catholic subjects, particularly the Catholic princes.

16. The newest periodizations of the Wars of Religion clearly acknowledge the failure of Nantes and the progressive denial of civil rights to Huguenots. See especially, Mack P. Holt, *French Wars of Religion, 1562–1629* (Cambridge: Cambridge University Press, 1995), who has rightly altered the traditional chronology to extend the period of religious wars to 1629 and the capture of La Rochelle, the Protestant stronghold. For the ensuing period, see Bernard Dompnier, *Le venin de l'hérésie: Image du protestantisme et combat catholique au XVIIe siècle* (Paris: Editions du Centurion, 1985), who analyzes the whittling away of Protestant privileges and rights. For a new *Realpolitik* approach to the development of religious tolerance in the early-modern period, see the collection of essays by Bob Scribner and Ole Peter Grell, eds., *Tolerance and Intolerance*, which focuses on reasons of state, "the pragmatic," and the political instead of the history-of-

ideas method of a classic such as Joseph Lecler, *Toleration and the Reformation*, 2 vols. (London: Longmans, 1960).

17. See Robert Descimon on municipal assemblies, "Les Assemblées de l'Hôtel de Ville de Paris" (unpublished paper) and Michel Demonet and Robert Descimon, "Politique municipale et espace civique: la représentation des quartiers aux assemblées de l'Hôtel de Ville de Paris (1552–1681) (unpublished paper); and Robert Descimon, "L'Echevinage parisien sous Henri IV (1594–1609): Autonomie urbaine, conflits politiques et exclusives sociales," in *La ville, la bourgeoisie et la genèse de l'état moderne (XIIe–XVIIIe siècles)* (Paris: CNRS, 1988): 113–50.

18. Henri Drouot, *Mayenne et la Bourgogne, 1587–1596: Contribution à l'histoire des provinces françaises pendant la Ligue*, 2 vols. (Paris: Picard 1937). Drouot first made this argument with evidence on the social support for the League in Burgundy. Richet and Descimon have adapted this model to the Paris League and have begun to define a socio-cultural component in the frustrations of this middling elite. Richet, "Sociocultural Aspects," and Robert Descimon, *Qui étaient les Seize? Mythes et réalités de la Ligue parisienne (1585–1894)*, vol. 34, Mémoires de la fédération des sociétés historiques et archéologiques de Paris et de l'Ile-de-France (Paris: Klincksieck, 1983).

19. "A oon uf die Ruman church," Irocmé Sweany, *Estienne Pasquier (1529–1615) et nationalisme littéraire* (Paris: Champion; Geneva: Slatkine, 1985), 10, citing Pasquier: "Je suis fils de l'Eglise Romaine."

20. The legal issues, such as the necessity for the Company of Jesus to acquire letters of naturalization so that it could legally receive funds from legacies in wills, brought *Parlement* into the contest: Henri Fouqueray, *Histoire de la compagnie de Jésus en France des origines à la suppression (1528–1762)*, vol. 1, *Les origines et les premières luttes (1528–1575)* (1910; reprint, Nendeln, Lichtenstein: Kraus Reprint, 1972), 164–65. The language of the debates, however, shows the nationalist sentiments involved. An early opponent of Jesuits, the Bishop of Mâcon, is reported as saying, "il savait quel était le fondateur du nouvel Institut, un certain Ignace, un espagnol, un ennemi de la France." Reported by the papal nuncio in 1549 to Loyola. See Fouqueray, vol. 1, 163.

21. Pasquier was appointed Henry III's *advocat-général* in the *chambre des comptes* in 1585.

22. For a detailed analysis of this episode from the perspective of a Jesuit institutional history, see Fouqueray, *Histoire*.

23. Bernard Chevalier, *Les bonnes villes de France du XVIe siècle* (Paris: Aubier Montaigne, 1982), and Robert Descimon, *Qui*, 26, 61ff.

24. For example, see Leon Bernard, *The Emerging City: Paris in the Age of Louis XIV* (Durham, N.C.: Duke University Press, 1970), chapter 3, "A City Takes to Wheels," p. 56, for the importance of *officiers* of the *Parlement* ceasing to ride mules and removing themselves to the private space of carriages. Bernard, citing Franklin, notes that in 1594 there were only eight carriages in all of Paris, but by the 1630s there were some 4,000. Personal nobility, which came with

purchase of an *office*, could not be passed on through lineage and blood lines, but, ultimately, the *office* as part of the personal wealth of the office-holder could be transmitted to heirs through a variety of expedients. The historiography on the evolution of the *bourgeoisie* and the *officer* class of Paris is vast. For the League era in Paris, the most important interpretations are the numerous studies by Mousnier, Richet, and Descimon, each with its own particular perspective. Henri Drouot's *Mayenne* first proposed the thesis of a frustrated second bourgeoisie, whose social mobility was blocked by the costs of venal office, as an essential factor for the development of the League in Dijon. For a general overview, see Joseph Di Corcia, "Bourg, Bourgeois, Bourgeois de Paris, from the Eleventh to the Eighteenth Century," *Journal of Modern History* 5 (June 1978): 207–33. Basic orientations may be found in Marcel Marion, *Dictionnaire des institutions de la France aux XVIIe et XVIIIe siècles* (Paris: A. & J. Picard, 1979), 52; Guy Cabourdin and Georges Vidal, *Lexique historique de la France d'ancien régime*, 2nd ed., rev. and cor. (Paris: Librairie Armand Colin, 1981); and Gaston Zeller, *Les institutions de la France* (Paris: Presses Universitaires de France, 1948), and Jean-Richard Bloch, *L'anoblissement en France au temps de François Ier, essai d'une définition de la condition juridique et sociale de la noblesse au début du XVI siècle* (Paris: F. Alcan, 1934). The most important recent contribution incorporating an anthropological perspective into the study of social structure and civic identity is Robert Descimon, "Le corps de ville et le système cérémonial parisien au début de l'âge moderne," in *Statuts individuels, statuts corporatifs et statuts judiciaires dans les villes européennes (moyen âge et temps modernes): Individual, corporate and judicial status in European Cities (Late Medieval and Early Modern Period)*, Marc Bone and Maarten Prak, ed. (Louvain: Garant, 1996), 73–128.

25. Colin Kaiser, "Les cours souveraines au XVIe siècle: morale et Contre-Réforme," *Annales: Economies, sociétés, civilisations* 37 (Jan.–Feb. 1982): 17–31.

26. Kaiser, 20, writes [my translation]: "Toward 1577, it became difficult to resist outside pressures. Just the year before, defamatory notices lampooning the judges of the court had appeared in the streets and the Guises had introduced the League into the capital." He then goes on to cite at length a text from a *mercuriale* of 1577 that he considers of the utmost importance for its emphasis on the necessity of *appearing* [my emphasis] to be a good Catholic [*bon catholique*]. The text emphasizes [my translation], "for the sake of religious devotion and to set an example, judges should be in attendance in their parishes at the chief masses [*grandes messes*] and by these demonstrations the people will be better instructed inasmuch as it does not suffice to be a man of good character and devout [*homme de bien et dévot*], but one must also be regarded as such."

27. Kaiser, 28. Cf. above, the organic links of penitential piety and asceticism as well as the distinctive combination of popular and elite asceticism that is most characteristic of League piety; cf. the penitential processions. The League flourished in an atmosphere of ascetic display and ascetic rituals.

28. This professional position makes Nicolas Pasquier an *officier* just as his father had been with his promotion to the *cour des monnaies*.

29. "On ne sçait plus que c'est du nom de Roy, dedans Paris. Non seulement on ne le sçait; mais qui pis est, on le deteste & abhorre. . . . Soudain qu'ils eurent advis de la mort des deux Freres, la revolte fut generale le propre jour de Noël; le lendemain, le Duc d'Aumale fut tumultuairement fait Gouverneur de Paris, en l'Hostel de ville; Estat qui, deux ou trois jours après, luy fut confirmé en plein Parlement, où il presta le Serment; le septième de janvier, les theologiens assemblez au College de Sorbonne, par conclusion Capitulaire, arresterent, qu'en consideration de ce qui estoit arrivé à Blois, les subjects estoient non seulement francs & quittes du serment de fidelité & obeissance qu'ils avoient au Roy; mais aussi que sans charge de leurs consciences ils se pouvoient armer, unir, & lever deniers contre luy; le tout toutesfois & avant tout oeuvre, sous le bon plaisir du Saint Siege. On n'a pas recours à sa Saincteté; mais sous le faux rapport de quelques prescheurs seditieux, non de cette remise et renvoy, ains d'une resolution absolue, les armes ont esté prises du jour au lendemain. Le Parlement mené en triomphe par un Bussi le Clerc & ses Complices, depuis le Palais jusques à la Bastille, où ils ont trié sur le volet tels Seigneurs qu'il leur a pleu pour y tenir prison close. . . . Mais considerez, je vous prie, comme ses mots de Bussi & de Clerc, sont fataux à la ruine de Paris; car celuy qui sous le regne de Charles VI introduisit le capitaine de l'Isle-Adam pour les Bourguignons par la porte de Bussi, s'appelloit le Clerc " Pasquier, *Lettres historiques pour les années 1556–1594*, Livre XIII, Lettre IX, ed. D. Thickett (Geneva: Librairie Droz, 1966), 394–95. Pasquier spells the name Bussi le Clerc; however, the modern historical standard is Bussy le Clerc.

30. Pasquier, *Lettres historiques*, 396: "Je vous ay cy-dessus raconté la desbauche du Parisien. . . . "

31. See Denis Crouzet, "Recherches sur les processions blanches 1583–1584," *Histoire, économie et société* 4 (1982); and Denis Richet, "Politique et religion: les processions à Paris en 1589," in Richet, *De la Réforme à la Révolution: Etudes sur la France moderne* (Paris: Aubier, 1991), on these processions.

32. There is an extensive literature on the socio-professional and cultural identity of the lesser men of the law. The term *basoche* is often used with much imprecision. Technically the term *basoche* refers to young law clerks. In the literature on the League, and elsewhere, it is extended to include an extremely varied group of essentially non-noble legal professionals: in descending order, *avocats* (in Cotgrave: an advocate or a counsellor at law; or, commonly now, a barrister), *procureurs* (attorneys), *notaires* (notaries), *greffiers* (clerks of the court), *huissiers* (process-servers), and, by extension, lesser enforcement officials: *sergents à cheval* (mounted sergeants) and *sergents à verge* (sergeants bearing a staff). See Roland Mousnier, *Les Institutions de la France sous la monarchie absolue*, vol. 2 (Paris: Presses Universitaires de France, 1980), p. 303ff., on the "auxiliaires de la justice"; for a socio-professional analysis of the legal profession in the later *ancien régime*, see also Kagan, *Past and Present* 68 (1975), and more recently, David A. Bell, *Lawyers and Citizens: The Making of a Political Elite in Old Regime France* (Oxford: Oxford University Press, 1994). In the analysis of these individuals and their pious practices, the less loaded terminology *gens de loi* (various

legal professionals and lesser officials of the court, all without the nobility conferred through ennobling office) is used. For the quantitative analysis the group
of *gens de loi* has been divided into four hierarchial strata: *1.* advocates (*avocats*),
who may claim nobility occasionally and who usually use epithets preceding
their names such as *noble homme maistre*, which indicate a certain social notability and professional ethos; *2.* notaries and commissioners; *3. procureurs*, frequently *honorables hommes maistres* or simply *honorables hommes*; and *4. huissiers*
and *sergents*, who use the term *honorable* or no honorable epithet at all preceding
their name. These epithets provide an initial rough index of social notability.
On the ultimate importance of the *gens de loi*, see the discussion below of
Descimon's finding that the *gens de loi* made up some forty percent of the known
Seize. For this four-part division of the *gens de loi*, see Descimon, *Qui*, 91.

33. Cotgrave, *Dictionaire*, s.v. tumultuairement, "rashly" or "disorderly" and
by extension, "seditiously."

34. Pasquier, *Lettres historiques*, 394: "La revolte fut generale le propre jour
de Noël; le lendemain, le Duc d'Aumale fut tumultuairement fait Gouverneur
de Paris." Note here: *tumultuairement*, which Cotgrave renders as "rashly or disorderly." The Duc d'Aumale, Charles de Lorraine [a first cousin of the slain Guise
brothers, the Duc de Guise and Louis, Cardinal of Guise, and of the youngest
Guise, Charles, Duc de Mayenne (1554–1611)], was made governor of Paris by
popular acclamation. See Appendix B. See the primary source account in *Journal historique de Pierre Fayet sur les troubles de la Ligue*, ed. Victor Luzarche (Tours:
Imprimerie Ladeveze, 1852), 43ff. Luzarche has written extensively on Tours,
the site of the royalist *Parlement* during the League years. His editorial notes
suggest that he was favorable to the *politique* position.

35. " . . . avant tout oeuvre, sous le bon plaisir du Saint Siège," 394, and
"*prescheurs seditieux*," 395.

36. Bussy le Clerc was a *Seize* activist widely detested by opponents of the
League. See below and the detailed prosopographical portrait in Descimon, *Qui*,
169–70.

37. Many more instances of memorable *politique* critiques of processional
behaviors could be invoked. See the Epilogue, which deals with the processional fate of the flagellant in the early Age of Enlightenment.

38. Pasquier, *Lettres historiques*, 396: "On a dit aussi que les Seze, des plus
seditieux de Paris, gens de basse condition, y ont empieté toute authorité &
puissance, que l'on appelle le Conseil des Seze. C'est une vraye anarchie. . . . " It
is well worth remembering that Pasquier himself had only just emerged from the
milieu of the *basoche* (broadly construed) when he was promoted to the office of
avocat général des comptes in 1585. I would like to thank Robert Descimon for
pointing this date out to me.

39. "Le Parlement mené en triomphe par un Bussi le Clerc & ses Complices,
depuis le Palais jusques à la Bastille, où ils ont trié sur le volet tels Seigneurs qu'il
leur a pleu pour y tenir prison close. . . . " Pasquier, *Lettres historiques*, 395.

Interestingly, Cotgrave, *Dictionarie*, gives several meanings for *complices*, including "companion (in a leud Action)."

40. The definitive refutation of Pasquier's social portrait of the *Seize* appeared in 1983, with Robert Descimon's *Qui*. He provided a very detailed prosopography of 225 *Seize* activists drawn from seven major socio-professional groups. (These percentages have been rounded for convenience.) See Descimon, *Qui*, 230–31, for details: *1.* sovereign courts, 10%; *2.* non-sovereign courts, 2%; *3.* chancellery & finances, 8%; *4. gens de loi*, 40%; *5.* merchants, 29%; *6.* artisans, 10%; *7.* unknown, 1%.

41. Other key contributions to identification of the Parisian leaders of the League and the *Seize* in particular include: Peter M. Ascoli, "The Sixteen and the Paris League, 1585–1591" (Ph.D. diss., University of California–Berkeley, 1972); J. H. M. Salmon, "The Paris Sixteen, 1585–1594, The Social Analysis of a Revolutionary Movement," *Journal of Modern History* 44 (1972): 540–576; Barnavi and Descimon, "Débat et combat: La Ligue à Paris (1585–1594): Une révision," *Annales: Economies, sociétés, civilisations* 37 (January 1982): 72–130; Descimon and Barnavi, *La Sainte Ligue, le juge et la potence: L'assassinat du président Brisson (15 novembre 1591)* (Paris: Hachette, 1985); and the numerous other studies by Richet as well as the opus of Descimon's studies on the militia.

42. For the significance of inversion rituals in sixteenth-century popular culture see Natalie Davis, "Women on Top," in *Society and Culture in Early Modern France* (Stanford: Stanford University Press, 1965), and Robert Scribner, "The World Turned Upside Down," in *Städtische Gesellschaft und Reformation*, ed. Ingrid Batori (Stuttgart: Klett-Cotta, 1980).

43. Pierre L'Estoile, *Journal de L'Estoile pour le règne de Henri III (1574–1589)*, ed. Louis-Raymond Lefèvre, 6th ed. (Paris: Gallimard, 1943), 557.

44. "Quels sont ces traitres qui parlent de paix? *Je veux de mes mains leur arracher le coeur.*" The reference is to the famous *politique* protest called "Du pain ou la paix" (Bread or Peace) that took place on August 8th during the greatest hardships of the siege of 1590 when hundreds, perhaps thousands, were dying of starvation. This protest was one of the few armed contests between *politiques* and Leaguers on the streets of Paris. The protest turned violent and cost the life of one of the most famous *Seize* leaders, Robert Le Goix, the husband of one of the most interesting Leaguer testators, Tassine de Compans. Bussy le Clerc's comment places the torture of bodies in an immanentist perspective characteristic of Catholic activists and of Catholic militants to different degrees. The emphasis on corporeality shows the judicial and religious cultures of the medieval period were linked by beliefs in the physicality of innocence and guilt and belief in the corporeality of the sacred.

45. Richet, "Sociocultural Aspects," 197; and on the superstitions of popular Catholicism and the gulf separating elite and popular religion, see 194. Richet mentions people seeking miraculous cures at the site of a hawthorn blooming out of season in front of a chapel dedicated to the Holy Virgin. Compare Calvin's dictum that the Age of Miracles is over and Pasquier's on God's own true miracles.

46. Richet, "Sociocultural Aspects," 210, n. 75, as cited by Descimon from Pigafetta, *Mémoires de la fédération des sociétés historiques et archéologiques de Paris et de l'Ile-de-France*, vol. 2 (1876), 76; Descimon, *Qui*, 169.

47. Estienne Pasquier, *Lettres historiques*, ed. D. Thickett (Geneva, 1966), 395–96: "Il n'est plus question de guerroyer la nouvelle Religion; tout le but de la ville de Paris, est la vangeance que tous les officiers ont jurée & signée; mesme quelques-uns, de leur propre sang. Sur cette devotion, hommes & femmes font processions en chemise, reçoivent leur Createur tous les dimanches, se trouvent au service divin depuis le matin jusques au soir, non pour apaiser l'Ire de Dieu, ains pour la provoquer contre leur Roy; n'ayants autre Foy & Religion dans leurs Ames, que la passion; non de nostre Seigneur Jesus-Christ, ains la leur; estimants furieusement que la mesme passibilité tombe en ce grand Dieu impassible."

48. Compare this experiential and theological contextualization of processional culture to the debates about the Stoic revival of the late sixteenth century. See Denis Crouzet, *Les Guerriers de dieu*, 2 vols. (n.p.: Champ Vallon, 1990), and in general Gerhard Oestreich, *Neostoicism and the Early Modern State* (Cambridge: Cambridge University Press, 1982).

49. For further insights into the Reformation's critique of the projection of the human family onto the Holy Family, see John Bossy on the cult of Saint Anne in *Christianity in the West: 1400–1700* (Oxford and New York: Oxford University Press, 1985), 93–97. Bossy's analysis makes clear the religious and secular legal parallels between Protestant and *politique* notions of religious and political transcendence.

50. For L'Estoile see *Journal de L'Estoile pour le règne de Henri IV (1589–1600)*, ed. Louis-Raymond Lefèvre, 4th ed. (Paris: Gallimard, 1948), and the collection in the *réserve* of the Bibliothèque Nationale, *Belles figures et drolleries de la Ligue*.

51. Denis Richet, "Socio-cultural Aspects." The full implications of this contradiction and ambiguity are analyzed in the Epilogue.

52. L'Estoile, *Journal . . . Henri IV*, 1:548: "tous les hommes d'esprit."

53. L'Estoile, *Journal . . . Henri IV*, 1:547–48: "En ce temps et pendant ce mois, à la suscitation et par exhortation de quelques prédicateurs de Paris et du capucin Brûlart, entre autres, qui prêchait les Avents à S. Etienne du Mont, fut proposé de porter le S. Sacrement par les rues, sous un poêle (à la mode d'Espagne), avec pareille pompe et cérémonie que le jour de la *Fête Dieu*, et que quand on irait sonner la cloche de la paroisse, que les paroissiens seraient avertis de sortir pour le venir accompagner et lui faire l'honneur qui lui était dû; aussi que devant les maisons par où il passerait, il y aurait toujours quelqu'un à la porte, qui se tiendrait là, avec une torche ardente à la main, pour l'éclairer. Cette nouvelle façon et cérémonie fut autorisée par le nouvel évêque de Paris, encore qu'eu égard au temps où vivons, elle fut jugée par tous les hommes d'esprit, quelque grands catholiques qu'ils fussent, une cérémonie de sédition plus que de dévotion."

54. L'Estoile, *Journal . . . Henri IV*, 1:548.

55. L'Estoile, *Journal . . . Henri IV*, 1:548: the ceremony "fut jugée par tous les hommes d'esprit . . . une cérémonie de sédition plus que de dévotion."

56. L'Estoile, *Journal . . . Henri IV*, 1:548.

57. Robert Descimon has documented the Chartreux connection in compiling the dossier on the *Seize* Jehan Hennequin, in *Qui*, 157. The younger generation of this illustrious family, known for its Leaguer ties, gave its support to the Jesuits and to the Feuillants, as the will of *noble homme maistre* Pierre Hennequin, son of the *sieur* de Bermanville, indicates (notary Claude I de Troyes, April 7, 1590).

58. L'Estoile, *Journal . . . Henri IV*, 46. Did women, either lay or nuns, also process? The sources, so far, have been silent on this important question.

59. "Messieurs, assurer se faut, Puisqu'à la mi-mai on voit faire du mardi-gras le mystère, D'avoir carême bien haut." To gloss, it may be said that "carême bien haut" is an oxymoron, intended to convey, just as Palma Cayet and Pasquier did in their satires, the profound sacral and political misbehavior *politiques* perceived in the communal revolution of the *Seize* and their clerical and noble allies. Lent was intended, of course, to bring penitential humility, not arrogance.

60. "Hamilton, écossais de nation et curé de Saint-Côme, faisait l'office de sergent, et les rangeait, tantôt les arrêtant pour chanter des hymnes, et tantôt les faisait marcher; quelquefois il les faisait tirer de leurs mousquets. Tout le monde accourut à ces spectacles nouveaux, qui représentaient, à ce que les zélés disaient, l'Eglise militante. Le légat y accourut aussi et approuva par sa présence une montre si extraordinaire et en même temps si risible; mais il arriva qu'un de ces nouveaux soldats . . . voulut saluer le légat qui était dans son carrosse . . . tira dessus et tua un de ses ecclésiastiques, qui était son aumônier." L'Estoile, *Journal . . . Henri IV*, 1:46.

61. I consulted the manuscript version of this text, Bibliothèque historique de la ville de Paris, ms. 533.

62. "A quoy nous commercerons à la monstre qui fut ioüee environ le mois de Juillet l'an 1590 ou une grande quantité de prestres & moines (ie ne dis pas religieux) & novices en forme de goujats la seiziere accompagnee d'un grand nombre de pedants le tout de divers ordres et nations armez a la legere, sur le moule du pourpoint de l'antiquité catholique, a peu pres de l'encoleure de ceux qui gardent le sepulchre en Avignon, qui dançans au son et cliquetis le tabourin de biscaye a l'imitation du mardi gras se faisoient voir en ce follastre & risible equipage par les rues de Paris au grand regret & mescontentement des gens de bien. "Apres eux cheminoit faisant l'arriere garde, un assez malostte personage que l'on disoit estre un advocat fol arme de mesme comme si ce mesme jour il eust a combastre les pigmeans sauvages a qui les roitelets et autres oysillons du ciel font la guerre a toute reste." "Les singeries de la Ligue," Bibliothèque historique de la ville de Paris, ms. 533: *Recueil de pièces sur la Ligue*. For the complex history of the many representations and misrepresentations of the Armed Procession, see Eugène Revillout, "Le Tableau de la ligue: dans ses rapports avec la Satyre ménippée," *La montagne Sainte-Genevieve*, vol. 1 (1909–1912): 117–51.

63. "Un sergent de bande un cornet de verre pendu en sa ceinture qui disoit avoir apporte de sainct Mathurin de l'archant en la faveur duquel il faisoit accourir une infinie de badaux de Paris, ja plus qu'a demy desbauchez de ces nouvelles adventures ausquels a petit bruict & basse notte predisoit comme il s'ensuict, que ceste *mommerie* [my emphasis] n'estoit autre chose que les signes et appeaux d'un nombre infiny de detresses & malheurs a advenir." Variant editions have been published: for example, see the *Histoire abregee des singeries de la ligue, dediee a messieurs de Paris*, in *Satyre Ménippée de la Vertu du Catholicon d'Espagne et de la tenue des estatz de Paris*, rev. ed. (Genève: Slatkine Reprints, 1971), 102–21.

64. "La fable de la Ligue 'populaire' . . . rend impensable la reproduction du vieux système de la ville médiévale." Descimon, *Qui*, 26.

65. See above chapter 1, the account of Pierre Delamer.

66. "Ce jour même, par l'avis de tous messieurs de la Faculté de théologie de Paris, fût publié un voeu à Notre-Dame de Chartres pour y aller à pied, au cas que la ville ne fût prise, car en ce cas la vertu de la bonne Dame expirait, comme ayant changé de parti et étant politique." L'Estoile, *Journal . . . Henri IV*, 104.

67. For the relationship between the *Université* and the *Ville*, embodied in the procession linking Saint-André-des-Arts and Saint-Jacques-de-la-Boucherie, see chapter 6.

68. "Mais mes amis dit-t-il [Aubry] je vous assure que si jamais ce méchant relaps et excommunié y entre, soit par cette porte ou autre, qu'il nous ôtera notre religion, notre sainte messe, nos belles cérémonies, nos reliques; fera de nos belles églises des étables à ses chevaux; tuera vos prêtres et fera de nos ornements et chappes des chausses et des livrées à ses pages et laquais. Et cela est aussi vrai, et je le sais bien, à fin que vous y preniez garde, comme est vrai le Dieu que je vais manger et recevoir là-dessus. Lesquelles paroles offensèrent beaucoup de gens de bien de sa paroisse [Saint-André-des-Arts]." L'Estoile, *Journal . . . Henri IV*, 103. Virtually no written sermons of the League preachers have survived.

69. During the early stages of the Protestant Reformation at a time when the precise liturgical and ritual identity of what would become divergent confessions was not yet defined, the concept of adiaphora played an important role for Lutherans and even for Erasmus. Adiaphora literally means those things that make no difference to one's salvation. For Leaguers such a notion of neutral elements of ritual was unthinkable. See the conclusion of this chapter, where the *royalist* L'Hôpital clearly does embrace the notion. It is also interesting to note that the term adiaphora does not even appear in the *Dictionnaire d'archéologie chrétienne et de liturgie*. See, however, the *Dictionnaire de théologie catholique*, s.v. adiaphorites, as a Protestant term. Vol. 1, part 1, col. 396ff.

70. Michel de L'Hôpital (c. 1505–73) was Chancellor of France from 1560 to 1568. The quotation is Michel de L'Hôpital writing to Claude d'Espence, "On Christian Piety," in Louis Bandy de Nalèche, ed., *Poesies complètes du Chancelier Michel de L'Hospital* (Paris: 1857), 34; cited by Edmond Morton Beame in "The Development of Politique Thought During the Wars of Religion (1560–1595),"

(Ph.D. diss., University of Illinois, 1957), 35. Although they held widely varying political and religious views, many *politiques* shared L'Hôpital's disdain for
what they considered superfluous ceremony.

Chapter 5

1. For an overview of the kinds of information found in Parisian wills and
the way it was entered into the quantitative database for this book, see Appendix K. See Appendix L for the macro-social information on four testator populations (91 Leaguers in 1590, a reference populuation of 636 "non-Leaguers,"
159 testators for 1543–44, and the population of 344 testators for 1630).

2. Since in the north of France customary law governed the disposition of
most forms of property, wills did not designate heirs. As part of the canonical
final reckoning, the church required wills to list debts owed by and to the
testator. For an overview of Parisian wills and the law and the technical evolution of wills see Antoinette Fleury, *Le Testament dans la coutume de Paris au XVI
siècle* [Thesis, Ecole Nationale des Chartes] (Nogent-le-Rotrou: Imprimerie
Daupeley, 1943), the manuscript of which Antoinette Fleury kindly allowed me
to consult; Philippe Ariès, *The Hour of Our Death*, trans. Helen Weaver (New
York: Alfred A. Knopf, 1981); and H. Auffroy, *Evolution du testament en France
des origines au XIIIe siècle* (Paris: Thèse de doctorat ed., 1911).

3. See Table 5.3, "Comparison of Numbers of Pious Requests in All Testator Populations."

4. See Ariès, *Hour*; Pierre Chaunu, *La mort à Paris aux XVIe, XVIIe et
XVIIIe siècles* (Paris: 1978); Michel Vovelle, *Piété baroque et déchristianisation en
Provence au XVIIIe siècle: Les attitudes devant la mort d'après les clauses du testaments* (Paris: Plon, 1973); Pierre Chaunu, "Un nouveau champ pour l'histoire
sérielle: Le quantitatif au troisième niveau," in *Mélanges Fernand Braudel*, vol. 2
(Toulouse: Privat, 1973); and Jacques Chiffoleau, *La compatabilité de l'au-delà:
Les hommes, la mort et la religion dans la région d'Avignon à la fin du moyen âge (vers
1320–vers 1480)*, vol. 47 (Rome: Collection de l'Ecole Française de Rome,
1980).

5. See especially Chaunu, *La mort*, 318 and *passim*, on the fate of the soul
separated from the body at death. Caroline W. Bynum, *The Resurrection of the
Body in Western Christianity, 200–1336* (New York: Columbia University Press,
1995) signals the corrective in the historiography that is currently underway.

6. For example, Alain Croix, despite his extraordinary achievement, argues in *La Bretagne aux 16e et 17e siècles: la vie, la mort, la foi* (Paris: Maloine,
1981), vol. 2, 975: "les variantes de libellé interdisent un décompte précis. [The
variations in wording make a precise count impossible.]" Others have assumed
testamentary discourse is highly formulaic. While, in fact, a significant portion
of it is, this objection ignores the considerable interest of change in the formulas
themselves. Most importantly, a sampling technique that considers all extant

wills in selected years (rather than some wills from specific years) may be the best way to find strategic testators who diverge from aggregate trends, but who are guides to how cultural change occurs. Divergence from the aggregate may signal an avant-garde supporting change or a traditionalist resisting change.

7. Table 5.1 divides the 1590 testator population into I) a reference group that initially shows no indication of League affiliation, II) key subpopulations thought to have League affinities, and III) a League-identified population, which clearly has the highest rates of performative religious engagement. Four chief categories of ritual engagement are displayed: 1) performativity, 2) immanence, 3) mentions of the body of Jesus Christ (*corps Jésus Christ*), and 4) concern with liturgical details. For an explanation of the precise requests and the will language considered as markers of these sorts of ritual or performative engagement, see Appendix C.

8. For a detailed analysis of the ninety-one Leaguers, see Appendix D. The information for each of the ninety-one testators includes testator's notary, present parish, health, and burial institution; any request for a special burial location; use of a sacralizing heading (such as "Jesus and Maria") in the will; examples of testator performativity; nature of League connections; and testator's socio-professional category and profession as stated in the will (italics indicate a direct quotation from the will). See Appendix L, which compares the characteristics of 1590's Leaguers and non-Leaguers using these and other basic variables such as sex and literacy.

9. The form "1590's" will be used to refer specifically to the testators of the year 1590, not the decade, which is why the form was chosen.

10. The twenty-six testators who made bequests to the Jesuits, Capuchins, or Feuillants were most likely among the avant-garde of Catholic reformers. A separate study of all these individuals is underway. Of these twenty-six individuals, five are unquestionably *Seize* activists: Charles Fustel, Genevieve Rolland, Jehan Dampmartin, Pierre Hennequin, and Marye Thiersault. All these family names will be well known to historians of the League, but no previous work has been done on the women in this group. See Appendix K, for a comparison of pious requests mentioning monasteries made by Leaguers and non-Leaguers.

11. Appendix K shows how relevant variables were applied to a specific case, master maker of cold cuts, Augustin Gueret. Readers interested in the mechanics of the code book and its application should consult Appendix K, which provides examples of the variables discussed in this chapter. Appendix C provides details on all the variables used to analyze immanence, performativity, and reform and shows precisely what kind of language from the wills corresponds to a specific variable and its specific values.

12. For a historical overview of the term *bourgeois de Paris*, see Joseph Di Corcia, "*Bourg, Bourgeois, Bourgeois de Paris*, from the Eleventh to the Eighteenth Century," *Journal of Modern History* 5 (1978): 207–33.

13. Chiffoleau, *La compatabilité*; Chaunu, *La mort*.

14. This is examined in detail in Table 5.6.

15. For details on the eight key variables see Appendix C. Only the first of these eight variables is discussed in detail in this chapter. This variable is called the Performativity Index, and it contains nineteen different values arranged in a hypothetical hierarchy as explained below.

16. Because of the great diversity in individual Leaguers' pious engagement, Appendix D presents each of the 91 Leaguers in a brief prosopographical sketch. Among simple macro-social traits, Leaguers were more likely than were non-Leaguers to be in good health when they drew up their wills. The nature of the bonds between League testators and League-affiliated notaries is discussed in Chapter 6.

17. Of these seven, four were Leaguers; each used a different notary: Arragon, Raoul Bontemps, P. Cothereau, Ferrant, Herbin, Landry, and Mahieu. The wording varied from "honestement" (in a worthy, decent, or even handsome manner), to "posement" (in a stayed and unrushed manner), to Gueret's request of "devotiement" (devoutly). Each distinct term was coded in a distinct value of one initial variable. Only value 3 (devoutly) was retained and recoded as a value in the Performativity Index, "Strict Comportment of Celebrant."

18. Examples of obviously wealthy high-profile Leaguers who insist upon liturgical and performative rigor are discussed in Chapter 7.

19. A typical "funeral package" may have included: a convoy, services, lights, prayers, speeches, burial, and perhaps a service one year after death. Gueret also provided important information concerning bell-ringing that was coded as the variable for the *sonnerie* (the sounding of bells).

20. The instances of Marian and Christocentric piety in Gueret's liturgical requests were unexceptional. The Marian and Christocentric variables await further refinement.

21. There are nineteen types of performativity, i.e., ritualized performance, or symbolic behaviors. Table 5.4: "Performativity Index for the Three Sample Periods, Including a Breakdown of the 1590 Leaguer Population" shows the frequency of these behaviors in the general testator population (GTP) of each sample period. Generally, as one moves up the hierarchy of performative behaviors, Leaguers are responsible for an increasing percentage of the performative population for each type of performativity. The Leaguer overrepresentation in the performative population is even more evident in Table 5.5: "Performativity Index: 1590 Population Compared with 1590 League Population Percentages." It is crucial to note, however, that Leaguers predominate in the more traditional performative behaviors as well, e.g., banqueting or aural and visual symbolic community. Here we have the foundations of a quantitative demonstration of the explanation of the puzzle of the Janus face of the League, which looks both backward and forward in time. Tables 5.4 and 5.5 are discussed in more detail below on 216–17.

22. When establishing foundations, i.e., investments for services to be performed in perpetuity, the wording of these bequests nearly always included the phrase "avec pain et vin." This means that the testator engages to pay the cost in

perpetuity of the bread and wine for the mass. Each of these phrases was coded at the initial variable, but not retained for the performativity analysis as this was clearly formulaic language in all the sample years, saying little about the affective intensity accompanying the bequest.

23. The testator Leon Le Cyrier used the notary Crozon, M.C. étude XLIX, 22 (1 January 1543). The second testator is Jehan Marion, notary Jourdan, a League-identified testator discussed in detail in Chapter 6 as a novice entering the Feuillant monastery in 1590.

24. John Bossy's analysis helps clarify the use of horizontal for social and anthropomorphic and vertical for more deocentric. See his analysis of change in traditional Catholicism in *Christianity in the West: 1400–1700* (Oxford and New York: Oxford University Press, 1985). Bossy argues that Protestant reformers sought to eliminate the social "bonds of affinity" (95), which had served to give the medieval Christ his "proper complement of kin" (9–10). He summarizes this argument: "There were scholarly reasons for casting off the web of human relationships which pre-Reformation *pietas* had spun around the figure of Christ; but they drew their force from a revision which deprived Christ's kinship to man of its status as a necessary axiom of reason in the story of the Redemption. The multifarious kindred of St. Anne would no longer be an absorbing object of contemplation" (95). See also Moshe Halevi Spero, *Religious Objects as Psychological Structures: A Critical Integration of Object Relations Theory, Psychotherapy, and Judaism* (Chicago: University of Chicago Press, 1992), especially chapter 5, "A Model for Anthropocentric and Deocentric Dimensions of Psychological Experience." Compare below on the possible significance of the given name Cléophas for the notary who has the highest number of testators among the 1590 notaries (forty-one cases). Cléophas, an unusual name, was the second husband of Saint Anne, the mother of Mary, who married Joseph. The name Cléophas thus especially evokes the notion of holy kinship ties and the horizontal bonds of confraternity that are the matrix of League conceptions of community affiliations. Generally large numbers of testators for a given notary in 1590 correlate with a known League orientation for the notary. In the case of Peron, besides his forty-one cases, the name Cléophas may provide an additional clue as to Leaguer affiliation. The early childhood socialization of Leaguers may have been distinctive.

25. "Fille majeure, demeurante en l'hostel et au service de Madame de la Ville." She gives "son cotillon de velours à ramage à fondz blanc . . . pour estre ledict cotillon employé à faire ung deslee au dessus du saint sacrement . . . ," Notary Turgis, 26 September 1630.

26. On banqueting, see the extensive analysis of the will of *noble homme* Georges Bucholicq, notary Ph. Cothereau, in chapter 5; for the overall high performativity ranking for his notary, Ph. Cothereau, see Appendix F. Bucholicq, from Dalmatia, is from the entourage of the late Cardinal of Lorraine. I would like to thank Martha Newman for her insights into medieval pilgrimage.

27. On the separation of the liturgical meal from the eucharist proper and its final disappearance see Theodore Klauser, *A Short History of the Western Liturgy: An Account and Some Reflections*, 2nd. ed., trans. John Halliburton (Oxford, New York: Oxford University Press, 1979), 8, and Josef Andreas Jungmann, *The Mass: An Historical, Theological, and Pastoral Survey*, ed. Mary Ellen Evans., trans. Julien Fernandes (Collegeville: Liturgical Press, 1976). Klauser cites from First Corinthians and John on this problem and also emphasizes the tension with the Gnostics. Klauser and Jungmann both comment on efforts to "spiritualize" the eucharist.

28. There is now a rich historiographical tradition of such research that had its roots in works such as Natalie Davis's essays, particularly "The Reasons of Misrule," in *Society and Culture in Early-Modern France* (Stanford: Stanford University Press, 1965), and Yves-Marie Bercé, *Fête et révolte: Des mentalités populaires du XVIe au XVIIIe siècle* (Paris, 1976).

29. See, for example, chapters 22–26 of the episcopal Constitutions of the great reforming bishop of Verona (1524–43), Gian Matteo Giberti, which define correct comportment for clerics at funeral banquets and stresses their educative role: "we direct that not frivolous stories but words of a sacred reading be heard. For by this means souls are edified for the good, and needless stories are barred. The clergy acting thus, whether summoned to the office of the dead or to solemn feasts, will edify the laity more than if the laity hears they are disparaging those absent or grumbling at them or injecting obscene talk." See below for the concerns with purity and the regulation of female sexuality in particular.

30. This effort is measured by categorizing and analyzing any mention a testator makes of his or her own body, especially when the testator emphasizes the placement of his body in front of the crucifix as, for example, requesting the *vexilla regis* to be sung with the testator's body placed in front of the crucifix. In one 1540's will, the testator, Estiennette Versoris, notes that the *vexilla regis* is also known as the "salut de la passion." This vernacular reference does not reoccur in either 1590 or 1630.

31. See A. Vacant and E. Mangenot, eds., *Dictionnaire de théologie catholique* (Paris: Librairie Letouzey et Ané, 1920), s.v. "cierges."

32. René Benoist, *Catholicque et utile discours des chandelles, torches et tout autre usage de feu en la profession de la foy et religion chrestienne* (Paris, 1566).

33. Benoist, *Catholicque et utile discours des chandelles, torches et tout autre usage de feu en la profession de la foy . . .*, "[rien] plus propre pour signifier la saincté de Iesus Christ, et la pureté de la Vierge, que le cierge duquel matière est faicte sans commixion de masle et femelle . . . comme la sacrée humanité de Iesus Christ a esté formée de la vierge sans aucune copulation et souillure."

34. See Chapter 3 on the Tridentine analysis of the *Fête-Dieu* (the Feast of Corpus Christi and its processions).

35. Donna Spivey Ellington, "Impassioned Mother or Passive Icon: The Virgin's Role in Late Medieval and Early Modern Sermons," *Renaissance Quarterly* 48, no. 2 (summer 1995): 227–61.

36. For a discussion of the early monastic origins and significance of these *livres martirologes* and their connection with the development of the liturgy, see Auguste Molinier, *Les obituaires français au moyen âge* (Paris: Imprimerie nationale, 1890). See Eamon Duffy, *Stripping of the Altars: Traditional Religion in England 1400–1580* (New Haven and London: Yale University Press, 1992), 334, on the way the bede-roll shaped a commemorative community at the parish level. The Reformation abolished bede-rolls.

37. This reorientation of social and cultural history grew out of the French school of the history of mentalities. The great landmarks in the history of death for the medieval and early-modern period are the writings of Philippe Ariès, *The Hour of Our Death*, originally published as *L'homme devant la mort* (Paris: Editions du Seuil, 1977); Vovelle, *Piété baroque*, and *La mort et l'Occident de 1300 à nos jours* (Editions Gallimard et Pantheon Books, 1983); Chaunu, *La mort*; and Chiffoleau, *La compatabilité*.

38. This analysis draws upon the extensive literature of the *ars moriendi*. For a stimulating analysis see Richard Wunderli and Gerald Broce, "The Final Moments before Death in Early Modern England," *Sixteenth Century Journal* 20, no. 2 (1989): 259–75, which emphasizes testator individualism.

39. For a modern statement of "sacramental realism" see Charles Davis, *Theology for Today* (New York: Sheed & Ward, 1962), 272–73: "Our share in Christ's life comes to us through our union with his life-giving body. The sacramental economy means that it is through our bodies that the life of Christ is conveyed to us, and in each sacrament our bodies are brought into vital contact with the power of Christ's risen body. . . . The effect is not confined to our souls, and Scripture and tradition emphatically tell us that the resurrection of the body is due to the Holy Eucharist." For the complex evolution of the last sacrament, see Joseph Avril, "La pastorale des malades et des mourants aux XIIe et XIIIe siècles," in *Death in the Middle Ages*, edited by Herman Braet and Werner Verbeke (Louvain: Leuven University Press, 1983), 88–106; and the classic studies by Peter Browe, "Die Letzte Ölung in der abendländischen Kirche des Mittelalters," *Zeitschrift für katholische Theologie* 55 (1931): 515–61, and "Die Sterbekommunion im Altertum und Mittelalter," *Zeitschrift für katholische Theologie* 60 (1936): 1–54. Browe points to the practice of erecting altars in sick rooms so the mass could be said in conjunction with the administration of communion to the sick and to the dying. It is crucial to note that the Council of Trent (at the 22nd session, 1562) forbade the practice of saying masses in private homes. This decisive 22nd session addressed in yet another fundamental way the permissible boundaries between the sacred and the profane.

40. This directive asking that her body not be cut open appears in her 1579 will but is not repeated in the 1590 will.

41. Tassine de Compans, notary Croiset VIII, 404, and Margueritte Dugué, notary Lybault, CV, 136.

42. See Table 5.7 for a detailed analysis of the pious directives concerning the offertory procession. The term in French is *offrande*.

43. Klauser, A *Short History*, 8.

44. For the performativity ranking of notaries see Appendix F, where the top three notaries in the ranking of general performativity were de Troyes (82% of clients' wills contained performative requests), Arragon (73%), and Monthenault (73%), all League-connected notaries.

45. Values 14–18 in the "Performativity Index" are discussed in detail in Chapter 7 when evaluating the reformist engagement of Leaguers and testators making bequests to the Jesuits, Capuchins, or Feuillants.

46. The testator is damoiselle Marie de Gourgue, May 3, 1630, whose mother was a Séguier. Her father is *Monsieur le premier président du Parlement*. This holograph will on the occasion of her entering the Carmelite monastery in Paris is discussed in detail in Chapter 7 on reformers. On female monastic professions see Elizabeth Rapley, *The Dévotes: Women and Church in Seventeenth-Century France* (Montreal & Kingston: McGill-Queen's University Press, 1990); Barbara Diefendorf, "Pious Women and the Roots of the Catholic Reformation in Paris: The Problem of Asceticism," working paper presented at the Conference on Early Modern History, The University of Minnesota, May 1993; and Diefendorf, "Give Us Back Our Children: Patriarchal Authority and Parental Consent to Religious Vocations in Early Counter-Reformation France," *The Journal of Modern History* 68.2 (June 1996): 265–307; and for a later period, during the reign of Louis XIV, Sarah Hanley, "Women and the Body Politic in Early Modern France," *Proceedings of the Annual Meeting of the Western Society for French History* 16 (1989): 408–14. Hanley outlines the coercive element of a "Family-State Compact," which used the monastery as a site of confinement and enforced penitence. See especially pp. 409, 412. The debate over the rules of enclosure for all female orders following the decrees of Trent was one of the most controversial aspects of Tridentine reform.

47. The concerns of testators about the intelligibility of the mass and sacraments for celebrants and for the laity are discussed in detail in Chapter 7 on reformist testators.

Chapter 6

1. See the comments on Crouzet below. Robert Descimon, *Qui étaient les Seize?* (Paris, 1983), and Elie Barnavi, *Le parti de dieu* (Louvain, 1980), explicitly examine the changing nature and social composition of the *Seize* and League leaders respectively (1585–94). The conflicting evidence, even for this narrow time period, means that these historians do not agree on the nature of the Holy Union. Moreover each historian approaches the sacred differently. Descimon excludes League clerics from his analysis of the 225 *Seize* but emphasizes the importance of "integral Catholicism" to the movement as a whole, whose purpose he defines as the restoration of the "medieval urban system" (26). Barnavi includes clerics in his analysis of League leaders, but views the movement as the

prototype for a radical totalitarian regime. For the crucial segment of Descimon on the relations of the clerical League and the *Seize* and the reasons for excluding the clerics from his analysis, see *Qui*, 45–50.

2. Descimon and Barnavi are particularly attentive to these changes and how to analyze them. While differing, these two historians also co-authored a study of the most radical phase of the League, the murder of Brisson, the first *president* of the *Parlement*, in November 1591. See Elie Barnavi and Robert Descimon, *La Sainte Ligue, le juge et la potence: L'assassinat du président Brisson (15 novembre 1591)* (Paris: Hachette, 1985). See also Michael Wolf, *The Conversion of Henri IV: Politics, Power, and Religious Belief in Early Modern France* (Cambridge, Massachusetts: Harvard University Press, 1993).

3. For Crouzet's critique of "a history without God," see *Les guerriers de dieu*, 2 vols. (Champ Vallon, 1990), 1:61ff. Crouzet's method of reinserting "God" into historical analysis relies on an innovative treatment of the gestural culture of Catholicism. For an example, see *Guerriers*, 1:75: "La gestuelle a été envisagée comme expressive du sens que pouvait avoir pour les fidèles leur relation à Dieu." For further references to the problem of "a history without God," see Crouzet, *Guerriers*, 2:287ff. For Crouzet's insistence on the reality of "the League of the people" ("la Ligue populaire n'est pas seulement 'fable' royaliste"), 2:295; also 296: "Le 'peuple' est, avec Dieu, un autre oublié de l'histoire."

4. Crouzet, *Guerriers*, 2:427.

5. See especially Crouzet, *Guerriers*, 2:496ff.

6. Crouzet, *Guerriers*, 2:502: "c'est par la tension vers Dieu, dans la célébration du deuil des princes lorrains et la piété penitentielle que l'Union sera accomplie."

7. See Crouzet, *Guerriers*, 1:47, 2:295, and 2:382 for the use of these terms.

8. Crouzet, *Guerriers*, 2:435, stresses that only in a second phase does the institutional church capture this emotional élan.

9. See Crouzet, *Guerriers*, 2:376 for the concept of mythic time.

10. Crouzet, *Guerriers*, 2:317 and 2:367.

11. Crouzet, *Guerriers*, 2:295.

12. "La Ligue cléricale est indissociée de la Ligue laïque. . . . Les Seize ont, en eux, la même puissance sacrale que les prédicateurs. . . ." Crouzet, *Guerriers*, 2:296–97: "L'engagement religieux n'est pas affaire de clivages sociaux." Also on 2:297: "La Ligue ne s'explique ni économiquement, ni socialement, ni politiquement. A la différence de l'engagement militant catholique du temps des premiers troubles, ce n'est pas non plus par sa violence rituelle qu'elle peut être analysée."

13. Crouzet, *Guerriers*, 2:403.

14. Crouzet, *Guerriers*, 2:433.

15. Crouzet, *Guerriers*, 2:433.

16. Crouzet, *Guerriers*, 2:435.

17. Crouzet, *Guerriers*, 2:367, rejects the "specificity" of the *Seize*: he denies any specific social, economic, or political motivation. "The motive forces of

Seize militancy are those of an enchanted catholicism." ("Les schèmes moteurs du militantisme Seize sont ceux du catholicisme le plus enchanté.")

18. Crouzet, *Guerriers*, 2:507, "Pleurer les Guises n'est pas un acte passif, mais est une extraordinaire tension d'intériorisation en soi de leur pureté sanctifée."

19. Crouzet, *Guerriers*, 2:510.

20. "Invasion mystique" of Brémond.

21. Crouzet, *Guerriers*, 2:396: "La procession exprime un vouloir corporel et spirituel d'atteindre Dieu."

22. Crouzet, *Guerriers*, 2:314.

23. Crouzet, *Guerriers*, 2:511–12: "un amour mystique qui est vécu collectivement; l'Union se réalise sotériologiquement en lui."

24. Crouzet, *Guerriers*, 1:75.

25. I would particularly like to thank Lionel Rothkrug and the cultural-mapping initiative sponsored by Lewis Lancaster for an introduction to the concept of cultural mapping.

26. See Crouzet, *Guerriers*, 2:433, where Crouzet specifically points to a fusion of the clerical League and the lay League of the *Seize*.

27. See Claude de Seyssel, *La monarchie de France et deux autres fragments politiques* (Paris: Librairie d'Argences, 1961), and the discussion by William F. Church, *Constitutional Thought in Sixteenth-Century France: A Study in the Evolution of Ideas* (New York: Octagon Books, 1969). The two other restraints were justice and "*la police*," the latter an elusive concept meaning the total of the body of regulations which establish civil order.

28. A general introduction to this subject may be found in C. H. Lawrence, *The Friars: The Impact of the Early Mendicant Movement on Western Society* (London and New York: Longman, 1994), and in his bibliography for chap. 6, "The Mission to the Towns." For the details of the early period before a *modus vivendi* was established between the University and the friars, see John Moorman, *A History of the Franciscan Order from Its Origins to the Year 1517*, especially chap. 13, "The Friars and the Universities" (Chicago: Franciscan Herald Press, 1988). For a brief overview and introduction to the early-modern period, see Henri-Jean Martin, *Livre, pouvoirs et société: Paris au XVIIe siècle (1598–1701)* (Geneva: Droz, 1969), 1:37–44; esp. 37–40, on the competition the University faced from the founding of the Collège royale in 1530 and the Jesuit Collège de Clermont in 1564. See also Jean Baptiste Louis Crévier, *Histoire de l'Université de Paris, depuis son origine jusqu'en l'année 1600* (Paris: Desaint and Saillant, 1761).

29. See Pierre L'Estoile, *Journal de l'Estoile pour la règne de Henri IV (1589–1600)*, ed. Louis-Raymond Lefèvre (Paris: 1948), 38–39, on Leaguer meetings at the Augustinian friary, a site where the officers of the *Parlement* also met. Raoul Busquet refers to the Collège de Fortet as the "berceau de la Ligue [the cradle of the League]": Raoul Busquet, "Etude historique sur le collège de Fortet (1394–1764)," *Mémoires de la Société de l'Histoire de Paris et de l'Ile-de-France* 33 (1906): 187–290 and 34 (1907): 1–151.

30. The BN ms. 2751, folio 201ff. [A List of those asked to leave Paris before the entry of Henry IV on 5 March 1594], indicates that the prior of the Carmelites of Place Maubert and Guillaume Rose were among those intransigents exiled in 1594 from the *quartier* of the *quartenier* Carel in the University. From the *quartier* of Huot (also the University) the *curés* of Saint-André-des-Arts, Saint-Côme, and Saint-Benoît were also exiled. See Appendix G for an overview of the clerics of the League. The notaries with practices situated on the Place Maubert are Jean Charles and Mathurin Périer. The practice of Jean Charles shows again the correlation between known Leaguer affiliation of a notary and large numbers of the testators of the 1590s. Jean Charles, with thirty-four wills, has one of the highest will counts for a 1590 notary, second only to Cléophas Peron. See Appendix L. There are five Leaguer testators among Charles's clients (see the "Master Notary Chart, 1590" [Appendix E] for their identities).

31. The Cordeliers were the largest of the mendicant houses in Paris and possessed a vast network of buildings and schools. In 1570, the General Chapter meeting of the order was held in the refectory building in Paris, where 1,200 Cordeliers elected as the General of their order Scipion Gonzagua of the illustrious Italian family. For the strong Italian influence in the mendicant houses, see A. Renaudet, "Paris de 1494 à 1517: église et université, réformes religieuses, culture et critique humaniste," in *Courants religieux . . . Colloque de Strasbourg 9–11 mai, 1957* (Paris: Presses Universitaires de France, 1959): 5–24; esp. 12, on the "transalpine" character of the movement for reform of the older orders in the sixteenth century. The presence of so many Italians may well have been a source of anti-Italian sentiment in Paris (note the large chapter meeting in 1570 just two years prior to the massacres of Saint Bartholemew's Day). For the strong Italian influence among the Cordeliers, see Laure Beaumont-Maillet, *Le grand couvent des cordeliers de Paris: Etude historique et archéologique du XIIIe siècle à nos jours* (Paris: Champion, 1975), 133ff., on the reforming efforts of Paul Pisot de Parme, minister-general of the Cordeliers. The imposition by Francis I of quotas limiting the numbers of Italians permitted in Parisian monastic communities suggests their sizeable presence was resented by some. The Cordeliers heartily resisted Italian-imposed reforms in the seventeenth century as well. Beaumont-Maillet documents this from very revealing primary sources on 142–51. Louis XIII was obliged to provide armed guards for the General of the Parisian house, Bénigne de Gênes, whom he supported as a strict reformer of the Cordeliers.

32. See Philippe Ariès, *The Hour of Our Death* (New York: Knopf, 1981), for some introductory remarks on the place of the mendicant orders in lay urban economies of salvation. The works of Jacques Le Goff, "Merchant's Time and Church's Time in the Middle Ages," in *Time, Work, and Culture in the Middle Ages*, trans. Arthur Goldhammer (Chicago: University of Chicago Press, 1980), and *The Birth of Purgatory* (Chicago, 1984), address the way the new penitential system and the emergence of purgatory bound the laity and the institutional church together while, at the same time, reshaping the religious culture according to the needs and mental world of "merchant time."

33. There has been no socio-cultural study of the way in which these allies of the League (*basoche* and mendicants) adapted to the new cultural system imposed by royal absolutism.

34. See Bernard Chevalier, *Les bonnes villes de France du XIVe au XVIe siècles* (Paris: Aubier Montaigne, 1982), 247.

35. "Confession publicque de chacun bourgeois tant ecclésiastique que séculier."

36. All citations are from BN ms., fr. 2751, "Copie de la Request présentée par le clergé à Mr. le duc de Maienne avec la response à icelle avec la forme de jurer l'Union reçue le 14 . . . 1590," folio 48, verso 49. The manuscript adds that the petition was accepted by Charles de Lorraine and that it was agreed that all collators and provisors would also be required to take the Oath of Union. The French reads, "inhibitions seront faites a toutes courtz et siège de jurisdiction chapitres & collèges ecclésiastiques et congrégations tant de universitez que autres approuvées de recevoir aucun office ou bénéfice [prior to taking] le serment d'union . . . comme tous les autres cytoyens."

37. See Chevalier, *Les bonnes villes*, 247ff.: "Ce sont les membres de la Compagnie de Jésus, qui se firent les agents non du métissage religieux et culturel, mais d'une épuration radicale des idées et des mœurs dans l'esprit de la Contre-Réforme."

38. Emond Auger, *Metanoeologie* (Paris: Jamet Mettayer, 1584).

39. Gincestre, a Gascon, has many variant spellings of his surname: Lincestre and Wincestre also are encountered in the sources and secondary literature. See also Appendix G.

40. The holograph will dated May 17, 1590, was written shortly before Hervy's death in June 1590. The deaths of Hervy and Pigenat are recounted in scathing terms by L'Estoile in the *Journal* entries for June 1590. Hervy was a doctor of theology from the University of Paris, with close ties to the College of Navarre. See Appendix G for the remarkable details of his devotional loyalties. Hervy's will was witnessed and signed by Guillaume Rose, who, next to his signature, wrote "evesque, à présent banny de Senlis pour la religion." Of two other signing witnesses one is Hervy's *vicaire*, Jehan Jibray, who must have just administered sacraments to Hervy. The invocation to the will concludes with the following ringing words: "Considerant que j'ay nul moyen de salut que par le sang esperdu a l'arbre de la croix. J'espere que pardon ma este octroie au jourduy par la saincte commu[nio]n du presieuse corps et sang de n[ot]re *seigneur* et en ceste confiance je deteste toute erreur n'ay jamais consenti n'y favorise a l'heretique." Descimon, "La Ligue à Paris," *Annales* 37 (1982), 106, indicates Hervy was a neutral cleric. This needs to be revised in light of Hervy's will, which also mentions a sum from Madame de Guise of fifty *écus* that Hervy bequests to the Feuillants.

41. Although Crouzet argues that in their mystical state Leaguers existed as "confraternal brothers . . . living out a ritual identity of supplication and adoration," he associates the formation of Holy Sacrament confraternities in Paris with a decline of mystical élan, *Guerriers*, 2:414, n. 99.

42. It should be noted that as part of his concept of the interiorization of piety, Crouzet actually speaks of the League era as a time of "demobilization."

43. Table 6.2 indicates testators from the three sample periods who wished to be buried at a mendicant house.

44. Although the twenty-seven testators of Philippe Cothereau are not analyzed here, Cothereau clearly had a variety of ties to the League and particularly to the *Seize*. Notarial evidence from the 1570s shows that Cothereau worked with the notary Raoul Bontemps in drafting a religious foundation for the confraternity of the Holy Sacrament, located in what was to become one of the most radical Leaguer parishes: Saint-Benoît. In 1590, four of Cothereau's twenty-seven testators were Leaguers. Among these was the mother of Pierre Acarie, Marie Catin, the widow of Symon Acarie. The language of her will is replete with penitential self-imagery, stressing her own iniquity. Furthermore, six of the Cothereau testators, or twenty-two percent, were *gens de loi*. See Appendix H, which indicates all testators classified as belonging to the University milieu.

45. For this analysis, the "University milieu" is defined according to a hierarchy of criteria. See Appendix H for the types of testators included and their names and biographical data. Testators enter this category based on their links to the University: by profession or education. A second set of criteria, based on bequests and on choice of notary, define a more broadly construed group of University-related testators. The performativity of this broader group of University-related testators is displayed in Table 5.1: "Performativity in the 1590 Testator Population" (subpopulation, "University milieu"), which is broken down by profession and education but adds testators who make bequests to an institution of the University; finally, a third criterion includes testators using a University-based or -affiliated notary and testators not resident in the University quarter but seeking out a University-based or -related notary.

46. Notary François Herbin, CVIII, 23, parish of Saint-Gervais, known for its Leaguer activism. See the "Master Notary Chart, 1590" (Appendix E), and "Criteria for League-Identified Testators in 1590" (Table 5.2).

47. See the 1580 incident over the papal bull *In Coena Domini*, which reveals a closely informed reading public in the University quarter and Gallican concerns over papal claims. The personal insignia of the printing house of Merlin, who published and displayed the bull defending papal rights, is a swan, a cross, and the motto "In hoc signo/cygno vinces" [the French for swan is *cygne*]. There is no more perfect example of the quintessentially Leaguer-like imbrication of the sacred within the profane than this very motto, with its play on words *signo* and *cygno*. See Philippe Renouard, *Répertoire des imprimeurs parisiens* (Paris: M. L. Minard, 1965), 304, and Victor Martin, *Le Gallicanisme et la réforme catholique: Essai historique sur l'introduction en France des décrets du concile de Trent (1563–1615)* (Paris: Picard, 1919), 174ff., for a discussion of the 1580 incident over the papal bull *In coena domini*.

48. AN, *Min. cen.* XLIX, 225 [Clément Bernard] (3/10/1590), will of Pierre Brotin. Jehan Boucher (c. 1550–1641), *curé* of Saint-Benoît, was the League's

most dynamic and strategic link to the student and professional population of the University. Supporting the evidence in Busquet, "Etude historique," the account in Louis Moréri, *Le grand dictionnaire historique, ou Le mélange curieux de l'histoire sacrée et profane* . . . (Utrecht: 1692), claims that the first gathering of the 1585 League occurred in Boucher's room in the Collège de Fortet. At that time Boucher was rector of the University of Paris. On Boucher's performativity, note his ringing of the tocsin (bells) of his parish on December 2, 1587, to encourage popular protest against the monarchy. He fled Paris with the Spanish garrisons on March 23, 1594, just prior to Henry IV's entry into the capital. The *politiques*, in a kind of retaking of public space, responded with a performative gesture of their own: Boucher's sermons were publicly burned at the *Croix du Trahoir* on the very day Boucher escaped the city. On the central role of Dijon as the initial powerbase of the Duke of Mayenne (leader of the Guise-Lorraine faction), upon whom Paris pinned its hopes after the Blois murders of 1588, see the classic study that initiated the modern social history of the League, Henri Drouot, *Mayenne et la Bourgogne: Etude sur la ligue (1587–1596)* (Paris: Auguste Picard, 1937).

49. Brotin stresses, "le danger qui est . . . encore à présent sur les chemins au moyen des guerres civiles qui augmentent de jour en jour en ce royaulme la multiplicité des infirmitez de malladye."

50. "allant et venant journellement par les rues de ceste ville de Paris et aux eglises pour ouyr la parolle de dieu et assister à son divin service."

51. For a fuller discussion of the evolution and significance of these two elements of Christian worship see references in Chapter 5 to the historian of liturgy, Theodore Klauser. The very wording of these distinctions calls to mind the key demand of the 1576 *Twelve Articles of the Sainct Union* for the restoration of "the divine service," which "is a law of God" in the perception of the 1576 Leaguers. Brotin helps us see the direct connection between liturgy (performativity) and right order in the world (the shape of community and its relation to God). Liturgy is thus the fundamental element in the symbolic construction of community.

52. Eyewitness accounts are all in accord on the critical role of preaching and religious ceremonies in sustaining morale. BN ms., fr. 3919, "Les choses passees au siege de Paris a la delivrance de Paris," folio 234, recounts that "les predicateurs precherent deux fois le jour quasy en chacune eglise durant tout le siege avec telles vehemences qu'ils ont conformé ce peuple a ce cette resolution de vouloir plustost mourir que de se rendre . . . le Navarrois mesme a confessé de sa bouche plusieurs fois . . . que tout son mal luy vient des predications et des curez."

53. Besides the views of L'Estoile, Palma Cayet, and Pasquier, whom we have already encountered as primary sources (Chapter 4), the only monograph devoted exclusively to the preachers of the League is Charles Labitte, *De la démocratie chez les prédicateurs* (1841; reprint, Geneva: Slatkine Reprints, 1971), an immensely polemical work that offers a scathing condemnation of League preaching for its subversive, anti-national tendencies and ribald content. Labitte's

political bias is strongly *politique*. His attack on League preaching for its conflation of the sacred and the profane (the confusion of theater and preaching) and its "macaronic" style places him clearly in the camp of nineteenth-century reformers of popular culture. Labitte is also the *locus classicus* for the condemnation of the intellectual tradition of the League preachers. See pp. xxxiii–xxxiv on the "Schools" (i.e., scholasticism) as "une société finie." He equates the "école scholastique" with the "école grotesque" and "une scolastique barbare." Labitte condemns the preachers' embrace of a regicidal popular sovereignty. Labitte, nonetheless, sees the League as a revival of the feudal spirit (the Guise) and the old communal spirit of revolt (17). He blames the civil war in France on the combination of these forces, and denounces them for their virtual destruction of the monarchy.

54. See Geoffrey Parker, *The Army of Flanders and the Spanish Road, 1576–1659* (Cambridge: Cambridge University Press, 1972), fig. 6, p. 51. Dijon (in Burgundy) lies just west of Besançon (in Franche-Comté), a Hapsburg recruiting ground within the Empire.

55. Although Jean-Marie Constant downscales Guise dynastic ambitions, his assessment of the "Letter of David" (which purported to characterize Guise's design on the French Kingdom based on the lineage to Charlemagne) agrees with my interpretation of Brotin and his milieu. Constant argues that the content of the letter (whose authorship is still unclear) "suggests the existence at this time [the League era of 1576] of a radical ultramontane religious current, desirous of transcending nations in order to return to a mythic Christianity, of medieval allure, governed by the pope." The point of Brotin's will and the argument of this chapter is not that such radical ultramontanism constituted the dominant view in Paris in 1590, but rather that it was a crucial subculture with deep historic roots in which the League's alternative political geography thrived. To dismiss the evidence in Brotin's will and its connections to the "Letter of David" as too marginal, or "mythic," or purely ideological, is to miss the cultural complexities in Paris that made the League possible. See Jean-Marie Constant, *Les Guise* (Paris: Hachette, 1984), chap. 10, "Le duc de Guise a-t-il voulu être roi de France?" 193–209, and esp. 208–9. For more on Jean David's papers as a possible Huguenot forgery, and on David as a secret agent of the Guise, see J. H. M. Salmon, *Society in Crisis: France in the Sixteenth Century* (New York: St. Martin's Press, 1975), 200–201. Note David's profession of *avocat*, a group strongly mobilized for the League.

56. Descimon found the inventory after death of Marie Lamyral (Garlin's wife and Philippe Lamyral's daughter) in the papers of the notary Jean Cothereau (C, 127) dated May 7, 1593. More neighborhood loyalties are revealed here: J. Cothereau practiced in the rue de la Harpe (parish Saint-Séverin) between 1583 and 1597. There is only one will in the 1590 corpus from Jean Cothereau, Ignace de la Croix, a *paieur de la gendarmerie* with multiple connections to the world of the *gens de loi*. It is possible that Jean Cothereau was for de la Croix a

notary of conviction, since this testator was resident in the *Cité* (Saint-Germain-le-Viel) and not in the University where J. Cothereau's practice was located.

57. Descimon, *Qui*, 148: "La profonde implantation politique de la Sainte-Union à Paris repose sur cette réserve, cette seconde ligne de meneurs 'seize' dont Garlin est représentatif."

58. On Mademoiselle de Montpensier, see Abbé Jean Lebeuf, *Histoire de la ville et de tout le diocèse de Paris* (Paris: 1883), 1:112, where he cites Piganiol. Mademoiselle de Montpensier has also left memoirs. She sought and received a special permission from the Archbishop of Paris, Monsieur de Péréfix, to regularly attend mass at Saint-Séverin although she lived in the Palais de Luxembourg.

59. The variable General Performativity Level (Perform Level) (for Laurent, value 7; and for Rolland, value 11) offers a general measurement of overall performativity, but it does not count specific incidences of each of the other cluster variables and, therefore, is not a cumulative sum but rather a more general indicator. Genevieve Rolland makes bequests to the Capuchins and Feuillants and is thus discussed in more detail in Chapter 7 on reformers.

60. In the cases of John the Evangelist and John the Baptist, with whom so many of the penitential confraternities had a close association (e.g., the Black Penitents of Avignon), we find echoes again of the twin poles of Leaguer piety as Brotin first introduced them to us earlier in this chapter: "the service of the Word [Logos]" and sacramental and even sacrificial aspects of worship ("son divin service") associated with John the Baptist, who embodied and presaged the very sacraments that form liturgical communities: baptism and reception of the eucharist in memory and enactment of the passion itself. These particular votive orientations are echoed in the invocation of saints that are uniquely associated with the clients of Philippe Cothereau.

61. The other Lamiral testator not resident in the University quarter is the brother of *noble homme* Georges Bucholicq, discussed in detail below for his revealing ties to the Augustinian monastery. This brother (*noble homme maistre* Nicolas de Bucholic [sic], *bachelier en la faculté du droit*), living "au bout du pont Saint-Michel" in the small parish of *la Cité*, Saint-Barthélemy, whose *curé* was the Leaguer memoirist Jehan de la Fosse, speaks in his will of September 19, 1590, of his deceased brother Georges Bucholicq, buried at the Augustinian monastery, where he, too, wishes to be buried. Nicholas Bucholic is himself clearly a cleric, not simply because of his University affiliation (which conferred the nominal status of minor orders) but rather because the only law instruction at the University of Paris was in canon law. This makes Nicolas de Bucholicq a specialist in the jurisdictions and dominion of the sacred that the Leaguers understood so well. Nicholas Bucholicq is also in good health at the time of drawing up his will and speaks of his letters of naturalization granted by the deceased King Francis I. Like his brother he was a native of Clissa (or Clessa) in Dalmatia. His will, which is co-signed by Saint-Vaast, names as executor *noble et discrette personne maistre* Henry de Montreden, *grand vicar de monsieur* le Cardinal

de Joieuse (Joyeuse). The League affiliations here are unmistakable. AN, *Min. cen.* XXXIII, 207 [Philippe Lamiral] (19/9/1590), will of Nicholas de Bucholic.

62. AN, *Min. cen.* XXXIII, 207 [Philippe Lamiral] (25/9/1590), will of Marie Laurent.

63. LITURG# is the counting variable used for Table 6.4 that sums the occurrences of such directives with special liturgical detail.

64. The variable used for Table 6.4 that counts activities (including liturgical requests) where the location of the body is specifically stated is BODY2#.

65. "avec son corps devant l'image du crucifix [elle] veult estre dit et chanté à hault voix par les prebstres qui assisteront à sondict convoy et enterrement, *vexilla regis prodeunt.*"

66. "incontinent que sondict corps sera enterré il soit . . . prier pour son ame et celles de ses parens ains vivans et trepassez et à mesme instant dit et chanté à hault voix *salve regina domine non secundum, de profundis*, et les oraisons accoustumez."

67. Marye Laurent also received two counts for mentions of the body of Jesus Christ (CJC#) in her two bequests, one to her vicar and one to her chaplain "qui luy administeront les sainctz sacrements."

68. In Lamiral's practice there are wills co-signed with the notaries Saint-Vaast, Fardeau, and Belot. The notary Saint-Vaast had a distinctive clientele, including one of only two reformist-oriented testators who were not also part of the milieu of the new religious orders discussed in Chapter 6. This Saint-Vaast testator is a young noble student, René de Mombron, a *seigneur* of Saint-Aignan in Brittany, which was a province controlled by the League noble, the Duke de Mercoeur. Saint-Aignan is located not far from Nantes where Mercoeur's government was established. This testator makes a gift in perpetuity of communion bread for the annual Easter communion of the parish where he is *seigneur* and funds a catechism school in his parish (will of 20 September 1590).

69. Lamiral names his son-in-law Claude Garlin as executor. "Lequel il prie que sesdictes funerailles soient les plus succintes que faire ce pourra sans aucunes pompes ny armoiries. [Let the funeral services be as brief as possible without any pomp and with no escutcheons.]" Will LXXIII, 142, 2 November 1590.

70. See Yves Metman, "*La vie économique à Paris pendant le siège de 1590, Bibliothèque historique de la ville de Paris*," ms., C.P. 6589, originally "*Thèse presentée à l'Ecole des Chartes*" (Paris, 1947), typed manuscript, for the non-payment of housing rents and the abandonment of housing during the siege, 100–123.

71. G. D. S. de Soulas, *Discours au Roy pour la reception du Concile de Trente: contre ceux qui s'efforcent de l'empescher. Ou il est prouvé que l'un des meilleurs moyens d'arrester le cours des heresies, est de faire valoir Conciles Generaux* (Paris, chez Jean Petit-pas rue S. Iacques l'Escu de Venise pres les Mathurins, 1615), 43. The copy I examined (Mazarine, ms., 37202) was bound in a volume bearing the dates 1546–1690 and contained some twenty items, each a small pamphlet published individually with the earliest dating from 1546 and the most recent from 1690. Testators linked to the Mathurins either by bequests or choice of

burial number only ten. The other testator requesting burial there, besides Lamiral himself, is a Lamiral client, *venerable et discrete personne maistre* Gilles Richer, a priest (*prebstre habitué* of the church of Saint-Benoît). Richer lived in the College of Baieux and made a living celebrating daily mass in the chapel of Saint Roch at the Mathurins, which was the exact place where he wished to be buried. It is striking that in the entire testator population of 1590 the only testators living outside the University quarter who make bequests to the Mathurins are both testators from the Leaguer parish in the *Ville*, Saint-Jacques-de-la-Boucherie, which is known for its *curé* Julien Pelletier who played an active role in organizing the League.

72. *La grand salle* of the Augustinians served as the traditional meeting place for civic leaders and later for Leaguers as well.

73. Further evidence is summarized in Chapter 8 of this book in the discussion of the changing use of number symbolism by the testators of the 1590s and its possible meanings for them.

74. Chevalier, *Les bonnes villes*, speaks of an "*épuration radicale*," 247.

75. Cf. Cotgrave, *Dictionarie* on "union," cited in Chapter 1.

76. I borrow here from Carl F. Schorske, who sought the sources of the late-nineteenth-century flight from mimesis and rationality when he spoke of politics in a new key in late-nineteenth-century Vienna: *Fin-de-Siècle Vienna: Politics and Culture* (New York: Alfred A. Knopf, 1980). See especially chap. 3, "Politics in a New Key: An Austrian Trio," which called into question the replacement of religion by science, the possibility of national cohesiveness in a multinational state, and the progress of "the spread of a rational culture [which] would one day provide the prerequisite for a broadly democratic order," 117. The era of the League shares with the period Schorske studies markedly increased tensions about the boundary-setting authority of religion, science, nationality, and democratic principles. Cf., particularly, how L'Estoile might reply, if he could, when questioned about his views (his ontologies) on reason, science, religion, and popular culture.

77. Frances A. Yates, "Dramatic Religious Processions in Paris in the Late Sixteenth Century," *Annales musicologiques, Moyen Age et Renaissance* 2 (1954): 215–70, esp. 239.

78. This phrase is taken from Jean-Christophe Agnew, *Worlds Apart: The Market and the Theater in Anglo-American Thought, 1550–1750* (Cambridge: Cambridge University Press, 1986), 7.

79. Cf. John Bossy, cited in Chapters 1 and 4 concerning the interpretation of Saint Anne and the projection of human bonds onto a sacred Holy Family: *Christianity in the West: 1400–1700* (Oxford and New York, 1985), 93–97.

80. See L'Estoile's account for December 1574 on the procession of Penitents (*Battus*) in Avignon and the death of the Cardinal of Lorraine, *Journal . . . ,* 53–54.

81. One other of the twenty-nine Cothereau clients, Loys Pichon, does make a bequest to a penitential confraternity, the *Congrégation du Tressainct*

Crucifix (the Black Penitents). Besides Pichon, there are three testators in 1590 who make bequests to penitential confraternities: Jehan de Vabres, notary Edme Parque, makes a bequest to the White Penitents; a testator of Raoul Bontemps, Mathurin Egert, also bequests to the Black Penitents; finally the testator entering the Feuillant monastery in 1590, Jehan Marion, of Toulouse, makes a bequest to the confraternity of *Miséricorde* that may well be a penitential confraternity related to *La Confrérie des Pénitents noirs de la Miséricorde* of southern France. Marion, discussed in detail in Chapter 7, was a canon in the cathedral of Carcassonne and the *curé* of the parish of Fanjeaux, located thirty kilometers from Carcassonne in the Aude, southwest of Toulouse. Robert Descimon has reminded me of the strong Protestant and earlier Cathar presence in Fanjeaux.

82. The statutes of the confraternity, "*La congrégation des pénitentes de l'Annunciation de Notre-Dame*," were composed by Auger and are reprinted in H. L. Cimber and F. Danjou, *Archives curieuses de l'histoire de France* (Paris: 1836), 10:437–58.

83. "honorablement et sans superfluité."

84. One of the best examples is the recent work of L. Michael White. See his "Askesis: Cure of the Passions and Medicine of the Soul in Antiquity" (unpublished paper), and "Jews and Christians in the Greco-Roman World," public lecture, University of Texas at Austin, 1996.

85. "ung gigot de mouton et [à] d'eulx tant prebstres que novices ung pain blanc poisant douze onces et une choppine de vin et quelque chose d'avantage pour le prieur et pour les docteurs et officiers dudict couvent tant que pourront suffire quinze escuz soleil a chancun desdictz repas."

86. Psalm 129 (Vulgate) [130, Lutheran Bible]: "De profundis clamavi ad te, Domine . . . "

87. "Entrans en ce branle de Penitence, nous ne sçaurions longuement estre menés à la cadence du Saint Esprit que nous ne facions veoir à tout le monde une harmonie sainte de toutes bonnes oeuvres." Yates, "Dramatic Religious Processions," 246, citing from Auger, *Metanoeologie*, 110. Frances Yates's gloss of the quote suggests part of the meaning: "The rhythm for the dance of penitence is set by the cadence of the Holy Spirit to bring forth the harmonies of charity." (The word "branle" is an older term for dance.) Yates's article makes powerful suggestions relevant to my arguments about the centrality of performativity (in its medieval roots) and the issue of ontological tensions in understanding the experience of the League. Given the remarkable insights in her article, it is all the more a testament to the power of meta-narrative imperatives that, in her conclusion, she reverts to the statist traditions of vilification of the League: "The League made seditious use of those emotional processions which the King had himself fostered, and the penitent confréries were used by the League as militant associations. . . . The deplorable role played by some of these associations during the League . . . had the result that, after the pacification of the country by Henry IV, they were discouraged in Paris and took refuge again in their place of origin, the south," 261. In fact, following the defeat of the League, penitential confraterni-

ties were outlawed by *Parlement* in the north. The North–South tensions, which are so crucial to understanding League historiography and the development of seventeenth-century French "classical" culture, are evident here as well. The *arrêt* of *Parlement* banning flagellant confraternities in the North was the work of the lawyer Servin, author of the 1601 decision (*arrêt*).

88. Yves-Marie Bercé has spoken of this transition: "On imposa alors une religion difficile, intellectualisée, sans miracles et sans médiations familières." *Fête et révolte: des mentalités populaires du XVIe au XVIIIe siècle* (Paris: 1976), 128. Although the elimination of miracles applies best to Calvinism, the cultural changes by both Catholic and Protestant reforms have many long-term parallels. The popularity of the "miraculous host of Saint-Jehan-en-Grève" continued in Paris throughout the seventeenth century.

89. "Cy gist Claude Blosseau vivant lieutenant du cappitaine Saint-Just lequel fut blecé d'ung coup de mousquet es faulxbourg Saint-Laurent le douziesme jour de May an VC IIII xx et dix duquel il est deceddé pour la defense de nostre saincte religion et de sa patrye." Will of Claude Blosseau, notary M. Bontemps, LXXIII, 219, May 24, 1590. We could add that this request for the pot of holy water recalls the essence of all penitential aspirations for purification and in its immanence realizes the words of the most familiar of the penitential psalms (Psalm 50/51): "Lavez-moi de plus en plus de mes souillures et purifiez-moi de mon peché." In English the psalm continues "Purge me with hyssop, and I shall be clean. . . . " Hyssop is a reference to the ceremony of sprinkling in Exodus 12:22–24, "You shall observe this rite as an ordinance for you and for your sons forever." Again we hear an echo, this time of Brotin and the League Articles, that sought to legislate divine ordinance in a world whose laws were embodied in liturgy. Blosseau is among a small number of non-elites closely tied to the League who continue to use service-related number symbolism in 1590. He requests a "service complect avec vigilles, recommendaces 3 hautes messes et 13 basses messes," technically banned by Trent. See Chapter 8 for an analysis of the testators of the 1590s who used the service-related, forbidden number symbolism.

90. This information comes from the *Constitutiones Antique Ordinis Fratrum Predicatorum*, ed. H. Denfle, ALKG I, p. 197, cited by C. H. Lawrence in *The Friars: The Impact of the Early Mendicant Movement on Western Society* (London and New York: Longman, 1994), 81.

91. This information comes again from C. H. Lawrence, *The Friars*, 81, drawing on the account in W. R. Bonniwell, *A History of the Dominican Liturgy* (New York: J. F. Wagner, 1945), 148–66. See also B. M. Reichert, ed., *Acta Capitulorum Generalium Ordinis Praedicatorum*, in *Monumenta Ordanis Fratrum Preadicatorum Historica*, vol. 1 (1898).

92. Pierre Christin, the client of the notary Lybault, elects to be buried at the *Augustins*. See Appendix G.

93. Certain key testators, such as Genevieve Rolland discussed in Chapter 7, seem to bridge the two populations. Their behavior, which embraces traditional and reformed patterns of performativity, helps show how religious change occurs.

94. Members of Holy Sacrament confraternities, who as a group are highly mobilized for the League, are more likely to be artisans, small-scale merchants, and some *gens de loi*. There is no example of a testator who makes bequests both to a Holy Sacrament confraternity and to any of the new religious orders of the League period that are discussed in Chapter 7.

95. The Capuchins, for example, play such a pivotal role in the League and the subsequent reform era because their devotional style integrates the pathos and eschatological anguish of the older communal and penitential piety with new, activist eucharistic devotions (e.g., Bellintani da Salò) and, thus, facilitates the transition from sixteenth- to seventeenth-century devotional styles. Just as the transition from League piety to the seventeenth century cannot be expressed adequately through the simple binary opposition of exteriority and interiority, so, too, it is the changing interrelation of penitence and the eucharist within the gestural economy of the wills that is most telling. See the article by Creighton Gilbert on a basic shift of emphasis from depictions of the Crucifixion to ones of the Last Supper on the walls of Renaissance refectories: "Last Suppers and their Refectories," *The Pursuit of Holiness in Late Medieval and Renaissance Religion: Papers from the Michigan Conference*, Studies in Medieval and Reformation Thought, vol. 10, Charles Trinkhaus and Heiko Oberman, eds. (Leiden: Brill, 1974), with comments by Clifton C. Olds, "Queries on 'Last Suppers and their Refectories,'" and David Wilkins, "Interventions," 403–8.

Chapter 7

1. Norman G. Tanner, *Decrees of the Ecumenical Councils*, vol. 2, *Trent to Vatican II*, eds. G. Albergio, J. A. Dossetti., P. Joannou, C. Leonardi, P. Prodi., and H. Jedin (London and Washington, D.C.: Sheed and Ward, Ltd., Georgetown University Press, 1990): "ad reformationem cleri et populi christiani," 660.

2. The seven values distinguish among seven different indicators of reform. The seven indicators of reform were: *1.* bequests that made explicit educational investments ("Cognitive concerns and educational investments"); *2.* investments to increase administration of the sacraments; *3.* contributions to build or improve churches or chapels; *4.* calls for confraternal reform; *5.* concerns expressed about clerical discipline or absenteeism; *6.* statements requiring a cleric with good moral character and an adequate understanding of liturgy and doctrine (i.e., competent) to intercede on behalf of the testator; and *7.* calls for the reverential care of sacred objects. For the actual language of examples of each type of reformist request beyond those discussed in detail in this chapter, see Appendix C, which shows the eighth variable used to analyze performativity. See Table 7.1, "Reformist Testators in Three Sample Periods," which indicates the number and type of reformist pious directives in each sample period and the names of testators making the reformist request.

3. The ratio of men to women in the general testator populations of all these years underwent no such shift. For the sex of testators among Leaguers and non-Leaguers in 1590 and in the testator populations of 1543–44 and 1630, see Appendix L.

4. Of the four *faubourg* residents, one is Damoiselle Margueritte Tronson, residing in the *faubourg* of Saint-Germain-des-Prés, in the parish of Saint-Sulpice, the wife of *noble homme maître* Pierre de Champin, *sieur de Roissy*, a *conseiller du roi* and *président* in the *court des monnaies*. The second of the more elite *faubourg* residents is Claude Petit, *escuyer, sieur de Saint-Aulnois, escuyer de la grande écurie du roy et gentilhomme et servant de la Royne à Saint-Germain-des-Prés . . . en l'hostel de monseigneur le Prince*. Claude Petit chooses burial at one of the new reforming orders of the early seventeenth century, the *Carmes deschaussez*, and establishes a perpetual foundation of catechism classes to be held by the chaplain of the chapel of Notre Dame de Sablons, who is also charged with saying a memorial mass of the dead (*messe des trespassez*) every Saturday before the Sunday catechism classes "pour l'instruction de la jeunesse à la foy crestienne et catholicque."

5. See endpapers for the placement of new ecclesiastical institutions.

6. "Et se veult et ordonne iceluy testateur que le jour dudict service soyt envoyé au principal maistre de la grant escole dudict Péronne cent solz tournois pour estre distribués par luy aux pouvres estudiants lesquels il advisera sans faveur et l'aumosne estre bien employés et pour faire ladicte distribution et inciter lesdicts estudians à prier pour l'âme dudict testateur iceluy testateur luy donne dix solz tournois." AN, *Min. cen.* XX, 16 [Jacques Mussart] (31/8/1543), will of *honorable homme maistre* Valerend Choquet, "advocat en la ville de Péronne filz naturel et legitimé de feuz Jehan Choquet et Marie de L'Espine, natif de Saint Valery sur Somme diocese et baillage d'Amyens." Is it a mere coincidence that one of the reforming testators from 1543–44 comes from Péronne, the very site of the founding of the first League of 1576? Only further research in regional as well as Parisian archives could provide an answer.

7. "Item donne et laisse ledict testateur au maistre ou vicaire qui luy administrera ses sacremens ung escu priant iceulx sacremens luy estre tost administrez ce premier que perdre usaige de raison mesme estre admonesté de la foy, de la passion de nostre seigneur et choses salutaires et à son decez estre leue ladicte passion." Will of Valerend Choquet.

8. In Parisian wills of the period, requests like Choquet's for the "passion" usually refer to the singing of the hymn "Vexilla regis prodeunt," often sung over the body as it is placed in presentation in front of the main crucifix inside the church.

9. Choquet's stress upon the concept of sacrifice was noted in Chapter 2, in "The Meaning of Sacrifice." Compare this with the theme of "passibility" in the discussion of Pasquier in Chapter 4.

10. "Item veult et ordonne ledict testateur son enterrement et services estre faictz sans aulcunes pompes mondaines le plus simplement qu'il sera possible et

à iceulx estre invitez *trente pouvres gens de bonne vie, les cinq des plus pouvres desquelz que ses executeurs choiseront sans faveur porteront chacun une torche* et à chacun diceulx *cinq* donne ung escu d'or soleil et au seurplus desdictz pouvres à chacun *cinq* solz tournois en l'honneur des cinq playes" (my emphasis). Will of Valerend Choquet. Although Trent explicitly sought to ban the superstitious use of number symbolism, it provided no criteria for distinguishing between superstitious and non-superstitious forms of use. From *Decrees*, 737, and Chapter 8 below.

11. Whether salvation history should be constructed on the basis of Kantian rationality or the more ancient kinship of a shared human suffering has been an unspoken debate within the history of early-modern Catholicism. On the devotion to the five wounds facilitating late-medieval kinship with its gods, see both Eamon Duffy, *The Stripping of the Altars: Traditional Religion in England 1400–1580* (New Haven and London: Yale University Press, 1992) and Richard W. Pfaff, *New Liturgical Feasts in Later Medieval England* (Oxford: The Clarendon Press, 1970), who also stresses the affinities of devotion to the five wounds with devotion to the name of Jesus discussed below in the portrait of Jehan Paluau.

12. Consider for example the following excerpt from the services Paluau requested at the mendicant orders (my emphasis): " . . . at the cordelliers *ten* masses of the trinity, *ten* of the holy spirit, *five* of our lady, and *five* masses, at the jacobins *ten* of all saints, *ten* of the angels, *five* of the apostles and *five* of all virgins, at the carmelites *five* of all martyrs, *five* of all confessors, *five* of the cross, and *five* of the apostles, at the augustinians five of the passion, *five* of the ascension of our Lord, *five* of the holy sacrament and *five* of the epiphany and of the aforesaid low masses let them be said by the poorest of the friars chosen and selected by the guardians and priors of the aforesaid monasteries." For asking that the poorest celebrate his masses Choquet was coded for value 13 on the Performativity Index, "Celebrant of Symbolic Importance." The French reads " . . . aux cordelliers *dix* messes de la trinité, *dix* de sainct esprit, *cinq* de nostre dame et *cinq* de requiem, aux jacobins *dix* de tous sainctz, *dix* des anges, *cinq* des appostres et *cinq* de toutes vierges, aux carmes *cinq* de tous martres, *cinq* de tous confesseurs, *cinq* de la croix, et *cinq* des apostres, aux augustins *cinq* de la passion, *cinq* de l'assencion nostre seigneur, *cinq* du sainct sacrement et *cinq* de l'epiphany et que lesdictes basses messes soient dictées par les plus pauvres religieux au cheoix et ellection des gardiens et prieurs d'iceulx coventz."

13. For a brief history of devotion to the name of Jesus, see Louis Châtelier, *La religion des pauvres: Les sources du christianisme moderne, XVIe–XIXe siècles* (Paris: Aubier, 1993), 21. The activities of the Franciscan Bernadino of Sienna (1389–1444) in propagating this devotion by the inscription of the name of Christ everywhere and the use of the monogram IHS [in hoc signo] is a perfect example of immanentist-oriented behavior. For the history of this devotion in Leaguer Paris see the article by Christopher Stocker on the Confraternity of the Holy Name of Jesus, which was founded in 1590 by ardent Leaguers, in *Confraternities and Catholic Reform in Italy, France, and Spain*, ed. John Patrick Donnelly, S.J., and Michael W. Maher, S.J. (Kirksville, Mo.: Thomas Jefferson University Press,

1999). The Jesuits were severely criticized for taking the name Society of Jesus; see Henri Fouqueray, *Histoire de la compagnie de Jésus en France des origines à la suppression (1528–1762)*, vol. 1, (1910; reprint, Nendeln, Lichtenstein: Kraus Reprint, 1972), 160–61.

14. Bonhomme's son, Thielman II Kerver, marries a Marie or Marguerite Palluau/Paluau. See Philippe Renouard, *Répertoire des imprimeurs parisiens* (Paris: M. L. Minard, 1965), 41 and 227. Thus the Paluau, Bonhomme, and Kerver families are closely linked not only by marriage and profession, but by intense University-related zealous Catholicism as well.

15. Readers wishing to know the relative frequency of this type of performative gesture in all the sample periods should refer to the "Performativity Index," Table 5.4. For 1543–44, only 7.2 percent of testators whose wills were drawn up by a notary had a sacralizing gesture. See Appendix L for the frequencies of special sacralizing headings in all sample periods.

16. "Item pour ce qu'elle ne scait si à l'heure de son . . . trespas le . . . usage de raison luy demoura, [elle] proteste que quelque temptation et illusion que luy pouroyt advenyr et avoyr à l'article de la mort, elle veult mourir en la vraye foy de nostre seigneur comme ung bon crestien doit faire et que ladicte temptation ne puisse prejuger au salut de son ame." AN, Min. cen. LXXIII, 5 [Jean Cruce] (21/2/1544), will of Yolland Bonhomme.

17. See Appendix K, which shows Saint-Vaast is the notary for René de Mombron, one of the reformers of 1590 discussed briefly below.

18. See Chapter 5.

19. For the further importance of this link see the discussion of the use of number symbolism by the 1590's testator Gilles Richer, a priest of Saint-Benoît who makes bequests to the Mathurins, who is one of only twenty users of the service-related number symbolism forbidden by Trent at session 22. Moreover, the Leaguer notary Philippe Lamiral drew up Richer's will.

20. " . . . pour estre employez et convertiz à faire faire une crosse quatre pilliers garniz d'anges le tout de cuyvre et les bares de fer qu'il conviendra pour les entretenir l'un à l'autre lesquelz anges porteront les armoiries de la passion et le tout estre mis et assis, assavoir ladicte crosse sur le grant autel et lesdictz quatre pilliers devant ledict grant autel d'icelle esglise." This is a particularly immanentist gesture. The concept of the escutcheons or family coats of arms of the Passion (*armoiries*), discussed in Chapter 1, is another example of the way militant Catholicism combines with notions of passion-centered kinship in order to create bonds to the Holy Family.

21. As Table 5.3 indicates, only two testators made this request in 1540. In 1590, as Table 5.4 indicates, Leaguers account for nearly one-half of those (forty-three percent or three of seven testators), a ratio far exceeding the Leaguer percentage of the 1590's testator population.

22. "Escriprir et enregistrer ledict obit au livre et martologe d'icelle communauté affin de memoire perpetuelle . . . [et] assister audict obit depuis la premiere leçon dudict obit jusques à la fin dicelle et ou ilz ou l'un d'eulx ne

assisteront audict obit comme dit est ilz n'auront aucune distribution." The forms of performativity just mentioned (sacralizing gestures, aspersion with holy water, and explicit requests for mention in the *livres martirologes* of the parish) are thus all closely correlated with known Leaguers in 1590. See Table 5.4.

23. See below the case of Jehan Marion, where the money intended for absent clerics is to be redistributed to the poor.

24. There is an extensive bibliography for the Parisian foundations by Jesuits and Capuchins in the seventeenth century. The history of the Feuillants in Paris in the sixteenth and early seventeenth centuries still remains to be written. See Pierre Gayne, "Un de nos compatriotes oubliés: Le moine-ligueur Bernard du Montgaillard," *Bulletin de la Société archéologique du Tarn et Garonne* (1967–1970): 51–78. Montgaillard is usually called "le petit Feuillant" and is the target of processional satire by League opponents because of a deformity causing an irregular gait. See also Louis J. Lekai, *The Rise of the Cistercian Strict Observance in Seventeenth-Century France* (Washington, D.C.: Catholic University of America, 1968).

25. The notary Claude Jourdan had a total of five wills for 1590. The other League-engaged testator, Jehan de Peyere, was the "maistre d'hostel de Madame la Mareschalle de Joyeuse." As further evidence of the multiple webs of affinity that connected distinct micro-worlds of Leaguers, the testament of the Duke of Joyeuse was drawn up by the *Seize* notary Raoul Bontemps. The loyalties of the Joyeuses after the death of Henry III require reexamination.

26. *Dictionnaire de théologie catholique*, and *Dictionnaire d'archéologie chrétienne et de liturgie*, s.v. "communion des saints."

27. "Pour le regard de sesdictz biens temporelz en premier lieu a donné et legué et laissé à l'eglise paroissial Nostre Dame de Fanjeaux la somme de vingt escuz soleil pour une foys paiée pour estre employee en l'achapt d'une livre d'argent propre pour servir à mectre le sainct sacrement pour porter en procession ensemble ung reliquare pour y enchasser les reliques de sainct Ganderic et autres qui sont dans la sacristie de ladicte eglise de Fanjeaux non encore enchassez et ce de meilleure matiere et façon qu'il se pourra faire. . . . " AN, *Min. cen.* IV, 17 [Claude Jourdan] (5/2/1590), will of maistre Jehan Marion.

28. "inciter les prebsters d'icelle [église] à y faire leur residence et le deu de leurs charges."

29. At the close of his will Marion leaves all of his remaining property to this confraternity, which he identifies only as "la confrairie de la miséricorde fondee à Thoulouze." The interpretation that this is a penitential confraternity is based on the special devotion Marion has for John the Baptist, who was the patron of other meridional penitential confraternities. See Frédéric Meyer, "A Avignon au XVIIIe siècle, la Confrérie des Pénitents noirs de la Miséricorde," *Etudes vauclusiennes* 29 (January–June 1983): 9–14.

30. See, however, Larissa Taylor's recent assessment of preaching, which did not find apocalyptic themes. "The Good Shepherd: François Le Picart," *Sixteenth Century Journal* 28 (1998): 793–810.

31. This account appears in Luke I:5–23, where angels tell Elizabeth and Zechariah, the parents of John the Baptist, that they will have a son, John, "who will make ready for the Lord a people prepared" (Luke I:17). This account of the birth of John the Baptist is followed immediately in Luke I by the announcement by the angel Gabriel to Mary that she will bear a son, Jesus—hence the Annunciation. This juxtaposition in Luke further clarifies Marion's choice of feast days, for he in part follows precisely the account in Luke I of the life of John the Baptist, which immediately precedes one of the more beloved accounts of the Annunciation to Mary and the nativity of Jesus.

32. See Frédégard Callaery, "Infiltration des idées franciscaines spirituelles chez les Frères Mineurs-Capucins au XVIe siècle," in *Miscellanea Francesco Ehrle* (Rome, 1942), 394, concerning Bellintani da Salò and the introduction of Capuchins into Paris.

33. In the wills analyzed, sanctions against absent clerics also change. Yolland Bonhomme gave the portion forfeited by absent clerics to the clerics present for the whole service. Marion instead gives the forfeited portion to the poor. Meyer, in "La Confrérie des Pénitents noirs," has pointed out that the charitable mission of the Avignon Confraternity of the Black Penitents of Divine Mercy evolved from devotion to poor prisoners in the seventeenth century to care of the insane in the eighteenth century. John the Baptist was himself termed "demon possessed."

34. Marion gave the very substantial amount, 250 *écus*, to buy income-producing land the sum of whose revenue should "soict en grins ou argent estre distribuee . . . durant lesditz *libera* ou *de profundis* que ceulx qui auront este assistans ausdictes offices de matines et laudes de telle sorte que la pars des absens ne soit donnee ne distribuee aux presens mais qu'elle soit donnee pour dieu aux pauvres malades. . . . "

35. "Pareillement fonde ledict testateur et veult que à chacun diceulx jours soit faict et dict un sermon sur la solemnité du jour par le recteur ou par quelques uns des prebsters d'icelle eglise, [ou] par quelque religieux du couvent Sainct Dominique ou aultre. . . . " Will of Jehan Marion.

36. "Item veult et ordonne que . . . ledict recteur de Fanjeaux present et advenir ou ses vicaires soient tenus sortans de l'eglise pour aller porter l'extresme onction à quelque malade [et] faire tainter quelque cloche pour advertir le peuple que c'est pour leur signifier de prier Dieu pour quelque malade auquel on va porter ladicte extresme onction." AN, *Min. cen.*: IV, 17 [Claude Jourdan] (5/2/1590), will of Jehan Marion.

37. In the French, "bien et deument instruire la jeunesse de ladicte ville de Fanjeaux."

38. "Et en faisant de ce lors de sa reception sera tenu, oultre l'examen ordinaire de sa doctrine et moeurs, faire profession de foy selon la teneur du Sainct Concile de Trante [sic] devant le recteur ou ses vicaires en la presence des consulz ou des baillis et administrateurs. . . . Sera pareillement tenu pendant l'exercice de sa charge amener tous les jours s'il se peult faire ou faire conduire

tous ses escolliers a l'eglise pour ouyr la messe et à l'entree de l'escole leur faire dire un *veni creator* et à l'issue dicelle un *salve regina* semblablement sera tenu ledict regent tous les vendredis leur faire aprendre quelque chose du cathechisme et le dimanche apres vespres leur faire rendre dans ladicte eglise devant le recteur en la presence du vicaire des autres prebsters et du peuple qui y vouldra assister ce qu'ilz auront apris dudict cathechisme, lequel recteur, vicaire ou prebster en fera une briefve exposition ou instruction tant pour eulx que pour le peuple." Will of Jehan Marion.

39. See Table 7.3, "Monastic Professions in the Three Sample Periods." Note in particular the increase in professions by women in 1630, and see below the micro-portrait of *mademoiselle* Marie de Gourgue, based on her will drawn up in her own hand on May 7, 1630.

40. See Colin Kaiser, "Les cours souveraines . . . ," on "ascétisme professionnel," as discussed in Chapter 4.

41. See again Tables 7.1 and 7.2 for these two testators.

42. Marillac's marriage to Marie de Sainct Germain took place in 1601. Marie de Sainct Germain was a widow from a previous marriage to Jean Amelot, a *president* in the *Enquetes*. See Elie Barnavi, *Parti de Dieu: Etude sociale et politique des chefs de la Ligue parisienne* (Louvain: Nauwelaerts, 1980), 99. Amelot's role in Thiersault's will is discussed below.

43. "Item donne et laisse à la femme dudict Sieur president Amelot, sa niepce, une croix d'or en laquelle sont enchasés dix diamendz et une perle au bout d'icelle croix pour l'amitié qu'elle luy porte et aussy qu'elle s'asseure qu'elle aura souvenance d'elle en ses prieres et l'en requis de bien bon coeur." AN, *Min. cen.* XXXIX, 21 [Jacques Landry] (6/10/1590), will of Marye Thiersault, 46.

44. Robert Descimon, *Qui étaient les Seize?* (Paris: Klincksieck, 1983); Pierre Thiersault, no. 218, 223.

45. " . . . une âme espagnol." See Descimon, *Qui*, Estienne de Nully, no. 176, pp. 197–98. These characterizations of Nully come primarily from L'Estoile, *Journal . . . Henri IV*, 236, entry for 6 April 1593. See also L'Estoile, 280, where Nully is counted among those opposed to the famous *arrêt* Lemaître of 28 June 1593 that held for the Salic Law. L'Estoile defined the debate as centered on "liberté française contre la tyrannie espagnole"—again privileging constitutional and national issues over religion.

46. See Descimon, *Qui*, no. 130, p. 171, on François Chantereau-Lefebvre.

47. Signers include *damoiselle* Anne Bouer, the groom's mother; Claude Lecoigneux, wife of the *Seize noble homme maistre* Loys de Sainctyon (see Descimon, *Qui*, no. 205); and Jehanne de Sainctyon. The marriage contract: AN, *Min. cen.* LXXXVII, 431, notary Jean Lenormant (with Monthenault), 31 August 1612. Barnavi, in *Parti de Dieu*, discusses the Sainction family as an example of the resentment and social stagnation experienced by *avocats* in the later sixteenth century, pp. 104–5. Such social resentment along with religious convictions helped fuel participation in the *Seize* movement.

48. For Charpentier, see Descimon, *Qui,* no. 33. In a final telling detail in her will, Thiersault gives both Amelot and Baquet "chacun un acoustement de doeuil complet de serge de Fleurance."

49. "Et premierement a recommandé et recommande son ame à dieu nostre createur sauveur et redempteur en toute humilité et reverance le remerciant tres humblement d'une infinité de biens qu'elle a receuz de luy en ce monde mortel mesmes de la participation de ses sainctz sacrements confessant l'avoir griefvement offencé en plusieurs grandz et griefz pechez lesquelz elle espere que par le benefice de la saincte passion de Jesus Christ son filz ntr sauveur et par l'intercession de la ste et sacree Vierge Marye sa mere et de tous les sainctz et saintes de paradis de les luy remectre et pardonner de sorte que Sathan ne se puisse prevaloyr allencontre de son ame ainsi que de ce elle a supplye et supplye nostre dieu et createur."

50. For the initial idea of the contrast between the more medieval penitential piety of the penitential confraternities and the "modern Catholicism" ushered in by Tridentine reform, see the conclusion to Marc Venard's seminal article, "Les confréries de pénitents au XVIeme siècle dans la province ecclésiastique d'Avignon," *Mémoires de l'académie de Vaucluse,* 6th series, vol. I (1967), p. 76, where he speaks of a transition, "selon une pulsation qui me paraît être une des lois de l'histoire du christianisme—d'une phase longue charactérisée par le pessimisme de la Croix, à une phase longue qu'anime l'optimisme de l'Eucharistie." The idea of quantifying and analyzing the changing modes of Christocentrism expressed in the language and gestures of the wills is in part an attempt to explore Venard's insight through the application of quantitative techniques. A beautiful example of how sacramental confidence works its way into the language itself of 1630 wills can be found in the unique wording of the opening of the will of *honorable femme* Louise de Gastines (notary, Belin, LVII, 46; May 25, 1630). After an especially fervent affirmation of faith and mention of the merits of Christ, she states in the first clause of her will: "Item desire ladicte testatrice mourir en bonne Catholicque apostolique et romaine comme elle y a vescu et entende vivre le reste de ses jours et estre munye a sa mort des sainctz sacremens de l'eglise." The key word here is "munye," armed, fortified, and prepared by virtue of the sacraments.

51. One could argue for a third option, penitential preaching, but its classical outdoor site occurs primarily in missions to the countryside in the seventeenth century. See Jean Delumeau, *Sin and Fear: The Emergence of a Western Guilt Culture, 13th–18th Centuries,* trans. Eric Nicholson (New York: St. Martin's, 1990), Part II. Note also how extremely carefully the issue of preaching is treated at Trent. The *Decrees* spell out the precise lines of hierarchy and authority over who may preach, and prophetic preaching is explicitly condemned. See *Decrees* 667–70.

52. For the theoretical analysis, see Victor Turner on the "multivocal quality" of ritual symbols and the polarization of their referents between physiological

phenomena (here the physical agony of the Passion and human form of Christ's body) and another "normative" or "ideological" pole whose messages range from humility to glory, implying different affects and structures of organization. Victor Turner, *Dramas, Fields and Metaphors: Symbolic Action in Human Society* (Ithaca and London: Cornell University Press, 1974), 55.

53. See Marc Venard, "Les confréries de pénitents," on the shift from anguish to optimism.

54. For ways of analyzing the different poles of eucharistic and penitential piety, see Creighton Gilbert, "Last Suppers and Their Refectories," *The Pursuit of Holiness in Late Medieval and Renaissance Religion: Papers from the Michigan Conference*, Studies in Medieval and Reformation Thought, vol. 10, Charles Trinkhaus and Heiko Oberman, eds. (Leiden: Brill, 1974), 371–407.

55. Cf. the episcopal *Mandement pour le règlement des processions et prières publiques pour chacun jour de la sepmaine, durant ce sainct temps de Karesme* of February 11, 1589, which prohibited spontaneous nighttime processions in favor of parish-based processions led by the *curé*. Cited in Denis Richet, "Politique et religion: Les processions à Paris en 1589," in *La France d'ancien régime: Etudes réunies en l'honneur de Pierre Goubert* (Toulouse, 1984). This preference is a repetition of the same structures of authority that René Benoît endorsed in his support of parish-based Holy Sacrament Confraternities over traditional confraternities. See René Benoît, *De l'institution et de l'abus survenu ès confrairies populaires avec la reformation necessaire en icelles* (Paris: 1578). The literature on penitential piety is vast. See in the Bibliography, especially Andrew Barnes and Robert Schneider.

56. "se asseurant qu'ils en feront honestement ce qu'il conviendra faire."

57. The mention here of *faulx bourdon* (literally bagpipes) is a request for these hymns to be chanted in *falsobordone*, a harmonized choral chant. For example, the *falsobordone* might contain one prayer harmonizing while also underscoring, both musically and textually, the liturgical contents of the main chant. See John Harper, *The Forms and Orders of Western Liturgy from the Tenth to the Eighteenth Century: A Historical Introduction and Guide for Students and Musicians* (Oxford: Clarendon, 1991), 160, and Fouqueray, *Histoire*, vol. 2, 193–94, note 3, on the types of chant the Jesuits provided.

58. While this richness of liturgical detail relates directly back to Trent's affirmation of "tradition" and its defense of "ceremony" against vitriolic Protestant attacks, much more study is needed to evaluate the relationship between the local liturgical culture of Paris and the new Tridentine prescriptions.

59. Turner, *Dramas, Fields and Metaphors*, 57.

60. Thiersault's will, p. 36.

61. Marion, explaining the solemnity of the day, founded "un sermon sur la solemnité du jour."

62. See *Decrees*, chapter 5, session 22, p. 734, on the necessary role of ceremony to arouse the devotion of the laity, which was cited and discussed in Chapter 3.

63. See Table 7.4, "Liturgical Standardization and Its Relation to the Decline in Number Symbolism in the Three Sample Periods." The decline in the number of distinctive verbal expressions testators used in requesting masses is correlated with the precipitous decline in the liturgical use of number symbolism, discussed in the Conclusion. The experiential question is to try to understand the meaning of these changes to the testators involved, for such changes represent a transformation of a symbolic system that is part of a profound cultural change separating late-medieval from early-modern Catholicism. Table 7.4 offers another perspective on the decline in liturgical options for most testators.

64. Cited by Reinold Theisen, *Mass Liturgy and the Council of Trent* (Collegeville, Minn.: Pontificum Athenaeum Anselmianum, 1965), 28.

65. See Louis Brochard, *Saint-Gervais: Histoire de la paroisse* (Paris: Firmin-Didot, 1950), 292–96. Brochard does not provide a precise chronology concerning the custom of founding *saluts*. The examples he gives, however, clearly suggest a greater frequency in the second half of the seventeenth century.

66. Georges Duby and Robert Mandrou, *Histoire de la civilisation française* (Paris: Librairie Armand Colin, 1968), 2:22–23.

67. "Item veult and ordonne lors de sondict convoy et enterrement soient habillés treize vrays pauvres à chacun desquelz sera baille une robbe et ung chaperon de drap noir d'ung escu l'aulne avec lesquelz ilz seront tenuz asister a sondict convoy avec une torche qu'il leur sera baillé et ledict convoy faict, laissant lesdictez robbes et chaperons en l'hostel de ladicte damoiselle testatrice et leur soient baillé à chacun dix solz tournois et à la huictaine ensuivant entend ladicte damoiselle estre faict son service du bout de l'an tant au coeur que à la paroisse dudict sainct Germain ou asisteront lesdictz treize vrays pauvres habillés comme desus chacun desquelz emporteront apres lesdictz services leur robbe et chaperon et leur sera baillé à chacun d'eulx dix solz tournois."

68. This type of service, literally meaning "at the end of the year," was moved increasingly close to the actual death in the hope that earlier suffrages and prayers would speed the soul's release from purgatory.

69. Will of Thiersault, 1590.

70. See Callaery, "Infiltration," 395, writing about Bellintani da Salò. See note 32 above.

71. Callaery, "Infiltration," 396–97, describes the writings that influenced Bellintani da Salò's *Historia capuccina*. Callaery's main point is to show how deeply Bellintani da Salò was influenced by the ideas of the spiritual Franciscans.

72. See Duffy, *Stripping of the Altars*, 210, on the seven penitential psalms (6, 32, 38, 51, 102, 130, and 143) and the evolution of monastic liturgy.

73. See Appendix E, which indicates the co-signing notaries for all of Raoul Bontemps' twenty-two testators: Lybault and M. Bontemps, League-affiliated notaries, and Barthélemy Dumarc, about whom little is known. The date strongly suggests this will, like Marguerite Dugué's, dated 21 March 1590, was a response to an unexpected apocalyptic struggle against Henry IV, perceived as Antichrist, that seemed likely after the defeat of Mayenne at the battle of Ivry earlier in March.

74. "Et premièrement comme crestien rachepté du sang et par la passion de nostre seigneur sauveur et rédempteur Jésus Christ régénéré par son sainct baptème en son église a recommandé son âme à Dieu par les prières de la tréssacrée et glorieuse Vierge Marie, mère de Dieu, à son bon ange et Monsieur Sainct Laurens et de Saincte Geneviefe, ses intercesseurs, à ce qu'il luy peult tandis qu'il se trouvera en bas dans son corps et depuis la louange tousiours transporté en la béatitude éternelle de son corps coadjuteur de son âme à l'acquisition de la gloire du ciel." For *louange*, see Cotgrave, *Dictionaire*, glorie. AN, *Min. cen.* XXIII, 95 [Raoul Bontemps] (16/3/1590), will of Laurens Malescot.

75. "une lecture publique des cas de conscience"

76. " . . . la congregation Notre Dame de Lyon qui s'assemble aux Jesusistes dudict Lyon 12 écus soleil pour estre employés en petitz catheschismes et chappelletz pour la distribution du pauvres. . . . "

77. "pour leur bon traitement, honneur et amitié que luy on porté."

78. "pour ayder à l'entretien aux ecolles et pour subvenir à ses necessitez."

79. See the entry for Fardeau in Appendix E and the high performativity ratings for Fardeau in Appendix F. Fardeau's two Leaguer clients are Nicole Ledanoys and Aymé Saultier. See also Appendix D. Fardeau also has a testator, Julien Perrier, who makes a bequest to the highly politically mobilized Confraternity of the Holy Sacrament.

80. See Appendix B for the posthumous son: Francis-Alexander-Paris, Knight of Malta.

81. Denis Crouzet, *Les guerriers de dieu* (Paris: Champ Vallon, 1990), 2:498. Crouzet describes the sense of the miraculous that surrounded the birth of this son, who is said to have been born with his hands held in prayer. This segment of Crouzet's argument explicitly speaks of a complete imbrication of the civic with the social in "une experience spirituelle de douleur . . . " The child's godparents are the entire cities of Paris, Orleans, and Amiens. In Crouzet 2:533, the same evidence suggests to me a complete identification of the civic and the sacred: hence the role played by the chief alderman Rolland, a relative of Genevieve Rolland.

82. "Et premierement comme bonne et vraye catholique a recommandé et recommand son ame en toute devotion et humilité à Dieu notre pere, createur saulveur redempteur Jesus invocquant, suppliant, et requirant son omnipotence et infinie bonté et [demande de] luy pardonner les pechez et offences qu'elle a contre luy commises et perpetué pendant sa vye et quant son pauvre ame sera separée de son corps la prendre et luy donner la beatitude eternelle. . . . " AN, *Min. cen.* XXXIII, 207 [Lamiral] (29/3/1590), will of Genevieve Roland.

83. " . . . pardon et miséricorde de sesdicts pechez et offenses rendant grace à Dieu des biens luy a donnez et prestez en ce mortel monde." For an interesting hypothesis concerning the more frequent reference to "biens . . . prestez" (lent worldly goods) among women than among men, see Pierre Chaunu, *La Mort à Paris: XVIe, XVIIe et XVIIIe siècles* (Paris: Fayard, 1978), 301ff., drawing on the master's thesis of Michelle Massucco, Paris-Sorbonne. The correlation remains to be tested in language analysis of a large sample of wills.

84. "Plus que incontinent qu'elle aura receu le corps de notre seigneur que luy soit baillé ung prebster, homme de bien, pour tousiours estre proche d'elle et icelle admonesté de son salut jusques à ce qu'elle soit decedée et que par ledict prebster soict dit et celebré pour le salut de son ame tous les jours [une] messe, et pour ce faire veult et ordonne que pendant ce temps il soit honnestement nourry [et] couché et à icelluy baillé ung cierge de cire blanche et paié par chacun jour qu'il y vacuera vingt livres tournois y compris sadicte messe. Aussy veult et ordonne que par le susdict prebster soit mis en son lieu aultre prebster pour l'assister pendant le temps qu'il dira et celebrera sa messe et qu'à icelluy soict aussy paié chacun jour pour son assistance et sa vacation dix solz tournois."

85. See Table 5.2, especially values 18 and 19.

86. "pour redimer et liberer de pauvres prisioners . . . qui seront conduitz au lieu de ma sepulture . . . et exortez de prier pour le salut de mon ame. . . . " The testator is Germain du Boys, *procureur au Parlement de Paris*, whose holograph will was deposited with the notary Périer (co-signing notary: Saulnier), XI, 125, 24 October 1630. This testator also places notable limitations on his funeral cortege.

87. Item donne et legue à Madame de Montmartre pour l'oeuvre de son monastere la somme de soixante livres supliant très humblement ladicte dame de faire communier toutes ses religieuses à l'intention de ladicte testateur le jour ou le lendemain de son decès et tous les ans au mesme jour la vie de ladicte dame de Montmartre. AN, *Min. cen.* CXVIII, 856 [Fontaine] (2/1/1630), will of *honorable femme* Jehanne Marchant.

88. "à la charge qu'elles prieront Dieu pour son ame et feront la sainte communion une fois la sepmaine durant un an pour la mesme intention."

89. "Plus donne et legue à cinq pauvres filles en l'honneur des cinq playes de nostre seigneur, qui seront choisies par sesdictz executeurs cy apres nommez la somme de deux cent cinquante livres qui est pour chacune d'icelles cinquante livres, à la change que le vendredy devant ou apres qu'elles seront mariées elles feront celebrer une messe de la passion ou la passion sera dicte . . . et feron la saincte communion et prieront Dieu."

90. See Table 5.4, value 19.

91. "Au nom de la tres saincte trinité pere, fils et sainct esprit randant graces a son infinie bonté de tant de tant (*sic*) dé benefices reçus de sa saincte et liberale main et de ce qu'il luy a pleu me donner la cognoissance et le desir de son service et en l'honneur de Jesus Christ nostre seigneur et de la vie tres humble et pauvre qu'il a menee sur la desirant l'himiter (*sic*) en ceste estat par le mespris des biens et comodités de la vie et me randre a sa parole et au desire qu'il me donne de les abandoner et renoncer pour son amour à cet effet ie me despouille de tous mes biens par ceste miene disposition et testament aisy (*sic*) qu'il ensuict." AN, *Min. cen.* LIV, 515 [Haultdesens] (7/5/1630), holograph will of *damoiselle* Marie de Gourgue.

92. Her name as *religieuse* (Marie de Jesus) is a perfect emblem of the spirituality of Bérulle. It would be interesting to trace the lines connecting all the testators using the headings "Jesus+Maria" in all of the sample years.

93. "Premierement je donne & legue a Monsieur le president Seguier mon oncle en recognoissance de la singuilliere afection qu'il m'a tousiours portee tous les meubles, choses, cencees et reputees meubles a moy appartenans avec tous les acquetz et le tiers de mes propres le tout a moy advenu et escheu par la succession de feu Monsieur le premier president de Gourgue mon pere et generalement tout ce que par droit et coustume ie luy puis donner et leguer des biens provenantz de sa dite succession au quel legs ainsy par moy faict je veux et entans estre compris et en tant que besoign seroit je luy donne et legue la somme de cent mil livres qu'il a plus au Roy accorder a feu Monsieur le premier president mon pere pour la recoingnance de sa charge de premier president par brevet expedié en sa faveur."

94. " . . . comme testament codicille ou donation a cose [sic] de mort, . . . escripte et signee de ma propre main au monastere de l'incarnation de l'ordre des Carmelites sis au fauxbourg Saint Iacques le Paris le septieme iour du present mois de may mil six cents trente."

95. "novice Carmelite indigne."

96. The nature of links between different Leaguer milieux and the world of the seventeenth-century *dévot* is suggested by the will of the wife of the notary Haultdesens, *honorable femme* Jehanne Maret, who had her will drawn up by the 1590's Leaguer notary Lybault on 9 March 1590. Lybault, it will be recalled, helped to draw up the exile procurations of 1594 for the most intransigent Leaguers.

97. See the articles of Andrew Barnes on penitential confraternities in the Bibliography.

98. *Decrees*, 660.

99. Refer to Appendix G for information on Gincestre, Jehan Hervy, and François Pigenat. Also it is clear that the preacher Christin was linked to the clientele of the notary Lybault, who helped to draw up the exile procurations of 1594.

Chapter 8

1. Eamon Duffy, *The Stripping of the Altars: Traditional Religion in England 1400–1580* (New Haven and London: Yale University Press, 1992), 116.

2. *Decrees of the Ecumenical Councils*, vol. 2, *Trent to Vatican II*, ed. Norman P. Tanner, original text established by G. Albergio, J. A. Dossetti, P.-P. Joannou, C. Leonardi, and P. Prodi in consultation with H. Jedin (London: Sheed and Ward, Ltd., Washington, D.C.: Georgetown University Press, 1990), 737.

3. An important exception is the most recent work of Carlos Eire, *From Madrid to Purgatory: The Art and Craft of Dying in Sixteenth-Century Spain* (Cambridge: Cambridge University Press, 1995), since Eire has been most responsible for rekindling interest in the phenomenon of immanence in the English-speaking world. See Carlos Eire, *War Against the Idols: The Reformation of Worship from*

Erasmus to Calvin (New York: 1986). This rekindling is consonant with his important reorientation of the study of early-modern religion and religious reform. The discussion of number symbolism concerning masses and candles by Jean-Baptiste Thiers, *Traité des superstitions qui regardent les sacremens* (Paris: Jean de Nully, 1704), 3:123ff., provides a crucial framework for my investigation.

4. *Decrees*, 737. Cited in full in Chapter 3.

5. My examination of synodal legislation affecting Paris in the sixteenth and seventeenth centuries found no discussion of this prohibition.

6. See Table 8.2 for the breakdown on which symbolic numbers were used in the three sample periods.

7. In 1543–44, the most popular symbolic number for numbers of masses was 13. For example, the following directives were encountered: "ung service complect assavoir est vigilles, a neuf pseaulmes et neuf leçons, laudes, recommendaces avec treize basses messes," or "ung service complect avec treize basses messes, vigilles, laudes, et recommendaces au nom des treize apostles." The significance of the thirteen Apostles is discussed in detail below. See also Abbé Thiers, *Traicté des superstitions qui regardent les sacremens*, 3:121ff., on the use of particular numbers of masses and synodal legislation prohibiting this practice. Only the example of a "superstitious" preference for thirty-three rather than thirty masses is discussed, but with no reference whatsoever to the symbolic meaning of 33, which is the number of years Christ is believed to have lived on earth.

8. The chief exclusion was the number 12, for which a separate study could be undertaken. Its use in requests for masses was not as significant as 13's in 1543–44. The use of 12 in pious directives designating numbers of persons was significant in all sample years and in fact increased by 1630. It was explicitly associated with "honor for the 12 Apostles," and was throughout the most frequently requested number of candles for the funeral bier, although in the latter setting never with explanatory wording. One could associate the pervasiveness and persistence of the number 12 with the orthodoxy of Apostolic succession and the ascendancy of an ecclesiological view of community. The numbers 1, 2, and 3 were excluded because of their ubiquity and general lack of accompanying explanatory wording, although 3 could, of course, refer to the Trinity. The number 100 gains in popularity in 1590 in designating poor persons as recipients of bequests, but without explanatory wording. It was also excluded.

9. " . . . ung service complect avec treize basses messes, vigilles, laudes et recommendaces au nom des treize apostoles." AN, *Min. cen.* LIV, 133 [R. Contesse] (14/5/1543), will of Michel Vincent.

10. See note 21 below, however, for Adolph Franz's mention of the *Notmessen* consisting of thirteen masses. Does the appearance of the thirteen-mass sequence in a local Parisian Missal of 1576 represent a negotiation over legitimate symbolic actions vis-à-vis Tridentine norms? I would like to thank Lisa McClain, who has pointed out that in *The Spiritual Exercises of St. Ignatius Loyola*, in the concluding segment entitled "Scriptural Texts for the Meditations on the Life of

Our Lord," there are meditations covering what are referred to as thirteen apparitions of the resurrected Christ prior to his Ascension forty days after his crucifixion, yet Loyola chronicles only twelve apparitions. The apparitions have
traditionally been used as one of the scriptural foundations of strict apostolic
succession, despite Christ's first appearance before Mary Magdalene, which Loyola
refers to as the Second Apparition. McClain is currently preparing a paper on the
significance of these differences and the importance of number symbolism in
Loyola's numbering of the apparitions.

11. For a detailed analysis of this testator and her membership in a Holy
Sacrament confraternity see Ann W. Ramsey, "From Ontology to Religious Ex-
perience: Civic and Sacred Immanence in the Holy Sacrament Confraternities
of Paris During the Catholic League," in *Confraternities and Catholic Reform in
Italy, France, and Spain*, eds. John Patrick Donnelly and Michael W. Maher,
Sixteenth-Century Essays and Studies, vol. 44, 1999).

12. Rolland's use of service-related number symbolism gives us insight into
a broader aggregate finding that high performative behaviors are associated with
individuals with ties to the University by either bequest or notary location. See
Table 5.1 on the high performativity rates of testators belonging to the University milieu by bequest and by notary location. This is important evidence of the
interrelation of the case study and the aggregate evidence.

13. For a more detailed identification of testators using service-related number symbolism in 1590, see Appendix J.

14. Rolland specified: "deux services completz de vigilles a neuf pseaulmes
et neuf lecons, laudes, recommendaces et trois haultes messes et a chascunes
d'icelles treize basses messes." The request appears on page 4 of her will dated
March 29, 1590, drawn up by Philippe Lamiral and co-signed by Jacques de
Saint-Vaast, strongly *Seize*-identified notaries.

15. If we look further into the future we must note that in the declining years
of the *ancien régime* Enlightenment values caused the abandonment of this communal graveyard for reasons of hygiene. Another example of the dominion of
medicalization can be found in the Epilogue of this book.

16. See Table 5.7, "The Offertory Procession and the Leaguer Construction
of a Liturgical Community."

17. The Compans family is one of the most prominent of the *Seize* faction.
Robert Le Goix, the husband of Tassine de Compans, was killed in a *politique*
protest during the siege of 1590. He drew up the liturgical order for the Guise
funerals. Tassine de Compans is the only major Leaguer among our elite Leaguer
testators who is not associated with the Jesuits, Capuchins, or Feuillants in any of
her bequests. Her bequests tie her to the University milieu.

18. For example, one testator, Michelle Gugane, the widow of a tailor
living in Saint-Sauveur, one of the poorer parishes, requests that five *solz* be
distributed to up to nine hundred persons on the day of her burial. Will of
Michelle Gugane, 23 July 1630, notary Huart, *étude* IX, 362. She specifically
states the poor be *pauvres honteux* (the shamed-faced or deserving poor). More

research is needed on the details of charitable distributions in this period to evaluate what portion of the parish poor those nine hundred individuals would represent.

19. Even among the world's experts in sacred numerology, most admit that the origins of the negative associations with 13 pre-date the Christian experience and are shrouded in uncertainty. See for example Annemarie Schimmel, *The Mystery of Numbers* (New York and Oxford: Oxford University Press, 1993), original German edition 1984, and Nelson Pinkston Shankle, "Number Symbolism in Religion and Philosophy," master's thesis, the University of Texas at Austin, 1932. In one of the typically unhelpful presentations, see the illustrations that accompany the article "cierges" in the *Dictionnaire d'archéologie chrétienne et de liturgie* (Paris: Letouzey, 1914), volume 2, part 2, p. 1620, which reproduces an altar decorated with thirteen candles but offers no explication except to indicate the source of the engraving: an altar at Reims, taken from the work of Rohault de Fleury, *La messe*, vol. 6, p. 37. I believe that, much like some of the fundamental beliefs of Menocchio studied by Carlos Ginzburg, the popular associations with 13 have deep roots whose precise origins we may never know. In this sense 12 and 13 are diametric opposites, as 12 stands for the official ecclesiology (Apostolic authority and succession) and 13 represents the popular "other." None of the standard encyclopedias of religion that I consulted offered any firm guidance on the pre-Christian origins of the cultural meanings of 13.

20. There is also the possibility that the number 13 is an inclusion of Paul among the count of the apostles. This would be in interesting reflection of the relative importance of Pauline theology in the Reformation era.

21. See Appendix I, on testators and service-related number symbolism in 1590, and Appendix J, on testators using symbolic numbers in bequests to the poor in 1590.

22. Much more could be said about the more private penitential practices such as flagellation practiced in the dark (see Epilogue) or in the secret Jesuit Marian congregations of the *Aas*. See Louis Châtellier, *Europe of the Devout: The Catholic Reformation and the Formation of a New Society*, trans. Jean Birrell (Cambridge and New York: Cambridge University Press, 1989), originally published as *L'Europe des dévots* (Paris: Flammarion, 1987); and the writings of the Jesuit father Jacob Gretzer, who was a director of the *Aas* and wrote in defense of flagellation.

23. In the nineteen general performativity indices of Table 5.4, entering a monastery is the final and highest hierarchical value.

24. See Adolph Franz, *Die Messe im deutschen Mittelalter: Beiträge zur Geschichte der Liturgie und des religiösen Volkslebens* (Darmstadt: Wissenschaftliche Buchgesell- schaft, 1963), 277–79, on "Die dreizehn Notmessen," which are important in the French context since Franz's evidence comes from the Abbé Thiers, who describes such a mass cycle based on a Parisian Missal of 1576 where the cycle is called "missae de gratia." It is crucial to note the date at which this appears in a Parisian Missal, 1576. The key dates for Tridentine liturgical reform

are the reform of the Breviary in 1568, the Missal of 1570, the new Martyrology in 1583, the Gregorian calendar of 1582, the reform of the Pontifical in 1596, and the last book to be released, the Ritual of Paul V of 1614 (note also Borromeo's preceding work); Sixtus V instituted the permanent Roman Congregations in 1588 (with the "Congregation quinta," defined as "pro sacris ritibus et caeremoniis." This Congregation of Rites is the institutional mechanism for imposing Tridentine uniformity, as noted in Niels Krogh Rasmussen, "Litury and Liturgical Arts," *Catholicism in Early-Modern History: a Guide to Research*, volume 2, *Reformation Guides to Research*, ed. John O'Malley (St. Louis: Center for Reformation Research, 1988), 273 98. Note also that Rasmussen calls for much more work on the Congregation of Rites; see 280.

25. Baslé is one of three testators who left wills with the notary Thévenin in 1630. All three of these testators are non-signers from the popular milieu (a *maistre jardinier*, a servant, and a widow of a merchant from Beauvais who lives in the cloître Notre Dame. Both Baslé and the master gardener, Pamain Laisinier, request that the curate be present at their funeral. Laisinier requests burial "in the place where he customarily sits to hear the service, near his own seat" ("au lieu ou il a accoustumé de se mettre pour l'entendu du service, proche son banc").

26. See Philip T. Hoffman, "Wills and Statistics: Tobit Analysis and the Counter Reformation in Lyon," *Journal of Interdisciplinary History* 14, no. 4 (Spring 1984): 813–34 and Daniel Milo, "La Rencontre, insolite mais édifiante, du quantitatif et du culturel," *Histoire et Mesure* 2, no. 2 (1987): 7–37.

Epilogue

1. Abbé Boileau, *Histoire des flagellans ou l'on fait voir le bon et le mauvais usage des flagellations parmi les Chrétiens*, translated from the Latin (Amsterdam, 1701). Boileau identifies himself as a *Docteur de Sorbonne*.

2. Abbé Jean-Baptiste Thiers, *Critique de l'histoire des flagellans et justification de l'usage des disciplines volontaires* (n.p.: 1703). Thiers was also a doctor of theology and the *curé* of the town of Vibraye. Given what we learned in the preceding chapter about devotion to John the Baptist, it is interesting to reflect on the socialization process of a child named in honor of this saint.

3. Thiers was used to advantage, for example, in two early and crucial works on early-modern popular culture: N. Z. Davis, *Society and Culture in Early Modern France* (Stanford: Stanford University Press, 1965), and Yves-Marie Bercé, *Fête et révolte: Des mentalités populaires du XVIe au XVIIIe siècle* (Paris, 1976).

4. This is despite the fact that both Thiers and Boileau are cited in the bibliographies for the articles on "flagellants" in the *Dictionnaire de spiritualité* (article written by Paul Bailly) and in the *Dictionnaire du théologie catholique*, vol. 6, ed. A. Vacant and E. Mangenot (Paris, 1920).

5. In this context it is interesting to note that the edition of Boileau that I consulted contains the handwritten notation that the owner of the book had been one "Hatte, medecin (medical doctor), 1801."

6. The terms appear in the following context: "Il est contre pudeur et la bienséance, tant pour les hommes que pour les femmes de se foüeter sur les fesses." (Boileau, *Histoire*, chap. 10)

7. Boileau, *Histoire*, 254, 280.

8. Boileau, *Histoire*, 282, "quod ab altro fiat et moderate et sine scandalo et ostentatione, ac sine sanguine."

9. Boileau, *Histoire*, 291: "la sect se renouvella sur la fin du dernier siècle et au comencement du nôtre." This places the revival towards the end of the sixteenth century and beginning of the seventeenth, the period of the League and the years immediately following. Boileau's treatise was obviously written at the end of the seventeenth century and published in 1701.

10. The example Boileau uses comes from Jacques Auguste de Thou and is cited at the end of Chapter 8.

11. One of our reforming testators in 1630 makes a bequest to the Capuchins to go preach in the countryside, while another 1630's testator, Marguerite Lefevre, helps organize a confraternity devoted to Carlo Borromeo.

12. The exception, of course, is the quantitatively much smaller world of mystic asceticism that has been the focus for the definition of seventeenth-century spirituality.

13. One of the most important findings to emerge from Thiers's account is the number of key, new associations founded during the Counter-Reformation which practiced self-flagellation. He comments on Borromeo, the Capuchins, the Feuil- lants, the Oratory of Bérulle, the Carmelites, all key elements within *dévot* piety.

14. Thiers, *Critique*, 149. See also pp. 156–58, which point out that chapter 8 of Borromeo's statutes calls for administration of self-discipline not only for the sins of the confrères but for the collective sins of the people.

15. Paul Bailly, "Flagellants," in *Dictionnaire de Spiritualité*, 404. Thiers, *Critique*, 390–91, cites from a life of Borromeo by Jussano [Juffano?], which, as Thiers said, "assure que S. Charles Borromée se châtoit toute l'année si severement avec des rudes disciplines, qu'à sa mort les marques y paroissoient très evidente en son cors." This was also mentioned in the bull of his canonization by Pope Paul V in 1610: "accedebant frequentes corporis flagellationes aliaeque id genus corporales mortificationes . . . "

16. Cited by Paul Bailly, "Flagellants," 406.

17. Denis Richet emphasized that L'Estoile's limited approval of the penitential processions revealed the basis for a latent cultural consensus among elites who had opposed each other during the League. See "Sociocultural Aspects of Religious Conflicts in Paris during the Second Half of the Sixteenth Century," in *Ritual, Religion, and the Sacred: Selections from the Annales, Economies, Sociétés,*

Civilisations, ed. Robert Forster and Orest Ranum, trans. Elborg Forster and Patricia M. Ranum, vol. 7 (Baltimore: The Johns Hopkins Press, 1982), 205–6.

18. "Il [Borromeo] leur enjoint en outre de faire en sorte que tous les confrères assistent aux Processions avec modestie et en leur bon ordre, et qu'ils se disciplinent eux-mêmes par devotion sans substituter à leur place des gens se disciplinant pour eux," cited by Thiers, *Critique*, 225.

19. Bailly, "Flagellants," 408, gives numerous instances from the statutes and constitutions of new religious orders or those reformed in the seventeenth century. For example, the *Statuta* of the Premonstratensians, revised in 1630, call for discipline "in passionis Christi memoriam majoremque sui mortificationem," based on a decision of the chapter in 1574.

20. Both examples in Bailly, "Flagellants," 408.

21. Louis Chatellier, *L'Europe des dévots* (Paris: Flammarion, 1987), 57. He describes in detail a procession organized in Augsburg in the early years of the seventeenth century when the city was still largely Protestant. The dramatic enactment of the passion appears to be very similar to the one led to Chartres by Père Ange de Joyeuse with the Capuchins in 1588.

22. Further research into the history of flagellation in the seventeenth century should help pinpoint when arguments about the immodesty of flagellation were first raised and by whom.

23. "Et c'est pour cela [pudicité] qu'aujourd'hui les religieux et les religieuses prennent la discipline sur les épaules, sur les reins, audessous, ou sur les cuisses, toutes nûës, mais hors la vûë de leurs Freres ou leurs Soeurs soit en particulier dans leurs cellules ou à la porte de leurs cellules . . . mais toutes les fenêtres fermées. Et toutes les lumieres éteintes: ce qui ôte l'indécence qu'il pourroit y avoir de se donner la discipline à crû. . . . " Thiers, *Critique*, 170ff.

24. Boileau, *Histoire*, 5: "oposée à la veritable piété et à la pudeur même."

25. Boileau, *Histoire*, 5.

26. Boileau, *Histoire*, 303–8.

27. The extent to which flagellation continued to occur in public has also not been much commented on. For example, flagellation had in the medieval period been part of the ritual by which an excommunicant was reintegrated into the church. I have not seen historians of the League comment on the fact that for the reintroduction of the excommunicant Henry IV into the church, the Pope prescribed a ritual of flagellation. In the negotiations with the papacy Henry refused to submit himself to flagellation as demanded but agreed that two of his procurators would receive flagellation instead.

28. Rules governing penitential rituals cited by Abbé Thiers, *Critique*, 239–44.

29. Jacques-Auguste de Thou, *Histoire universelle de Jacques-Auguste de Thou, depuis 1543, jusqu'en 1607*, ed. and trans. Pierre-François Guyot, M. l'abbé Desfontaines et al. (London: 1734).

Bibliography

I. Minutier Central

[Brackets denote notaries for whom there were no wills to code, or whose wills were incomplete, damaged, or otherwise inaccessible.]

Notaries for 1543–44

ALART, Jean. VIII, 476.
    rue Saint-Denis, devant l'église Saint-Jacques-de-l'Hôpital, à l'Ecritoire. 1542–75.
[ANGIRARD, Jean.]
BASTONNEAU, François. VIII, 290–92.
    rue des Marmousets. 1526–47.
BERGEON, Hervé. LXVIII, 2.
    rue Saint-Denis, paroisse Saint-Merri. 1543–73.
[BERTHE, Gilles.]
BOISSELLET, Philippe. VIII, 141.
    rue Saint-Denis (partie moyenne). 1523–57.
[BOREAU, Claude.]
[BOREAU, Jean.]
BOULLE, Michel. CXXII, 83.
    rue Neuve-Saint-Merri. 1541–44.
BOULLE, Pierre. CXXII, 183.
    rue Saint-Martin. 1539–48.
[BOURGEOIS, Yves.]
BRAHIER, Nicolas. VIII, 165–66.
    rue Saint-Honoré. 1533–51
BRUSLE, Etienne. VI, 14.
    rue Jean-de-l'Epine. 1542–84.
CARTAULT, François. XI, 5–6.
    place Maubert. 1539–61.
CHAMPIN, Nicolas. CXXII, 103–4.
    rue de la Harpe. 1540–44.
CHARLET, Pierre. CXXII, 75.
    rue des Arcis. 1541–54.
[CHENU, Simon.]

CONTESSE, Nicolas. CXXII, 1091 bis.
    rue Saint-Germain-l'Auxerrois. 1522–47.
CONTESSE, René I. LIV, 133–34.
    rue Saint-Germain-l'Auxerrois. 1543–86.
CORDELLE, Jean. LXXXV, 14–16.
    paroisse Saint-Jacques-de-la-Boucherie. 1539–52.
COUSIN, Philippe. LXXXVII, 4–5.
    rue Saint-Denis. 1539–55.
CROZON, François. XLIX, 22–24.
    rue Saint-Jacques, paroisse Saint-Benoît. 1528–60.
[CROZON, Jean et Pierre.]
CRUCE, Jean. LXXIII, 5.
    rue Saint-Jacques, au Lion d'Argent. 1539–71.
[DELARCHE, François.]
[DUGUE, Charles.]
DUNESMES, Etienne. LIV, 19–20.
    rue de l'Arbre-Sec, près la Croix-du-Trahoir. 1528–63.
DUPONT, Thibaud. CXXII, 1349.
    rue Saint-Martin, paroisse Saint-Nicolas-des-Champs. 1544–63.
FARDEAU, Catherin. XXXIII, 29.
    rue Saint-Jacques. 1539–73.
[FELIN, Michel de.]
FILESAC, Jacques. IX, 1–4.
    rue Saint-Martin, près la rue aux Ours. 1543–89.
[FRANQUELIN, Claude.]
FRENICLE, François. CXXII, 131.
    rue des Prouvaires. 1539–68.
HALLE, Claude. XCI, 18–19.
    paroisse Saint-Nicolas-des-Champs. 1529–55.
[HAMELIN, François.]
[JACQUESSON, Dominique.]
[LEBARGE, Simon.]
LE CHARRON, Germain. 159.
    rue Saint Honoré. 1539–64.
LECLERC, Jacques. CXXII, 49–50
    rue Saint-Honoré, paroisse Saint-Eustache. 1540–64.
[LENORMAND, Claude.]
LENORMAND, Claude. CX, 4.
    rue du Petit-Pont. 1539–60.
LEROY, Pierre. CXXII, 31.
    rue Saint-Germain-l'Auxerrois. 1517–47.
[LESCUIER, Hector.]
LE TELLIER, Michel. CXXII, 197–210
    rue Saint-Denis. 1542–60.

L'OLIVE, Mathieu de. CXXII, 1295.
    rue des Noyers. 1539–44.
[LOUVENCOURT, Jean de.]
LOUVENCOURT, Jean de. VI, 6, 10
    paroisse Saint-Gervais. 1524–61.
[MAHEUT, Jean.]
MAUPEOU, Vincent. VIII, 290–91.[1]
    maison du Chapeau rouge, près de l'église de la Madeleine-en-la-Cité.
    1534–71.
MERAULT, Michel. CXXII, 1298.
    paroisse Saint-Gervais. 1540–47.
MONTIGUE, Pierre. XLIX, 71, 73.
    près la porte Saint-Germain. 1539–46.
MUSSART, Jacques. XX, 16–18.
    près les Halles. 1537–49.
NICOLAS, Guillaume I. CXXII, 1313–14.
    rue Saint-Denis. 1539–62.
PALANQUIN, Philippe. CXXII, 136.
    rue Saint-Denis, paroisse Saint-Sauveur. 1540–59.
PAYEN, Guillaume. XIX, 87–88
    rue Saint-Antoine. 1530–59.
[PAYEN, Guillaume et Jean.]
PERIER, Thomas. XI, 24.
    place Maubert. 1543–89.
POUTRAIN, Pierre. LXXXVI, 14.
    rue de la Ferronnerie. 1531–74.
[QUETIN, Jean.]
ROGER, Olivier. CX, 12–13.
    rue du Petit-Pont. 1539–75.
[ROGER, Olivier.]
[SAINCT-YON, Adrien de.]
THURET, Pierre. III, 55–56.
    à la porte Baudoyer. 1540–68.
TROUVE, Jean. XIX, 164–66.
    rue Sainte-Antoine, devant le Petit-Saint-Antoine. 1533–78.
TROUVE, Jean. CVII, fragments.
    rue Saint-Antoine, devant le couvent du Petit-Saint-Antoine. 1536–80.
TURPIN, Pierre. VI, 11.[2]
    paroisse Saint-André-des-Arts. 1543–55.
[VALET, Pierre I.]
VIAU, Mathurin. CXXII, 1246–47.
    place Maubert. 1539–46.
YMBERT, François. XX, 37.
    rue Saint-Jacques-de-la-Boucherie, à la Chaise. 1542–75.

Notaries for 1590

ARRAGON, Louis. LXXXV, 90.
  rue Saint-Jacques-de-la-Boucherie. 1587–1622.
AYMERY, François. III, 356.
  près l'église Saint-Eustache. 1585–94.
BEAUFORT, Claude de. XLII, 23.
  rue Saint-Honoré, paroisse Saint-Germain-l'Auxerrois. 1568–1605.
BECQUET, Jean. CXXII, 1494.
  rue Saint-André-des-Arts. 1587–90.
BERGEON, François. LXVIII, 61.
  rue Saint-Denis, paroisse Saint-Merri, puis rue Barre-du-Bec (1601). 1573–630.
BERNARD, Clément. XLIX, 225.
  rue de la Harpe. 1582–1600.
BONTEMPS, Mathieu. LXXIII, 218–19.
  rue Saint-André-des-Arts. 1585–1621.
BONTEMPS, Raoul. XXIII, 95.
  rue des Canettes, paroisse de la Madeleine. 1569–1617.
BRUYÈRE, Marc. CXXII, 1184.
  à Saint-Germain-des-Prés. 1585–91.
CHAPELAIN, Sébastien. XXI, 56.
  rue Saint-Martin, au coin de la ruelle de Venise. 1586–1612.
CHAPELLAIN, Jean. XXXV, 15.
  l'aîné, seigneur de Billy et de Louvainville, pointe Saint-Eustache. 1580–1623.
CHARLES, Jean. XVIII, 114.
  place Maubert. 1581–1635.
CHARTAIN, Lambert. LXXXVII, 63.
  rue Saint-Honoré, place aux Chats. 1553–90.
CHAUVET, François. VIII, 545.
  au bout du pont Saint-Michel. 1582–91.
CHAZERETZ, Jean. I, 18.
  rue Saint-Denis. 1577–1605.
CHEFDEVILLE, René. V, 17–18.
  près les Halles. 1577–1602.
CONTENOT, Nicolas. XVI, 169.
  rue Saint-Honoré, au coin de la rue Tirechappe. 1587–1603.
CONTESSE, René II. LIV, 230.
  rue des Fossés-Saint-Germain-l'Auxerrois. 1586–1644.
COTHEREAU, Jean. C, 118.
  rue de la Harpe. 1583–97.
COTHEREAU, Philippe. XXIX, 87.
  rue de la Calandre. 1578–1613.
CROISET, François. VIII, 404.
  rue de la Vieille-Draperie. 1559–1601.

DES QUATREVAULX, Antoine. XXIV, 176.
   rue de l'Arbre-Sec, au coin de la rue d'Avron. 1579–1617.
DOUJAT, Pierre. LXI, 104.
   rue Comtesse d'Artois. 1583–1623.
DUMARC, Barthélemy. LXXIII, 141.
   rue Saint-Jacques, paroisse Saint-Benoît. 1569–90.[3]
DUNESMES, Jacques II. LIV, 127.
   rue de l'Arbre-Sec, près la Croix-du-Trahoir. 1590–96.
FARDEAU, Jacques. XLIX, 179.
   rue Saint-Jacques, paroisse Saint-Séverin. 1581–1629.
[FARDEAU, Nicolas.]
FERRANT, Charles. VII, 46.
   rue Saint-Honoré, au coin de la rue des Bourdonnais. 1582–1611.
FILESAC, Claude. IX, 165.
   rue Saint-Martin, paroisse Saint-Nicolas-des-Champs. 1589–1611.
GIRAULT, Alexandre. LXXVIII, 165.
   rue des Marmousets, paroisse de la Madeleine. 1588–1604.
GOGUIER, Henri. CIX, 81.
   place Baudoyer. 1576–91.
HAULTDESENS, Laurent. VIII, 350.
   rue de la Fontaine-Maubué. 1552–96.
HERBIN, François. CVIII, 23.
   rue Saint-Antoine, paroisse Saint-Gervais. 1569–92.
JACQUES, Martin. XXIII, 152.
   rue des Marmousets, paroisse de la Madeleine. 1581–1605.
JOURDAN, Claude. IV, 17.
   rue Saint-Honoré. 1576–1606.
LA BARDE, Simon de. VI, 147.
   rue Saint-Christophe, puis au Marché-Neuf. 1588–1604.
LAMIRAL, Philippe. XXXIII, 207.
   rue Saint-Jacques. 1555–90.
LANDRY, Jacques. XXXIX, 21.
   rue de la Tabletterie, au coin de la rue de la Harengerie. 1568–1600.
LE CAMUS, Jean / CHANTEMERLE, Denis. LIX, 11.
   son beaupère, rue des Prouvaires, à la Corne de cerf, en association. 1578–1601.
LEMOYNE, Olivier / BABYNET, Hugues. CX, 29.
   rue et paroisse Saint-Séverin. 1580–90.
[LENOIR, Nicolas.]
LENORMANT, Jean. LXXXVII, 412.
   le jeune, place Baudoyer. 1586–1618.
LE ROUX, Pierre. XX, 138.
   pointe Saint-Eustache. 1589–1630.
LEROY, Nicolas. XLI, 21.
   rue Saint-Germain-l'Auxerrois. 1571–1610.

[LE VASSEUR, Arthur.]
LE VASSEUR, François. XVI, 9.
  rue du Temple, paroisse Saint-Nicolas-des-Champs. 1582–1620.
LUSSON, Jean I. LXXVIII, 142.
  rue des Marmousets, au Chef Saint-Jean. 1566–99.
[LUSSON, Regnault / LUSSON, Jean.]
LYBAULT, Hilaire. CV, 136.
  rue Barre-du-Bec. 1580–1621.
MAHIEU, Martin. CV, 59.
  rue des Arcis. 1569–1612.
MAIGRET, Jérôme. LIV, 443.
  cloître Sainte-Opportune. 1575–96.
MONTHENAULT, Laurent de. XXVI, 12.
  rue des Barres. 1579–1619.
MOTELET, Jean. LXXXIV, 30.
  rue de la Verrerie, près le Petit-Saint-Antoine, puis au carrefour Guillori,
  paroisse Saint-Jean-en-Grève (1601). 1588–1614.
MURET, Jean. XXXIV, 3.
  rue Saint-Côme, puis rue Comtesse d'Artois. 1585–1614.
PARQUE, Edme. LXXXVI, 131.
  rue de la Ferronnerie. 1565–1603.
PERIER, Mathurin. XI, 74.
  place Maubert, au Cheval blanc. 1589–1626.
PERON, Cléophas. XCI, 96.
  rue aux Ours. 1555–99.
POCHE, Jean de. CXVII, 32.
  à la porte Baudoyer, paroisse Saint-Gervais. 1579–98.
PRIVE, Nicolas. LXII, 15.
  rue Saint-Antoine, près le cimetière Saint-Jean. 1581–1604.
ROBINOT, Nicolas. LXXXVIII, 2.
  rue du Temple, paroisse Saint-Nicolas-des-Champs. 1588–1646.
ROSSIGNOL, Pierre de. XIX, 327.
  rue Saint-Antoine. 1578–1613.
SAINT-FUSSIEN, Valeran de. XCIX, 53.
  rue de l'Arbre-Sec. 1585–1610.
[SAINT-LEU, Léonor de.]
SAINT-VAAST, Jacques de. LXXIII, 142.
  rue Saint-Jacques, paroisse Saint-Benoît. 1589–1637.
[SEVESTRE, Nicolas.]
THEVENIN, Jean. XCI, 147.
  rue aux Ours (1599) puis rue Saint-Martin, paroisse Saint-Merri. 1588–
  1631.
TROUVE, Claude. CVII, 61–62.
  rue Saint-Antoine. 1566–1606.

TROYES, Claude I de. CXXII, 1523.
  rue Saint-André-des-Arts. 1583–1623.
TULLOUE, Philippe. XXIV, 72.
  rue Saint-Germain-l'Auxerrois, au coin de la rue des Lavandières. 1576–1618.
VACHOT, Philippe. XXXVI, 57.
  rue de la Chanvrerie. 1586–1604.
VIARD, Pierre. CV, 283.
  rue Saint-Antoine, paroisse Saint-Paul. 1588–1623.

Notaries for 1630

BAUDOUIN, Claude. CVII, 134–35; no wills for 1630.
  rue Saint-Antoine, devant le Petit-Saint-Antoine. 1608–43.
BAULDRY, Nicolas. XIX, 400–401.
  rue Saint-Antoine, près la porte Baudoyer. 1623–56.
BEAUFORT, Pierre de. CXIII, no wills for 1630.
  rue Saint-Honoré, paroisse Saint-Germain-l'Auxerrois. 1626–56.
BEAUVAIS, Michel de. XCVI, 18–19.
  rue Saint-Honoré. 1618–63.
BEI IN, Jacques. LVII, 46.
  rue de la Calandre. 1619–53.
BERGEON, François. LXVIII, 115.
  rue Barre-du-Bec. 1573–1630.
BLOSSE, Pierre. LXXV, 16–17.
  rue Sainte-Avoie. 1622–36.
BONOT, Edme. LXVII, 78.
  rue de la Verrerie, près la rue des Arcis. 1619–63.
BOUCOT, Claude. VI, 208–9.
  rue Saint-Séverin. 1614–48.
[BOUQUIN, Joachim.]
BOURGEOIS, Richard. C, 159.
  rue Saint-Séverin. 1598–1634
BRUNEAU, Jacques. XC, 30–32.
  rue du Temple, paroisse Saint-Nicolas-des-Champs. 1620–64.
CAMUSET, Denis. XXXV, 121–32.
  rue Saint-Denis, paroisse Saint-Leu-Saint-Gilles. 1629–41.
CARON, Claude. XXIII, 268.
  rue de la Harpe. 1619–39.
CARTIER, Thomas. XIII, 11–12.
  rue Saint-Germain-l'Auxerrois. 1625–45.
CHAPELLAIN, Jean I. XXIV, 328–30.
  rue de l'Arbre-Sec, vis-à-vis la rue d'Avron. 1610–40.
CHARLES, Jacques I. XVIII, 247.
  place Maubert. 1624–30.

CHARLES, Jean. XVIII, 184.
place Maubert. 1581–1635.
CHARLET, Simon I. IV, 63–64.
rue de la Poterie. 1608–52.
COLLE, Vincent. CV, 563–64.
rue des Arcis. 1614–31.
CONTENOT, Nicolas. XVI, 227.
rue Saint-Honoré, au coin de la rue Tirechappe. 1605–36.
CONTESSE, René II. LIV, 286.
rue des Fossés-Saint-Germain-l'Auxerrois. 1586–1644.
CORNILLE, Eustache. CVIII, no wills for 1630.
rue Saint-Antoine, paroisse Saint-Gervais. 1628–65.
COTHEREAU, Bon. XXIX, 149.
rue de la Calandre. 1613–30.
COUSINET, Jérôme. LI, 485.
rue Sainte-Avoie. 1627–69.
COUSTARD, Jean. XXIX, no wills for 1630.
rue Saint-Christophe, puis rue de la Calandre. 1626–34.
CRESSE, Nicolas et Pierre. VII, 127.
place Maubert. 1625–35.
CRESSE, Pierre. XXXIII, 258.
place Maubert. 1625–36.
CUVILLIER, Richard. XV, 73.
rue Comtesse-d'Artois, au coin de la rue de la Grande-Truanderie, à la
Licorne. 1593–1630.
DAUVERGNE, Claude. LVIII, 49–51.
carrefour du pont Saint-Michel. 1612–59.
DELACROIX, Martin. XLI, 89.
rue Saint-Germain-l'Auxerrois. 1606–55.
DEMAS, Jean. XXI, 116–17.
rue Saint-Martin, au coin de la ruelle de Venise. 1613–66.
DESNOTZ, Jean I. CXII, no wills for 1630.
rue des Arcis, paroisse Saint-Merri. 1602–30.
DESTRECHY, Clément. XLI, 156–57.
rue Saint-Honoré, de l'autre côté des Piliers-des-Halles, à la Croix-de-Fer.
1621–47.
DUBOIS, Claude. CV, 443–44.
rue Saint-Antoine, paroisse Saint-Paul. 1623–36.
DUBOIS, Marin. LXXIII, missed.
rue Saint-Jacques, paroisse Saint-Benoît. 1589–1637.
DUCHESNE, Guillaume. CV, 377–79.
rue Saint-Antoine. 1608–46.
DUPUYS, Jean. XXXIV, 50–51.
rue de la Vieille-Draperie. 1616–48.

FIEFFE, Pierre. LXII, 125–26.
  rue Saint-Antoine, paroisse Saint-Paul. 1605–51.
FONTAINE, Jean. CXVIII, 856–57.
  rue Saint-Germain-l'Auxerrois. 1613–32.
FOURNIER, Mathurin. III, 544–45.
  rue de la Tisseranderie. 1630–43.
GARNON, Absalon. LXIV, 46–47.
  rue de la Harpe. 1606–31.
GAULTIER, Olivier. LXVIII, 116.
  rue Barre-du-Bec, paroisse Saint-Merri. 1630–34.
GERBAULT, Etienne. II, 131–32.
  rue Saint-Jacques-de-la-Boucherie, au coin de la rue du Crucifix, au Crucifix
  Saint-Jacques. 1605–60.
GRANDRYE, Pierre I. V, 74–75.
  rue de la Tisseranderie, près la ville de Troyes. 1608–45.
GROYN, Michel. CXVII, 493.
  rue Saint-Antoine, devant le Petit-Saint-Antoine, puis porte
  Baudoyer. 1623–63.
GUERREAU, Pierre. LXXXVI, 211.
  rue de la Ferronnerie. 1599–1630.
GUYON, André. XXX, 12.
  rue Vieille-du-Temple, paroisse Saint-Gervais. 1618–68.
HAGUENIER, Martin. X, no wills for 1630.
  rue Saint-Denis, près l'église Saint-Leu-Saint–Gilles, associated with Pierre
  Huart. 1606–38.
HAULTDESENS, Laurent. LIV, 515–16.
  rue de la Verrerie. 1596–1632.
HERBIN, Guillaume, le jeune. LI, 93–95.
  rue Sainte-Avoie, paroisse Saint-Merri. 1600–36.
HUART, Claude. IX, 360–63.
  rue Saint-Martin, au coin de la rue Garnier-Saint-Ladre. 1609–31.
HUART, Pierre. XLIX, no wills for 1630.
  rue Saint-Jacques, paroisse Saint-Séverin. 1629–79.
HUART, Pierre. X, no wills for 1630.
  rue Saint-Denis, près l'église Saint-Leu-Saint-Gilles. 1606–42.
JOLLY, Nicolas. XXXVI, 122.
  rue Saint-Denis, devant les Saints-Innocents. 1590–1631.
JUTET, Fiacre. VIII, 630–32.
  rue de la Vieille-Draperie. 1622–32.
[LE BOUCHER, Nicolas.]
LE BOUCHER, Nicolas. LXXVIII, 231–32.
  rue des Marmousets, paroisse de la Madeleine. 1604–57.
LE CAMUS, Jean. LIX, 86–95.
  no address. 1628–34.

LE CAMUS, Louis. XIV, 36.
 rue du Temple, paroisse Saint-Nicolas-des-Champs. 1605–37.
LE CAT, Philippe. XVI, missed.
 rue des Prouvaires, à la Corne de cerf. 1629–62.
LECONTE, Louis. LXX, 93–94.
 Saint-Leu-Saint-Gilles. 1597–1630.
LEGAY, Jacques. XCII, 59–60.
 rue des Boucheries, paroisse Saint-Sulpice. 1605–53.
LE MERCIER, Simon. VII, 19.
 rue de l'Arbre-Sec, près la Croix-du-Trahoir, à côté de la Chèvre-qui-paît.
 1611–46.
LEMOYNE, Antoine. XXIX, 38–39.
 rue Saint-Séverin. 1563–1639.
LEMOYNE, François. CX, 76.
 carrefour Saint-Séverin. 1609–40.
LEMOYNE, François. XXXIII, l'Hôtel Dieu wills only.
 rue Saint-Séverin. 1614–38.
LEOMON, Etienne. LXXXVII, 101.
 rue Saint-Honoré, place aux Chats, paroisse Saint-Eustache. 1591–
 1637.
LE ROUX, Guillaume. XX, 196–97.
 pointe Sainte-Eustache. 1630–63.
LE ROUX, Pierre. XX, 175.
 pointe Saint-Eustache. 1589–1630.
LEROY, Claude. LXXVII, 460–63.
 rue Saint-Antoine, devant Saint-Paul. 1618–69.
LEROY, Etienne. VI, 441–42.
 rue des Fossés-Saint-Germain-des-Prés. 1609–41.
LESTORE, Charles. LXXXV, 130.
 rue et paroisse Saint-Jacques-de-la-Boucherie. 1622–55.
LE VASSEUR, Claude. XXXV, 208.
 pointe Saint-Eustache. 1599–1645.
LE VASSEUR, Claude. XX, no wills for 1630.
 pointe Saint-Eustache. 1609–41.
LEVASSEUR, Jean. XLV, 167.
 rue Saint-Honoré, paroisse Saint-Eustache. 1629–85.
LEVOYER, Claude. XII, 60.
 rue de la Tisseranderie, à la porte Baudoyer. 1587–1637.
LYBAULT, Martin. CV, 279–81.
 rue Sainte-Avoie, paroisse Saint-Merri. 1607–31.
MACE, Jacques. CV, no wills for 1630.
 rue aux Ours. 1628–37.
MARION, Gilles. CXV, 59–60.
 rue Saint-Germain-l'Auxerrois. 1617–51.

MARREAU, Jean. XCVII, 105–6.
    rue Neuve-Saint-Lambert, paroisse Saint-Sulpice. 1627–61.
MENARD, Claude I. XXIX, 62.
    rue Saint-Denis, au coin de la rue Aubri-le-Boucher. 1611–45.
MONTHENAULT, Jean de. XXVI, 55.
    rue des Barres. 1619–55.
MONROUSSEL, Antoine de. CIX, 156.
    rue Saint-Jacques. 1609–39.
MOREL, Jacques. XLII, 77–78.
    rue Saint-Honoré, paroisse Saint-Germain-l'Auxerrois. 1605–52.
MOTELET, Nicolas. XC, 192.
    rue de Poitou, au coin de la rue d'Orléans. 1619–30.
MOUFLE, Simon I. LXI, 180.
    rue Comtesse d'Artois, au carrefour de la pointe Saint-Eustache. 1604–38.
NOURRY, Nicolas. XVII, 210–13.
    rue Sainte-Geneviève, devant les Carmes, à la Petite Pomme rouge. 1592–
    1644.
OGIER, François I. LXXXIII, 12–13.
    rue Saint-Honoré, paroisse Saint-Eustache. 1622–31.
PAISANT, Etienne. LXVI, 59–60.
    rue de la Vieille-Draperie, paroisse Saint-Pierre-des-Arcis. 1611–60.
PARQUE, Jacques. VI, 325–26.
    au Marché-Neuf. 1605–40.
PARQUE, Pierre I. LXXXVI, missed.
    rue de la Ferronnerie. 1612–63.
PERIER, VENANT, Michel, and LE SUEUR, Martin. CXIV, no wills for 1630.
    banlieue (?). 1601–56.
PERIER, Philippe. XI, 125.
    place Maubert, au Cheval blanc. 1626–44.
PERLIN, Claude. CV, 579.
    à Saint-Germain-des-Prés, paroisse Saint-Sulpice. 1618–31.
PETIT, Simon. LXX, 105.
    rue du Temple, paroisse Saint-Nicolas-des-Champs, rue Neuve-Montmartre.
    1630–39.
POICTEVIN, Louis. XLIII, 7–8.
    rue Saint-Jacques, au cloître Saint-Benoît. 1624–35.
POURCEL, Louis. LXIX, only 18 documents for whole period; skipped.
    rue aux Ours. 1623–31.
REMOND, Guy. XVI, 60–61.
    rue Saint-Martin, près la rue Maubué. 1620–63.
RICHER, Charles. LI, 158–60.
    rue Sainte-Avoie. 1607–58.
ROBINOT, Nicolas. LXXXVIII, brevets only.
    no address. 1624–45.

ROBINOT, Nicolas. LXXXVIII, 90–91.
  rue du Temple, paroisse Saint-Nicolas-des-Champs. 1588–1646.
SAINT-FUSSIEN, Jacques de. XCIX, 129–31.
  rue Saint-Martin, paroisse Saint-Nicolas-des-Champs. 1614–35.
SAINT-VAAST, Charles-François de. LXXIII, 320–23.
  rue Saint-André-des-Arts. 1621–67.
SAINT-VAAST, Jacques de. LXXIII, 199.
  rue Saint-Jacques, paroisse Saint-Benoît. 1589–1637.
THEVENIN, Jean. XCI, 199.
  rue Saint-Martin, paroisse Saint-Merri. 1588–1631.
TOLLERON, Etienne. LXXII, no wills for 1630.
  rue Saint-Antoine, paroisse Saint-Paul. 1615–40.
TRONSON, Germain. I, 99–100.
  carrefour du pont Saint-Michel, à l'Ecu de Vendôme. 1598–1657.
TROYES, Hector de. CXXII, 1619–20.
  rue Saint-André-des-Arts. 1625–31.
TULLOUE, Robert. XXIV, 395.
  rue Saint-Germain-l'Auxerrois, au coin de la rue des Lavandières. 1606–38.
TURGIS, Denis. XLV, 50–51.
  rue Saint-Honoré, au cloître de l'église. 1603–33.
VASSETZ, Thomas. LXXXIV, 88–89.
  rue des Marmousets, au coin de la rue de Perpignan. 1618–42.
VAUTIER, Renault. CXII, 15–16.
  rue Saint-Séverin. 1623–57.
VIGEON, Antoine. LXII, 66.
  rue Saint-Antoine, paroisse Saint-Paul. 1618–40.

II. Other Primary Sources

Auger, Emond. *Metanoeologie*. Paris: Jamet Mettayer, 1584.
———. *Les Statuts de la Congrégation des penitens de l'Annonciation de Nostre Dame,
  par le commandement et privilege du roi*. 1583. Reprinted in *Archives curieuses de
  l'histoire de France*, vol. 10. Ed. H. L. Cimber and F. Danjou. Paris: Beauvais,
  1836.
Benoist, René. *Catholicque et utile discours des chandelles, torches et tout autre usage
  de feu en la profession de la foy et religion chrestienne*. Paris: G. Chaudière, 1566.
———. *Traicté de la messe qui est le sacrifice evangelique*. Paris: N. Chesneau, 1564.
Boileau, Jacques. *Histoire des flagellans, ou l'on fait voir le bon et le mauvais usage des
  flagellations parmi les chrétiens*. . . . Amsterdam: François van der Plaats, 1701.
Bonnardot, François, ed. *Registres de délibérations du bureau de la ville de Paris (1586–
  1590)*. Vol. 9. Paris: Imprimerie Nationale, 1902.
Bourbon, Cardinal. *Pardon octroyé par monseigneur le reverendissime cardinal de Bour-
  bon à la maison de la charité chrestienne establie ez faubourgs Saint Marcel*. In

Histoire de la Ville de Paris, vol. 3. Ed. Michel Félibien and Guy-Alexis Lobineau. Paris: G. Desprez and J. Desessartz, 1725.

Bourgoing, Edmond. *Discours veritable de l'estrange et subite mort de Henry de Valois.* . . . Lyon: Jehan Pillehotte, 1589. Lb[34]793.

Bullarum diplomatum et privilegiorum sanctorum romanorum pontificum taurinensis editio locupletior facta collectione novissima plurium brevium, epistolarum, decretorum actorumque S. Sedis a S. Leone Magno usque. . . . Turin: Seb. Franco and Henrico Dalmazzo, 1870.

Calvin, Jean. *Petit Traicté de la saincte cene de nostre seigneur Jesus Christ.* In *Three French Treatises.* Ed. Francis M. Higman. London: The Athlone Press, 1970.

———. *Short Treatise on the Holy Supper of Our Lord Jesus Christ.* In *John Calvin: Selections from His Writings.* Ed., trans., John Dillenberger. New York: Anchor Books, 1971.

Cayet, Palma. *Chronologie novenaire contenant l'histoire de la guerre et les choses les plus mémorables advenues sous le règne de Henri IV (1589–1598).* In *Nouvelle Collection des mémoires relatifs à l'histoire de France.* Ed. J. Michaud and B. Poujolat. Vol. 11. Paris: Féchoz and Letouzey, 1854.

———. *Chronologie novenaire contenant l'histoire de la guerre et les choses les plus mémorables advenues sous le règne de Henri IV (1589–1598).* In *Collection complète des mémoires relatifs à l'histoire de France.* Ed. M. Petitot. Paris: Foucault, 1823.

———. *Chronologie septenaire de l'histoire de la paix entre les roys de France et d'Espagne* . . . *(1598–1604).* Paris: Jean Richer, 1605.

Cheffonteines, C. de. *Apologie de la confrérie des penitens erigée et instituée en la ville de Paris.* . . . Paris: Michel Jouin, 1588. Lb[34]216.

Collin, N. *Traité des confréries.* Paris: 1784.

Copie de la requeste présentée par le clergé à Mr. le duc de maienne. . . . MS fr. 2751, Bibliothèque Nationale, Paris.

Cotgrave, R. *A Dictionarie of the French and English Tongues.* 1611. Reprint, 2nd ed. Columbia, S.C.: University of South Carolina Press, 1950.

Cromé, François. *Dialogue d'entre le Maheustre de le manant: Contenant les raisons de leurs debats and questions en les presens troubles au Royaume de France.* Ed. Peter M. Ascoli. Geneva: Droz, 1977.

de Soulas, G. D. S. *Discours au roy pour la reception du Concile de Trente: Contre ceux qui s'efforcent de l'empescher. Ou il est prouvé que l'un des meilleurs moyens d'arrester le cours des hérésies, est de faire valoir Conciles Generaux.* Paris: Chez Jean petit-pas rue Saint-Jaques à l'Escu de Venise près les Mathurins, 1615.

The Despatches of Michele Suriano and Marc Antonio Barbaro, Venetian Ambassadors at the Court of France: 1560–1563. Publications of the Huguenot Society of London, vol. 6. Lymington: The Huguenot Society of London, 1891.

Exercices spirituels pour les confrères et soeurs de la Confrérie du Très-Saint Sacrement première érigée en l'église paroissale de Saint Jacques de la Boucherie. Bibliothèque historique de la ville de Paris, 1718.

Fayet, Pierre. *Journal historique de Pierre Fayet sur les troubles de la Ligue.* Ed. Victor Luzarche. Tours: Ladevèze, 1852.

Félibien, Michel, and Guy-Alexis Lobineau. *Histoire de la ville de Paris*. Vols. 2–3. Paris: G. Desprez and J. Desessartz, 1725.

———. *Recueil de pieces justificatives pour servir à l'histoire de Paris*. Paris: G. Desprez and J. Desessartz, 1725.

Fosse, Jean-Baptiste de la. *Journal d'un curé ligueur de Paris sous les trois derniers Valois*. Ed. Edouard de Barthélemy. Paris: n.p., 1866.

François of Paris. *Journal de François, bourgeois de Paris, 23 décembre 1588–30 avril 1589*. Ed. Eugene Saulnier. Paris: E. Léroux, 1913.

Génébrard, Gilbert. *Excommunication des ecclésiastiques*. Paris: Gilles Gourbin, 1589. Lb³⁴661, Bibliothèque Nationale, Paris.

Gondy, Henri, Cardinal de Retz. *Réglemens faicts de l'authorité de Mgr . . . Cardinal de Retz . . . contenans l'explication de quelques articles des statuts synodaux de son diocése*. Paris: François Julliot, 1620. In *Synodicon* 1674.

Gondy, Pierre de. *Statuta a Petro de Gondy, episcopum Parisiensem, in synodo parisiensi renovata, anno 1585*. MS fr. 5570, Bibliothèque Nationale, Paris.

———. *Statuta reverendi in Christo Patris domini Petri de Gondy, episcopi parisiensis edita in syncdo anno D. 1582*. MS fr. 4719, Bibliothèque Nationale, Paris.

Grégoire, G. *Explication des cérémonies de la Fête-Dieu d'Aix-en-Provence*. Aix: Esprit David, 1770.

Haton, Claude. *Mémoires de Claude Haton contenant le recit des événements accomplis de 1533 à 1582, principalement dans la Champagne et la Brie*. Ed. Felix Bourquelot. Paris: Imprimerie Impériale, 1857.

"Histoire abregée des singeries de la Ligue, dediée à messieurs de Paris." In *Satyre ménipée de la vertu de catholicon d'Espagne et de la tenue des estatz de Paris*. Rev. ed. Geneva: Slatkine Reprints, 1971.

Histoire des singeries de la Ligue. "Recueil des pièces sur la Ligue." [Sixteenth-century collection of satirical material.] MS 533, Bibliothèque historique de la ville de Paris.

Houel, Nicolas. *Advertissement et declaration de l'institution de la maison de la charité-chrestienne . . . (1580)*. In *Histoire de la Ville de Paris*. Ed. Michel Félibien and Guy-Alexis Lobineau. Vol. 3. Paris: G. Desprez and J. Desessartz, 1725.

Instruction pour les confraires de la confrairie de S. Sacrement de l'autel, estably à Bordeaux, avec les articles, qui doivent estre gardez par tous ceux qui sont de ladite confrairie. Bordeaux: S. Millanges, 1577.

"Journal d'un bourgeois de Paris." *A Parisian Journal, 1405–1449*. Trans. Janet Shirley. Oxford: Clarendon Press, 1968.

Lamoignon, Guillaume de. *Recueil des arrêts de M. le premier président de Lamoignon*. Paris: Chez Merlin, 1772.

L'Estoile, Pierre de. *Journal de l'Estoile pour le règne de Henri III (1574–1589)*. Ed. Louis-Raymond Lefèvre. Paris: Gallimard, 1948.

———. *Journal de l'Estoile pour le règne de Henri IV (1589–1600)*. Ed. Louis-Raymond Lefèvre. Paris: Gallimard, 1948.

Livre et registre de la Congrégation du Monastère de St. Bernard des Feuillants. MS fr. 11767, folio 24, Bibliothèque Nationale, Paris.

Moréri, Louis. *Le grand dictionnaire historique, ou le melange curieux de l'histoire sacrée et profane.* . . . Utrecht: F. Halma and P. Mortier, 1692.

Ordonnance et advertissement de m. l'archevesque de Vienne à tous medecins, chirurgiens, apothicaires et barbiers de ses diocese, province et primace servant d'addresse, publication et intimation, à la bulle de feu pape Pie V . . . ce qu'ils doivent observer envers les malades, pour cooperer au salut des ames. Lyon: Jean Pilehotte, 1593. Bibliothèque Ste. Geneviève Réserve, 1.712 E 3.101.

Pasquier, Etienne. *Lettres historiques pour les années 1556–1594.* Ed. D. Thickett. Geneva: Droz, 1966.

Piganiole de la Force, Jean-Aimar. *Description historique de la ville de Paris et ses environs.* Vol. 2. Paris: Les Libraires associés, 1765.

Savaron, Jean. *Traitté contre les masques.* . . . Paris: Périer, 1608.

———. *Traitté des confrairies.* Paris: Périer, 1604.

Serment d'union de la Ligue. MS 3737, Bibliothèque de l'Arsenal.

Thiers, Jean Baptiste. *Critique de l'histoire des flagellans et de justification de l'usage des disciplines volontaires.* Paris: Jean de Nully, 1703.

———. *Traité des superstitions qui regardent les sacremens.* Paris: Jean de Nully, 1704.

Thou, Jacques-Auguste de. *Histoire universelle de Jacques-Auguste de Thou, depuis 1543 jusqu'à 1607.* Basle: Jean Louis Brandmuller, 1742.

———. *Histoire universelle de Jacques-Auguste de Thou, depuis 1543, jusqu'en 1607.* Ed., trans., Pierre-François Guyot, M. l'abbé Desfontaines, et al. London, 1734.

Valois, Charles, Ed. *Histoire de la Ligue. Oeuvre inédite d'un contemporain.* Vol. 1, *1574–1589.* La Société de l'histoire de France, 365. Paris: n.p., 1914.

III. Secondary Sources

Adam, Antoine. *Sur le Problème religieux dans la première moitié du XVIIe siècle.* Oxford: Clarendon Press, 1959.

Agnew, Jean-Christophe. *Worlds Apart: The Market and the Theater in Anglo-American Thought, 1550–1750.* Cambridge: Cambridge University Press, 1986.

Alberigo, G. "The Council of Trent: New Views on the Occasion of its Fourth Centenary." *Concilium* 7 (1965): 38–48.

Allier, Raoul. *La Cabale des dévots, 1627–1666.* 1902. Reprint, Geneva: Slatkine Reprints, 1970.

———. *La Compagnie du très Saint-Sacrement.* Paris: Armand Colin, 1902.

Anderson, Benedict. *Imagined Communities: Reflections on the Origin and Spread of Nationalism.* 2nd ed. London and New York: Verso, 1991.

Anquetil, Louis. *L'Esprit de la Ligue ou histoire politique des troubles de la France pendant les XVIe et XVIIe siècles.* Paris: Janet et Cotelle, 1818.

Ariès, Philippe. *The Hour of Our Death.* Trans. Helen Weaver. New York: Alfred A. Knopf, 1981. Originally published as *L'Homme devant la mort.* Paris: Seuil, 1977.

Artonne, André, Louis Guizard, and Odette Pontal. *Répertoire des statuts synodaux des diocèses de l'ancienne France du XIIIe à la fin du XVIIIe siècle.* Paris: CNRS: Documents, Etudes et Répertoires, 1966.

Ascoli, Peter M. "The Sixteen and the Paris League, 1585–1591." Ph.D. diss., University of California–Berkeley, 1972.

Aubert, Félix. "Le Parlement et la ville de Paris au XVIe siècle." *Revue des études historiques* 71 (1905).

Auffroy, H. *Evolution du testament en France des origines au XIIIe siècle.* Thèse de doctorat. Paris, 1911.

Avril, Joseph. "La Pastorale des malades et des mourants aux XIIe et XIIIe siècles." In *Death in the Middle Ages.* Ed. Herman Braet and Werner Verbeke. Louvain: Leuven University Press, 1983.

Bailly, Paul. "Flagellants." In *Dictionnaire de spiritualité.* Paris: G. Beauchesne, 1937.

Bakhtin, Mikhail. *Rabelais and His World.* Trans. Hélène Iswolsky. Bloomington, Indiana: University of Indiana Press, 1984.

Barel, Yves. *La Ville médiévale, système social, système urbain.* Grenoble: Presses Universitaires de Grenoble, 1975.

Barnavi, Elie. *Le Parti de Dieu: Etude sociale et politique des chefs de la Ligue parisienne, 1585–1594.* Louvain: Nauwelaerts, 1980.

Barnavi, Elie, and Robert Descimon. "La Ligue à Paris (1585–1594): Une révision." *Annales: Economies, Sociétés, Civilisations* 37 (1982): 72–130.

———. *La Sainte Ligue, le juge et la potence: L'assassinat du président Brisson (15 novembre 1591).* Paris: Hachette, 1985.

Barnes, Andrew E. "Cliques and Participation: Organizational Dynamics in the Penitents Bourras." *Journal of Interdisciplinary History* 19 (1988): 25–53.

———. "De poenitentibus civitatis Massaliae: The Counter Reformation, Religious Change and the Confraternities of Penitents of Marseille, 1499–1792." Ph.D. diss., Princeton, 1983.

———. "Religious Anxiety and Devotional Change in Seventeenth-Century French Penitential Confraternities." *Sixteenth Century Journal* 19 (1988): 389–405.

———. "The Wars of Religion and the Origins of Reformed Confraternities of Penitents. A Theoretical Approach." *Archives de sciences sociales des religions* 32 (1987): 117–36.

Baumgartner, Frederic J. *Henry II, King of France, 1547–1559.* Durham, N.C.: Duke University Press, 1980.

———. *Radical Reactionaries: The Political Thought of the French Catholic League.* Geneva: Droz, 1976.

Beame, Edmond M. "The Development of Politique Thought during the French Religious Wars (1560–1595)." Ph.D. diss., University of Illinois, 1957.

———. "The Politiques and the Historians." *Journal of the History of Ideas* 54 (July 1993): 335–60.

Beaumont-Maillet, Laure. *Le Grand Couvent des cordeliers de Paris: Etude historique et archéologique du XIIIe siècle à nos jours.* Paris: Champion, 1975.

Bell, David A. *Lawyers and Citizens: The Making of a Political Elite in Old Regime France.* Oxford: Oxford University Press, 1994.

————. "Unmasking a King: The Political Uses of Popular Literature under the French Catholic League, 1588–1589." *Sixteenth Century Journal* 20 (1989): 371–86.

Benedict, Philip. "The Catholic Response to Protestantism: Church Activity and Popular Piety in Rouen, 1560–1600." In *Religion and the People, 800–1700.* Ed. James Obelkevich. Chapel Hill, N.C.: University of North Carolina Press, 1979.

————. *Rouen during the Wars of Religion.* Cambridge: Cambridge University Press, 1981.

Benichou, Paul. *Man and Ethics: Studies in French Classicism.* Garden City, N.Y.: Anchor Books, 1971.

Bercé, Yves-Marie. *Fête et révolte: Des mentalités populaires du XVIe au XVIIIe siècle.* Paris: Hachette, 1976.

Berman, Morris. *Coming to Our Senses: Body and Spirit in the Hidden History of the West.* London: Urwin Paperbacks, 1989.

Bernard, Leon. *The Emerging City: Paris in the Age of Louis XIV.* Durham, N.C.: Duke University Press, 1970.

Bloch, Jean-Richard. *L'Anoblissement en France au temps de François Ier: Essai d'une définition de la condition juridique et sociale de la noblesse au début du XVIe siècle.* Paris: F. Alcan, 1934.

Boggis, Robert James Edmund. *Praying for the Dead: An Historical Review of the Practice.* London, New York, Bombay, and Calcutta: Longmans, Green and Co., 1913.

Bordo, Susan R. *The Flight to Objectivity: Essays on Cartesianism and Culture.* SUNY Series in Philosophy. Albany, N.Y.: State University of New York Press, 1987.

Bossy, John. "Blood and Baptism: Kinship, Community and Christianity in Western Europe from the Fourteenth to the Seventeenth Centuries." In *Sanctity and Secularity: The Church and the World.* Studies in Church History, vol. 10. D. Baker, ed. New York: Barnes and Noble, 1973.

————. *Christianity in the West: 1400–1700.* Oxford and New York: Oxford University Press, 1985.

————. "The Counter-Reformation and the People of Catholic Europe." *Past and Present* 47 (1970): 51–70.

————. "Holiness and Society." *Past and Present* 75 (1977): 119–37.

————. "The Mass as a Social Institution 1200–1700." *Past and Present* 100 (August 1983): 29–61.

Boucher, Jacqueline. "Société et mentalités autour de Henri III." 4 Vols. Ph.D. diss., l'Atelier de Réproduction des Thèses, Université de Lille III. Paris: Champion, 1981.

Bourgeon, Jean-Louis. "Pour une histoire, enfin, de la Saint-Barthélemy." *Revue historique* 282 (1989): 83–142.

Brémond, Henri. *Histoire littéraire du sentiment religieux en France: Depuis la fin des guerres de religion jusqu'à nos jours.* 1923. Reprint, 11 vols. Paris: Librairie Armand Colin, 1967.

Briggs, Robin. *Communities of Belief*. Oxford: Clarendon Press, 1989.

Brochard, Louis. *Saint-Gervais: Histoire de la paroisse*. Paris: Firmin-Didot, 1950.

Broutin, P. S. J. *La Réforme pastorale en France au XVIIe siècle: Recherches sur la tradition pastorale après le concile de Trente*. Paris, Tournai, New York, and Rome: Desclée, 1956.

Browe, P. "Die letzte Ölung in den abendländischen Kirchen des Mittelalters." *Zeitschrift für katholische Theologie* 55 (1931).

———. "Die Sterbekommunion im Altertum und Mittelalter." *Zeitschrift für katholische Theologie* 60 (1936): 1–54; 210–40.

Brown, Peter. *The Body and Society: Men, Women, and Sexual Renunciation in Early Christianity*. New York: Columbia University Press, 1988.

Brunet, Emmanuel. *Les Compagnies de charité*. Thèse, Paris, 1903.

Bruno, Jésus Marie de. *Madame Acarie, épouse et mystique*. Paris: Buges & Paris, 1937.

Bryant, Lawrence M. *The King and the City in the Parisian Royal Entry Ceremony*. Geneva: Droz, 1986.

Buisseret, David. *Henry IV*. London and Boston: G. Allen and Unwin, 1984.

Burke, Peter. "How to Be a Counter-Reformation Saint." In *Religion and Society in Early Modern Europe, 1500–1800*. Ed. Kasper von Greyerz, 45–55. London: German Historical Institute, 1984.

———. *Popular Culture in Early Modern Europe*. London: Temple Smith, 1978.

Busquet, Raoul. "Etude historique sur le collège de Fortet (1394–1764)." Parts 1 and 2. *Mémoires de la Société de l'Histoire de Paris et de l'Ile de France* 33 (1906): 187–290; 34 (1907): 1–151.

Butler, Judith. *Bodies That Matter: On the Discursive Limits of Sex*. New York: Routledge, 1993.

Bynum, Caroline Walker. *Fragmentation and Redemption*. New York: Zone Books, 1991.

———. *Holy Feast and Holy Fast: The Religious Significance of Food to Medieval Women*. Berkeley and Los Angeles: University of California Press, 1987.

———. *The Resurrection of the Body in Western Christianity, 200–1336*. New York: Columbia University Press, 1995.

Cabourdin, Guy, and Georges Vidal. *Lexique historique de la France de l'ancien régime*. 2nd Ed. Paris: Librairie Armand Colin, 1981.

Callaery, Frédégard. "Infiltration des idées franciscaines spirituelles chez les frères mineurs-capucins au XVIe siècle." In *Miscellanea Francesco Ehrle*. Vol. 1. Rome: Biblioteca Apostolica Vaticana, 1943.

Carrière, Victor. *Introduction aux études d'histoire ecclésiastique locale*. Paris: Letouzey et Ané, 1934–1940.

Centre de Pastorale Liturgique. *Le Mystère de la mort et sa célébration*. 1956.

Chatellier, Louis. *L'Europe des dévots*. Paris: Flammarion, 1987.

———. *The Europe of the Devout: The Catholic Reformation and the Formation of a New Society*. Trans. Jean Birrell. Cambridge: Cambridge University Press, 1989.

———. *La Religion des pauvres: Les sources du christianisme moderne, XVIe–XIXe siècles*. Paris: Aubier, 1993.

Chaunu, Pierre. *La Mort à Paris: XVIe, XVIIe et XVIIIe siècles.* Paris: Librairie Arthème Fayard, 1978.

———. "Un Nouveau Champ pour l'histoire sérielle: Le quantitatif au troisième niveau." In *Mélanges Fernand Braudel.* Vol. 2. Toulouse: Privat, 1973.

———, ed. *The Reformation.* New York: St. Martin's Press, 1990.

Chauvet, Louis-Marie, and François Kabasele Lumbala. "Liturgy and the Body." *Concilium* 3 (1995).

Chenu, M. D. *Nature, Man, and Society in the Twelfth Century. Essays on New Theological Perspectives in the Latin West.* Ed., trans. Jerome Taylor and Lester K. Little. Chicago and London: University of Chicago Press, 1968.

Chevalier, Bernard. *Les Bonnes Villes de France du XIVe au XVIe siècle.* Paris: Aubier Montaigne, 1982.

———. "L'Etat et les bonnes villes en France au temps de leur accord parfait (1450–1550)." In *La Ville, la bourgeoisie et la genèse de l'état moderne (XIIe–XVIIIe siècles). Actes du Colloque de Bielefeld, 30 novembre–1er décembre 1985.* Paris: CNRS, 1988.

Chevalier, Pierre. *Henri III.* Paris: Fayard, 1985.

Chiffoleau, Jacques. *La Comptabilité de l'au-delà: Les hommes, la mort et la religion dans la région d'Avignon à la fin du moyen-âge (vers 1320–vers 1480).* Collection de l'Ecole Française de Rome, vol. 47. Rome: n.p., 1980.

Christian, William A. Jr. *Local Religion in Sixteenth-Century Spain.* Princeton, N.J.: Princeton University Press, 1981.

Church, William F. *Constitutional Thought in Sixteenth-Century France: A Study in the Evolution of Ideas.* 1941. Reprint, New York: Octagon Books, 1969.

Citron, Suzanne. *Le Mythe national: L'histoire de France en question.* Paris: Les Editions Ouvrières, 1989.

Clark, George Norman. *The Seventeenth Century.* New York: Oxford University Press, 1961.

Cochois, Paul. *Bérulle et l'école française.* Paris: Seuil, 1963.

Cognet, Louis. *Les Origines de la spiritualité française au XVIIe siècle.* Paris: Fayard, 1949.

Commission des travaux historiques. *Répertoire des travaux publiés par les sociétés d'histoire de Paris du 1er janvier 1912 au 31 décembre 1980.* Paris, 1987.

Constant, Jean-Marie. *Les Guise.* Paris: Hachette, 1984.

———. *La Ligue.* Paris: Fayard, 1996.

Crévier, Jean Baptiste Louis. *Histoire de l'Université de Paris, depuis son origine jusqu'à l'année 1600.* Paris: Desaint and Saillant, 1761.

Crimando, Thomas I. "Two French Views of the Council of Trent." *Sixteenth Century Journal* 19 (1988): 169–86.

Croix, Alain. *La Bretagne aux XVIe et XVIIe siècles: La vie, la mort, la foi.* Paris: Maloine, 1981.

Crouzet, Denis. *Les Guerriers de Dieu.* 2 vols. n.p.: Champ Vallon, 1990.

———. *La Nuit de la Saint-Barthélemy: Un rêve perdu de la renaissance.* Paris: Fayard, 1994.

———. "Recherches sur les processions blanches 1583–1584." *Histoire, économie et société* 4 (1982): 511–63.

———. "La Représentation du temps à l'époque de la Ligue." *Revue historique* 548 (1983): 297–388.

———. "La Violence au temps des troubles de religion (vers 1525–1610)." Exposé de soutenance de thèse de doctorat d'Etat, Paris IV–Sorbonne, janvier 1989. *Histoire, économie et société* 8 (1989): 507–25.

———. *La Violence collective en France à l'époque des guerres de religion*. Mémoire de Maîtrise. Université de Paris–Sorbonne, 1975.

Cuthbert, Father O. F. M. *The Capucins: A Contribution to the History of the Counter-Reformation*. London: Sheed & Ward, 1928.

Dagens, Jean. *Bérulle et les origines de la restauration catholique (1575–1611)*. Bruges: Desclee de Brouwer, 1952.

Davis, Charles. *Theology for Today*. New York: Sheed & Ward, 1962.

Davis, Natalie Zemon. "Missed Connections: Religion and Regime." *Journal of Interdisciplinary History* 1 (1971): 381–94.

———. "The Sacred and the Body Social in Sixteenth-Century Lyon." *Past and Present* 90 (February 1981): 40–90.

———. *Society and Culture in Early Modern France*. Stanford: Stanford University Press, 1965.

de Certeau, Michel. *The Mystic Fable*. Vol. 1 of *The Sixteenth and Seventeenth Centuries*, Trans. Michael B. Smith. Chicago and London: University of Chicago Press, 1992. Original edition, Paris: Gallimard, 1982.

Delaruelle, Etienne. *La Piété populaire au moyen-âge*. Ed. R. Manselli and A. Vauchez. Turin: Bottega d'Erasmo, 1975.

Delaruelle, E., E. R. Labande, and Paul Ourliac, eds. *L'Eglise au temps du grande schisme et de la crise conciliare (1378–1449)*. Vol. 14 of *Histoire de l'église depuis les origines jusqu'à nos jours*. Paris: Bloud & Gay, 1962.

Delumeau, Jean. *L'Aveu et le pardon, les difficultés de la confession, XIIIe–XVIIIe siècles*. Paris: Librairie Arthème Fayard, 1990.

———. *Catholicism between Luther and Voltaire*. Trans. Jeremy Moiser. London: Burns and Oates, 1972. Originally published as *Le Catholicisme entre Luther et Voltaire*. Paris: Presses Universitaires de France, 1971.

———. *Un Chemin d'histoire: Chrétienté et christianisation*. Paris: Librairie Arthème Fayard, 1981.

———. "Une Histoire totale de la Renaissance." *The Journal of Medieval and Renaissance Studies* 22 (1992): 1–17.

———. *Histoire vécue du peuple chrétien*. Toulouse: Privat, 1979.

———. *Rassurer et protéger. Le Sentiment de sécurité dans l'occident d'autrefois*. Paris: Librairie Arthème Fayard, 1989.

———. *Sin and Fear: The Emergence of a Western Guilt Culture, 13th–18th Centuries*. Trans. Eric Nicholson. New York: St. Martin's, 1990.

Denis, Philippe. *Le Christ étendard: L'Homme-Dieu au temps des réformes (1500–1565)*. Paris: Ed. Cerf, 1987.

Deregnaucourt, Jean-Pierre. "Le Dernier Voyage: L'ambulation funèbre à Douai aux 14e et 15e siècles." *Actes du Colloque: La sociabilité urbaine en Europe du Nord-Ouest, Douai 1883, Mémoires de la Société d'Agriculture, Sciences et Arts de Douai* 8 (1883): 81–88.

———. "La Symbolique et sa signification dans le discours testamentaire des bourgeois de Douai à la fin du Moyen-Age." *Les Amis de Douai* 7 (1979): 224–29.

Deroo, André. *Saint Charles Borromée, cardinal réformateur, docteur de la pastorale, 1538–1584.* Paris: Saint-Paul, 1963.

Descimon, Robert. "Les Assemblées de l'hôtel de ville de Paris (mi-XVIe–XVIIe siècles)." *Mémoires de la Fédération des Sociétés Historiques et Archéologiques de Paris et de l'Ile-de-France* 30 (1987): 39–56.

———. "Les Barricades de la Fronde parisienne: Une lecture sociologique." *Annales: Economies, Sociétés, Civilisations* 45 (1990): 397–422.

———. "Le Corps de ville et le système cérémonial parisien au début de l'âge moderne." In *Statuts individuels, statuts corporatifs et statuts judiciaires dans les villes européennes (moyen-âge et temps modernes).* Ed. Marc Boone and Maarten Prak. Louvain: Garant, 1996.

———. "L'Echevinage parisien sous Henri IV (1594–1609): Autonomie urbaine, conflits politiques et exclusives sociales." *La Ville, la bourgeoisie et la genèse de l'état moderne (XIIe–XVIIIe siècles). Actes du Colloque de Bielefeld, 30 novembre–1er décembre 1985* (1988): 113–50.

———. "Henri III et Henri IV: Le triomphe dynastique." *L'Election du chef de l'état en France . . .* (1988): 45–61.

———. *Qui étaient les Seize? Mythes et réalités de la Ligue parisienne (1585–1594).* Mémoires de la Fédération des Sociétés Historiques et Archéologiques de Paris et de l'Ile-de-France, vol. 34. Paris: Klincksieck, 1983.

Desmarthes, Alice. *Histoire de la confrérie de la passion.* Paris: Ecole des Chartes, 1939.

Desmaze, Charles. *Le Châtelet de Paris, son organisation, ses privilèges: Prévôts, conseillers, chevalier de guet, notaires, etc.* Paris: Didier, 1870.

Deville, Raymond. *L'Ecole française de spiritualité (Bérulle, Condren, Olier, Saint Jean Eudes).* Paris: Desclée de Brouwer, 1987.

Dewald, Jonathan. "The 'Perfect Magistrate': Parlementaires and Crime in Sixteenth-Century Rouen." *Archiv für Reformationsgeschichte* 67 (1967): 284–300.

Deyon, Pierre. "Sur certaines formes de la propagande religieuse au XVIe siècle." *Annales: Economies, Sociétés, Civilisations* 36 (1981): 16–25.

di Corcia, Joseph. "*Bourg, Bourgeois, Bourgeois de Paris,* from the Eleventh to the Eighteenth Century." *Journal of Modern History* 5 (1978): 207–33.

Dictionnaire d'archéologie chrétienne et de liturgie. Paris: Librairie Letouzey et Ané, 1914.

Dictionnaire de la langue française du seizième siècle. Ed. Edmond Huguet. Paris: Librairie M. Didier, 1952.

Dictionnaire de théologie catholique. Ed. A. Vacant and E. Mangenot. Paris: Librairie Letouzey et Ané, 1920.

Dictionnaire historique de la langue française. Ed. Allain Rey. Paris: Dictionnaires le Robert, 1994.

Diefendorf, Barbara B. *Beneath the Cross: Catholics and Huguenots in Sixteenth-Century Paris*. New York: Oxford University Press, 1991.

————. "Give Us Back Our Children: Patriarchal Authority and Parental Consent to Religious Vocations in Early Counter-Reformation France." *The Journal of Modern History* 68 (1996): 265–307.

————. "Myths about the St. Bartholomew's Day Massacres, 1572–1576." *American Historical Review* 94 (1989): 782–83.

————. "Prologue to a Massacre: Popular Unrest in Paris, 1557–1572." *American Historical Review* 90 (1985): 1067–91.

————. "Recent Literature on the Religious Conflicts in Sixteenth-Century France." *Religious Studies Review* 10 (October 1984): 362–67.

————. Review Article, "The Catholic League: Social Crisis or Apocalypse Now?" *French Historical Studies* 15 (Fall 1987): 332–44.

————. Review of "Les Guerriers de Dieu: La violence au temps des troubles de religion, vers 1525–vers 1610, 2 vols." *American Historical Review* 99 (1994): 241–42.

Dompnier, Bernard. "Un Aspect de la dévotion eucharistique." *Revue d'histoire de l'eglise de France* 67 (1981): 5–31.

————. "Les Confréries des pénitents du Saint-Sacrement au XVIIe siècle: Essai de définition." *Cahiers d'histoire* 30 (1985): 263–88.

————. "Exercice et oisiveté chez les capucins." *Archives des sciences sociales des religions* (1994): 199–212.

————. *Le Venin de l'hérésie: Image du protestantisme et combat catholique au XVIIe siècle*. Paris: Le Centurion, 1985.

Douglas, Mary. *Purity and Danger: An Analysis of the Concepts of Pollution and Taboo*. London: Routledge & Kegan Paul, 1966.

Drouot, Henri. *Mayenne et la Bourgogne, 1587–1596. Contribution à l'histoire des provinces françaises pendant la Ligue*. Paris: Picard, 1937.

Duby, Georges, and Robert Mandrou. *Histoire de la civilisation française*. Vol. 2. Paris: Librairie Armand Colin, 1968.

Du Cange, Charles du Fresne. *Glossarium mediae et infinae latinitatis*. Graz, Akademische Druck- und Verlagsanstalt, 1954.

Duffy, Eamon. *The Stripping of the Altars: Traditional Religion in England 1400–1580*. New Haven and London: Yale University Press, 1992.

Dumoutet, Edouard. *Le Désir de voir l'hostie et les origines de la dévotion au Saint-Sacrement*. Paris: Gabriel Beauchesne, 1926.

Du Plessis, Robert S., and Martha C. Howell. "Reconsidering the Early Modern Urban Economy: The Cases of Leiden and Lille." *Past and Present* 94 (1982): 49–84.

Durkheim, Emile. *The Elementary Forms of Religious Life*. London: Allen and Unwin, 1961.

Duval, A. *Des Sacrements au concile de Trente*. Paris: Cerf, 1985.

Eire, Carlos M. N. *From Madrid to Purgatory: The Art and Craft of Dying in Sixteenth-Century Spain.* Cambridge: Cambridge University Press, 1995.

———. *War against the Idols: The Reformation of Worship from Erasmus to Calvin.* Cambridge: Cambridge University Press, 1986.

Ellington, Donna Spivey. "Impassioned Mother or Passive Icon: The Virgin's Role in Late Medieval and Early Modern Sermons." *Renaissance Quarterly* 48 (1995): 227–61.

Evennett, H. Outram. *The Cardinal of Lorraine and the Council of Trent.* Cambridge: Cambridge University Press, 1930.

———. *The Spirit of the Counter-Reformation.* Notre Dame and London: University of Notre Dame Press, 1968.

Faire croire: Modalités de la diffusion et de la réception des messages religieux du XIIe au XVe siècle, table ronde. Rome: Ecole française de Rome; Torino: Bottega d'Erasmo, 1981.

Farge, James K. *Biographical Register of Paris Doctors of Theology, 1500–1536.* Toronto: Pontifical Institute of Medieval Studies, 1980.

———. "Early Censorship in Paris: A New Look at the Roles of the Parlement of Paris and of King Francis I." *Renaissance and Reformation* 13 (1989): 173–83.

———. *Orthodoxy and Reform in the Early Reformation in France: The Faculty of Theology of Paris, 1500–1543.* Leiden: Brill, 1985.

Fischer, David Hackett. *The Great Wave: Price Revolutions and the Rhythm of History.* New York: Oxford University Press, 1998.

Febvre, Lucien. "Une Date: 1534. La Messe et les placards." In *Au Coeur religieux du XVIe siècle.* 2nd ed. Paris: Ecole Pratique des Hautes Etudes, 1957.

Feret, Pierre. *La Faculté de théologie de Paris et ses docteurs célèbres: Epoque moderne.* Paris: Picard, 1900.

Ferté, Jeanne. *La Vie religieuse: Dans les campagnes parisiennes (1622–1695).* Paris: J. Vrin, 1962.

Fleury, Antoinette. *Le Testament dans la coutume de Paris au XVI siècle.* Thèse, Ecole Nationale des Chartes. Nogent-le-Rotrou: Imprimerie Daupeley, 1943.

Forster, Marc. *The Counter-Reformation in the Villages: Religion and Reform in the Bishopric of Speyer, 1560–1720.* Ithaca and London: Cornell University Press, 1992.

Fosseyeux, M. "L'Assistance parisienne au milieu du XVIe siècle." *Bulletin de la Société de l'Histoire de Paris et de l'Ile de France* (1916): 83–128.

———. "Les Premiers budgets municipaux d'assistance." *Revue de l'histoire de l'église de France* (1934): 407–32.

Foucault, Michel. *Discipline and Punish: The Birth of the Prison.* Trans. Alan Sheridan. New York: Pantheon Books, 1977.

———. *Folie et déraison: Histoire de la folie à l'âge classique.* Paris: Plon, 1961.

Fouqueray, Henri. *Histoire de la compagnie de Jésus en France des origines à la suppression (1528–1762).* Reprint, Nendeln, Lichtenstein: Kraus, 1972.

France Métropolitaine Départements d'Outre-Mer. *Dictionnaire des communes.* Paris: Berger-Levrault, 1977.

Franklin, Alfred. *Paris et les parisiens au seizième siècle*. Paris: Emile Pul Frères, 1921.

————. *Les Rues de Paris sous Louis XIII*. Paris: Editions de Paris, 1988.

————, ed. *Dictionnaire historique des arts, métiers, et professions exercés dans Paris depuis le treizième siècle*. 1906. Reprint, New York: Burt Franklin, 1968.

Franz, Adolph. *Die Messe im deutschen Mittelalter: Beiträge zur Geschichte der Liturgie und des religiösen Volkslebens*. Darmstadt: Wissenschaftliche Buchgesellschaft, 1963.

Freedberg, David. *The Power of Images: Studies in the History and Theory of Response*. Chicago: University of Chicago Press, 1989.

Freud, Sigmund. *The Interpretation of Dreams*. Trans. James Strachey. New York: Basic Books, 1965.

Froger, J. "Le Concile de Trente: A-t-il prescrit de donner des explications en langue vulgaire pendant les cérémonies liturgiques?" *Ephemerides liturgicae*, 1959.

Gadille, J., D. Julia, and M. Venard. "Pour un Répertoire des visites pastorales." *Revue d'histoire de l'église de France* 55 (1969): 49–67.

Galot, Jean. *Le Coeur du Christ*. Tournai: Desclée de Brouwer, 1958.

Galpern, A. N. *The Religions of the People in Sixteenth-Century Champagne*. Cambridge: Harvard University Press, 1976.

Garrisson, Janine. "Tocsin pour un massacre: La saison des Saint-Barthélemy." Paris: Centurion, 1968.

Gascon, Richard. *Grand Commerce et vie urbaine au XVIe siècle: Lyon et ses marchands*. Paris: SEVPEN, 1971.

Gastaldi, Nadine. "Les Dévots laïcs au XVIIe siècle: usage et perception du temps." *Bulletin de la Société Française d'Histoire des Idées et d'Histoire Religieuse* 6 (1989): 15–36.

Gayne, Pierre. "Un de nos compatriotes oubliés: le moine-ligueur Bernard du Montgaillard." *Bulletin de la Société Archéologique du Tarn et Garonne* (1967–1970): 51–78.

Geertz, Clifford. *The Interpretation of Cultures*. New York: Basic Books, 1973.

————. *Local Knowledge: Further Essays in Interpretive Anthropology*. New York: Basic Books, 1983.

Geremeck, Bronislaw. "Paris: Moral Anxiety and Fear." In *Poverty: A History*. Trans. Agnieszka Kolakowska. Oxford: Blackwell, 1994.

Gibson, Ralph. "Rigorisme et liguorisme dans le diocèse de Périgueux, XVIIe–XIXe siècle." *Revue d'histoire de l'église de France* 75 (1989): 315–42.

Giesey, Ralph E. *The Royal Funeral Ceremony in Renaissance France*. Geneva: Droz, 1960.

Gilbert, Creighton. "Last Suppers and Their Refectories." In *The Pursuit of Holiness in Late Medieval and Renaissance Religion. Papers from the Michigan Conference*. Studies in Medieval and Reformation Thought, eds. Charles Trinkhaus and Heiko Oberman. Vol. 10. Leiden: Brill, 1974.

Ginzburg, Carlo. *The Cheese and the Worms: The Cosmos of a Sixteenth-Century Miller*. Trans. John and Anne Tedeschi. Harmondsworth: Penguin Books, 1980.

Godefroy, Frédéric. *Lexique de l'ancien français*. Paris: Champion, 1990.

Godefroy de Paris, Père. *Les Frères-mineurs capucins en France: Histoire de la province de Paris*. Paris: Bibliothèque Franciscaine Provinciale des FF. Min. Cap. de Paris, 1937.

Grégoire, Louis. *La Ligue en Bretagne*. Paris: J. B. Dumoulin, 1856.

Grell, Ole P., and Robert Scribner, eds. *Tolerance and Intolerance in the European Reformation*. New York: Cambridge University Press, 1996.

Guenée, Bernard. *States and Rulers in Later Medieval Europe*. Oxford: Basil Blackwell, 1988.

Guerin, Paul. *Registres des délibérations du Bureau de la Ville de Paris, vol. 8, 1576–1586*. Paris: Imprimerie Nationale: 1896.

Guibert, Louis. "Les Confréries des pénitents en France et notamment dans le diocèse de Limoges." *Bulletin de la Société Archéologique et Historique du Limousin* 27 (1879): 5–193.

Guiffrey. "Nicolas Houel, apothécaire parisien, fondateur de la maison de la charité chrétienne, et premier auteur de la teinture d'Artémise." *Mémoires de la Société de l'Histoire de Paris et de l'Ile de France* 15 (1898): 3–94.

Gutton, Jean-Pierre. *La Société et les pauvres: L'exemple de la généralité de Lyon, 1534–1789*. Paris: Société, 1971.

Haidu, Peter. *The Subject of Violence*. Bloomington: Indiana University Press, 1993.

Hamon, Auguste. *Histoire de la dévotion au sacré-cœur de Jésus*, 5 vols. Paris: Gabriel Beauchesne, 1923–1939.

Hanley, Sarah. "Women and the Body Politic in Early Modern France." *Proceedings of the Annual Meeting of the Western Society for French History* 16 (1989).

Harding, Robert. "The Mobilization of Confraternities against the Reformation in France." *Sixteenth Century Journal* 11 (1980): 85–107.

———. "Revolution and Reform in the Holy League: Angers, Rennes, Nantes." *Journal of Modern History* 53 (1981): 379–416.

Harper, John A. *The Forms and Orders of Western Liturgy from the Tenth to the Eighteenth Century: An Historical Introduction and Guide for Students and Musicians*. Oxford: Clarendon Press, 1991.

Heers, Jacques. *Fêtes, jeux, et joutes dans les sociétés d'occident à la fin du moyen-âge*. Paris: Vrin, 1982.

Hillairet, Jacques, ed. *Dictionnaire des rues de Paris*. 2 vols. Paris: Minuit, 1963.

Hoffmann, Philip T. *Church and Community in the Diocese of Lyon, 1500–1789*. New Haven: Yale University Press, 1984.

———. "Wills and Statistics: Tobit Analysis and the Counter Reformation in Lyon." *Journal of Interdisciplinary History* 14 (Spring 1984): 813–34.

Holt, Mack P. *The French Wars of Religion, 1562–1629*. Cambridge: Cambridge University Press, 1995.

Hopper, Vincent Foster. *Medieval Number Symbolism: Its Sources, Meaning, and Influence on Thought and Expression*. New York: Cooper Square Publishers, 1969.

Hsia, R. Po-Chia. *Social Discipline in the Reformation: Central Europe, 1550–1750*. London: Routledge, 1989.

Huizinga, Johan. *The Waning of the Middle Ages: A Study of the Forms of Life, Thought, and Art in France and the Netherlands in the Dawn of the Renaissance.* Trans. Rodney J. Payton and Ulrich Mammitzsch. Chicago: University of Chicago Press, 1996.

Iserloh, Erwin. "Das tridentinische Messoperdekret in seinen Beziehungen zu der Kontroversetheologie der Zeit." In *Wege der Forschung.* Vol. 313, *Concilium Tridentium.* Ed. Remigius Baumer. Darmstadt: Wissenschaftliche Buchgesellschaft, 1979.

James, M. E. "Ritual, Drama, and Social Body in Late Medieval English Towns." *Past and Present* 98 (1983).

James, William. *Varieties of Religious Experience.* New York: Modern Library, 1902.

Jedin, Hubert. *Geschichte des Konzils von Trient.* Freiburg im Breisgau: Herder, 1951.

———. *History of the Council of Trent.* London: Nelson, 1957–1961.

Jones, Cheslyn, et al., eds. *The Study of Liturgy.* New York: Oxford University Press, 1992.

Jouanna, Arlette. "Excommunication et mobilité sociale selon les ecclésiastiques ligueurs à Paris (1588–1594)." In *Les Eglises et leurs institutions au XVIème siècle: actes du 5ème colloque du Centre d'Histoire de la Réforme et du Protestantisme.* Ed. Michel Péronnet. Montpellier: Université Paul Valéry, 1978.

———. *L'Ordre social: Mythes et hiérarchies dans la France du XVIe siècle.* Paris: Hachette, 1977.

Julia, Dominique. "La Réforme posttridentine en France d'après les procès-verbaux de visites pastorales: Ordre et résistance." In *La Società religiosa nell'età moderna.* Naples: n.p., 1973.

Jungmann, Josef Andreas. *The Mass: An Historical, Theological, and Pastoral Survey.* Ed. Mary Ellen Evans. Trans. Julien Fernandes. Collegeville: Liturgical Press, 1976.

———. *Missarum Sollemnia: Eine genetische Erklärung der römischen Messe.* 2 vols. Vienna: Herder, 1952.

Jütte, Robert. *Poverty and Deviance in Early Modern Europe.* Cambridge: Cambridge University Press, 1994.

Kaiser, Colin. "Les Cours souveraines au XVIe siècle: morale et contre-réforme." *Annales: Economies, Sociétés, Civilisations* 37 (1982): 17–32.

Keating, L. Clark. *Etienne Pasquier.* New York: Twayne Publishers, 1972.

Kelley, Donald R. *The Beginning of Ideology: Consciousness and Society in the French Reformation.* Cambridge: Cambridge University Press, 1981.

———. *Foundations of Modern Historical Scholarship: Language, Law, and History in the French Renaissance.* New York: Columbia University Press, 1970.

Keylor, William R. *Academy and Community: The Founding of the French Historical Profession.* Cambridge, Mass.: Harvard University Press, 1975.

Klauser, Theodor. *A Short History of the Western Liturgy: An Account and Some Reflections.* 2nd ed. Trans. John Halliburton. Oxford and New York: Oxford University Press, 1979.

Koenigsberger, H. G. "The Organization of Revolutionary Parties in France and the Netherlands during the 16th Century." *Journal of Modern History* (1955).

Labitte, Charles. *De la Démocratie chez les prédicateurs de la Ligue*. 1841. Reprint, Geneva: Slatkine Reprints, 1971.

La Borderie, Arthur de. "Les Chiens dans l'église au XVIIe siècle." *Revue de Bretagne et de Vendée* (1894).

Ladner, Gerhart B. *The Idea of Reform: Its Impact on Christian Thought and Action in the Age of the Fathers*. Cambridge, Mass.: Harvard University Press, 1959.

Lawrence, C. H. *The Friars: the Impact of the Early Mendicant Movement on Western Society*. London and New York: Longman, 1994.

Lebeuf, Abbé Jean. *Histoire de la ville et de tout le diocèse de Paris*. Vol. 1. Paris: Féchoz, 1883.

Lebigre, Arlette. *La Révolution des curés, Paris 1588–1594*. Paris: A. Michel, 1980.

Le Bras, Gabriel. *Etudes de sociologie religieuse*. Paris: Presses Universitaires de France, 1955.

Le Bras, Gabriel, François de Dainville, and Jean Gaudemet. *Répertoire des visites pastorales de la France*. Paris: CNRS, 1977.

Lecler, Joseph. *Toleration and the Reformation*. 2 vols. London: Longmans, 1960.

Le Goff, Jacques. *The Birth of Purgatory*. Trans. Arthur Goldhammer. Chicago: University of Chicago Press, 1984.

———. *Faire de l'histoire*. Paris: Gallimard, 1974.

———. *Time, Work, and Culture in the Middle Ages*. Trans. Arthur Goldhammer. Chicago: University of Chicago Press, 1980.

Lekai, Louis J. *The Rise of the Cistercian Strict Observance in Seventeenth-Century France*. Washington, D.C.: Catholic University of America, 1968.

Lemaître, Nicole. "Visites pastorales sous logiciel." *Histoire moderne et contemporaine informatique* 8 (1986): 7–35.

Lenient, Charles. *Satire en France, ou la littérature militante au XIVe siècle*. 2 vols. 1886. Reprint, New York: Burt Franklin, 1963.

L'Epinois, Henri. *La Ligue et les papes*. Paris: Société Générale de Librairie Catholique, 1886.

Les Archives nationales. Etat général des fonds. Vol. 4, *Fonds divers*. Paris: Archives Nationales, 1980.

Little, Lester. *Religious Poverty and the Profit Economy in Medieval Europe*. Ithaca: Cornell University Press, 1978.

Lorcin, Marie-Thérèse. "Les Clauses religieuses dans les testaments du plat pays lyonnais aux XIVe siècle." *Moyen-Age* 78 (1972): 287–323.

———. *Vivre et mourir en Lyonnais à la fin du moyen-âge*. Paris: CNRS, 1981.

Lousse, Emile. *La Société d'ancien régime: Organisation et représentation corporatives*. Etudes présentées à la Commission internationale pour l'histoire des assemblées d'états. Louvain: Bibliothèque de l'Université, 1943.

Lukken, Gérard. *Per visibilia ad invisibilia: Anthropological, Theological, and Semiotic Studies on the Liturgy and the Sacraments*. Ed. Louis van Tongeren and Charles Caspers. Kampen, the Netherlands: Kok Pharos, 1994.

Luria, Kenneth. *Territories of Grace: Cultural Change in the Seventeenth-Century Diocese of Grenoble.* Berkeley and Los Angeles: University of California Press, 1991.

Maertens, Thierry, and Louis Heuschen. *Doctrine et pastorale de la liturgie de la mort.* Bruges: Apostolat Liturgique, 1957.

Mâle, Emile. *L'Art religieux de la fin du XVIe siècle.* 2nd ed. Paris: A. Colin, 1951.

Marion, Marcel. *Dictionnaire des institutions de la France aux XVIIe et XVIIIe siècles.* Paris: A. & J. Picard, 1979.

Markus, Robert A. *The End of Ancient Christianity.* Cambridge: Cambridge University Press, 1990.

Martin, Henri-Jean. *Livre, pouvoirs et société: Paris au XVIIe siècle (1598–1701).* Geneva: Droz, 1969.

Martin, Victor. *Le Gallicianisme et la réforme catholique: Essai historique sur l'introduction en France des décrets du concile de Trente (1563–1615).* Paris: Picard, 1919.

McLaughlin, Megan. *Consorting with the Saints: Prayer for the Dead in Early Medieval France.* Ithaca: Cornell University Press, 1994.

McManners, John. *Death and the Enlightenment: Changing Attitudes toward Death among Christians and Unbelievers in Eighteenth-Century France.* Oxford: Clarendon Press, 1981.

Mellor, Philip A., and Chris Shilling. *Re-Forming the Body: Religion, Community, and Modernity.* London: Sage Publications, 1997.

Metman, Yves. *La Vie économique à Paris pendant le siège de 1590.* Thèse, Ecole Nationale des Chartes, Paris, 1947.

Meyer, Frédéric. "A Avignon au XVIIIe siècle, la confrérie des pénitents noirs de la miséricorde." *Etudes vauclusiennes* 29 (January–June 1983): 9–14.

Miles, Margaret R. "Theology, Anthropology, and the Human Body in Calvin's *Institutes of the Christian Religion.*" *Harvard Theological Review* 74:3 (1981): 303–23.

Milo, Daniel. "La Rencontre, insolite mais édifiante, du quantitatif et du culturel." *Histoire et Mesure* 2 (1987): 7–37.

Molinier, Auguste. *Les Obituaires français au moyen-âge.* Paris: Imprimerie nationale, 1890.

Mollat, Michel. *Etudes sur l'histoire de la pauvreté, moyen-âge: XVIe siècle.* Paris: Publications de la Sorbonne, 1974.

Monter, William. *Ritual, Myth and Magic in Early Modern Europe.* Athens, Ohio: Ohio University Press, 1983.

Moorman, John. *A History of the Franciscan Order from Its Origins to the Year 1517.* Chicago: Franciscan Herald Press, 1988.

Mousnier, Roland. *Les Institutions de France sous la monarchie absolue, 1598–1789.* Vol. 1, *Société et état.* Paris: Presses Universitaires de France, 1974.

———. *The Institutions of France under the Absolute Monarchy, 1598–1798.* Vol. 1, *Society and the State.* Trans. Brian Pearce. Chicago and London: University of Chicago Press, 1979.

———. *Paris au XVIIe siècle.* Paris: CDU-SEDES, 1969.

————. *Recherches sur la stratification sociale à Paris aux XVIIe et XVIIIe siècles.* Paris: A. Pedone, 1976.

————. *La Vénalité des offices sous Henri IV et Louis XIII.* Rouen: Maugard, 1945.

Muchembled, Robert. *Popular Culture and Elite Culture in France, 1400–1750.* Trans. Lydia Cochrane. Baton Rouge and London: Louisiana State University Press, 1978.

————. *Société et mentalités dans la France moderne, XVIe–XVIIIe siècles.* Paris: Colin, 1990.

Mullett, Michael. "Popular Culture and the Counter-Reformation." *History of European Ideas* 11 (1988): 493–99.

Obelkevich, J. M., Lyndal Roper, et al. *Disciplines of Faith: Studies in Religion, Politics, and Patriarchy.* London: Routledge and Kegan Paul, 1977.

Obelkevitch, James. *Religion and the People.* Chapel Hill: University of North Carolina Press, 1979.

Oestreich, Gerhard. *Neostoicism and the Early Modern State.* Cambridge: Cambridge University Press, 1982.

Ozment, Steven E. *Mysticism and Dissent: Religious Ideology and Social Protest in the Sixteenth Century.* New Haven: Yale University Press, 1973.

————. *Protestants: The Birth of a Revolution.* New York: Doubleday, 1992.

————. *Reformation Europe: A Guide to Research.* St. Louis: Center for Reformation Research, 1982.

————. *The Reformation in Medieval Perspective.* Chicago: Quadrangle Books, 1971.

Pallier, Denis. *Recherches sur l'imprimerie à Paris pendant la Ligue (1585–1594).* Geneva: Droz, 1975.

Parker, Geoffrey. *The Army of Flanders and the Spanish Road, 1576–1659.* Cambridge: Cambridge University Press, 1972.

————. *Philip II.* London: Thames & Hudson, 1975.

Pecquet, Marguerite. "Des Compagnies de pénitents à la compagnie du Saint-Sacrement." *XVII Siècle* 69 (1965): 3–36.

Pfaff, Richard W. *New Liturgical Feasts in Later Medieval England.* Oxford: Clarendon Press, 1970.

Phythian-Adams, Charles. "Ceremony and the Citizen: The Communal Year at Coventry, 1450–1550." In *Crisis and Order in English Towns 1500–1700.* Ed. P. Clark and P. Slack. Toronto: University of Toronto Press, 1978.

Po-Chia-Hsia. "Civic Wills as Sources for the Study of Piety in Münster, 1530–1618." *Sixteenth Century Journal* 14 (1983): 321–48.

Potonniée, Simone. "Les Confréries dans l'ancien régime d'après les statuts synodaux." Thèse, Faculté de Droit et des Sciences Economiques, 1960.

Prak, Maarten. *Individual, Corporate, and Judicial Status in European Cities (Late Middle Ages and Early Modern Period).* Louvain: Garant, 1996.

Prunel, Louis N. *La Renaissance catholique en France au XVIIe siècle.* Paris: Desclée de Brouwer, 1921.

Puyol, Pierre Edouard. *Edmond Richer: Etude historique et critique sur la rénovation du Gallicanisme au commencement du XVIIe siècle.* Paris: Th. Olmer, 1876.

Quine, Willard van Orman. *From a Logical Point of View: Nine Logico-Philosophical Essays.* 2nd ed. New York and Evanston: Harper and Row, 1961.

Quinn, William A. *Jongleur: A Modified Theory of Oral Improvisation and Its Effects on the Performance and Transmission of Middle English Romance.* Washington, D.C.: University Press of America, 1982.

Ramsey, Ann W. "From Ontology to Religious Experience: Civic and Sacred Immanence in the Holy Sacrament Confraternities of Paris During the Catholic League." In *Confraternities and Catholic Reform in Italy, France, and Spain.* Ed. John Patrick Donnelly and Michael W. Maher. Sixteenth-Century Essays and Studies, Vol. 44. Kirksville, Mo.: Thomas Jefferson University Press. 1999.

———. "Towards a Definition of League Piety and Its Relationship to Seventeenth-Century Catholic Reform in Paris." *Proceedings of the Annual Meeting of the Western Society for French History* 16 (1989): 23–36.

Ranum, Orest. "The French Ritual of Tyrannicide in the Late Sixteenth Century." *Sixteenth Century Journal* 11 (1980): 63–81.

———. *Paris in the Age of Absolutism: An Essay.* New York: Wiley, 1968.

Rapley, Elizabeth. *The Dévotes: Women and Church in Seventeenth-Century France.* Montreal and Kingston: McGill-Queen's University Press, 1990.

Reinburg, Virginia. "Liturgy and the Laity in Late Medieval and Reformation France." *Sixteenth-Century Journal* 23 (1992): 526–48.

Renaudet, Augustin. "Paris de 1494 à 1517: Eglise et université, réformes religieuses, culture et critique humaniste." In *Courants religieux . . . Colloque de Strasbourg 9–11 mai, 1957.* Paris: Presses Universitaires de France, 1959.

———. *Préréforme et humanisme à Paris pendant les premières guerres d'Italie (1494–1517).* Paris: E. Champion, 1916.

Renouard, Philippe. *Répertoire des imprimeurs parisiens.* Paris: M. L. Minard, 1965.

Rheinhard, Wolfgang. "Gegenreformation als Modernisierung? Prolegomena zu einer Theorie des konfessionellen Zeitalters." *Archiv für Reformationsgeschichte* 68 (1977): 226–52.

Richard, Jean. "Royal 'Enclaves' and Provincial Boundaries: The Burgundian Elections." In *The Recovery of France in the Fifteenth Century.* Ed. P. S. Lewis. Trans. G. F. Martin. New York and London: Harper and Row, 1971.

Richet, Denis. "Les Barricades à Paris le 12 mai 1588." *Annales: Economies, Sociétés, Civilisations* 45 (1990): 383–95.

———. *De la Réforme à la Révolution: Etudes sur la France moderne.* Paris: Aubier, 1991.

———. "Politique et religion: Les processions à Paris en 1589." In *La France d'ancien régime: Etudes réunies en l'honneur de Pierre Goubert.* Toulouse: Privat, 1984.

———. "Sociocultural Aspects of Religious Conflicts in Paris during the Second Half of the Sixteenth Century." In *Ritual, Religion, and the Sacred: Selections from the Annales, Economies, Sociétés, Civilisations.* Ed. Robert Forster and Orest Ranum. Trans. Elborg Forster and Patricia M. Ranum. Baltimore: Johns Hopkins University Press, 1982.

Richman, M. "The Sacred Group (1937–39): A Durkheimian Perspective on the Collège de sociologie." In *Bataille: Writing the Sacred*. Ed. C. Bailey Gill. London: Routledge, 1995.

Robiquet, Paul. *Histoire municipale de Paris*. Paris: Hachette, 1904.

———. *Paris et la Ligue sous le règne de Henri III: Etude d'histoire municipale et politique*. Paris: Hachette, 1886.

Roelker, Nancy Lyman. *One King, One Faith: The Parlement of Paris and the Religious Reformations of the Sixteenth Century*. Berkeley and Los Angeles: University of California Press, 1996.

Rogier, L.-J., R. Aubert, and M.-D. Knowles, general editors. *Nouvelle histoire de l'église*. Vol. 3. Paris: Seuil, 1966.

Roper, Lyndal. *Oedipus and the Devil: Witchcraft, Sexuality and Religion in Early Modern Europe*. London and New York: Routledge, 1994.

Rosenwein, Barbara, and Lester K. Little. "Social Meaning in Monastic and Mendicant Spiritualities." *Past and Present* 63 (1974): 4–63.

Rubin, Miri. *Corpus Christi: The Eucharist in Late Medieval Culture*. Cambridge: Cambridge University Press, 1991.

Rutherford, Richard. *The Death of a Christian: The Order of Christian Funerals*. Collegeville, Minn.: Liturgical Press, 1990.

Sahlins, Peter. *Boundaries: The Making of France and Spain in the Pyrenees*. Berkeley, Los Angeles, and Oxford. The University of California Press, 1989.

Salmon, J. H. M. "The Paris Sixteen, 1584–1594: The Social Analysis of a Revolutionary Movement." *Journal of Modern History* 44 (1972): 540–76.

———. *Society in Crisis: France in the Sixteenth Century*. New York: St. Martin's Press, 1975.

Schmitt, Jean-Claude. *La Raison des gestes dans l'occident médiéval*. Paris: Gallimard, 1990.

Schneider, Robert A. *The Ceremonial City: Toulouse Observed, 1738–1780*. Princeton: Princeton University Press, 1995.

———. "Mortification on Parade: Penitential Processions in Sixteenth- and Seventeenth-Century France." *Renaissance and Reformation* 10 (1986): 123–46.

Schorske, Carl F. *Fin-de-siècle Vienna: Politics and Culture*. New York: Alfred A. Knopf, 1980.

Schramm, Percy Ernst. *Herrschaftszeichen und Staatssymbolik: Beiträge zu ihrer Geschichte vom dritten bis zum sechzehnten Jahrhundert*. Munich: Monumenta Germaniae Historiae, 1978.

Scribner, Robert. "The World Turned Upside Down." In *Städtische Gesellschaft und Reformation*. Ed. Ingrid Batori. Stuttgart: Klett-Cotta, 1980.

Selznick, Philip. *The Moral Commonwealth: Social Theory and the Promise of Community*. Berkeley: University of California Press, 1992.

Seyssel, Claude de. *La Monarchie de France et deux autres fragments politiques*. Paris: Librairie d'Argences, 1961.

———. *The Monarchy of France*. Trans. J. H. Hexter. New Haven: Yale University Press, 1981.

Shankle, Nelson Pinkston. "Number Symbolism in Religion and Philosophy." Master's thesis, University of Texas at Austin, 1932.

Spence, Jonathan D. *The Memory Palace of Matteo Ricci*. New York: Penguin Books, 1984.

Spero, Moshe Halevi. *Religious Objects as Psychological Structures: A Critical Integration of Object Relations Theory, Psychotherapy, and Judaism*. Chicago: University of Chicago Press, 1992.

Stocker, Christopher W. "The Confraternity of the Holy Name of Jesus: Conflict and Renewal in the Sainte-Union in 1590." In *Confraternities and Catholic Reform in Italy, France and Spain*. Sixteenth Century Essays and Studies, vol. 44. Ed. John Patrick Donnelly and Michael W. Maher. Kirksville, Mo.: Thomas Jefferson University Press, 1999.

Swanson, Guy E. *Religion and Regime: A Sociological Account of the Reformation*. Ann Arbor: University of Michigan Press, 1967.

Sweaney, Suzanne Trocmé. *Estienne Pasquier (1529–1615) et nationalisme littéraire*. Paris: Champion; Geneva: Slatkine, 1985.

Sypher, G. Wylie. "Faisant ce qu'il leur vient à plaisir: The Image of Protestantism in French Catholic Polemic on the Eve of the Religious Wars." *Sixteenth Century Journal* 11 (1980): 59–84.

Tallon, Alain. *La Compaignie du Saint-Sacrement (1626–1667): Spiritualité et société*. Paris: Cerf, 1990.

―――. *La France et le concile de Trente (1518–1663)*. Palais Farnèse: Ecole Française de Rome, 1997.

Tanner, Norman G. *Decrees of the Ecumenical Councils*. Vol. 2, *Trent to Vatican II*. Ed. G. Albergio, J. A. Dossetti, P. Joannou, C. Leonardi, P. Prodi, and H. Jedin. London and Washington, D.C.: Sheed and Ward, Georgetown University Press, 1990.

Taveneaux, René. *Le Catholicisme dans la France classique, 1610–1715*. Paris: Société d'Edition d'Enseignement Supérieur, 1980.

Taylor, Larissa. *Soldiers of Christ: Preaching in Late Medieval and Reformation France*. New York: Oxford University Press, 1992.

Theisen, Reinold. *Mass Liturgy and the Coucil of Trent*. Collegeville, Minn.: Pontificum Athenaeum Anselmianum, 1965.

Thickett, D. *Bibliographie des oeuvres d'Estienne Pasquier*. Geneva: Droz, 1956.

Toussaert, Jacques. *Le Sentiment religieux en Flandre à la fin du moyen-âge*. Paris: Plon, 1963.

Trexler, Richard. "Reverence and Profanity." In *Religion and Society in Early Modern Europe*. Ed. Kaspar von Greyerz. London: German Historical Institute; Boston: Allen & Unwin, 1984.

Trichet, Louis. *Le Costume du clergé: Ses origines et son évolution d'après les règlements de l'église*. Paris: Cerf, 1986.

Trinkhaus, Charles Edward. *In Our Image and Likeness: Humanity and Divinity in Italian Humanist Thought*. Chicago: University of Chicago Press, 1970.

Troeltsch, Ernst. *The Social Teaching of the Christian Churches.* Trans. Olive Wyon. Chicago and London: University of Chicago Press, 1976.

Turner, Victor. *Dramas, Fields, and Metaphors: Symbolic Action in Human Society.* Ithaca and London: Cornell University Press, 1974.

Uvarov, P. Yu. "La Radicalisation dans les villes à l'époque des guerres de religion en France et sa tradition médiévale." *Kultura et Obscestvennaia Mysl'* (1988): 230–41.

Valois, Charles. "Un des Chefs de la Ligue, Jacques de Cueilly, curé de Saint-Germain-l'Auxerrois." *Mémoires de la Société de l'Histoire de Paris et de l'Ile-de-France* XXXVI (1909): 83–118.

Van Engen, John. "The Christian Middle Ages as an Historiographical Problem." *American Historical Review* 91 (1986): 519–52.

Venard, Marc. "Les Confréries de pénitents au XVIe siècle dans la province ecclésiastique d'Avignon." *Mémoires de l'Académie de Vaucluse,* 6th ser., 1 (1967): 55–79.

———. "Le Répertoire des visites pastorales (suite)." *Revue d'histoire de l'église de France* 55 (July 1969): 279–89.

———. "Les Visites pastorales dans l'église de France au XVIème siècle: Evolution d'une institution." In *Les Eglises et leurs institutions au XVIème siècle: Actes du 5ème colloque de Centre d'Histoire de la Réforme et du Protestantisme.* Ed. Michèle Péronnet. Montpellier: Université Paul Valéry, 1978.

Viguerie, Jean de. *Le Catholicisme des français dans l'ancienne France.* Paris: Nouvelles Editions Latines, 1988.

Vovelle, Michel. "Histoire sérielle ou "case studies": Vrai ou faux dilemme en histoire des mentalités?" *Histoire sociale, sensibilités collectives et mentalités: Mélanges Robert Mandrou.* Paris: Presses Universitaires de France, 1985.

———. *La Mort et l'occident: De 1300 à nos jours.* Paris: Gallimard, 1983.

———. *Piété baroque et déchristianisation en Provence au XVIIIe siècle: Les attitudes devant la mort d'après les clauses des testaments.* Paris: Plon, 1973.

Wachtel, Nathan. "L'Acculturation." In *Faire de l'histoire: Nouveaux problèmes.* Ed. Jacques Le Goff and Pierre Noria. Paris: Gallimard, 1974.

White, Hayden. *The Content of the Form: Narrative Discourse and Historical Representation.* Baltimore: Johns Hopkins University Press, 1987.

———. *Metahistory: The Historical Imagination of Nineteenth-Century Europe.* Baltimore and London: Johns Hopkins University Press, 1973.

White, Michael. "Askesis: Cure of the Passions and Medicine of the Soul in Antiquity." (forthcoming)

Wolfe, Michael. "The Conversion of Henry IV and the Origins of Bourbon Absolutism." *Historical Reflections/Réflexions historiques* 14 (1987): 286–309.

———. *The Conversion of Henri IV: Politics, Power, and Religious Belief in Early Modern France.* Cambridge, Mass.: Harvard University Press, 1993.

Wood-Legh, K. L. *Perpetual Chantries in Britian.* Cambridge: Cambridge University Press, 1965.

Wunderli, Richard, and Gerald Brose. "The Final Moment before Death in Early Modern England." *Sixteenth Century Journal* 20 (1989): 259–76.

Yardeni, Myriam. *La Conscience nationale en France pendant les guerres de religion (1559–1598)*. Louvain and Paris: Nauwelaerts, 1971.

Yates, Frances A. "Dramatic Religious Processions in Paris in the Late Sixteenth Century." *Annales musicologiques, moyen-âge et renaissance* 2 (1954): 215–70.

Zeller, Gaston. *Les Institutions de la France au XVIe siècle*. Paris: Presses Universitaires de France, 1948.

Zika, Charles. "Hosts, Processions, and Pilgrimages: Controlling the Sacred in Fifteenth-Century Germany" *Past and Present* 118 (1988): 25–64.

Notes to Bibliography

1. *Les Archives Nationales: Etat général des fonds*, vol. 4, *Fonds divers* (Paris: Archives Nationales, 1980), 23, mistakenly attributes this section to François Bastonneau.

2. *Fonds divers*, 20, mistakenly attributes *liasse* 10 to Pierre Turpin.

3. *Fonds divers*, 86, incorrectly lists Dumarc's practice as ending in 1589, when in fact AN, *Min. cen.*, LXXIII, 141 contains wills for 1590. Most important, Barthélemy Dumarc, whose practice was located in the Leaguer parish of curate Boucher, co-signed 11 of Raoul Bontemps's 22 wills for 1590. See Appendix E, under the notary R. Bontemps.

Index

Liturgy, Politics, and Salvation: The Catholic League in Paris and the Nature of Catholic Reform, 1540-1630 analyzes the contest between the Catholic League and the sovereign authority of the French crown from the perspective of the culture wars that were part of the European Reformation. In Paris, the partisan politics of the period were inseparable from broader religious debates in which Huguenots, Politiques, and zealous Catholics clashed over the proper relations between the sacred and the profane. Ramsey employs a new method for the analysis of symbolic behaviors to reveal the relations between political and religious engagement and cultural change at a crucial moment in the development of the French nation. This approach to liturgy from the late middle ages to the baroque also highlights the personal experience of Catholic reform and offers surprising insights into the sources of our modern gestural culture and sensibilities.

ANN W. RAMSEY is a specialist in late medieval and early modern cultural history. She has taught in the Department of History and the Religious Studies Program at the University of Texas at Austin.

"*Liturgy, Politics, and Salvation* sets the study of early modern religion, and most particularly the significance of the French Holy League, in a wholly new light and direction of understanding. It is an extremely original, thought-provoking treatment of long standing problems central to our efforts to come to grips with the past: the relationship between religious belief and action among average people; the shifting, ever ambiguous nature of the boundaries set by institutions of church and state; and, lastly, the complex metamorphosis of religious experience from the late Middle Ages on through the eve of the Enlightenment."
—Michael Wolfe, Associate Professor of History,
Pennsylvania State University, and author of *The Conversion of Henri IV*

"The breadth of Ramsey's scholarship, the depth of her understanding of complex and highly nuanced ideas, and the daring of her reach . . . present the large issues in a manner that sweeps across a broad spectrum of interests. *Liturgy, Politics, and Salvation* appeals to a wide and varied readership."
—Lisa Ferraro Parmelee, author of *Good Newes from Fraunce:
French Anti-League Propaganda in Late Elizabethan England*

Ecclesiastical Map of Paris ca. 1665. (Bibliothèque historique de la ville de Paris. Photo: Gérard Leyris.)